D1604833

Interior Design in the 20th Century

Allen Tate

C. Ray Smith

HARPER & ROW, PUBLISHERS, New York
Cambridge, Philadelphia, San Francisco, London,
Mexico City, São Paulo, Singapore, Sydney

Interior Design in the 20th Century
© 1986 Allen Tate and C. Ray Smith

Sponsoring Editor: Fred Henry
Copy Editor: Naomi Lucks
Designer: Michael A. Rogondino
Production Supervisor: Pearl C. Vapnek
Compositor: Graphic Typesetting Service
Printer and Binder: Kingsport Press

Cover Photograph: Philip Johnson Associates. The Four Seasons Restaurant, New York City. 1959. Photograph © Ezra Stoller/ESTO, 1960.

Library of Congress Cataloging-in-Publication Data

Tate, Allen, 1930–
    Interior design in the 20th century.

     1. Interior decoration—History—20th century.
2. Interior decoration—United States—History—20th century. I. Smith, C. Ray, 1929–   . II. Title.
III. Title: Interior design in the twentieth century.
NK1980.T37 1985   729   85-24872
ISBN 0-06-046584-0

86 87 88 89 90   10 9 8 7 6 5 4 3 2 1

Contents

Acknowledgments

The history section of this textbook, Part 3, was made possible by a grant from the Graham Foundation for Advanced Studies in the Fine Arts, under the direction of Carter H. Manny, Jr. To him and to his trustees, I am deeply grateful for having supported an extended final revision of the text and for their expression of confidence in the history.

The idea for a modern interior design textbook was initiated by Harper & Row, and I am indebted to editors Earl Shepherd and Fred Henry, who foresaw the need for coverage of twentieth-century interior design as a companion to available interior design textbooks. It was Allen Tate, then chairman of the Department of Environmental Design at the Parsons School of Design in New York City, who devised the three-part outline of the book. An interior design educator for more than twenty years, he understood the necessity of twentieth-century interior design history as part of his concept outline for the textbook of which we are co-authors. And it is to him that I gratefully credit the idea of such a history. To many people, that assignment would suggest merely a history of the modern movement as it affected interior design. My view of the assignment was more inclusive.

To all those designers whose own personal preferences advanced the field of interior design in the twentieth century—as well as to their associates, friends, and families who opened their files, records, and memories to make this history more accurate, complete, and understandable—I am deeply indebted.

To all the scholars and historians whose previous research and evaluations about individual designers and movements have informed my work, I am fundamentally indebted. Many of their works appear in the Suggested Reading lists that follow each chapter in Part 3. I am fundamentally indebted to Edgar Kaufmann, Jr., whose learned scholarship in interior design and architecture has been an unattainable model.

To all the magazine editors and journalists who reported on the works of their day, I am, like succeeding historians, indebted. For, maligned by historians as journalists often are, their daily reporting is among the first-source research material of history.

To all the photographers who recorded the work of interior design, along with the many manufacturers and museums that provided photographs, I am both indebted and in admiration; for without them, the designs of this ephemeral art would be virtually lost. I especially appreciate Erica Stoller's professional management of ESTO, and the cooperation of August Lotito and the Hans van Nes Studio.

Among the interior designers and architects who gave to Part 3 extended readings and interviews and who shared their knowledge and memories most generously are Peter Andes, Benjamin Baldwin, Richard Callahan, Jack Conner, Michel

B. de Turck, Roger Ferri, Albert Hadley, Anthony Hail, Robert D. Kleinschmidt, George Nelson, William Pahlmann, Mrs. Henry Parish II, Charles Pfister, Edward J Wormley, and Edward Zajac. I am also grateful to the practicing designers represented in Part 2 for granting interviews.

Among the educators and historians who read sections of Parts 2 and 3 in different stages and versions of revision, and for whose special care in directing sensitive emphasis and avoiding egregious errors I express gratitude, are Stanley Barrows, David G. De Long, Fabio Fabiano, Gilbert M. Foley, Jody Greenwald, John A. Huff, Archie Kaplan, Kerwin Ketler, Roger M. Kramer, Charles F. Lewis, Frank Morigi, Aristeides Papadakis, Guido Stockmann, Elaine Thomas, Christopher Wilk, and Kingsley K. Wu.

Other readers gave extended time, insight, and knowledge, and dealt with suggested corrections with experience, charm, humor, and perspective. To them and to a host of others—friends, professional associates, librarians, and many more—I am indebted for assistance in opening their funds of information to me and providing much-appreciated support and encouragement along the seemingly unending way: Alexandra C. Anderson, Suzanne Stephens, Everett Brown, Lyman Martin, Luiz Rey; Roger and Edith Tuckerman, Carol and Richard Selle, Lester Grundy, John B. Wisner, John Fitler-Ellis, Carleton Varney; Melanie Kahane, Mary Jean Alexander, Harriet Morrison, Marion Gough, Jacqueline Beymer, and Anita Welch of the Decorators Club of New York; James Amster, Arthur E. Smith, Mrs. Charles Gleaves, Robert Modaff, Ann Wright, Peter Keibel; Ralph Caplan, George Finlay, James Wines, Gerard F. McCauley, Channing Blake, Sherman B. Emery, Stanley Abercrombie, James Earl Jewell, Howard B. Leighton, Ralph Cutler, Eileen Seidelbach, Ariane Breitling, Abigail Sturges, Mr. and Mrs. James F. McClelland, Jr.; Elaine Kirkland and Jacquelyn Kavanaugh of the Atlanta Historical Society; Sarah Cecil, DePuy Warwick Reed, Katherine E. Boyd; Michael Vincent, Ruth Weinstein, Louis Tregre, John H. Timothy, Stephen Kirschenbaum, Paul Blyth Hill, Kathleen Kirk, Claiborne Jones, Charlotte Sunday, Richard Oliver, Ricardo Regazzoni, Christine Rae, David Pelt, Nicole Richards, John-Michael Amato; Thomas A. Heinz, Herbert E. Walker, Leo Goldsmith, Jr.; the librarians at the Parsons School of Design: Sharon Chickanzeff, Catherine Fukushima, Claire Petrie, Howard Wood; Lisa Taylor, Peter Scherer, Eileen White, Katherine Martinez, and the Cooper-Hewitt Museum Library; Elaine Greene, Denise Otis, and the librarians at *House & Garden*.

And especially I express my gratitude and appreciation to those who worked directly with me and for long periods on the task: my research team—Marian Page and Timothy G. Morrell; those who collected photographs for me— Janet Marks, Stephen Jones, Jill Sanchia Cowan, and Elizabeth Childs-Johnson. The illustrations in Part 1 were ably rendered by Amy Samuelson-Moore. Kathy Maschke and Kevin Wolfe put Allen Tate's Part 1 on diskette. T. LaRossa transcribed the case-study interviews in Part 2 from tape. Parts 2 and 3 of this text were written entirely on an Osborne 1 computer, without which the project would have been an insuperable task. Michael Dembo expedited my learning to write on the Osborne. Karl Sandin and Diane Moran at Harper & Row offered many generous acts of assistance. Pearl C. Vapnek's shepherding of the text through the production process has been invaluable. To all these mainstays I offer my sincerest and most indebted expression of gratitude.

Finally, I express my thanks to Marcel and Jean Grignon, in whose house the original chance connection with Harper & Row was made, and to my son Scott, who patiently and genially gave up hours of our recreation time together.

C. Ray Smith

January 1986
New York City

To the Student

Any study of interior design succeeds or founders on how much of the subject is considered—on how broad and far-reaching are its boundaries and limitations. Some people consider interior design to be the selecting, assembling, and arranging of items to furnish a room. To others, interior design means designing furniture and other furnishings. Still others approach it first as affecting a space—designing the envelope, the enclosing walls, floors, and ceilings—then planning the items. A certain few embrace all these activities—designing the architecture of spaces as well as designing the furniture and furnishings; then assembling and arranging all these components into a cohesive, functional, and psychologically appropriate whole.

Here, we consider the latter approach, that is, the total process of designing interiors as it relates to a classroom studio. This book provides a guide for making interiors. It introduces beginning students to the most fundamental means with which to organize interiors. The aim is that students' designs be rational, intelligent, orderly, usable, and appropriate.

Part 1, "The Making of Interiors: An Introduction," therefore, offers a guide to *how* things are done—not *what* should be done or *what* should be designed, but the process of *how* designs are arrived at. The uniqueness of this section is its approach to the problem of design concept. Unless there is an all-encompassing attitude and concept, regardless of how much technical data a student has in the essential areas of drafting, construction, detailing, drawing, and visual presentation, a design solution will be devoid of content and character.

This section answers the following questions: Where do concepts come from? How does a student find a design approach to solve a problem? How does a student make a choice when more than one concept is possible? In answer, Part 1 discusses how the concept for an interior must arise from the existing architectural plan. Since almost all interiors are designed within existing buildings, this approach to concept and concept development becomes critical both to study and to the future practice of professional interior designers. Although the stylistic outlook of the authors is based on the Modern movement in design, the text explores a procedure that is ageless, timeless, and without regard to idiom. The objective is to provide a survey of design methodology and design influences that constitute the fundamentals of twentieth-century design.

Part 2, "The Design Process in Practice: Case Studies," includes answers to questions put to practicing designers of interiors about their design processes. Process, as these case studies reveal, is a development and distillation of each designer's past experience in education and professional practice. The authors believe that despite the different personal approaches and specializations of the different designers, the case studies reveal an underlying methodology that is relatively consistent in broad outline and gives credence to the theoretical guidelines offered in Part 1.

Part 3, "Interior Design in Twentieth-Century America: A History," presents a historical survey of twentieth-century interior design. It begins with precursors and outlines the evolution of the twentieth-century interior, then continues through each decade of our century to present the design contributions of the principal design directions and the principal personalities who contributed to them.

The historical precedents for twentieth-century design have been published repeatedly. No other interior design textbook concerns itself exclusively with today's design. Nevertheless, the legacy from the past is delineated, and the foundations of twentieth-century interior design are outlined. This history has attempted to survey the full range of twentieth-century interior designing—not just the Modern movement, but also the traditionalist residential designers, the industrial designers, and the space planners who have made recognized contributions in our time. It should provide the background necessary to assist students in the search for solutions and sensibilities appropriate to the problems of interior design today.

What Is Interior Design?

In the popular mind, interior design is thought to deal mainly with items—objects only. In the best interiors designed today, these items have had only a minor part in the success and significance of the finished design. That part is not unimportant, but it is not the first priority. To consider items first is to leap from shore to midstream, leaving the primary problem of interior design unexamined. This textbook concentrates on the methods of decision making that give strength to design concepts. It explains why those usual items are of secondary importance and must first be put aside in order to consider the spatial problems relating to plan, elevations, and the architectural volume or character described by them.

Since the activity of designing interiors began as a profession, the confusion of talent or "flair" with the ability and desire to learn has prevented some students, at the outset, from useful analysis and decision making that could develop into method. Talent is elusive at best. A more reliable attribute—analytical ability—will prove far more meaningful in learning how to design interiors. Then the necessary human attribute of intuition can contribute its quality to the process.

This book demonstrates that all successful design results from an examination and understanding of what is appropriate, what is possible within the confines of an existing space—not *What do I want?* but *What can be done?* The process of designing interiors must be largely intellectual so that study is possible; when design decisions are largely emotional, there is little opportunity for the beginning of objectivity.

Some Essential Definitions

An **interior** is a space that is enclosed by walls, floors, and ceilings. It has one or more entries/exits, and usually one or more openings, such as windows, for light and ventilation. Those enclosing elements may be composed of any number of materials and formed of countless shapes.

"Interiors" are distinguished from "spaces," which can be fully outdoors, as in landscapes or the infinite cosmos, or partly enclosed, as in plazas or open-roofed atriums and courtyards. Interiors are distinguished by their ceilings, which provide the essential shelter against weather and the elements.

To **design** is to conceive, envision, plan, delineate, and compose things. The design method includes communicating the concept to the client-owner and to the craftspeople who will build or execute those designs. It includes appropriate use of materials, attention to scale, and attention to functional and psychological appropriateness.

Interior design has been defined as the creation and organization of interior spaces to perform specific functions within an architectural environment. Such interior spaces must combine the functional, technical, and economic aspects of design with the human, aesthetic, and psychological considerations needed by the intended users.

A formal definition of interior design, formulated by the National Council for Interior Design Qualification (NCIDQ), has been developed to help unify the varied directions and professional activities in the field today. The definition has been accepted by the major national design organizations in the United States and Canada as well as by the International Federation of Interior Designers/Interior Architects. It has also been adopted by the U.S. Government's Office of Personnel Management as the official standard classification of an interior designer:

> The Professional Interior Designer is a person qualified by education, experience, and examination who:
>
> 1. identifies, researches, and creatively solves problems pertaining to the function and quality of the interior environment;
>
> 2. performs services relative to interior spaces, including programming, design analysis, space planning, and aesthetics, using specialized knowledge of interior construction, building systems and components, building codes, equipment, materials, and furnishings; and
>
> 3. prepares drawings and documents relative to the design of interior spaces in order to enhance and protect the health, safety, and welfare of the public.

Today's interior designers are involved in creating a remarkable array of different interiors—not only residences, clubs, and yachts, including large country houses and small urban apartments; but also palaces for rulers and the wealthy, seats of government and world headquarters, cathedrals and shrines, princely corporate office and production complexes, libraries and educational facilities, hospitals and hotels, airplanes and ocean liners. The scope of endeavor and the breadth of involvement for twentieth-century interior designers are enormous and exhilarating.

Decoration is an essential part of the design process. It involves the consideration of color, texture, and ornament. This consideration is an important part of all architecture and all interior design. The degree of concentration on this aspect of the design process is critical. Modern architects believed that inherent colors, textures, and the graining in natural materials were adequate decorative contributions to their architecture and interiors. Some practitioners have specialized in this aspect of design, and have considered it to be the primary activity if not the totality of the design process. Interior decorators have often been primarily concerned with the decorative effects or results of a combination of components in an interior. Interior designers aim to be essentially occupied with interior spatial effects.

Throughout this book, we refer to designers of interiors as "designers," whether they personally classify themselves as architects, decorators, or otherwise. We have attempted to avoid distinguishing "interior designer" from "decorator" and "architect," except where those titles clarify legal professional standings. In Part 3 this has not always been possible or appropriate. The objective is to concentrate on the activity of designing interiors, not to distinguish ranges of activity or specialization or to stoke the fires of controversy or parochialism. For some, this middle-profession label will be equally inflammatory, perhaps; but they might ask if "designer" is not a better designation than calling all designers of interiors "architects" or "decorators." The term "designer" focuses on the activity discussed.

Assembling is used in this book to denote that phase of furnishing an interior that involves selecting, shopping, specifying, and arranging already designed elements within an interior.

Style has been broadly defined by the critic Meyer Shapiro in relation to its scholarly and cultural definitions.

> By style is meant the constant form—and sometimes the constant elements, qualities, and expressions—in an individual or group. The term is also applied to the whole activity of an individual or society, as in speaking of a "lifestyle" or the "style of a civilization." . . . in general the description of a style refers to three aspects of art: form elements or motives, form relationships, and qualities (including an over-all quality which we may call the "expression").[1]

More simply, style is what a designer—or indeed any person—develops as a way of presenting himself or herself. It is not an overlaid thing, but an integral aspect developed over the years. As the critic of writing style William Strunk has observed,

> Style has no . . . separate entity; it is nondetachable, unfilterable. The beginner should approach style warily, realizing that it is himself he is approaching, no other; and he should begin by turning resolutely away from all devices that are popularly believed to indicate style—all mannerisms, tricks, adornments. The approach to style is by way of plainness, simplicity, orderliness, sincerity.[2]

Style, then, results from a search. It comes not at the beginning of a career, but, if at all, during—perhaps even after—the long development of design practice.

Taste has always been elusive of a universally acceptable definition. It is an ability to discriminate and distinguish appropriateness, quality, style, craftsmanship, and personality of contribution. It can be acquired, perhaps, only through interest and exposure, experience and practice. It is said that it cannot be learned. Yet it is not inborn in the same way that sensory ability to taste flavors is inborn, nor is it made and developed the same way as tastemaker critics help to fashion the "taste of the day." These three different kinds of taste—discrimination, the sense of flavors, and fashion-making—if borne in mind—can help students arrive at their own acceptable definitions of taste.

Function is the word designers use to mean "the activity performed." That activity can be performed by human action or by a working part, such as the action of a drawer, or the action of a chair in providing support. Structural engineers use the term to mean the ability of a structural member to support something. Students are counseled to distinguish failures in function, which might cause physical disasters, from failures of comfort, which may be mere nuisances and inconveniences.

Aesthetics is the study or philosophy of the beautiful. Theories about what constitutes the beautiful have been numerous throughout history. The aesthetic aspects of interior design are, essentially, the visual and psychological appropriateness to the functional requirements of the specific interior under consideration.

The relation between *function* and *aesthetics* is one of the fundamental balances to be achieved in the applied art of interior design. For interior design is unlike the fine arts of painting and sculpture, which have no requirement to function for any human or mechanical activity. Interior design must apply its art to the required functions of a client or clients. That makes it an applied art, and creates the delicate balance between function and aesthetics that is a matter of endless discussion in the field.

Modern has two meanings to us today. The first generally connotes the modern sensibility, the Modern Age, the modern world and lifestyle as we know it in the twentieth century. The other, a more specific use of the term, designates the Modern movement in design. That movement, described in Part 3, began in the first decade of this century and developed an antihistorical and purposely abstract approach. It is based on the ideals, goals, and aesthetic of the Industrial Revolution, with its respect for the machine.

Modern interiors are, therefore, those interiors that include not only the elements assumed under the above definition of an interior, but also the developments since the Industrial Revolution that we have come to consider essential in our shelter and architecture. Those elements are plumbing, sanitation, ventilation, heating, functional efficiency, privacy, and personal possessions, including furniture.

Modern interior design as a profession is practiced by a wide variety of people. They include interior designers, architects, industrial designers, decorators, furniture dealers, and graphic designers; and the design staffs of department stores, of corporations, and of federal and state governments. Other professionals who actively contribute to interior design include engineers; lighting designers, acoustical and audiovisual specialists; food facilities consultants; behavioral scientists; programmers and planners; draftsmen, detailers, and renderers; exhibit designers; colorists; furniture and textile designers, manufacturers, and suppliers; specification writers; photographers, graphic artists, painters, and sculptors; landscape designers, contractors, management consultants, and accountants.

What Makes a Professional?

We live in the age of professionals. The politician and the actor are called professionals, as are athletes who receive a salary. Few people recognize that to be a professional means something more than "to be in a business." That something has to do with what you do, why you do it, and also how you become equipped to do it.

In a commencement address at Brown University in the 1930s, Chief Justice of the United States Louis Brandeis defined a "profession": First, the necessary preliminary training is intellectual in character, involving knowledge and, to some extent, learning, as distinguished from mere skill. Second, the occupation is pursued largely for others, not for oneself. Third, it is an occupation in which the financial return is not the only accepted measure of success.

Certainly the training of interior designers fits into this definition. If we accept it, however, we see that the athlete, whose work is largely skill, does not qualify as a professional. Neither does the fine artist, who may have had a rigorous education, but whose work is done largely as self-expression and not for others.

Financial return seems to be the accepted criterion for determining a profession, and many professionals do make vast incomes. When criticism is leveled at interior design as a profession because the work is said to be undertaken primarily for the affluent, we can answer that the same can be said for the professions of law and medicine when the client or patient is rich. However, when a service is needed, and professional assistance is available, the amount of money spent for the assistance or earned as a fee for the service is not a viable criterion for judging professionalism. When a designer plans interiors for a hospital, a school, or a public library for a fixed amount of money, the same level of expert contribution is expected—and is compensated in the same way—as when a designer plans a residence on a limited budget or a palace for a potentate.

Still, a career is best undertaken for motivations other than profit. Not the least of those better motivations is that one truly *likes* the activity in which one plans to spend the time and energy of one's life. The Brandeis definition may be too idealistic for all of us, but it is good to take its high ideals at the beginning. Its direction will give breadth and scope to our work and will give us, like the angels, a long way to fall.

As a profession, interior design—even at this late point in the twentieth century—is new and still emerging. It has gained credibility in every educational region of the United States. In each region one or more schools offer programs in interior design that lead to the granting of a degree; some schools offer graduate work in the subject.

Around the profession of interior design, recognized organizations have formed. National organizations investigate and qualify interior design programs by establishing minimum standards. Other national and regional groups have attempted to create standards for professional practice. These organizations also provide forums for discussion on problems of design as well as information on products, methodology, technology, and the psychological implications of interiors as an important part of the manmade environment.

Among those groups that investigate and qualify interior design programs and that develop educational standards in America are the National Council for Interior Design Qualification (NCIDQ), the Foundation for Interior Design Education Research (FIDER), the Interior Design Educators Council (IDEC), and their sponsoring national professional societies: the American Society of Interior Designers (ASID), the Institute of Business Designers (IBD), the Institute of Store Planners (ISP), and the Interior Designers of Canada (IDC). Many of these groups have been represented on a committee working with the American Institute of Architects (AIA) to establish and refine a standard contract document for interior design work.

The Need for Interior Designers

Before the twentieth century, the range of interiors made considerably simpler demands on designers in terms of functional planning. The technologies and processes of each activity and profession were less categorized and specialized. Around the turn of the century, countless elaborations of procedure—in hospital and laboratory spaces for the practice of medicine, in courts and prisons for the practice of law, in department stores for retail trade, and in offices for corporate administration—brought greater and greater needs for more specific and knowledgeable planning and provision of interior equipment. The twentieth-century interior designer, therefore, arose to focus on these constantly developing subprocedures and subcategories of activity. Throughout the twentieth century the practice of interior design has itself witnessed a steady development of specialization.

Interior designers are needed to concentrate on this specialization. But further, as any number of historians see it, technical and professional innovations have always been the result of someone's initial desire to make something beautiful. The current thinking is that bronze was developed for jewelry and urns before it was used for weapons. Iron was used for the wrought-ironmakers' craft before it was a construction material. Pottery and ceramics were developed for decorative objects before they were used for purely practical purposes.[3] Interior designers can recognize that aspiration to the beautiful, and they can take pride in the fact that their aspirations reflect the roots of our civilization.

The Act of Creation

The old adage that creation is one-tenth inspiration and nine-tenths perspiration has a majority of believers. It also has interpreter-philosophers of a much more heady bent. Benedetto Croce's tenet that "expression is intuition" summarizes the belief that we have not thought out something until we have expressed it. Whether in words or stone, painting or drawing, expression and thinking go hand in hand. We must put down or put out our thoughts before they are realized. All of our past experience comes to bear in this self-conscious realm, where we piece it all together in a dream state. Until this dream-state thinking is realized in some physical form, we have not created.

In its simplest form the act of creation is an interaction of the mind with a handcraft in materials. For interior design students those materials are drawings and models, and for them the work of expressing a thought—a concept—in drawings and models is the act of creation. Indeed, for most designers, drawing is designing. The two are virtually synonymous and inseparable.

Drawing is not only creative expression, it is thinking itself. Drawing is essential to conceptualization. A drawing may not be superb as classically pure drafting; however, it can convey necessary information. Sometimes, even at the early stage of development, a student's drawing may also be expressive and convey feeling and the emerging character of an interior. All students of design must draw, but not all of them will become outstanding in that craft. Still, at each line of the pencil, the possibilities change and new thoughts are germinated; for drawing is thinking.

Most students do not easily grasp what the act of developing a concept is, because they have not been through this process often enough to recognize it. But they should begin thinking at an early stage that a concept is something that always changes and becomes something new. They should begin to understand that a concept is a whole without parts. When designers become one with their drawings, we say that their nerves come out of their fingertips, that they get the idea into their hands. This is the methodology for arriving at a physical, form-making concept of design.

This textbook, then, in Part 1 offers a guide to acquiring a methodology that will help students arrive at concepts for their studio problems and will further help them to realize those concepts. Through Part 2, the text also provides an insight into the approaches, outlooks, inspirations, enthusiasms, and special techniques of a distinguished group of practicing contemporary designers of interiors. Finally, in Part 3, the book presents facts—names, dates, locations, theories—from the past and present that every serious student of design should be familiar with, and that every enrolled student has made a commitment to be responsible for.

The Student's Need for History

For all students of interior design, the history of twentieth-century interiors is essential to understanding today's practice. Students at the beginning of their careers need to know where the traditions of their field have come from, for several reasons. First, new professional careers are built on the foundation of inventive genius in the past. That foundation includes both an understanding of the events that contributed to design progress as well as a knowledge of the names, dates, and locations associated with those original inventions. Second, history itself influences the future and provides a basis for aesthetic judgments. As the philosopher George Santayana warned, "Those who do not remember history are destined to relive its mistakes." Learning from the mistakes of the past, in other words—including learning from what we do not like—is essential to making progress in the future.

The Scope of This History

This history of interior design in twentieth-century America aims to demonstrate that interior design is a tangible record of the values, technology, economy, regionalism, and genius of its evolving culture. Much of that culture has been influenced by European design movements, and those influences are part of twentieth-century interior design in America. Therefore, Part 3 of this text is not merely a history of styles and personality designers, but is also a history of plans, materials, functional changes, design influences, and idioms—and therefore of society.

It outlines the concurrent development, within the profession of interior design, of several directions that have often been considered mutually exclusive. For the history of twentieth-century interior design in America is both the history of the Modern movement and the history of traditional decorating during that time. Modern architects and designers have created significant interiors throughout our century and have made original and lasting contributions to twentieth-century interior design. Twentieth-century decorating arose, not as a new activity in our century, but as a new and separate profession. The decorators who work in that tradition have had much immediate influence on the total spectrum of interior design in America. The development of these professional directions has been concurrent, if sometimes conflicting.

Both directions—the Modern movement and traditional decorating—are part of this history of the profession that designs interiors. That is one of the aspects that makes this history different from other interior design histories. In addition to these two directions, Part 3 also surveys the contribution of a third professional direction—that of industrial designers and the later space planners. The specific contributions of each direction and how they have related to each other are outlined here.

This history also aims to describe three levels or strata of design activity and interest within our population. Along with the innovative, original concepts of vanguard designers—those concepts and images that have changed the vision of our age—this history also describes what was most popular in each decade. What was most popularly seen, understood, and desired is compared with both vanguard original invention and the mainstream of design practice and design education.

The Format and Organization of This History

Part 3 begins with a survey of the precursor developments that led to the modern interior. After this introduction, the history is organized by decades; that is, a chapter is devoted to each decade of the twentieth century. Following each chapter is a list of recommended further reading.

This chronological division was made for convenience—for understanding and for study—rather than being based on actual divisions in design development. Development in design history, as in the rest of life, is gradual. It spreads out across decades—as across countries—drifting and filtering slowly from single vanguard inventors in one decade to professional acceptance in the next decade. These time lags in understanding and acceptance are such, in fact, that design inventions may not become supported by existing technology until two decades later. And sometimes acceptance by the broadest sector of the population occurs as late as three decades after the invention by the original genius. This is the historical progress of ideas. This history aims to provide an outline of that progress in the field of interior design in our century.

Because of its broad scope, this history may offend both camps: the Modernists, to whom the decorators may seem minor personalities; and the traditionalists, whom the architects may consider as having missed the point. Modernist architects may say, "Just delete all the minor personalities and concentrate on the major form-givers"—by which they mean Modern architects, regardless of their influence on or contribution to interior design. Traditionalist decorators may say, "Just leave out all the architects and tell us what the decorators did"—by which they may mean women and traditionalism, regardless of their overall influence on or contribution to interior design.

My goal, however, was to be inclusive. The decade of the 1980s was, perhaps, the first of this century in which such an overview of interior design could have been possible. Before, the crusade of the Modern movement and its taboo against historicism and decoration so polarized architects and interior designers against decorators that none of those camps would have wanted to be included with another in the same book. The two approaches were so antithetical that neither was willing to acknowledge, much less associate with, the other. Some of that feeling of singlemindedness still obtains.

However, for more than twenty years the direction has been increasingly toward inclusiveness in design. Since the mid-1970s this pluralism has become predominant—more interior designers are espousing the Modern movement, while more and more architects are re-adopting historicism and decoration. It is most apparent, from any reading of twentieth-century design history, that there has been a continuous pluralism of individual expression and approaches, from decade to decade. All are part of the full palette of interior design.

In this history, then, all candidates are considered as part of the force contributing to interior design advancement. There is no polemic, no taking sides with either Modernism or traditionalism, with architects or decorators. Indeed, it has been my aim to present the contributions of each designer or individual, of each school or idiom, on its own merits. There is, therefore, little critical evaluation from today's or the author's point of view of the work of any designer or idiom—except the fundamental criterion for selection and inclusion in the history. Instead, I have tried to present, as accurately and fairly as I see it, the goals, aims, and ideals of each: how *they* wanted to shape the world or the interior; not how *we* think of what they thought, not how the world of today may evaluate their success or the validity of their goals.

What I have tried to include in this history of interior design in twentieth-century America, therefore, are the objective facts of history. The evaluation of those facts will change from year to year, or at least from decade to decade. Critical opinion on almost all of the idioms, developments, practitioners, and works has varied—wavered—cyclically throughout the century. I have tried to say what each aimed to do, what each wanted to do, and what seems to have been positively accomplished in that direction.

Because evaluations will change again, I have avoided criticizing the obviously negative points, evident omissions and commissions of various designers—for example, the actual comfort of much innovative furniture, or the significance of Surrealism in interior design, or the lasting benefits of office landscape. Instead, I have aimed to describe and present as palpably as possible what innovative furniture has been, what Surrealism in interiors has been, and so on. The objective facts will, I trust, remain unchanged.

Nor must this be taken to indicate that all the objective facts about interior design in our century are stated here. There is a wealth of data and information on engineering, construction, manufacture, and installation elsewhere. The Suggested Reading lists following each chapter of the history section direct attention to many of those sources. So it will be the responsibility of each reader—teacher and student alike—to evaluate the facts presented in terms of their own day, in terms of the idiom prevailing in their schools or communities, in terms of the personal preferences of the moment.

Notes

1. Meyer Shapiro, "Anthropology Today," *A Modern Book of Aesthetics*, ed. Melvin Rader (New York: Holt, Rinehart and Winston, 1960).

2. William Strunk, Jr., and E. B. White, *The Elements of Style*, 3d ed. (New York: Macmillan, 1979).

3. Cyril Stanley Smith, *A Search for Structure* (Cambridge: MIT Press, 1981).

Interior Design in the 20th Century

The Making of Interiors: An Introduction

Chapter 1

Interior Design Problem Assignments

The Design Studio

In the interior design department of most schools, almost without exception, the design studio (or laboratory, as it is sometimes called) is the heart of the curriculum. The studio is not so much a place for receiving instruction—although there is instruction given in a studio, but, like a laboratory, it is the place where experimentation—search and discovery—takes place.

The studio is an ideal place to search for solutions to the problems of interior design. Architectural design, painting and sculpture, and the various crafts are traditionally accomplished in studios.

With its student group and teacher-critics, the studio offers an atmosphere that is conducive to a free exchange of ideas. It is an atmosphere that is sometimes quiet and orderly, sometimes noisy and chaotic. Historian Colin Rowe, who had many years of exposure to the architectural design studios at Cornell University, felt the studio system was such a splendid way to learn that he advocated the adoption of the same procedure by other departments.

In the studio the learning process is learning-by-doing, not the learning-by-listening done in a lecture hall. Each student has the opportunity to speak directly with the teacher or to overhear a teacher's discussion with another student. A student may share ideas with one classmate or with many.

The studio system, therefore, is in a sense peripatetic. It is not so much a literal moving around or walking about, in the way Aristotle did with his students; but, like reconnaissance trips, the coming and going in a studio is noticeably different from the lecture hall and other kinds of classroom learning. Students move about in a studio to discuss design problems with each other; they go out of the studio during class time to seek information in a library or from an outside source firsthand or from on-site observations.

Most of all, a studio is a room in which to work. When filled with the collective energy of a group of students working in conjunction with a teacher-critic to find solutions to design problems, it is a setting conducive to study. Something is always taking place, work is always in process, design problems are being solved.

What Is an Interior Design Studio Problem?

The Type and Complexity of Problems

For students, interior design problems are theoretical explorations, as opposed to the real design problems of professional designers. Each problem is assigned to require a special solution for a specific type of interior; each assignment is planned to include an increasing level of complexity.

Each design exploration exposes a student to another type of problem, and another level of experience. As students move on to the next problem, another level of complexity in another type of interior is explored. The complexity of a problem may include a larger-scale interior, or greater detail, depending on the teacher's view of which would best help students to accumulate information through problem solving.

During the period of study (from two to four years, or more) design problems are usually given in ascending complexity. In some schools early studio problems may be as rudimentary as the selection and arrangement of furniture, color, and materials for a single room. The next level may require modest architectural changes, or the design of several rooms that are sequential. A higher degree of complexity may include architectural additions or deletions, as well as complete proposals for furniture, color, and so on. More advanced problems will focus on space planning for open floors, or multiple floors in high-rise buildings. The variety of design problems is of ever-increasing dimensions and complexities.

Over a period of time, assigned problems will cover a variety of design conditions. Residential or domestic interiors, offices or corporate interiors, and public interiors such as schools, hospitals, libraries, and theaters may be assigned. Commercial problems such as shops, stores, and restaurants are also typical kinds of interiors that, by the nature of their requirements, make particular demands on students' abilities.

Individual or Group Projects

Individual projects are the rule in most schools. Each studio problem is assigned on the basis that a solution—called a project—will be accomplished by a single student under the critical direction of a teacher. In this case the student is solely responsible for his or her own design project; all of the design ideas originate with the student; all development of the ideas are the student's; all drawings submitted for review are the student's alone.

Some schools occasionally assign studio problems to groups of students. In such cases groups of students are formed, and each is instructed to arrive at a single solution to the design problem and to execute the required drawings together. They will, of course, work under the direction of a teacher.

Group projects are assigned for two reasons: First, a problem may be too large in scope or in the amount of research required to be assigned on an individual basis in the time available. The problem may have a level of complication that can best be solved by several students. Another reason is that, since design has social connotations—as well as being an aesthetic and functional discipline—interaction in a group causes a somewhat broader reaction to a problem than a single student can provide working alone.

Working in groups has its special internal problems of personality, but much can be gained when several minds focus on one problem. It is typical in group projects for each member to take part in gathering information prior to and preparatory to the conceptual phase. After the research period information can be consolidated, preliminary ideas can be explored, and a direction for exploratory designs can begin.

What Is the Given Information?

Before work on an interior design project can begin, students need information about the problem. All interior design problem assignments require programs or programmatic information in written or verbal form. In addition, all problems require information in the form of drawings of the existing architectural plans into which the interior is to be designed.

Design Programs: Written and Verbal

A written design program sets forth an outline of what is required for the interior problem assigned. The outline may be a brief general statement of what is needed, or the program may outline in detail all that is required. Programs for students are similar to professional programs in the level of given detail. For most professional design work the client provides the designer with a list of what is wanted or needed. That is the client's program. Some of these are sketchy, broad ideas; some are specific and intricate. Architect Robert Venturi once received a residential program from a client that ran to eleven written pages; it set out specific demands for each room in a seaside house. Other designers say they need or want only a brief verbal description to understand a client's needs.

Other projects require not only programming, but pre-programming. This is often undertaken by experts outside the design professions. Pre-programming is needed for extremely large-scale, complicated corporate, industrial, commercial, or complex multi-unit housing projects.

For students, the highly detailed program may include data on location, climate conditions, site description, or notes on a building's history. Interior requirements may be listed item by item and may include the number of people who use the interior, whether or not any architectural additions or deletions are allowed, whether windows can be changed, doors moved or blocked, plumbing relocated, ceilings opened, and so forth.

In residential projects the detailed program will say how many people are expected to sit in a living room, how many must be seated at a dining table, how often special entertainment takes place, and what character these occasions will have. More information may describe the client's education, occupation, recreational interests, and, sometimes, taste level.

If the problem is for a commercial interior such as a shop, the program will give its location, type of product sold, and the kinds and numbers of customers expected. Requirements may state the number of running feet needed for shelf storage or stockroom square footage.

Programs for corporate design projects will spell out various relationships between one employee and another—whose office needs to be near another to ensure maximum efficiency, who must have privacy, if a conference room is necessary, how much space is required for clerks and for secretarial pools. The public image of the corporation may be described in the program, as well as information about how the manufactured product or available service benefits consumers.

Some interior design departments insist that teachers prepare written programs. Others prefer that program information be given verbally.

Verbal programs for student design problems are usually less detailed, and may loosely describe design requirements. In this case there is more freedom to interpret, but there is also a risk for students because of that freedom—or ambiguity. However, some professional designers say that even the most detailed, written program requires interpretation and investigation. Some say that clients seldom know what they need, that they only know what they want. The reasoning-out of requirements by students, therefore, can be good experience for future practice. But students must make certain how fixed a program the teacher intends the assignment to be.

For example, when a verbal program for a domestic project suggests that a living space should include the usual seating as well as accommodation for dining and study, the student must reason out not only the disposition of the parts, but also the number of people other than the occupants who might use the space. Sometimes this kind of program will give minimum-maximum square footage rather than a specific amount.

One part of the design problem assignment that is often included in the written program—simply because it also must be written out in detail—is the requirement of drawings to be presented, or the "presentation requirements." Both verbal and written programs will give information on what is required of each student concerning the physical presentation of the design solution. Either program type may say that students must produce "sufficient drawings to show the major concept of the design." This general statement means that students will decide on the number of drawings. The "sufficient drawings" stated in the assignment must be interpreted in relation to the individual student's project. Some design concepts may need only a few drawings; others will require several more in order for the concept to be understood, or to bring out the best parts of a design.

Many design programs include lists of specific requirements for presentation. These programs say, for example, "Plan at 1/4 inch = 1 foot 0 inch; elevations of all major spaces; one major perspective (or two or three) of the main space; and sufficient details to explain special features."

The requirement for materials—the wood, paint, fabric, and so forth—to be shown in the presentation varies from school to school and from teacher to teacher. Some schools in large cities require actual material samples to be selected by students, since local suppliers can make those materials readily available. Schools at some distance from suppliers try either to keep collections of materials for student use or to make fewer demands that materials be shown with presentations. (Students should be prepared for reluctance on the part of some suppliers to provide samples to students because of the cost of the samples, and because giving a student a sample will not bring direct compensation.)

Architectural Drawings

Whether the assignment is in written or verbal form, architectural drawings of existing conditions will be needed to complete the given information for a problem assignment. Some teachers give each student a set of basic architectural drawings and make available to the studio a complete set of working drawings for use when needed. Other teachers provide only one set of drawings and prefer that each student prepare a copy by transferring dimensions or by tracing paper overlays. This method, although time-consuming, has one advantage—it gives the student immediate familiarity with the information in the drawings. Either procedure will provide the necessary information. These drawings are essential for all but the simplest decorative interior design projects.

Some teachers occasionally give problem assignments that do not require detailed architectural plans of existing conditions. Those problems will be primarily concerned with completing existing spaces and will not involve changes in the construction. Plan information given in these cases will be in the form of simple line drawings without structural details.

The Duration of Project Assignments

Over the period of an academic quarter, trimester, or semester, teachers usually schedule design projects of various lengths. The length of a project may range from a few hours to a few days to several weeks. Short-term projects are usually called sketch-projects; long-term ones are usually called major projects.

Short-Term or Sketch-Projects

The sketch-project is given in many schools for several reasons. This type of assignment requires that a student generate a design quickly, prepare drawings quickly, and present a design quickly.

Sometimes sketch-project assignments deal with large-scale design issues. In this type of assignment the student's solution may remain largely conceptual. There will not be enough time to carry it further, and the design will of necessity be an unfinished, if creative, idea. This type of sketch-project does not ask for details.

Other sketch-projects may deal with small-scale design issues. These will ask mainly for details rather than concepts. Short-term sketch-projects also offer a break from the in-depth assignments that constitute longer major design projects.

Major or Long-Term Design Problems

Major design problems may last from two to six or more weeks. Within the academic time schedule, whatever that may be, some teachers prefer to assign major problems that cover a maximum time; others prefer a somewhat shorter length of time. Whatever duration is preferred, major design problems always require that students solve the problem as completely as possible.

Major design problems are assigned to cover the conventional types of interior design problem. Conventional interior design problems are of several types—domestic or residential interiors that include houses and apartments; nonresidential interiors such as offices and shops; and public spaces such as schools, libraries, hospitals, theaters, clubs, entertainment spaces, and the like.

Some interior design teachers also assign highly imaginative problems that fall somewhat outside the expected province of interior design. These problems may seem far from the central concern of interior design students; but they are assigned to stretch and expand students' thinking, to pique their imaginations and help them see design in larger perspectives. This type of assignment may ask for the design of an outdoor space, a terrace, garden, or open plaza. Or an assignment might be an exhibition design including a display system that can be packaged and shipped to another town and reassembled. A teacher might ask students to design the triumphal end to a marathon run, a theme for a birthday celebration, or a centennial event to mark a city's founding.

All these projects have as their creative goals the making of form, just as the goal of making an interior is creating form. Professional designers are often asked to answer problems of this type.

Major design problems are therefore concerned with major design issues. The selection of a covering for a bed is not a major problem, but only a part of the larger problem of designing a bedroom. However, a bedroom may be considered a major design problem when all of its parts, materials, and details are included in the assignment. The bedroom assignment has a series of complications that need resolution in the same way that much larger interior spaces have interrelated complications. The difference is in the scale of the two problems and in the level of complexity, but both may be considered by a teacher as major design problems.

When major problems are assigned, students are almost invariably asked to give a full and complete treatment, a full complement of functional and aesthetic answers to the implied design questions. Sometimes the conceptual idea that a student produces is so strong, so filled with natural talent and imagination, that even though the design may not be fully detailed, the teacher evaluates it highly. However, in major problem assignments, it is the full development that is asked for, that all students should aim for and complete, and for which all teachers look.

Process Drawings: What Is Expected?

In the study of the making of both large- and small-scale interiors, students should understand that the drawing process is inextricably connected with the design process. When design assignments are made and program and architectural drawings are received, students are then ready to begin process drawings.

Thinking and drawing are intimately interrelated. Some practitioners say that thinking begins first. Others are convinced that until lines are put on paper, no real thinking occurs. Some designers say that the two should happen simultaneously.

Like practicing designers, students are individuals and they will develop this aspect of their design procedures naturally from their own personalities.

Sketches: Rough Plans, Elevations, and Perspectives

With plans and program in hand, students are ready to begin generating design ideas. The ideas must be externalized—put on paper—so that both student and teacher together can examine their validity (see Figure 1). Design ideas that are not externalized remain thoughts only.

Design is a visual, physical activity; design ideas must be made visible—understandably visible. This can be accomplished by students only through drawings and models. At this stage teachers do not expect beautiful drawings (although some gifted and practiced students do make beautiful rough sketches). These early sketches may have all the seeds of the finished design, but lack small details.

The usual procedure (though some teachers proceed in other ways) is to start rough sketches on tracing paper laid over the existing architectural plan at the beginning of a problem assignment. These lines will be made freehand, and many ideas can be generated in a short time. At this point both the drawing process and the design process have begun.

When a rough freehand plan is sketched, it is advisable to carry the idea into freehand elevations. Elevations will tell more about the idea. Rough perspective sketches will carry the idea still further and keep the process moving.

Students are responsible for producing the most complete idea possible at every phase of a design project, even in its earliest stages. The number of sketches and their completeness are essential to convey as much information as is known at

1. Process Drawings

From the given architectural plan to the final stages of design development, process drawings indicate changes in thinking. Nevertheless, movement toward a concept is the desired result. Preliminary design stages are studied with rough, loosely scaled drawings of plans, elevations, and perspectives. Different shapes and sizes change the configuration of the interior without necessarily affecting the existing architecture. Notions on color and materials may emerge as contrasting dark-light, rough-smooth situations — information that begins to influence the finished design.

a particular time. Most teachers insist that each discussion with a student must be based on sketch-plans, elevations, and perhaps rough perspectives.

For interior design students it is almost imperative, at every stage, to make rough perspectives to explain a design. As the design process continues, drawings must become greater in number and in detail. The first lines, though they may be somewhat abstract, will become more and more descriptive. These sketch drawings of plans, elevations, and perspectives will move toward finished drawings that will be assembled with all the information required for the final design presentation.

Often at this stage, a student will be caught up in purely functional problems and forget that aesthetic considerations are always equally the concern of studio work, as in all design. Or the student may consider only aesthetics while the physical comfort, convenience, or usability of the space is overlooked. A design idea that appears to be strong may be weakened if aesthetic criteria are placed above program requirements. Ideally, both aesthetic and functional necessities come together. When this occurs, the project is illuminated through the student's ability to synthesize both. Program requirements must be met; but they serve as information, not creative concepts. However, concepts for interiors do come from the promptings in the program of requirements.

Scale Drawings: Plans, Elevations, and Sections

All rough sketches translate into scale drawings. Rough plans and elevations will become precise, measured drawings. Architectural sections are usually required when a project includes major renovation or involves multiple floors. Sections are not required in all projects at all schools, but they are required in most schools where interior design is considered as part of architectural design.

At this stage in the design process the drawings should begin to suggest materials and the values of light and shade. Some students will begin to consider color and may make partially colored drawings or renderings as a next step in moving the design toward final presentation.

During this phase of the process, students will continue to discuss their design ideas with teacher-critics.

Models: Sketch and Finished

Frequently, a student will find it informative to make a rough, three-dimensional sketch-model. Models provide another way to visually represent an interior space or series of spaces. Some teachers only suggest that sketch-models should be made for each project during the early stages of the design process. Others insist on sketch-models, and may make finished or sketch-models a requirement for the final presentation.

Sketch-models are usually made from inexpensive board. They can be put together quickly, and the effort is worthwhile. Such rough models may be used during the design process to assist students in judging matters of function as well as aesthetic problems of scale and proportion, color and texture. Models can give a more exact position-relationship in three dimensions of the component parts that make up the whole of the design (see Figure 2A).

Finished models, which are much more specific in the quantity and quality of design information they provide, require more time to build (see Figure 2B). Better-quality materials will be used. Some teachers insist on finished models; but when this is a specific requirement for presentation, the teacher will probably not require finished perspectives as well. However, this procedure varies widely from school to school.

2. Interior Models

A. A rough model of existing architectural conditions clearly describes the volume of the interior. Experimentation with size, shape, and aesthetic principles continues. All components remain movable except the fixed architecture.

B. In a finished model, one that may be used as part of a presentation, the final relationships are revealed. All design decisions have been made and all of the components are in place.

A

B

Final Drawings and Other Presentation Materials

As the design process continues, all required drawings and models move toward a level of finish. Final presentations that include models and material samples require that students consider those components of the assignment at as high a level of design finish as their drawings.

Chapter **2**

The Components
and Materials for Interiors

Several levels of components are necessary in the design of interiors. Some of the component areas are of greater importance than others. The architectural ones, for example, are essential to every design concept. Some of the items within a component area, such as fine art or portable lighting, may be of small importance in some interiors.

The elements of architecture are walls, floors, ceilings, doors, windows, and light. In his four-volume work, *Eléments et théorie de l'architecture*, the nineteenth-century theoretician Julien Gaudet explained that the elements (that is, components) of architecture are not the classical Greek orders and their accompanying parts set forth in strict proportions.

It is interesting to note that the great pieces of architecture from the past are composed of these elements. This holds true for their interiors as well. Many historical rooms are known to us today only as empty spaces, devoid of furniture, furnishings, and art. Still, many of these rooms seem to be complete as design concepts because they are in some sense furnished by their architectural components.

In most Modern interiors, the walls, floors, ceilings, doors, and windows have so little architectural treatment that without the inclusion of all (or at least some) of the components, there is nothing but an empty void. Therefore, with few exceptions, Modern interiors are more dependent on component items for conceptual wholeness than were most historical interiors.

Architectural Components

Walls

The enclosing walls of caves were the first protection offered by nature for human beings. As we know from preliterate history, these protecting walls were soon given a gift in return for the safety that they offered—the beautiful drawings such as those at Altamira, and even the childlike drawings at Lascaux. From this prehistoric time to the present, walls and their meaning—their presence—have occupied the thoughts of humankind, in particular the thoughts of builders, architects, and makers of interiors.

Ancient Greek temples with walls of solid blocks of sparkling marble; medieval fortified cities with massive walls, smoke-blackened, crenellated, and forbidding; the gloriously treated walls of the Renaissance master builders, so lovingly decorated with columns, pilasters, cornices, and pediments—all offer proof of the continuing preoccupation, throughout history, with the wall. The need, the importance, and the preeminence of the wall as the component of first consequence in artistic efforts to define interior space are clear. Without walls, there is no interior—no house, no church, no temple, no school, no inside at all. Even if a space is marked only by vines and trees or pebbles in the sand, the ghost of the concept of the wall as enclosure is present (see Figure 3).

Walls have the power to evoke both good and bad feelings, positive or negative emotional responses. Walls can be interpreted as keeping danger away, or as limiting freedom. They can protect the beauty of a tranquil garden, or hold in the

3. Walls

The visual character and the structural integrity of a wall are established by method and material. The appearance of some walls reveals precisely how they are made. In others a treatment may obscure a structure, but it may still be acceptable as well as expressive.

A

B

A. These Paleolithic paintings in the Lascaux Caves in Dordogne, France, make the rock walls more visible. The animal pictures add a presence beyond that of the natural form. Painted over time for symbolic purpose by a succession of artists, the figures accommodate themselves to the shape of the wall surface.

B. Carvings that relate important events are depicted on walls of the eleventh-century Temple of Hathor in Dendera, Egypt. The linear incising completely covers the plane of the heavy wall, and the pictures stand out sharply in the steady, intense sunlight.

C

D

E

F

G

C. The Greeks used marble blocks laid up without mortar to build temples. This produced a fine surface of great regularity. In a side-wall segment from the interior of the Temple of Apollo Epicurius at Bassae, Arcadia, about 450 B.C., the columns stand in relation to the slight outcropping of the wall plane. This projection isolates the columns and also relates them to the wall.

D. At Compton Wynyates Hall in Warwickshire, England, around 1520, the size of available wood suggested the size limitations of a screen wall design. Organized in rectangular parts, some are filled in with carved panels, others are left open where doorways are needed. The plane of the wall, though made up of separate parts, presents an articulated, unified appearance.

E. A seventeenth-century marble elevation in the period style of Louis XIV is built as a separate design in front of heavy, masonry construction. The design of the elevation uses rectangles, squares, geometric segments, and columns in proportions based on classical models. A cornice of multiple moldings crowns the wall and joins it to the ceiling.

F. This 1907 house designed by Frank Lloyd Wright for Isabel Roberts in River Forest, Illinois, has plaster walls that mold the interior. The wall segments of the living space travel at different angles from the floor to the ceiling plane. Wood banding emphasizes the edges of the segments and is carried upward through the volume.

G. The glass-walled Tugendhadt House at Brno, Czechoslovakia, was designed by Mies van der Rohe in 1930. The principal space is loosely, but precisely articulated by a freestanding screen wall made of unadorned slabs of onyx. This is set in relation to spatial needs and to the slim, structural columns.

horror of a Minotaur, as did the labyrinth of walls built by Daedalus for King Minos in the Greek myth. Poets have used the connotative quality of fence walls to bring up feelings, as Robert Frost does in his poem "Mending Wall":

> Something there is that doesn't love a wall,
> That sends the frozen-ground-swell under it,
> And spills the upper boulders in the sun;
> And makes gaps even two can pass abreast. . . .
> Something there is that doesn't love a wall,
> That wants it down.

The famous last line, "Good fences make good neighbours," sees the good in a wall. Frost's earlier poetic question asks, "What I was walling in or walling out." This is perhaps the ultimate philosophical question about walls, and one to which the designer of buildings and interiors must know the answer without question. The problem for the designer, however, is to be sure that *what* is walled in—and *how* it is walled in—causes only the intended responses.

The walls, more than any other component, seem to be the principal means of making interior spaces, regardless of what mode of spatial perception is at work in the mind of the designer. The walls hold in or mold the space. The walls allow for doors and windows. The walls lend support to the ceilings and define the floors. In one sense it is the walls that "make" the interior, that give it its form and special shape. When Mies van der Rohe exclaimed "There is a wall" when he stepped back to examine the onyx wall in the Tugendhat House, he expressed not only his respect for the wall he had designed, but also his admiration.

This is a very different idea from that stated in an interview with Michael Graves. He says that one comes "face to face with a wall," revealing a confrontational attitude. (He calls a wall the emotional part of a room. "The plan is intellectual," he says.) Art critic Brian O'Doherty says in *American Masters* that Mark Rothko's paintings, like blank walls, have a "stare" when viewed frontally. This seems to be the reason why so many High Modernist architects and interior designers employ the plain or blank wall in interior spaces: The blankness gives a power when "unrelieved by incident."[1]

In many of Frank Lloyd Wright's houses, the walls—though they be composed of many planes, turning and shaping a space, or pierced by many windows—hold their visual strength and scale. This is usually due to their treatment, which includes wood bandings and moldings that move around windows and accentuate the wall planes as they carry lines up onto the ceiling. This gives the increased height needed for the monumental yet domestic scale of such Wright interiors as the Isabel Roberts and Francis Little houses. In most of Wright's interiors two components do not merely meet at a junction of a change of planes; the walls and ceiling have much more of an interrelationship.

Materials for Walls   In any interior, walls constitute more square footage than any other interior component. Their construction materials, whether they be structural bearing walls or nonstructural partitions, are expressive means in design. For example, a bearing wall made of stone always projects an impression of weight, strength, and solidity. We know by experience that stone walls have these qualities. We also know that stone is cool and granular in texture. A wall made of wood or metal framing and covered with lathing, brown-coat, and finish-coat plaster presents itself in another way. We sense strength and solidity, we know from both

---

[1]Brian O'Doherty, *American Masters: The Voice and the Myth* (New York: Random House, A Ridge Press Book, 1974).

sight and touch that it "feels" a certain way, a way different from a stone wall. If both walls are finished with a skin of paint, we will still receive the essential information through the construction and the material.

Other materials produce different results. Laying up a bearing wall of marble is essentially the same as laying up a wall of concrete or glass block. Here we are most concerned with the effect of the construction material, not the method of construction, although the method of construction produces the effect under consideration.

Integral Wall Materials   Of the four materials mentioned above—stone, plaster over framing, concrete, and glass block—all are integral wall materials. Other materials that can be considered integral are few—sheet glass and plastic, brick (including adobe construction), and wood, in limited ways. With each of these the material is the wall, the wall is the material. However, because most of today's construction is accomplished with non-bearing walls (with the exception of single-family housing), these integral bearing walls become exceptional.

Walls made of integral materials have special, innate characteristics. When used in interiors, they need a treatment and a consideration that recognizes this specialness. For example, it is unlikely that a wall made of marble would interact compatibly with a picture hung on its surface. Both the wall and the picture would probably suffer. Glass block would present a similar aesthetic problem, as would concrete block—unless it has been given a painted finish, or if the picture hung on its face is of a character that mutually benefits both wall and picture.

In these examples it should be clear that walls of special, integral material are not suitable as mere backgrounds for other components. The one exception may be in historical renovations, where there are precedents for the use of precious materials as background. Today, however, such materials as marble and other stone, wood, glass in several forms, metals, and even brick and real plaster are too scarce, too expensive, and too difficult to handle with the current dwindling craft in the building trades to be thought of as anything but special. These materials must be honored and used in significant ways in interiors to retain their richness and to draw from them their sumptuous character.

Some integral wall materials may be appropriately finished in a skin of paint. (Marble is the one exception; but at least one minor example of painted marble comes to mind from the work of Skidmore, Owings & Merrill—SOM. On that occasion unfinished white marble was used as a base for a plaster wall and painted out with the wall. The idea was that if the paint on the baseboard chipped off during maintenance, only white would show through.) Paint has a long history of use over materials. It is justifiable to paint these materials for two reasons: (1) for protection, and (2) for aesthetic continuity with an interior scheme.

When paint is applied to the surfaces of such materials as brick, concrete block, and wood, it focuses attention on the material's texture, rather than on the pattern resulting from construction methods. Painted finishes on these materials have some of the richest potential of any type of wall. Infrequently, paint may be used as a covering skin on sheet glass and plastic: The flawlessness of their surfaces becomes noticeable in a different way than when seen as transparent planes. Smooth plaster walls are painted for protection and to cover certain flaws of surface. Textured, rough plaster is painted for protection as well, but here the paint tends to draw the surface together in a cohesive textural effect. Any poorly made wall of integral material can be made to seem less poorly made when painted, particularly if the paint is fairly dark in color value.

Lightened and Dematerialized Walls   Architects and designers of interiors have always had the capacity to build massive, protective walls of enclosure. The mate-

A

rials themselves—solid stone, solid wood—have the necessary weight and density to make solid wall planes. To lighten these materials is another design challenge (see Figure 4).

The first attempt to lighten solid walls (other than with such necessary openings as doors and windows) occurred in the late Romanesque–early Gothic churches in England and Northern Europe, especially in France. Such Gothic cathedrals as Notre Dame (1163–1235) and Laon (1160–1225) exemplify the medieval builder's efforts to accomplish both height and lightness when making walls. Architectural historian Sir Banister Fletcher notes that "Emboldened by success (in vaulting roofs and successfully maintaining the greatest amount of elasticity compatible with stability), they even ventured to cut granular stone as thin as fibrous wood."[2] This allowed for the vast number of openings in the side walls of churches and admitted the expanses of darkly stained, glowing colored glass. Though these ritual spaces were filled with gloom, the walls had nonetheless been made lighter for the first time.

Throughout the Renaissance there was a reliance on classical models for all buildings and their interiors. One period in which lightening and dematerialization as an interior concept is unmistakable: the eighteenth-century style known as Rococo. In *Creation of the Rococo* the architectural historian Sidney Fiske Kimball defines the style as a development not of architecture, but of the decorative arts. He says, "the primary sphere of the movement was, to a degree almost unique in artistic history, in the realm of decoration: in the interior, whether domestic or religious, and in ornament, chiefly the ornament of surface."[3]

Wylie Sypher describes this use of ornament as "architectural" when used by designers such as Pierre Lepautre and Oppenord. The paneled walls became "a field for the ornamental motifs that required exquisite workmanship—finely executed bands, interlaces, palm branches, leafage, stems, acanthus scrolls, flowers, sprays, and tendrils carefully presented upon a neutral plane." The overlaying of the panels with these naturalistic arabesques, cut fine and fragile, spread over the panels to create a frontal layer of decoration. Then, according to Sypher, the decoration "pushed the solidity of the walls into the background." He says further,

---

[2]Sir Banister Fletcher, *A History of Architecture on the Comparative Method* (New York: Charles Scribner's Sons, 1950).

[3]Sidney Fiske Kimball, *The Creation of the Rococo* (Philadelphia: The Philadelphia Museum of Art, 1943).

4. Lightened Walls

A. It was necessary to lighten Gothic walls in order to build them higher. To do this, stone was cut into thin, linear members, as shown here in England's eleventh-century Lincoln Cathedral. Openings — as windows — further reduced the weight of the walls and, later, developed into the characteristic Gothic window of colored glass.

B

C

D

B. The dimensional designs on French eighteenth-century paneled walls created a frontal plane over the flat panels and pushed them back. The decorations became a shimmering screen of carved treillage, leafage, and tendrils finished in gleaming, reflective silver or gold. If mirrors were added, the space of the room began to dematerialize and vanish.

C. In the twentieth century reinforced concrete skeleton construction allowed columns to carry the entire weight of the roof, or of the floors above. Since walls no longer needed to be load-bearing, they could be placed in positions that answered functional or aesthetic planning needs. The walls themselves could be mere partitions or transparent glass curtain walls. This construction method, developed by Le Corbusier in 1915, provided the means for the development of open planning in interiors.

D. Dematerialized walls reach their zenith in the work of Mies van der Rohe. This interior, the lobby of the 1947 Promentory Apartments in Chicago, is enclosed in intersecting, transparent glass planes held in a steel framework. Partial- or all-glass buildings developed from the architect's earlier pavilion-like experimental houses.

"To heighten the fictional quality of Rococo space the architects often used mirror . . . Mirrors not only empty the walls but wipe away volumes until one seems to move through a constantly changing infinity."

Although Rococo spaces are symmetrical, and the paneling is also, the decoration is developed with "occult balance rather than mathematical symmetry . . . one side of a panel never exactly repeats the design of the opposite side; there is equivalence, not mere restatement."[4] The walls in Rococo rooms meet the ceiling plane in decorated coves, blurring the usual hard lines and furthering the imperceptibility of the walls in a way similar to the more "flamboyant Gothic."

We know that twentieth-century Modernism has its roots in the enlightenment of eighteenth-century French thought. With the advent of periodicals, there arose a new reading public; the rise of the middle class, which at least at its upper edges commingled with the aristocracy, had an ever-growing interest in literature, and continuing advancement was made in the arts and sciences. It is not surprising, then, that a few years into the twentieth century (after the multitude of nineteenth-century historical revivals in architecture and the visual arts) it was in France that an architect led the way in lightening methods of building construction. Cubism is also French by location, even though it was Picasso, a Spaniard, who made the first Cubist painting; and many historians attribute the whole of Modernism in architecture and the arts to the Cubist beginnings in the Paris of the 1920s.

In 1915 the architect Le Corbusier (a Swiss transplanted to Paris) made the drawing that Sigfried Giedion describes as the "real starting point of Le Corbusier's career." The drawing shows how he used reinforced concrete columns, developed by engineers from the nineteenth century forward, as a means of architectural expression. The pillar, left free to rise through the open space of a dwelling, left nothing for the walls to support, thus giving the structural skeleton and the wall functional independence. Now both exterior walls and interior partitions could be placed with freedom where aesthetic needs demanded. Le Corbusier, according to Giedion, was able to "create a house of unprecedented lightness and to carry still farther the kind of 'open planning' which Frank Lloyd Wright had begun."[5]

The Villa Savoye (1928–30) exemplifies Le Corbusier's lightened construction. The exterior walls are almost paper-like in their crisp weightlessness; the interior living spaces flow into the enclosed, but open terraces; the roof holds the blue- and rose-colored, abstractly shaped wind screens open to the sky: The entire concept of the house is directed toward lightness.

During the same period in Germany, Mies van der Rohe was lightening his buildings in another way. While Le Corbusier made solid walls lighter, Mies was making walls transparent, perhaps the ultimate dematerialization. The German Pavilion at Barcelona and his pavilion-like houses all use lightened and dematerialized materials or employ the materials in lightened ways. Thin, polished-metal posts carry roof slabs; interior walls become screens of travertine, marble, wood, and various shades of tinted or clear glass. Often the interior partitions are held up off the floor plane on slender, polished-chrome posts, furthering the aspects of lightness. Dignity and nobility in design had historically been brought about with weighty materials presented in weighty ways; now, however, modern means allowed these characteristics to be had through lightness, also admitting daylight and air into the free-flowing interiors.

As the Modern movement continued into the mid-twentieth century, and as lighter and lighter construction became accepted in building, lightness in interiors

---

[4]Wylie Sypher, *Rococo to Cubism in Art and Literature* (New York: Vintage Books, A Division of Random House, 1963).

[5]Sigfried Giedion, *Space, Time and Architecture* (Cambridge: Harvard University Press, 1963).

was seen as a necessary quality of modernity. Interior partition walls, though now mostly made of metal studs and sheetrock even in the best buildings, have been made to appear even lighter by painting them in high-gloss paint finishes. The high-gloss paint not only shimmers with its own luminescence, but reflects daylight back into a space. In some applications it acts as a vague mirror-like surface where people and components at close range are dimly reflected.

Mirrored walls in interiors, as Sypher notes, wipe away walls and multiply volumes and duplicate all components within the mirror's sight lines. For this reason it is imperative that when large planes of mirror are used, what is reflected must be worthy of being seen twice: the real components and those seen in the mirror as reflections.

Applied Wall Finishes: Paint   Paint is the most widely used finish applied to walls. Paint is almost integral, because it bonds with the wall surface and becomes one with it. It is durable, comparatively inexpensive, and can be maintained in areas of hard usage. Painted wall finishes are appropriate in any interior.

The best-quality paint is always an oil-based solution. It is best primarily because it lasts longer and remains in better condition than plastic, synthetic-based paints. Synthetic paints tend to attract airborne soiling agents. Pigments for coloring matter in almost all paint are of the aniline dye type. Deep colors require more pigment and are therefore more expensive than the lighter colors, which require less pigment.

Wall Coverings: Paper, Fabric, and Novelty Coverings   Paper coverings for walls are probably the most popular way to treat wall surfaces. However, in most cases wallpaper is an inappropriate wall treatment because the patterning usually obscures the wall, rather than making it more apparent as a spacial component of major importance.

Some few wallpapers have patterns that present the wall plane in a clear, dignified way. Most, however, obscure it in a welter of pattern, creating visual chaos. Most wallpaper patterns are poorly designed and of inferior quality. When wallpaper is used in an interior, the scale of the pattern must be considered first, even before color.

There are certainly interiors in which paper is a good choice as a wall covering, and there are papers that have well-designed patterns. Some old, or antique, pictorial papers also make successful wall surfaces, but they must be carefully considered and used as special parts of a room. Some of these papers can be used instead of picture art. As with any other two-dimensional work of art, they require special settings.

Floors

The horizontal floor plane, the bottom-most part of every interior, is the only architectural component that is both seen and felt in all conditions of use. The other architectural components are felt—or, more correctly, touched—only by accident. The eyes see all of the components, but the foot "sees" (that is, it feels) the floor. The foot also has a memory, just as all of the body has memory. Sensory information received in the foot is transmitted upward. Foot in contact with the floor, body memory, and physical movement over a surface, as well as the visual, physical presence of the floor plane, gives this component a special prominence: It supports every thing in every interior.

The floor is the only architectural component that naturally makes sound when used. All floors except those covered by the densest carpets and traversed by the lightest footfall have the potential for sound. This potential should be considered first as a positive one for incorporation in the design of interiors, and only as a negative one when acoustical problems are present. (Steen Eiler Rasmussen speaks of "hearing architecture" in his discussion of interior sound. He says that sound in architecture can add to our experience of space, and further that acoustical attributes have contributed to the development of certain musical forms over centuries of changing methods of construction.[6])

It should be remembered that the very first physical contact each of us has with architecture is the floor. This takes place during the creeping-crawling stages of infant development. Much speculation and some real psychological evidence indicate that the floor plane on which infants spend time needs special attention. Both visual and tactile deprivation can occur for infants and children in the floor-level environment that is drained of richness by an insistence on "style," or the fear that an antiseptically clean surface is the only acceptable plane on which infants can safely play. Those parts of a room that touch the floor can also add to environmental richness for infants. Such parts as the legs of furniture, the bottoms of draperies and other window treatments, as well as the incidental objects that rest on the floor can contribute to a visual and textural experience.

Perhaps more than any other architectural component, the floor plane can unify a space or a series of spaces. Furniture components can be connected visually by the design treatment of the floor plane.

In existing or new spaces where organic connections are part of the design concept, the absence of door saddles and the allowance of a continuous flooring material that moves from space to space without interruption can bring together disparate rooms in a more fluid spatial connection. The presentation of the floor as a continuous plane designed without any break gives the connection to both eye and foot.

Plain materials are the most effective floorings to accomplish this idea. Continuous floorings, such as carpet, various tiles, and linoleum, are good choices because of their evenness of texture and color and the absence of line or grain direction. Natural materials may be used as well; however, they make the point less apparent. Their grain and pattern often have a line direction that will tend to confuse the flow of the floor plane desirable in an organically conceived interior.

The treatment of the floor plane can separate spaces and components as well as connect them. The floor plane can make visual spatial divisions by a change of material or color. The possibility of changing the coloration of a single material or of using more than one contrasting material juxtaposed to another one can produce visual closure and spatial separation without more extravagant architectural means.

Materials for Floors Flooring materials are usually divided in two broad and generalized categories: resilient and nonresilient. The category of resilient materials includes carpet, wood, linoleum, and the various composition tiles; however, the only truly resilient material in the group is carpet. With variation in use, all of the other resilient flooring materials have a low resilience factor. All show dents, scratches, scuffs, and so forth. The nonresilient materials—stone, brick, tile, concrete, and terrazzo—are not so easily damaged. In both categories, maintenance is important.

---

[6]Steen Eiler Rasmussen, *Experiencing Architecture* (Cambridge: MIT Press, 1964).

Another division—and perhaps a more meaningful division of flooring materials—should be considered by designers: those materials that are a part of or are intended to be a part of the architectural construction, and those that are added to the surface of the constructed floor. The first category includes concrete and terrazzo (either poured in place or precast), all of the stone materials, clay tile, brick, and wood. These materials are considered to be as permanent and as enduring as all of the other architectural components. They make rich floors that age well. In many situations these materials become more beautiful with age, developing a kind of patina that comes about only through time and use. The maintenance requirements of these materials are somewhat lower than might be expected, because they hold up under conditions of less than perfect care. Long periods of neglect can be counteracted by various methods of cleaning, restoring them to a newness of color, texture, and brightness.

Permanent materials for floors are appropriate in almost any interior, domestic or otherwise, but some of them project associative qualities that must be considered. For example, marble floors connect unmistakably in our minds with grandeur, formality, and nobility; brick is seen as offering warmth (although its actual temperature is about the same as marble), domesticity, and casualness, perhaps because of its humble origins as a handmade craft product. Certain clay tile patterns make sophisticated flooring and may have an association with a country of origin when the pattern and color have a history of place. Concrete and, to some extent, terrazzo are often associated with nonresidential interiors, and may remind us of office, government, or factory buildings.

Among the permanent flooring materials, wood has the ability to present widely differing characters, depending on how it is used. The random-board floors of American Colonial interiors have one connotative quality; the sumptuous design of French parquet has an entirely different quality. Although the other materials in this group can be designed in contrasting ways, it is wood that has the most potential for differing effects. Not only can wood be designed in many patterns, it can also be finished in several ways. Stains and varnishes can deepen the natural color; bleaches can lighten it. Tinted stains can give a dark, almost black wood, and with aniline dyes wood floors can be colored to almost any hue. In some special situations wood floors can be painted; however, this method of finish requires frequent refinishing to be kept at its peak.

Of all the materials that can be added to the surface of floors, carpeting is the most versatile and now the most widely used. Although all carpeting must be periodically replaced, high-quality carpets may last for decades. Alone of all the other materials in this group, carpeting can be laid without visible seams over an expanse of floor; all other flooring material has seams that will be visible. Even the hairline joints of linoleum will darken and become quite visible after a short period of use and maintenance.

Another point in favor of carpeting is its acoustic quality. With much of the lightened construction of twentieth-century building, the porous texture of carpet can reduce the often too-live bounce of sound in an interior. Poor quality or unevenness of wood floors in existing interiors can be hidden by carpeting. Carpeting is available in many textures and color hues.

Some past design theorists, and some current practitioners, say that the floor plane should be treated with fairly neutral or dark colors. This idea is attributed, they say, to the general coloration of the earth's surface. They posit that light or bright floor color creates an uncomfortable response. Further, these designers have applied the same theory to walls and ceilings, saying that walls should be a medium tone and ceilings should be the lightest tone. Dark-colored ceilings, they say, give the sensation of heaviness. This would, of course, invalidate all of the dark, heavily

A

B

C

5.   Ceilings and Floors

A.   Dark-colored beams do not necessarily lower the visual height of a ceiling or cause it to appear heavy. Either may happen, however, depending on the effect of a design concept on the existing architecture.

B.   In interiors with light-colored ceilings and floors, dark walls tend to recede. The lighter horizontal planes gain emphasis by value contrast and the reflection of light.

C.   Dark-colored ceilings and floors tend to push light-colored wall planes outward, away from the center. The walls begin to appear thin and weightless because light is reflected mainly from their surfaces.

beamed ceilings in several periods of history. With this theory as the operative idea, no floor could be white and no walls black (see Figure 5).

Ceilings

In earlier historical periods ceilings, almost without exception, either exhibit structural members (such as beams, coffers, or vaults); or are expansively decorated with painted pictures, plasterwork, or wood carvings; or are treated with coves and moldings. Modern ceilings tend to be the least-considered component in interiors. Most of the domestic masterpieces of the Modern movement have plain white, undecorated plaster ceilings (although some examples can be cited where structural beams are exposed, and a few have ceilings of wood). During the second half of the twentieth century the ceilings in commercial interiors became the component in which mechanical systems were housed—heating and air-conditioning ducts, and much of the electrical conduits.

Lighting attached to the ceiling has grown from candles in a chandelier, to a centrally located lighting fixture, to the whole ceiling as lighting fixture with the advent of the "luminous ceiling" in the late 1950s office boom. (This went out of fashion rather quickly when it was discovered that the overall plane of luminosity was not good to work under and that it effectively washed out shadow, flattening out most of the dimensional quality of the interior.)

The hung or false ceiling has become usual in all but domestic interiors where plaster in older structures, or sheetrock in newer ones, is usual. In multistory buildings (now even in high-rise apartment buildings) the floor slab acts as a plane from which the ceiling below hangs. The space between the floor slab and the hung ceiling is then used as duct space, the air between acting as a sound barrier.

These ceiling planes are composed of one of several types of porous acoustical tiles inserted into a thin metal framework that is suspended from the above-floor slab on other metal hangers. The acoustic quality is a plus; the aesthetic, a minus. If the tiles are given a painted finish, the sound-deadening ability is vastly reduced; if left in their available colors, they are neutral or characterless.

As with floors, appropriate coloration for ceilings is debatable. Some designers insist that all ceilings be light in color value to escape the idea that a deep value would make the ceiling appear to be pressing downward. However, dark ceiling planes can be effective in some interiors, even when there is only average ceiling height. Dark-colored ceilings tend to push side walls outward from the center of an interior. In some interiors a very dark ceiling will tend to disappear when other architectural components support such a concept. A dark ceiling plane and dark flooring of the same value can make light-colored wall planes seem paper-thin, as shown in Figure 5.

When considering strong color hues for use on a ceiling plane, it should be remembered that with some lighting conditions certain hues have a tendency to "bloom" onto other surfaces. That is, a red ceiling may bloom pink on side walls, a yellow ceiling may turn white side walls cream-colored, orange can bloom to peach, and so forth.

Reflective finishes on ceiling planes are possible with metallic paints or papers. Gold and silver metallic paper can make effective, low-level patterning on ceilings in certain kinds of interiors, and metallic tiles are available.

Wood in several forms can be used for special ceilings. Planes of wood, wood slats or louvers, and lattice work can make texture and pattern.

Some novelty finishes may—in exceptional interiors—be effective. Ceilings painted to resemble cloud-filled blue sky, or sky-colored with painted stars, can give ceilings an importance that may be necessary in a spatial concept. Such painted ceilings add an element of delight in some cases, but this type of ceiling treatment must be undertaken seriously. Other unusual treatments of the ceiling include such materials as mirror, or mirror-like plastics; heavy textures; or banners of fabric, plastics, or wood.

One particular spatial possibility should be remembered with regard to ceilings. When one space has a lower-than-average ceiling, the space next to it—even though its ceiling height may be average—will appear higher. If one space has a dark ceiling plane, and its adjoining space a lighter one, the lighter ceiling will appear higher by contrast.

Columns

Structural columns can rarely if ever be removed in the design of interiors in existing buildings. So much present-day construction is based on supporting columns that in all but the simplest domestic and nondomestic architecture this component brings the greatest pressure on interior planning. In large high-rise apartment buildings, in office towers, and in department stores and shopping malls, the placement of structural columns—whether freestanding or outcropping from partition walls—not only sets restrictions on interior planning, but also may aid in the development of design concept.

Most buildings based on columnar structure of necessity place all of these vertical components at regular intervals. The interval, or bay, repeats precisely across the building's width and depth; or, in less regular building plans, across one direction with one bay-column dimension, another dimension in the other direction. Irregularly planned or poorly designed buildings may allow columns to occur in what seem to be eccentric locations. Sometimes this arrangement of column placement is necessary to maintain structural integrity, and sometimes it results from a weak structural concept. In either case the interior designer must find some rational means of acknowledging exposed structural columns.

Given the option, most interior designers and architects would prefer column-free space. Because this option seldom exists, acknowledgment of columns must start at the beginning of conceptual thinking. Columns often can be incorporated into a design concept to bring all of the necessary components into a balanced cohesion of aesthetic and functional satisfaction and wholeness.

The structural function of columns aside, it is not only their plan-placement, but their insistent verticality that must be considered. This verticality can never be completely hidden except when columns are enclosed within new walls. Attempts to disguise columns in other ways never work. When columns are dematerialized by mirrors attached to their sides, we are informed by our sensibilities that there is a column "hidden" behind the mirrors. Likewise, a column only in the rarest circumstances can be used as an integral part of a furniture component. Desks, tables, or seating wrapped around or engaged with a column invariably make strange furniture forms. In all cases the column is aesthetically degraded. The relationship between columns and other architectural and furniture components, however, is crucial.

All architectural and all furniture components must relate to columns with deliberate, conscious purpose (see Figure 6). Even when the visual connection is a seemingly casual one, the decision must be undertaken with due consideration for the aesthetic and functional solutions sought in the design concept.

Spatial axes and center-and-edge alignments of other components can allow freestanding or outcropping columns to gain importance and to maintain their identity. However, columns must always relate most apparently to other architectural components.

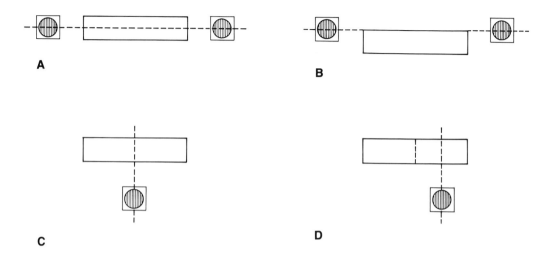

6. Columns

Columns, almost always immovable in existing spaces, need special relationships with the new components of a design concept. Sometimes columns can be hidden in an interior; but when they remain visible, they are powerful elements to be considered.

A. The center of a component—architectural or otherwise—aligns with the centers of the columns.

B. A component aligns its edge with the center of the columns.

C. The center of a component aligns with the center of a column.

D. The center of one-half of a component is aligned with the center of a column.

Materials for Columns   All materials for the treatment of structural columns are surface materials, unless columns are of reinforced concrete or prestressed steel left in an exposed state. Some materials appropriate for treating column surfaces may appear to have structural properties and make handsome finishes—marble and wood, for example.

Sometimes it is necessary to apply a sheath of cladding (usually called furring) to columns as an aesthetic consideration. But sometimes it is necessary to apply furring to bring all of the freestanding columns into alignment with one another. In some building schemes one or more columns are heavier than others to ensure that structural loads are distributed properly. "Wet columns," which carry piping as well as structure, are always larger than other columns. In all high-rise commercial buildings (office or residential) wet columns supply pipes for plumbing connections to the various floors of a building.

The importance of structural columns can be suppressed in a design scheme by giving them a finish that is the same as or similar to other components. Columns may be expressed in a design concept through contrast. This can be accomplished in several ways. For example, when other architectural components are light in color, columns in a dark color will be more visible. Or, if ceiling, wall, and floor planes are highly textured, columns faced with a smooth, polished finish will stand out in contrast.

Stairs

Stairs provide vertical circulation in interiors. They can be hidden away as completely functional, separated components, or they can be fully integrated to become a most dramatic part of an interior.

A number of special terms are used in stair design (see Figure 7). Some important ones are listed here:

1. Tread. The horizontal member of a stair on which the foot is placed when going up or down.

2. Riser. The vertical member partially supporting the treads. (This member is sometimes missing in stair design, most noticeably in Modern interiors where lightness is sought.)

3. Stringer. The structural support for treads and risers. Stringers run diagonally underneath a stair.

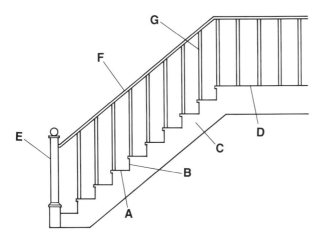

7. Stair Parts

Stairs form an integral part of many interiors. The scale of a stair may be suited to a monumental space or to one of the smallest dimension. Proportions of the parts must relate to each other and to the functional and aesthetic whole of an interior.

A. Tread

B. Riser

C. Stringer

D. Landing

E. Newel post

F. Handrail

G. Baluster

4. Baluster. The member that supports the handrail and is attached to the stair treads.

5. Handrail. The member that runs diagonally and parallel to the angle of the stair; it is intended for safety.

6. Newel, or newel post. The member that ends the run of a stair, usually much larger, sometimes more decorative than the balusters.

7. Landing. An intermediate plane or platform between two or more floors. Also the floor at the beginning and end of a stair flight.

The proportioning of stairs is critical. The relationship of the depth of treads to the height of the riser is one that has evolved through long experimentation. The maximum height for risers in either public or private spaces is approximately 8 inches or less; treads need to be a depth of approximately 9 inches or more to accommodate the foot comfortably. These dimensions are general ones, and must be adjusted to fit a given situation within a building as well as to suit the character of the interior.

The proportion of a stair determines how comfortably and how slowly or quickly a person will travel on it. In general, a stair with low risers and deep treads will suggest that a person walking on it will walk more slowly; the foot lifts up less high to negotiate the riser, the sole of the foot finds an excess surface of tread. The low risers mean more treads in the run of the stair. This type of stair is considered to be appropriate in formal or monumental interiors.

A more usual stair proportion—7-inch riser, 9-inch tread—suggests an optimum pace of up or down movement. Dimensions larger than 7 inches for risers make climbing stairs tiring; less than 9 inches for the tread dimension means that only the ball of the foot will be accommodated, and this too is uncomfortable.

Tread and riser relationships have a functional safety factor, the same relationship that makes for aesthetic proportions in stair design. Most stairs require a sturdy handrail. In some interiors a stair can be designed without a rail, but never in public spaces. It is often a requirement in public interiors that a handrail be supplied on both sides of a stair, one forming the outer edge barrier, the other attached to the building wall. Freestanding stairs—those not connected on either side to a wall—require double handrails.

Materials for Stairs   Stairs are designed of stone (marble, granite, and so forth), wood, metal, and various combinations of these. Handrails, balusters, newels, and so forth are designed of similar materials.

The finishes for stairs (when a finish other than the material used for its structure is needed) include tile, various plastics, rubber, and carpet. Safety again must be considered. This small group of finishing materials presents few safety problems. An exception is carpet that has a long pile. Long-pile carpet should be avoided on stairs because it can roll over the edge of a tread and cause the foot to slip. The same is true of carpet with very dense, deep pile.

The preferred carpet for stairs has a dense but short pile. This type will not cause safety problems and will not "grin" (when the carpet pile opens up as it turns over the edge of a tread).

Doors

Doors can prohibit or invite entry, they can reveal or conceal. The first doors were probably animal skins hung over the openings of caves to provide some degree of protection from the wind and the cold. Today, doors still offer protection. Too seldom do they invite entry.

Doors often carry literal messages—"Do Not Disturb," "Office of the Principal," "Entrance," "Exit," "Stairway," "Men," "Women," "No Entrance," "Keep Out," "Employees Only," and so forth—that tell us unmistakably how to respond.

In architecture, doors have always had a specialness other than mere protection. The front doors of palaces, churches, and houses announce special places. Many times they are raised up, or protectively covered with porch roofs; often they are crowned with fan-lights or emphasized with decorative columns, moldings, and cornices. The doors themselves receive special attention—their size, material, and design carry connotations way beyond the idea of protective closure (see Figure 8).

In some early architecture, doors were often made less than the height of the average person so that stooping was necessary to gain entrance. In other building design, door heights were so great that giants could enter with ease. And enter they did, those who saw themselves as giants—noble, powerful people who did important business behind imposing doors. The business of the church, the business of government, the business of a ruling family took place (and still does) behind the walls of large buildings entered through doors of great importance.

In other buildings, however, doors were of average size, but severe and imposing in their treatment, surrounded with carved stone embellishments and flanked by windows in a composition of strict symmetry that focused at the center-door entrance. Wood doors were sometimes covered with bronze, or the panels were decorated with carvings.

In today's standard-size buildings with standard-size interiors, doors too have become standard. The usual interior door in today's interior is standardized at 6

A   B

feet 8 inches high, and from 2 feet 0 inch to 3 feet 0 inch in width. It is usually of wood made on the hollow- or filled-core principle of construction, distinguished by an extremely flat, planar surface. In one sense this is the quintessence of the Modern door: Its flatness would be impossible to create without twentieth-century technology.

Materials for Doors   Wood, glass, and metal are the principal materials used in the design of doors. In interiors, doors of wood paneled or flush-faced are by far the most usual. Glass in combination with wood or metal or all-glass doors are common; all-metal doors can also be used effectively.

If the natural grain of wood is desired, the door should be selected for color and pattern. Mahogany, ash, and birch are among the woods commonly used. The standard wood door, paneled or flush, can be finished with clear varnish or with paint. The finish should be determined by the design concept of the interior.

Hinged, sliding, and folding doors comprise the possibilities for movable interior closure. Special sizes can be designed. The available, standard-size door can, however, be used effectively when attention is given to placement and finish.

Windows

Daylight admitted into interiors through windows is discussed in Chapter 7. This section will confine itself to window size and shape, the characteristics that affect interiors and their components.

Planning in most interior situations is first influenced by the location of columns and doors. The other component that makes an impact on interior plans is windows—their placement, sizes, and shapes. Windows are less standardized than doors. Consequently, the interior designer is likely to find many variations in window type and configuration.

The basic window types are double-hung, sliding, casement, awning, and glass jalousie (see Figure 9). They are available in a variety of designs, depending on the manufacturer. Double-hung windows of the most ordinary type are readily available in several wood or metal models. These will be available with single panes of glass, 6-over-6 or 4-over-4 panes. Similarly, casement windows are made in several types, as are sliding, awning, and jalousie designs.

8. Doors

A. The size of this Renaissance doorway implies that what or who is inside its portals has some degree of importance. Arriving or leaving through such a door becomes no small event.

B. The Modern standardized door, on the other hand, has few distinguishing characteristics aside from the fact that it is quite flat, light in weight, and cheap. Nevertheless, these doors must receive every design consideration when they are a given component of an interior.

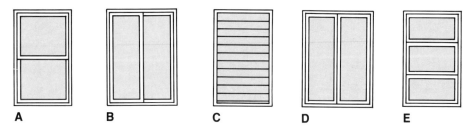

A   B   C   D   E

9. Window Types

Like doors, windows have become standardized. These are the most basic window types, but variations are extensive. It must be remembered that when a change in the window is permissible, both the interior and the exterior scale may be affected.

A. Double-hung   **C.** Jalousie   **E.** Awning

B. Sliding   **D.** Casement

For many centuries windows have been modified punctures through the wall. Early glazed windows were fixed in position before methods were devised for making them movable. The technology of the twentieth century that gives us ventilation and air-conditioning from mechanical means also allows windows to be either fixed or movable. The mechanical devices, as well as the manufacture of sheet glass, brought the possibility of the all-glass wall into prominence. Now the window of past times could change from a hole-in-the-wall to being the wall itself. Not only did this new window wall introduce more daylight into interiors than ever before, it also had a profound effect on interior planning and furniture placement. At this time the indoor-outdoor connections first conceived in the design for the Hall of Mirrors at Versailles came to fruition. The maximization of glass use as a way of making windows now gives a designer the full range of size in designing. With this flexibility, however, come several problems that should be considered.

An assessment of windows in an existing interior must include aesthetic and functional questions. If new windows are to be designed, the following questions should be reviewed:

1. Will the new windows improve both exterior and interior aesthetics regarding proportions, size, shape, and material?

2. Do the new windows and their positions permit better interior planning?

3. If the windows are used in linear sequence, is there a need for a section of wall between each window?

4. What is the proper height for the windowsill?

5. How does the height of the sill relate to the needs of the possible furniture plan?

6. Does the new window design solve problems or create new ones?

7. Does the new window design create better overall organization?

Window design can be changed to suit a design concept only if the client owns the property. In rental apartments or offices, changing windows is usually impossible. In some rental properties designers have been permitted to change the glazing within window frames—single panes for multiple panes—for a more modern appearance. This had led some critics to observe that in some buildings, so much new glass has been introduced that the entire scale of the building has been altered.

Although windows need to relate to all components in an interior, especially architectural ones, it is most important that windows have an aesthetic relationship with doors. Whether or not that relationship is satisfactory, the heights of the doors and windows still have a relationship. Also, the segments of wall between doors and windows may be awkward areas in some spaces, particularly if they are small ones. If a furniture component is placed there, the furniture, the door, and the window as well may become cramped.

The treatment of windows with shades, curtains, blinds, and so forth (discussed later in this chapter) suggests a range of possibilities and problems. The untreated window, a possibility when privacy is not a problem, presents the notion of an aesthetic advantage to be considered when appropriate: Untreated windows become black mirrors at night. These can reflect images of light and shape, just as true mirrors can. If such an effect is supportive in an interior, the planning of the space should consider how best to manipulate components that bear being doubled as reflected images.

Fireplaces

Although in most contemporary buildings fireplaces serve no essential functional purposes, they are valued as interior components in almost every type of space. In urban centers fireplaces in apartments and offices are considered luxurious; in country retreats they are thought of as elegantly rustic. Fireplaces waste heat, create continuing expense, take up space, and are used somewhat less than one percent of the time during cold weather. In spite of these drawbacks fireplaces are important to people, and they are important to interior design.

Any space with a fireplace has an anchor in the position of that component. In most rooms a fireplace will be located in the center of a wall, perhaps the longest wall in the space. This physical center will also be the natural focus of the space. It is best for a designer to recognize this focus and support it conceptually. Even small, awkwardly placed fireplaces draw attention and require full consideration from a designer.

Several types of fireplaces are common in interiors (see Figure 10):

1. Projecting. The breast of the fireplace projects into the room from a surrounding wall.

2. Flush-face. The breast lies in the same plane as the surrounding wall. It usually has no mantel shelf.

3. Hooded. Projecting or flush type with no mantel shelf.

4. Corner. Sometimes the corner is filled in with masonry; sometimes the firebox hearth and hood are separate.

5. Freestanding. Not incorporated into a wall, open all around, flue hangs directly over firebox.

In many fireplace installations the functional parts (such as the flue and damper) are covered with a structure called a chimneypiece. A chimneypiece has no relation to the way a fireplace functions; it is a conventional, decorative part that surrounds the opening. It can be designed of several materials—wood, marble, granite, metal—that harmonize with other architectural features in a space. Unlike other parts of a fireplace, the chimneypiece can be removed without affecting function. The chimneypiece acts as a transition between fireplace and wall. Like furniture, these pieces can be purchased or designed.

10. Fireplace Types

Although the types of fireplaces are few in number, their design composition is limitless in its variety. All fireplace designs should consider the scale, proportions, and material of the interiors they help to complete. A fireplace design may contrast or repeat the design of other components of an interior.

A. Flushface

B. Projecting

C. Chimneypiece

D. Hooded

E. Freestanding

F. Corner

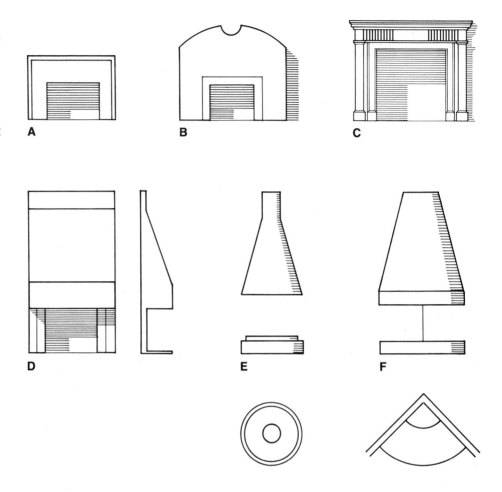

A   B   C

D   E   F

Closets

A closet is not considered to be part of the elements of architecture—the wall, floor, ceiling, columns, door, and window, as well as stair and fireplace. However, since a closet is usually a part of a spatial envelope and a necessity in most interiors, it is worthy of consideration along with the more elemental parts.

Clothing, all types of equipment, box storage, cleaning material, maintenance machines, tools, and various kinds of goods and property must be stored within the confines of closets. Without closets such storage has to be accommodated in movable furniture components.

In almost all interiors, until well into the nineteenth century, closet-type storage was accomplished in movable furniture. The cupboard, armoire, cabinet, chifforobe, chiffonier, chest of drawers, and so forth, were designed to house the necessities of daily life and work. Later in the century, as aspects of modern living emerged, closets were introduced in new interior plans and into existing interiors. Often in the existing room the newly added closet bit out a corner at the juncture of adjacent walls, making a different room shape, and frequently creating an awkward new shape, even when two were paired in opposite corners. Still later, all interiors (at least all that were planned well) included built-in closets designed to be functional and aesthetic at once.

Existing Closets In many plans of existing interiors the closets should remain in place when their size and location fit within a new design concept. These closets may only need new insides. New parts can refurbish a closet easily. Resurfaced walls, lighting (when necessary), improved clothes poles, and new built-in shelving in both domestic and nondomestic spaces are some of the usual parts to be improved or added. Stored items must be as convenient as possible, within limitations.

Existing closet doors often need to be repaired, rehung, or replaced, since old doors may be damaged. Some may have warped or sagged over time. The outer face of a closet door is a visible component in an interior and is important in a design scheme.

New Closets   Some existing interiors have closets that must be removed. When a design scheme will not be possible if existing closets remain, it is generally all right to remove them. Their structure rarely bears on the structural integrity of a building, and therefore makes demolition feasible and relatively minor in most situations.

Interiors with no closets must have them added—and this must be done in the conceptual stage of design. Closet storage is too important in size and function to be left to secondary thinking in a scheme. No interior can work to its best advantage without at least one closet—if not within a space, then adjacent to it.

Closets can be suppressed into the architectural framework of an interior. They can become cavity walls and used to define large, open spaces, or built as new faces against old walls. The face of new closets may be designed entirely as doors in series butted together side by side, their height extending from floor to ceiling to make a plain, seamed wall of doors. Also, doors can be designed as single or multiple components that are cut into walls. Freestanding closets should be considered in some interiors. However, because of their size, their first relationship is still to the architecture, not the furniture.

Closets that occur in private dressing or changing rooms may be designed without doors. Here, the space above and below the clothes poles can be organized as open or closed storage to house specific items. Open closets in such rooms offer easy accessibility for the user; but if they are not kept in good order, they can quickly become unsightly.

All exposed hardware—doorknobs, exposed hinges, hooks, racks, and so forth—and all hidden hardware, both outside and inside, is part of the design of closets. Whatever makes a closet function best must also have the desired aesthetic. The two should be considered together.

Fixed Furniture Components

In any interior environment, those components of furniture that become fixed are second in importance only to architectural components. Fixed furniture falls into two categories: (1) fixed in place—that is, attached to the architectural envelope; and (2) components that, by reason of their size, cannot be accommodated in other position-relationships within a space, or whose moving or repositioning requires major upheaval.

Fixed-in-place furniture components should be considered as an extension of the architecture; they may almost *be* architecture when their size, scale, or importance in the concept has been developed as part of a major theme. However, size is not the determining factor when making the decision to fix a component. The principal reason should be an unshakable means with which to organize rooms or spaces.

Sometimes, fixed furniture should be conceived in the same or similar color and material as the surrounding architecture; sometimes the components need to contrast in the extreme. The same degree of consideration is required in either situation. Aesthetic and functional requirements must also be met, and shape and material are paramount.

Seating

Fixed-in-place seating has a history much older than the Modern movement. When chairs or benches were made of stone, there was obviously little possibility of moving them. In later times, even when the piece of furniture was small in size and weight, it might be attached to a wall, as were the delicate seating banquettes used in some Greek Revival rooms.

However, fixed seating is a predominant part of Modern interiors. Not only does fixed seating have the potential to extend and strengthen the existing architecture but, perhaps surprisingly, it may be more economical than seating specified from a manufacturer. Manufactured seating is almost completely size-standard and offers a limited variety in form as well, except for certain variations in detail and upholstery. It is possible to incorporate mass-produced seating into a fixed-in-place framework; however, this is the long way round. The selection of furniture first, without doubt, hampers conceptual thinking.

Lounge or sofa seating, the standard centerpiece of most domestic living rooms, is always conceived of (with the possible exception of a very few Modern pieces) as a base with legs supporting a structural framework to hold seat upholstery (see Figure 11). The upholstery incorporates a backrest and armrests. Although the latter two parts are not always present, the fundamental form of a sofa is quite easily designed. The very quantity of upholstery makes this piece of furniture easier to conceive and to design than the chair form.

It should go without saying that seat depth and height are the critical dimensions for lounge seating. Incorrect seat height and depth makes for two poor conditions for comfort: (1) If the seat is too high and shallow, the user is forced to sit bolt upright, losing the main characteristic of a lounge piece. (2) If the seat is too low and too deep, the user is strained for a leg thrust to comfortably lower or rise with ease.

In the latter condition, while sitting, the user is in either one of two awkward positions: feet and legs thrust forward and fully extended; or legs drawn in, knees pushing up above the waist and chest height. Either of these positions is less than comfortable and, to be sure, will subtract from physical grace when used. This discussion, however, is not to be taken as an effort to limit certain experimentation with sizes in seating components. Some spaces may in fact be best with seating dimensions that are in the too short and high or too deep and low category. Seating in rooms for special purposes may well demand that human dimensions be con-

11. Fixed Seating
The essential parts of a fixed-in-place sofa are: a base, a back, and appropriate upholstery. Seat height and depth are critical issues for comfort, but length and overall height may be any dimension that suits a design concept.

A. Top view

B. Front view

C. Side view

A

B

C

stricted or stretched, to create an atmosphere different in character from more usual spaces.

Fixed seating is often conceived as a part or extension of walls, the wall plane serving both as wall and as support for the backrest. At other times the sofa type of seating is designed to give separation in a space. In either case this component should be seen as architecture and conceived in relation to the existing architectural envelope. The other furniture components, those that are movable, become almost incidental to spatial organization.

Another quality of fixed-in-place seating is its lack of detail. In the planar interiors of Modernists, fixed-in-place components must have the same degree of weight or monumentality as the architecture to make the correct fit or extension from what exists in the original elements of the room or space. Too much detail and articulation in these components would lessen their planar form. In most instances the fixed-in-place components have a slab-like character, just as plain wall slabs have. All aspects of linearity are expunged whenever possible. The structural elements of these pieces are slab-like, as are the upholstered parts, which are thickly padded and usually have little or no texture in the fabric covering.

A critical issue in the design of fixed-in-place seating is its relation to the floor plane. Unless the base of the component touches the floor, the component will separate from it. This is also true of large chairs, such as club chairs. When their bases sit directly on the floor plane, they lock into place visually and retain their apparent weight. But even the smallest reveal at the base will cause them to separate and lighten.

Horizontal Furniture Surfaces: Tables, Counters, Ledges, and Shelves

After fixed-in-place seating, horizontal surfaces offer the next most important interior design component. "Tables," as Florence Knoll has said in her effort to reduce that component to its most basic characteristic—function—"are to put things on."

Open shelves, ledges, counters, and work tops are the other components that make up the vocabulary of usable horizontal surfaces that are used to "put things on." These components are essential in almost every interior, domestic or otherwise. Each of them, by its nature, will be fixed in place (or appear to be fixed in place). Ledges and shelves are always fixed in place because they depend on vertical surfaces for support. (Even movable shelves are considered fixed within the limits of vertical adjustment ranges and have only a limited adjustability.) (See Figure 12.)

Tables   Tables have only one critical dimension—height. The height of a table is determined by its purpose. A table for dining is one height, a table for writing another, for coffee yet another height. Conference or kitchen work tables, desks, and drafting tables require other height adjustments in relation to specific use.

The size of tabletops is not subject to any rule of dimension. A table to hold a lamp may be a minimum size just large enough to hold its lamp, or it may be as large as a space permits and be accommodating to other objects as well. In all periods of history tables have been made large and imposing, immovable and monumental, as well as tiny conceptions of the most diminutive scale. Marble tables occupied Roman rooms and held the floor plane down, so to speak, with a weight of stone. Robert Adam conceived little console tables of the most delicate scale and proportions, and attached them to the walls in many of his eighteenth-century rooms.

The most common mistake in determining table height is not relating it to the height of the chair seats. For example, it is more comfortable when eating to have the tabletop at a height that allows the forearm to be parallel to it. Most

12. Fixed Horizontal Furniture Surfaces

These components relate structurally and aesthetically to either vertical or horizontal architectural components, or to both. In one sense, they are parts of architecture.

A. Fixed table surfaces. The top is supported on a base, or pedestal. This is attached to a base plate that is fixed to the floor, or countersunk into it. The plate is concealed under the flooring material. Larger tables may need larger or multiple pedestals.

B. Counter surfaces. Counters may be parallel to a wall (sometimes designed as alcoves); perpendicular to a wall (sometimes called peninsula types); and free of walls on all sides (the island type).

C. Shelves. One thick shelf slab can organize a wall in a significant way, or multiple shelves can create a new forward face on a wall.

D. Ledge surfaces. A ledge may be enclosed beneath the surface. This suggests that the wall has been folded out into a surface, with a forward plane below. A ledge that runs the full length of a wall divides it into three distinct parts. A ledge that is shorter than a wall will gain importance from the surrounding plane of the wall.

A

B

C

D

tabletops are too high to allow this relationship; the user is made to feel that he or she is sitting in a slight depression, and the forearm is made to thrust upward at the table edge. It is important to understand that the chair seat can be of several heights; it is the table that can be adjusted up or down. Chair forms, the classic problem for all designers for all time, cannot be adjusted (except where the chair is made to do so as part of its design).

Fixed-in-place tables in residences are not as usual as fixed seating. Nonetheless, there are times and reasons for fixing tables, just as there are for seating. First, again, is the potential for tightly controlled organization when tables cannot be moved around. Second, there is the reduction of furniture legs and feet touching the floor. Fixed-in-place tables can be supported on one central, columnar base: The stabilization can be accomplished with a concealed plate hidden under carpet, tile, or wood floor.

Materials for Tables   The most common, the most useful, and some say the most appropriate material for tables is wood. Tables have been made from all manner of materials: stone—marble, granite, onyx, and alabaster; metal—iron, steel, aluminum, brass, and copper; glass and plastic—molded, bent, plain, and decorated; and such humble stuff as paper and cardboard as well as endless combinations of these materials. But wood, since ancient time, has been used more consistently, with more imagination, and with greater simplicity. While the French kings ate from tables of lacquered, ormolu-adorned wood, French peasants put planks of scrubbed wood on top of wooden barrels to have their meager diets.

It is not only the plentitude of wood that has made it the material of choice throughout the centuries. Wood offers several other qualities, inherent in its character, that make it especially desirable for tables. Wood is easily worked, it is available in many patterns and colors, it can be milled and finished in a variety of ways, and it has the unmistakable asset of being pleasant to the touch. With use, even very hard use, it ages well.

Tables can be made of any appropriate material, and some of the most beautiful tables ever designed have no wood in them at all: The material must suit the use. Inappropriate material for a tabletop results in unusual problems. Stone tops are beautiful, without doubt; but in a cool room, they become funereal to the touch of the hand, arm, or elbow. Transparent dining tables have a most unpleasant and disconcerting aspect: They show all the legs and feet, clothing and whatever, underneath. Metal is also cold and has its own special problem—any light in a room will be reflected back from its surface, into the user's eye. A prominent, internationally known and lauded designer made his own beautiful desk from a dull-finished metal, only to find it completely unsuitable for work. One restaurant in New York City has glass tops without cloths on all its tables. Between courses, the customers are treated to the slight dampness and the smell of glass cleaner when the waiters clear up the crumbs and the spills.

When Florence Knoll made her assessment of tables, she did not limit them to the merely utilitarian. For tables can also be objects of beauty in themselves, holding much or nothing at all, left bare—and standing ready to hold what is needed, from a demitasse to an assortment of briefcases, mail, books, handbags, and the transient things of everyday life. Tables may also hold treasures: A table may be loaded with precious objects or display goods for sale, or serve as a surface for sculpture or plants.

Counters   A counter is a plane that may be freestanding within a space, available for use from both sides, or attached to both wall and floor. The top of a counter may be of a material and color in contrast with its base (if there is a base) or the floor and wall plane, or it may be made in a material and color that continues the color and material of the parts of the space. Invariably, countertops must be of a material that is maintainable, but this should not limit the possible range of material that is considered for use.

Counters are invariably a component of domestic interiors, particularly in kitchens, but are useful in other rooms as well. Nonresidential interiors, such as stores, offices, banks, hospitals, and schools, also have counters of one kind or another. Many counters have storage components underneath, but this is not a requirement. The prerequisite for counters is the ability to use the top as a surface.

When a storage component is part of a counter, bulk is added, both physically and visually. This should be given considerable attention.

The storage part of counters—usually called under-counter storage—may be composed of open shelving, closed cabinets, bins, and so forth. These can make up a most useful part of this component. Again, the material and color may be in contrast to what surrounds the counter, or may continue the material that is established by the architectural elements near it.

When counters are attached to wall planes, they may be seen as extensions of the wall, as fixed-in-place architectural furniture components. When freestanding, they are furniture-like as well, but must also be related to the architectural volume. In either instance, height and depth must suit task-performance and accommodate the necessities of storage and user convenience.

Ledges   A ledge is a horizontal surface, a projecting ridge, or raised edge along a vertical plane. In architecture and interiors, as in nature, the ledge is inseparable from the vertical plane.

Ledges in interiors project from the plane of a wall. They are usually designed to read as a projection from or outcropping of the wall, are supported by the wall, and cannot exist without the wall. Even the narrowest ledge makes a strong line of horizontal weight when seen against the wall plane.

When a ledge travels across the face of a wall, no matter what its height or depth, the proportions of the wall are changed. If the ledge-outcropping is extremely thin, it will be read as a line that divides the wall into two parts; if the ledge is a thick one, its face may be read as a forward plane, making the wall into three parts. If the ledge depth cuts back under to the lower wall part, a deep shadow will occur under it. If the face of the ledge continues downward to the floor, the lower wall plane will be thickened, or a cutback of any selected dimension may be desirable when the necessities of construction or the consideration of aesthetics is a major issue.

Materials for Ledge Surfaces   Maintenance is a concern in the decision to include a ledge surface in conjunction with a wall plane. Since the ledge, by its nature, is part of the wall, it is usual to make it of the same material as the wall. This creates a problem in the maintenance on the surface of the ledge and at the connection or seam of the ledge and wall plane. Very quickly, the horizontal corner will darken from soil and cleaning residue. This is true no matter what material is used; but it is more pronounced when the material is of a light value, particularly if the wall and ledge have a painted finish.

Sometimes the maintenance problem can be solved by placing a removable, separate top on the ledge, if that is appropriate to the overall materials concept. For example, a sheetrock wall and ledge might have a ledge top of wood, marble, or glass, for emphasis, to separate it from the wall plane and to improve its maintainability.

When the ledge top changes material or color, or is different in finish from the wall plane, the top is emphasized as the most important part of the elevation and the horizontal line takes over no matter how high the wall plane is. Therefore the length of the wall is emphasized, but it is secondary to the ledge because the ledge is always in front of the wall plane.

A ledge that is the same length as a wall will emphasize the wall's length; a ledge that is shorter than a wall will put emphasis on the ledge, as will a ledge finished in a contrasting material or color. A ledge finished in the same material, color, and texture as its wall will put emphasis on any object placed on the ledge.

It would not be inappropriate to include ledges in a list of architectural components, because all ledges are dependent on the wall. However, because the primary purpose of a ledge is to serve as a surface, it is grouped with other furniture components.

Shelves   There is a slight, but noticeable difference between ledges and shelves. Whereas all ledges are an inseparable part of a wall plane, shelves are usually attached, or fastened to it. However, they can also be designed as an integral part. Shelves can be used singly or in vast numbers so that, in fact, they become an existing wall's face.

Since all shelves are designed to hold something, their construction as sturdy components is mandatory. The best shelves are designed to hold specific things, but this is not always possible. For this reason many shelves are designed to be adjustable. Although this is a functional aid, it is often the reason that shelf design is unsatisfactory.

Shelf size can be determined exactly when designed for specific use. Books, for example, are produced in a number of sizes; therefore bookshelves should be measured by book size. If diverse objects or collections are to be stored or displayed on open shelves, some optimum dimension must be found. In all cases depth and height will be set by use. Shelf thickness, the thin face of the shelf, is determined in another way.

Almost without exception the face of the shelf, its thickness, will be an aesthetic decision. For example, one thick slab of a shelf can visually hold down a huge expanse of wall; or an entire wall of relatively thin shelves can make a strong forward face for a wall.

It should be remembered that the horizontal line of all shelves gives a horizontal direction to a wall and to a space or room. If horizontality is not desirable within an interior, shelves should not be used, or they must be covered with doors, panels, shades, or placed out of sight so that they do not become dominant.

Materials for Shelves   Shelving material, always a functional-aesthetic problem, can range from the most ordinary to the most elegant. Shelving material must be appropriate to the architectural components and sympathetic to what is shelved. Leatherbound volumes may be appropriately housed on marble shelves, paperback books may not be. Shelves covered in chamois or silk may be the perfect solution to display a collection of delicate objects, but those materials would be wrong for pots and pans.

The construction of all shelves, aside from the purely structural necessities, can be seen as a study in the problems of proportion as well as the art of display.

The size of the shelves is determined by their use; the proportion must be determined by other architectural components in an interior, and in consideration of what is placed or housed on their surfaces. The arrangement of shelved things, then, becomes of equal importance to the housing. Because shelves are usually in series, many things are placed on them; many books, many objects, many utensils. The sheer number of things makes them, their arrangement, and their organization significant.

The things that are housed on shelves need special organization to keep them from becoming messy or too dominant. No matter what is on the shelf, it is the face of the shelf that has the most power in an interior. The exception to this is when shelves are completely held on three sides and especially lighted to pull forward the back plane or to push forward the housed objects. In this situation the face of shelves must be considered as secondary and the other parts of the component—back, sides, things—become dominant.

Because shelves are used continually, they require maintenance on a regular basis. It is well to keep this in mind when designing them as a major component. Shelves in storage rooms are much less a problem. Storage shelves in storage rooms are usually organized in purely functional ways: depth, height, and strength of construction being the primary considerations.

13. Fixed Storage

Although these components are usually seen as movable furniture, they can be fixed in the architectural framework of an interior. The visual importance of such components in a design scheme can be suppressed or can be made to appear more dominant.

A. Cabinet

B. Cupboard

C. Chest

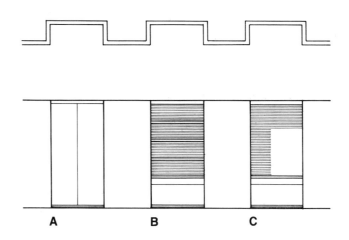

A   B   C

Storage

In any interior, storage is a major design problem. Small amounts of storage may be accommodated in such furniture as desks, tables, and accessory pieces; but this discussion is centered on components that are for housing quantities of goods, supplies, and personal or business effects. Fixed-in-place furniture for storage may include cabinets, chests (equipped with drawers or doors), and cupboards (see Figure 13).

Cabinets   Although cabinets are usually thought to be cases or boxes with doors, cabinets may also hold drawers. The American furniture industry is predicated on the making of boxes, and a great variety of them are available for purchase. However, as with other manufactured furniture, case pieces fall within a narrow range of sizes—usually determined by the standard dimensions of the American living room or bedroom and by the problems of shipping; the variety comes in the finish and the detailing of the case. Consequently, built-in case pieces can serve interior designers in a special way when solving storage problems.

Chests   The most usual chest contains drawers, as with the chest of drawers. Chests may also have shelves, open or concealed behind doors or panels. Built-in chests usually become part of a wall plane or a wall recess. They can be detailed to read in the same plane as the wall, or they may be finished in sharp contrast to it. When existing conditions permit, chests may be completely submerged into the architectural components. When suitable to a design concept, chests may become like thickened wall peninsulas of whatever height and depth is appropriate in a space. Drawer or shelf depth and height should be designed to fit use, with standard sizes of clothing, paper, or utensils acting as the guide.

Cupboards   Cupboards may be walked into or not, but they are somewhat different from cabinets or chests because they are more usual as built-in components. Recessed and corner cupboards have long been a part of many period interiors. They serve for storage as well as display, part being open to view, part closed. Cabinets are always closed completely; cupboards may be open or closed, or a combination of open and closed compartments.

Materials for Storage Components   Built-in storage components are constructed like architectural components, as opposed to cabinetwork, which connotes more refinement, greater finish. Wood, sheetrock, and several types of wood composition board are common materials. Finishes include paint, wood veneer or solid wood, plastic laminates, and novelty materials such as paper, fabric, or metal.

Interior finishes of storage components—the drawers or shelves—are usually painted wood or left natural, or covered in a plastic laminate. Drawers and shelves may be lined with paper or fabric when appropriate; and shelves may be made of glass or marble, or laminate over wood or wood composition board.

Sometimes it is necessary to give the interior of storage components a high degree of finish, especially when doors are a major part of the piece, or when doors are apt to be left open, thus becoming a part of the visual experience of the room or space.

Sleeping

Components for sleeping usually make up the single largest bulk of any fixed furniture piece in domestic interiors. For this reason beds form another particular problem for the designer. The design of a bed does not begin with its covering or bedspread.

In historical rooms beds were really small rooms in themselves; the French *lit clos*, or closed bed, was a recess in a wall usually closed with curtains or wood doors. During centuries of poor heating in Europe and America beds were enclosed in layers of drapery, complete with many hangings (this ensemble was sometimes called "bed furniture") to shut out cold drafts and make comfortable sleeping possible. Today this kind of "decorated" bed is used as the centerpiece of bedrooms, and fine ones are magnificent objects in themselves. For Modern interiors modern beds are not usually physically fixed, but their bulk makes them effectively so. The problems of how to stay warm have been dealt with. Dealing with bed bulk has become the important consideration.

Like sofas, beds are the simplest kind of construction (see Figure 14): a base—with or without spring construction—and a mattress, which is made of various

A　　　　　　　　**B**

C　　　　　**D**

14. Beds: Fixed and Movable

A. Older or antique bed designs have unusual proportions because of higher frames and mattresses. These parts were intended to lift the sleeper up, away from drafts.

B. A bed design can be extremely light and thin in construction. Foam material for mattresses makes springs unnecessary.

C. A bed with a boxed frame makes a solid component. The frame can be visually submerged with the floor plane by finishing the two parts in the same material and color.

D. When a mattress rests on a platform, it becomes fixed with the architecture on a raised floor plane. A platform for sleeping should extend in one or more directions around the mattress.

materials in several thicknesses. Some beds have legs, others have a boxed base. A most Modern bed is one composed of a mattress resting on a platform base connecting its bulk to the architectural components and reducing its furniture-like character. Some platform beds include a storage component in their design to house bedclothes and, occasionally, seldom-used clothing or paraphernalia.

Beds can be turned into seating components with the addition of back cushions. They can be converted into lounge-like pieces with backrests and cushions that are removable. This kind of design is often necessary in small residences so that the sleeping room can also be used as a living room.

As to bed coverings—the spread—several approaches may be considered. When a bedroom is used only for sleeping, it is sometimes unnecessary to use a traditional bedspread. Many designers prefer to design the bed to be covered only in appropriate sheets and blankets or comforters as part of the overall scheme of the room. Luxurious effects can be achieved in this way. Others always choose to make the bed with some type of covering—unusual quilts; handmade blanket spreads; specially designed covering in appropriate fabrics from lace to rough wools; with leather; or in uncontrasting plain fabrics that will diminish the bulk of the bed by not causing the eye to stop to look long at its surface. Commercially available bedspreads are not usually special enough to do anything but hide the sheets and blankets.

Bed covers in domestic situations warrant special design solutions. In hotels and motels bed construction and bed coverings are crucial. The commercial bedroom has become almost nothing but a room filled with beds. Two double beds, queen-sized, king-sized, both often in pairs, fill up most of these rooms. Because they are sat on, played on, jumped on, and slept in, bed construction must be of the most durable quality. Here bed height must be standard—not lower, even though lower bed height reduces bulk—because the height facilitates daily changing of the sheets. Bed coverings in these rooms need to have as much character as the designer can summon, as well as high durability.

Raised beds such as double-decked or loft types have limited use and must be carefully considered when made the central part of sleeping-room concepts. Their higher-than-usual character makes for a certain flexibility of design, but also reduces the ease of maintenance. Lowered or sunken beds have similar good and bad characteristics.

Movable Furniture Components

Although movable furniture comes in an endless variety of shapes and sizes, the basic forms of this component group are few: beds, chairs, sofas and other lounge pieces; tables; and case pieces comprise the group in its entirety. American, European, and Asian manufacturers create an endless supply of these basic furniture forms in a spectrum of materials, most of it poorly designed and constructed, highly fashionable, and transient in shape—and therefore lacking in true style. For that, we must turn to the contract market of the closed showroom—open to designers, architects, and their clients, and closed to the general public.

In the closed furniture showroom, the best of what is available is displayed. Whether it is new furniture or reproduced from historical models, the quality is, without exception, better than that sold at retail; it has consistent, superior design and construction.

Antique furniture is also an important part of interior design. There are open showrooms and closed showrooms in this vast market. Good pieces are available at retail, but the unique or important pieces of antique furniture still must be found in the to-the-trade, closed-to-the-public stores. Auction galleries are also important sources for all manner of antiquities.

Chairs

In the whole lexicon of furniture, from earliest history to today, the chair occupies a unique position apart from any other furniture form. It is the connotative quality of the chair form that gives it its potency and power to evoke feeling from us; to relate it to ritual, past experience; and to power, love, and safety.

The earliest form of true furniture was the chest, according to the French historian Fernand Braudel. He said that its importance lay in its storage capacity and its portability. The first chairs were small chests with a back added, sometimes with arms. These were reserved for use by important personages; all others had to make do with chests as stools. Even early cupboards were chests with legs added. But the chair took on an immediate presence when used by the privileged, the wealthy, and the royal. The throne chair, the liturgical chair, father's and mother's chairs, host and hostess chairs, the nursery rocking chair, ladies' and gentlemen's chairs, university chairs, all contribute to the connotative quality of this component, whether it is complex or simple in design, humble or exalted in origin (see Figure 15).

In most design schools a chair problem is given as a major project. The investigation of chair form-making is always considered difficult to conceive, particularly when a degree of original design is set as a criterion.

Lounge Chairs With the exception of chairs intended for royal or ritualistic purposes, the low or lounge chair has most occupied the thinking of Modern architects and designers, as well as those from historical periods who have designed such chairs. Students should understand that lounge chairs—indeed all chairs— can be the single most important pieces of movable furniture in any space, domestic or otherwise.

It is probable that the lounge chair was invented in France during the late seventeenth century, when the royal court began to include more informal social arrangements. When comfort became important (Sherill Whiton says that "Rococo furniture was designed to fit human dimensions and not intended for pomp and pageantry"), lounge chairs were conceived to give it. Whiton also says that the French cabinetmakers of the period developed so many new types of furniture that "they left few possibilities to their successors."[7]

The bergere, or closed armchair, and the chaise longue are French lounge chairs. The fauteuil, or open armchair, is also comfortable enough to be considered in this category. All other countries followed the French designers in their efforts to create comfortable seating, some with high levels of success through many years of development. In the early twentieth century both European and American architects designed chairs to be made in factories. Many of these important early-twentieth-century chairs are still made today, and with improved methods that allow for fewer hand operations and more perfect finish.

It should be noted that chairs designed by craftsmen and architects are almost always highly articulated, like the buildings that they or others of their time were designing. The large lumps of upholstery that laymen usually think of as lounge chairs bear little resemblance to these masterworks. Their purity of expression and exquisite use of materials rival the chairs of any earlier century.

Chaises Longues The chaise longue—literally, long chair (not lounge chair)— is another eighteenth-century French invention. The chaise longue was first designed for use in the new and smaller boudoirs used by ladies of the court of Louis XV. The ladies received their friends and admirers seated *en déshabillé* on their *chaises*

---

[7]Sherill Whiton, *Interior Design and Decoration* (New York: J. P. Lippincott, 1974).

15. Movable Seating Types

Chairs, like storage furniture, developed from the portable chest. The chest made a seat when the lid was shut; with a cushion it was more comfortable. When a backrest and later arms were added, the chair form emerged. Raised up from the floor, a chest became a cupboard or a cabinet.

A.   Lounge chair: front view, side view

B.   Chaise longue: side view

C.   Side chair: front view, side view

D.   Armchair or pull-up chair: front view, side view

E.   Posture chair, adjustable: front view, side view

F.   Small lounge chair: front view, side view

G.   Bench: top view, front view

H.   Stool: top view, front view

I.   Sofa: front view, side view

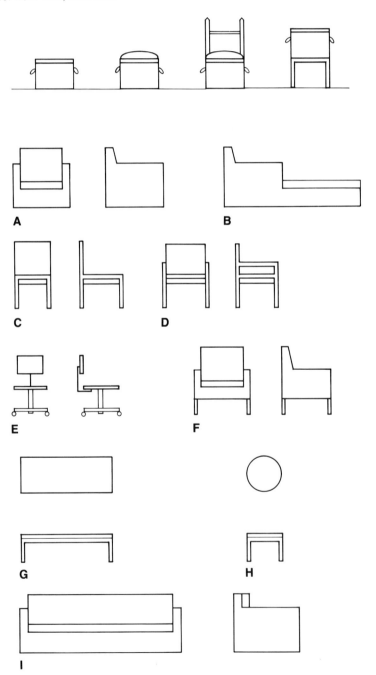

longues while perfuming, applying rouge, or placing a beauty spot on their cheek. Today the chaise longue is used in the bedroom for somewhat less elegant activity— simple rest.

The chaise longue is, perhaps, the most restful of all chairs. Though intended for boudoirs and bedrooms, some designers include them in other rooms as well, because they occupy the same amount of floor space as a lounge chair with a footstool. Most chaises are fully upholstered, but some are all wood or have a wood frame with caning on the seat and back. Most have arms, but some are armless. The contemporary poolside chaise, made of metal, wood, or plastic, developed from this eighteenth-century idea.

Miscellaneous Chairs   Several types of chairs fit into this group. They are often used interchangeably, and almost every interior will need some of them.

Side Chairs   The side chair has no arms. This is its principal difference from an identical type of chair that has arms. Side chairs are usually light in weight, easily moved, and useful in numerous interiors such as offices, dining rooms, living spaces, and conference rooms. They may be fully upholstered, but will have exposed legs; some only have a hard upholstered seat with wood or metal construction.

Armchairs   The armchair is a side chair with arms. Armchairs are not the same as lounge chairs, because the seat is usually too high for more comfortable sitting (although the arms make it somewhat more comfortable over time). This chair is often used at residential desks, for dining, or in entryways. In offices and commercial projects it is a usual choice; not too comfortable, but better than a side chair.

Pull-up Chairs   Most offices need pull-up chairs. They have this title because they are literally pulled up to desks on the opposite side from the office's occupant. In general, pull-up chairs should offer more comfort than side chairs; a soft or saddle seat, and shaped or upholstered arms and back help with this criterion. Pull-up chairs must be easily movable so that minor position adjustments can be made by the user during meetings in offices.

Conference Chairs   For conference rooms, chairs should give both comfort and body position flexibility. They can be somewhat heavier than pull-up chairs, because the tendency at conferences is not to move chairs around to any great extent. Many designers prefer to use fully upholstered chairs in all conference rooms, but there are some all-wood chairs that have almost the same degree of comfort because of their shaping.

Posture Chairs   These chairs are lifesavers for office workers. Executive and secretarial posture chairs make sitting all day bearable. They give support to the lower back, and almost all of them are adjustable in the back and seat—up, down, forward, and backward. All posture chairs have swivel bases in order to make them serviceable. Secretarial chairs never have arms, because arms interfere with typing. Executive posture chairs almost always have them.

Benches and Stools   Benches and stools, like the earliest chests, are chairs without backs. Some benches do have backs but this seems to be the exception rather than the rule; some also have arms. Stools do not.

Benches   Benches seat two or more people. A main characteristic of benches is the shallowness of the seat; therefore a bench is always longer than it is deep. This furniture component serves well in all rooms, especially narrow halls and corridor-like rooms. Although benches give little real comfort, they make useful short-term places to sit.

Materials for bench construction include wood—a traditional favorite—metal, and plastics. Bench tops may be upholstered with tight seats, with loose pads, or be left unsoftened. When benches have backs and arms, these parts are usually light in character, often made of multiple spindles or splats, and sometimes fully upholstered.

Stools   Stools are intended for one-person use, never more. In ancient times stools seem to have been the favored piece of furniture for sitting. The stools found in the tombs of Egyptian pharaohs were many and magnificently designed. All subsequent historical periods, up to and including the twentieth century, have continued to produce stools in quantity.

Like the early chests that were used as seats, stools are easily the most transportable seating pieces. Some stools, developed from military campaigns, fold for easy storage and movability. Stools offer comfort when well designed, and they have one advantage over chairs—they can be sat on from all four sides.

Footstools are usually lower than stools intended for sitting and they accompany many lounge chairs. Some lounge-chair designs are much more comfortable when used with a footstool. Children like using footstools because they can move them and sit on them with feet well on the floor instead of dangling in midair.

Ottomans, an Eastern form of footstool, are much less leggy than Western designs; indeed, most ottomans have no legs at all. They rest their bottom surfaces on the floor, giving them great stability. Ottomans are usually stuffed with dense cotton or packed animal hair, which makes them quite heavy. Coverings range from leather or carpet, sewn or wrapped, to any desired fabric.

Materials for Chairs   The first chairs or stools, anthropologists say, were stones pulled up in caves around a fire. Stone chairs are still made in this century, but wood has been the preferred material throughout history. Wood—in combination with other materials such as cane, rush, webbing, slings of leather or fabric, and upholstery—is still the most commonly used material. Metal has a long history of use for chair design. Plastic, whether molded into shape or folded from sheets, has frequently been made into expressive chairs, particularly by American and Italian designers today. New chair designs in heavy paper were conceived by product and interior designer Spiros Zakas in the late 1960s; in 1982 architect Frank Gerhy introduced paper chairs into retail stores. Folding chairs developed as part of the equipment used in military campaigns in early centuries. The most famous of these was originally a wood-frame, leather-sling chair. It was popularized in the late 1940s in a metal version with a canvas seat known as the Hardoy, or Butterfly Chair.

The design of chairs—the Modern chair in particular—has often come from a need to solve a seating problem, to extend a design concept in an interior, and the wish to work with an available material. The Barcelona Chair, the Breuer Chair, and the chair designs of Thonet were investigations of these needs. Current design explorations by designers, architects, and manufacturers all share in this continuing design problem.

Sofas

This component must have at least an upholstered seat to be termed a sofa. If no upholstery is included, the component is something else—a bench with arms, a settle with a back—not a sofa.

Many terms are used to describe the sofa component: Chesterfield is an English term used to describe a sofa that is usually tufted and/or buttoned; davenport is an American term used to indicate any type of lounge; a Lawson-type sofa is one that, more often than not, has loose seat cushions and sometimes back cushions as well; a settee is a small sofa; a love seat is a two-person settee (originally a double chair).

All these sofa types developed before our own century, but several more have been added during it. The club sofa, so named because of its use in men's clubs, is a blown-up version of the chesterfield; the sleep-sofa is a twentieth-century solution for small houses and apartments that create the need to sit and sleep in the same room.

Many historical designers had their own sofa designs. Modernist designers and architects, such as Hans Knoll, Charles Eames, and Eero Saarinen, also contributed several. Late seventeenth- and eighteenth-century French designers developed numerous distinctions in sofa designs, including the then new ideas of comfort that could be gained by softly upholstered furniture.

Materials for Sofas   Sofa construction is usually a wood-frame structure, sometimes with innersprings, covered with stuffing or batting. Loose cushions can be filled with various materials, such as foam rubber, plastic foam, feathers, Dacron, or goose down, depending on the degree of softness, resilience, and luxury that is desired. Some sofa frames are made of metal; some of molded, rigid plastic.

Fabrics used to cover sofas are virtually limitless, but maintenance can be problematic on wear points, especially when light-colored. This problem can be reduced with a protective, dirt-resistant impregnation.

Tables

Every interior needs tables or something that serves as a table. No chair in any interior should float in a space without an accompanying table. With a very low chair, even a tray on the floor will provide the idea and place of table as long as extreme arm stretching is not necessary. Movable tables come in an unending supply of sizes and shapes (see Figure 16). Other than those problems of correct and appropriate height that all surfaces must have, it is size and stability that are paramount when designing movable tables for an interior.

Some of the criteria for making decisions on table height have been noted in the discussion on fixed-in-place furniture. With movable tables, those criteria hold.

The size of the table can vary from extremely small to extremely large. It is doubtful that any table can actually be too large if its center can be comfortably reached and if it fits well within the spatial concept of the design. However, many tables are too small for convenient use. Nonetheless, a table intended to hold only one small vase or a coffee cup can be smaller than usual—even a table of 6 inches in diameter can be adequate. Size, as well as height, must suit purpose.

Tables can bring people together or keep them apart. A dining table, for example, can make dinner a warm, friendly event when the number of people fits well with the table size; a table of a much larger size may separate the same number of people, giving a sense of austerity or stiff formality. The same emotional responses arise from conference tables (international political incidents have occurred over the size and shape of conference tables when great powers and heads of state were involved). Because all interiors carry not only visual weight and make connotative impressions, it must be clear to design students that all of the furniture and furnishings carry emotional weight, for good or otherwise. Tables, when used for daily meals, special dinners, or matters pertaining to business and professional life, also

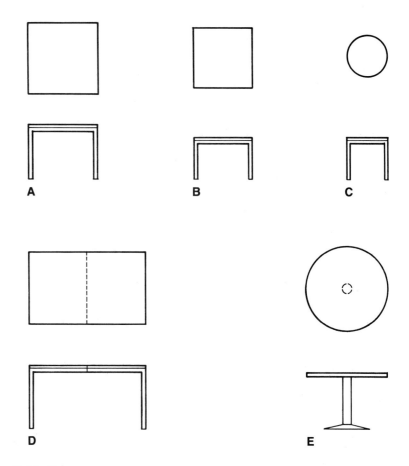

16. Table Types

The types of tables are few, but the variety of their size, shape, and material is limitless. Proportion can distinguish the plainest table design.

A. Dining or conference table: top view, front view

B. Low or coffee table: top view, front view

C. Side or lamp table: top view, front view

D. Extension table: top view, front view

E. Pedestal table: top view, front view

carry an emotional load that the designer of interiors must be aware of and must take into account when design decisions are made.

Materials for Movable Tables   There is little need to go beyond the discussion on materials for fixed-in-place tables, with two exceptions: (1) when the table must be truly movable on a daily basis, and (2) when there is the question of legs versus a center pedestal.

When tables are intended to be moved around—that is, rearranged—it is necessary that they be fairly light in weight and convenient to pick up with one or two hands. This type of table would never be more than 18 inches across the top, and can be much smaller. Often such tables can be improvised from small cubes, drums, or jars that are pressed artfully into service. They are not important items in a design concept, but can be incidental components that make using an interior more comfortable. They add textural material and reduce the scale of more usual table concepts.

Desks   Like other kinds of tables, desks have two important dimensions: height and dimensions of the top. Desk height is determined first by purpose, and second by the height of the desk-chair seat. Nothing is more uncomfortable than working at a desk that is too high or too low in conjunction with chair-seat height. If there is no way to make a satisfactory adjustment, it is better to have a chair seat somewhat on the low side; pads or cushions can make the necessary correction.

Most desks are too small in top dimensions. Consider all of the items that are needed on a desk: file folders; writing paper; an appointment calendar; a dictionary or other books; a briefcase or folio; pencils and pens; a typewriter; adding machine or calculator; good portable lighting; a growing plant or cut flowers; family photographs or other mementos. The list is long. Only a desk used occasionally for writing a personal, brief note can be small and do an adequate job.

In the home where there is no study or workroom, desks can be used as part of other spaces and can serve more than for desk work only. Desks in offices must be designed or specified with greater criteria.

Desks used in offices are of several types, and all of them have noticeable differences (see Figure 17). Reception desks, secretarial desks (usually with a typing runoff), executive desks, desks used for office machines, and other highly specialized desks are a partial list of particular desk needs in offices. Most of these will have drawers of several kinds: pencil drawers, side or pedestal drawers, and sometimes file drawers.

Except in executive offices, desks are more likely to be fixed-in-place, though not necessarily attached to the floor plane. Once a design scheme is settled between the designer and the corporate client, most of the furniture remains in the exact position prescribed in the furniture plan. Executive spaces can sometimes be arranged to allow the desk to be placed in more than one position, but this is not usual.

More often than not, reception desks are designed to impress. Any office reception room will be designed to give a specific impression, and that may range widely according to what image a corporation wishes to project. The reception desk is an important item that can assist the image. Large or modest, this is a special part.

In large secretarial-pool spaces, desks always remain in place; sometimes they are attached to the floor. Floor space is usually at a premium in pool spaces and rearrangement is not feasible unless the entire space is redesigned. Secretarial desks are equipped with drawers and a "modesty screen."

Executives—corporation presidents and vice presidents, board chairs, and junior executives of all kinds—require the proper desk. These desks must serve the work as well as the executive image.

Many top-ranking executives prefer table desks—that is, desks without pedestal drawers, perhaps only pencil drawers built into the apron of the table. Storage for this kind of office is then accommodated in side units or back units (sometimes called credenzas). Such executive storage units may be related to the desk as furniture, or they may be designed in close relationship to the architecture, making them into background pieces. Table desks accommodate pull-up chairs with ease.

Many shapes other than the usual rectangular ones can be designed for executive use. Square-shaped table desks work well when more than three pull-up chairs are needed; round table desks, with one side flattened for the executive's chair position, are more friendly and allow pull-up chairs to be shifted easily. (The leg room needed for pull-up chairs is, in fact, the reason for the preference for table desks, and is a main concern for the designer unless the discussions that take place in an office take place in a lounge or conference area.)

17. Desk Types

The design of desks varies widely with the needs of visual and functional requirements, but there are only a few basic types. When desks must be repeated in an interior, the rectangular ones usually prove to be the more appropriate shape. When required, modesty panels may be added to the front of most desk designs.

A. Table desk, apron pencil drawer: top view, front view

B. Double drawer-pedestal desk: top view, front view; also as single drawer-pedestal with a panel end

C. Center-pedestal desk: top view, front view

D. Secretarial desk, typing extension or runoff: top view, front view; may also be equipped with a drawer-pedestal

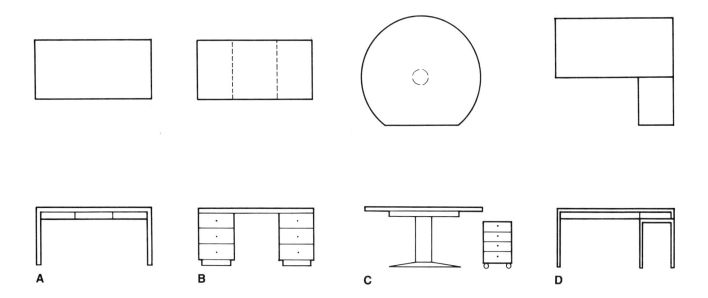

A   B   C   D

Case Pieces

Case pieces are essentially boxes made with some attention to detailing. Not every interior needs them, because other methods of storage are possible; but cases do serve a real purpose in interiors. Types of case pieces are called by names such as china cabinets, buffets, sideboards, credenzas, nightstands, hutches, curio cabinets, and the like (see Figure 18).

The most familiar case piece is the chest with drawers, or chest of drawers. This furniture component is available in many different heights and lengths, with the depth fairly standardized at between 13 and 15 inches, and up to 18 inches in some large-sized ones. Furniture manufacturers who design for the retail market tend to be more standard as to size than contract manufacturers.

18. Case-Piece Types

The evolution of case pieces from the ancient movable chest is apparent. The chest form differs in individual pieces only in size and detail. Each component is equipped with drawers, shelves, or both. The cupboard, now a clothes press or armoire, usually has a hangrod and a dust shelf.

A. Cabinet

B. Chest of drawers

C. Chest-on-chest

D. Cupboard, or armoire

E. Buffet, or sideboard

F. Double chest of drawers

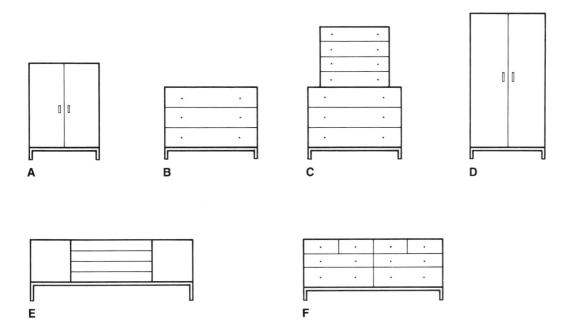

Because all case pieces are made in basically the same way, and a simple way at that, it is often worth considering that this type of storage component be a special design and fit within a concept, be an exact length, perfect height, and in the finish and material that suits the purpose. Also, other solutions for storage can sometimes suit a purpose better than the traditional drawer. Alternatives should be considered when there is any doubt.

Beds

Beds, whether they are individual pieces of furniture or fixed-in-place components, are always in standard sizes. The sizes have been established over time and are based on two sets of dimensions: (1) human dimensions, and (2) the dimensions of sheets and blankets. If the standardized dimensions are not adhered to, the necessary bedclothes will not fit.

The standard sizes of beds are as follows: (1) cot or bunk, 30 by 75 inches; (2) twin, 39 by 75 inches; (3) three-quarter, 48 by 75 inches; (4) double, 54 by 75 inches; (5) queen-size, 60 by 80 inches; (6) king-size, 72 by 80 inches. These sizes may vary slightly in length or width, but the variation does not cause a problematic misfit with bedclothes. Nevertheless, the exact dimensions of a mattress should be selected before the design of a bedroom is finalized.

A bed is composed of three parts: (1) a bedstead, the structural frame; (2) the springs, coiled or flat, which rest on the bedstead; and (3) the mattress resting on the springs. Old or antique beds tend to be high off the floor plane, probably to avoid cold drafts. Modern beds are closer to the floor because drafts are less of a problem. Also, the lower the bed, the less the apparent bulk, as shown in Figure 14.

Movable beds can be designed as large, imposing creations or they can be light and linear. Large bedsteads, those with headboard and footboard, posts, perhaps a canopy or tester, are object-like because of their shape and parts; smaller beds with simple bedsteads or none at all are more easily submerged in the architectural framework of a bedroom.

Beds should be placed so that they are convenient to make up. A bed cramped into a corner, its long side against a wall, is awkward to maintain. If such placement is unavoidable, it is best to have the bed frame on casters for easy bed-making. Also, if beds are too high or too low, all maintenance is difficult at best. It is possible for a designer to create an aesthetically satisfying bedroom that also makes the daily necessities (such as bed-making) less of a problem for the users.

Furnishings

In most professional design practice the components that are not architectural, or that are not strictly furniture, are referred to as furnishings. This discussion of furnishings includes both functional and decorative accessories, portable lighting, paintings and other two-dimensional art, and sculpture. Window coverings and loose floor coverings are included here, although in practice they should be considered as part of the earlier stages of conceptual development.

Rugs

Loose rugs that overlay other flooring materials are often needed in interiors. When used over hard floors, they offer softness to the foot and some acoustical control. They can give pattern and texture, and some degree of spatial definition.

Modern rugs are usually made in more or less standard sizes that are compatible with standard-sized rooms. For this reason they can be difficult to relate sensitively to the special requirements of designed interiors.

The placement of rugs is more important to a design concept than their fineness. Color, texture, and pattern are always considered when rugs are used, but their proper placement in an interior is often overlooked. Two problems of rug placement must be considered: (1) their relationship to furniture components and to architectural components; and (2) their placement must always fulfill aesthetic and functional requirements.

When rugs are used in direct connection with furniture, there are three acceptable position-relationships (see Figure 19): (A) the entire dimension of the furniture component sits within the boundary of the rug; (B) the entire dimension sits outside the boundary; or (C) the front legs sit on the rug in relationship to its edge.

Rugs in relation to walls, columns, doors, windows, and fireplaces must have connections to visual centers, or to the edges of these components. Haphazard placement of small rugs in relation to architectural components can destroy order. The center and edge alignments of large rugs must also be considered, because even small areas of flooring around the rug must become a part of the design of the floor plane.

A   B   C

19. Rug/Furniture Placement Relationships
The placement of rugs in relation to architectural components is a necessary design consideration. Further, furniture must relate to rugs in equally particular ways.

Window Coverings

In the name of good design, more bad judgment is exercised on window coverings than on any other part of interiors. The systems for window treatments that control light and privacy are few, and include shutters, shades, blinds, and curtains. The variations on these systems are many.

From the earliest periods of building, window coverings were a necessity. The first window was a mere unglazed opening in a wall; its covering was all that kept out light and cold. Later, wood panels made into shutters, sometimes in combination with oiled skin or oiled paper, covered window openings. Still later, glass became the main material.

Until the late eighteenth century all window coverings were made to be movable and retractable. They functioned as a necessary part of environmental controls. When this type of control became less necessary, window coverings in the form of curtains became ossified into stationary draperies that act only as decorative frames for windows. The frozen character of these draperies has never added to the vitality of any interior: their only asset, purely an accidental one, is to absorb sound. When any part of an interior is conceptually intended to function and then becomes nonfunctioning, the quality of static deadness is unmistakable. This type of window treatment can never be a part of a well-conceived interior.

Otherwise, all of the systems for window coverings are legitimate as devices for the environmental control of light and privacy. The differing characters of each device should be considered when choosing a window covering, because each of them offers an appearance and convenience quite different from the other. Each device is unique in construction; each affects the window and the daylight passing through it in a different way. Each subsequently affects the whole of an interior.

The following discussion identifies each type of window covering and gives some conceptual clues on the results of its use in an interior. It is not the intention of this discussion to explain the details of fabrication or construction. Here, as in other parts of this book, it is the form of the component that is considered to have the major impact of an interior concept.

Shutters   Shutters are always fitted inside the frames of windows. They offer the possibility of solid closure over the entire opening. Shutters do not change the proportions of a window. They can shut out the light and view; or, if they have sections that are louvered, allow for some outside penetration when the louvered section is opened.

When shutters are used to cover glass walls, their principal relationship is to the adjacent wall and floor plane. Walls of shutters covering walls of glass become, conceptually, walls. Shutters should be used as working devices, not as decorative trim. Usually made of wood, they can be finished as natural or painted surfaces.

Shades   Window shades are the simplest covering for windows. They are always fitted into the frame of the window, exposing all the face of the frame. They can be designed to draw down or pull up.

Shades can be made of several materials to suit functional and aesthetic needs. Plastic and fabric shades, plain, textured, or patterned, are possible and they may be used as matching or contrasting color components. Window shades should be seen conceptually as retractable planes, either translucent or opaque.

Blinds   A blind is a component made up of many thin parallel horizontal or vertical slats that can be set simultaneously at any angle to control light and give privacy. Horizontal blinds can be raised or lowered; vertical ones are retractable from side to side.

Horizontal venetian blinds are always fitted within a window frame; however, whole walls of glass can be covered with them. The size of the slats varies from approximately 1/2 inch to about 2 inches. Venetian-type blinds can be made with wood, metal, or plastic slats. They are available in many colors; bicolored venetian blinds, however, should be avoided.

Vertical blinds, a development from the blind in use since ancient Egypt, are a mid-twentieth-century device for window covering. These blinds have a strong architectural character and are most effective when used as large planes that cover both window and surrounding wall. The slats (called vanes) are available in different widths of opaque plastic, whitish in color. They pivot from a track at the top rather than on the sides, as do venetian-type blinds.

Some manufacturers make vertical blinds in translucent plastic, or plastic-impregnated translucent fabric, as well as in novelty textures of luxury materials like leather. All of these have a rather curious effect when hung over windows or walls, seeming either too light or too heavy. The eloquence of the vertical blind is its simple architectural character. It is therefore best used in its simplest form.

Curtains   It is best to refer to all fabric sewn into soft folds that is used for window coverings as curtains. The nomenclature used to differentiate the several types of curtains is unnecessary here, and in most practice as well. However, the vocabulary of curtains and curtain accessories that has developed over centuries is fascinating in its peculiarity.

Unfortunately, curtains have been so misused for so long a time that a prejudice against them has developed among many interior designers. Curtains can serve a real purpose in many interiors, however.

Two major problems must be confronted when curtains are used as window coverings: (1) their design and (2) their fabrication. The design of curtains—even very simple curtains—is complex. Their fabrication is equally difficult, almost a lost craft.

The intimate connection between curtain and window suggests that they are best when related to the architectural components of an interior. They must be proportioned to the window, to the wall of the window, and to the volume of the interior (see Figure 20). The fabric and necessary hardware must be appropriate. The design of a curtain can adversely affect the scale of the window and, consequently, the scale of the wall and of the whole interior.

There is a perpetuated myth surrounding window curtains. Some texts on interior design and many practitioners say that curtains are needed to soften a room, to soften or blur the line between window and wall. If this condition truly exists, it is doubtful that curtains will correct it; the fault is in the architectural

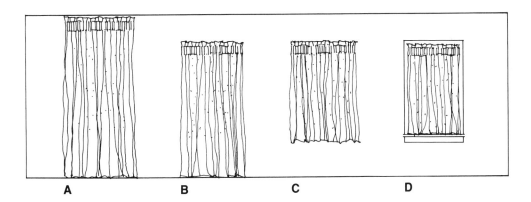

A   **B**   **C**   **D**

20. Curtain Proportions

Curtain styles change with each historical period. Basic curtain proportioning, however, does not change. Width-to-height and part-to-part proportions must still be considered when designing them. If a decorative treatment is added to the basic curtain — a swag, lambrequin, valance, trimming, or the like — the sizes of these must be decided based on the proportions of the parts as they relate to the size of the whole.

A. The curtain hangs from ceiling to floor and covers the entire width of the window.

B. The curtain hangs from the top of the window casing to the floor.

C. The curtain hangs from the top of the window casing to cover the apron.

D. The curtain hangs within the window casing, exposing all of the trim.

components, which should be given more serious consideration than to disguise the fault with curtains.

Of all the components in an interior, curtains have the most potential for projecting a sense of luxury, perhaps even a kind of visual poetry. The connotation of revelation and concealment, the sumptuous, elegant history of curtains, and their veiled relationship to clothing give them significance beyond mere function. That curtains have been degraded into ready-made department store "drapes" does not altogether diminish their capacity.

Window curtains can never be bought as ready-made items for designed interiors. They never fit exactly the aesthetic or the intended function.

Real skill is needed to make curtains, skill that might be similar to that needed to make the best clothing. Fabric that hangs must be treated differently than fabric that lays over another component. The measuring, cutting, seaming, gathering, or pleating; the inner linings, facings, and weighting; and finally the hanging of curtains require time, care, and attention to detail. If these things are not considered, the finished component is sad indeed. Of all window components, curtains are the most difficult and the most costly way of treating windows.

Accessories: Utilitarian and Decorative

Every interior needs accessories. Some interiors only need utilitarian (that is, functional) accessories; others need both utilitarian and decorative ones. If accessory components are left out in the design of an interior, the finished design will appear unfinished.

Some designers say that they are "not very good with accessories," that they are unsure of how to select them, to organize them, or to arrange them. This insecurity causes these designers to leave out accessories and thereby to leave the interior incomplete.

For students, the scale of drawings and models done for studio design projects often precludes experimentation and inclusion of components of the scale that is usual to accessories. Even so, students should include—in their thinking—these small but necessary parts. Though accessories may not be shown in a presentation, they must be included in a fully developed interior design concept. In professional practice, accessories, whether many or few, take on a level of greater importance. It is best to consider that importance now.

Utilitarian Accessories   This category of accessory is comprised of useful objects, the things without which people can't function easily in an interior. Utilitarian accessories are necessarily included in domestic as well as nonresidential projects. Some interiors, such as offices, require more functional accessories than others. In a typical office for a desk alone, a designer would specify a file tray, pen and pencil holder, calendar, telephone, ashtray, and picture frames for personal photographs. The office would also need a waste receptacle and perhaps a clock and an umbrella stand. These same accessories may be needed in a number of rooms in a residence, but other items will be needed there as well.

In a residence the number of functional accessory objects necessarily increases to aid in the flow of daily needs. Kitchens are filled with an array of functional equipment sometimes selected by a designer; bathrooms need wastebaskets, tissue boxes, hand mirrors, soap holders. Living rooms and bedrooms will have accessory objects such as clocks, vases, candlesticks, and trays for holding smaller objects. Dining rooms or eating areas usually need the greatest number of utilitarian accessories: dinnerware, flatware, glasses, and table coverings.

Dining room accessories need two considerations: first, the beauty of their function; and second, because they are transient objects, their ease and convenience of storage.

Decorative Accessories   The objects in an interior that cannot be described as having a "real" function are described as decorative. Often these objects are the "things" that have no use at all. They are eschewed by some interior designers.

Some designers do not favor decorative accessories, saying that these kinds of things do not fit or extend their spatial aesthetics. Others make no provision for them because of budget limitations ("the budget was spent for construction and furniture"). Still other designers are too uncomfortable with accessories to use them as part of the components of an interior. However, these same designers like to specify plants—at least one, strategically placed, carefully selected for shape and color—and plants, of course, are decorative accessories.

The types of utilitarian accessories referred to previously may, in all likelihood, be appropriately seen as having decorative possibilities and qualities. However, their presumptive use separates them from the purely decorative things that have no use.

The only need to justify the inclusion of decorative objects in an interior is delight—that aspect of an accessory that does nothing but provide visual pleasure.

The list of accessories is limited only by the imagination, but there are a few categories: personal collections comprised of one type of object, memorabilia or mementos, individual objects of unrelated form or origin. This type of accessory may exist at the outset of the design project. In other cases all accessories will be selected by the designer. In each situation the inclusion of these objects in an interior concept is a somewhat different problem for a designer.

When accessory objects exist at the start of a project, they may influence the overall project, particularly if the objects are large in size or many in number. These must be considered fully at the beginning of conceptual thinking, not added on at the end. Their number, shape, size, and color will become inseparable from the larger, spatial thinking.

If a designer is responsible for selecting decorative objects, another advantage and another problem will occur. Part of the positive quality in accessories (particularly collections) is that when they are collected over time, they have a direct connection to an individual or to a family. They may be a part of the past with associative powers. This type of object adds a special quality to an interior, especially when everything else in it is new. If a designer must select all accessories, this quality is missing, albeit through no fault of the designer.

However, the special accessories selected by a designer have the potential for an unmistakable relationship to a design concept. Just as architectural and furniture components come out of an initial design concept, the accessories chosen by a designer can extend and complete that concept. A designer who can select accessories as needed exercises the greatest control in an interior, from the largest to the smallest part.

Some of the principles of aesthetic composition may apply directly to the inclusion of accessories in interiors. Objects can affect interior scale; large-scale accessories in small spaces; small-scale accessories in usual-scale spaces. Symmetry in architecture and furniture can be made more emphatic by symmetrical accessories. Repetition can make accessories stronger in impact—many plants of the same species repeated in a configuration; a collection of one type of object displayed in one location—not scattered about; or the accessories may repeat a color or a material, becoming submerged in the overall character of a space. Some interiors benefit from accessories that contrast sharply with other parts. These stand out clearly and add points of color, shape, or texture, especially when they are the termination of a planned vista or the center object of symmetrical composition.

Organizing functional and decorative objects is similar to organizing other components. They impart richness and texture, they can add comfort and identity. The manner in which a designer arranges such components can give them dignity, elevating their qualities. They may also be handled in a thoughtful, but offhand way with a subtlety that requires the viewer to discover them. Particular interiors require particular accessories and particular organization, just as other parts need such consideration.

Plants and Flowers as Accessories   For centuries growing plants and living flowers have been a valued part of interiors. They offer one of the most varied, readily available forms of accessories.

Growing plants must be evaluated on three criteria for inclusion in an interior: (1) Can the plant be maintained in good condition in its interior location? (2) Does the form of the plant complement the location and introduce pattern, if that is desired? (3) Does the inclusion of the plant actually extend the design concept?

Not every interior needs plant material. Many designers think plants must be included in every interior as a significant part. However, this is like saying that every interior needs carpeting, or window curtains, or table lamps. Some do, some do not. Most interiors of great historical importance were designed without a single plant. Each interior must be evaluated individually for the appropriateness of plants. Arid climates in interiors are valid, as are tropical ones.

Arranging plant material of large scale becomes architectural in concept. As visual components, large plants require large amounts of space to display their forms. They should not be crowded into tight spaces or corners.

Smaller plants may be grouped together to make arrangements of a size. These should be selected as to plant type—not too many varieties with conflicting shapes—that look well in groups.

Living flowers are probably the most luxurious accessories possible. Their cost is high if purchased, and they last only a few days. But well-designed, appropriate flowers give an interior vitality and freshness.

In some interiors huge arrangements of flowers are needed to meet an established scale. In other spaces quite small arrangements are correct or, as is popular today, only a single flower or leaf may be a solution.

When cut flowers are given prominence in a space, it is essential for a designer to recognize that unless they are consistently replaced with new ones, some other accessory must be planned to take their place. It is possible that if the flower container is sufficiently interesting as an object, it may serve alone.

Fine Art

The cave paintings at Altamira and Lascaux bear witness that art has been a part of our living environment for centuries. Through all the great periods of architecture and interior design—Egyptian, Grecian, Roman, throughout the Middle Ages, and into Renaissance Europe—the fine arts of painting and sculpture have been a major contributing part of development (not part of their structural development, but the visual extension of evocative, emotional responses that are possible in interiors). Through our own period as well, painting and sculpture adorn important interiors—government, religious, domestic, public, commercial. Some designers of interiors are satisfied to have no fine art in their spaces; others say that no interior is complete without it.

How to include fine art in interiors is often debated by theorists and aestheticians. The philosopher Susanne Langer posits that "Pictures, treated by 'interior decorators' as embellishment for a room, may remain disassociated from it or even hostile."[8] Yet a picture in an interior becomes, at least partially, at least visually, an embellishment if it is the right picture presented in the right location and contributes to the visual structure of an interior.

Because each interior is a unique creation, each work of art within it occupies a unique position in that interior creation. However, in every interior where fine art is included, similar questions of design principles should be asked. The answers will vary according to each question. For example, should the color of a picture match other colors in an interior, or is it better that contrasting colors be used? Should large wall planes hold large paintings, or is it possible to display a small one there? Is it necessary that all pictures be hung at standing eye level, or are other eye levels appropriate in some interiors? Must all pictures be hung as single components or in pairs, or can groups of pictures hang together?

The matching of painting to interior color scheme is a distinctly twentieth-century question. In past periods the color of a painting always "matched" interior colors—indeed, in all types of interiors, the painting often was the color motif. This does not suggest that a red and orange painting is needed for a red and orange room, but that compatibility is required. However, compatibility may be a color scheme that is in contrast to the picture. A predominantly blue picture, hung on a blue wall, over a blue sofa will, in all likelihood, create a poor environment for the picture as well as an interior that is less than vital. The matching of a picture's color to that of a room will cancel a special contribution that art can make, and the matching runs the risk of draining away the picture's life.

A growing cliché is the so-called "sofa-sized painting." This implies that the sofa is against the wall and that the sofa requires a large picture on a large wall. This is a question of scale (as well as appropriateness). Only an analysis of an

---

[8]Susanne K. Langer, *Feeling and Form: A Theory of Art* (New York: Charles Scribner's Sons, 1953).

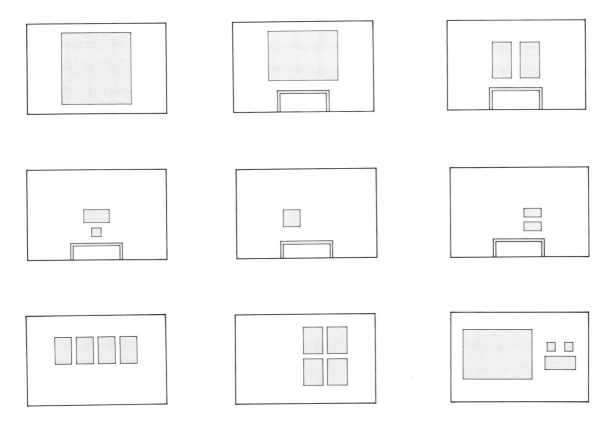

21. Picture Relationships

To place pictures singly, in pairs, or in groups, a center-line axis is helpful so that either symmetrical or balanced arrangements are in equilibrium. Only some of the possible conditions are suggested here, since these will differ in every interior and with every picture.

interior can determine the desirability of a large painting and an accompanying sofa. Perhaps only a small painting is needed, perhaps no painting at all.

Where to hang a picture is important, but all pictures do not have to be hung in relation to furniture (see Figure 21). Sometimes the best location, even for a small painting, is on a wall near no furniture, isolated on an otherwise empty plane.

Pictures should be hung where they are best seen. This means that most pictures will be hung somewhere close to standing eye level (5 feet to 5 feet 6 inches at the center of a picture). This general rule cannot always work, as with very large paintings, but it does work with small- and average-sized pictures. Sometimes it is best to place pictures much lower than standing eye level. This may occur when a picture will be viewed adjacent to a seating component. When pictures are hung over mantel shelves, chests, tables, or fixed-in-place storage components, it is best to place them only a few inches above the surface of the component. If placed too high above a surface, a picture will separate from the whole composition. If at all possible, objects placed on a surface should not obscure the picture.

Pictures, whether they are prints or paintings, should be treated with dignity, not merely as decoration. When pictures are hung in groups, the problem of picture-as-decoration begins (this does not include pictures intended by the artist as a group, or series). There is a fashion for hanging diverse sizes and subjects of prints or paintings together, sometimes regardless of compatibility. Such arrangements can be effective, but they are singularly difficult to accomplish. When a pair of pictures is hung together, they may be hung one directly over the other, or side by side, depending on their proportions. Pairs of pictures should never be hung in a staggered, stair-step arrangement. When two pictures of different size are placed together, it is usually best to hang one above the other rather than side by side. Also, the larger picture should be hung above the smaller to prevent a pyramid effect. Subject matter, shapes, and colors should be compatible and non-conflicting in pictures that are hung together.

Sculpture in historical interiors had an importance at least equal to that of painting. Often the sculpture was integral, commemorative, and decorative at once. Sculpture in Modern interiors is rarely so, even though many contemporary spaces accommodate it with grace. Langer comments that it takes "strong self-sufficient interiors" to "afford sculpture"[9]; not that it is assimilated, but that it is intimately compatible.

Nonresidential interiors—banks, shopping malls, schools, and government interiors—are thought to be ideal spaces for sculpture, much of it commissioned from the artist. Sculpture in domestic interiors is not usually large in size, but can make a significant impact on a space.

If large-size sculpture is used in usual-size spaces, domestic or otherwise, scale contrast will be evident. Oversized objects, like very big jars or vases, can create similar effects on interior scale. Large-size sculpture will be most effectively exhibited if it is shown sitting on a large plane—floor, table, or wall. Lighting should bring out the shape, color, and texture of a piece.

Some types of sculpture require bases or pedestals. These bases should complement the sculpture in color, shape, and material. Small sculptures can be displayed on tables or shelves in locations where they can be viewed at close range.

---

[9]Ibid.

Chapter 3

Design Presentation

The physical presentation of a project in interior design is the last stage of creative activity in student study or professional practice. For the student, the presentation is the evidence of a design concept "presented" to a teacher or to a design jury for review. The professional designer's presentation is reviewed by a client. For both, design presentation has one objective: to provide information. To be understood, information in any form must be organized, correct, and direct; even with complicated subjects it should be presented in an accessible way. Interior design presentation is complicated information. Students must therefore prepare that information to convey the design clearly, simply, completely, and eloquently.

What to Present

Drawings

Many drawings are generated during the design process. Some of them will develop into parts of the presentation; some will be incorporated into finished drawings. Process drawings are not usually included with the final presentation. In a typical interior design project the variety of drawings may include floor plans, elevations, sections, and some form of projected drawing—perspective, isometric, or axonometric. These will be prepared in finished form to become a part of a presentation. (Sometimes a reflected ceiling plan is also necessary.)

All drawings must meet the requirements set out in a design program. Some teachers specify that all drawings be presented in a particular medium; pencil or ink is typical. Most programs insist that a given scale be used; 1/8-, 1/4-, and 1/2-inch scales are typical, though larger-scale drawings may be required for a particular project.

The drawings in a presentation are a language. That is, they are "read" in order to be understood. Therefore drawings in a presentation must agree with each other: the information in a plan must be the same information extended in the elevations. The elevations amplify and explain the plan.

Two problems consistently hamper presentation: too little information or, surprisingly, too much. In drawings done to scale, students tend to leave out certain detail that is essential to the strong portrayal of a design. Such graphic information as texture or pattern may be essential to understanding a plan or an elevation.

These drawings appear unfinished, underdone, and incomplete, although that was not the student's intention. Often a student will have information in mind, but will not transfer it into drawn lines, into the external, visual presentation. A lack of information in the lines makes a presentation hard to read and understand.

Some students attempt to give more information than can be understood or accepted within the format of a presentation. Here the drawings are so crowded with information that the larger issues of a concept are lost in a gathering of detail. Such drawings will be difficult to read because of an overabundance of information in the lines.

The way to avoid such problems may appear oversimplified: Look at the drawing in progress! Many times a student is so intent on accomplishing a drawing (and the drawing is done at close range) that a look from a distance does not take place until the drawing is completely finished and too late to change. Looking from a distance offers an opportunity for an objective appraisal. The distance helps the student to see the strength of the drawing's information. Being too close to a drawing can distort the reality it represents.

A readable drawing always has contrasting light and dark lines as well as contrast in line weight, or thickness. It is the lines themselves that make for readability. If a drawing is too light, important lines may be darkened to increase line weight and add visual strength. Readability means not only that a drawing can be understood, but that what is understood is what a student intended to convey.

Perspectives, isometrics, and axonometrics require the same level of readability, but their information is a step closer to reality than the abstraction of plans, elevations, and sections. A projected drawing is more easily understood by non-professionals; and although there is a degree of inexact information in it (because "artistic" license is often taken), a projection drawing is an excellent way to show an interior.

The simple type of presentation is executed as line drawing. Sometimes the entire presentation can be done in line only, a difference in line weight being the only differentiation necessary to bring out important parts (see Figure 22A). In such a presentation visual strength is fully dependent on line weights in each drawing, and each drawing must be in sympathy with the overall composition.

Line-drawing presentations may also include areas of color, if that is desirable (see Figure 22B). When color is added to such a drawing, it can be applied to whatever parts a student wishes to call attention to. Color may be applied with pencil, ink, watercolor, tempera, or collage, from photographs. Such color additions can enliven drawings in pencil or ink. This technique can be used on plan, elevation, section, and all projection drawings. Care must be exercised to prevent the color additions from becoming confusing when all or several of the drawings have them. Everything in a presentation must aim to clarify information.

Another presentation method using line is the type that is drawn and rendered with lines. In this type of presentation the line drawings are given texture, shades,

A. A freehand and hard-line perspective drawing

22. Five Variations of Perspective Presentation

Depending on the requirements in a design program, each of these variations is applicable. One method is not necessarily preferred over another, although some methods provide a greater depth of information. Still, some interiors may be described best when the presentation of the perspective drawing is kept quite plain.

shadows, and materials—all indicated by the variety and character of lines (see Figure 22C). The character lines should bring out the important shapes and materials in the interior. Such drawings may be only partially rendered, leaving much in outline. The addition of some texture and some small areas of solid dark can bring out form and focus attention. When it is done well, this type of drawing can make a handsome presentation that has a sparkling, brilliant surface.

A third type of presentation is a combination of line drawing and color rendering (see Figure 22D). Sometimes such a presentation is designed to have a full-color plan with elevations, sections, and projection drawings in black and white. Another possibility is to color only the projection drawings, leaving the remaining ones in line. This type of presentation can present an interior with strong information and visual richness.

Some projects require another type of presentation—one that is completely rendered (see Figure 22E). When this procedure is required (or selected), a student must remember that fully rendered presentations take on visual weight as no other type does.

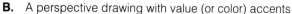

B. A perspective drawing with value (or color) accents

C. A perspective drawing with values and textural treatment

The drawings in a presentation may be simple line drawings or drawings that are fully rendered; they may be combinations of line and color or a combination of freehand and straightedge lines. Whatever method is chosen, the information given in the presentation must be in such a form that it is supportive to the design concept, the presentation of the concept being the reason for the existence of the presentation. Students therefore should avoid using too much "technique" if that technique overshadows a design. All technique in drawing and rendering is at the service of design.

The point of view of projection drawings should always be the most advantageous. When the drawing is a perspective, the view should always be taken from a realistic position. Often that position is at a doorway entrance, the point from which the built space would be viewed. It is a disadvantage (as well as unrealistic) to remove a wall or hang outside a window to draw a perspective. Interiors are never seen from those views. Though the drawing may be effective, it will not assist in understanding a concept or its realization.

Perspectives of interiors should, whenever possible, show three walls or boundaries of a space. Perspectives that show only two walls tend to become decorative vignettes concentrating on furniture components or furnishings. Perspective views explain architectural relationships better when a view or glimpse of another space is seen. This kind of drawing is perhaps more complicated, but it is also more explanatory.

D. A partially rendered perspective drawing

E. A fully rendered perspective with no lines visible

Models

Models are often required for final presentations—sometimes alone, sometimes with drawings. In either case models are a special way to present design. They are still abstract, but are one step closer to reality because they are three-dimensional.

Depending on the degree of detail required, models of interiors may be as small as 1/8-inch scale or as large as 1-inch scale. The size of the interior will probably determine the scale model. Smaller models require less detail; larger ones need greater detail.

Models of interiors are excellent means for showing spatial relationships within a single space or in sequential spaces. They also provide a superior means of showing volume, mass, and weight.

There are several problems for students when models are used in presentation: cost, time, and skill. The cost of model-making is high. Board, paper, and other supplies are expensive. Models require considerable time to build; and when a model is only one part of a presentation, it takes time away from other parts. Some students have weak model-building skills because of inexperience and are therefore insecure with them. Unfortunately, not much can be done to change the problems of cost and time; but skills can be improved with practice.

For all students, another (and more important) problem comes into being when models are made. This is the question of how much reality to put into an abstract model. In most cases a high level of reality injected into a model will give it the characteristics of a dollhouse, the counterpart that comes to mind—everybody's mind. No student would want this comparison, because it is one that would not support the seriousness of a design project.

The dollhouse appearance can be avoided in interior design models by simplifying all or most shapes, and by carefully selecting the materials used to build and finish the model. Each model maker must decide on these questions, basing decisions on the design to be presented.

Real materials are also to be avoided. Many times a student will think that using real fabric, real wood for paneling, real carpet or floor covering will make the model more convincing. But real materials are never in scale, and therefore overwhelm the scale of the model. Real manufactured patterns never work in models; patterns must be simulated to make them a compatible scale.

At their most effective, models of interiors should be relatively plain so that they describe conceptual thinking in a direct manner. The plain model, with sufficient information, will convey the spatial relationships and exhibit the characteristics of volume, mass, and weight.

Materials for the Interior

When sample materials are required in a presentation, they, by their nature, pose a different problem than drawings or models. When material samples are handled well, they make a rich and informative contribution to a presentation. Poorly shown, they will detract more emphatically than any other element because they are always outside the realm of abstraction. Samples are real; drawings represent the real.

Two general procedures apply when materials are shown in a presentation: (1) They may be shown on a board in combination with drawings, or (2) they may be presented separately on a board. Either way, the materials must be designed into the presentation.

When materials are shown on a board in combination with drawings, they must not intrude on the visual connections between the various drawings. Often, in this type of presentation, the samples can be arranged along the bottom edge of the board, or at one side. It is seldom advisable to place samples at the center.

If materials are shown on a separate board, this will conform to the visual format of the overall presentation. A separate board for materials can be handsomely designed.

Although there may be some disagreement on this, it is preferable to place each sample so that it is surrounded by blank board (and usually it is best to use white or a pale, neutral color for this). If samples are placed so that they touch each other, the nature of the sample can make for a messy connection. Also, because there is no alternative, samples must be shown as two-dimensional, not in the three dimensions for which they are intended. Having them touch will still not give the full impression of the materials-color relationship in an interior (all materials in a built interior are separated by space, distance, or shadow). So, even with samples of real materials, a level of abstraction exists within the format of a two-dimensional presentation.

A generous amount of blank board (or "air") around materials will usually show them to best advantage. Crowding samples on a board will do them no justice.

Almost all material samples that are collected for a presentation must be physically prepared before they are assembled. Materials such as marble, glass, and stone will probably be left in whatever size they are obtained. Everything else will require attention. Paint, paper, and other wall finishes must be trimmed to size, as must samples of carpet and floor covering. Photographs of furniture and furnishings should be trimmed and, if necessary, cropped to remove extraneous portions not pertinent to the presentation.

Fabrics require special handling to look good in a presentation. All identifying tags should be removed. Each fabric sample should be backed with masking tape pressed down firmly; tape and fabric are then trimmed (with scissors) together. This procedure will ensure that the sample will not unravel or fuzz at the edges; also, the backing allows a better glueing surface and prevents the glueing agent from bleeding through to the face of the fabric. The saw-toothed or pinked edge on fabric samples should always be removed.

How to Design the Presentation

As previously discussed, all design becomes external, visual, and subject to review. Presentation is the culmination of student design work. No matter how strong the concept, it will be undervalued if it is shown in a weak presentation.

Strict presentation requirements may be stipulated. If so, follow them to the letter. If there is only a suggestion of presentation requirements (such as "drawings sufficient to show the design concept," or some similar direction), the student may choose the type and number of drawings needed to show a project to best advantage.

Certainly, there will be a plan. Probably there will be elevations, at least one major projection drawing, and, in some projects, a transverse or longitudinal section. These diverse drawings must be arranged together, designed into one cohesive composition—the presentation.

The various drawings will be organized within the boundary of boards or sheet sizes (see Figure 23). These surfaces should complement the project design. Some schools prefer all work on board, especially if there is a full-color rendering or colored drawing required, as well as rendered plans and elevations. Other schools prefer original drawings on paper or prints, mounted or unmounted. The overall size of the sheets or boards is important. Standard board sizes may be the wrong proportions for a project, but these can be improved by trimming. A typical 20 by 30-inch board placed on its long side makes a horizontal format for a presentation. If three of these are used in a presentation, the overall length will extend to 7 1/2 feet. This is fine, but only if a critique or jury space will permit.

When multiple boards or sheets are needed in a presentation, each must be prepared in the same directional format; all vertical or all horizontal. Never have some boards vertical and some horizontal—a presentation is *one* composition. Even if a square sheet size is used, each board should be composed to fit into one compositional unit.

The critique or jury presentation will almost invariably begin with an examination of the plan. Because in our culture we read groups of words from left to right, it is conventional to read groups of architectural drawings the same way. Whenever possible, the plan—always the first drawing to be examined—should be at the left side.

If a scale for the plan has been specified (remember that large-scale drawings need more detail), they require more time to prepare. If allowed, choose a scale that shows your design to best advantage. The plans, when possible, should orient the major entrance to the lower edge or toward the center of the sheet. With the entrance in one of these positions, one may "walk" into the space easily. Never orient a major entrance toward the top edge of the sheet. With the entrance in that position, one must, so to speak, turn upside down to get into an interior.

Elevations are best located at close proximity to the plan. This provides an easier way for plan and elevation information to be compared. If the elevations are stacked one above the other, they should align at the center. They may also be strung out side by side adjacently and, sometimes, edge-aligned flush left.

Never try for "interesting" arrangements of the parts of a presentation. The words on the page of a book are not arranged in an "interesting" way; the words

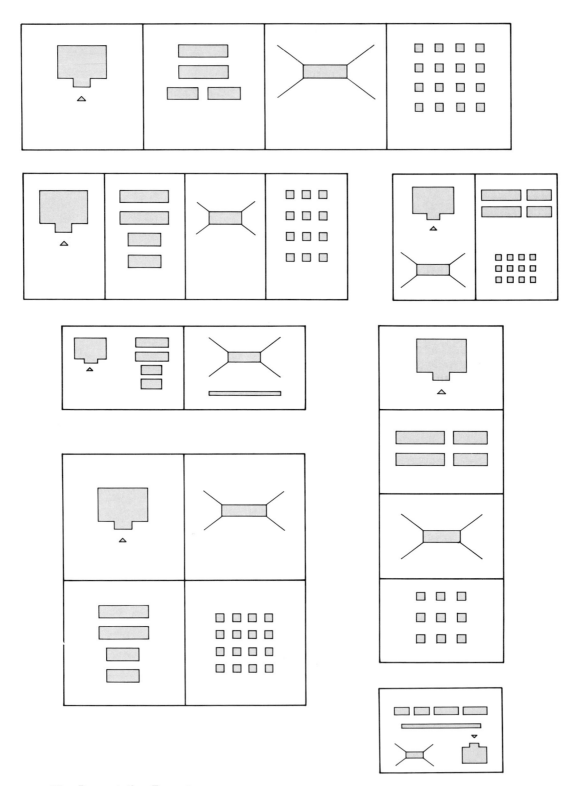

23.   Presentation Formats

When presentation requirements in a design program permit, the format can be organized in one of several ways. One variation may suit a particular project best, and each variation can be adjusted. The parts of the presentation must be shifted into positions that accommodate diverse sizes and weights of plans, elevations, perspectives, detail drawings, materials samples, and the rest. It is always necessary to juxtapose certain drawings or parts to convey information easily—the only reason for the presentation.

themselves are interesting enough. If drawings are not of interest, perhaps the design is weak. No fanciful arrangement of drawings will make a design stronger if the concept is weak to begin with.

When you lay out all of the sheets, try to visualize how the finished presentation will look and how it will read. Remember that all drawings and all presentations are done so that design can be understood. Always keep this in mind. Design a simple, uncomplicated presentation. Particular weight can be given to one part, but try for balance, distribution, and open space on the sheets. This gives the possibility for being eloquent without being elaborate or fussy.

Architectural lettering is part of every presentation. Never underestimate the importance of good lettering. If a student cannot letter well, practice will improve the skill. Leave enough time so that the lettering work will not be rushed. Some students resort to the use of press-on lettering. This is invariably a mistake. First, the use of such instant letters prevents further practice; and second, the manufactured product is at odds with the hand-done quality of the presentation. (Sometimes press-on lettering can be used when it occurs in a title block, separated from the rest of the presentation by a box or border.)

A lettering checklist should include the following:

1. All projects must have a title. Be sure you have the title words correct. Check for correct spelling.

2. All plans must have a North arrow.

3. All plans must have an arrow at the major entrance.

4. All drawings must have a scale notation.

5. Identify each drawing. Be consistent.

6. If a legend or notes list is included, check the wording and organize it as part of the overall composition.

7. Check all drawings to determine if something has been overlooked.

8. If lettering is very difficult for you, try making it a smaller size. If the usual 1/4 inch is too large for you, try 3/16 or 1/8 inch.

The aesthetic principles that apply to the design of an interior also apply, in part, to the design of the presentation of that interior. Such principles as axis and alignment, balance, repetition, and rhythm can be directly applied. These compositional devices must, however, be used in support of relationships that convention has bestowed and necessity demands of architectural drawings. Otherwise the readability, clarity, and ultimate purpose of a presentation are lost.

Oral Presentation

Some schools require students to present projects orally. This provides an opportunity for a student to justify what is seen in the visual presentation. Sometimes what is not seen (or is unseen) can also be described.

Above all, oral presentations must be prepared in advance. It is never appropriate to speak about a project in an extemporaneous or improvised manner. You may forget important points or meander from critical issues.

Verbal presentation has one major issue—amplification of the design conceptualization in the visual presentation. Verbal presentation should attempt to bring out ideas. It is not a listing or recitation of what can be readily seen. For example, in the plan of an interior it is not necessary to point out that there are five rooms, four chairs, two tables, and two sofas. This can be seen. However, it is important to explain why those particular parts relate in that particular plan in a particular way. In other words, not *what* but *why* a situation exists, why it is designed that way. To count out the furniture (or the walls, or the colors) is a waste of time. Your ideas are of interest—your ideas about the furniture, the walls, the colors.

Keep in mind that a design project solves a design problem. Verbal presentations allow you to explain how the problem was solved. In most designs the solution is at the core of the concept, that center from which everything else extends. This is what you will want to explain.

At some point in a presentation questions may be asked—usually by jury members or teachers, sometimes by other students. If a question is asked and you have no answer, it is best to say, "I don't know." If you do not know, some member of the audience may know. This way an exchange of information can occur. On the other hand, you should make a concerted effort to have all of the necessary information about all of the major issues in a project. The issues include not only the concept, but such parts of the design that support and extend that concept. For example, the program requirements that influence the concept initially, contextual constraints that may dictate materials and colors, and the theories projected out onto a design; these may need amplification throughout the verbal presentation.

You should not feel constricted by the beginning-middle-end order of most information-giving presentations, although this format has proven workable over time. It is necessary, however, to inform an audience in such a way that it can easily grasp what you wish to make clear. For this reason, after opening comments are made, it is best to proceed with an exposition of the overall plan. The exposition—that is, the meaning or the purpose of the design found in the plan—includes conceptual design issues. Next, the individual parts of the plan should be discussed. These parts may properly include the order of entrance, movement, the disposition of rooms or spaces, and special features.

Some students find verbal presentation a particularly trying part of interior design study. Other students become quite expert in this performance aspect of presentation. In either case it is best to remember that the visual design work is the more important part of the presentation. Drawings, not words, are what make design. Students who have trouble with spoken information should keep their comments brief and pointed toward specific aspects of the project. For these students, presenting generalized information is a mistake because it leads to longer, often poorer, commentary. For all students, planning specific comments is critical.

Charrette

The French word *charrette* literally means cart, or barrow. To design and architecture students, however, it means much more.

The term "charrette" comes down from the nineteenth-century French Ecole des Beaux-Arts, the leading school of art and architecture of that period. There, on the day projects were due, students drove to the school in small carts called *charrettes*. Students worked in their own studios away from school, sometimes at distances too far to walk. When design projects were due (and students had been working late, until all hours, probably all night and possibly for several nights), the charrette would be sent from the school to pick up students and projects and be driven at top speed back to the school in order to meet the deadline. During the fast ride, it is said that the enterprising students used the time to put the finishing touches on the meticulously rendered sections and elevations that have come to typify Beaux-Arts presentation. So the final rush to complete a presentation came to be known as a charrette.

If the nineteenth-century story is somewhat apocryphal, the twentieth-century charrette for students is in no way a fiction. The fast ride today is a real last surge, a final push toward completion of a project. Students work up to the last minute to finish at as high a level as possible. The charrette is the time when the design concept comes into final form, is finalized, and is completed.

All design projects assigned to students have due dates. Some schools have one due date for a project and a later due date for the review of the project or jury. Other schools have both due date and jury on the same day. No matter how long a design project runs, there always seems to be less time than is needed or wanted. (This is true in professional practice also, where dates of client meetings set the deadline.)

The pressure of time is what has created the need for charrette in both school and practice. There seems to be no way a charrette period can be avoided. It is something designers and architects accept as a given, another convention associated with design activity over time, a tradition in fact. It is not necessarily an honored tradition, but one accepted of necessity.

Some schools allow students on charrette to stay in the design studio until very late or, in some cases, all night. Other schools, particularly those surrounded by large cities, never allow late working hours. The studios close at a consistent hour. This may create problems for some students—such as the need to have a proper work space in student quarters. This necessitates duplicate equipment, or transporting a large project on boards or in model form from student room to school studio when the due date arrives. This can occur in strong winds, rain, or in a snowstorm. Students must be prepared to meet these unpredictable circumstances.

In spite of problems surrounding charrette, the time period—whether overnight or for many days—can be a positive one. Some further planning may help to ensure a trouble-free charrette.

When the charrette period arrives, most design decisions—certainly all major ones—have been made. Some things may change, but these will come naturally as the presentation process goes on. What is important now are supplies: art and drafting material for the design project and supplies of energy for the student.

Supplies for the project include everything that will be needed to finish, especially if this period will run overnight, or over a weekend when stores are closed. Make a checklist to be sure that nothing is forgotten. If you are charretting with a classmate, some supplies may be used in common, such as a large container of glue. But other items—knives, extra blades, pens, and the like—should be held on an individual basis. In every case, plan ahead.

The physical energy supply needed to push through a charrette should come from prior good health habits. However, if you are not in the habit of good exercise and good food, you can still help yourself by eating certain foods, avoiding others, and by physically relaxing or walking at intervals in this strenuous work period. To keep energy high, the blood-sugar level must be kept high. This is done not by eating sugar, but by eating such foods as fresh fruit and fruit juice, whole grains, nuts, milk, cheese, and yogurt. This suggestion does not presume that students will give up junk foods. However, the foods listed here together with regular meals will provide you the energy needed to get through a charrette. If you are tired, an orange will give a lift that is better and longer-lasting than a cup of coffee; you may still have the coffee, but have the fruit also.

Finishing a project on charrette is not always thought to be appropriate. Some schools do not favor it at all. Others would not expect their students to complete their projects in any other way. Ultimately, planning to meet deadlines—despite other commitments and emergencies—is as critical a part of student work as it is of professional practice.

Chapter 4

Understanding Studio Criticism

At the start of serious study in interior design it is sometimes difficult for students to grapple with studio criticism along with everything else. They struggle, all at the same time, with new course material, with new design critics, with fear of failure, and with anxiety over having to expose their work to instructors and peers. Good critical discussion, however, is the best means of developing discipline in any creative area.

In the studio, where criticism is given, learning takes place through the process of doing. It is a trial-and-error method that offers the almost immediate possibility of "seeing" one's thinking. Results can be examined and considered, can be put aside for the moment and returned to when needed. Therefore, for design students, the externalized thought—a sketch, a kind of drawn thought—provides the basis on which critical discussion is built. Teacher-critics respond to drawings and, throughout critiques, concentrate on these visual thoughts, only occasionally looking at students. Communication between students and teachers takes place around the medium of the drawing. This discussion is the process of studio criticism.

Criticism is directed through the drawing to the student's thinking. The drawing is the student's thinking. It is therefore not the student that is being criticized, but the work—the evidence of the student's thinking.

When this principle is not adhered to or not understood, it results in weak criticism from instructors (who often do not want to offend students), and students who feel abused when harsh criticism is leveled at their design. The process of criticism, even when it is painful, must be worked through or both teacher and student will become dissatisfied, complaining, and malcontented.

The Essential Process of Studio Criticism

Certain procedures during an individual critique are conventional and should be held to rigidly; understanding them will make the process easier. Not every student understands this procedure, nor does every instructor or critic follow it. Essentially, it is basic courtesy.

When an instructor arranges to give a critique, you should rise from the drafting table, offering that central position to the instructor. The gesture makes it possible for the critic to confront the work head-on. Sharp, soft pencils and a roll of tracing paper should be at hand for the critic to use, as should a scale, possible reference materials, and program requirements. It is polite as well as helpful if everything is as convenient as possible for the instructor's work. This attention lets the teacher know at once that you are prepared for a serious critical session.

You can signal readiness for criticism in several ways. You can go up to the teacher, raise a hand, or put your name on a list (if that is the procedure set by the teacher).

The teacher may make a decision about which student needs attention. It may be decided mutually that you need attention later—to allow time to develop more drawings and be prepared for a more definitive critique session.

Some instructors will insist on doing some drawing themselves while talking through a critique; some instructors cannot really explain unless they draw. Others will give a critique with words alone. In either case you must pay close attention. Instructors are experienced in appraising student work and in pointing out problems, and will be able to grasp the form of the concept quickly. After all, instructors have learned design through much the same studio procedure. They are aware of what is at stake.

Criticism as Discussion or Exchange

Critique sessions in the studio are a time of discovery for both student and teacher. Students discover their growth as form-makers; teachers begin to see students' potential as designers. Mutual discovery and trust continue with the growing complexities of problem solving. This procedure has the benefit of two minds at work on the same problem.

During studio criticism you must be prepared to talk as well as to listen. If a critic wishes to speak first, you should listen carefully without interruption. You should not say, at the first negative comment, that the critic does not understand. The critic should be permitted to make a point before being questioned—or challenged.

If you have more than one preliminary design concept, this should be mentioned at the beginning of a critique session. An instructor should not be permitted to speak at length on one concept and, finding it less than superior, then be surprised with another one.

In most cases only one concept should be undertaken for development. If you have several very preliminary concepts under consideration, it is best to choose one or two at most. Several meaningful critiques should result in a scheme suitable for development. This decision is usually made jointly by the student and teacher. The decision will be based on which concept is considered the most significant or which offers the strongest possibility and opportunity for full exploration. If you feel that two concepts have good potential, you may decide to develop both somewhat further. At the next critique period you should then present both simultaneously. One of the schemes will be chosen for full development. This scheme is the one that will be expected to be presented for final review or jury. In no case should you carry two schemes to a higher level (unless this happens to be part of the assignment).

Don't be discouraged if most of what you hear are questions about what remains unanswered in the work. It is perhaps unfortunate that most criticism is negative, or at least has a negative sound; but that is the nature of much critical comment—its line of least resistance and perhaps its sternest pedagogy. Praise, seldom given except at the end of a critique, is usually brief and almost always occurs at the point when the critic has finished.

Sometimes a teacher finishes a critique by saying, "You should continue with the development of this scheme." This may not mean that the teacher thinks the scheme is really worth development. But if you offer no alternative idea, the critic has little choice but to hope for the best—at the next session something may have developed.

In this case you must carry forward to make some progress before the next critique. The work must never stop during the duration of the project. Never waste time waiting for an instructor's attention, or for a decision to formulate itself. Waiting time should be spent in some productive manner—by making more sketches, or preliminary decisions about materials or color. Sitting and waiting for a teacher is both irritating and wasteful.

The relationship between student and critic does not always work. A critic may say, "I don't think this concept can be developed," and the student says, "Well, I think I would like to try." So the critic may then say, "Well, you can try it, but I do not think you will be able to do it in a clear way—it will be difficult or you will end up with a great confusion at the end." Sometimes the critic is wrong, and the student can develop the scheme. Students don't always throw out a scheme because the critic tells them to. Sometimes a student will hold onto the concept against all advice. This is one of the great problems between student and critic, but it is also the great value in having a critic.

Critics constantly talk about the difficulty of getting students to listen to what is being said. One reason is that some students will not believe that any teacher who gives negative criticism understands the concept, because so much of the idea is still in the mind of the student or not enough sketches have been done to show the idea. But most of the time critics do understand. They are experienced; their principal work is teaching design. But getting students to give up their preconceptions is often quite difficult.

Some teachers will insist on seeing each student at every studio meeting; others will give only one or two lengthy critiques during the run of an entire project. The number of critiques, or the number of hours spent on a project, is no guarantee of its success. The completeness of concept drawings is paramount. The more complete your visual thinking is, the more thorough the instructor's critique can be.

Critical comment may include specific instruction. For example, an instructor may comment that a principal entrance is in the wrong location to allow direct circulation from one area of the plan to another. Because of a particular disposition of parts in a scheme, the instructor may say, "The entrance should be located to the east." This is specific instruction and needs no further discussion or questioning. However, if the observation is that "The entrance is poorly defined," ask for clarification; for "poorly defined" can be construed in several ways. If an instructor does not choose to elaborate on such an observation, you are nevertheless expected to explore further, and to arrive at an entrance solution that will be evaluated as "well defined."

Only rarely will an instructor throw out a scheme at a late point in the run of a project, although this will occasionally happen. This means that, even though the project's due date is imminent, the scheme is so faulty that no amount of development will improve it and you must begin again.

Although this situation is bound to be discouraging, you must start again. The charrette period will be most difficult. You should make every effort to arrive at a new concept quickly, have at least one critique, and get on with the basic drawings required for presentation. If time is too short to do a complete presentation, you will have to decide what must be done and what cannot be done. At least try to produce enough drawings to explain the new concept, even if they remain in fairly rough form.

Responses to Criticism

When you have spent time on a project, there is an accompanying emotional investment: You care about the work. For this reason, when harsh criticism is leveled at a particular scheme, some students, rather than choosing to understand that criticism is a discussion as well as an essential part of design education, become angry and hurt. Remember that a teacher also has an investment in the success of his or her design students. The teacher's aim is to see that the students succeed to the highest level of their abilities. In a very real sense the student is the product of the teacher's influence: If a student produces fine work, a teacher succeeds. It has been said that in the best teaching the student surpasses the teacher.

When you receive criticism from your instructor, your response can be positive or negative. Some of the positive ways to respond are these: First, you must understand the suggestion (as in "try it the other way") and then investigate to see if that thinking can work in that situation. Even if you do not think that the teacher's suggestion can work, some attempt should be made to investigate the suggestion—through sketches and more elaborate drawings, if necessary—to see if the idea will work. This is a direct, positive way to respond to criticism. In some cases you can make direct use of the suggested way of doing it; sometimes clarification is necessary.

If the teacher comments that he or she cannot understand the intent because there are not enough drawings, you may feel angry or neglected. But you should respond by making the additional drawings suggested by the teacher and making them clear enough so that the teacher knows you are interested in your work and that you care enough to produce information that the teacher can understand.

Another criticism that you may get is, "The drawings should be turned into a sketch-model, and it will be helpful to put that together now so that we can move some of these parts around." You can say, "I don't see why I have to make a model now when nobody else has to," or "That's not part of the problem," or "Ah, maybe that's what a professional does and I ought to do the sketch-model because he's not trying to be mean by assigning the model; he's assigning it because that's the way professionals work and he knows that's a way of visualizing a space more closely to a real situation and showing relationships that may not show in a drawing."

A critic may say that you should see what Palladio did in his designs for villas, or that you should read what Robert Venturi has to say about a design attitude the critic may feel is beginning to be apparent in your project. Or a critic may tell you to look at what Le Corbusier did in the Ville Savoye, when he turned the landing of a stairway or was joining one color to another. A teacher may also suggest that you examine a certain material or the way a material was used in another interior. A teacher might say, "Find four ways of laying stone," or "Find three patterns of brick for use on a floor," or "Find different textures in fabric that could be developed." What the teacher really is saying is that you ought to consider other ways of using existing methods or details. The value of this procedure is not that those forms or ways of doing should be transferred into the project in a literal way, but that they might be considered as ways to extend thinking about how to resolve a problem.

It is not unusual for students to get stuck—not knowing where to go next in a project or even what to do in considering suggestions from a critic. At that point, the critic might recommend that the student consider looking at the current professional literature in the field—in magazines, recent books, and the publications of other designers' works—for other solutions and to give some hints.

For beginning students it is not so necessary that a concept be brilliant or unique or "different." What is desirable is a concept that can be developed into a straightforward, well-ordered, workable scheme, humane in form and deferential to the demands of the program. If what you strive for is to be different, the chances are that is all the scheme will become. And different, more often than not, will translate into strange, peculiar, and inhumane.

The Final Review or Design Jury

For the final evaluation of design projects, most schools have open critiques or juries. Frequently, these include visiting critics from the profession or faculty members other than the instructors responsible for the project.

Procedure during a jury is fairly standard. Either all student projects are displayed on the walls simultaneously so that all jury members can make a preliminary appraisal, or each student's project is hung singly for review. In either case some introduction of the problem will be made, usually by the responsible instructor, the teaching assistant, or a selected student.

Each student in turn presents work with verbal commentary prepared in advance. Then, questions and comments from the jury will begin.

The final presentation of a project is the first occasion when a studio project is complete and can be given complete evaluation. Prior to this the project has been in constant flux through all the preliminary stages of concept development, working through details, and finished drawings that are the results of the student's thinking.

Jury is difficult for some students, but the occasion is also highly informative. Here the student's work is given full attention by well-informed, professional designers. Give them your attention, take notes if you wish. Valuable information on the design process can be learned, even when work other than your own is being discussed. Criticism of another student's work allows you to be more objective—not only in hearing the comment, but in its possible application to your own project.

A project "singled out for praise" is a comment that all design students want to hear. It is seldom heard, however, and its absence need not be taken to mean that no work or no learning is taking place.

Chapter 5

Three Perceptions of Interior Space

To students of interior design or architecture the word "space" usually means an enclosed volume of a particular dimension or an amount of measurable square footage. Late-twentieth-century minds think too of outer space. However, our sensory perception of space—the way we think about it, the way we think of "making" space (or building or designing it)—is preceded by information that is less measurable than such characteristics as dimension or amount, or the advances of space science.

Designers and architects speak of shaping, organizing, and articulating space. They say that they do this in order to make the space, to give it form in a shape that will allow for use and endow it with meaning. Meaning gives space identity; it is what makes us see that a space is a place—a particular place. Place, in a nongeographical sense, has been defined by philosopher Susanne Langer as

> a created thing, an ethnic domain made visible, tangible, sensible. As such it is, of course, an illusion. Like any other plastic symbol, it is primarily an illusion of self contained, self sufficient, perpetual space. But the principle of organization is its own: for it is organized as a functional realm made visible—the center of a virtual world, the "ethnic domain," and itself a geographical semblance.[1]

This semblance (or similarity), this outer form of seeming spatial reality created in the plastic arts, in architecture, in interiors, has at its artistic foundations his-

---

[1]Susanne K. Langer, *Feeling and Form: A Theory of Art* (New York: Charles Scribner's Sons, 1953).

torical theories and subsequent spatial perceptions of science. It would seem that scientific spatial investigation always precedes artistic spatial conception.

Scientific perception of space—and artistic conception and the consequent depiction of it—has changed over time in relation to theories on the structure of the universe. Since the beginning of the recorded history of the advances of science and art, there have been three theories of the space of the universe: the Greco-Egyptian Ptolemaic system held by both the ancient and medieval West; the Copernican system of the Renaissance; and the relational theories of the twentieth century.

The theories of scientific speculation and investigation are transferred as perceptions—through the senses—into artistic creations. These creations become the depictions or constructions that are the visible, physical characterizations of centuries. Time indicates that once a scientific view of the universe becomes pervasive in a culture, it permeates that culture through creative, artistic work. It also exerts an influence on the popular mind. Therefore it is not only the artist whose perception is changed; the sensibility of the architect and the interior designer is influenced as well. It is apparent that once an artistic spatial conception comes into being it never falls into complete desuetude.

Ages, epochs, and periods do not end with the death of a king, the overthrow of a government, or the turning of a calendar. Great chunks of time are required for the design and production of the myriad stuffs that make up the physical artifacts that characterize a period.

Even the onrush of the twentieth century does not wipe out the validity of differing spatial theories. When a theory continues to have meaning, it can be used over and over again as both concept and realization. Past spatial perceptions in the creative mind may be called up when needed. They will not return to use as new theories and concepts, but they can make for renewed visions of what artistic creations might become.

The Ancient/Medieval Concept

The Greco-Egyptian Ptolemaic system (323–30 B.C.) maintained that the Earth was the fixed center of the universe and posited that the sun and the stars rotated around it. According to some architectural historians, the architecture of Greek temples is monolithic in origin and concept; they express no awareness of containing space (see Figure 25A). The ancient temples were solid structures, their interiors designed to conceal the statue of a god or to hide a sacrificial altar. Their spaces had no suggestion of direction or movement: they stood quite still, much as in the Ptolemaic order of the universe the Earth stood still.

The concept of Earth as the universal center prevailed into the later years of the Roman Empire. Architecturally, the concept culminated in the most perfectly preserved of all ancient buildings—the Pantheon—built when Rome was at its imperial height, around 120–24. In this temple the curved canopy of heaven, some say, is represented in the hemispherical dome that rises over the circular-planned rotunda. The Pantheon's interior is representative of the ancient idea of the universe, in which everything revolves around one point (see Figure 24). That one point is found on the unseen diameter of the section at the spring line of the dome. And if the circumference line of the dome were continued, completing the arc, the other half of the hemisphere would make a perfect sphere just tangent to the temple floor. Thus the entire building revolves around a single, invisible, but all-important geometric point. Within the shell of the temple the great sphere is the whole concept.

24. The Pantheon, Rome, circa 120–24, Plan and Section

A. In the closed interior, light enters only from above through a giant occulus. The volume of the interior exhibits a powerful and elegant geometry of pure forms.

B. In the section, the uppermost band of the vertical wall-cylinder marks the diameter line of the hemispherical dome. If the arc of the dome is continued downward, the corresponding lower arc touches the temple floor to make the ancient, symbolic shape of the Earth—a complete, perfect sphere.

Centuries earlier, before the high civilizations of Greece and Rome, the Pharaohs who ruled Egypt for thirty centuries gave their heavenly aspirations the physical form of the pyramids (see Figure 25B). The great forms were symbolically shaped to resemble artificial mountains. Along with the ziggurats of Mesopotamia, these gigantic forms spreading out over the flat land are the first truly monumental buildings. Interior space within them is by comparison almost nonexistent (although admittedly no "activity" took place within). Egyptian temples, entered through huge pylon walls, led into grand hypostyle halls, their enormous volumes filled almost to capacity with superscaled stone columns. The interior spaces of these temples are always filled up, occupied by columns (see Figure 25C).

Later, as the system of the Earth as the center of the universe continued to prevail, the medieval mind continued to think of the Earth as fixed and flat. As a consequence, painters of the period depicted nature, people, buildings, and interiors as flat, fixed, and static (see Figure 25D).

Throughout the Middle Ages the collective spirit and the universal ethos of religious and social sanctions expressed a turning inward. Not only was that turning inward to be seen in the attitudes of religion and the strictures of secular daily life; it was expressed in unmistakable form in the built environment. In this period the fortified city developed: Houses were closed to the street; small windows were like islands in large areas of wall (see Figure 25E); the great churches allowed light to enter through dark stained glass, but no light escaped back out into the open air. Interiors, whether in sacred churches or secular palaces, were closed into themselves. They had only necessary physical connections with adjoining interior spaces. Domestic interiors had little light, little comfort, and little visual delight (see Figure 25F). "Somber grandeur" might describe most of the interiors of this period.

The symbol of the Middle Ages is the Gothic cathedral (see Figure 25G). This building has most often been described as having an interior space designed to progress toward the altar. It is true that Gothic churches display progression in the repetition of the arched bay; but the Gothic bay is essentially a method of constructing vertically rather than a conscious application of aesthetic progression.

Rather than moving forward, Gothic cathedral interiors always seem to be striving upward, an expression of the medieval preoccupation with entering heaven. Still, these interiors hold space in, making it finite, self-contained (much as Greek or Roman interiors were self-contained), and unable to make the final, upward leap to heaven. The finials that give the Gothic style its visual expression of aspiration are further symbols of the aspirations of the period. They serve no structural necessity, but reinforce, as outward symbols, the wish to turn heavenward. Nevertheless, the upward movement in this style of architecture, though it typifies spiritual aspirations, does so in forms whose main physical effect is that of inert stability.

25. The Ancient/Medieval Spatial Concept

A. Temple plan: The Parthenon, Athens, 447–32 B.C. This great building, made of solid stone, presents a quality of perfect stillness. The exterior is fully expressed, while the interior shows limited spatial development.

B. Pyramid-type tomb section: Egypt, 4th Dynasty, 2680–2565 B.C. A section diagram indicates the disproportionate amount of building material used to produce a small interior space.

C. Hypostyle hall plan: Temple of Ammon, Karnak, Egypt, 1550–323 B.C. Heavy material for walls and columns was required to build halls of the type. The diameter of the columns is almost equal to the width of the intervening spaces.

D. Painting: *A Life of Christ,* detail, Giotto, 1266–1337. The concept of Earth as flat and static was depicted by painters. The figures of men and sheep show little dimension. The curtain-like stone background seems to float weightlessly.

E. Fortified-type construction: England, circa eleventh century. For safety, the medieval building was fortified. Few windows were possible in the forbidding walls, and little light could penetrate into the dark interiors.

F. Domestic interior: England, circa 1300. The Gothic hall begins to articulate space with openings and exposed construction. Gloom remains, but daylight is consciously brought inside.

G. Religious interior: Lincoln Cathedral, England, 1185. Gothic cathedrals expressed the spiritual aspirations of the age. The height pushed people and space heavenward. The great upward reach of these interiors is "restless," but it is a static restlessness.

A

B

C

D

E

F

G

Sir Banister Fletcher observed that the Gothic cathedral is a complex, restless structure composed of many vertical features, but that the restlessness never achieves a true leap, movement, or direction. Gothic space is both depiction and perception of static restlessness. In his television series *Civilization,* Sir Kenneth Clark observed that Gothic space "culminates" in stillness.

So splendid and so numerous are the examples of the Gothic cathedral that one cannot select a single building as the crown of the period. Each country had its own best example—in France, Rheims, Chartres, and Notre Dame; in England, Wells, Salisbury, Lincoln, and Westminster Abbey; in Italy, Milan, Florence, and Sienna; in Spain, Toledo, Seville, and Barcelona; and in Germany, Cologne cathedral (finished in 1880). All share the best of Gothic ideas.

Movement toward a finite altar, the bays of naves pacing a measured beat; the upward struggle to heaven is unmistakable in the "vehement verticalism" and balanced "high tension" described by Nikolaus Pevsner.[2] The pointed arch, the flying buttress, and the vault combine technically with the glorious colored glass to set these inert masses trembling with mysterious spatial emotion. More than any other creation, the interiors of these buildings are the almost miraculous achievement of the Middle Ages.

Interiors built on the ancient/medieval concept of space are distinguishable from those that followed in later ages. The distinguishing characteristics are exhibited similarly where the interior is large or small, important or obscure. With some variations the concept follows through in the design of tomb, temple, cathedral, or house. In general the interiors of this long period were designed as separate entities, functioning with minimal connections to other spaces within the same building. Indeed, the building itself, in most instances, has the quality of independence.

These interiors contain not space, but statues, royal remains, relics, treasure, ritual, or throngs of people. Just as the ancients' view of the universe said that it was contained in a single, unchanging pattern, so interiors reflected that same notion (although it is unlikely that the application was a conscious one).

The contained interior, one planned as a separated, isolated space, can possess its own form. Its architectural components, furniture, color, and materials need have no relationship to adjoining spaces. In such interiors there is little point made of doorways to connect spaces. Their size and embellishment are not primary. Likewise, windows are usually small, unimportant openings, moderate in size and frequently few in number. Such windows let in light and admit air, but they are not intended to make physical connections with the landscape or to visually bring in the out-of-doors. In addition, the large windows in the cathedrals and their expanses of stained glass were developed to lighten the walls, to reduce actual weight—not to bring light into the interior or to connect it with a surrounding view.

Some contained interiors receive light only through skylights or glass domes. These roof openings allow no exterior connections at all—no view and no sidelight. The Pantheon of antiquity and Frank Lloyd Wright's twentieth-century Guggenheim Museum are spaces that exemplify the concept of containment, each appropriate to its purpose.

Certain inherent advantages accrue to the designer who employs this type of spatial concept. By their forms, contained spaces offer a sense of separateness, of a place apart. They are spaces isolated from distraction with a subsequent focus that results from the very nature of the form. These interiors leave the outside world behind and gather in the comfort of solitude, of stillness. The qualities of

---

[2]Nikolaus Pevsner, *An Outline of European Architecture* (London: Penguin Books, 1977).

the concept of containment developed in ancient/medieval interiors make for a concept that is strong enough and desirable enough that we find this spatial notion in continuing use. Though often blended or merged with later concepts, the ideas are still appropriate for some interiors by some designers in the late twentieth century.

The Renaissance Concept

The ancient system of understanding the universe remained in effect both in science and in art until it was superseded by the discoveries of Copernicus in the late fifteenth and early sixteenth centuries. Copernicus (1473–1543) overturned the ancient view of the Earth-centered universe and instead posited that the sun is the fixed center and that its planets, including Earth, revolve around it. The Copernican system completely altered our view not only of the universe, but of our relationship to it. The notion that the sun was at the center of all heavenly motion was the first view in hundreds of years that questioned the view of the universe derived from Ptolemy. The proposal was debated for decades by the scientific community and by the Church as well, the "Earth as center of the universe" being more in accord with biblical Scripture.

The Copernican discovery was a revolutionary theory that not only affected the scientific perception of the universe, but also transformed the artistic creation of space in painting, architecture, and interiors. In the artist's mind the new ideas of space were made visible through the development of linear perspective. From the moment of its discovery, perspective was used without hesitation; and for the next four centuries it was the dominant force in creative thinking in all the arts. The scientific Copernican theory related the parts of the universe; the perspective system of the artist related the parts of a visual whole to a particular standpoint. Both systems sought to make things knowable from a distance.

Perspective principles were not the invention of any single artist; they were developed collectively as a means of expression by the whole of the Renaissance. It became the means of organizing pictorial space as well as the space of buildings, their interiors, and whole cities. The artists, architects, and designers of all the great paintings, buildings, and interiors of the Renaissance relied on perspective as a way of conceiving three-dimensional space.

The first full-blown use of perspective was in painting (see Figure 26A). Long before any Renaissance interior had been designed, the fifteenth-century artist Masaccio used perspective to organize his fresco *The Holy Trinity with the Virgin and St. John* (1425) in the church of Santa Maria Novella in Florence. Trinity pictures had been painted over and over again in Florence; but this one, with the new perspective system applied, found a new way of depicting space.

Masaccio composed the picture from a very low station point, looking up past the figures of the Trinity into the receding form of a painted barrel vault. The vault dominates the picture, encircles it. The perspective pierces the surface of the flat wall. With its heavily coffered, painted vault, the fresco becomes a two-dimensional triumphal arch. The barrel vault in this picture suggested one of the major solutions to the problem of architectural vaulting in the whole of the Renaissance. It took, however, some forty-five years for such a solution to be attempted. In the Church of St. Andrea in Mantua (1472–1514) Leon Battista Alberti used the barrel vault both in the exterior and interior as the controlling device of the design (see Figure 26B).

The Copernican theory of space and the new possibilities of perspective, coupled with euclidean geometry, make up the backbone of Renaissance composition. Artists made drawings that linked proportion to geometry. In Germany Albrecht Dürer, in Italy Leonardo da Vinci, and others throughout Renaissance Europe studied the symbolic connections between human and geometric proportion. The information from these intellectual studies was added to the dramatic potential of perspective in the creation of paintings, architecture, and interiors (see Figure 26C). In these the outer world is seen in three dimensions from the point of view of the individual ego, a single point of view. Paintings and buildings and their interiors were planned specifically to take advantage of the principles of perspective. Indeed, there was no other way the creative mind of the artist could conceive of the visible world in these centuries, and further expressions for the use of perspective were found over and over again.

In the new interiors the application of Renaissance perspective gave way to rooms planned in sequence, a dramatic change from medieval interiors that were designed in relative isolation from other parts of a building. Elaborate schemes were devised in connected room plans so that the longest vista, or the most complex relationships in geometric progression, could be incorporated. In the previous epoch the most important building and its interior was the church. Now, although religious buildings remained significant, secular architecture and design took on an importance not seen before. Churches, palaces, and public interiors all acquired the new device of perspective. Three-dimensional space, an idea fully developed in the period, translated itself into great rooms with plans shaped as circles, ovals, octagons, hexagons, and squares—euclidean geometry put to the service of art. Often these rooms were made to connect physically and artistically with elegant halls or corridors. These led into other geometric rooms, creating suites and apartments of great impact.

In the churches the new scientific evidence of infinity could be embodied in the nave designed to stretch out toward the altar, the wall behind the altar—much like Masaccio's original picture—pushing away still farther in painted perspective. And over and over again designers used the device in ever more inventive ways. Even quite small interiors were made to seem deeper, higher, or wider when per-

26. The Renaissance Spatial Concept

A. Perspective. *The Holy Trinity with the Virgin and St. John,* circa 1425, Masaccio, Church of Santa Maria Novella, Florence. Perspective, as a compositional device, appears for the first time in this picture. More than thirty years elapsed before the device was applied to building; then it was applied to all of the arts as an important means of organization.

B. Vaulting. Church of St. Andrea, 1472–1514, Alberti, Mantua. The perspective composition of Masaccio's fresco is interpreted in the façade and carried in the interior of the church. The receding barrel vault was used throughout the Renaissance as a recurrent form.

C. Proportion. *Illustration of the Proportions of the Human Body,* circa 1485–90, Leonardo da Vinci. The proportions of the human body are compared to those of geometric form. Before recorded history, the circle symbolized the universe; the square represented the Earth. Similar studies were made by artists all over Western Europe.

D. Scale and geometry. Partial plan, St. Peter's Basilica, 1506–1622, Bramante, Michelangelo, and others, Rome. Circles, squares, ovals, hemispheres, and segmented portions of these geometric forms make up the plan and the space of the interior. All of the parts are large, almost stupendous in scale. This scale is heroic and identifies the building as the most important one in the Renaissance.

E. Mathematical proportions. Plan, Villa Capra, 1550–51, Palladio, near Venice. The space of the plan is organized around an equal, double axis. Each room's size, shape, and proportion are based on the relationship to its neighbor. All rooms are in ratio to each other, and to the central hall. With variations, the architect investigated the theory of such concepts for some fifteen years.

A

B

C

D

E

spective principles were applied. Then as never before, space was manipulated and molded to produce effects. Some of these effects were created from the imagination as had happened in the past; however, many of the effects came from the overwhelming interest in the science of mathematics.

Isaac Newton (1642–1727), the scientist of this new "world order," had developed a primary system of the laws of motion. The Newtonian system, based on mathematics, even inspired a religious movement—deism—that had God-as-mathematician at its head, just as Newton's universe is entirely mathematical in construction.

Mathematics as a way of thinking became the international mode in the eighteenth century: The Enlightenment is based on the scientific ideas of Newton and René Descartes, its leading mathematician. Bernard Fontenelle deduced from their theories that the geometrical spirit is not so tied to geometry that it cannot be detached and carried into other branches of knowledge, suggesting to us that everything can be understood through mathematical calculations.

In his efforts to reassure us that the world is absolute and that it has a "truth so clear and apparent" it cannot be questioned, Descartes said that a square can only have four sides. Unfortunately, in this simplification of information he also found it necessary to take away color and scent from reality—the sensuous qualities—and said that each and every body (as its own separate identity) was only the mathematical idea of that body; that all bodies could be measured in length, width, and height. The Cartesian world is a reality that is not the physical world as we see and feel it, but one in which everything is reduced to an amount that is measurable. The Cartesian world is our measurable, thinking notion of it; feeling is to be put aside as suspect and not trustworthy.

Although secular architecture and interiors gained more and more attention as projects for Renaissance designers, ecclesiastical projects received the creative genius of the period. The centerpiece of religious structures in the Renaissance is St. Peter's Basilica in Rome (see Figure 26D).

St. Peter's Basilica (1506–1622) is the largest and most important building of the period. When it was finished, it was the product of many artists including Bramante, Michelangelo, Maderno, and Bernini. The Basilica, piazza, and Vatican complex comprise a group of vast proportions. The Basilica itself covers 25,230 square yards. The dome with its lantern is 452 feet high, 137 feet in diameter.

The space is so large that the size of the interior is hard to estimate. Not only are the structural piers of stupendous scale, but sculptures of saints and cherubs are colossal—16-foot-high saints and 7-foot cherubs. To gaze into the vastness of the space, onward and onward toward the baroque altar, is awe-inspiring and sublime. Fronting the cathedral is the great outdoor room designed by Bernini. This colonnade-enriched piazza is, as Banister Fletcher said, "The greatest of all atriums before the greatest of all churches in Christendom."[3] The oval piazza leads to a square stair-court; the Basilica is composed of square, circle, and triangle in both the plan and the articulation of the exterior and interior volumes. These shapes visually and structurally support the great circular dome of Michelangelo. Geometry and perspective are everywhere in this composition.

Renaissance perspective and geometry joined classical ideas of mathematical proportion and were applied to houses as well as to churches. Andrea Palladio typifies Renaissance concern with measurement in the country houses he built in Northern Italy.

---

[3]Sir Banister Fletcher, *A History of Architecture on the Comparative Method* (New York: Charles Scribner's Sons, 1950).

All of Palladio's villas include symmetry and mathematical proportioning as governing principles. He used certain rules from which he never departed. A center hall always served as the central axis for the plan, and rooms of lesser importance on either side were matched in size and proportion to the central room. Pevsner states that Palladio's villas, planned over a period of about fifteen years, were all "derived from a single geometrical formula." Harmonic ratios were applied, not only within each room, but in the unseen, felt ratios of one room in relation to another.

In the Villa Capra at Vicenza, known also as the Villa Rotonda, a circular dome centers on a cruciform hall (see Figure 26E). Rooms on either side are symmetrically planned and in ratio to the central hall and to each other. Each door in this progression of rooms is aligned with its opposite neighbor; windows in the rooms on either end connect on the same axis and extend the vistas into the open landscape. The original plan for the villa extended and connected well into the open land. Pevsner says that, "To get the totality of a Palladian countryside composition one has to add to such a nucleus the curved colonnades and low outbuildings by which the villa takes in the land around."[4] This embracing attitude proved to be of the greatest historical consequence. Here, for the first time in Western architecture, landscape and building were conceived as belonging to each other, as dependent on each other. Here, for the first time, the chief axes of a house are continued into nature.

At about the same time, Michelangelo planned a similar vista for the Farnese Palace in Rome. He suggested that the palace be connected with a perspective vista to the Farnese gardens on the opposite side of the Tiber River.

In France too, infinity in science and religion became a part of the conceptual underpinnings of design at Versailles, the palace of Louis XIV. The architecture, the grand interiors, and the elaborate gardens all stretch out along perspective axes as far as the eye can see. The Galerie des Glaces (Hall of Mirrors), discussed in Chapter 7, is a rich and significant peak in this concept of interiors.

The Modern Concept

In the twentieth century, science, through the work of Herman Minskowski, discovered a new structure of the universe. This new concept saw the universe in four dimensions with space and time coming together to make an invisible continuum. By about 1830 a new geometry had been created that employed more than three dimensions. Space in modern physics was then conceived as relative to a moving point. The single, fixed point of Renaissance open space no longer made scientific sense. Modern science could now see the element of space-time as an unlimited, but relational continuum.

Mathematics, evolving through the relativity theories of Alfred North Whitehead and Albert Einstein, became an expression of a new landscape—the landscape of time and space. This scientific thinking was quickly made visible in the art of the newly developing cinema and in the Cubist movement. Architecture and interior design, together with industrial and product design, shared in this important influence.

In the continuum of time and space modern people, according to early twentieth-century scientists, would need to develop the ability to move among diverse perspectives in the cosmos, an idea extended by the modern Spanish philosopher

---

[4]Pevsner, *An Outline of European Architecture.*

José Ortega y Gasset. He said that "perspectivism" indicates to us the complex and ambiguous nature of our own existence, and that it shows the unmistakable artificiality of Renaissance euclidian geometry.

The twentieth-century scientific world of four dimensions found its first artistic realization in painting, just as the artistic keystone of the Renaissance had been in painting. With the Cubist revolution (around 1910) art broke with the Renaissance principle of the single viewpoint in perspective and instead employed aspects of Einstein's theories of relativity and simultaneity in the portrayal of objects. The new way of seeing allowed all parts of an object to be seen together, including those parts that are invisible from a single viewpoint (see Figure 27A). When Picasso painted a face, several sides were revealed together. The flat canvas plane was no longer seen as something to be given perspective depth, but as the limitless depth of space-time.

Like the painters, the writers of the period made Cubist-relativist novels, plays, and poems. Gertrude Stein wrote her version of random simultaneity by repeating words and phrases, such as "a rose is a rose is a rose" and her description of New York's Rockefeller Center as the best architectural complex she had "ever seen ever seen ever seen." Writing about Picasso, Stein said that "because the way of living had changed the composition of living had extended and each thing was as important as any other thing."[5] Her statement reiterates the relative importance between one thing and another thing.

Simultaneous occurrences and simultaneous narratives were also used by Aldous Huxley and Phillip Toynbee in their novels, and Pirandello used the device, he said, as a "way beyond art" in his plays. In *Six Characters in Search of an Author* Pirandello said, "A character has a life of his own . . . is somebody. A man may be nobody." The flux and uncertainty of life then became part of his art. Wylie Sypher observed that Cubist writers, like Cubist painters, and like the scientists, "accepted reality as a continual transformation where fiction impinges on fact, where art intersects life."

Filmmakers of the period also used Cubist techniques. Cinematographer Sergei Eisenstein explained film montage as "a complex composed of film strips containing photographic images" that are arranged, two or more, so that "the polyphonic structure achieves its total effect through the composite sensation of all the pieces as a whole." He said further that "in our new perspective—there is no perspective."[6]

The principle of synchronization is the basis of mechanization in the twentieth century—synchromesh gears bring parts together at varying speeds: Cinema is a primary art of this century because it synchronizes thinking, feeling, space, and time. The assembly-line technique is a symbol of American "know-how" in mass production. The automobile is a whole concept realized by the assembly of a collection of parts.

Twentieth-century kinetic sculpture synchronizes changing forms into patterns where time is a function of space. This is apparent not only in the mobiles of Alexander Calder (see Figure 27B), but in such early works as Boccioni's stationary sculpture *Bottle Evolving in Space*, which showed composite views of the solid bottle by means of syncopation (see Figure 27C). And syncopation is Jazz movement, the inherent tempo of the early years of the century.

---

[5]Wylie Sypher, *Rococo to Cubism in Art and Literature* (New York: Vintage Books, A Division of Random House, 1963).

[6]Ibid.

Twentieth-Century Organic Space

Twentieth-century architects and designers were greatly influenced by the new scientific and artistic ideas. Einsteinian theory in physics and the new emotional concepts of the psychologists encouraged them to exploit the ideas and make them evident in physical space. Now the rooms that were previously so separated, so geometrically complete in themselves even when planned in sequential relationship, became unified overlapping spaces that flowed from one "area" to another "area." Interpenetration and interrelationship, concealment and exposure, within and without, were the shifting, drifting, connecting, and contrasting means by which new spaces were given shape. This perception of built space has been called "organic." It is the interrelated, relational mode of the twentieth century, and it came from the new scientific understanding of the universe.

The pioneer in exploring this modern concept of interrelated interior space was the American architect Frank Lloyd Wright. It was he who called this conception of space "organic," a word adopted from his teacher, architect Louis Sullivan.

The interconnection between inner and outer spaces, and the interior as one room, were explored by Wright for many years. The interrelationship, or "interpenetration" as it was called, of manmade building and nature appears early in Wright's houses. The plans stretch out into the land, grow in and out of natural surroundings, become part of nature. The houses merge into the landscape, with plants packed in close. Vines trail over the outer walls and intertwine with projecting eaves and cantilevers, increasing the connection between house and nature. Whenever possible, materials inside were used as they came from nature—unfinished timber, rugged stone, and rough, unpolished granite.

Wright's domestic interiors have flexible, open plans. As much as possible, a whole house is sometimes conceived as one room with the parts interrelated. Built in Chicago and vicinity, the Isabel Roberts House (see Figure 27D), the Robie House, and the Coonley House are among Wright's designs that exhibit organic interiors. Full integration of public spaces such as entry, living, and dining rooms was the goal. As Giedion reports, Wright said he designed "the whole floor as one room, screening various portions in the big room for certain domestic purposes—like dining or reading, or receiving a formal caller."[7]

The European counterpart of Wright's explorations finds its clearest expression in the early work of the German architect Ludwig Mies van der Rohe. In the German Pavilion for the 1929 International Exposition in Barcelona, Spain, Mies van der Rohe manipulated the space in a manner similar to Wrightian ideas (see Figure 27E). The pavilion, however, is completely open internally with only the most economical use of screens to differentiate areas.

The roof of the pavilion is a thin plane supported on slender, shining steel shafts; the outer walls are the severest planes of transparent and opaque material. The pavilion's interior spaces are loosely defined by screens of pale-green-tinted glass and onyx, which, precisely placed in contrasting juxtaposition to one another, create moving interplay of space and light. Shimmering pools—planes of blue-green water—add to the floating lightness of the interior, the water sending reflections onto the screens and ceiling. The luxurious materials—marble, onyx, steel, and glass—contribute to the polished elegance of the pure, unadorned character of this new design in the early twentieth century.

In France too, the new way of looking at space took shape in the work of architect Le Corbusier. His houses were designed on the basis of the new concepts

---

[7] Sigfried Giedion, *Space, Time and Architecture* (Cambridge: Harvard University Press, 1963).

of organic and interrelated spaces and the use of new materials developed since the outset of Cubism—ferro-concrete, sheet glass, extruded steel, and the like. In what is perhaps his most famous design—the Villa Savoye at Poissy—Le Corbusier's concern for integrating interior and exterior is shown in a way that is quite different from Wright or Mies.

Le Corbusier was himself a painter and, like the Cubists, the new space conception is many-sided. The villa can be looked at from all four sides, from below (since it is freed from the ground) and from above (from its roof terraces).

This house stands up from the ground, on piers that elevate the enclosed volume of the space, putting it aloft into the sun, air, and breezes (see Figure 27F). This building cannot be understood from only one point of view. There is no front or back; no one façade is more important than another.

The interior of Savoye is fluid space, molded by geometric shapes that move out into the terrace spaces accessible through glass and sliding walls. Interior and exterior connections from floor to floor are by ramp. Curves are used sparingly.

Later in Le Corbusier's development, his investigations of space led to Ronchamp, the chapel near Bescanon, France. What had been an interplay of geometric planes that are pure, mechanical, and intellectual at Savoye, become organic, free, and imaginative at Ronchamp. There the forms are molded, as Nikolaus Pevsner has said, "in formal acrobatics."[8] Curving walls and ceiling planes combine with penetrations of daylight that sparkle and wash the surfaces, imparting to the volume of the interior a floating and mysterious presence.

These Modern interiors, like the grand spaces of the Middle Ages and the Renaissance, exhibit the great sweep of human imagination. A commingling of art

---

[8]Pevsner, *An Outline of European Architecture.*

27. The Modern Spatial Concept

A.   Simultaneity. *Les Demoiselles d'Avignon,* circa 1907–10, Picasso, Paris. The Cubist painters expressed the scientific theories of relativity in artistic forms. Now, more than one view of a person or an object could be shown simultaneously from a single point of view.

B.   Movement. *Janvier,* 1950, Alexander Calder. Mobile sculpture uses kinetics as the conceptual basis for the balancing of shapes in open space. All of the parts move, but in relation to each other.

C.   Syncopation. *Bottle Evolving in Space,* circa 1911–12, Boccioni, Italy. The artist applies American Jazz rhythm to the sculpture to convey movement and energy. We cannot know with certainty, despite the title, if the form is in the process of becoming or dissolving.

D.   Interpenetration. Isabel Roberts House, 1907, Frank Lloyd Wright, River Forest, Illinois. The arms of the parts of the ground floor reach out into the landscape, joining it and drawing it inward. The public rooms flow together, lessening traditional boundaries. Nature is deliberately linked to the interiors.

E.   Transparency. Plan, German Pavilion, 1929, Mies van der Rohe, Barcelona. Structural needs and spatial definition do not depend on solid walls. Thin steel columns carry the weight of the roof, and walls are freed to become sheets of glass. Exterior boundaries allow the outside to come in. Interior spaces are loosely demarcated.

F.   Lightness. Villa Savoye, 1928–30, Le Corbusier, Poissy, France. Lifted up on piers, both house and ground are freed. In spite of the enclosed, box-like volume, the house appears to be light, almost like folded paper. There is no front or back, the bottom is in view, and the top is used as an open terrace. Each part of the house is given equal importance.

A

B

C

D

E

F

and science has enriched creative output in every age. In some instances the combination is deliberate, a conscious part of the conceptual act of making interiors. In other moments art and science combine in a designer's mind as an unconscious response to information and data, as well as to soft, sensate feeling and intuition.

These concepts are lasting—indeed, enduring. So far, they are all we know of how to make interior space: the ancient interior concept, contained and separated from outside forces; the geometric, infinite interior concept of the Renaissance; or the Modern interior concept—organic and relational. Combinations of these three spatial perceptions occur throughout history, each succeeding one added to a previous one again and again. Today such combinations are still being made and are still valid. Ancient, Renaissance, and Modern spatial perceptions now exist together in our imagination. They are constant and recurrent ways of mastering conceptions for interiors.

The Application of Spatial Perceptions

In summary, we can make the following statements.

1. If the Earth is contained in a finite universe, as the ancients believed, completely determinable (except heavenward) and if we live in that universe, our view of the space of the Earth must, by consequence, also be finite, contained. Indeed, we cannot perceive it any other way and our artistic creations will reflect such a view. Such a view will continue, as it did throughout the Middle Ages, until, through science, another view is made possible.

2. In the Renaissance, when a new perception of the universe came into being through science, people began to see their relationship to the space of the Earth in connection with that new science. If the new universe is three-dimensional, is infinite, then we must view ourselves (as well as the space we conceive artistically) as connected to that world. And we try to make the manmade world reflect that view. Artistic experiment uses whatever means of expression is at hand.

3. If yet another space perception is postulated by science, saying that there are more than three dimensions, that space and time connect to make an unending but relative continuum, then again our view of what is possible, of what is necessary artistically, will be expressed as conceptions grow in accord with the influence of a new science.

When perceptions change in the making of interior spaces, the previous perception does not die out: It continues to be used whenever appropriate. Scientific perceptions become obsolete, but artistic spatial perceptions of one age are added to the next and become part of a rich, universal spatial vocabulary. At the height of the Renaissance, for example, Gothic-like interiors were made. In the twentieth century some eloquent examples of Modernism use spatial concepts that are clearly more medieval than organic.

Wright's Guggenheim Museum is essentially a one-room contained space within which an organic ramp moves. The glass ceiling, however, seemingly explodes almost to infinity. Today, Post-Modernists are reviewing the geometry of the Renaissance with increasing enthusiasm. Some make only classical application of Renaissance geometric principles. Others use the principles in looser, more playful ways, but with the discipline found in classical thinking.

One theory of conceptual space may be no better than another, even though the scientific thinking from which a concept springs becomes useless and passé. A scientist is not free to choose which theory of the universe is valid; but a designer, reaching for aesthetic goals, may choose whatever suits a condition, whatever meets a need of the time.

Chapter **6**

Conceptual Design Thinking

What Is a Concept?

In all sizes and situations of designing interiors—from a single room to a complex series of interrelated spaces, from small domestic projects to corporate interiors involving multiple floors—design thinking springs from one notion, one all-encompassing idea. This is called a concept.

A concept is an idea held in the mind. It is an idea or notion—however small, or however incompletely detailed—that is a first thought, or series of first overall thoughts about a project. It is an idea that often comes spontaneously and is accessible perhaps only briefly. It is a generalization that is seen in the mind's eye as a whole, without particular parts.

In design, as in all activities that involve creation, conception is a beginning. Sometimes that beginning is found through information, and sometimes that beginning is touched off by inspiration—the mind's ability to make quick conclusions from facts, experiences, or from the need to solve a problem.

Interior design concepts should aim for the ideal, but only in terms of the limitations imposed by the realities of the program requirements and the restrictions of existing plans. The ideal can be only what is best within the confines of a given space. For example, column-free spaces may facilitate planning; but if a row of columns exists, removing them is usually not quite feasible. When columns exist in a plan, they are structural. It is best to consider them right away as a crucial part of the concept, and possibly the most worthwhile existing element to assist conceptual thinking.

A valid interior design concept cannot arise unless it springs from the program requirements, as well as from the existing plans. Interior design concepts always are provoked by external human needs—those physical requirements of daily life. This is different from concepts in the fine arts, which spring from the internal needs of an individual artist, the need to externalize internal feelings. The artist can decide to "design" or paint anything at all—apples on a plate, cows in a meadow, a picture of mother.

External human needs, on the other hand, are those required for function; and these are provided by the designer within an aesthetic frame. The functional needs are defined by the program of design requirements. You don't design a room for books if what is needed is a room for pots and pans. This is fundamentally the case, although, in theory, designers may experiment with all manner of ideas about making form, creating effects, looking at how materials can be used, and trying out combinations of shapes and colors. Indeed, until a problem is assigned to a student or a commission is given to a professional, all effort is in the realm of theory. How these external needs are turned into space for that specific activity—sleeping, eating, working—requires the mind's ability to transfer conceptual thinking into tangible solutions.

Design Concepts in Drawing Form

How does the mind transfer those concepts into form? When you have the idea in response to the program and the existing plan, it has to be turned into a drawn idea on paper. You may visualize a very intricate form in your mind. When you externalize that idea, it may just be a circle or a square or a line. How does that shape or line become a wall that defines a space, gives it a shape? How does it become a corridor or a piece of furniture? You may think that there must be some component to separate this from that. It may be a wall, it may be furniture, it may be a change in material on the floor plane, it may be the lowering of a ceiling plane.

The more you put down—that is, the more you draw and begin to develop—the closer you get to having a concept. This brings us to the brink of a concept that can push further into developmental phases.

Design Concepts in Written Form

Visual design concepts can be put down in words as well as drawings. A concept statement can be a brief declaration of what will be attempted in physical form. For example, the concept for a library could be described as "a well-lighted space for reading" or as "a quiet retreat for study." Either description may be an appropriate way to think about libraries; either description may help to arrive at a successful concept.

Certainly, the two approaches bring up different mental pictures of forms, materials, colors. One description begins to depict a space that is open, expanding, crisp, stimulating, bright. The other indicates, although vaguely and without any detail, a library that we picture as muted, muffled, soft, distant, and dim. One student may see certain shapes; another may see spaces as dark or light, smooth or textured; still another may visualize color of maximum contrast or no contrast at all. We are beginning to think conceptually when we translate plan and program into form. These are spatial concepts.

Concept as Theme

Concept in interiors, therefore, means some dominant characteristic; and this characteristic may be thought of as a theme. In every complex work of art there is a dominating characteristic. It may be a series of notes in a musical composition, or a shape on a fabric, which, when repeated, makes a pattern. In painting, the theme may be made of line and color. In architecture, each style in history has its own characteristic theme of colors and materials, and ways of shaping a volume. We recognize Gothic buildings primarily by the structure of the pointed arch. We recognize Modern buildings by their planar walls or glass curtain walls.

Establishing a dominant characteristic, or theme, is necessary for the design of every interior. The theme may have several levels of dominance: preeminent shape that can be repeated at a smaller or larger size; or a color that is at full intensity in one material or location, and only a tint or shade in another. This can begin to set the conceptual theme. There is a danger to be foreseen in the use of the word "theme" as a substitute for concept, since theme is often taken to mean decorative theme only—as in a "garden theme." This thinking usually results in a recitation of clichés, such as garden benches, fabric printed with leaves and flowers, treillage, brick-patterned flooring, and so forth. When such clichés are applied in a room, when the attempt is to re-create a garden rather than to evoke the characteristics that are in the idea of a garden, the goal of a spatial concept has been bypassed.

True theme, or concept, is a major element that sets a design direction. That element may be a way of treating the volume of space, a particular element to effect the scale, or a means of improving circulation. Every good interior is built up of one or more lines, shapes, and colors that establish its theme-concept.

Architect I. M. Pei has told how he arrived at the design concept for the East Wing of the National Gallery in Washington, D.C. Many weeks had been spent in attempts by him and his associates to make a beginning on the project and to suggest valid approaches. One day Pei walked to the drawing board, picked up a pencil, and "drew one line." That line connected the corner of the old gallery building to the farthest point of the triangular site. That one line became the concept for the project. All subsequent parts of the design honored, acknowledged, and extended the idea of that line, and brought out possibilities that expanded the conceptual thinking. We could say Pei's professional experiences, his direct confrontation with the program requirements, and his study of the site plan, all combined to make that first conceptual line. There was no preconceived idea of the line. Inspiration happened in a moment when pieces of experience and pieces of information came together simultaneously.

Conceptual Objectivity

Together with the existing plan—the first lines that you sketch from the idea in your mind—it is possible to begin an objective view of the concept that existed only a moment ago in your mind. These first ideas in sketch form take only a few minutes, but may result in important information about the space. The lines may also be, in an almost literal sense, the lines on which you "hang" the design in its entirety.

For beginning students—and for advanced ones as well—it is not necessary that the concept be unique, brilliant, or "different." What is more desirable is a concept that can be developed into a straightforward, well-ordered, workable scheme, and one that is deferential to the demands of the program. If what a student strives for is to be different, the chances are that is all the scheme will become. Differentness for its own sake, more often than not, will translate as strange, peculiar, and inhumane.

One of the criteria of mature design is to attain the greatest effect possible from the seeming least means. We call this "economy of means." This economy would, of necessity, have to include physical effort as well as the amount of material, or the number of elements, or more.

Concepts are not preconceived ideas that you carry around in your head. Philosopher Susanne Langer says, "Conception is the first requirement for thought."[1] A preconceived idea, as interior designer Robert Bray said in an interview, is "carrying around in your head a visual image of 'wouldn't this be beautiful, if I get the opportunity I'll use this.'" That is not appropriate to conceptual thinking, he says. A predisposition toward particular shapes, colors, or materials may or may not be appropriate or useful to a project. That favorite combination of colors, or the desire to use a favorite shape or material—one that is favored before the design problem is known—must be put aside.

The problem is that if the notion is preconceived, it does not relate to the need to find a particular solution to the work at hand. It does not spring from the need to solve this particular problem. Concept, in relation to interior design, must relate to the actual problem.

Conceptual Thinking as Process

Conceptual thinking is a process. It is thinking through a problem. Langer has also said, "Conception [is] giving form and connection, clarity, and proportion to our impressions, memories, and objects of judgement—it is the beginning of all rationality. Conception itself contains the elementary principles of knowledge: that an object keeps its identity (as Aristotle put it, 'A = A'), that it may stand in many relations to other things, that alternative possibilities exclude each other, and one decision entails another."[2] In the studio process this means (1) that after students are assigned a project, even the smallest interior is too complex to allow quick and easy solution; and (2) that concept in interiors, as in all other acts of creation, must be inclusive enough to maintain the initial idea, to build upon it, and to keep it clear from the beginning phase through the presentation of the final design.

Answers to problems in design come slowly, even though the first conceptual notion may be the inspirational flash. And what of inspiration? What does that mean as we engage our minds in conceptual thinking? Inspiration is a taking in, as of air into the lungs. In design, inspiration is the taking in of information— quickly. From this intake comes a stimulation that causes expiration, or response. Inspiration, however, can only stimulate our thinking. A flash of it may be the beginning, but that beginning requires detailed decisions that must be considered, delineated, and adjusted.

How the Concept Arises from the Existing Plan

Drawing as Thinking

This is the procedure design students should take when first starting on a new project. First, examine the plans and other architectural documents. Then look away, as if to daydream, to think; a spontaneous response to the plan will occur. Try out this daydream idea by making a quick sketch. More often than not you will say, "I see that won't work," probably because of some mistake in scale assumptions about the existing space. Look away; then turn again to the plan.

You look away in order to look inward, to visualize the volumes in the existing plan. This inward look must be externalized by drawing. Unfortunately, most

---

[1] Susanne K. Langer, *Problems of Art: Ten Philosophical Lectures* (New York: Charles Scribner's Sons, 1957).

[2] Ibid.

students think about the project and discard the idea before it has been tried out—before it has been externalized in a sketch.

Study the plan, become familiar with its characteristics—its parts, its shapes, its general configuration, even its specific measurements—then look inward, get a flash of an idea, and externalize it. The moment an idea is externalized, you can say—and the teacher can say—that won't work or that will work. But since this is only a briefly entertained idea, that sketch can be put aside and the same procedure followed through again. Again: First think inward, make a sketch of the idea, put that sketch aside, and go on to the next idea.

Within a short time you have a compilation of concept notions for the project at hand. You have read the program and are familiar with the requirements. You know the major characteristics of the plan. Then you begin making form within the space to accomplish whatever the needs are. It may take only a few seconds to superimpose a form on the existing plan on tracing-paper overlay. Do it again and again. These ideas may be in undifferentiated forms to begin with; but as the process continues, you will be compiling a stack of ideas, a vocabulary of possibilities.

Then you may run dry. But you say, "Wait a minute—I have all these ideas in my stack and I can go over them again. Each one of these sketches is a concept—perhaps unworkable, but a concept nonetheless."

The Synthesis of Existing Plan and Conceptual Thinking

There may be a synthesis of ideas in that stack of sketches, or you may select one idea that can be carried further for a few minutes. Whichever you find, the spatial concept must come from the existing plan whether the building is completed, is undergoing reconstruction or renovation, or is new construction in the planning stage. The degree of the designer's influence on the space may vary, but in each case the concept must come from the plan.

A new interior plan will take cues from what is possible within the space rather than from an idea imposed on the space. The attitude that should prevail is not "What do I want?" but rather, "What will this building allow?" The "What do I want?" attitude will result in a kind of insult imposed upon the building's form, and can lead to endless inappropriate conclusions. In this purely subjective way, the emotional feeling overrides the need for intellectual interpretation. At its best, a new plan concept will not cause what exists to suffer insult, but will draw out those qualities of strength that do exist even in less than superior architecture.

What are the cues in the existing architecture? The first is the building as a whole—its location and context, its form and materials; then the structure of the building as reflected in its external character and interior spaces, and its rationale. What is the building's purpose? Is it domestic, is it public, is it undergoing conversion from one purpose to another? All architectural elements—bearing and partition walls, columns, openings, doors, windows—can offer clues to spatial analysis. Quick overlays on tracing paper will generate several possibilities of form within the existing conditions. The location of mechanical systems, entrances, plumbing, ceiling heights, will affect the design at the outset. In even the simplest rectangular spaces many cues exist. Cues are in the formal properties of the building. They can be named, called out, used with the purpose of provoking new thinking based on the facts that exist within the boundaries of the plan.

The design may have many subordinate parts, but all of these will relate to a dominant theme. The parts make the whole and the whole is made up of parts, but all relate to one idea, one notion, one concept.

Concept Development

There is no magic moment that signals the end of conceptualization and the start of development. The concept is the "one line." Development sometimes begins when the second "line" is drawn. But it may not begin until adjustments in inches are made as firm decisions. Since design is a process—always growing, always ongoing—conceptual design development usually has a nebulous boundary and a vague moment of beginning.

However, as development continues, each new part must support the initial concept. This necessarily includes elements of scale, proportion, materials, and their contribution to the emerging form. Concept development begins when specific decisions are made.

Giving New Form to the Existing Space

New interior form is essentially the direct outgrowth of the existing volumes of the architecture. It can best be accomplished with fixed architectural components (as opposed to movable furniture), but these components need not necessarily have a direct bearing on the building's construction: The new components will give shape and configuration to the existing plan.

Most design assignments require reshaping the existing interior spaces. This may mean the redirection of circulation, or it may mean that the entire plan needs spatial reorganization. The components used to accomplish reorganization may be in the form of walls or fixed-in-place furniture that become part of the architecture. When there is a variety of formal elements to be considered, it is necessary to arrange all of them, disparate though they may be, into a single cohesive design.

New architectural elements used to reshape existing space may be simple in form, they may be quite submerged into the existing frame of the interior; but their effect on the space will be felt unmistakably. All additions should promote better organization, clearer form, and aesthetic integrity.

Sometimes the apparent form of an interior space is in contradiction to its essential structure. This may necessitate the peeling away of certain elements that obscure the better qualities that are hidden.

The philosopher-aesthetician Max Eastman has said, "Art is a matter of choice and selection"[3]; and that means inclusion, exclusion, and deletion as well. In design it is not only inclusion—allowing what is in the concept to develop—but the exclusion of parts that do not support or extend the concept. One thing must involve the next thing; one decision must lead to the next decision.

With the best interior design, we speak of the physical, material realization of a mental concept, and concept realization is a necessary goal. From mental concept to each and every part in an interior, we aim for an ideal whole where nothing wants subtraction, nothing wants addition.

The Appropriateness of the New Scheme

All interior spaces are designed for a purpose or function. That implies that character should be developed in the space. What is appropriate for one activity will fit that need; another need suggests another kind of spatial character. The activity to be characterized comes from the requirements of work, or the way of living suggested by the daily routine of the occupants. These are noted in the program. Character comes not only from the forms in the space, but from the way the forms are made; that is, the materials of the forms express something.

---

[3]John Dewey, *Art as Experience* (New York: Capricorn Books, G. P. Putnam's Sons, 1958).

Interiors must be appropriate to the buildings that enclose them. A simple house will look strange if its interior is made to resemble a Tudor castle. An office in a gleaming steel-and-glass tower will seem foolish if treated to Colonial American paneling and furniture or a theme otherwise out of context with its architectural character. Even if the interior is in a building of undistinguished design, it is the first obligation of the designer to attempt integration, harmony, and cohesion within. That is what appropriateness means in any activity. What is suitable for one condition or circumstance will be unsuitable for the next. Certainly the designer should try to reconcile what has been done with what needs to be done, a careful consideration of old and new. As the Renaissance architect Alberti put it, "One wants to improve what has been built, and not . . . spoil what is yet to be done."

Many examples can be cited where a style has been imposed on an interior made within a house or building designed in another style. There is no doubt that this is common practice. Yet it must be remembered that the interior creations we admire most, which have become the ideal we aim for, are all produced from a fusion of thinking that is intimately related to a particular time and place. Creations that express an age are always of that age and no other. That is not to imply that interiors inserted into existing buildings must be carried out in exactly the same style as the building, but in a sympathetic spirit to bring out its good qualities and at the same time improve its weaknesses.

Chapter 7

The Principles of Aesthetic Composition

Some practitioners and some teachers say that there are no rules to follow in the making of interiors. Still, there are aesthetic principles older than civilization that all designers of interiors must know.

What is usually absent—and what surely shows—in the interiors of those untrained in the practice of design is the ability to compose an overall interior. A totally composed interior is organized to fulfill its function and spatial purpose, and at the same time offers a visually unified and coherent aesthetic statement. Such a statement endows an interior with a sense of place.

"Place" in interiors is what makes the form of one space distinguishable from the form of another. Such interior forms are distinguishable not by their differentness, but by their conceptual wholeness or completeness, by their essential characters and structures. All interiors—like all works in the arts—can be conceived and examined in the theoretical terms of aesthetic principles. Anthropologists speculate that some of the principles, such as symmetry, pattern, and balance, were discovered by accident. Others have been developed through deliberate search to make existing phenomena understandable, as with the theories of proportion and color. Still other principles have evolved over centuries of exploration.

This chapter explores some of the principles that will help student designers to develop concepts and exploit the best attributes of the spaces in which their designs are realized. All of the principles discussed serve to support concepts. Some of them are concepts in themselves. The application will be evident in all phases of a project, from initial concept to final presentation.

Interior design students will find that many of these principles are inherent in the existing architecture of the projects assigned to them. Recognizing their existence will assist in those early stages of conceptual thinking. As the design process continues in later professional practice, the principles will become assimilated and internalized in a designer's method, and will be there to be drawn upon almost as second nature. However, their conscious use is better. Conscious application provides reason and justification for use.

Without guiding principles and conscious application, there is only subjectivity, copying, or guesswork. With only those to serve, there is small possibility of creating rational interiors. The use of the principles is necessary in all interiors—not all of them in any one project, but one or more will be used in every project.

Form, Shape, and Configuration

In the visual arts, in architecture, and in interior design, the terms *form, shape,* and *configuration* are often used interchangeably. Many aestheticians and others writing on the creative process in art and design present different and often conflicting definitions on the subject. Design students should attempt stricter distinctions of these terms. In doing so they will see more potential use and impact of the principle that each word designates.

A

28. Form: Parts Suggest the Whole

A. Statues from the Parthenon, East Pediment, 447–32 B.C., Phidias, Athens. Even when essential body parts are missing, we see human form.

Form

Form is the generic idea—the arrangement of parts that differentiates one object or identity from another. Form indicates the whole idea—both the internal structure and the external parts integrated into the whole.

In our visual world there are both natural and manmade forms. Natural forms are animal, vegetable, or mineral, including human form. Though each type of natural form is the same in its fundamental character, each is also distinguished by individual traits or features. The human body is made up of feet and legs, a torso, hands and arms, neck and head. The body form is recognized as human even when some of the parts are missing (see Figure 28A). In many damaged Greek sculptures of human form, the missing parts have little effect on our perception of the humanness of the depiction. The stick figures in children's drawings often delete all detail, but the essential parts are enough to indicate human form. Artists draw trees with great intricacy, showing trunk and limb formations and growth pattern of leaves. But children's drawings, with mere suggestion, can portray the form, the idea, the character of a tree (see Figure 28B).

Manmade things make up other classifications of forms. Manmade forms include all of the visual arts, such as painting and sculpture; music in all of its compositional modes; poetry, the novel, and drama. Buildings, interiors, and products are manmade forms that are, at times, the highest expression of civilization.

28. Form: Abstraction

B. The external human body is recognizable from its whole form made up from the shape of its parts. (1) Artistic interpretations of the body, whether from master painters (2) or from children (3), carry the same identifying characteristics: the form of the whole and the shape of its parts. A naturalistic tree (4), an artistic abstraction of a tree (5), and a reductivist tree drawn by a child (6)—all carry critical information on tree form. In each, the parts are the same. Though vastly different in shape, each is unmistakably the form of a tree.

B   4   5   6

Form always has content—the internal, or unseen, yet felt component of external form. Content does not exist without form; form can never exist without content. If form changes, content changes. Form is what is physical, what is seen; content is interpretation, the meaning of what is seen. Sometimes the meaning with which we endow form comes from past experience, from what we have seen in the visual world or have heard in the world of sounds.

Form in nature is always thought to be beautiful. It is beautiful for many of the same reasons that some manmade form is thought to be beautiful. The general characteristics of manmade—or aesthetic, or beautiful—form are defined as possessing a quality of unity (sometimes called organic unity). This unity implies that the form embodies all necessary elements and contains no elements that are not necessary. The beautiful aesthetic form is organized externally and internally. When we look at such a form, we do not wish to change it by addition or deletion; we see the form as whole, and we accept it as complete. Arriving at such forms for the designer of interiors is a problem similar to the creation of other forms. All of the remaining principles in this chapter contribute to qualities that are necessary to interior form-making.

Form in Interiors Form gives identity to space. Without form, space is amorphous, unstructured, and boundless. Form makes space measurable, a necessity in developing interiors. But since form includes external and internal features, that which is seen or perceived and that which is unseen or felt, the final evaluation may become aesthetically unmeasurable.

Interior spaces can be formed in an infinite number of arrangements. All of the components needed to complete an interior can be selected or designed by the same process by different people, yet each interior will be a form recognizable as a particular type of interior. If the interior is, for example, an office, each design scheme will be different. Each scheme will have its own plan of measurable space; each will have appropriate equipment, materials, and so forth; each will have an arrangement of all the parts necessary to an office. The form of an office is not the same as the form of another type of interior. The form, or idea, of an office is prescribed in such a way that we recognize its characteristics just as we recognize other forms, either human form or plant form.

Shape

Shape is the characteristic that gives individual identity to form. Physical shape is determined by the outward boundaries of an object. The boundaries refer to the outer contour, or outline. Although it is the outer edge that characterizes shape—as a circle describes a plate, or a flower—shape also carries indications of mass, or body. But shape is primarily concerned with external features (see Figure 29).

Without shape, space is formless. Without the possibility of giving shape even to outer space, our visual concept of it would be formless. If we do give shape to outer space in our mind's eye, we usually visualize it as a dome or an arc. However, this "roof" shape is poetic and artistic, not real.

The limitless number of shapes can be divided into two classifications: (1) natural (or organic), and (2) geometric. Natural shapes are characterized by softness and irregularity. Manmade geometric shapes are, with some exceptions, usually distinguished by hardness, and appear regular and rectangular. Natural shapes and manmade shapes complement each other. In interiors these qualities are contrasted, for example, when natural plant material is placed within highly controlled planar environments.

Shape, like form, has meaning or significance; that is, shape tells us something. A circular shape in a geometric equation only tells us that the shape is the

29. Shape

A. The form of a geometric circle, with small additions, can become a plate, a flower, or a wheel. Individual identity is given to form by shape.

B. Human form is also made specific by shape: a large, heavy body has a shape vastly different from a small, thin one.

C. Sculptures of the body can be shaped to suggest inner feeling, physical fact, or concern for the human condition.

problem. But a circular shape that defines a living room has a meaning larger than the simple geometric circle. All living rooms have similarities in form, but not all have the same shapes. Shape is specific identity. "Living room," no matter what shape describes its plan, has some meaning for everyone. Shape is specific identity. All living rooms have places for people to sit and tables to put things on. All living rooms are communal places that offer hospitality and welcome, conversation and comfort—usually the best room in the house. Form in interiors is a generic idea.

The meanings carried through shape into form are, in large part, the reason people care so much about their houses. If this were not true, designers of interiors would have fewer problems when the problems deal with "home." Since home is a "nest," the place of protection, safety, and nurturing, and since it is also everyone's idea of a "castle" no matter how humble, be it small or large, its importance rests in the idea of home. That idea rests in the form.

When we see created form, its essential characteristics can be grasped at once. We can describe the characteristics in quite basic but telling terms indicative of shape. We will say that an object is curved, roundish, rectangular, squarish, angular; that the shape is soft or irregular, hard or regular. The use of such shapes in the design of interiors leads to identity through form-making.

The use of both natural and geometric shapes can produce interiors that are either simple or complex. But either result must embody orderly structure. Whether simple or complex, order in an interior is accomplished by the similarity of repeated shape. Every shape within an interior has a relational effect on its form. Even small-size components must fit within an order to ensure aesthetic completeness. Shapes can be repeated almost endlessly, since a given shape can be varied by a change of size, color, texture, or its position-relationship with other shapes. Aestheticians call this "thematic variation" (see the discussion under "Repetition and Rhythm" later in this chapter).

Thematic variation means that once the shape (theme) is stated, it is repeated in another way. For example, if an interior has a plan in the shape of a perfect square, other squares can appear as components of wall or furniture. Some parts of that interior may be designed as double squares or half squares. The square shape can be varied by the color and texture of material. The stated theme-shape can be given positive tension by the introduction of a contrasting shape (see the discussion under "Contrast and Opposition" later in this chapter).

Configuration

Configuration is specific and detailed external shape resulting from the disposition of different parts. The relationship between the parts, whether related or unrelated, creates configuration. In a configuration, all parts are relational. Configuration is detailed relationship.

In interior design, configuration is the relationship between all components in the volumetric whole of a space (see Figure 30). Architecture, furniture, and furnishings work together in an interior composition. Their arrangement in an interior creates "filled" and "empty" places within the volume. The filled places are occupied by specific components—a wall, a table, a chair—while the places between those parts are empty. Some of these empty places are pathways, or circulation routes, because they also fulfill that functional need. In addition, those places also have shape; and that shape is of similar compositional importance in the design of every interior.

Whether an interior has many parts or few parts, is simple or complex, each component becomes part of its configuration in both horizontal and vertical planes. Horizontal configuration relates to the shape that results from the placement of parts in plan; vertical configuration includes the heights of all components and

A

B

 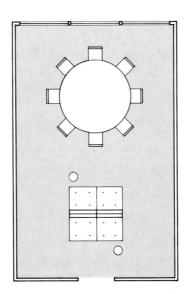

C

30. Configuration

A. A rug, a table, and a chair are set together in a composition. The relationship between the parts creates a specific configuration. If the relationship of the parts is changed, the configuration is changed.

B. A table with chairs becomes a different configuration when the shape of the table is changed. The space around each shape is also changed.

C. Two interior plans use the same component parts. A rearrangement of some parts makes a new configuration. Emphasis shifts to another part of the space of the room. The "filled" and the "empty" portions of a plan will alter how the interior is used, and how it is perceived.

their relative placement to each other. Consequently, all components in an interior relate regardless of proximity, because all of the parts relate to the same configuration in the same interior.

Size, Scale, and Proportion

Problems of scale and proportion have occupied the attention of artists for centuries. Scale and proportion have been written about, talked about, subjected to investigation, and codified over time.

Size

When the American painter Georgia O'Keeffe was asked why she painted her flowers so big, she answered that no one ever asked her why she painted the river so small. Was this question about the size of the flowers? Or was it about scale? Is the painter's reply a counter-comment on scale or on size?

Both scale and proportion relate to size. Scale compares the size of one thing to another: the size of a metropolis to the size of a hamlet. Scale seeks to determine the size of one thing in relation to another thing. Proportion, on the other hand, seeks to decide the size of one part to another part of the same thing.

The flowers in the Georgia O'Keeffe paintings are large in relation to the size of the flowers that grow in nature and in relation to the space of the painter's canvas. Flowers do not generally grow to the size O'Keeffe has depicted them. We do not expect to see one flower that fills the dimensions of a canvas, such as in her *Red Poppy*, painted in 1927 (see Figure 31). So we measure the flower against our senses developed from our past experience with poppies, and we say that the flower is large in scale—large in relation to nature and larger than expected in relation to a canvas.

Within O'Keeffe's poppy, all the parts are in proportion to each other. The parts are in botanically correct relation to each other. The size of the petals is in relation to the size of the center stamen as we know from nature. However, the painted flower is out of scale with what we know about poppies. And this increase in scale makes us look at the flower in a special way. The artist has chosen to make the poppy as large as possible in the format of the canvas. If the flower were painted the usual size, a good painting could still be produced; but we would look at it in the usual way, without the special feeling we have for O'Keeffe's idea about this poppy.

Further, we know that it is possible to make a picture of a poppy without changing its size; that a poppy can be painted in the same size found in nature. But how can we paint a river at its actual size? A river is too large even for the format of a very large canvas. The answer, for the artist, is to make the river smaller in size than we normally think a river is. We expect rivers to be painted small in the format of a picture, so that in comparison to real rivers the smallness of the painted river is acceptable to us.

Scale

Whenever the word "scale" is used, the size of something is being compared with the size of something else: painted flowers to real flowers; painted rivers to real rivers. We compare what we see with what we remember and expect when we say "scale."

When we speak of a "large-scale" interior design project—a corporate interior covering several floors in an office building—we are comparing it to the "small-scale" interior of a studio apartment. One is clearly larger in size than the other. With the use of the word "scale" rather than "size," we emphasize the component of comparison that is always present in discussions of scale.

Although scale is not the same thing as size, still it relates to size—relative size—the size of something *relative* to something else. The scale notation on architectural drawings is, in one sense, a comparison of the building drawings to the size of the real building.

What are the sizes of things relative to scale? How are these sizes determined? We speak of monumental scale, miniature scale, human scale. Scale must not exclude any of the possible meanings, but must find what is common in all of the ideas of scale.

31. Scale

Painting, *Red Poppy,* 1927, Georgia O'Keeffe. The painted poppy is large compared to poppies in nature. In the small format of the 7- by 9-inch canvas, the flower is still large in scale.

We use human scale as the most common comparison. If things in an interior do not function within some relation to the size of the human body, within some human scale, we cannot use the interior. For the purpose of human use it is necessary for sizes to be determined by maximum or minimum limits. For example, if a doorknob is larger than the human hand can grasp, we cannot open the door. The door itself may be restricted by a less than minimum size. Below a certain height, we could not comfortably pass through it. Everything intended for use in an interior—doors, stairs, beds, chairs, sofas, tables, shelves, and so forth—is determined by human use, and each must have a relation to human size. Only in relation to their use do the things that are of human scale have a precise meaning.

Within loose limits, most things have a usual size. When things are much larger or much smaller than we expect, we see them as having bigger or smaller scale. However, this sense of scale is determined or measured only by our experience of how things usually are.

Our expectations of size have much to do with our evaluation of scale. We expect that a doorway will have a large enough dimension for us to pass through without bumping into the top or sides. We can pass with physical ease through a doorway that is a standard size of 30 to 36 inches wide and 6 feet 8 inches high. The passage is so easy that we take no notice of it. But if a doorway is only 1 foot 6 inches wide and 5 feet high, the difficulty of getting through it makes us abruptly aware of its size. Something is "out of scale" with something else. We compare our human size (the average size of human beings) to the usual door size, the size of a doorway that will allow passage through it. We find the size of the doorway "small in scale." If, on the other hand, the doorway is larger than usual, say 12 feet wide and 25 feet high, we may feel that it is too large in comparison to our human size. Still, this doorway may be "in scale" with the size of the room of which it is a part (see Figure 32A).

Scale carries psychological connotations. When we pass through a doorway of usual, expected size, there is not much to note in terms of experience. But if a doorway is the size of one in the Medici Palace, or of the entrance doors to St. Peter's in Rome, we notice it because it is so much larger than usual. In relation

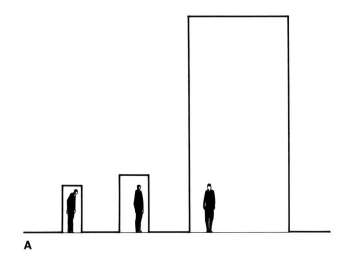

A

32. Relative Scale

A. Comparative door scales. We take notice when an undersized doorway makes entry forbidding, and passage through it may be difficult, if not impossible. A standard doorway of average size allows passage that is comfortable, but unremarkable. Great height and width in a doorway can seem to diminish our own size, and at the same time signal entry to an important place. Each opening has a size that is "in" or "out" of scale with human size, but each may also have an effective scale in a particular interior.

B. Bedroom interior, 1983, Robert Bray and Michael Schaible, Museum Tower Apartments, New York. A standard-size bedroom uses large-size components to affect the scale of the space. A bow-front chest takes up the entire length of a wall and projects into the room by almost one-third its width. The chest appears to be a raised portion of the floor, but serves instead as a seating, storage, and display component.

B

to human size and to the usual size of doorways, we may feel diminished by the magnitude of implications (see Figure 8). The scale of these doors, therefore, indicates that something important is taking place, some important event, something larger than ourselves; something solemn, formal, ritualistic, awesome, or in some way unusual. The very size of such a doorway produces a feeling of grandeur and calls our attention to the action of passage through it, because our usual relationship with doors has been altered.

Scale is of consequence for both large- and small-size interiors, even though there is a tendency to put more scale emphasis on the large interior. In small space, scale can be employed as an important design principle.

At the Frick Collection in New York, there is a small room in which everything is small in scale. The room is representative of the small rooms that became popular in eighteenth-century France. Small sofas and chairs and small tables easily rearranged furnish the room comfortably. The walls are paneled to hold Boucher's paintings of figures in a landscape. These are drawn at about one-quarter life-size. In this intimate room all the parts are in scale with each other: The volume of the room is in scale with the furniture, the paintings, and the fabrics and rugs.

Another small room, designed in the late 1950s by Gerald Luss, uses scale in a different way. This room is used for private telephoning and adjoins a conference room. Everything in the room is large in scale in comparison with the size of the room. Three walls are plain white plaster; the fourth wall is all windows covered with curtains made of translucent woven horsehair in natural gray, black, and white. Adjacent to the windows is a low shelf of broad-grained rosewood that runs the full length of the wall. The shelf holds one red telephone. One chair, the largest lounge chair by Charles Eames, is next to the telephone shelf. The room seems to be filled by the components of shelf and chair that hover over thick, plain carpeting. The plainness of the walls and floor, and the bigness of the furniture, contrast with the light horsehair curtains. Another minor but important scale change occurs in the curtain. Because horsehair grows only to a limited length, the material had to be seamed horizontally to cover the window height. This causes the scale of the window to decrease.

In the Boucher room at the Frick Collection, scale is used as a continuum: The size of the furniture and the furnishings matches the scale of the room. The room designed by Luss contrasts large-scale furniture components against the comparatively small-size room.

If one chair in a room is much larger than other chairs in the same room, it does not matter what the actual size of either is. Like the poppy on the canvas, another scale has been introduced, and the larger-size chair indicates that there is something special to be noted. The specialness may indicate the importance of the chair, or of the user of the chair.

The size of the furniture in a room relates to the whole of the room and exerts a scale influence on its volume. Large-scale furniture in an average-size room can change our visual perception of the interior volume—it may appear smaller. Small-scale furniture in the same room will also affect our perception of the room—it may appear larger.

Appropriate Scale   The question of appropriate scale is of ultimate concern in design. The scale of the Washington Monument is appropriate to the size of the monument. The same scale would not be useful in deciding the size of a dollhouse. Although dinners for two may be eaten at a table 20 feet long, a more appropriate scale for the table would help to promote an atmosphere of intimacy.

Manipulating Scale   In interiors, when a change from what is considered usual scale is desirable, the scale can be modulated or altered in several ways. Several scales may be mixed together so that there are multiple scales at work within one space or in a sequence of spaces. When multiple scales are used, two or more components are used together at different sizes and in different relationships to the whole. Because the two scales are in contrast to each other and to the whole, the juxtaposition can create a desirable tension within the volume.

Very large and very small furniture components placed together in usual-size spaces, or usual-size furniture components in contrast with large-size works of art, begin to use scale manipulation effectively. In spaces where architectural components are large, a contrast in the size of furniture components will emphasize the difference in scale.

Discussing the manipulation of scale in his book *Dimensions*, architect-author Gerald Allen describes the use of scale alone and in combination with shape as it can occur in interiors:

> Sometimes the variation in size is between things with the same shapes—not only windows and doors, but furniture and moldings and floor boards—and sometimes it is between things of different shapes. For example, all the parts—furniture, doors, windows, walls, floors, and ceilings—can be sized in a usual way, thus having a normal and orderly relationship to each other and to the whole. But this hierarchical chain can be interrupted by some additional thing—a fireplace, for instance—that is dramatically bigger or smaller than one would expect. What is the whole of which this different element is a part? Which whole is more vivid—the one we see, supported by the scale of everything else in the room? Or the one we can't see, suggested by the surprising size of the dissonant object?[1]

Because every part of an interior has to have a size, scale manipulation should be experimented with in every interior. Scale combinations are endless, and relationships can change in every part of every interior.

Most interior designers tend to make everything "in scale." This may be a natural consequence of considering interiors as filled with components that are meant to be used in the usual way: Average-size rooms are usually furnished with average-size things—things that can be purchased through distributors or manufacturers. Because things for interiors are made in standard sizes, few items of mass-produced furniture have anything but usual scale.

Further, because most interior design takes place within preconceived space—space determined by builders—these also tend to have standard dimensions. If scale is to be an effective design device, designers must find some means by which scale can be exploited beyond the usual idea of usual scale.

A remarkable example of the scale of a part in relation to the whole is in the bedroom designed by Bray-Schaible in the Museum Tower Apartments in New York (see Figure 32B). What must be one of the largest chests of drawers ever designed holds down both wall and floor of this interior. The entire length of the space and almost one-third the width of the floor is taken up by this bow-front storage component. The effect of this component is as if another floor level is pushing out into the width of the room. But this level is intended for storage. It also makes a place for sitting and for display. The size of this component is like no chest of drawers ever seen before. It so affects the scale of the room that at first it is not perceived as furniture. This component accomplishes two needs within the room: (1) The functional requirement for storage is provided, and (2) the aesthetic need to affect the scale of the room is satisfied in an appropriate, dramatic manner. Without seeming to be forced—though it is obviously forced—scale has been employed as the major principle of spatial organization.

Gerald Allen says that when questions arise regarding which relationships of scale are worthy of emphasis, he would propose a solution in the form of a question. He asks, "What do you care to measure?" He answers the question with another question, "What relationships do you care to call attention to?"[2]

Proportion

After Le Corbusier returned to France from his 1936 trip to America, he wrote his views of Americans and American architecture in *When the Cathedrals Were White*.

---

[1] Charles Moore and Gerald Allen, *Dimensions: Space, Shape, and Scale in Architecture* (New York: Architectural Record Books, 1976).

[2] Ibid.

A

B

C

33. Proportion

A. Greek proportion. Ideal form was investigated through the invention and application of the golden section, the ancient system of proportion. In that system, for example, the longer side of a good, or ideal, rectangle is related to the shorter side, as the sum of both is to the longer.

B. Palladian proportion. This method sought relationship between each part of a building. Palladio felt that the rooms in a building should share common ratios with the exterior. This plan of the Villa Foscari shows that when the long wall of one room is twice the dimension of the short wall of the room next to it, or when the size of a smaller room is half the size of a larger, the parts reach for ideal relationship through their proportions to each other, and with the proportions of the larger whole.

C. Measured proportion. Le Modulor, a system developed by Le Corbusier in the early twentieth century, used ratios from the golden section for smaller dimensions. Larger ones were based on the measurements of parts of the human body. From a combination of these measurements, the height of ceilings, doorways, and furniture could be decided. It seems, however, that each systematically determined ratio then needed intuitive adjustment.

There, he questioned, "Proportion? What is it? The nothing which is everything and which makes things smile."[3]

Nothing? Everything? Smile? Likely he is saying that proportion, though unseen, is crucial to artistic creation and offers delight.

The principles of proportion have been investigated from the ancients to our time: the Greeks, through Pythagoras and his disciples; through all of the Renaissance artists, including Michelangelo and Palladio; and theoreticians and designers today. This is a search for a formula to ensure ideal—meaning beautiful—proportions through some means other than intuition.

Greek philosophy aspires to apply aesthetic "ideals" to the conditions of the real. From Aristotle, Greek philosophers sought to define the ideal in every part of the human condition: Politics and politicians, education, gymnastics, poetry, painting, music, friendship, growth, and the social structure of city-states were subjected to the most meticulous examination in their efforts to approach an ideal condition. Ideals were often formulated into laws. The laws could be followed and the perfection of the ideal would be inculcated in the lives of citizens. When citizens became ideal people (that is, people who knew the laws), the perfect city, the ideal place, could be attained.

After all this striving for perfection, it is no wonder that Greek philosophy reached into Greek art. Several centuries of Greek sculpture portray not just a form representing a god or goddess, a ruler or statesman, a warrior or athlete, but the ideal, perfected form of each.

In architecture, the aims of the ideal developed into rules of proportion called the golden section, or golden mean. But limitations of the ideal proportions were discovered. They found that strict application of the laws of the golden section produced a total deadness, and that it was necessary to make corrections intuitively to produce visual satisfaction.

The Golden Section   According to Steen Eiler Rasmussen in *Experiencing Architecture*, the golden section is the fundamental Greek analysis of proportion (see Figure 33A): "A line segment is said to be divided according to the Golden Section when it is composed of two unequal parts of which the first is to the second as the second is to the whole. If we call the two parts A and B, respectively, then the ratio of A to B is equal to the ratio of B to A plus B."[4] This means that if we want to design a particularly good (ideal) rectangle, the subdivision of the golden section may be applied: That is, the longer side is related to the shorter side as the sum of both is to the longer.

The Greeks applied the golden section of proportion to a full range of their artistic creations—from temples, to sculpture, to the design of the smallest molding. Their most discussed application is the specific manner of proportioning the columns that signal the three major temple styles of Doric, Ionic, and Corinthian orders.

Another version of a systematic attempt at proportional codification is discussed by Sir Herbert Read in his introduction on the creative process in *The Forms of Things Unknown*. His summation explains why a particular organization of material elements in a composition has aesthetic appeal. He writes of the early Greek philosophers' attempts to "relate the measurements of art to the measurements of nature, and to see in the proportions of a crystal, of vegetation, of man himself,

---

[3]Le Corbusier, *When the Cathedrals Were White* (New York: McGraw-Hill, 1947). (Translated from the French, *Quand les cathédrales étaient blanches*, by Francis E. Hyslop, Jr.)

[4]Steen Eiler Rasmussen, *Experiencing Architecture* (Cambridge: MIT Press, 1964).

the prototypes of proportions discovered in the work of art." Further, Read says that he uses the word "discovered" because:

> . . . though the Greek architects and sculptors . . . and others today, began to make conscious use of natural proportions, the significant fact is that these proportions appear without conscious intervention in all those works of art that can be characterized as "beautiful." This, perhaps, is no more than an hypothesis which has yet to be proved, and certainly a few traditional concepts of natural proportion, such as the Golden Section, do not suffice to explain all the phenomena of art. Form, that is to say, is not necessarily so obvious that it can be expressed in a single formula such as the Golden Section.[5]

Nonetheless, throughout the ages, efforts were continual to find clearer approaches to proportional arrangement in the visual arts. More often than not, the search was made by architects.

The Fibonacci Series   The Fibonacci series, or Fibonacci sequence, named for the most distinguished mathematician of the Middle Ages, Leonardo Fibonacci, was used as further evidence that the golden section was valid. Fibonacci brought Arabic numbering to the West. He found that nine figures (1,2,3,4,5,6,7,8,9) were the most satisfactory method for his calculations.

The Fibonacci series is similar to that of the golden section in that, as each number is added to the next, the third number is the combination of the first two. Thus the formula that has 1 as its first number (called a term) is 1,1,2,3,5,8, and so forth. The golden-section ratios are not the exact figures of the series, but they are close. Furthermore, the Fibonacci sequence is found in the spiral arrangement of petals on certain types of flowers, as well as in the branch and leaf arrangement of certain trees.

In later centuries the series also was found to be in the spiraling ratio arrangements of snail shells, animal horns, sunflower heads, pinecones, and related logarithmic spirals. The twentieth-century architectural theoretician Anne Ting has discovered corresponding proportional arrangements in the configuration of the planets as well as in the molecular structure of hemoglobin pigment of the red corpuscles of vertebrates.

Palladian Proportion   The importance of proportion as a concern in the arts has never been solved entirely by formula, but formula together with intuition has produced more than a few masterpieces. When Palladio returned from Rome, where he had studied ruins of ancient buildings, he was convinced that he had a mission to create architecture that was as sublimely proportioned in composition as that of antiquity. He saw that each part of a building, and its interior, could be integrated in such a way that each part of a façade, and each portion of a room, and each room in ratio to all the other rooms, could present an "ideal form" within the form of the larger whole.

The Villa Foscari (also called the Villa Malcontenta), built on the mainland near Venice, is a prime example of Palladio's system of proportioning. Based on the system of the golden section as he understood it, each room at Foscari has been given a precise and definitive plan (see Figure 33B). The central space is the shape of a cross, and at either end of that cross-armed hall is a square room 16 by 16 feet. On either side of these rooms is a larger and a smaller rectangular room: One is 12 by 16 feet; the other is 16 by 24 feet—or twice as large as the smaller room. The smaller room has its longer wall in common relation with the square room; the

[5] Sir Herbert Read, *The Forms of Things Unknown* (New York: World Publishing Company, 1960).

larger room has its shorter wall as the common relationship. Foscari, like his other villas, demonstrates Palladio's repeated search for the perfection of form through the use of mathematic ratio, the simple use of geometry transformed and applied to architectural form.

Although we do not consciously experience these proportions as actual measurements, we sense them physically and intuitively. Here we have the same underlying notion of Read's explanation of aesthetic appeal that exists in all of the phenomena of art. He says that this phenomenon exists whether it has been produced by conscious calculation—as with the Greeks and Palladio—or from the intuition at work in the unconscious mind. Either means may result in a firmly integrated composition where each part is an ideal form in relation to the created whole. The artist's aesthetic operates through perception and sensation, and refers back to form made up of measurement, volume, shape, and scale: Parts organized in particular arrangements in particular relationships are the essence of proportion.

Le Modulor of Le Corbusier   Early in the twentieth century, Le Corbusier's concern with the problems of proportion was developed into a measuring system, which he called "le Modulor" (see Figure 33C). The golden-section ratios were used for smaller measurements; larger ones were based on the human body.

In le Modulor, the height of the average man (a height that had to be changed according to nationality) was divided in ratios provided by the golden section. Like Leonardo da Vinci, Le Corbusier found that the division corresponded to the distance from the floor to the navel. The navel height was divided in the same way, and the division was continued until a harmonic series of smaller and smaller measurements was obtained. Le Corbusier also found, as Renaissance artists had, that human height with an upraised arm was double the height of the navel. He used these dimensions for different purposes or functions, such as the determination of heights for ceilings, counters, desks, tables, and different types of chairs.

Le Corbusier attached importance to the dimensions he had worked out in le Modulor. It offered him help in making decisions, and there is good evidence that every measurement that he arrived at intuitively was corrected so that it corresponded to one of the measurements in le Modulor. Some of his critics, however, say that his best work was done when he paid less attention to his rules of proportion, that his work was more powerful when the measurements were not fixed, but relied on artistic intuition.

Appropriate Proportion   Just as there is a need for appropriate scale in design, so also there is a need for appropriate proportion. The proportions of domestic interiors may be of large scale in a big house. However, appropriate proportion in that situation is different from the large scale of a hotel, or of a hospital. The scale of the house may include many rooms, some large and some smaller, according to their intended purpose. In a hospital, built for health care for many people, the scale also will be large; but the proportions of the rooms will vary in accordance with the special needs that health care demands. The proportions of rooms in houses may be determined by the occupants' needs for interaction, or for privacy. In a hospital, proportions will be determined by a more measurable component— a bed, that unit of measurement on which the hospital is founded. The unit of measurement in this case is not determined by a highly generalized or universal system, but on a more specific unit. The resulting proportions may not be "ideal" in the sense of "ideal beauty," but will be useful in a more fundamental way.

Proportions in interiors can be influenced by three criteria (or determinants): aesthetic, functional, or material. In some situations, all three of these will be used; in most situations, all three should be considered.

34. Symmetry in Ancient Design
Carved fragment, 2685 B.C., Ur, Sumeria. An early artist composed a symmetrical design with symbolic meaning. The equilibrium of symmetry is achieved by placing a human figure in the central, axial position and on each side, in the equivalent left and right halves, matching animal figures. The human center, though already in a key position, gains importance when flanked by the pair of animal figures.

Equilibrium: Symmetry and Balance

In any form of aesthetic creation there are only two means of establishing equilibrium—symmetry and balance. Equilibrium in any composition is an even adjustment, an equality between two opposing parts. The principle of symmetry was developed through conscious workings of the mind; balance came about through artistic experimentation and intuition. Both principles are thousands of years older than recorded history.

Symmetry

According to Sir Herbert Read, the first principle of aesthetic composition to be discovered was symmetry. The principle is most apparent in the natural world, since we carry its model in our own bodies and observe it objectively in the bodies of animals. As long ago as Paleolithic times, artists represented the human body with symmetry as the pictorial means. Later, in some Neolithic statues, symmetry is consciously exaggerated, making it a deliberate compositional device, an isolated principle.

Apparently such symmetrical designs developed when those early artists needed to symbolically depict people and animals together in carvings or paintings (see Figure 34). Sometimes one person is centered between two animals; sometimes one animal is between two people. The center motif changed according to symbolic, artistic needs. Read notes that if only one animal figure was used, the results would seem to indicate that the animal was attacking the man. It took two animals, one on either side, to convey the idea of symbol.

Once this means of pictorial organization became a conscious device, it was used continually. Symmetry was applied to all manner of creations for the rest of prehistory, throughout all of the great periods of recorded history, and into the present time. Symmetrical composition is used in most of the arts, including the visual arts, architecture, interior design, music, and, perhaps surprisingly, drama.

In the visual arts, symmetry requires a centerline with matching left and right sides. The same parts are required when it is used in music, either in an ABA form of composition, or when two instruments speak to each other as in a double concerto. The dramatist Robert Wilson, creator of *Einstein on the Beach,* used symmetry as the organizational device in his teleplay *Stations,* the thirteen-part play he described as having at its center a depiction of a dense forest. Part one, fire, he set in opposition to part thirteen, water. These, Wilson said, were of equal weight, adding that fire and water have traditionally always been complementary to one another.

Equilibrium is desirable in every creation, and symmetry is a direct way to achieve it. Sometimes it is the most appropriate way, especially when the desired result of a composition is that it exhibit formality and simplicity, and be easily understood.

Symmetrical compositions always require matching parts equally distributed on opposite sides of a centerline. The matching parts in the left and right sides establish the equilibrium.

Strict symmetry has been considered a satisfactory means of organization for centuries, most constantly in architecture and interior design. Rudolph Arnheim comments that, "Architectural design has in all cultures so insistently relied on symmetry because buildings serve as an element of stability and order in the midst of human experience, which is pervaded by struggle, accident, discords, change, and irrationality."[6] Here the principle itself serves as symbol—the symbol of stability. This is certainly at least one of the reasons that so many religious buildings are designed as symmetrical creations. In them, the design also reinforces ritual. Every detail culminates at a central altar, the central aisles designed for ceremony, procession, solemnity, and grandeur.

All symmetrical interiors have a centerline, or axis. This middle is always visible. It may be seen in various architectural components—doors, windows, projections or depressions in a wall plane. Restatement should occur in furniture, furnishings, and art.

In symmetrical interiors there will be an equality of tension that pulls toward the center. That tension is brought to repose by the matching components fixed in corresponding sides, twin reflections of each component. Pairs of identical components again and again support the center. The focus is unmistakable.

Symmetry in design emphasizes the center in the way that symmetry of the human body emphasizes the head. The strongest center for a symmetrical composition in an interior is a component of architecture. In residential interiors this component is quite often a fireplace, the space between a pair of windows, or a pair of doors. In houses, centered fireplaces become the center of the home, both as physical place and in psychological feeling. We hang our best pictures over these hearths; our best furniture is arranged there. Some interiors planned around the principle of symmetry have their emphasis weighted on the left and right sides, with insignificant centers. This weakens the symmetry. The center must be supremely dominant in a symmetrical composition, particularly when it is the controlling principle of an interior volume in its entirety. Dominant may mean large or small size, but power and dominance must be asserted—whether by height, weight, shape, or color.

Since antiquity, symmetry has been a recurrent device used for organization. Often, it has been the dominant device in city planning, in architectural design of not only religious buildings, where ceremony demanded it, but government and commercial complexes, palaces, and other residential structures. The interiors of all these building types have consistently been internally planned, furnished, and finished as symmetrical designs.

Perhaps the most insistent employment of symmetry is from the mid-eighteenth century, when the then new discoveries of Pompeii and Herculaneum led to the Classic Revival in France and England. In France the Louis XVI style was greatly influenced by the excavations in Italy and the subsequent publication of

---

[6]Rudolph Arnheim, *Art and Visual Perception* (Berkeley and Los Angeles: University of California Press, 1974).

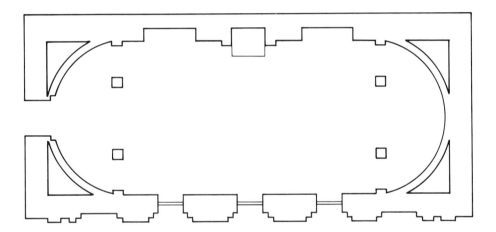

35. Symmetry in an Interior

Library interior, Kenwood House, 1767–68, Robert Adam, near London. The volume of the interior is organized by the repeated use of pairs. These are placed around longitudinal and transverse axes in unmistakably symmetrical arrangements. Each elevation has an almost mirror image. The fireplace, the center of the transverse axis, is also the pivotal center of the design. Though smaller in size than some other architectural components, it holds its importance in the scheme because it is the single unrepeated part. A picture—the only one in the room—further strengthens the center.

Piranesi's engravings. In England the book *Antiquities of Athens* by Stuart and Revett, published in 1762, was studied by practicing architects and designers, as well as painters, craftsmen, and the public.

The English architect Robert Adam produced his finest work using classical forms. These he applied to the design of large houses and their interiors. At Kenwood, a country house just outside of London, classical symmetry is applied to the façades, to the interior plan, and to the design of the interior spaces. In the library at Kenwood (1767–68) Adam created symmetrical compositions in both the length and width of the room (see Figure 35). The shape of the room, with its curved ceiling leading into curved, apsidal ends, each marked by a pair of classical columns, is a shape often used by Adam. The long walls are also symmetrically designed. The garden elevation has three windows; it is mirrored by the opposite wall, which has a central fireplace and a pair of flanking arched recesses. The center fireplace is designed as the single unrepeated component in the room; over this central component is the room's only painting. The recesses hold pairs of sofas matched on the opposite wall by another pair.

In the design of twentieth-century interiors, symmetry can be seen in the early work of Frank Lloyd Wright and Mies van der Rohe, as well as in the work of Modernist and Post-Modernist architects and designers. For interior designers today, the consequences of the discovery of symmetry for use as a formal compositional device are second only to the discovery of balance.

Balance

In symmetry there must be a strict regularity of parts, a pure intellectual or mechanical application. A more subtle, intuitive, and variable means of relating the parts of a whole is found in the principle of balance frequently called asymmetry. In symmetrical designs we say that the design is right; with balanced compositions we can only say that a design feels or seems right.

When the principle of balance is applied, equilibrium is brought to creation by combining *unlike* components acting with *like* strength upon a composition. The parts of such a composition can be assembled in infinitely different ways. The number of parts may be many or few. In balanced compositions the distribution of weight may be dominated by a single strong component; or several smaller components may be arranged in a series or gradient from the most important to the least important. Balance requires no aspect of symmetry: no matching pairs, no central emphasis. A centerline may be implied in balanced arrangements and such arrangements may have vertical or horizontal direction.

Balance as a compositional principle can be traced to an early prototypical design—a limestone plaque found in Sumeria from about 2900 B.C. (see Figure 36). This composition is almost entirely instinctive in its design. The positioning of the figures is done to tell a story (the function of the piece) and to control the aesthetic appearance in a manner that the artist felt was best. No formal, intellectual analysis is relevant: What is important is that the composition feels right.

36. Balance as a Compositional Device

Limestone plaque, circa 2900 B.C., Sumeria. The figures are composed in a deliberate, balanced arrangement. They are accommodated to the size and shape of the surface around a central aperture. This may have served some functional purpose, but the relationship of the figures to the background is only in the service of aesthetic composition.

Balanced compositions may be said to be a precept of the whole of Modernism. In painting (with the exception of portraiture and paintings on religious subjects, where a strong symmetry prevails), balance has continually been the supreme organizational principle. In Modern architecture and interior design, balance is the underpinning of the principle of organic unity, the theory of spatial organization developed by Louis Sullivan and Frank Lloyd Wright.

In highly stylized eighteenth-century Rococo interiors, French designers of the period planned overall interiors on symmetrical schemes. Importantly, and according to such experts as Wylie Sypher, the surfaces of Rococo interiors use "occult balance" rather than "mathematical symmetry." In the symmetrical panel designs, balanced arrangements are overlaid so that one side of the decoration never quite matches the opposite side. Sypher describes the interior architecture of Rococo interiors as basically "geometric abstraction," while the face of the wall became "organic."[7] In interiors, from the eighteenth century forward, balance never disappeared as an organizational means.

The historically significant 1930 Tugendhat House in Brno, Czechoslovakia, designed by Mies van der Rohe, brings the principle of balance to a high level of refinement. The main space of the first floor is composed of an open plan of living, study, and dining rooms. The three spaces are separated by screen-like walls—one a flat plane, the other circular. Furniture within the spaces is arranged in a delicate equilibrium within the open space. A few pieces of furniture stand in elegant isolation. Two furniture components find a centerline: The dining table and the living room table find the middle of their respective spaces. However, balance is the underlying principle for the organization of the whole of the interior plan.

Combinations of the Principles of Symmetry and Balance

As in Rococo interiors, aspects of both symmetry and balance are used in combination in the design of all other types of interiors. In some interiors the furniture plan may be clearly symmetrical, while the design of the elevations will show a balanced composition. Such is an office space designed by Alexander Girard in Columbus, Indiana, around 1962. The plan of this room could not be more simple: A centered executive desk is accompanied by two pull-up chairs, a swivel chair, and a wall-hung back shelf; all are symmetrically placed between the side walls. However, one side wall is plain, with only doors at each end; the other wall holds four very different components. This wall manages to control, through balanced organization, the diverse needs of a clock, a fireplace, a photo display unit that is continuous with an enclosed bookcase, and a television recess. The clock and television recess have a common vertical centerline; the upper line of the fireplace opening aligns with the horizontal center of the television recess (see Figure 37).

Combinations of symmetry and balance can be employed, but designers must remain conscious of the tensions that may result. Sometimes the desired result is positive tension, as when Modern furniture is placed in balanced arrangements within symmetrical, historical interiors. This procedure can be effective when a pronounced separation is wanted, when the designer wants to let the existing volume of the architecture maintain its own identity and also let new components maintain their identity.

In conclusion it can be said that symmetry and balance have always been essential principles of aesthetic composition. Certain historical periods have favored

[7]Wylie Sypher, *Rococo to Cubism in Art and Literature* (New York: Vintage Books, A Division of Random House, 1963).

37. Balance in Interiors
Office interior, 1962, Alexander Girard, Columbus, Indiana. Although the furniture plan is symmetrical, it is juxtaposed to a wall of balanced components. The clock and television set are related through a common, vertical centerline.

A. Plan

B. Elevation

one over the other; at other times combinations of the two principles have assisted in the creation of diverse arts. It seems that when one principle falls into disuse, it returns at a later time with renewed vigorous applications (see Figure 38).

Axis and Alignment

All interior plans have an axis, but not all of them exhibit aspects of alignment. Axis pertains to a centerline; alignment concerns edge.

Axis

As with the Earth, where everything revolves around its axis, so in the volume of an interior every part relates to (or revolves around) an imaginary axis in space. An axis implies direction; it is often at or near the center of a plan.

In an interior an axis is not real or seen; it is felt or sensed. Interiors of even the most ordinary character have at least one axis, though it may not have been consciously planned. For example, a usual-size living room, say 12 by 20 feet, will have a major axis down its length and at, or near, the center. Other minor axes may exist in such a space, particularly where doors (and sometimes windows, depending on their design) are cut into walls, or where a major architectural component, such as a fireplace, crops out of a long wall. Secondary axes are not necessarily in competition with major axes, and can be incorporated or absorbed into the design concept.

In symmetrical interiors an axis is most apparent; it is obvious and easily found. In center-aisle churches, for example, the symmetry springs from the center axis to which all of the components in the left and right halves refer. The center is marked with entry door, aisle, altar, and choir. The left and right halves will be

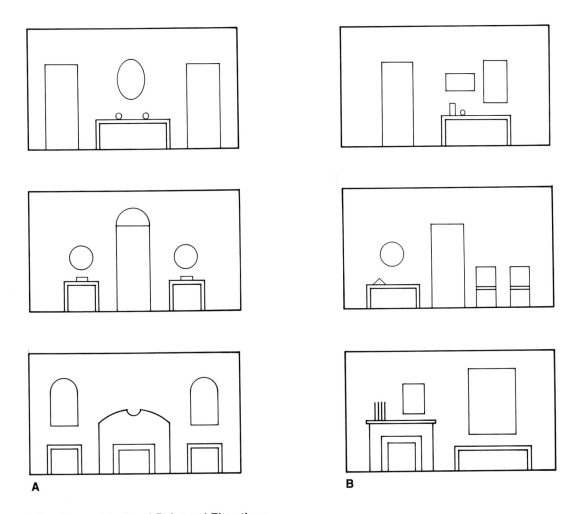

A

B

38. Symmetrical and Balanced Elevations

A limited number of design possibilities is shown in these examples. In each, the architectural components — the walls, the doors, the fireplaces — are taken as predetermined: therefore, the components of furniture and art must accommodate to them. That accommodation must be accomplished in either a symmetrical or a balanced composition.

A. Symmetrical elevations

B. Balanced elevations

of matching design, each part referring back to the center axis. If the plan of the church includes a cross-aisle, another axis exists. Although various components support the axis, it is mainly the thrust, or direction, of the space of the interior that indicates the location of the axis. Axes are present even when an interior is without furniture or furnishings (see Figure 39).

In urban design one of the most dramatic uses of axis as a design principle came about when the court of the seventeenth-century French king Louis XIV moved from the capital city of Paris to rural Versailles. A road was designed to run straight from the heart of the old city to the new "city" of Versailles and, it is said, into the king's bedchamber. The road-as-axis provided the physical and emotional link between the city and the king, and it served as the design references for all of the buildings and parks.

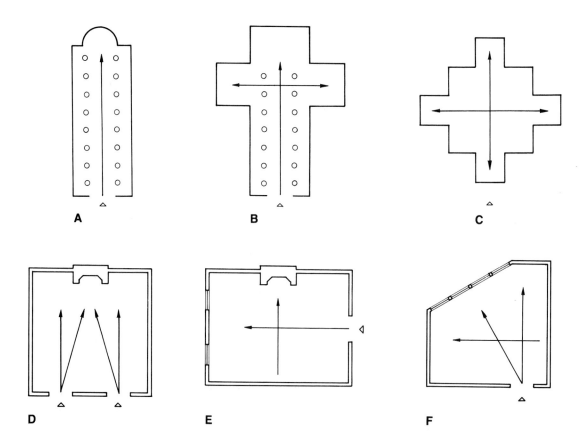

39. Typical Interior Axes

A. In a single-axis plan, each component must lead to the same point. The design of such an interior will focus at the termination of the axis.

B. A transverse and a longitudinal axis crossing will put emphasis on this point. The crossing must not only acknowledge, but reemphasize the point.

C. Equal axes thrust out from the center with equal force. The center is further strengthened by this thrust.

D. An axis occurs from each doorway. Each equal axis is equally focused toward the center of the opposite wall.

E. Two axes cross each other in the center of a room. Gaining strength from the centered fireplace, the shorter axis begins to have an importance equal to the longer one.

F. In this plan several axes create equal tensions. One of them can be made stronger and more important by a design concept.

So pervasive was the use of the axis in late Baroque design—it was the supreme design principle of the period—that it was referred to during that time as *"la culte de l'axe."* The principle was used to set the concept for the design of everything from lace to town planning, especially for the great, formal parks and gardens that became so important in the seventeenth century. In these situations the use of an axis became the means to relate nature to manmade buildings.

Although axes occur in symmetrical interiors as a result of their bilateral design, spaces with balanced, nonsymmetrical plans also have discernible axes. In balanced plans an axis may be somewhat obscured by irregularities in the volume of the interior. Nevertheless, axes must be found so that new components of architecture and furniture can be distributed in aesthetic relationship.

An examination of Mies van der Rohe's 1929 German Pavilion at the Barcelona Exhibition reveals that several axes occur in various subdivisions of the interior. The building is designed with regularly spaced steel columns that support the flat roof. The columns divide the interior into three long bays across the width. An axis clearly runs along at the center of the space longitudinally between the two rows of columns. However, Mies sets up a contradiction to this axis by placing wall-screens off the center of the axis in a free arrangement. In the process he creates several other axes. Thus the main axis created by the columns is slightly obscured. Each of the resulting spaces differing in size and proportion has its own axis. The spare, but elegantly designed furniture acknowledges these axes and plays off of them in balanced arrangements.

Once the principal axis has been established in an existing space, it may be desirable to conceal it. Another axis can be created in opposition to the more apparent one. But this is done only if it contributes a new vitality or positive tension in the interior.

Although most spaces are rectangular in shape, some of these may be more effective if a diagonal axis is created. The problem with diagonal axes is the resulting triangulation of the interior. Often an axis on the diagonal results in a plan with strange, sometimes unusable cutoff corners when a designer attempts to use triangulation as a repeated principle. However, when used as a single dominant direction, diagonal axes can assist in the creation of dramatic interior concepts.

Alignment

In aesthetic composition alignment is a principle relating the edge (or corner) of one component to the edge (or corner) of another component. Alignment also relates the center of a component to the center of another component. Edge and center alignment is a principle used in building construction, and as a guide for the arrangement of architectural additions and furniture components (see Figure 40).

In architecture the whole practice of construction relies on the alignment of centers. The post-and-beam method of construction could not exist without the alignment of columns. In well-made buildings, columns also have all the edges in alignment (with the exception of high-rise structures, where wet columns carry plumbing).

The length and width of new architectural components in an existing space can be determined by considering alignment. Existing breaks in a wall plane, structural columns that project out into a space, doorways, and windows can be used as a guide for visual connections between old and new components. The visual link needed can be provided by the edge alignment of an existing architectural component with a new component of architecture, or furniture can accomplish visual connection between parts.

The above alignment conditions and possibilities can be seen readily in interior plans, but this principle can also be used to determine height in interiors. Height alignment may come from ceiling height, door height, the top or bottom of a window, or the height of an existing fixed-in-place appliance or furniture component. Any existing height in an interior may be used as a guide for height alignment. Sometimes the need is for nonalignment, but this procedure should still use alignment as its basis for determination.

Furniture components must always consider height alignment. The late Van Day Truex suggested that the height of the horizontal surfaces in an interior—window sill, table tops, case pieces—should match, when function permits, to give

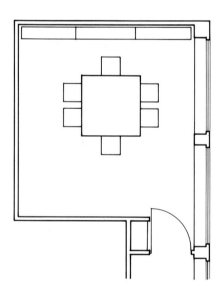

40.   Alignment

A.   Assuming that the columns in an interior are fixed, the walls must be placed in relation to them in either aligned or unaligned positions.

1.   The edges of the wall align with the columns.
2.   The edge ends of the walls align with the columns.
3.   The edge ends of the wall length are not aligned with the column spacing, but remain in a parallel relationship to the columns.
4.   The wall planes do not align with the columns, but have a position relationship to them.

B.   Center alignment produces an immediate, stable relationship between differing components.

C.   In an office each horizontal component is of a different material; wood desk, plastic laminate shelf, steel-wire back unit. These are put into a closer relationship through the alignment of their heights.

a room a feeling of tranquillity. He felt that too many different heights made rooms restless and discomforting. For the same reason, Truex also recommended that pictures on opposite as well as adjacent walls should have either their top or bottom edges in alignment.

Nonalignment in Interiors   New construction in interiors must acknowledge existing edges and, for the sake of an organized spatial aesthetic, recognize those components that are best when aligned. If edge alignment is overlooked, the size and placement of components may be haphazard and appear as a mistake. Alignment must be exactly precise, not almost precise.

In some design concepts for interiors, alignment is not an appropriate principle, because it is too rigid to accomplish what a designer wishes to project spatially. In such interiors, nonalignment can be employed. After alignment has been explored, nonalignment can be considered; however, nonalignment must be as deliberate as alignment. It is best to make the nonalignment—the slip—as a precisely measured dimension. The dimension of the nonaligned component must still relate to other dimensions in an interior. Nonaligned components are more noticeably separate in a space; they take on importance as special, significant parts.

Repetition and Rhythm

In art and design, repetition is the planned recurrence of a component. The components that are repeated must have a maximum of sameness and a minimum of difference in order to establish visual continuity firmly. In music, repetition brings back a melodic phrase; in dance, the structure of movement depends on repetition. Poets use repetition in the lengths of alternating lines and in rhyming sounds; in rhetoric, it is reinforcement and elaboration. Repetition can be used to establish rhythm, as we shall discuss later in this section.

Repetition in Structure

Repetition makes structure possible. Structure in the visual arts—painting, sculpture, architecture—as in poetry, music, dance, and drama, requires repetition. Without repetition these arts would be formless. Repetition made it possible for people in prehistoric societies to make objects of utility—shelters, baskets, woven cloth, and to formulate ritual.

In architecture all columned structures use a strict repeat of vertical members so that horizontal members can be supported; clay bricks are made into walls by repeated use of similar bricks (see Figure 41A). Throughout history some of the great periods of architecture are recognized in part by a repeated component that has become characteristic over time: Greek columns, Roman arches, the pointed arch in the Gothic period; the pure geometric circles, squares, octagons, and ovals of the Renaissance; and the smooth, planar walls of the Modern movement.

The repetition of parts has allowed the whole method of modular design to become systematized in the twentieth century. The great period of American cast-iron architecture was a precursor of modular design. In that system, as in the systems of today, various parts were repeated in multiples that match in dimensions of height, width, depth, and material.

Consistency in Repetition   To be effective in design, repeated components must recur with as much sameness as possible. Without sameness, the parts repeated in the design will not connect visually. Each stone column, or each wood panel, must have the same physical characteristics: They must "match" as closely as

A

B

C

D

E

F

G

41. Repetition and Rhythm

A. The patterning of bricks set into a bond produces a rhythmic variation when the long side (or stretcher) is placed next to the short end (or header). All brick bonds are made by repetition; some carry aspects of rhythm.

B. A static consistency is produced when equal-size shapes are repeated with equal spaces between them. Continuous beats of one-one-one do not produce rhythm, only repetition.

C. When shapes vary, even though the spacing between does not, a rhythm begins to form: one-two, one-two.

D. When the shape and number of shapes are varied, a more pronounced rhythm emerges: one-two-three, one-two-three.

E. This column spacing produces the beat of a staccato rhythm: solid-void, solid-void; or one-two, one-two.

F. Paired columns make this rhythmic repetition: one-two three, one-two three; or solid-solid void, solid-solid void.

G. Repeated arches can slow rhythm to a fluid, more lyrical movement.

possible even if each is made by a different pair of hands. With machine production, the matching of parts is assured.

When a component is "like" another component, a designer is wise to consider duplication—sameness—as the best decision. When two or more components should be identical, the decision to use merely similar ones will likely be taken as a mistake.

Consistency of size, shape, color, and material must be given attention in any repeated component. This assures that each one maintains all of the necessary characteristics and will create the strongest possible relationship. This notion holds true for components within one space or in adjacent spaces.

Variation within Repetition Sometimes continuous repetition needs variation (see Figure 41B,C,D). Several means of variation are possible when other principles are included, such as size, shape, color, texture, still maintaining minimum differences. For example, if the size of a component is varied, the material may remain the same. This was the principle used by Mies van der Rohe in the structure of the building and furniture in the German Pavilion at Barcelona. The columns of the pavilion are X-shaped in plan; the Barcelona Chair uses an X on the side; the glass-topped table has its X on the horizontal. Each X is a different size, but each is the same material and each is used in a different direction (see Figure 42A).

Color can be used as a powerful means of repetition with variations. A pure hue used in an interior can be repeated in identical intensity, but on different components; or a color may be used as a pure hue with a tint; or as a shade. Furniture components of different shape can be finished in the same color to connect them visually. The same color may appear in an interior in various textures or in different materials.

Another way to bring variety to repetition is through alternation. Alternation is used in interiors when several components are part of a composition. Two or more shapes, two or more colors, are used—first one, then the other—for example, square-circle-square, or red-green-red. The shapes and the colors may repeat in the same position relationships, or the position relationship may also alternate.

Horizontal and vertical repetition of components may create a unifying theme in an interior, as C. F. A. Voysey did in his own house in Hertfordshire, England, in 1900 (see Figure 42B). Two parts of the interior clearly are linked together by their linear design—the stair screen and the fireplace. The screen-wall of the stair is composed of thin vertical strips of wood to create a kind of veil. This vertical motif is repeated in the fireplace design of intense blue tiles that are stacked on end. The tiles and the joints have a marked verticality, the dark tiles in high contrast with the light mortise joints.

Practicing interior designers often use repetition—not only as a means of organization, but as a way to reduce the number of shapes, materials, and colors. This procedure can simplify an interior in the most direct manner. For example, in such an interior—even though quite large—the designer may specify one flooring material that continues throughout all the spaces and in one color; one fabric for all soft upholstery; one device for window coverings; one principal chair form, appropriate for use in a variety of spaces; one table form that can be made smaller or larger according to need. This method of using the principle of repetition is a precept of the type of spatial organization known as organic unity—the interrelationship of adjacent spaces, the interconnection between all spaces that exist under one roof, or are related through function and purpose.

Rhythm

Repetition can produce rhythm. Rhythm is movement. It can move the body, and it can move the eye. Its force is powerful because of its connection to human biology, its roots far down in our primordial existence. Rhythm is in the pumping of our blood back and forth; in the breathing in and out of our lungs; in the pace of our footfall, and the swing of our arms. We can feel rhythm; we can see it in ourselves.

Rhythmic repetition hits an emotional peak when groups of people perform the same physical movements, or make the same sound. This type of rhythm is made by a great mass of marchers on parade; by a line of dancers stretching across a stage executing the same high kicks; the 200-voice choir singing the same word with variations in tone, or in countermeasure one against the other. However, in the strict aesthetic sense, rhythm in interiors exists only when forms or objects are separated by spaces. These must be measurable. The measurement is usually repeated

A

B

42. Repetition

A. Furniture, 1929, Mies van der Rohe, from the German Pavillion, Barcelona. The roof of the pavillion was supported on X-shaped columns of steel. The shape was repeated in the furniture, also made of steel. In the design of the low table, the X appears in the top view. The chair and stool structure places the X on the sides.

B. Domestic interior, 1900, C. F. A. Voysey, Hertfordshire, England. The linear trim of the wall planes is repeated in two other ways in two components. In the stair screen, linearity is apparent in the repetition of thin lines of painted wood. They are made into a semitransparent, veil-like design. In the face of the fireplace the solidity of the dark, vertically stacked tile is contrasted with a web of the light mortar joints. In this room repetition is varied by changes in scale, color, and material.

exactly; but looser dimensions of the spaces are sometimes acceptable and artful, except with load-bearing structure. There inexact measurements would be unacceptable for a system of construction, or would be visually disturbing.

In the arts, rhythm as a creative principle is most clearly observed in music and poetry. The notes in a musical composition are arranged to produce forms that are the rhythms of a waltz, a tango, a movement, or a whole symphony. In these, as well as other musical forms, notes make the sound. But between the sound of the notes are rests where there is no sound. This rest—or rhythmic silence—is equally important to the composition. Similarly, in poetry, rhythm is necessary. In prescribed poetic form, rhythm is mandatory; it is what makes the form. The rhythm is in the length of a line and the fixed number of rhymes in the composition of many poetic forms.

In architecture, too, the spacing of components can set a rhythm. The columns of a portico make a rhythm by the repetition of the regularly sized column separated by open space (see Figure 41E,F,G). The column makes a solid "beat"; the space between columns makes a void that is another type of beat. Rasmussen says that this is a rhythm that "represents a regularity and precision found nowhere in nature, but only in the order man seeks to create." Rasmussen also observes that the simple rhythm—one-two, one-two—will never be obsolete, that it has been used by designers in equally appropriate ways from the rock tombs of Egypt to the present.[8]

Rhythm in Interior Design Some rhythms expressed in the external features of a building are evident in its interior. Columns may occur inside a building; windows or doors in series can set up rhythms. If recognized, the existing architectural components can be reinforced by the interior components. Color, lighting, and furniture may be designed to strengthen rhythms that are present in existing spaces. All existing architectural rhythms should be considered as assets to conceptual thinking.

Most twentieth-century interiors have little or no rhythm in their architecture: Most of these interiors have little architecture at all, let alone rhythm. In them, windows are only in pairs, most doors are single ones, walls are flat, embellishment is absent. However, visual rhythm of a sort and kinetic rhythm—the movement through spaces—can be a part of such interiors.

The arrangement of furniture in interior plans can produce only a limited rhythmic repetition except in large, public spaces. Residential interiors usually contain relatively few furniture components that can be rhythmically repeated, and rhythm can be produced only by several "beats"; one "beat" is not rhythm.

Kinetic rhythm is often overlooked when interior design concepts are devised. This type of rhythm, the movement through interior spaces, must be consciously injected. Movement through a space can be influenced to progress at a slow or rapid pace. Moving through an interior in which rhythm is part of the design can cause the eye and the foot to pause, to slow down, or to hasten movement. This can be accomplished by a change in flooring material, or a change in level in the floor plane. Hard surfaces tend to cause rapid movement; soft surfaces slow us down. When both hard and soft surfaces are used on the same floor plane, our movement is affected to a certain extent because the foot responds to each material in a slightly different way. Of course, any change of level will cause us to pause, or slow down.

Movement through spaces, and movement in and around furniture components, should be considered as having the potential of rhythmic design rather than

---

[8]Rasmussen, *Experiencing Architecture.*

as "traffic patterns." Traffic patterns, studied so earnestly by many designers, are more appropriate to moving automobiles, trucks, and buses than to people in interiors. Rhythmic movement can be efficient as well as aesthetic in public, corporate, or private interiors.

Repetition and Rhythm in the Hall of Mirrors

Perhaps the most monumental use of repetition and rhythm in interiors is in the Hall of Mirrors at Versailles. The hall (1678–84), designed by Jules Mansard with painted decorations by Charles LeBrun, connects two wings of the palace. It was designed with the most sumptuous materials—marble, wood parquet, gold leaf, frescoed plaster, and the newly available sheets of glass and mirror. The dimensions of the impressive hall measure 240 feet in length by 34 feet in width. The ceiling is 43 feet high, designed as a single barrel vault.

Every component is repeated in the long elevations—pilasters, arches (filled with either mirrors or windows), and carved decorations. The rhythm established by these parts develops down the length of the hall as a three-to-one ratio: three arches of mirror, or glass, and one flat panel between. The rhythm is reemphasized by the repetition of the marble pilasters inserted between each arch.

One of the more subtle repetitive motifs is the reflection of the lavish formal gardens through the windows into the mirrored arches opposite. By daylight, the boundaries of this space begin to dematerialize in shimmering, reflected garden images that are slightly distorted in the sections of mirror. At night gilt bronze chandeliers light the hall and repeat the rhythm of every third arch, their light reflected in the now dark glass and pale mirrors. These lighting components, with their huge bunches of candles, pace the intervals of the arches and reemphasize the processional character with rhythmic repetition.

Contrast and Opposition

The aesthetic principle of contrast offers the satisfaction of differences. Contrast places interior components in relation to each other so that when seen side by side the components exhibit their individual diversities to the best advantage. Opposition is a similar principle with one variation: The components must exhibit equality in such characteristics as weight, height, color value, and shape.

Contrast

Contrast is familiar in our daily lives because it exists naturally in the world of the senses: light against dark, sweet against salty, smooth against rough, warm against cool, soft against hard, and sound against silence. Without these contrasts the world of the senses would be flat, indeed, indistinguishable.

In all artistic creation, contrast is essential to composition. In music a symphony is conducted with a slow or adagio movement, set in contrast against a faster or allegro movement; sometimes against a moderately slow, flowing, andante movement. String sounds contrast with wind instruments, and high treble notes play against low bass notes.

In painting, contrast is seen in the juxtaposition of one color to another color, whether the two shades of white in a Malevich painting, the black-on-black paintings of Ad Reinhardt, or a multicolored still life by Matisse. The painter Wassily Kandinsky wrote in his *Reminiscences:* "I saw that there was nothing magical about any large surface by itself and that any such surface revealed at once its derivation from the palette; but through another surface, opposed to it, this surface acquired

A

B

C

43. Contrast and Opposition

A. Light and dark values exhibit maximum contrast. Equal amounts of color hues in equal values oppose each other.

B. Two differing textures are in low contrast to each other. Polished, smooth textures against ones that are rough produce greater textural contrast.

C. Patterns may contrast by a difference in scale, but still be related by similarity in shape.

D

E

F

D. A circular plan is in contrast to square-shaped furniture: one large circle in contrast to many small squares.

E. A standard-size wall and fireplace are in contrast to a small-size picture.

F. A low, horizontal table is in contrast to the vertical candlesticks.

G. A standard-size wall is in contrast to a large-size picture.

G

indeed a magic power, so that its origin on the palette seemed unbelievable at first impression."[9]

In architecture the contrasting effects of solids and voids are essential parts in the design of a building. Contrasting textural effects are essential, as are contrasts such as the use of one color adjacent to another (see Figure 43A,B). Contrasts in daylight and shadow bring life to a building by differentiating planes and materials.

Contrast in Interiors   Contrast in interiors provides emphasis. If one wall plane in an interior is rough-textured and all of the others are smooth, the rough-textured wall plane will dominate. In a spatial composition, whatever components are most unlike the other components will by contrast be emphasized and acquire importance (see Figure 43D,E,F,G). A solid door set in a glass wall takes on importance by the contrast of opaqueness and transparency; a door painted black set into a white wall gains importance by the contrast of value.

The white wall planes and dark-carpeted floor planes of Modernist interior designers use contrast to distinguish vertical from horizontal. Both walls and floor may be relatively free of textural difference, but the contrast is emphasized by maximum contrast in color value. If only one color is modulated from dark to light in a monochromatic scheme, there can still be contrast in value and texture. Not every use of contrast has to be at the maximum: Black and white makes a dramatic difference, but subtle contrast between two shades or tints of the same color can also be effective.

Contrast can provide the means of spatial separation. Within a single space, the separation of parts can be accomplished through contrasting color, texture, pattern, scale, and shape or configuration (see Figure 43C). The same contrasting means can be used to separate adjacent or sequential spaces. Several contrasts can be used simultaneously to increase differences and further identify spatial boundaries.

A kind of spatial emphasis through separation, which uses the light against dark and small against large, is seen in the design of many Italian squares. For these outdoor "rooms" the entrance (often more than one) is through a narrow street bordered by buildings that put the passageway into deep shadow. A burst of light occurs on arriving at the square, with its brilliant "roof" of bright sky; the contrast becomes exhilarating. This principle can be used to good effect even in modest-size interiors. A corridor or fore-room can have its small size emphasized with deep color, while the larger room can be emphasized with a light, contrasting color.

Interiors that are architecturally symmetrical can be contrasted by an asymmetrical, balanced plan of furniture components. In this type of interior planning, architecture and furniture coexist, but each is allowed its own identity. The contrast provides a positive tension between the parts of the interior.

Furniture from historical periods can be used in contrast with Modern interior architecture; Modern furniture can be juxtaposed to historical architectural styles. Linear furniture may stand in contrast to planar walls.

Opposition

Opposition occurs when one component is contrasted in equal strength—or seemingly equal strength—to another component. For example, an amount of red is in opposition to an equal amount of green. A horizontal beam presses its weight on the equal, upward push of a vertical post. In symmetrical compositions identical components repeated on either side of a central axis are equally weighted, the left

---

[9]Nina Kandinsky, *Concerning the Spiritual in Art* (New York: George Wittenborn, 1947).

and right halves existing in opposition to each other. Components that are equal in size, weight, and color value produce equilibrium through opposition.

Complementary colors are opposites. When equal amounts of opposite colors of equal value are placed next to each other, they are in competitive opposition, one against the other (see Figure 43A). With equal amounts of each, red is in opposition to green, orange opposes blue, yellow opposes violet. Every tint of red opposes every tint of green when both amount and value are equal.

DeWitt Parker, in his treatment of this principle, says:

> Opposition or contrast is never absent from balance, for even in symmetry, where the balancing elements are alike, the directions of these elements are opposed right and left. But contrast is never by itself aesthetically satisfactory, for the contrasting elements must offset each other, they must balance. . . . The essential thing about balance is equality of opposed values.[10]

Vista and View

Many laymen use the terms "vista" and "view" interchangeably to mean an overview from a roadside stop, or a panoramic view from a mountaintop. Interior designers, however, must distinguish the two terms as having opposite effects. Still, both imply distance.

View means looking at space from right to left, up and down, ranging over distance, taking it in visually. Vista, on the other hand, is a controlled and delimited view. A vista focuses on a single object and culminates in a single point or place. Both vista and view are used to create a visual extension.

Vista

Vista leads the eye in a clear linear path directly to another point or place. The path of a vista directs us to a destination easily attainable. In interiors the termination point may be a work of art, an arresting architectural feature, a place to sit, or an object presented in a celebratory way. The object at the termination point, if the distance is long, may not be fully revealed until the path of the vista is traveled.

In landscape design a vista may be defined by trees, hedges, arcades, columns, or walls in parallel rows set at the limiting edges of the path. The focus of such a vista is often a garden seat, sculpture, or building part.

Interior vistas can be created in several ways. Corridors offer an obvious possibility; the side walls provide the means of focusing on a climactic component placed at the terminus of the length. When a corridor ends at the entrance to another room, the vista can be extended and pushed to the far wall of that room by centering a component there.

Rooms connected in series offer another condition where vista may be employed. When two or more rooms are connected by doorways or openings centered on an axis, the path along this axis can be seen as a potential vista. Here the vertical sides of the doorways provide the parallel control. The termination will, again, be climaxed in some particular component of architecture, furniture, or art.

In Western history the vista came into prominent use in eighteenth-century French Rococo art and design. Wylie Sypher notes that the "pompous alleys" at Versailles became quiet, poetic, intimate vistas, and were particularly apparent in paintings by Watteau.[11]

---

[10]DeWitt Parker, *The Analysis of Art* (New Haven: Yale University Press, 1926).
[11]Sypher, *Rococo to Cubism in Art and Literature.*

In the Louvre Museum in Paris, the sculpture of the Venus de Milo is the point of climax at the end of a vista. The Venus stands in isolation, centered within the width of several openings, its height increased by a pedestal. It can be seen from a long distance through several galleries that precede it. The importance and distinction of the sculpture are greatly enhanced by the long approach.

The Post-Modernist architect Michael Graves often treats corridors to create vistas (see Figure 44; see also Figure 22). In them he designs the side walls with column-like components that repeat down the length and terminate in an arresting object—sometimes a doorway decorated with moldings and cornices that opens into another room to extend the vista, sometimes in a piece of sculpture or a pedestal holding an arrangement of flowers. Graves's vistas make deliberate allusions to historical interiors, such as those of the classical Baroque or French Rococo, where perspective encourages the idea of continuing toward a significant destination.

To be effective, vistas need not be long. The termination need not climax in a world-famous sculpture. The effect of vista may be accomplished within a few feet, as long as the width of the path is controlled and a component of interest is placed at the termination point.

View

Circuity, obstruction, and pause are qualities of view. The viewer must go around or look around something to get to what is seen. Interior views can be created in small rooms, and the pause can be brief. From an entrance, the view of a room

44. Vista and View

Interior vista, 1982, Michael Graves, Sunar showroom, New York. The termination of a vista may be marked by a component of architecture, furniture, art, or decoration. This corridor vista directs its linear path to a door. Along the path, wall segments and columns hold light sconces that mark the direction of the focus. (See also Figure 22.)

may be over a low wall that intercepts the path, or across a group of furniture to the opposite wall. At a very small scale, a view may be created on a table surface when looking over, across, or around one or more objects in order to see another, perhaps larger object. These examples begin to suggest that the device of view can create a layered, enriching effect, and cause the eye to move from one place or object to another.

The layering effect of view—seeing more than one space, plane, or shape overlaid on another—is used frequently in the vocabulary of twentieth-century interior design. Adolf Loos employed the principle of view in the Moller House in Vienna (see Figure 45). From the dining room he planned a view through a

A

B

45. View

Domestic interior view, Moller House. 1928, Adolf Loos, Vienna.

A. From the dining room, a view down into the lowered music room also creates a view in reverse. Access between the rooms is possible only by a small, folding stair encased in the threshold.

B. A reverse view is created from the music room up to the dining room. In this design, as in all planned views, pause, obstruction, and circuity—the characteristics of view—are exploited.

wide opening down into the music room, which is about two feet lower than the dining room. To get from one room to the other, it is necessary to fold down stairs that were fitted into the threshold. The impact of this design is explained by Loos's contemporary, architect Willy Hofmann, who wrote, "This may appear absurd, but it has been done with such a fine feeling for spatial effect, with such a supreme mastery in the exploitation of view, that what might otherwise have easily seemed ridiculous, compels reflection from sheer force of personality."[12] From almost every space in this house, Loos offered a view into another room; in almost every case, the room viewed is reached by a circuitous route.

Frank Lloyd Wright's organic interiors exemplify layered views. Not only from one space onto another, but within spaces, he has layered intersecting horizontal and vertical planes and added layers of built-in-place furniture and objects as well.

More recently, aspects of view have been used to create rooms-within-rooms, as architect Charles Moore did in his 1962 house in Orinda, California. There the interior is a single space, but within it there is a remarkable variety of form. Two pyramidal domes, each resting on four 10-foot-high Tuscan columns, which were salvaged from a San Francisco demolition, define two square areas—a living area under the larger dome, and a bathroom with a sunken tub under the smaller. The domes, like inverted funnels, pull light down into the areas they define. They and their supporting columns define the smaller rooms within the larger room. Views from each are seen from the other, as well as panoramic views over the open space.

Texture, Pattern, and Color

Because they are so closely related, texture, pattern, and color are always considered together. This discussion outlines the contribution each makes to interior design, and the approaches to each that should be considered for investigation.

Texture

Every material used in an interior has texture. Texture is present in materials whether they are made from natural or manmade substances. Although texture is often thought to mean the characteristic of a surface, texture is more often indicative of construction. Surface texture can be felt with the fingers, but the eyes can teach things about both surface and construction without tactile assistance. Some materials appear to have more texture than is actually present in either surface or construction. Such materials as printed fabric, wallpaper, plastic laminate, and synthetic floor covering often appear highly textured and dimensional when seen, but on closer examination reveal that their surfaces are quite smooth to the touch, their texture a fiction.

Texture is often a result of contruction. The texture of a straw basket is a consequence of a natural material shaped by a weaving technique (see Figure 46A). Woven cloth similarly gets its texture from the character of the yarn together with the method of construction (see Figure 46D). Clay made into pots or bricks still retains the essential nature of the raw material.

Some natural materials such as wood and stone are textured by the method used to finish them for use. Wood can be given a smooth and glistening surface, or it can be left in a rough, unfinished condition (see Figure 46F). Metal can glow or gleam softly (see Figure 46E). Stone can be polished to a mirror-like sleekness,

---

[12]Ludwig Munz and Gustav Kunstler, *Adolf Loos: Pioneer of Modern Architecture* (New York and Washington: Frederick A. Praeger, 1966).

A

B

C

D

E

F

A. Straw. The stems or stalks of grains such as oats, wheat, rye, and some grasses are dried, cut to size, and woven into straw. The type of straw and the type of weave together create material of distinct character. Fine straw may take on a fabric-like quality when woven, but still retain its natural identity.

B. Marble. A quarried stone, marble is a material for building, for interior architectural components, and for parts of furniture. The less-veined marbles have a capacity for structural use. Those with more patterning are more decorative, and are prized for that reason. Colors deepen when polished to a high, glass-like sheen.

C. Rock. The grainy surface of cut rock has an uneven, textural richness. Though never used for bearing construction, fine-grained rock has an ancient tradition of use as roof tile, flooring, and furniture tops. Protective finishes darken and deepen its color tones.

D. Fiber. Cotton, silk, flax, animal hair, and manmade fibers are woven into fabrics. These are suitable for exterior or interior use, as well as in industry. The qualities of woven fibers are so distinct that they remain identifiable even when dimmed by inappropriate designs.

E. Metal. Reflective metals may have surfaces of a low sheen or be polished to a brilliant, slick shine. Patterns can be added to give a layer of imposed texture. Metal is characterized by hardness, coldness, and, in some forms, strength.

F. Wood. Dressed wood can have a finish that is lustrous, satiny, glossy, or dull in texture. The graining is a pattern-like texture that ranges from fine to bold, depending on density. New wood has a freshness and vibrancy. It ages with dignity and refinement.

46. Texture

Materials are rarely usable in interiors in a completely natural state. When processed to make them appropriate for use, their inherent properties are altered and may become hidden or enhanced.

dressed to a soft sugar-like surface, or rusticated to a burly roughness (see Figure 46B,C). Textures must be selected deliberately as support for concepts.

The Japanese stone garden provides such an example. Although these garden rooms are not "used" in the ordinary sense, they are "used" by the eyes for visual contemplation. In these designs there is only slight contrast in color value, but each component of the garden has a textural identity and consideration that heightens the organizational scheme. The contrasting textures of raked sand, stone, pebble, and wood are composed in arrangements of great refinement. The materials, all taken directly from nature, are used with discretion. The control of the design is obvious in each chosen component; even the natural sand is controlled by a raked, manmade texture.

When changes in color are undesirable as support for a design concept, changes in texture become critical and may need to be exaggerated. In a small New York apartment, the design was based entirely on textural contrast. Every component in the apartment was white. Matte-white painted walls contrasted with gloss-white painted woodwork and ceiling moldings. White enamel covered the floors in contrast with a white goat-hair rug. All of the wood furniture was painted white; upholstered furniture was covered with white fabric. Functional and decorative accessories were silver-white metal or transparent glass.

In this design the concept superimposes an organic scheme on a series of geometric rooms. Form and shape have been deliberately reduced in their importance; color is almost absent. Texture combined with light and shadow differentiates the parts of the rooms. One room flows into another room with varied textural differences providing the visual and tactile interest. The whiteness of the rooms tends to wipe out architectural boundaries.

The characteristic of texture that is most apparent for exploitation is the feel, or "hand" of a material. We usually think of feeling with our fingers, and, to be sure, fingers are the main implements that tell us how smooth or rough, soft or hard, a material is. If a fabric is selected for use in a scheme, the decision will be based on color and texture together. The selection will also be based on the contrast of one texture to another. Tweed fabric is noticeably different from silk fabric, even though both may be the same color. In the surface of the tweed fabric, light is absorbed; in the silk fabric, it is reflected. The method of construction used in each fabric is different; therefore, each reacts differently to dye color and to light.

In some interior situations textural contrast is seen, felt, and heard. Hard, nonresilient floors give the foot and ear different sensations from soft, resilient floors. The click of shoes on hard surfaces can seem refreshing when heard in contrast to the muffled sound of soft surfaces.

Textural contrast does not always have to be extreme to be effective. In a New York apartment designed in the early 1960s by Paul Lester Weiner and Ala Damas, there is a striking use of polished-smooth and matte-smooth material. In the living room, flat-woven silk in descending order of color brightness is the material for upholstered furniture and curtains. These are in full-saturation colors of yellow and purple. A pure red wool felt, also flat in surface texture, covers one wall. The other walls are painted white. The terrace doors and the tables in this room are glass. The floor is covered in a dense, low-pile tan wool carpet. Visible from the living room is the dining area, which also has smooth-textured materials. The floor is black marble; ceiling recesses are painted a clear blue. Dining chairs are black leather on steel supports; the table is polished white marble.

In this interior, although each material has smoothness as its main characteristic, the slight difference in surface texture has been heightened by color. Each material has not only its own texture, but each has its own color. The softest components receive the brightest color: curtains, upholstered furniture, soft covered wall. The floor contrasts dark, hard stone against light, soft carpet.

Texture Selection In every interior several materials are used; therefore, every interior has several textures. As textures are selected, they must also be compatible with each other and with the component for which they are selected. A texture may be too fine (that is, too small) to *hold* visually if it is used on a large component such as a wall or floor. A coarse texture may overwhelm a small piece of furniture. Combinations of textures within an interior may need to be at opposite extremes of smoothness and roughness when the form differentiation calls for that difference. Other interiors may need only slight degrees of contrast.

Textural Patterns When some textures are increased in size, they become pattern-like. A finely woven basket may remain a texture only, but one woven of coarser material begins to show patterning. Clay made into a pot or brick exhibits textural form, but bricks made into a wall become patterned texture.

Pattern

Pattern is the planned repetition of a motif. The repetition of form, shape, and outline is a necessary component of pattern. These are what make a composition: form, shape, and outline repeated. Pattern used as a formal principle in composition had to be discovered. Pattern is a human creation.

Pattern can be the result of structure. Certain weaving techniques lead to pattern; architectural construction techniques such as those used in brick bonds, stone masonry, and tile work, interior construction of wood floors or synthetic tiles, produce the repetition of a shape that makes a pattern. These patterns are a result of the necessity of structure.

Origin of Pattern On a small block of bituminous stone in the Louvre Museum are the sculpted figures of two men, one on either side of an animal figure. Above the clasped hands of the men is another motif: two interlaced serpents (see Figure 47A). This is perhaps the earliest example (approximately the third millennium B.C.) of an important compositional device that was to have unending progeny.

Several centuries later—around the twenty-fourth century B.C.—a stone lamp lid from Neo-Sumeria is carved with the same interlacing motif. Sir Herbert Read points out that

> The idea may have been suggested by the natural habit of snakes. But snakes do not normally interlace themselves into symmetrical patterns. It could have arisen only from activities such as basketmaking, or weaving, that induce an archetypal pattern—the consciousness of a pattern as a thing-in-itself—by abstraction from the repeated action of interlacing. [See Figure 47B.][13]

Read says further that the resulting effect, the "effect of aesthetic pleasure," is the same as that produced from plaited straw. The snakes, plaited in the same manner, convey the same aesthetic pleasure because they repeat the same pattern. Why a plaited pattern produces a reaction of pleasure is not known; but it does. And *that* it does was first discovered by Sumerian artists five thousand years ago. Theorists say that the discovery of pattern—meaning the abstract idea of it—gave birth to form, and that its application to the representation of natural objects held incalculable consequences for the history of art.

Integral Pattern Integral pattern is produced from the essential character of a material, the manner in which the material is employed, as well as its shape and

---

[13] Sir Herbert Read, *Icon and Idea* (New York: Schocken Books, 1964).

finish. Integral pattern is inseparable from a component part; it is a result of material and structure.

The sources of integral patterns are both natural and manmade. Walls or floors of stone (see Figure 47C), brick, or wood (see Figure 47D) make patterns as a result of the manner in which the materials are used in making the wall or floor. A floor of wood planks creates a repeating linear pattern; wood laid in squares makes a repeating pattern called parquet. In each case the pattern results from the planned repetition of the material and the way the material is employed. Various methods of fabricating a brick wall create different patterns—called bonds—each of which has a distinct character. Stone is laid in several patterns—called uncoursed, rough-coursed, or coursed—that exhibit individual characteristics. The weaving processes of many fabrics were invented to create particular patterns, including damask, brocade, gingham, and tartan; without the process these patterns could not exist (see Figure 47E,F).

Surface Pattern Surface pattern does not depend on structural process. It is applied to a finished woven material for decorative effect or embellishment. Surface patterns derive both from sources such as nature in abstract shapes and from geometric shapes developed over time. To make the pattern, the shapes—called motifs—are repeated at regular intervals along the surface (see Figure 48). These can be applied by hand or by machines. The size of the motifs can vary because their size does not affect the actual structure of the material. Fabric and wallpaper are the most common materials to receive surface patterning by printing.

Repeated geometric patterns used for surface decoration figured at an early date in human artistic expression. From at least before 3000 B.C. these patterns were applied to pottery; and no organic explanation can be given to the designs, which are purely abstract.

The early discovery and the subsequent continuous use of pattern are considered by anthropologists and art historians alike as an artistic compositional device equal to the discovery of symmetry and balance. As a means of offering aesthetic pleasure, pattern is more likely to have a wider appeal than any other device, even when poorly conceived. If proof of this is needed, we have only to examine the overwhelming growth of patterning from preliterate cultures onward. Whether or not this means the embellishment was used as symbol or as decoration, its continued use today is evident in handmade and machine-made articles for every conceivable type of product. Motifs abstracted from nature or purely geometric continue to offer the same visual pleasure today as they must surely have given to early artistic creators and the users of the product of their art even before recorded history.

Interior Application of Pattern Ideally used, pattern should make us more aware of surface, should call attention to a surface and give it importance. That pattern can make things more visible is one of its unmistakable characteristics. This characteristic is evident in many of the products of modern technology, as well as in ancient crafts.

The application of pattern in interiors can be used as a device to give variety. Many designers think that a room without at least one patterned component is unsatisfying and unfinished. Others prefer only the natural patterning found in wood or the veining in marble to supply pattern when manmade, applied patterns are thought to be inappropriate.

Scale in patterns is of special importance. If a pattern is a bold, large-scale design, it can overwhelm. Large-scale patterns tend to break up surfaces. They can become contradictory by making a form or a surface seem to be something other than it is. In general, the scale of a pattern should be evaluated against the scale

A

B

C

D

E

F

47. Pattern

A. In this bituminous stone carving from the third millennium B.C., interlaced serpents are composed in the earliest known pattern.

B. A stone lamp lid from Neo-Sumeria, twenty-fourth century B.C., also uses snakes, but in a repeated, symmetrical pattern.

C. The veining of marble, repeated in tiles, produces an integral, natural pattern.

D. Wood graining in matched flitches of veneer becomes patterning when repeated over a surface.

E. Weaving two or more yarn colors creates such patterns as gingham.

F. Damask can be woven of cotton, linen, silk, or wool. The pattern derives from a mixture of flat and twisted yarn.

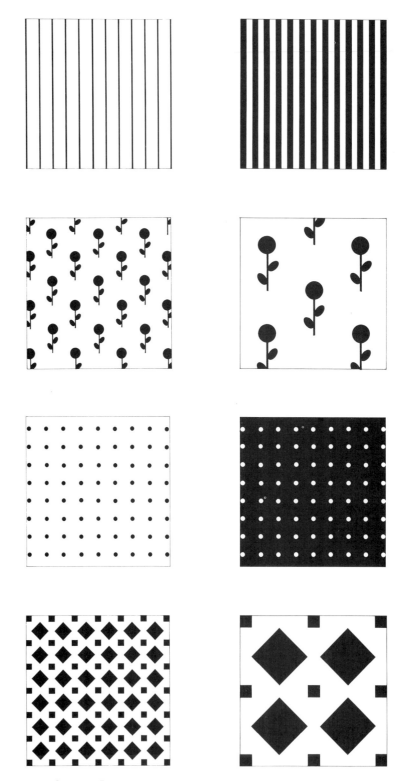

48. Surface Pattern

The application of a pattern to a flat surface such as paper or fabric has few restrictions. The shape of a pattern does not rely on the construction of a ground, but on aesthetic invention only. When the scale of a pattern is changed, the pattern is changed, even though the same motif is repeated. Pattern designs are limitless; but the basic ones, such as stripes, dots, flowers or other vegetation, and geometric constructions, are few.

of the host component. On the other hand, small-scale patterns tend to become submerged into textural patterns when seen at even short distances. Small patterns do not break up surfaces or submerge form. Small-scale patterns are less arresting visually, and more of them can be tolerated in interiors than can large-scale patterns.

Some practitioners argue that pattern is a device that can be used to correct problems in an interior, to hide faults in architectural components, to affect proportional changes, to camouflage shape or boundary. Good pattern that is appropriate to use is not used as a disguise. It is employed as a conscious means to make things more visible.

Color

Color is generally considered the most potent device available to an artist in any aspect of aesthetic composition. It influences shape, size, weight, and temperature. Color is expressive because it carries with it the idea of symbol. In baby clothes, for example, color tells us something. Pink for girls and blue for boys are recognized symbolic associations of gender while pale yellow and white are said to carry no gender connotations for our society.

The symbolic connotations of color have developed over time, from repeated application in rituals, seasons, and forms, as well as in the way color exists in the natural world. We commonly use color names to make our verbal descriptions more vivid. We speak of golden sunsets, blue heavens, fiery reds. But without qualifying factors these colors can mean very different things. The yellow used to describe a sunset is also a color that has often been used to connote cowardice. Blue is often used by song writers to symbolize sadness; red, more often than not, indicates anger or danger. We say that we are "green with envy," but grass is not envious. Purple may mean royalty or it may represent rage in some cultures. The Bauhaus teacher and painter Wassily Kandinsky taught that yellow was akin to the shape of a triangle, that red related to a square, and that blue was best as the symbol of a circle. In some cultures yellow symbolizes splendor, but in others it is the color of shame and contempt.

Some contemporary designers of interiors also use the symbolic quality of color as a means of expression. For Michael Graves color references recall natural elements such as blue for sky, brown for earth, and green for foliage. In an interior by John Hejduk, as Deborah Nevins describes in *200 Years of American Architectural Drawing*, "The kitchen is yellow, symbolizing energy, the dining area green for nourishment, the bedroom black for night, the living room brown for earth, the study gray to signify the twilight one enters between reality and nonreality while in the process of reading and thought."[14] John Saladino contrasts the mottled, verdigris colors of ancient materials with clear, flower-like colors. Other designers say that they use color schemes from historical periods to relate contemporary interiors to the past. Whatever procedure is used, each is an attempt to apply theories of color symbolism to interiors.

Color Theories   For centuries color has been investigated by scientists and artists. They have explored the minutiae of color phenomena and color harmony. Systems for color harmony have been prescribed by Aristotle, Isaac Newton, Goethe, and Schopenhauer. Their prescriptions were attempts to classify all color into a single standard, an objective system of values. The earliest designs of the systems were two-dimensional. These showed sequences and some interrelations of color

---

[14]Deborah Nevins and David Gebhard, *200 Years of American Architectural Drawing* (New York: Whitney Library of Design, an imprint of Watson-Guptill Publications, 1977).

hues by two-dimensional shapes such as circles or polygons. At a later time it was recognized that color could be determined only by at least three dimensions or variables—hue, value, and saturation—and at that time three-dimensional models were introduced.

All color experts seem to agree on three characteristics of all color: hue, value, and saturation or chroma.

1. *Hue* is the classification of a color by name—red, yellow, and blue are the fundamental Primary color hues; orange, green, and purple (or violet) are the Secondary color hues. Mixtures of two Primary colors will produce one of the Secondary colors: Red and blue mixtures produce purple; red and yellow mixtures produce orange; yellow and blue mixtures produce green. Intermixtures of Primary and Secondary hues produce the intermediate (Tertiary) colors—red-orange, yellow-orange, yellow-green, blue-green, blue-violet, red-violet.

2. *Value* in color classification is the lightness or darkness of hue produced by the introduction of black or white intermixed with Primary, Secondary, or Tertiary color hues. Tints are made by intermixing white; shades (sometimes called tones) are made by intermixing black. Grayed hues are produced by intermixing small amounts of an opposite color. A gray-green is produced by intermixing small amounts of red, a gray-blue is produced by intermixing a small amount of orange, and so forth.

3. *Saturation* indicates the purity of a hue—one that is unadulterated by another hue. Pure Primary hues are neither cold nor warm, despite popular notions. Pure blue of a saturation equal to that of a pure red cannot properly be called cold; pure yellow in saturation equal to pure blue and red is clearly neither cold nor warm. This characteristic is that of temperature.

According to Rudolph Arnheim, when colors are intermixed (he calls it "admixture"), the added color tends to dominate. For example, when red is added to blue, producing a reddish blue, it will look warm; conversely, when blue is added to red, producing a bluish red, it will look cool. When equal amounts of two primary colors are intermixed, they tend to produce gray shades that are neutral or ambiguous. Being less characteristic of one or the other hue, they will have less tendency toward warm or cool temperature. Arnheim goes on to say, "If my approach is viable, it may apply more generally to the expressive qualities of colors. Perhaps it is not so much the dominant hue but its 'afflictions' that give a color its character."[15]

Harmonic Color Systems The question of how colors relate to each other is the search for harmony. Early attempts at systematic color harmony generated several theoretical models, some still in use today. They were intended to assist in determining color combinations that produced harmonic relationships, colors that "fit" together, that blended. The most influential of the color systems were designed by Wilhelm Ostwald, and by the painter Albert Munsell in 1915. Their systems were designed to classify color (that is, to identify it), and to indicate—objectively—which colors could be employed together in harmony. Although each of these men based his theories on a somewhat differently shaped model, the various color classifications were all based on the same principle.

The simplest and probably the most useful tool for the creation of color harmonies is the two-dimensional color wheel (see Figure 49). The divisions of the

---

[15]Arnheim, *Art and Visual Perception.*

49.   The Color Wheel

Colors placed in the design of a simple wheel relate the basic, foundational hues and their derivations. Red, blue, and yellow make up the Primary color group; orange, green, and violet are the Secondary colors. The intervening Tertiary colors take their dominance from adjacent hues, as when red-orange takes its dominance from red; or yellow-orange takes its dominance from yellow; and so forth to yellow-green, blue-green, blue-violet, and red-violet.

The lettered keys in the wheel are as follows:

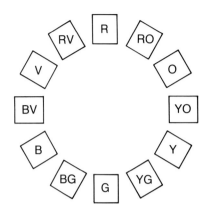

R, red	G, green
RO, red-orange	BG, blue-green
O, orange	B, blue
YO, yellow-orange	BV, blue-violet
Y, yellow	V, violet
YG, yellow-green	RV, red-violet

color wheel make twenty-four identifiable hues—termed Primary colors, Secondary colors, and Tertiary colors. As shown on the color wheel, the basic divisions are:

1. Primary colors: red, yellow, blue.

2. Secondary colors: orange, green, violet.

3. Tertiary colors: red-orange, yellow-orange, yellow-green, blue-green, blue-violet, red-violet.

Knowing the relative position of a color on the color wheel allows a designer to select effective color combinations such as complementary, analogous, monochromatic, double, or split complementary categories. If red is selected for use in a scheme, the following combinations could be devised from the arrangement of hues on the color wheel:

1. Red complementary color scheme. A pure red would take as its complement pure green, the hue that is directly opposite on the color wheel.

2. Red analogous color scheme. A pure red can move away from itself in either direction—toward orange or toward violet.

3. Red monochromatic color scheme. A pure red changed only through tints and shades by adding white or black to the original hue.

4. Double complementary color scheme. A pure red used with either red-violet or red-orange complemented by green used with either yellow-green or blue-green.

5. Split complementary color scheme. A pure red is joined with a pair of colors of equal intensity at either side of red's true complement green—blue-green and yellow-green.

Another basic concept for color schemes taken from the color wheel is the triangular or triad scheme. Here, three colors are given equal importance; for example, red-yellow-blue or green-orange-violet in Primary or Secondary colors; or the triad may come from the intermixes of the Tertiary colors.

Color in Interiors Harmony of the colors selected for interiors is necessary. All colors in a composition must fit together. The color theory systems provide a method by which we can identify and group colors objectively. But the interaction of one color with another is also influenced by factors of size, location, juxtaposition, light, and texture. Most interior compositions of any type are too complex to rely solely on a color system. In a composition where every color fits with every other color, all relationships exhibit the same systematic conformity or sameness. A system may serve when only a simple harmony is needed, but a color system cannot be relied upon in most situations unless a designer is willing to reduce the power of the expressiveness of color. If the colors in an interior are derived from a simple sequence, a designer risks little, but also tends to accomplish little.

In the past, many attempts have been made to specify the correct usage of color in interiors. Ostwald said in 1919 that fully saturated colors should be used only in small amounts. He said that the large surfaces of pure color used at Pompeii were "crude." An unknown German theorist described how color could be used to emphasize size and location. He said that floors should be dark, like the earth, to give an impression of gravity; walls should be colored in the values of trees or flowers. Ceilings, he said, should be light and airy like the sky and be painted in pale tints. The American etiquette authority Emily Post gave similar advice early in this century. The Victorian architect William White felt that color was a "luxury on which the eye can feast." He was convinced that the nerves are "excited by the presence of red, soothed by the presence of green, and deadened or numbed by the presence of blue." White postulated that the renunciation of worldly pleasure by monastic orders included the wearing of black and white or dull-colored clothing.[16]

Color formulas and color taboos of the past often seem dictatorial, if not silly, today. Now we know that in certain interior conditions fully saturated color is called for, and that in some cases a dark, heavy ceiling plane and the lightest-colored flooring material can best suit a design. However, we should also know that relationships of color in one set of interior conditions can produce undesirable results, while the same combination can produce harmony in another situation.

Every interior requires a new evaluation of the application of color. When one color makes a physical connection with another color in three-dimensional spaces, the interaction is quite different from when the same two colors are physically separated. The separation of color in interiors is as essential to composition as connection. The theories of color harmony are mainly useful for making connections.

No color system takes into account the question of material or the variable of changing light. Systems consequently remain useful primarily as tools for the investigation of color phenomena, for the identification of individual colors and color families, and for the designing of whole systems of paint and dye colors.

In an interior, however, color does not exist as a theoretical phenomenon. The color red, for example, is not an abstract idea in three-dimensional space; it is red brick, glass, mahogany, paint, or silk. Each of these materials has its individual texture. Red can exist in an interior only through a material, whether it is paint or fabric, structure or decoration. Color in interiors exists only as a direct result of material.

Some textbooks, and some designers, suggest that color can be used to correct problems in an interior. Color can affect the apparent shape of a room, its temperature, or the apparent size and weight of a component. These effects are based on particular characteristics of particular colors. For example, colors advance or

---

[16]Paul Thompson, *The Writings of William White*, from *Concerning Architecture*, edited by John Summerson and Allen Lane (London: Penguin Press, 1968).

recede according to their warmth or coolness; therefore, if we wish to change the apparent shape of a room that is long and narrow, the narrow end walls could be finished in a color that will advance, and the longer side walls will tend to recede when finished in a light color. By the same principle, small rooms can be made to appear less small if given light colors, and large rooms can be made to appear less large if painted dark, warm colors. The temperature of the color affects the perception of size.

Similarly, color has visual weight. So the apparent weight of a component can be made to appear heavier if colored in a dark shade, lighter if colored in a tint. The dark shade will make the component appear somewhat smaller along with the heavier weight; and the tint-colored component will appear somewhat larger, as well as somewhat lighter in apparent weight. It may or may not be coincidental that dark pigment colors actually have greater physical weight, because they require greater quantities of pigment.

The most widespread use of color as a means of altering situations or of correcting problems in an interior is the attempt to change the effect of prevailing natural light. This use says that rooms with warm south light can be made cooler by treating them to combinations of cool, light colors; north rooms with steady, cool, reflected light can be made to seem warmer when given colors that are warm. Thus south rooms are often painted in green or blue colors, while north rooms are painted in warm reds and yellows.

These ideas suggest that it is appropriate to use color to hide defects to correct problems in an interior. It is true that color can affect our perception of size and shape; it can be used to counteract temperature and weight. But is this the ideal use of so potent a device?

If one learns to use color only as a means to correct problems, the most expressive character of color—its ability to emphasize—may be overlooked or forgotten. With all the principles of aesthetic composition, one must attempt to find the best, most expressive use within the given circumstances. Design principles are best used to reveal inherent characteristics, to offer clearly what is there to experience.

There is nothing inherently wrong with the experience of being in either small or large spaces; both have positive qualities. Warm south light is beautiful in its way, as cool north light is in its way. When making color decisions for such situations as these, one must consider the effectiveness of using contrasting color application. Should warm south rooms be cooled down with blues and greens? Should north rooms be warmed with reds and yellows? Or should each orientation have its main qualities exploited? Rasmussen makes the case that "there is something unsatisfactory about such camouflage. It is irritating to discover that the thing is not what we expected." The "something unsatisfactory" is the contradiction between prevailing daylight and a chosen color scheme in an interior. Rasmussen continues:

> In good architecture, consciously designed, the small room appears small, the large room large, and instead of disguising this, it should be emphasized by the judicious use of color. The small room should be painted in deep saturated tones so that you feel the intimacy of the four walls closing about you. And the color scheme of the large room should be light and airy to make you doubly aware of the broad expanse from wall to wall.[17]

These points on the use of color in interiors should not, however, be taken as inflexible theory. In some interior concepts, for example, a red may be an appro-

---

[17]Rasmussen, *Experiencing Architecture.*

priate color choice for a north room. But the red should tend toward blue, becoming bluish red. In a room with south light, a blue should tend toward red, becoming reddish blue; or if green is the selected color, yellowish green. In each situation the best qualities of both color and daylight will be exploited.

This approach to color selection offers latitude in color concepts and allows a designer to accommodate the unalterable, natural conditions. Decisions based on this premise will increase the existing character of an interior and validate the scheme of selected color.

Light: Natural and Artificial

Light is reserved as the last aesthetic design principle—not because it is the most expendable or because it can be considered last in arriving at design concepts (though, lamentably, it often is in interior design). Rather, it is reserved until last because light makes all other principles possible. As the Bible tells us, light was the first act of creation, "And He divided the light from the darkness." Without light there is no life. Without light there is no vision, and without vision there is no design.

The phenomenon of light has been used in powerful ways by painters to evoke mystery, transcendence, and aspects of the divine. The Impressionist painters were obsessed with every aspect of light, from the light that gives shape to the majesty of a mountaintop, to the light that transforms the humble stack of hay, or the plate of ordinary apples. Van Gogh often saw daylight as swirling radiant pattern; Cézanne painted light as a means of making order.

Architecture is brought to life by light, and every interior is considered to be more desirable when windows bring in direct light and reflected light in abundance. Many interior designers consider the aesthetic problems of natural and artificial light as a major concern in the conception of interiors.

Lighting consultant and designer James Nuckolls says that "seven-eighths of all our perceptions are through sight . . . the way structures and objects in our world are illuminated makes a tremendous difference in the way they look to us and how we respond to them."[18] Light, then, is of importance to our perception in the real everyday world as well as in the world of painters. In either world, light informs on a subject in a particular way.

All the other aesthetic principles discussed are there for the choosing. Designers may choose to use a design principle or not, according to their needs, as support for conceptual notions. Some of the principles will assist in a particular concept; some will not. But light, like shape, texture, and color, must be a part of every design concept and every design solution.

Natural Light

Natural light in interiors is largely predetermined by the existing architectural framework. Daylight, as suggested in the previous discussion of color, may influence choices of hue or degree of brightness. Daylight adds its own color, and contributes its own moving texture and pattern to interiors that can make spaces vibrant or poetic. Other aspects of daylight need consideration along with color—quantity, quality (the character of light caused by environmental conditions), the position relationship of window to interior volume, and the type of window covering used to control daylight and to provide for privacy.

50. Light

Daylight illuminates and defines a typical seventeenth-century Dutch interior. Without the light, there is no color, no contrast, no texture or pattern, no shape, and no form.

---

[18]James Nuckolls, *Interior Lighting for Environmental Designers* (New York: John Wiley & Sons, 1976).

The quantity of daylight that passes into an interior through windows is first determined by the directional exposure—north, south, east, west, or the variations northeast, northwest, southeast, southwest, and so forth. Each of these exposures has its own intensity (as well as its own coloration) regardless of geographic location, although each is affected by the general environment. Southern exposures are always assumed to produce interior light that is constant, bright, and warm; northern ones produce steady, cool effects. Eastern windows bring in a fluctuating, coolish light; western light is changing and warmish. These effects are varied by the movement of the sun in its daily track across the sky, but the orientation of windows in relation to that solar path produces distinct overall effects.

The quality of natural light in interiors also relates to exposure. Artists have for centuries preferred to work in north light because of its steady character and because it adds less coloration to the pigments at hand. However, several environmental conditions may affect the quality of daylight admitted to an interior. When daylight is reflected from nearby forms or surfaces, light in the interior is altered. For example, a white wall adjacent to windows will sharpen and intensify light from any exposure; a red wall will reflect pinkish light in varying degrees, tending to warm up north light and to cool down south light. Trees that overhang a window or cut out a direct sky view will both dim the light and add cool, greenish overtones to it.

Other environmental conditions also influence light quality, among them clouds and airborne pollution, and the seasonal changes that bring leafless trees, snow, or heavy foliage. These transient, changing conditions are beyond the control of designers, but nonetheless must be considered as basic problems to be resolved.

The three pervasive architectural elements that admit daylight into interiors are (1) windows that bring light in from the side, (2) walls of glass (glass curtain walls and sliding or hung glass doors), and (3) skylights that admit light from above. Each type of light requires its own appraisal, because each affects an interior in a differing way.

Natural Sidelighting   One of the principal qualities of natural light in interiors is that it produces shadow. Sidelighting does this to particularly good advantage. When sidelighting is used well, it enhances shapes and their characteristics. With sidelighting the shadow brings out shape and heightens texture; shape becomes differentiated and clearer than when light falls from above, or from a frontal position. Considering this, a designer might decide to give particular prominence to components that are adjacent to windows producing sidelight—giving a special component that location, or a wall treatment.

Front light falling on a component tends to wash away all but the most pronounced texture, and shape may be almost completely lost. Sidelight strengthens the volumetric shape of an interior, especially when some of the entering light strikes adjacent walls. This effect shows most prominently in Dutch interiors as is evidenced in sixteenth- and seventeenth-century paintings by Jan Vermeer, Pieter de Hooch, and others. In those paintings the light entering an interior is a major compositional element, as it was in the real interiors of the period (see Figure 50). The typical Dutch window, from the sixteenth century until well into the nineteenth century, was screened by movable wooden shutters in its lower half, the upper part glazed with milky glass in small panes. Sometimes these upper areas were covered with opaque or translucent fabric.

Too often today designers cover sidelight windows with an array of curtains—draperies, over-draperies, glass curtains, and the like. These treatments are done, they say, for decorative effect, for privacy, and to soften the line between the edge of the window and the wall plane. Such designs overlook the advantages of natural light, and interiors with such window treatments will need artificial light both by night and day. Curtains can certainly be used at windows, but the application cannot be arbitrary. Windows that provide sidelight serve a purpose—to bring daylight inside—not to provide a hanger for decorative curtaining.

Walls of Glass Walls of glass, glass curtain walls, and walls composed of multiple windows are thought to be a prime component of design in the Modern movement. However, large expanses of glass are used less often than may be imagined, with the exception of the glass office tower. In such towers the glass curtain wall is the principal means of enclosure hung on the skeleton of the structure. Glass-walled structures allow the interiors to absorb the maximum amount of available light. The light varies from bright, at the top of the building, to moderate as the shadows from other structures fall across its lower faces. This condition, found in densely built urban centers, varies when a building stands in isolation. Isolated buildings with large expanses of glass are more apt to get a brighter light penetration throughout top floors and bottom floors as well.

With very few exceptions, any building with a maximum amount of glass requires some means of light control—both for quantity and quality. Sometimes daylight is so strong that it becomes glaring, so sharp that it prevents clear vision. This condition exists in tower interiors that have south or southeast exposures. In such interiors a designer can alter the effects of glaring light by creating an appropriate scheme of colors and materials. In most cases an appropriate light-controlling device will also be needed at the windows.

In interiors with extremely bright natural light, it is often necessary to adopt color schemes of low contrast. When direct sunlight enters an interior where high-contrast color has been used, the strong light will heighten the effect through casting very dark shadow. This can cause components to separate from each other in disconcerting ways.

Window coverings can control natural light where there is too much brightness. Curtaining of loosely woven cloth or sheer material will still allow daylight to enter. Where many windows make the wall plane, or in glass-walled buildings, it is difficult to control light by rigid opaque means such as shutters or wood panels. Although shutters or panels may seem like a workable idea, we associate them with single-light windows. Also, curtaining is the tradition set by early Modernist designers for glass-walled interiors. All of the most significant glass-walled interiors of the Modern movement—the Tugendhat House by Mies van der Rohe, the Glass House by Phillip Johnson—used retractable curtains of thin, unlined material—usually silk. When the glass curtain wall developed, curtains were there also. A possible theory for the use of curtains in Modern interiors is that the very softness of curtaining makes it visually less important as a component. Curtains can be retracted and are less noticeable when not needed for light control or privacy.

Natural Light from Above: Clerestories and Skylights Clerestory and skylight methods of bringing light into interiors are ancient devices. Clerestory windows were used abundantly in the Gothic period. Skylights—a type of unglazed window in the ceiling—were used by the ancient Greeks. Both types have been used repeatedly since their invention, and both became renewed in the Modern movement.

Le Corbusier used the clerestory (or ribbon window) in many of his houses, including the Villa Savoye. From the start clerestory windows have never produced clear, bright daylight. In the Gothic churches clerestories brought in dim daylight that sent light shafts shimmering down into the vast and dark interior of the church. In contemporary interiors the clerestory is used most when some natural light is needed, but when privacy must be a prime consideration. Still, the light from these high windows is not greatly effective as a tool in shaping interior space.

Skylights are often used in twentieth-century interiors to bring in quantities of daylight—a principal reason for their continuing popularity. In interiors with typical ceiling heights, skylighting is often an idea that seems good as a theory—raise the ceiling and simultaneously admit light. But when the total effects of ceiling light are studied, the effects can be less good in real situations. Daylight entering from above is, almost without exception, diffuse, and can spread over a space even through relatively small openings. This characteristic may seem a distinct advantage when quantity of light is desirable; however, a great profusion of daylight that enters through a skylight can wipe shadow away, and cause an interior to flatten out.

When designing interiors with skylights, it is advantageous to develop the space with high contrasts in color and texture. This procedure reintroduces the contrast lost in the downpouring daylight.

There are some few exceptions to the interior problems created by skylights. In large or vast spaces with unusually high ceilings, lighting from above is often dramatically effective, as in the Pantheon in Rome (see the discussion in Chapter 5). Natural light must become a basic conceptual consideration in all interiors. It is the one component of an interior that a designer cannot totally control, because it is always changing. Like the weather, we hope that available natural light will be effective. If the ever-changing effects of daylight are fully estimated, more effective form-making is possible.

Natural Light from Flame   Another means of "natural" light in interiors comes from flame—fireplaces and candlelight. These two light sources are often overlooked; however, each of them can augment artificial lighting. Light from a fireplace or from candles can create special, emotionally charged effects.

Today, fireplaces are not essential in any but the most primitive living conditions. In all other interiors a fireplace is an elegant luxury that most people think of as a desirable accoutrement. In preliterate societies fire represented warmth, safety (it kept away wild animals), and a degree of control over the blackness of night. It is put forth by some theorists that modern people respond similarly to fire. Aside from the physical warmth offered by a fireplace, the evocation of these primordial feelings is an asset worthy of consideration in many interior designs.

Candlelight, the method of lighting used for centuries of highly civilized living, is often forgotten as an effective means of providing visual warmth and vitality in an interior. Holders for candles must be safe, sturdy, and nonflammable. Depending on the purpose of an interior, they may be floor-standing, wall-mounted, or placed on table surfaces. The shape and material of candle holders must relate to the design concept, and their size and number must also be considered. Candlelight can contribute a compatible aesthetic to the overall lighting concept.

When candles are used on a dining table, their flame should be either below or above eye level. It is best to have one candle for every two or three people seated. The height, placement, and number of candles must not interfere with sightlines across the table. Very low or very tall candle holders (or candlesticks) are usually more effective than in-between heights.

Artificial Light

Although natural light is of critical importance in an interior, no interior can be successfully completed today without the detailed design of its artificial lighting. Lighting is of such importance that even the most perfectly integrated space can succeed or fail on the basis of the full development of its artificial lighting. At this time in the twentieth century, lighting design bears on interiors as in no other period; it is a technology raised to the level of art.

The techniques of lighting in Modern interiors change frequently in both form and method. Despite the current diversity in lighting technology, most residences are still lighted with table lamps—a base with a lightbulb, covered with a shade. This lighting device is often augmented with a floor-standing lamp for indirect up light or direct down light. Sometimes wall brackets or "pin-ups" with candle-flame bulbs or miniature shades are used, along with the most standard of all light fixtures—the overhead, ceiling-mounted light. From time to time these three lamp types change shape; more rarely does the light source ever undergo improvement.

In the best of early Modern interiors, these three types of fixtures can be seen in photographs. In such interiors we see the validity of the spaces and furniture, the shapes, proportions, and materials. What is strange in some of these historical interiors, however, is the lighting. Mies van der Rohe's Tugendhat House (1930) seems to have been lighted solely by underscaled ceiling fixtures. The fixtures are beautiful, to be sure, but they seem insignificant and "dated," not as timeless as the rest of the interior. A luxurious bedroom of the same period by Lilly Reich in the Berlin Building Exposition might have been designed today, except for the small pin-up lamp. In 1930 Le Corbusier, in the de Mandrot Villa living room, resorted to the "architect's lamp," a device still used today.

At one time modern lighting was considered to be any means that kept the ceiling plane fixture-free (the ceiling fixture was thought too traditional because it was reminiscent of the chandelier). Wall brackets were preferred and, like the ceiling fixture, they could be connected to wall switches. In the late 1940s, interiors intended to be "modern" would have no attached fixtures at all, except for those in the bathrooms and kitchens. Then all lighting would come from portable lamps. Some of these were formidable in size and design. Three-foot-high table lamps were not unusual, and several of these huge shaded giants might be the light source for one average-size room.

The last quarter of the century reveals yet another lighting design fashion. Interiors now display unobtrusive, linear table and floor lamps to supplement elaborately designed architecturally integrated lighting. Distinct advantages in lighting design are possible today. Previously, a designer might sacrifice a lighting effect for the lighting needed by the uses of a room; it was often not possible to accomplish both. Now, however, the mechanics and aesthetics of an interior, and the needs of its occupants to see properly, are no longer mutually exclusive.

As the aesthetics of lighting design change, so the theories of what constitutes "good" lighting also change from time to time. New information on the physiological act of seeing and the psychological effects of lighting can lead to better lighting design. The problems of proper vision for the aging eye and the influence of lighting on behavior are areas being studied by specialists in lighting in conjunction with specialists in the medical field. Some designers make careers as lighting designers, working along with interior designers, architects, and engineers.

Lighting Concepts in Interiors

At the beginning of study students may design projects that have no specific requirement for lighting. This will come at a later time, after separate instruction is given. However, it is best even for a beginning student to make lighting part of a design concept. This is possible without any technical data and without any specific information because every student has experience with artificial light.

Lighting concepts at the early stage of study cannot develop very far into finished designs. That will require technical information and the ability to make calculations. But just as the spatial concept relates to the characteristics in the existing architecture, so the lighting concept will grow from the emerging interior design concept.

A beginning student will know from past experience about portable lighting—table and floor lamps and several types of ceiling and wall fixtures, the items that comprise the popular vocabulary in purchasable fixtures. The more sophisticated lighting equipment used in architectural lighting and in the theater may not be known. How, then, is it possible to incorporate artificial light into the concept for an interior?

Because we have all had the experience of being in interiors, whether or not they were created by designers, we know that interiors may have seemed bright or dim, and that these levels of light have caused us to respond in different ways. From experiencing a campfire we know that it is more comforting to sit in a relatively dark area and look toward a lighter area: The dark at our backs makes a background for the circle of warmth from the firelight.

Conceptually, without knowing how to achieve a design criterion, lighting schemes are possible. Even in professional design practice it is the designer of the interior who sets the lighting concept when working in conjunction with a lighting design consultant. Lighting designer James Nuckolls states emphatically that "the initiative for creative lighting must come from an environmentalist, for it is this authority who assumes responsibility for the total structure."[19]

The beginning designer can decide that one area of an interior should be warm, dim, and shadow-filled; another area may require light that is cool, bright, and crystal-clear. Or a project may need a general, moderate amount of overall illumination with focused, specific light in some areas. This thinking—or speculation—is conceptual in lighting design in the same sense that spatial concepts arise at the start of a design project: It is the whole without the parts; it is thinking about the effects of the lighting perhaps without knowing how to achieve them.

The late Richard Kelly, a pioneer in lighting as a design discipline (instead of a purely engineering task), observed that psychologically and physiologically we need more artificial illumination in interiors during daylight hours than we do at night. This, he felt, was true except at such times of day when abundant natural light flooded an interior. The artificial light mixing with daylight was more comfortable, allowing less strain to nerves and eyes. Kelly's observations suggested that a balance between exterior daylight illumination and interior illumination made people feel better, more productive, less irritable. This was true, he found, whether occupants of the interiors were aware of light levels or not. People may often express what they feel about lighting as a desire for more of it, when what is actually being felt is the need for a different quality of light. Not the quantity, but the quality in conjunction with other factors in the combined natural and artificial light in the built environment.

Portable Lighting   Portable lighting requires no professional installation. It can be put into working order with its attached plug and a nearby duplex outlet. Portable lighting has limitations, however—it is available only in table and floor designs, considered by some designers to curtail the effectiveness of this lighting type. Other designers feel that portable lighting is the most effective means, especially in domestic interiors.

Certain interiors can be admirably lighted with portable lamps alone. The form of lamp base and shade can blend with other component forms to create successful environments. Because the form of a table lamp or floor lamp will have

---

[19]Ibid.

a particular shape, it is important that the shape be appropriate to the interior. The proportions of a lamp should be examined carefully; not only the base proportions together with the shade, but the proportions of the lamp, its overall scale, and its material must be assessed against the overall volume of an interior.

The scale of portable lighting is critical. A tall table lamp may give a good quality of light, but it may overwhelm an interior. A short, squat table lamp may be aesthetically appropriate in size, but the amount of light from it may be inadequate. Too much light from a single lamp may produce glare and wash out shadow. Too little light may make for a gloomy interior.

As a general notion of how to decide on the number of portable light sources an interior should have, some professionals say that even small rooms need three light sources. These tend to triangulate in a space and distribute light over the principal portions of the interior. If all three of the light sources have shades, their overall height should be approximate. This prevents a shade from becoming a too dominant form, particularly if it is of a translucent material.

Many decorative shapes are available in portable lamps, and these can be effective in some interiors. Other lamp shapes are less decorative and may be combined well with other shapes. Portable lamps should not be ruled out as good solutions for lighting.

Architectural Lighting   Architectural lighting is that which is affixed, or attached to a building—usually to the ceiling, sometimes to the walls. This type of lighting has slowly emerged since the early 1940s. By the mid-1950s architectural lighting design had become synonymous with the surge of office buildings that began during that period. Although lighting is now firmly established as one of the design disciplines, then lighting was considered the province of engineering. As practiced today, lighting designers (or, more correctly, lighting consultants) and engineers work together cooperatively, in particular when a project is large and multifaceted. The work of such a team would be done with an interior designer or architect as the initiator of the overall design concept, including the lighting.

In almost every nonresidential interior, architectural-type lighting is part and parcel of a design concept. In many new or renovated domestic interiors, architectural lighting is considered by interior designers as a necessary functional and aesthetic component—the one that can bring out the best qualities of the design, the one that completes a space and allows it to be used and experienced fully.

Though lighting design has become a recognized necessity by environmentalists, there is still controversy as to the most appropriate means of achieving good results. The controversy divides itself into two groups, each with a different approach. The two different approaches lead to vastly different results.

The first group concerns itself with the amount of light. Nuckolls calls this the "quantitative" approach. It includes the determination of the level of light that is considered correct in an interior; the selection of the lighting device needed to produce the desired light level; figuring the number of such devices required; and making a lighting plan that will ensure consistent levels of light throughout an interior. To an interior designer this method, without exception, is lacking in the essential aesthetic principles that make artificial lighting another tool in the making of interiors—a tool not possible to make use of when only numerical calculations govern the results, when uniformity is perhaps the main criterion.

Evenness of light levels was one criterion that led in the 1950s to the desire for the lighted or luminous ceiling, which became the rule in office interiors of the period. These ceilings, hung as lighted planes from the structural slab above, could produce smooth, equal amounts of light across the vast dimensions of an entire floor of a large building. Fluorescent light sources diffused by lightweight plastic (sometimes translucent glass) sheets were installed with ease and could be maintained without too much effort. As part of the visual design of an interior, the luminous ceiling could provide a plane of great elegance and simplicity; however, the effects of this type of light provoked adverse reaction from workers who sat underneath. The amount of light made spaces shadowless and reduced form differentiation. It made for a bland environment.

The formula approach exemplified by the proliferation of the luminous ceiling in nonresidential interiors still has its practitioners. Now, however, another more appropriate direction is becoming a far more useful method—the design approach to interior lighting.

The design approach to architectural lighting offers a range of possibility for domestic and nonresidential applications. The approach begins with the initial design concept of an interior, with the concept embodied in its component parts. The lighting design then becomes inseparable. It will be considerate of the specific needs relating to function and it can enhance an interior with such nonspecific characteristics as shadows, the modeling of shape, reflections, and contrasting light and dark effects.

Each application of the approach to architectural lighting is an individual one. Each interior is considered as an entity to which the design criteria for lighting are subsumed. Sometimes the most successful lighting in an interior will be almost unnoticed; sometimes the lighting design takes a major role in its visible form.

PART 2

The Design Process in Practice: Case Studies

Ward Bennett. Own house. Springs, Long Island. *Photograph © Peter Aaron/ESTO, 1978.*

Robert Bray and Michael Schaible. First National Bank. Hialeah, Florida. *Photograph by Norman McGrath.*

Barbara D'Arcy. Bloomingdale's. New York City. *Photograph courtesy Bloomingdale's Store Design Office.*

Angelo Donghia. Omni Hotel. Miami, Florida. *Photograph courtesy Donghia and Sonet Agency Ltd.*

Joseph Paul D'Urso. Apartment of Reed Evins. New York City. *Photograph © Peter Aaron/ESTO, 1978.*

David Easton. Residence. Lake Forest, Illinois. *Photograph courtesy David Anthony Easton Inc.*

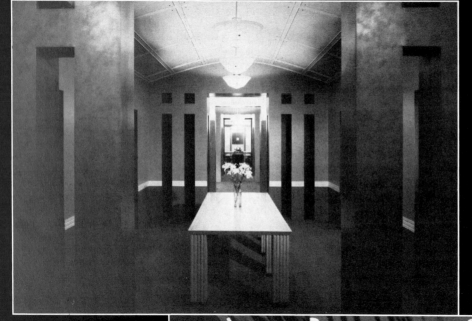

Michael Graves. Sunar showroom. Chicago, Illinois. *Photograph by Yuich Idaka, 1982, courtesy Sunar/Hauserman.*

ISD Inc. Law offices of Johnson & Swanson. Dallas, Texas. *Photograph by Nick Merrick/Hedrich-Blessing, courtesy ISD Incorporated.*

George Nelson. The L-shaped desk from Executive Office Group. *Photograph courtesy Herman Miller Inc.*

Paul Rudolph. Tuskegee Chapel. Tuskegee, Alabama. *Photograph © Ezra Stoller/ESTO, 1969.*

John Saladino. Conference room for Almay Inc. *Photograph by Jaime Ardiles-Arce.*

Lella and Massimo Vignelli. St. Peter's Lutheran Church. New York City. *Photograph © Peter Aaron/ ESTO, 1977.*

Chapter 8

Interviews with Practicing Designers

Theory about procedure—abstracted, distilled, and Latinate, as it often is—can raise questions and doubts about its authority and accuracy in the minds of students and inexperienced novices. Who made the rules, almost everyone asks at the beginning, and what makes them infallible or even right? Long experience, comes the answer, is the basis and background of theory, and it can authoritatively answer questions and confirm the reality of theoretical explanations.

A large and impressive body of experience is the evidence and testimony of the following case studies. They serve as object lessons to bear witness on the theory of Part 1. They reveal that despite the personal vagaries and idiosyncrasies of every designer, all follow an essentially consistent overall method of arriving at a concept and developing it. Most interior design books discuss what people design, more than how designs are created. For practicing designers this question is of endless curiosity and importance. For students, it is even more so.

Throughout history the act of creation has been much discussed. Stories abound: Archimedes in his bathtub shouting "Eureka!" when he found the displacement of water; Newton discovering gravity by watching an apple fall from a tree; Luther composing his Theses in his most private closet.

In literature, the blind poet Milton said that he composed whole cantos of *Paradise Lost* in his mind before he dictated them to his daughters. Dr. Samuel Johnson wrote down each chapter of *Rasselas* on a successive evening and sent it off the next morning to the printer, never to see it again until the entire volume was published. Flaubert, on the other hand, worked and reworked many drafts of each chapter in order to perfect his phraseology. Shakespeare, according to Ben Jonson, "never jotted a line," and Jonson thought he should have done at least a bit of tightening. Coleridge's work on "Kubla Khan" was interrupted when his tailor presented a bill, and he never thereafter could finish the poem. De Quincey tried writing under the haze of drugs a century before the hippie design experimenters of the 1960s thought it fashionable.

In music, Mozart wrote out full movements at the first draft—often on coach journeys—which were uncorrected, complete, and finished. Handel dictated compositions from the keyboard in his last years after he became blind. Beethoven wrote all of his Ninth Symphony after he became deaf. Stravinsky composed on an out-of-tune piano and said that it did not matter, because he heard the correct notes anyway. Such is the potential of the human mind for conceptualization.

What of interior designers? How do their procedures for realization and refinement of their concepts vary? Is there a consistent overall methodology of concept development, despite personal idiosyncrasies? To find out, we interviewed twenty prominent designers of interiors and asked them to recall and relate their methodologies.

The group represents a broad range of professional activities and involvements, styles and scopes, backgrounds and interests. It represents the wide variety of professionals who design interiors in the United States. They include vanguard architects and interiors specialists, traditional residential decorators, Minimalist interior designers, mainstream office space planning firms, industrial and furniture designers, and designers for retailing and display.

The designers included in our case studies are among the current established leaders in their respective areas of interior design. Collectively, they represent a body of work that is a furthering, an advancing, and a continuation of contemporary design. Each is a distinguished model for student observation.

Each designer was asked a similar set of questions organized around the three phases of the design process: the conceptual or inspirational phase, the design development phase, and the mechanical phase of final detailing. These phases outline the activities required to develop a design with refinement of process as well as refinement of taste.

We asked the following questions:

1. How do your initial concepts first reveal themselves or express themselves—as ideas, or as lines on paper, or in some other way?

2. When you are designing, does your thinking have to be externalized on paper?

3. Do you draw or sketch constantly? Daily?

4. Please give an example of how you arrived at the basic concept for a project you are working on right now.

5. How do you analyze a space from the drawings given to you? As you grasp the information on an existing plan, how do you determine what to eliminate and what to add?

6. Where does the client fit into this process?

7. Do you do what you want to do in spite of clients' wishes? Do you feel you know best?

8. Can you speak about preserving the concept by doing and by not doing things that are programmatic requirements?

9. In this process, is there a difference between working on interiors in existing buildings and working on newly created spaces? Is the process of conceptual analysis and realization materially different? How so?

10. Is there a difference in this process between work for public projects and work for private clients?

11. How do the different sizes of projects affect your methodology?

12. After you find out how a project must function, how do you develop a concept further? What methods do you employ for realizing this concept?

13. In the development of a concept toward realization, do you find that different phases change or affect the design, and in what ways?

14. How do you apply or consider the standard design principles and devices—for example, scale, size, and proportion; balance and symmetry—when designing your interior projects?

15. How does the consideration of materials affect your concept? And at what stages?

16. Is designing different from assembling? How so?

17. Is there one factor—budget, time, plan, mechanical systems, other—that is consistently more critical?

18. Do you seek consistency in the methodology by which you go about designing? Do you see any consistent methodology from project to project?

19. How does the procedure you have developed over the years you have been in practice differ from what you thought it was when you were a student?

20. Do you have any additional advice to give to students of interior design?

The questions are not always discussed in the same order, because of the flow of ideas peculiar to each of those interviewed. When a question is not answered or addressed, that omission tells us as much about the design process of that designer as lengthy discussion of a single aspect tells about another designer.

Where there have been disagreements between the designers and the authors, those disagreements have been reported. For example, we have made some attempt to distinguish the process of design—those who draw—from the process of assembling—those who purchase and arrange elements and objects. The reported disagreement on this matter may be the pivotal distinction between various designers' individual activities and talents.

The actual words of the designers and architects themselves are quoted as much as possible to give the flavor and personality of their ideas and characters as well as the facts about their methodologies. Students are advised to note these quotations carefully, and not search for the authors' interpretations. Many readers tend to gloss over quoted discussion, preferring to be told what their conclusions should be. One's own conclusions are the ultimate rationale for and outcome of education.

Among the questions raised by these case studies are the following: If the process is the same for traditional versus Modern projects, what causes the resulting designs to be different? How can such different things come from the same procedure? Similarly, if the process is the same, why are interiors by architects so often thought to be stiff, uncomfortable, poorly lighted, and devoid of historical reference, at least until recently? On the other hand, why are interiors by non-architects so often considered less interesting spatially, overdecorated, and less significant in terms of history?

Only one factor seems to alter the overall design process of these practitioners: the number of years they have been practicing their crafts. Cumulative experience, it appears, telescopes the process, condensing its timespan and its sequential nature. But such telescoping must remain a long-term goal of students.

From the recognized professionalism of these practitioners, that experience has produced some remarkably affecting statements. In addition, these case studies contain a wealth of advice on design areas and phases that have been valuable to each specific designer. Although the actual answers of the designers do not always state a consistent method of approaching conceptualization and realization, the insights we gain from the similarities indicate that the process of arriving at a concept and of developing it is identical to the process outlined in Part 1. Most students will not need further convincing that the surest way to become a professional designer is to gain the experience that only practice can bring.

Interiors for Study: Case Study Analysis

The following questions are intended to engage students in both inquiry and discussion of the issues raised by the case studies. Three subject areas are considered for analysis: (1) methodology, (2) theory, and (3) product criticism.

Methodology Methodology in design, as elsewhere, is understood to mean procedure or process. Once determined, a methodology can be repeated to produce a manner or way of working. Methodology attempts to carry forward in orderly form; it is often a framework applied to all projects. Such a methodology must be firmly established to give control, but open enough to allow for changes during the design process.

1. Do the completed projects discussed in the case studies reveal a design methodology?

2. If methodology is not apparent in a designed project, does that invalidate the product?

3. Does intuition accompany method?

4. Do all case study designers use a similar methodology?

5. Does a developed methodology change in relation to the type of project? Must a design method be applicable to all types of projects to be considered valid?

6. Among the case study designers, is drawing a consistent part of design method?

7. If a concept is "possible" in an existing space, does that possibility alone ensure the appropriateness of the completed interior?

8. If the designers are respectful of a client's wishes, how can a concept be preserved through the development process and remain consistent with such wishes? How can it still result in a project that we recognize as work from a particular designer?

9. Does methodology lead to individual style in an interior? Is style produced by method? Is a style discernible in projects of differing interior types by the same designer?

Theory Theory searches for ideal relationships. Theories develop from facts that have been analyzed; however, a resulting theory may not be provable—and need not be—to be useful. Theory in art and design is most often the contemplation of an idea, a speculation to be discussed, tried, or tested.

1. Do the completed projects described in the case studies reveal the conceptual ideas discussed by the designers?

2. Is it appropriate for an interior concept to come from a single material such as stone, wood, fabric, or a wallpaper pattern?

3. Can a concept arise from a need to change (that is, to transform or remove) an architectural component such as a wall, a floor, a ceiling, a door, or a window?

4. Is there a relationship between the success of a project and the amount of design effort expended? Or the amount of money spent?

5. Is there a link between a designer's education (formal or otherwise) and his or her formed sensibilities as evidenced in design practice?

6. Should the aesthetic principles applied in the design of an interior be visible or apparent, or should they be submerged in the conceptual and built framework?

7. Some designers say that the plan must be "beautiful." Does such a plan ensure the success of a built interior?

8. Some theorists say that the artistic responsibility of the creative personality is to produce work that is *of* an age, and the *best* of that age. Does the thinking in the case studies indicate that?

Product Criticism Product in interiors is either a project on paper or a built project. Each may be an end result: the theoretical or student project on paper, the built project of the professional. Each product is complete in itself and on completion is subject to criticism. Criticism is informed opinion. It is an attempt to judge the results of an activity, to evaluate a whole within a context. Criticism should seek to inform the creator as well as others.

1. Can criticism be purely objective?

2. Is aesthetic perfection a legitimate goal in an interior?

3. Can a critical assessment of an interior be made based on aesthetic merit alone?

4. Do interior design projects sometimes have moral implications? Might a project fail to succeed because of those values?

5. If a project is not successful, could a designer's process be responsible?

6. Must all projects judged to be successful have attained that success as a result of applied methodology, or is it possible to succeed through intuition only?

7. Which is the more valid critic—the user or the maker?

8. Is a search for originality evident in these interiors? Is originality (or differentness) presumed to be desirable?

9. Do the case study interiors make unmistakable connections between functional and aesthetic criteria?

10. Are there influences in the interiors described that are traceable to such arts as painting, sculpture, film, or theater?

11. Is it possible to analyze a concept from drawings and photographs without knowing a designer's thought process?

12. Is a concept truly revealed in plans, models, and other documents, or is a concept revealed only in a built project?

Ward Bennett

Ward Bennett has created a wide range of interiors, including residences, offices, showrooms, banks, and a series of hospital environments. His interiors show a Modernist simplicity with an emphasis given to the expression of space and light, the sculptural qualities of the building envelope, and the materials used, whether natural or industrial. Furnishings are sparingly placed in his interiors, juxtaposed as if they were objects on display in a museum.

Bennett has applied this direction to the construction of four houses in which he has functioned virtually as an architect. Whereas he is known best for his chair designs, he has also worked in fashion and in product design, creating china, glassware, silver designs, leather goods, carpets, lighting, and ceramics. Currently, he produces a line of furniture and fabrics for Brickel Associates.

Ward Bennett first worked as a fashion designer, including display and design work for the fashion firm Hattie Carnegie Inc., and on Broadway shows. During that time he helped Hattie Carnegie work with Syrie

Maugham in the refurbishing of Carnegie's Redbank, New Jersey, house.

Bennett studied drawing at the Porto Romano School in Florence, as well as in Paris with sculptor Constantin Brancusi, whom Bennett acknowledges as influential on all his later work. In New York he studied painting with Hans Hofmann and shared space at the Clay Club with sculptor Louise Nevelson. His sculpture has been exhibited at the Whitney Museum and other galleries. His jewelry designs have been exhibited at New York's Museum of Modern Art.

In 1947 he began designing interiors, and was catapulted into international prominence in the early 1960s by his work as design consultant to David Rockefeller on the interior furnishings and art collection for the Chase Manhattan Bank headquarters for which Skidmore Owings & Merrill were the architects.

How do your initial concepts for interiors first reveal themselves or express themselves? As ideas, or as lines on paper?

As space. I walk through the space; I sit in the space; I go to the space over and over again. It is the space that starts it all. Usually I rip out the walls in my head—without a pencil. I dream of the spaces I could make there. For me it is like making sculpture.

Do you draw or sketch constantly?

I work very little with pencil; I work with models. For furniture I work directly with models. I like working in the three-dimensional form. Some people love to draw. It is innately in them. They have to draw. You must do it your way. There are no rules.

After I have a sketch-model, I have a draftsman measure it up and we'll make a floor plan and find out what walls are bearing and what walls are wet walls. That is the way I usually start, and even before the floor plan arrives I can begin to feel what is happening.

Can you give an example of how you arrived at the basic concept for a project you are working on currently?

One penthouse apartment had a regular entrance hall, then another entrance hall and a living room beyond, from which you went through double doors to the dining room. I sat there and saw where the walls that had plumbing were, where the bathrooms and kitchen were, where the fireplace was. And I saw that the windows of the penthouse were just windows; there was only one door to the terrace. I knew immediately what to get rid of—everything. I saw that the beautiful terraces made the apartment like a wonderful Italian villa. And yet it had little windows. Automatically, I saw that it had to have

doors to walk outside. So I made every window into a door onto the terrace.

Then the space started to line up in my head, though I had to move one thing a little to the right and one to the left to get the room into nice proportions. Also immediately I knew that I wanted to remove the dining room wall, but still have some sort of division; and I saw in my mind a wall—not high, not to the ceiling. And because of a dark corner in the dining room, I put in a skylight. Then as soon as I got the plans, I immediately made a model. And that model of the concept is what I showed the clients.

What is the contribution of clients to this process?

The client comes first. The client does not understand certain things; that is why he or she hires a designer. Clients do not know how to do the job. They don't understand what to do with a space or circulation. They don't know about the height of a table or that the arm of a chair will hit the table if it is too high. The client comes to a designer as everybody goes to a doctor—to find out what the pain is, what you need. The designer comes in to show how to develop the space for the client's needs, whatever they may be. A designer has to find out the clients' way of life: their friends, the way they dress; do they read or don't they; if they don't, why are books lying out? It is an analytical process, a very deep one, to find out what these people are all about. It takes time and effort.

In my Chase Manhattan work, I interviewed thirty-five vice presidents—going into what their role was, what sort of communications they had with the outside world, who would come to see them, what their offices would be used for. It was a personal involvement.

I need my clients to participate. I give them choices and want them to decide what they really like. And when I leave them, they will have learned a lot about how they like to live and how they can live more fully in the future. Involvement is what you really want from a client. Then they really care.

They make lists of what they like, what buildings they like, whose houses they like, what room they like best, what furniture they like. And I ask what food they like. A dining room, for me, is not the furniture; it is food and conversation.

Sometimes clients don't really care about anything, have never been to a museum or seen a painting—or even know what is comfortable. And that is so important, to try to make it comfortable, whatever room it is. So often you go into a place and it is simply uncomfortable. And when you learn these things, there is a chance that the designer has to refuse the invitation to work on that project because it would not be right for that designer to be with these people socially for a year or two. They might not have much in common. In that case the client would be better off working with some other designer.

I find that the majority of our most successful designers today are doing interiors that are totally without any personality. They are very glamorous, but when you walk in, you don't know where you are: They could be stores; they don't look like homes. They have nothing to do with the people who are living in them, and one looks like the next. They have the same art, the same furniture. You could sell shirts or sheets there. I don't know that I have ever done a residence—other than my own—that I would live in. They are for someone else. And I hope they relate to the way those people live. Even the offices at the Chase Manhattan Bank work that way.

The process is not basically different for public clients. But in residential work you are really holding their hands and teaching them.

What methods do you employ for realizing your concepts?

After my clients in the apartment at Fifth Avenue and 83rd Street accepted my concept for the space, I couldn't tell them anything about the furniture. Only after the walls went up did I develop furniture for it. I really didn't think about the furniture before that.

I knew that the bed size they wanted would fit into the bedroom and that it could go either against the wall or in the middle of the room. I knew that I could get in either a round or a square dining table to seat twelve; I had tried that in the plan. But I didn't really think about the furniture. I didn't permit myself to think about it until I got the architecture established.

Then I saw a four-fold screen in Paris; they liked it and bought it, and that started the furniture going. I had the bed in the middle of the bedroom at an angle, with a footboard and headboard and a couple of lamps. I had found some stools to go at the end of the bed. In the library there was a sofa—a mattress with a table backed up to it, all in one piece; it is a unit that can rotate to face the TV or another direction. And there were two chairs, so that they can eat in there—and those chairs were not the final chairs, but borrowed from the dining room until the right ones were found. In the living room there was a daybed with a footboard and headboard in black.

I design most of the furniture also. And in the beginning I don't know what is going to happen. In this case I designed two chairs and showed them models over a year ago, and they were just being made two years after the project began.

How does the consideration of materials affect your concepts? At what stages are they considered?

In one of my apartment designs I did terrazzo floors with a terrazzo dining table. The living room had carpeting, except in front of the fireplace, but the terrazzo went right through the kitchen into the breakfast room. But that was not part of the original concept. I liked the terrazzo because then I could also do the dining table out of it.

Sometimes a space is a year-and-a-half in happening, and you go there a couple of times a week—always thinking about it. Then you might find a chair or a screen, and it starts something else. I found a Hoffmann chair for one apartment that both the client and I loved. We didn't know where it was going to go, but we loved that chair. In another case I found a Japanese screen in London that I thought would be fine in an apartment: The client went over and looked at it, and that developed the need for a shelf to put the screen on. This gold-leaf screen was just right for the space, right for the client, right for the golden afternoon sun. Incidentally, in that case, before I found the screen, the client had bought a very early Chinese vase, a primitive one. And that was something that told me about her, that told me I could consider a Japanese screen.

How do you go about incorporating the design principles and devices into your design work?

I don't even think about it. One of the most valuable design aids I have had is travel—everything is seeing, looking, observing everything on the street. I look at scale, proportion, relationships. I look at paintings, sculpture, museums. You cannot teach that. It is part of culture. You can only expose students to culture—music, literature, religion. It is part of our sensitivity. And when you have grown accustomed to looking at and observing these things, you don't have to think about them. You are in the habit of observing them.

How is designing different from shopping and assembling?

What we are talking about is architecture. Architecture is space, you see. And then you take these items and put them in the space to make it function—that is, to sit, to sleep, to eat, to cut vegetables. Good theater is wonderful—I like to design a good stage set, but it is not what anyone would want to live in. Theater settings do not have anything behind them; they are all cardboard. That is what I do not like about Post-Modernism.

How do you meld those two activities and results together?

You know your scales. A bedroom has to take the desired bed size; you need side tables, reading lights; you have to put your clothes away. These are functions. But it first starts with the walls, and the light, the exposure, the daylight. We aim to pull the daylight in. Frank Lloyd Wright was the genius in this. I learned more from Wright than from anyone else in interiors. I love his built-ins—not the chairs, necessarily, but nobody has made a better fireplace than Wright. And no one has ever used daylight as he did. When we talk about architecture, we are talking about walls and spaces and balconies.

But if interior design is part architecture and part furniture design, where are the dividing lines?

Years ago there was a unity to the two activities, and then they became more separate. I think there are more impersonal interiors today than ever—totally impersonal.

Is your design process different from what you thought it would be when you began?

We all grow, of course. But I still work as I was trained to work as a sculptor. I still work with models, even for my furniture. Making the models for my furniture or my flatware is very important. I sometimes make furniture models out of pipe cleaners.

Do you have any additional advice for students of interior design?

I believe students should be actually physically involved in building spaces. They should work for a building contractor for a year or so, so that they really learn how a building goes together; or they should work in an upholstery shop. That was how I learned. When I worked in the dress business, I learned how the fabrics go together. I actually cut the fabrics; I liked to cut right into them to see what happened to them on the bias, on the straight.

And I would certainly advise students to learn to draw and draft well. But the first thing to do is get a job. Get your foot in the door, even if it is for the first six weeks without pay. When I went to Hattie Carnegie, she didn't need a designer. I said, let me do the windows for nothing. And I did that for six weeks. Then all of a sudden her windows were in *Time* magazine. So I say, "Get a job." Work for the best.

Robert Bray and Michael Schaible

Bray-Schaible Inc. is an interior design firm that designs residential and corporate interiors in the Minimal idiom. The partners, Robert Bray and Michael Schaible, established their practice in 1969.

Robert Bray studied architectural engineering at Oklahoma State University and interior design at the Parsons School of Design. Michael Schaible received a B.F.A. from the University of Colorado, and also studied interior design at the Parsons School. Before opening their own firm, they had worked for several years with large interior planning organizations such as Ford & Earl Design and Saphier, Lerner, Schindler Environetics, where most of their experience was in corporate interior design. As Bray-Schaible they have also designed large corporate installations, retail stores and shops, banks, apartment and house renovations, as well as complete new houses, including the architecture and planning. Their firm is small and personal, and they seldom employ more than two assistants.

How do your initial concepts first reveal themselves or express themselves? As ideas, or as lines on paper?

Robert Bray: A good part of the conceptual thinking, in the case of existing plans, springs from the examination of the plan. Our question at that point is, "How can I give shape to this space?" And the range of things that we attempt varies. If the space is in a great building, we feel a responsible designer will show some allegiance to that building. There are times when you feel you owe no allegiance; there are times when you feel somewhere in between—and those in-between situations are confusing.

Michael Schaible: As in every other existing project, we first look for what we should eliminate—the clutter of details that destroys so many beautifully devised spaces. We try to take all of those details out to get back to the original shape.

Bray: It is a matter of looking for any way to see what concept is possible. Some designers superimpose a scheme they have been carrying around in their minds. If you carry around an idea with you, if you have visual images in your head, you often think, "Wouldn't it be beautiful if I got the opportunity to try this one?" That approach has very little meaning to me. If you are always superimposing some fantasy on something, it usually doesn't apply. And when you have something specific in mind, you cannot explore all the possibilities.

Still, sometimes we do start with an approach simply as a place to start. But when it goes on paper, and we start looking and resolving, then that preconceived idea usually gets eliminated. A designer often wants a certain type of visual imagery for his own reasons. But it doesn't always really work for what you are doing in that particular job. You are always searching, and it is sometimes in those blind stabs that you discover something new.

When do those blind stabs come? Are they ideas, visions, or lines on paper?

Bray: I am usually not working seriously until I make a mark on paper. I think about something for days and nothing happens. Then, once I make a line on the paper, it is usually not what I was thinking. We start with lines and all of a sudden we see relationships. Then we begin to look at what is there to find more of an order in it. We search until we arrive at some kind of order.

Schaible: In designing new interiors for existing buildings, also, there are many instances where we cannot visualize whether there is order on the paper, though I may be aware that it does indeed exist. Sometimes a visit to the site and seconds of looking are major moments of seeing things.

Where does the client fit into this process?

Schaible: Only the mundane physical requirements of the client apply to the concept. Our clients come to us knowing basically what we do and what we don't do. They see something in our work—although I don't know that they know exactly what it is. They are not going to ask us for French Provincial or Early American. We will do what a client insists on, but we will never agree with them if we think they are wrong.

Bray: The biggest fear we have is how is it going to work, not what is it going to look like. In the case of our design for the First National Bank of Hialeah, we first went to every department and learned what was in every file drawer. At the end we knew exactly how the bank worked. It was our functional activity analysis. In a residential project, we get feedback from everyone we can talk to—the children, the maid—and all that information is in our heads as we plan. No matter what clients may say about what they want or hate, whether you want to forget it or change it, you never forget their feelings.

Is this process different for public clients and private clients?

Schaible: For private clients the process is more tailored to personalities. We cannot talk about the people we deal with collectively, since they are all so diverse. We must deal with everyone as individuals—and that is more important than changes in the process.

What methods do you employ for realizing a concept?

Bray: There are numbers of rules that designers have learned or set up for themselves—rules or devices or theories—that have applied and continue to apply to changing spaces. Sometimes, as in our Hialeah project, a powerful symmetry exists, and we repeat every single detail—the wiring and cables—to get one connection right on the center of the axis. The existence of that symmetry was obvious from what the architects gave us in the beginning. But realizing that symmetry down to the finest details was extremely difficult.

How does the consideration of materials affect your concept?

Bray: You investigate many materials, but many times go back to the tried and known. Sometimes you see something you love but you know it's inappropriate. We select certain things for practicality and a sense of permanence; throw-away design is too expensive.

Schaible: In the case of the Hialeah bank we began to think of it as a small product, like an electric razor design, which we could really make precisely beautiful at large scale. We determined that the strength of the materials used on the exterior of the bank should be continued on the inside—the granite floors and teller cages, the columns, the thickness of the walls. We had come to love these materials for their sense of permanence.

And we wanted all the linear qualities of a drawing, the pencil lines of the design, to be visible in the bank when it was completed. To do that, the selection of materials was important. For example, the ceiling grille system goes right up to the line of stone, and we wanted it to be seen as an uninterrupted plane, like the granite. So the sprinkler heads and air-conditioning intakes are all behind the grille. We tried to keep the lighting on the other side of that surface also; but we could not hold the light levels we wanted that way, so we had to lose the flat surface by puncturing it for lighting. Otherwise, we maintained the linearity of the ceiling by the use of the grid or grille system.

[In a recent residential project, however, Bray-Schaible proposed glass block as the material surrounding a powder room in their first presentation drawings. When they saw what that presentation revealed, however, they decided to use another material. The drawing showed them they did not like it, so they changed their thinking and looked for a material that would work better.] It happens a lot between the two of us.

After developing this procedure over the years you have been in practice, do you consider it to be the same procedure you thought it was when you were a student?

Schaible: We were both idealistic in the beginning. We went on in spite of the fact that we didn't think we could do design our way. Then we found out that we could: You can practice in an idealized way. One of the biggest changes we went through was when all of those rules and theories we had learned and set up for ourselves started leaving us. Then we began to do it for ourselves, for the way we felt it ought to be done.

Barbara D'Arcy

Barbara D'Arcy specializes in the planning and design of retail stores.

Born in Manhattan, Barbara D'Arcy majored in art at the College of New Rochelle. After college she worked for a short time for the Alexander Smith Carpet Company on a promotion program that offered to readers of the firm's advertising a color scheme and a floor plan for any room in their house. "For two years," she relates, "I sat in a basement and drew 1/4-inch floor plans in brown india ink of everything from city apartments to farmhouses in Kansas—for two years, five days a week, all day long—floor plans. It was an invaluable aid. To this day floor plans are easy for me to do. I can do 1/4-inch drawings without a scale and come in within 2 inches on a very long span." Students who are just learning to draw may find this tale heartening.

D'Arcy joined the staff of Bloomingdale's department store in New York City in 1952—first as a junior decorator in the fabrics department, shortly thereafter in furniture, and then assisting on the design of the store's model rooms on the furniture floor. In 1957 she took charge of designing the model rooms herself.

In 1972 she became director of store design for all branches of Bloomingdale's corporate retailing organization across the country. She is now vice president and director of merchandise presentation, with the store planning, store design, and display departments reporting to her.

When Barbara D'Arcy designed the model rooms for Bloomingdale's, she had a staff of three assistants. Her present store planning and design department has nine designers and seventeen draftsmen. "This department is responsible for the look of Bloomingdale's," she explains. "The people in this department are responsible for the design of everything in all Bloomingdale's stores across the country that is not for sale—from the planning and design of new stores and the renovation of existing stores to every velvet pad on which a piece of fine jewelry is shown."

The main store in New York City accounts for a large amount of the renovation and redesign work owing to several seasonal shops that are changed every two weeks and one that is changed every four or five weeks. Many of these changes are not made purely for cosmetic reasons; in many cases an important designer becomes more popular, and the merchandising program must be constantly updated. At any one time her department may have well over a hundred projects going on—and all this must be arranged in conjunction with the schedule of the construction department.

How do your initial concepts first reveal themselves or express themselves? As ideas, or as lines on paper?

It isn't the same each time. It depends on the scope of the project. The redesign of the main floor of Bloomingdale's flagship store, now called B'Way, was a subject of discussion for four or five years—because it was just plain blah, nondescript, nothing, and no longer served the needs of the business. And I was groping with what to do with it, since I was the one that was going to have to redesign it.

It all started with the fact that we needed to have a

hard-surface floor material, strangely enough. The original travertine floor had become cracked and pitted, and a hard surface was needed that would withstand traffic by thousands of people daily. So the idea was to do marble. And I guess because I am a traditionalist I went back to the old concept of black-and-white marble. But I did it very quietly in my own head.

Where does the client fit into this process?

About two years before we started the actual work, a group of us was in India and I happened to be staying in an incredible room in an old palace that had a black-and-white marble floor. So I suggested that we have the next day's meeting in my room. And I said to Mr. Traub, the chairman of the board of Bloomingdale's, "What would you think about Bloomingdale's having a black-and-white marble floor?" For something as bold a pattern as that, I needed to have him as a partner. And he thought it was an interesting idea.

The purpose of the renovation was not just to change the aesthetics. The practical reason behind the change, and this is where the client comes in and is enormously important, was that Mr. Traub and the merchants felt that the potential growth of business had to be planned for in relation to the relatively small square footage of floor space available.

The idea was to create a shop concept for the main floor—to have a cosmetics shop, a perfume shop, a fashion accessory shop, a jewelry shop, a hat shop, a hosiery shop, and so on. And the next question was how to do this without putting up a lot of walls that would restrict traffic flow and sight lines. Then, because we felt that defining the shop spaces on the floor alone would not be strong enough visually, I felt there needed to be drops in the ceiling to define the shop spaces. Next, I felt that the drops in the ceiling should follow the marble floor to create a sense of direction. That gave birth to the light coves on either side of the aisles. The idea was that, in addition to the black ceiling, we would have white lighting coves leading you through the store from Lexington Avenue to Third Avenue.

[The discussion was veering into the area of programming, "but we don't call it that in our store," Barbara D'Arcy said. One of the designers in her department works on "block plans," which is what they call the preliminary sketch plan or feasibility study that shows the blocks of space that the various boutiques, departments, and merchants need, and the size of those spaces in relation to both business volume and traffic considerations. "That is the first stage in design development," she points out. The block plan has to take into consideration not only those factors but also the existing column arrangement and existing ductwork.]

So these things were worked over and over until the merchants and Mr. Traub felt that they had a plan that both made sense and looked to the future. And that block plan was done long before I did my first plan of the black-and-white marble floor.

Does that mean that in store design the client—store chairman and merchants as a team—does all the functional planning, since they know how it works, and the designer has to listen to them?

Yes.

Do you do what you want to do in spite of the client's wishes?

We try to work it out together. There is a lot of mutual respect. I will go back and say, "Supposing we did it this way because it answers my problems of balance or proportion, does it work for you?" Sometimes they'll say yes; sometimes no, and you have to go back and rework it. But we try to have both work together. The main thing is to remember constantly that we are a department store, that we are selling merchandise, and that the needs of the merchandise have to come first. Then you build the architecture and design around it. It is a challenge and there is absolutely no reason why it cannot be made to work. Sometimes it is the easier solution that thwarts the merchants; sometimes the demands they make on you force you to rethink and rethink until it gets better for you both.

Does this process differ when a store designer is planning model rooms where there is no client?

No live-in client. But there is a vast difference. When I was doing a model room, I was able to do the space in its entirety. When I left the room, it was complete—every color was as I wanted it, every accessory was in place, every pillow—and it was the best I could do in that given instance. But when you are designing a dress or sportswear department, you are creating a space that will help sell the merchandise. You need places to hang as well as display the sportswear. And you need to create a background that won't clash with the merchandise, but enhances it, a background that creates a mood that makes the customer feel comfortable shopping in that environment. But after you create that space, the merchants come in and fill it. You may try to go back and police it, but you don't have the final touch. You don't have complete control in a store design as you do in a model room design.

My feeling is that a design is not successful if it doesn't answer the function of the client.

Isn't the function in a model room purely the designer's conception of what it should look like?

Also to sell merchandise. [Barbara D'Arcy says that selling the merchandise is, or should be, part of the designer's conceptual image; but she also points out that some conceptual images don't sell.]

When it's time to start designing the model rooms, the merchants are very specific about which groups of furniture are to be drawn from. It is always a collection of furniture that forms the pivot around which a "look" is then developed. Special accent pieces can be added to carry out the look, but model rooms cost money, and in order to be financially successful they must be based on sound business and aesthetic decisions. When I was involved with the rooms, we always worked this out together.

Did you make working drawings for those model rooms?

I always drew 1/4-inch plans. I did not simply walk in and say let's put a bit of this here and some of that there. I drew everything, including elevations and sections. It is very easy to take the best corner of a room and do a conceptual design, but the trick is to do the total room and work out all of the problems that exist on the other side of the space. Conceptual renderings do not really figure out all of the details and pitfalls. So I always gave the drafting room detailed drawings to work from.

[Since she has been in store design, Barbara D'Arcy gets less time to draw—"I am more of an administrator now," she points out—but her training is still there to support her analysis of the drawings that the drafting room produces. And, for the B'Way renovation, she drew the first basic 1/4-inch-scale plan herself.]

How do you develop a concept?

In the case of the B'Way design, first I drew in the black-and-white marble floor on a plan—but this may have been as much as two years after the India trip. And during that time the programming phase—the development of the merchandising plan—went on spasmodically; it lasted four to five years. Meanwhile, I kept asking myself how all of this should relate to "What is Bloomingdale's?" What should the main floor be, was my investigation. It was agonizing, because I was terrified at performing this duty.

Then one day as I was crossing Lexington Avenue and looked up at our building, which is Art Deco, I thought that although we couldn't do an Art Deco main floor (because it would be too definite a style and inappropriate for a store that was aiming to be more contemporary), I did feel that the exterior architecture provided continuity

with what we were planning for the interior. So the steps in the ceiling are my answer to the Art Deco; they provide an Art Deco flavor that runs through the floor.

In this development phase I laid out the circulation, because it was complicated, and I worked at the scale of the marble squares that I thought would be appropriate to the scale of the floor. I laid out the pattern and colored in the black and white and worked out the borders so that there was a modulation. In order to design the ceiling I had to modulate the floor and fit in the walls, then try to make the ceiling work with it. Obviously, there was a lot of back and forth.

Is there a difference between working on interiors in existing buildings and working on newly created spaces?

There is a vast difference. But the same process evolves.

Do you consider the renovation and redesign that is done for the purposes of merchandising to be decorating or designing?

When I was doing the model rooms, I felt that I was decorating. When I came into store design, I felt as though I was doing architecture. [She describes the carrying out of a clothing designer's promotional image—photographs of polo players for Ralph Lauren's line—as] props to give flavor. In a cosmetic case for the Polo fragrance, the pad may be done in green felt, which is one of the colors that have been established as Lauren colors, and there might be a helmet and riding crop just for atmosphere.

Is one factor constantly more critical than another—the budget, the mechanical system, the time, the plan, the merchant, or some other?

I keep going back to the merchandise. It used to be that stores were able to have all kinds of exclusive merchandise; today, more and more stores have the same or similar merchandise. So a store designer really has to present it better than the fellow next door. The goal is to create an atmosphere—a total atmosphere to which our customer relates and in which our customers feel comfortable for shopping, and which includes the presentation of the merchandise, the displays, the shopping bags, and the advertising. [For corporate continuity, all these factors are then carried out in branch stores to make them reflect the downtown or pilot store.]

How do you consider and apply the standard design principles and devices?

Instantly, but it is not a checklist, just something that is innately in you. It is assimilated over years of experience.

But it is something you need to develop.

I had a classics background—Latin and Greek—both in high school and college. We were subjected in depth to the proportions of the Colosseum, all of the Greek temples, and the Egyptian temples. A broad base in the classics is invaluable and I think it is one of the sad things that is missing in the curriculum of our schools today. I can't tell you how many times I have pored through drawings of classic temples to see the proportions of a crown molding or whatever. Unlike a living room, a department store is loaded with columns and you just have to work out some form of symmetry or rhythm to incorporate or hide them—things based on the rhythm of classic architecture. There is definitely something to be learned from that.

Do you have any additional advice to give to students of interior design?

I advise them to gain a broad base of experience. I believe that design has to be approached in ten directions at the same time. You have to be thinking about what is going on everywhere in relation to a design, whether it is a store or a room. Few designers in school have their minds stimulated to the point where they think in all directions. I cannot tell you how many people cannot *see*. Most young designers just look at a wall. I say you never look at just that wall, you are always looking also at one corner and the other corner at the same time. You cannot look at an elevation and isolate it from the other elevation. So I say never design without looking in all directions. Think of the scale of spaces. Think of how it looks from this side, this side, and that side.

How is a student to get this vision?

It is exposure and background and experience on a high level. I find that some people have been fortunate in having their brains exercised more than others. Some who study design and along with it have a lot of scholastic studies have been forced into truly using their brains—into *thinking*. And this, I believe, is essential to the development of excellence in design. There are so many elements to be considered in the creation of a design—and it takes an orderly mind to put all those elements into proper perspective. The goal is to develop from each experience and use it to do a little bit better the next time—and grow.

Angelo Donghia

Angelo Donghia, who died not long after this interview in 1985, was a designer of interiors, furniture, textiles, and household appointments. In addition, he was one of the notable business talents in the design field.

Born in Vandergrift, Pennsylvania, Angelo Donghia studied interior design at the Parsons School of Design, both in New York and in Paris, before joining Yale Burge Interiors in 1959. In 1966 he became a partner in Burge-Donghia Interiors. From then on his business expansion was exemplary: In 1968 he organized his fabrics and wallcoverings division, Vice Versa. In 1970 Donghia Associates was formed; in 1976 Donghia Showrooms was established; and in 1978 the Donghia Furniture Company was initiated. In 1985 his nationwide personnel totaled one hundred.

How do your initial concepts reveal themselves or express themselves? As ideas, or as lines on paper?

As a visual image. When I walk into a space, I see something in my head. I then take it to a piece of paper—my own paper, not that of the drafting room. I sit at my bed, my kitchen table, my breakfast table, my desk, and I will do a very primitive little drawing. It may mean nothing to anyone else, but will mean something to me. And it is amazing to me to see how close I have been to the final product, in those primitive drawings, which came directly from my mental image picture.

Past experience is what brings that mental picture about—things that are in that experience—when something in an apartment or in a space triggers something from the past. It could be the view, it could be the sense of light, it could be the air, the coolness, or the warmth. It could be anything intangible. The feeling of the air could remind me of something I have seen, or trigger a feeling that I would like to experience in that space. I would have a different feeling about the space if it were freezing cold and if it were very warm.

Normally, I would not put something on paper instantly in the space. It would have to incubate—during the time of going back to my office—to get to the point of being prepared to do something about it.

For one thing, I am not a machine. I have found that my creative spirit has to be prepared to give off what it wants to. It cannot just give it off. So my preparation for that is to allow myself to be in the mood. I have to wake up feeling like I want to do that. I cannot be expected to do it. And I try to allow that freedom to the people who work for me. It is an enormous luxury, but it is a necessity if you are going to get what you have to get in the way of a design.

One's attention must be on that subject fully and you have to know fully what the problem is. Understanding the problem is what I mean—having a total understanding of the problem. One of the blocks to creative expression is not knowing what is expected of you and/or not knowing what your goal is. Somehow if you know that *that* is what I really have to do, and you know and understand the problem, it is then much more easily approached.

In school, when the problem is given, a student can either understand the problem or not understand it. But it is foolish to try to solve the problem if it is misunderstood. So the first thing to do when exposed to the problem is to ask a lot of questions, so that what is expected is totally understood. That little piece of the mind that is attached to not-knowing-exactly-what-the-problem-is wastes a lot of fuel. When 100 percent of the mind is sure of what it is doing, the mind is able to drive right on with security and knowledge, with no hesitation.

One of the biggest problems in our business, as in life generally, is that people don't ask enough questions. They are always afraid of looking like they don't know. The most important thing is to ask, ask until you fully understand what you are about to do. Once you understand what you are about to do, the solution is very close to the surface.

What about furniture design?

The process is the same. Both for me and for the furniture designers who work for me, we have to know what we are after—what kind of chair we want, what kind of people we think need this chair, in what kinds of circumstances this chair is going to be used, and budget and materials. If you know that those questions are part of the problem, then suddenly you can give a quick answer for each of the specifications and requirements.

Still, I cannot then just sit at my table and design that perfect chair the first time around. I now know that that can happen only by a miracle. What I have to do is try anything that comes into my head—not by sitting there and saying, "Now I must design the perfect chair," and judge myself on that chair. Rather, what I want to do is just open up my head to chairs—all chairs, the memory of chairs, chairs that I love, chairs that I feel would be attractive, chairs that I think are in dreams, from another lifetime, from China, from the Renaissance, from Venice, from Africa—chairs.

And then I just do quick drawings, without allowing myself to edit the drawings. I say, "OK, here is my target: I want to draw twenty chairs in ten minutes." So I time myself.

Do you actually time yourself?

I time myself. I want to design twenty chairs in ten minutes. That gives me half a minute per chair, and no time to correct. All I am going to get is a quick sketch. So I draw, draw, draw, draw. And what comes out is new things.

And these are the concepts for chairs?

Yes, this is my method.

What I then have there are twenty chairs—some ridiculous, some so absurd that they don't matter—but among them is going to be the spark of the beginning of an idea. And that is even before the concept. Because what I have done is churn myself up, I have turned on the chair mechanism. Then I can say, "Now I never thought of that one before, and there it is." Where it came from I don't know. I just jotted things down—without editing them. And then I review these quick silhouettes or outlines of chairs.

When I designed the Focal Chair, I first saw a shape like a sled, then I drew an arm like that, then a base like it. Then it began to develop. The final design is not what I started with, but as soon as I saw the profile that I liked, I asked, "Does it fit the set of requirements that I was working toward?" Whatever they were: I need a freestanding armchair, a dining room chair, a chair of metal, and it has to cost such and such and it has to fit in a presidential office—whatever the requirements to solve the problem.

For a chair design, who is the client to set out such requirements?

In the case of the Focal Chair, I was designing for Donghia Furniture, so I had fewer restrictions, because I am the ruler here. In the case when a designer works for me, I have to say whether a scheme is out of the price range, or whatever it is I see that does not fit the requirements. When we designed for Kroehler, they had to remind me constantly that the sofa had to sell for $400 retail and not $3,600 retail. It was the same process, but a different set of rules.

Do you draw or sketch constantly? Daily?

I sketch constantly. I can sit at the drafting board and get a floor plan done and I can do a perspective, but I am not a freehand drawer. My sketches are a language for me, and when I look at them, they say everything to me. And I do it all the time, I love it.

What is the contribution of the client to this process?

The rules of the game are set up by the client. The client has requirements—either known goals or unknown goals. Sometimes the designer has to be expert in figuring out the unsaid. And that can happen only with experience, knowing how to dig it out, how to draw out what they haven't even been thinking that they want.

Do you sometimes do things that the client does not want? Does the designer know best?

I feel I can recommend the best, and I feel that the client has to make the final decision. I never do anything against the client's wishes. But I always do my very best, and I think I am pretty convincing. It is important to convince the client that we are both right.

Then how can a concept be preserved?

If the client's requirements are such that they will change the concept, then it is very important to pull back—if you cannot convince the client that the requirements may not be necessary, that they may be a matter of whim. If that cannot be altered, and the requirements changed, then the concept should be changed—at the roots. The worst thing a designer can ever do is to nibble at the concept, to pull away its strength by pulling away various parts.

Does this happen to the same degree when designing furniture?

Yes. You don't want to compromise. If a manufacturer says, "Well we could make this chair better if we put the leg on the outside," then a designer has to say, "Then let's redesign the chair; let's do a new chair; let's throw that one out—it's no good." Don't try to shift the concept. The concept is the concept. And there is very little room for it to stay whole if you nibble at its parts.

Is this true because the concept is fragile and because its integrity is essential to the strength of the final design?

Right.

How do you analyze a space from the drawings given to you?

I am not that certain about space from a drawing. I would be certain of the space if I had conceived it and had it drawn. But it is difficult for me to get into a space from a drawing alone. If I have the opportunity, I prefer to *be* in the space before I begin to give my considerations.

Is there a difference between working on interiors in existing buildings and working on newly created spaces?

For the best result it is good to have the great luxury of being in the space before designing it. Knowing where the light is, how the air feels, and what the sense of space and scale is—these are essential. When coming from a drawing of a new space that does not exist, it is more of a gamble. Then you have to project what it might be, and it does not always end up being what you think it might be. Especially when it comes to light.

You have designed two Omni hotels, the Hotel Inter-Continental in New Orleans, and the Trump Tower lobby on Fifth Avenue, as well as numerous residences. Is there a difference between designing for private clients and for public clients?

With residential clients you usually have the luxury of an existing space; you have more flexibility, more time; you have more personal input, more personal rules coming from the client. [He says that the designer has more time because residential clients can afford to pay to have the time stretch out, and they are not so pressing; whereas the public project is on a fast-track or similarly rigid construction schedule.] The public project is less personal. It has to be much more documented in drawings and correspondence. And everything is more guesswork, yet there is no room for revision. [However, he adds, the different sizes or scales of project do not affect the methodology of design.] It is the same method for a one-room apartment as for a 500-room hotel.

What is your view of the boundaries or limits of your design practice?

My limits have increased over my years. When I first started I knew nothing, and each year that I practiced, I learned more and my limits grew. Today, after twenty-five years of doing what I do, I now have the energy and the desire to include an architectural approach that I have been allowing myself to take recently. I have begun to know more because I have asked a lot of questions, and because I feel I do have the ability. I have hired architects to work for me on the staff to support my own skills.

Students who have been trained to think conceptually have been trained to think of form; they have been trained to think of volume.

There is a bridge in the gap that separated the two professions for so ridiculously many years. There is definitely a bridge building, where the two professions are looking at each other with respect, more so than before.

How do you go about developing a concept further?

Developing a concept—after the rules are understood and the sketches have been done, and you know that you have a beginning—is when it is sent to the drawing boards to be refined and pinpointed. Then I begin acting essentially as a design critic, then I sit back and say, "Now develop this." I give direction up to a point.

In the case of the Trump Tower lobby, they gave me two slabs—top and bottom—and a mouth as the opening; that's it. And they said, "We want something elegant." Mr. Trump said to me, "I want something very luxurious, very Gucci, very Old World." Now, I am not making any judgments about what he was telling me, I am only telling what he told me. And I said, "What have you seen that you have always loved?" And he said, "The Regency Hotel lobby." That was a clear indicator to me, because I feel that the Regency's lobby is one of the best lobbies in New York City. It looks substantial, as if it has been there for years, and as if it always will be there. And that was when my mental image struck. I suddenly said, "Oh, I now know what I should do; I have it." And the first solution that came to me was that it must have a hard-finish surface—walls and floor. I wanted marble or some kind of stone, so that it would feel permanent. Then we discussed color. My original design was for gray and beige limestone—all tones of gray and beige in stone, and a little gold; and pale mohair furnishings, with maybe a glass table. They refused this gray color scheme. They hate gray, love burgundy, and deep rich colors. And they wanted large pattern in the marble.

So I then knew the rules—what I had to know. And I was either going to do what I was going to do in burgundy marble, or change my concept. Yet I had to keep it relatively simple since it had only an 8-foot 9-inch ceiling. So I developed a concept with these elements and the client accepted it. Then it went into development drawings and was combined with the architects' and engineers' requirements.

Do the different phases change or affect the design?

They don't change the design. But if you let them, they would change it. You have to be honest with yourself from the beginning and not specify something that is impossible because of the budget or other requirements. A designer has to have a sense of reality about his concepts at all times. The concept has to be realizable. If a budget is tight, you think about what is available instead of what can be custom-designed. If you have to produce a chair that has to sell for $300 retail, you should know what is available to make that chair happen before you get serious about thinking you can do it.

Is any one factor consistently more critical in this process?

Time. Time is the answer to everything. And the secondary critical thing is budget. The most important thing to say on any job is that we were on time and within budget.

How do you consider and apply the design principles and devices?

Whenever appropriate. They will appear as part of a designer's communication with himself. If he looks at a problem and thinks about all that, each will appear as a concern when it has to appear.

Is designing different from assembling?

I am a decorator and an interior designer. I design and I decorate. I assemble things and I conceptualize things. They are directly attached to one another, yet they can exist without each other.

I like to think of decorating as doing nothing more than prepping or dressing a room—taking this office and saying I think this room should be in a dark fabric with a floor of stripes and venetian blinds. Order it, and the room is redecorated. Now if I decide to change the shape of this room and decide to put in a wall of glass, and to make the ceiling with a special lighting system, then I decide to change the floors and that I need a staircase going to the room below, I would be changing the entire room so that you would not know you are in the same space. In other words, when the six-sided box is changed—ceiling, floor, walls—and the fenestration and portals have been changed, that is designing. Design goes deeper than the other.

Is your design procedure different from what you thought it would be when you were a student?

No. But when I started as a student, I thought I was expected to be a mechanic who came up with answers. You pressed the button, you were on; and when you pressed the button again, you were off. Then I had a teacher who used to say, "Don't think about it. Do it." The worst thing one can do is just sit and look at a piece of paper. The thing to do is to fill the piece of paper, even if it is something wrong, because out of that will come something that is right. That was the beginning of my understanding of this process.

The most singular influence was the experience during my formative years, when I went to the movies all the time. I saw all the Forties movies, in which they did a bigger-than-life story about the rich. They showed style through a magnifying glass. And that registered with me. It wasn't a true picture of the way all the rich really are, it painted the ideal rich. The movies made a Georgian room ten times the size a Georgian room really was, and when they made a detail on a door, they made it four times the size it really was. That affected my sense of scale.

My advice to anyone who is studying interior design is not to limit themselves to school. They should take it upon themselves to go out and see everything there is to be seen. And to absorb as much as they can. Students must go out with the desire to have a successful career. That desire should force them to see everything that has been done ever, and to read everything, and to absorb everything they can.

Joseph Paul D'Urso

Joseph Paul D'Urso designs residential and corporate interiors in a spare, minimalist idiom, for which he has been widely acclaimed from the very beginning of his career.

Born in Newark, New Jersey, he studied interior design at Pratt Institute in Brooklyn, then spent two years studying in England—first at the Royal College of Art in London, then as a fellow at the Manchester College of Art and Design. At both institutions he did projects in interior design. Immediately after, in 1968, he began his independent practice in New York, and since then has usually operated as a one- to three-person office. Recently, after a commission to design a large social and cultural club in Hong Kong, his offices there and in New York increased to six people.

How do your initial concepts first reveal or express themselves? As ideas, or as lines on paper?

We all have our own ways of looking at things. First you react to the space—this is what we are trained to do— then you start analyzing it quickly. You don't sit down with paper and pencil and make a list, though; it just happens, automatically and very quickly. To find a space you really must find the architecture first. Different designers react to different things at different speeds. But I wouldn't be surprised if, given the same space, you found strong planning similarities in the reactions to the same space from a group of different designers. However, the proportions and the use of materials are where you do your own thing.

When I first started doing interiors, the projects were not large and the budgets were modest, so obviously everything had to count. If I were to demolish a wall or install a skylight, it really had to be the right wall and the right placement of the skylight. It is a good way to begin, because it forces you to be intelligent, even clever, to be thoughtful. I became aware of how much can be done with very little. You can deal with form and space and with exciting dynamics with just a gesture or two.

In the beginning of a project I usually ask what I would do if I were living in the proposed space. If there is a family, I put myself among them and really design it for myself. I always identify personally with a space— and, of course, the spaces one likes the most are the most rewarding to work with. They are usually the ones that have something going for them architecturally—a good view, of course, and good natural light. Then you must imagine what it would be like to live there. It must be a personal involvement.

The enthusiasm of a client can lead me to get excited about a project, too, and vice versa, I'm sure. In a good situation, the client is continually the most interesting part. A client is someone you have to get close to immediately and to surround. Fortunately, I have had intelligent clients. There have been difficult ones, but they have always been intelligent. They have thought out what they wanted to do and have had wonderful ideas of their own. For a good client-designer relationship, there must be trust and a closeness of working together.

How do you put yourself into a client's position in order to understand the client's needs?

When someone has rented or bought an apartment or work space, they have already done a lot of work simply by choosing that space. And there is a lot you can glean from why they bought the space. At that point they are coming to the designer saying, "Look, this is what I have. What would you do?" Then, I don't think there really are too many questions one needs to ask them. A client with any sense of analysis of what it is to make a design work will tell you what is unusual about it—like, "I've got 650 garments to hang in the closet," or "I have an obsession with books," or whatever. You visit them in their present place and see if there is anything else unusual you might have to deal with, but other than that I don't think there are extraordinary differences between one residential project and another—other than what you can pick up in a very short time.

[Clients' needs for public spaces are a rather different matter, D'Urso says. The client of Hong Kong's I Club indicated that the discotheque would be the important program element. But when D'Urso analyzed what the club was all about—what kind of members it was going to attract, the amount of space available, and the management operation—he found that the restaurant ought to become the more important function. The client had made a reference to being in the restaurant and in the nightclub at the same time, but D'Urso found that there was no way to make that relationship of spaces possible. "Whoever wrote the program had not understood the nature of the particular space they rented," he explains. This is a telling illustration of how a designer must help clients reanalyze their needs and possibilities.]

Do you draw or sketch constantly? Daily?

I am not a drawing fanatic. [From the beginning of his career, D'Urso has relied on the impressions received from an existing space as a means of developing a concept, though he admits that many of his colleagues view his degree of commitment to drawing differently from the way he does. Still, he does not keep an organized sketchbook going all the time.]

I draw on tissue paper on the plane, in a hotel room, at home, or in the office. Usually as an overlay on the plan. I do most of my designing at 1/4-inch scale. At 1/8-inch you don't have enough room usually for details, and the scale of the space can fool you more. But you can be surprised at 1/4-inch scale as well. Sometimes you may think you don't have enough room for something you design, then you find when it is blown up in working drawings that you have too much. Of course, it happens the other way around, too.

Whenever you have a large project, you have need of a great quantity of drawings. Students, of course, usually don't have anything else to work with. They have to rely on drawings and models. When I taught, I encouraged my students to make models. Because students cannot go back to an existing space whenever necessary, models can show them much about the space that they cannot visualize or analyze in drawing form. You cannot visualize from a plan when you are new to the craft the way you can as you become more experienced. But in professional work I find that models get changed so frequently they are ultimately too reworked to learn from. And to have a model shop that can make a fresh model for each stage is a luxury that I do not have.

One of the best things about doing more and more work as one continues one's career is that you learn from what you have built, so that the next time you design something you really have an idea of what it's going to look like because you have seen it or something like it before. You don't have this experience when you are first starting out. There are so many considerations in design, and your relationship with your clients is so much more tense because you don't really have the confidence or the authority yet.

Now I can go into a space and quickly know how to begin. In my Hong Kong project, after I had a plan resolved, I laid out the entire space with strips of wood—both 4 inches and 3 inches wide, to indicate either high or low walls. I helped nail them down and we made the whole plan—159,000 square feet. It really helped me to see that one angle wasn't right and that another one was much better. When you see in this way, so many things tell you that there is another way to make it better.

In terms of the methodology of construction, however, the more complicated the job, the more the contractor must have complete drawings—or else must know the designer's work closely and the two understand and trust each other—or, as an alternate, the designer must spend a great deal more time in on-the-job supervision. That is what is wonderful about doing small projects. You can do it like a sculpture and start chiseling away or adding.

Is there a difference between working on interiors in existing buildings and working on newly created spaces?

Starting with a new building is completely different. Everything is under your control, everything is totally original; it doesn't exist. You can start with a big scheme, a plan or sketch, and in a sense you are starting at the same instant with the detailing. There is something amazing about that as opposed to working on an existing space. No matter how hard you try and how different you want to make it, there is still so much that was already there, so much you cannot do. When you are dealing with an existing orientation, like a window facing north, no matter how you try to make that space different the light is going to come from the north; whereas if you are designing from scratch, the combinations are infinite.

Can you imagine worrying about 159,000 square feet in the kind of detail I was used to considering in an apartment? In my early projects there wasn't an inch that wasn't thought out.

[In designing an apartment for shoe designer Reed Evins, D'Urso reacted first to several features of the space: the ceilings, which were not high and which had a textured surface, and a door that led from the main room into the kitchen.] I knew immediately that I had to close up that door and that I had to deal with the ceilings. These are simple things that one can do automatically, but those two features started my mind toward changing the space in a way that I could imagine liking it. That was the beginning of the analysis of the space, and it is easy to recall that beginning. It is another thing to know when I decided that there should be a single large table and that the closet should come out and be the location for the bed.

One thing I learned from the Reed Evins apartment was not to be afraid to make elements in a space as big as I sensed they should be, even though they appeared too large in plan. [The single large table in the living room, for example, virtually fills the conversation area and makes it perhaps the most integrated living-dining room of modern times.] Scale became the whole point of the apartment, since the only things in it were a bed, a chair, lights, and the table. It took courage for me to make the table that big and to put the bed in that proportion of space.

What is the contribution of the client to this process?

The I Club is something of an experimental project in that it is a combination social club and cultural center. The client's idea was to set up a private membership club that would incorporate contemporary design and art into its environment—not in a museum way, where you go and look at chairs but cannot sit in them; but employing a kind of history of modern design and furniture as an ongoing, useful exposure and experience. Modern artworks were also to be a part of this environment.

Among the activity functions to be provided in the I Club were a cocktail lounge and restaurant, game rooms, a library and seminar area, an art gallery, a discotheque, and a health club. These functions made it possible to envision furnishing the various areas with different classics of Modern furniture in each area. From a financial point of view, the furniture program is interesting. My client stated that instead of having five hundred of the same chair, there might be fifty of ten different chair designs so that if the client ever needed to sell them, he would have smaller lots. In addition, that would give the

members a chance to sit in many different types of chairs. All this was the client's program. He gave me a three-page typed program—it was like getting a student problem in that it was basic—and it was accompanied with existing plans of the space. Most of what he said made good sense to me from a conceptual point of view. He didn't know exactly what furniture or furniture designers were important; that was where I came in. But I really couldn't get going on it until I saw the actual space, because it was so large.

So I went to Hong Kong and started to analyze the program in the space. The club was to be in an existing office building space. The whole organization is new. So I had to piece together the program and make definite decisions about how these spaces should interrelate. When you get into the interrelationships of spaces that you cannot perceive from any single place, that's planning.

There was no single motif for the entire project. Each part has its own, and the separate parts were then joined. For this project I had to make sure that the space was going to work and there was a logical sequence between one area and another. It all flows as a varied sequence of social activities, and that is what generated the plan.

Next in the design process was the question, How do I make each space special? That is what is wonderful about this project—that the spaces could be so different. In the nightclub we could do one thing—red lips for sofas and wire mesh fencing and black carpeting and spaghetti chairs in black and white, maybe even chandeliers hanging down over the tables. In the restaurant we could do something else; more elegant—rosewood and leather banquettes, green marble, Wilton carpeting, black leather Breuer chairs. The library has gray carpet, Aalto furniture in ash wood, some Hoffmann pieces; it has marble floors and glass columns. Each space becomes a separate world. And that is really what is nice about doing a public space like this: it is not the same as doing an apartment where someone must live. When you come home, you want reality; when you go out, you want a fantasy world.

[D'Urso has learned from his years in practice that designing is different when a designer works with clients who are starting from scratch, as opposed to those who have existing collections of things.] A lot of my clients have been people who were essentially starting new lives, visually certainly. And they said, in effect, "OK, that was my life before; now I want to start new and fresh." Something I was doing answered those needs. So we did new things. But while I was answering those needs, I was somehow turning off or not communicating with a lot of people who already had ideas about the kinds of things they loved. They immediately thought what I was doing with these other people was a rejection of working with given elements. I am also very interested in working with collections, be it art, objects, whatever. If a space is beautiful, I even could get just as much pleasure from arranging good things as from restructuring the space.

How does the consideration of materials affect your concepts? And at what stages?

Right away. When I think of a floor, I think about what it is going to be made out of—automatically. It may not end up that way. Lots of things change, but materials are considered from the beginning and all along the process. When any good designer is planning, he is thinking in terms of all the elements—what it will be made out of, whether it is going to be dark or light, whether the surface will be continuous or seamed, and so forth. That is where concentration comes in, because there are so many things to think about.

Is your list of design devices ticked off at some point, like a checklist?

You have them in your head all the time, and if you are concentrating and really tuned in, they all happen automatically. And they get in your head by constant observation of how they work in the work of others, throughout history, in other countries, and in your own work.

Do the different phases change or affect your concepts?

It can change enormously. And if one isn't careful, it can run away with you. Again, it depends on the scale. For example, with mechanical systems, if you haven't researched all of it enough, suddenly your entire space can change when the requirements of the system become clear to you. Mechanical systems are often primitive things that can change the design from what you wanted—if you are not careful to plan in advance with great care.

Is your design process different from what you envisioned it would be when you were a student?

I was completely involved when I was a student, and I think I still am. If you are interested in taking on big challenges, you are involved in the full process of design from your student days and throughout your professional life.

Do you have any additional advice for students of interior design?

Students should be aware of the different aspects of the field of interior design. Residential work and commercial design work are very different. And where you begin often affects the overall direction of a career. Some people get set on a particular track that they cannot get off, without knowing in advance that this is a commitment, or that there were other choices. So I think students should observe the field carefully and decide where they want to work, in which areas of design they want to work, before they accept their first jobs.

I believe that good interiors are deliberate, that they are done with intensity and thoughtfulness, with passion and conviction. Anyone can respond to someone who is doing something that is really well done, whether it is somebody playing tennis or doing an interior. You play with conviction and experience and with the opportunities to display what you can do.

David Easton

David Easton, of the New York firm Easton & La Rocca, designs residential interiors in the tradition of English eighteenth-century decorating.

Born in Louisville, Kentucky, Easton studied at Pratt Institute, where he earned a B.F.A. He worked with interior designer Valerian Rybar briefly, and then worked for about three years with Parish-Hadley and with furniture and interior designer Edward Wormley, one of the deans of interior design in the 1950s and 1960s.

He started his practice with Michael La Rocca in 1973. Almost exclusively devoted to residential work, his office currently is involved more and more with architecture and building as well as interior design. Of the twenty people on the staff of Easton & La Rocca, seven are architects, or have had architectural training. "The unique part of our office," Easton says, surrounded by Georgian library ladders and fragments of cornices and moldings, "is the combination of decorating and building."

How do your initial concepts first reveal themselves? As ideas, or as lines on paper?

A concept is an idea that leaps from your mind to the paper. A good many design problems and their solutions come out of dreams. I can be baffled at work about problems I have to resolve, can go home and fall asleep, and afterward, almost unthinkingly, the pencil flows and the design happens.

There are three parts of a design project. One is the client and the client's desires, which are spoken. The second is the site of the house to be built or the apartment to be gutted. And the third is the designer's own education, sensitivity, ability, and the knowledge that he brings to the project. This threesome—the problem, the client, and the designer—really must work together. How it comes out is the magic of it all.

It can mean doing the preliminary sketches on an airplane, coming back to the office and putting them into 1/4-inch elevations, then giving those to the drafting room so they can dimension the plans and send back elevations at 3/4-inch scale so that no details are overlooked. I try to draw everything from there on so that the doors from room to room line up, the flooring patterns work, the air-conditioning vent doesn't show, the electric outlets are at the right height, and so on. I never lose sight of the flow of rooms from one to another, as well as the flow of indoors to outdoors. In traditional work, that is hard to do.

If I design a Georgian house, the moldings are correct, the proportion is correct, the flooring and mantles are correct, and it is indeed a very traditional house. Our houses look as if they had been built fifty years ago. We sometimes try to use the color and fabric of a period—it depends on the sensibility of the client. But I do not like to re-create previously existing rooms. I don't like it when a room looks like a museum piece. For me, interior design has to have a playful manner.

Here, when a floor plan is first done, the furniture is on it. I don't draw a plan without the furniture. That is where the decorating experience comes in handy. The balance of the upholstered furniture placed in a room is important. I don't like it all clumped together. When the windows are designed, I know what the curtains are going to be like. All those things happen at the first plan. In the process of drawing, we consider these things as we draw.

Does the first plan resolve everything?

It doesn't resolve the elevations or a change in plane. But essentially when the first plan is done, the design is all conceived at that point. I am very plan-oriented.

Do you draw or sketch constantly? Daily?

The pleasure I get out of drawing those lines to create space is immensely satisfying to me. To me that is the 10 percent of the job that's fun. The thinking process is indelibly connected to the pencil, at every stage. Something exists in your head, but you've got to draw it to prove it.

[He sketches often, if not constantly. On trips, he draws details of things that catch his attention; he also sketches garden plans to teach himself about landscaping. For clients, as well as for his design staff, renderings of all the major rooms are prepared to explain what "the architecture" will look like. Renderings, he notes, are also helpful in the decorating phase so that "clients can really sense what they will be getting."

[For a house in Tulsa, Oklahoma, Easton recalls that the site and his associations with it brought about the concept. The site was a hill overlooking a golf course and its pond.] I began to think of the house up on its hill as a boat, reflected in the pond. I drew on the plane coming back from Tulsa, on some scraps of paper. Then I took it into myself for a while and came in on a weekend and drew. I had a few ideas that were drawn in 1/4-inch plans. I had a sense of doing a house that had a quietude to it, a house that was not going to be offensive to its neighbors. It had a flow coming from the driveway, an entry court, then big doors, and from this a plan started to unfold. It all came from that first sketch I made on the plane.

Is there a difference between working on interiors in existing buildings and working on newly created spaces?

There isn't as strong a main idea that carries through in renovation work. The ideas are smaller. Usually the apartments we are involved with are in very good buildings where people gut only the kitchen and master suite. The rooms do not require change in terms of scale and detail. They have been so well thought out that there is no reason to gut them.

Many of the same things apply in apartment renovation—the site, the client, the problem, and, of course, the background of the designer.

How does the consideration of materials affect your concept?

The materials you use in a job are really considered when you're drawing the plan. When I'm drawing a floor plan, I have an idea of what all the materials will be.

How do you consider and apply the standard design principles and devices?

They are an aspect that you work at while you are forming a plan. They are part of a designer's craft, and one learns more about them as one gets older. All the elements must be considered simultaneously. But balance and proportion do not come naturally. You may have an eye for it, but it takes a great deal of work. I feel that the 3/4-inch elevations are helpful in controlling all of those concerns, because at that scale you can really begin to tell what the balance of a room will be.

The assemblage aspect of decorating is important because it gives a sense of ease, but it must have an underlying discipline. In decorating there is more feeling and emotion. There is a certain time when you begin to play with a scheme; things happen that are accidental, that you couldn't think out. They just have to happen. It happens in shopping when you see something and you know it is right. Assembly gives softness to decorating.

Where does the client fit into this process?

At a certain point in the germination of a design, it all comes together. All of the ingredients are there—especially the rapport between the designer and the client, who feels secure in backing you. The best clients are those who have a strong, leading idea and who have the intelligence to explain it. So many times designers are very much like psychiatrists who have to drag it out of a client. But for the designer, there are wavelengths that tell him about his clients—the way they talk, the way they dress, the friends they have. All these things give some knowledge of how they think and live. This is a critical aspect in getting the problem solved.

Maybe you see things their way and maybe you don't. But clients approach designers differently. Some are on the phone day and night because they don't want to give the designer any freedom. Sometimes you get swept along into their way of doing things and don't recognize it. You listen to a client, but all the time are still trying to get your own way. Hopefully, you get together.

Clients let you do a lot more with architecture than with decorating. Most clients think they know what the leg of a chair looks like or the color on a wall, but most don't understand space—no matter how careful you are with models and renderings.

So with architecture you have an advantage. The best clients are the ones who have had some experience. They require less teaching and see more easily what the designer wants to do.

What is the influence of the designer's background on the concept?

So many elements go into the makeup of a human being—physical and mental state of mind, receptiveness, where you come from, your family, education, and interests. It is a matter of the individual and his sensitivity to his surroundings, the matter of how you were brought up, how bright you are, and that certain sensitivity to life. Sensitivity is an important gift. Being brought up right and being bright don't necessarily give you the sensitivity you need.

My love of history and architecture has come from growing up in a very nice environment. And all of those things were important to me because they were a reference point for me to look back on. My liberal arts courses were important, I read Milton and learned Latin. My history courses opened my eyes. These experiences train and enrich the mind and are a point of reference. I have no respect for anyone who doesn't have a good grounding in a complete design education, including the disciplines of architecture and decorating and a thorough understanding of history. No one can design a good modern building unless they are rich inside.

When I taught interior design, I used to tell my students that studying history was like looking at a picture or seeing a movie or reading. All of this experience was being poured into oneself, and the creativity comes after all of this, when that mind controls the pencil and puts it on paper. Some of the students had to be pulled along so far because they had never had any experience. Yet how one got that experience was simply luck.

Can experience be equated with taste?

The word "taste" can be defined; it exists. Some of it is innate in people and some of it is trained. But it is something that helps define the line on a piece of paper. I always told my students to get themselves a big 6B pencil, because it flowed better on paper as the thought processes came out.

Do you have any additional advice to give to students of interior design?

Experience and taste cannot be left solely to luck and background. Students must strive to enlarge their spheres of reference and experience. An immense amount of discipline goes into what is done—more so in architecture than decorating. All of the education possible is of no value unless there is some discipline behind it. Discipline is the most important factor in the success of a job that has turned out well. You have to have a lot of it just to do the work—disregarding aesthetics and creativity. It is an immense part of a creative person.

Discipline can come from the fear of something not being right, fear of losing control of a job. I feel hurt when I walk into a job and see a design element that should have been done another way. I feel even worse if it is from a lack of attention on my part. You have got to control the job. There is so much detail involved. The

site, the people, the place, all filter through me, to create a design, although along the line it is affected by other people.

Michael Graves

One of the most versatile designers of our day, Michael Graves has designed houses, showrooms, furniture, textiles, and major civic and government buildings. His series of eight showrooms for the Sunar furniture and textile line and his products for that firm burst on the design scene just as he received his first major commissions as architect of public buildings. The Portland Building for the city of Portland, Oregon, has been one of the most discussed buildings of the 1980s.

Graves was born in Indianapolis, Indiana, and is a graduate of the University of Cincinnati and Harvard schools of architecture. He subsequently spent two years in Rome as a winner of the Prix de Rome before going to teach at Princeton, where he has lived and worked since 1962.

He describes the design procedure of his office as "very orthodox." As he outlines it, "I design the piece, whatever it is, not through schematics, but I make a sketch or series of sketches. Then I instruct somebody in the office on what to do in terms of the development of that concept into drawings. From that point on, I act as a critic, except for the major buildings, such as the one for the hospital services firm Humana. On a design like that the cycle will continue and continue, and I will get back into the project in a major way every month or so and spend a full week or so drawing. Then somebody else in the office will carry it forward for three weeks and do supplementary drawings. If there are problems, meantime, or consultations required with the engineers or others, or if something has to be redone, I do it."

How do your initial concepts reveal or express themselves? As ideas, or as lines on paper?

Always through drawings. That is the only way you can do it. I draw what I contend to be the thing or the series of drawings that lead to the scheme. I do many, many sketches that are pretty much finished.

[Graves developed his freehand drawing and sketching skills while he was a student at the American Acad-

emy in Rome. As he tells it, every day the other academicians would go to their studios and the composer would compose, the painter would paint, and the writer would write. But what, he thought, was he the architect to do without a client? He decided to go through Rome drawing as much as he could, especially the work of Borromini, which interested him.]

Then I started to recognize that it was not just the strength of the drawings that was important to me, but the act of making something; that the aesthetic involved in a particular event or artifact could be extant in the way it was described, whether in built form or in drawing or in words. A drawing does not duplicate a building. A drawing is a drawing. They don't necessarily imitate each other. But they have embodied in each other a way of looking or a way of understanding, a way of walking through, a way of perceiving. A drawing can be a tool for making a building, but its primary means of usefulness is one of a conceptual ambition.

I don't know how you do architecture without drawing. I think and have an intention when I draw. I cannot draw blindly. But when I have an intention, it is backed by other drawings and other observations. Almost everyone looks at pictures, but you are not copying pictures when you draw, you have images in memory. And you use those; they are brought up when you write something or when you draw something. So I draw and, as I have said, I don't know how to do architecture without drawing.

I externalize those images in memory as quickly as possible. If somebody says "design a chair," I am going to remember all the chairs I know of that have been designed and are appropriate to the particular issue.

Would you discuss the value of background and education in relation to "images in memory"?

It is curious that one would have to ask about that because for four thousand years one did not ask that question. But from the time of Walter Gropius at Harvard, we have had to ask that question because we have burned the books. So if a student says to me, "What should I do to prepare to be an architect?" all I can say is "Get smart. And read, and look and look and look, and read." So you get yourself to a library and look at those things that Gropius didn't want us to look at because he wanted to start from ground zero. For him every problem was a new problem. Well, for me it just isn't. The cultural background comes through—the culture of architecture, the culture of design and of making things. And looking at those things, recording them in one way or another, is the way for me. When I sit at the library, which I do pretty frequently, I will take my sketchbook and draw from what I see. Whether it is something I read or something I look at. And I am not just copying out a chair; I am looking at it to remember it by virtue of recording it graphically.

The concept is influenced by what you have available to you. In our office we work by type—type of scheme, type of materials, a centralized room versus a peripheral condition. These are all the things that Durand would teach us—the types of elements, how they influence what is active and static in an interior, the room versus the hall. [J. N. L. Durand, the nineteenth-century French architectural theorist, analyzed building types and their compositional forms in such books as *An Accounting of Ancient and Modern Buildings of All Types*.]

The concept is also influenced by what you have available to you. In the gypsum-board world of the Sunar showrooms, for instance, we leave 10 percent of our budget for what we call hot-rodding—decoration—at the end. And that helps. What you can do after the form of a room has been made is decorate. And that is about all you can do. You can paint. You can embellish. That is ultimately what gives the room its character, beyond the light and shade of that space.

Showrooms such as the Sunar showrooms are like little museums. Our effort is to get whoever it is that comes there to look at something and buy it. Another aim is to make a circulation route through the whole showroom and back out again in a path that won't repeat itself—a loop of some sort. And for the people who work there every day, another path is required. We locate work spaces for some of these employees in the showroom area. This is a symbolic function. It is a symbol of seeing things in their settings—settings that we have made for them with a variety of lighting and furniture arrangement.

[After determining such functional requirements of the program, Graves then "makes a *parti*." In line with his historical leaning he uses the French terminology of Beaux-Arts training.] A plan is like the musical score of a work. The plan is the score because it is the diagram of the intentions. I don't draw a perspective of the best or biggest or most important room. I draw a plan and the plan organization—the way its hierarchies work. That plan ought to elicit from our thoughts the descriptions of what is the most important, what is secondary, what is public, what is private, what is movement, what is rest. All of those things should come clear from the plan description.

Now that is often hard for a Modern architect to understand, because he is used to making a homogeneous world where everything is space, where there are wall divisions but where there are no names for the spaces anymore. There is just a flowing void. In fact Frank Lloyd Wright, Walter Gropius, and even Le Corbusier, with his free-plan concept, said, "Let's blow the walls down. Let's let the light and air into these dark, dank interiors." And they found a variety of technical means to do that—glass walls and free open space. But they lost a lot. They lost the divisions that gave us privacy, that gave us hierarchy, that allowed us to know one place from another, to have an intimate conversation in a room appropriate to five people rather than a room ten times that large. If we had all the walls down, would it be better? Not necessarily. I want to have the character of my bedroom different from my kitchen.

Can you elaborate on the distinction you make between the words "space" and "room"?

Rooms are all we have. Space is within the room. In the Modernists' theory, space became a concept that supplanted room. But space is just this void stuff here, and a room can have lots of it or little of it. Without the room I have no walls, and without the walls I'm a dead duck in terms of being an architect. If you don't need to enclose space, you don't need architects.

[The plan is the generator, as Le Corbusier called it, of Michael Graves's concepts. The plan does not yet take the concept into the third dimension, however.] People might say, "Why don't you draw a perspective to know what the room is going to look like?" And when I was in school, people would suggest drawing the image of the room or the building first, then drawing a plan. But I cannot draw a perspective without knowing what the plan is, the hierarchy of the whole plan, in which more than one room is considered—a society of rooms. It is important that the plan suggest the three-dimensional proposition. The two-dimensional diagram of the plan should be able to suggest the three-dimensional possibilities.

The intelligence of the interior or of the building relates to the plan. The emotion seems to me to relate to the vertical dimension, those things that we understand anthropomorphically. When we stand face to face with a wall, with the vertical surface, we see differently from the way we see the abstraction of the plan. One is down and horizontal, and the other is face to face with us. The plan is the intelligence because it is the outline, the scoring, the diagram of the dimensions. It is certainly not done out of emotion. A different kind of intelligence is used in describing the hierarchical relationships and the privacy levels than is used in describing the character of a room. So the activity of doing a plan is intellectual, as an activity. It is already abstract by nature. Then when you have eye contact, as you look across the room, the plan has been cast in perspective.

How do you preserve a concept by doing and by not doing things that are requirements of the program?

I don't preserve it. It gets modified all the time. It starts out as a diagram and proceeds to something that is modifiable rather than to something that is ever fixed. How much it is malleable is really the question. When do you throw it out? Do you start over? We do modify concepts; we start over rarely. We do not say, "This is the way it has to be." In practice you have got to be able to change. I often like that because I get a chance to design something else. If this doesn't work or the client doesn't like it, you do it again. It gets boring if you do it again and again; and you are never going to satisfy the kind of person that asks for that to be done. Usually we are the ones making the modifications, because it is not working for us, it is not working architecturally.

What is the contribution of clients to this process?

There are certain things the client knows best about and certain things that the designer knows best about. The client presumably knows what he wants and what he can and cannot do, and what he can afford. He brings those intentions and aspirations to the table. The designer brings a professional expertise to the table. If you haven't satisfied him after making the drawings and presenting the work, then you try again. But at the same time you are using persuasive means to describe why you are doing something. And these persuasive means not only come through drawings (which are difficult for anybody to read, let alone laymen), but through stories and verbalizing what you have drawn and what you think. No, we don't say, "We're going to do it our way or you don't do it." There are things that are more dear to you than others and there are things you struggle with. Ultimately, if it's not going to work for that client, it's never going to work.

Is there a difference between working on interiors in existing buildings and working on newly created interiors?

There is not a lot of difference for me in the general framework. There are local conditions that always influence me. Any project you work on has general ideas about it; they deal with one's experience in design and architecture and with one's intelligence in employing that experience and knowledge. There are also local ideas—whether it is a regional characteristic that one is implying or it is a particular interest of a client or a local material or adjacent building.

[Graves distinguishes the general characteristics of his own house from its particular characteristics. The house was built in Princeton, New Jersey, in 1926 by Italian craftsmen who came to work as masons on the university dormitories. And at the same time they built the house that Graves now owns. It is built in an Italian Tuscan style and looks, Graves says,] more like a farmhouse or a warehouse. The particular is all the stuff that is brought to it by those characteristics of its origins. The generals are the things you bring to any project, the intelligence you bring—your knowledge, your memories, your interests, your ability to make a plan. And the program is a little of both, usually. Is your house really going to be dramatically different from mine in the end? But if you have a collection of books and the next guy has not, you have a particular attitude about your library that he won't care about. And that becomes a particular.

I always consider the context, whether it is new or old. [He explains this statement in relation to his designs for the Sunar showrooms, which are always inside only.] We've hardly gotten out into the hall. It matters a lot less there to relate the design to Chicago or Dallas or anything. There might be some quotations in the plan or organization that are not terribly important. Instead, the context is the Sunar products that are on the site or the height of the ceilings.

Is there a difference in this process between work for public projects and for private clients?

One of them is a personal process and the other is a political one. When you are designing a building for a city in a democratic society, you must present your ideas to the city council or the mayor or various civic bodies that represent the city's well-being. You do the same thing with a private client, except it is a lot simpler. There you have only a couple of people to describe your work to; in a city organization you sometimes have one body of overseers disagreeing with another body—and not necessarily with you. So you may have to act as a mediator, for instance, between the city planning commission and the design review board. And that gets difficult. But you know that going in. A new administration can change the whole purpose of a building or an interior. And if you don't want to participate in that, you shouldn't do it, because it isn't easy.

How does the consideration of materials affect your concepts? And at what stages?

To some extent, materials do affect the concept and the process. In our Humana building, where the material is granite, it affects how we are thinking about thicknesses. In the Sunar showrooms, where everything is of gypsum board, and where it is not enough just to paint it, we textured it and made allusions to other materials without imitating them. We call it "ragging"; it is an old tradition.

Is one factor consistently more critical—the budget, the time, the mechanical system, the plan, or something else?

[Graves says that all the problems are more or less manageable, that a designer knows going into a project all the potential difficulties of mechanical systems and other factors]—except for the budget, and that probably is the greatest influence on a scheme.

How do the different sizes of projects affect your methodology?

They make it slightly longer. They don't affect the method.

How do you consider and apply the design principles and devices?

Classically.

Do you seek consistency in your design methodology?

It is a very strong plan of action, but it doesn't modify it very much. It is orthodox. One makes a plan; one makes perspectives and turns the plan into its vertical dimension; one builds models. All that time you are meeting with the client to show what you are doing. All of that is very orthodox, I think. But I don't bring the work back for my lieutenants to do; I do the design myself.

Do you consider your procedure the same as you thought it was when you were a student?

The process is very much the way I went about it when I was in school, except that in my early days of practice I did it all. Next it was a two-person office, then four. And now we are fifty.

Terrific!

I'm not so sure about that.

Do you have any additional advice to give to students of interior design?

Get smart. Know the literature. Get to the library. And draw, draw, draw.

ISD Inc.: Kenneth E. Johnson, Louis M. S. Beal, Joseph L. Rosen, Michael Pinto, and J. Harrison Lassiter

With offices in Chicago, New York, and Houston, the 130-person ISD Inc. is one of the country's largest space-planning and interior design firms. The organization was founded in 1960 as an interior design affiliate of a national architecture firm. Since 1973 ISD has operated as an independent corporation owned by its ten principals. Among them are Kenneth E. Johnson, president, headquartered at the Chicago office; Louis M. S. Beal, exec-

utive vice president, based at the New York office; Joseph L. Rosen, vice president in charge of planning and design at the New York office; Michael Pinto, vice president and chief operating officer, based in the Houston office; and J. Harrison Lassiter, vice president of marketing out of New York.

Kenneth E. Johnson is a graduate of the University of Nebraska in 1952. He worked first with architects Perkins & Will, then with Harry Weese & Associates, where he established the firm's interior design department. He joined ISD in 1961 as director of the Chicago office, became vice president in charge of the Chicago office in 1962, and president of the firm in 1967.

Louis M. S. Beal was educated at Harvard's Graduate School of Design, where he studied architecture under Walter Gropius. He then attended the Rhode Island School of Design, where he received his bachelor's degree in interior design. He first worked with Florence Knoll in the Knoll Planning Unit, then with Designs For Business. He joined ISD in 1961, was named vice president in charge of the New York office the following year, and was appointed executive vice president in 1967.

Joseph L. Rosen is a graduate of Pratt Institute with a B.F.A. in interior design. He joined ISD in 1968 and was made an associate in 1974, and vice president of the firm in 1979.

Among the interior design projects that ISD has been recognized for are office planning and design for major corporations; banks and other financial institutions; educational institutions; hotels, clubs, and restaurants; government and health care facilities; and one hundred major law firms. ISD has also been involved with some product design.

The most prominent of the firm's projects include interiors for the AT&T Building in New York City; the headquarters for PPG in Pittsburgh; the Chicago Mercantile Exchange; Boston City Hall; Heublein; Xerox Corporation; Mitchell Energy and Development Corporation; Vinson & Elkins; and international work in London and the Middle East. ISD has provided service to a number of leading architects, including Edward Larrabee Barnes, Marcel Breuer Associates, Johnson/Burgee, and Kallman, McKinnell & Wood.

In addition to space planning, ISD's services include selection, design, and specification of furniture, furnishings, and equipment; preparation of construction drawings and specifications; site observation, contract document administration, and coordination during project construction and installation. ISD also provides space programming and utilization studies, lease consultation for tenants, and exterior and interior signage. The firm works with building owners, leasing agents, and brokers in preparing space layouts and feasibility studies for prospective tenants. This broadly outlined view of services leads the partners' discussion of design methodology into somewhat different areas from many other interior design firms.

How do your initial concepts reveal or express themselves? As ideas, or as lines on paper?

Louis Beal: ISD works in a five-phase format, which is divided into program definition, schematic design, design development, contract documents, and contract administration. A principal is always in charge of a project and works with a project manager and the necessary designers and draftsmen. Sometimes the project manager and the project designer are one and the same, depending on the size and nature of the project.

[ISD communicates from office to office: There is an exchange of documents so that each office can see the solutions made to every project by other offices. If there is a traditional job, Beal or Rosen might be called in to consult. If there is a complicated programming phase, Michael Pinto and the Houston office may be called in for consultation.]

Michael Pinto: Conceptual or schematic designs are expressed in broad terms, since the time allocated to this phase of the design process usually represents no more than 10 percent of the total fee. [Consequently, ISD's initial concepts aim to] focus on an overview that will express the idea of how the project will function, what it will look and feel like, and how much it will cost. Within this broad outline, ISD conceptual design aims to include the plan; three-dimensional design thoughts including lighting; interior construction standards; colors and materials; furniture forms; art/accessories, plants, and signage; as well as probable costs/budgets.

ISD's background literature: The first step to be taken upon the client's acceptance of what ISD designers submit as the "project requirement" is to develop the necessary Block Plans or Stacking Diagrams that indicate how the client's functions will be situated in relation to one another within the space to be occupied. In developing these plans, consideration should be given to the stated adjacency requirements, in relation to the unique features that the architecture housing the client's functions provides. Views, floor sizes, bay spacing, core-to-window wall dimensions, service systems such as freight elevators, circulation patterns determined by core configurations and fire codes all will impact upon the placement of a client's function, and should be studied in order to provide for the best marriage of stated need to building architecture.

What is the contribution of the client to the design process?

Beal: Determining the scope of the project, the schedule, and budget has a great bearing on the concept. These questions are the ones that clients seem to have prime concern with.

Harrison Lassiter: This is what our marketing operation uses as a basis for its contract arrangements.

Beal: For us, the building has a tremendous bearing on it, particularly owner-occupied buildings. The building certainly establishes the concepts of layout.

Kenneth Johnson: We have seen an increasing sophistication in the design process from the 1950s to now. The changing organization of the client's team has affected that process considerably. In the Fifties we were more often than not dealing with a corporate purchasing agent, who was used to working with furniture dealers and major stores. A few of those stores had large departments that did contract design work, but were really acting as dealers. Now we have got up the ladder in the corporation to working with the vice president of finance or the facilities manager, which many corporations did not have back in the Fifties.

Beal: The facilities manager usually has nothing to do with aesthetics; he concentrates on bodies and numbers, people and amounts of space and money. It is usually the chief executive officer and the marketing people who have the image and aesthetics in mind.

Johnson: We have increasingly seen clients, including developers, come in early enough so that they can modify the core of a building—so they can change the dimension from the core to the window wall to make a more plannable space. In one project, for example, we were able to increase that dimension by 5 feet. And it happened to be the space that had the best view—so that it could accommodate the conference room, the reception room, and the key executive offices.

Joseph Rosen: When we have our initial meeting with a client, we try to glean as much information as possible about the way the operation functions and about the image that client wants.

Beal: This is the programming phase. We draw out of our clients a program, and we are able to put down in writing what they want and need—in numbers and facts. In order to be a good designer you have to articulate what you are doing. Then the aesthetic aspects are considered in a way that relates to these requirements of the client.

[ISD distinguishes two levels of design. First, the organizational structure of the client's organization as a committee or department. Such departments are equipped to deal with interior design needs and to represent management. Second, the designer's design team with their interest in spatial plasticity.] Plasticity is limited by the relation of the core to the perimeter wall, by ceiling heights, and by budget constraints.

We have gotten into writing programs before a client has any building in mind because we find that often a project is too far along to permit us to come up with a concept for what that client needs or wants. A building may establish a concept before a designer has had any input. And a designer can be caught between the require-

ments of the client and the limitations of the building. So we try to get involved in projects before clients have signed a lease and before they have hired a design team. Then we can make programming reports or building analyses for clients. Such reports determine what is the most suitable building. And this can have as much to do with what the concept of the interior should be for the occupants, as much as such physical restraints as square footage or amenities of any kind.

Rosen: The initial concept for AT&T was first expressed as an idea about how people would work there. When we were called in by the architects, Johnson/Burgee, they had shaped the building and gotten the directors to approve the general concept of the building. The architects had already generated a concept that included a dropped ceiling grid. From then on we worked together hand in hand. We all agreed what the potential of that ceiling could be—and we had a team of consultants working with us; it was an opportunity of working together to develop the concept.

For PPG's headquarters building in Pittsburgh, also by Johnson/Burgee, we were called in at a later stage than at AT&T, this time by the client. So the procedure on PPG was totally different. ISD developed a module for the PPG interior, and after several studies we were able to change the overall proportion slightly so that it worked to the functional advantage of the interior. We were brought in as interior architects when the systems of the building had already been created by the architects—the ceiling system, the partition system, the general lighting concept. As we got into it we were responsible for the total programming of the building, its projected requirements through 1995.

Beal: Other concepts come about from visiting and inventorying existing spaces. It is a psychological process that proceeds as you are interviewing people, seeing where they presently work. And this gives clues—perhaps negative—which may be completely contrary to what they are envisioning.

Rosen: The educational process is consuming. Because a good many corporate clients have been through this process before, they consider themselves "professional clients." And the professional client can be more difficult to work with than one who has never gone through the process, because they know too much and not enough. [That depends on their sphere of attention and interest, however.] Some facilities managers are concerned only about reordering desks and rearranging them; others have the broader vision of the chairman of the board. The best jobs are those where the chief executive takes an interest and spends time with his designers. The best procedure is to have direct contact with whoever is the real client, namely, the chief executive officer.

One of the key things on any major project today is that you must ask questions at the very beginning as to what budget you have to work with, so that you as a responsible professional are working within a real framework. It is not responsive to have grandiose ideas and go to a client with a concept that the client cannot afford.

Lassiter: To be able to establish in the mind of the client the influence that budget has on the project is part of ISD's early marketing strategy.

What is the effect of corporate office standards on your concepts?

Rosen: All major corporations today have office standards. They define the number of square feet each individual has at his level in the organization. Such standards developed during the office boom in the 1950s, when compartmentalization and the detailed consideration of who-gets-what developed. It developed along with the modular concept of designing offices, wherein each person, according to position in the corporate hierarchy, got so many square feet, so many ceiling tiles, and so many floor tiles. In some respects, architects forced this sense of standardization. And developers found that the modular concept was the least expensive way to put up a building. More and more today, however, everyone is trying to reverse that and to create a more personal sense of identity.

Johnson: Interiors are now also considered an inducement that clients can offer to lure better-qualified personnel.

[This discussion points out that sometimes sizes get set because of money and sometimes they get set because of function or aesthetics. They do not get set the same way all the time.]

Rosen: I would like to think sizes get set in relation to what the person will be doing, not because of other factors.

Beal: But most of the time they are already set if you are not in on the project early enough.

Rosen: The designer's penetration is set by the architecture. You have only so many columns and moldings you can attach things to. The rhythm is starting, it is rolling. What we try to do is to take a look at that rhythm and see how we can break it and still give a sense of identity.

How do you develop a concept further?

ISD's background literature: Upon acceptance of the Block Plans and/or Stacking Diagrams, the next step is to refine the Block Plans into Space Plans. These can be no more than a single line representation of a refinement to the Block Plans. It should serve to indicate to the client how the groups located on the Block Plan break down into

office and auxiliary space, and how circulation from one to another will occur. As one develops the Space Plans, consideration must be given to three-dimensional form, since the Space Plans must respond not only to functional relationships, but also to aesthetic ones. The molding of these forms, the balance of solids to voids, and the creation of the spatial statement all take place at this time, and more than any one thing, is the point upon which the design will or will not have visual clarity.

Beal: In offices, the concept is established by the sheets of paper that have to be filed—legal, letter, ledger, or computer size. That means you need so many cubic feet of storage, or you need the machine that prints on the paper, and you must provide certain dimensions for each machine that is used. Everything is analyzed in terms of space, whether it takes up floor space, tabletop space, storage space, drawer space, cubic space.

Johnson: It is all designed from the inside out. [All that is a part of a corporate designer's assimilated craft. Instead of thinking about symmetry and balance, ISD designers think about the physical accommodation of paper, machines, furniture, people, tasks, lighting, and storage. Then they go on to think about larger spaces for group encounters—conferences, reception, and so forth—that must reflect an image. These become the building blocks that build up the lines on the paper. These are the raw materials of ISD's office design—analogous to bricks and mortar. In many ways, ISD's work is accommodation of these factors.]

Beal: A good plan is like a three-dimensional organization chart. It gives you an initial point of view about adjacencies and can help you see how to stack the spaces vertically. These increments become the larger building blocks. For a hospital, the same applies: There are bed sizes, equipment sizes, and multiples of these. In a law firm the blocks are offices for partners, senior partners, retired partners, associates. For each type of project, then, one of the early questions is, What is the ideal floor size? given no already established site or building configuration. Next there is the consideration of flexibility.

Is there a difference between designing for private clients and public projects?

Rosen: In government and hospital work, the time from concepts to construction is so long that concepts get lost. New programs start to take over; new equipment comes to light; and the rooms of the original concept do not work for what they were planned for. That is not a satisfying design process for us.

Johnson: In the Sixties we did a lot of school work. Later in the Sixties banks came out from behind their teller cages, and we changed a great number of banks. Now, more recently, law firms are upgrading their interiors. You have to change your thinking when you are considering the budget of a law firm in comparison with the bare-bones budget of most school work. In the Sixties, for example, we knew that students were running around barefoot and would put their feet up on the upholstery; you don't find that with the legal profession.

Designing for a law firm, where there are more private offices, is very different from planning for an insurance company—where you are inclined to find a field of desks for the transfer of paper work as one of the main processes.

Rosen: Arriving at a concept for a hospital is not much different from the process of conceptualizing an office. Your concepts develop as you are doing your plan. When you design, you are designing three-dimensionally as you do your space plan. The one element that really sets the way of your planning is the program, which you take a hard look at when you start drawing.

[In the case of ISD's designs for PPG in Pittsburgh, after the planning was in progress for two years, the project was stopped because of economic reorganization. Several floors were cut from the structure, and the entire building had to be replanned. But this does not always have a negative effect: A law firm that ISD had planned six floors for decided, after the drawings were complete, that they wanted to take eleven floors. So the designers had the luxury of feeling that they were spreading out. "But the concept did not change," Rosen notes, "it only meant more development of the concept for a larger space. Often such a change gives more time to study our concepts and to come up with refinements that make them better. Sometimes schedules don't allow you enough time on your concepts." ISD feels that the effect of the reorganizations at AT&T and PPG made ISD's refinements better.]

Is there a difference between working on interiors in existing buildings and working on newly created spaces?

Rosen: Yes, because existing buildings can provide more of a concept than new ones. They are also more restrictive and at the same time more helpful.

[In their New York offices, the existing midtown industrial loft structure essentially fixed ISD's concept. The attitudes of the day, which in this case tended to respect "the existing," also had a strong influence on this concept. In previous decades the goal of "tidying it all up" rather than leaving it all exposed clearly created other design concepts. The matter of the mindset or attitudinal approach of each generation, period, or idiom can influence a design concept as much as site conditions.]

How does the consideration of materials affect your concepts?

Beal: Since the budgets for interiors invariably get cut as the costs of buildings rise, we try to keep a safeguard. We try to show our clients that in cutting the costs of things they are diluting the concept. It is a constant vigil on our part to preserve the quality and the concept, from the beginning to the end, to the completion of the art program and the planning of accessories and maintenance. If the concept is not maintained, the design can fall apart. It is a constant dialogue of educating and communicating with the client all the time.

Do you have any additional advice for students of interior design?

Beal: Students have to have what the profession as a whole needs. Designing from the individual user's point of view—what the individual's requirements are, what the occupants' requirements are—is the true goal. It is the people who are going to occupy and work in a building that are important. A building has to work for the occupants, and unless the building works for them it is not a successful building. Designing is working with people. It is a personal thing. You solve personal problems for people.

The best work results from a cooperative, not competitive attitude among the design team members. The best work also requires a respect for the fact that the client is going to occupy the space, not the architect or the interior designer. It is not the designer's project; it is the client's project.

George Nelson

One of the truly innovative furniture designers of this century, George Nelson has also designed interiors, exhibitions, products, graphics, and architecture. Among his furniture innovations are the L-shaped desk, the Storagewall concept, the pole-supported shelf system, and whole systems of furniture.

Born in Hartford, Connecticut, in 1908, George Nelson is a graduate of Yale College and the Yale School of Fine Arts in 1931; he studied architecture at Catholic University in Washington, D.C.; and the next year won the Prix de Rome in architecture. For the next two years he studied at the American Academy in Rome, and traveled throughout Europe. In 1934 he returned to the United States to become associate editor and, later, managing editor of *Architectural Forum*.

During this time he worked as both architect and author, collaborating with Henry Wright on the book *Tomorrow's House* (1945), in which they put forward the concept for Storagewall. In 1947 he left magazine work, opened his own office, and soon began designing furniture for Herman Miller Inc.

As design director of Herman Miller in the late 1940s, Nelson was instrumental in that firm's collaboration with both Charles Eames and Alexander Girard, two of the other geniuses of American furniture and interior design at mid-century. These three designers as a team made Herman Miller the leading design development laboratory of American furniture.

Besides his work as furniture designer and interior designer, his practice has brought him the architecture of houses and commercial and institutional buildings. With his sharp turns of phrase and of mind, with his wry and irreverent wit, he has produced five books, including *How to See* and *George Nelson on Design*, as well as numerous articles. In all can be seen the work of a mind that focuses neither on word nor line, form nor shape, nor on single items, but rather on overall systems. His furniture especially reveals his focus on systems of use, systems of manufacture (including storage and distribution), and above all systems of analysis—what he calls, with characteristic directness, "thinking."

How do your initial concepts reveal or express themselves? As ideas, or as lines on paper?

Most people think that anything is a concept—any notion. They think if you make it pink, that's a concept. But it is not. [He hesitates, saying that he does not know how to help students with this question.] I believe that this side of society doesn't have the faintest idea of what it is to think a thought. Some people are more talented than others, and there's not much anybody can do about that. But a lot has to do with preparation. For instance, if you can't read and write, there are certain disadvantages that you must try to get around. Students dealing with the problems of interiors have to learn the rudiments of their trade. In some schools they learn this. Then they have to learn something else that is extremely difficult, which is that it is not enough to copy the cover photo from some publication.

One of the problems a student has is to figure out how to tackle a problem like an interior. Inevitably, what they do is run to appetizing sources—furniture catalogues, magazines—and this is not new in our time. Then at that time they have to think—and nobody has ever taught them what thinking is, and they don't seem to have enough curiosity to learn on their own. A concept comes from thinking—and a lucky inspiration.

I have had occasion to learn a lot about thinking. I had six or seven years of Latin, which in those days you took for granted as what you were supposed to do. I happened to love it, so it was no problem.

How did you arrive at the concept for Storagewall?

It was anything but obvious until it happened. The process whereby you set up a problem so you can deal with it is not mysterious, however. I was working on *Tomorrow's House* with Henry Wright, in particular on the chapter about storage. We knew from our experience that at the top of every survey list was "Not enough closet space," so Henry and I thought deeply about this. We asked, "What is a closet? What other kind of storage is there?" We knew that a kind of "possessions explosion" had gotten under way and that people were buying all kinds of stuff they had never bought before. Naturally, they had to keep this stuff somewhere. And since most people live in old houses, the only place to store it was either in a bookcase in the library, which wasn't very good, or in closets, or in the garage. We continued our researches and recognized that there was a vast category of stuff that was left over, all of which could fit in a 10- or 12-inch-deep space.

So we had done all our research and, like a lot of people who are on the verge of a creative breakthrough, we were frustrated. We couldn't state the problem quite sharply enough, but we knew that something was wrong. I remember going into my office and throwing myself into a chair, nervous and frustrated. And as I stared at the wall, for no reason that I can recall, I asked myself what was inside that wall. And my answer was, "air space." And the next thought was, "If you expanded the amount of air, which is what storage is before you use it, just thicken any wall or partition in any part of the house on both sides by 3 inches (which would not be noticed by the occupants), then you'd get hundreds of feet of storage for all the stuff we hadn't been able to find a place for." In a split second the whole Storagewall concept presented itself—a double-sided partition-wall that incorporated storage space. It was like shooting off an electronic flash or something. And soon a great many architects were writing "Storagewall" on their plans. We had distinguished 24-inch-deep closet space from 10- to 12-inch Storagewall space. Well, that's how that one happened.

But it wouldn't have happened if we hadn't done our homework, and it wouldn't have happened if we had not been blocked. What is missing with most designers is that they don't do their homework; therefore they don't have a chance to get frustrated; therefore they're not goaded into letting the problem, somehow, present itself in a light that is more manageable and simple.

Most designers, when you talk to them, don't know what you're talking about if you mention frustration, being blocked or stepping back. They think you're conning them, or they reject it because it is so much work. That is the three-word phrase I hear most often, "so much work." So, needless to say, they wallow around drooling with envy over the people that make it, and whose work they copy from the magazines. But it never occurs to them to emulate the simplest thing that those people do—which is their homework.

How is it that, since your college days, you have so often seen what the real problem is and how it should be solved afresh—always cutting through to something new, instead of accepting the traditional modes?

The idea never got to me that the truth was really a fixed quantity and not something subject to respectful investigation. The idea that there was any immorality in questioning the status quo never got to me. So this habit of asking questions, which I think any kid is born with, probably was constantly encouraged in me. [And that

inquiry, he indicates, is what creates concepts in design.]

I certainly wasn't unique. People have had creative ideas back to Archimedes—like to what extent the gold in the king's crown was adulterated with silver. If he weighed it, he got a composite weight. Nobody could measure a crown. So he got into his bathtub one day for the ten-thousandth time, frustrated, and he noticed that the water went up, which he'd missed every other time he'd ever gotten into the tub. And this time he saw it, so he thought, "Well, my body is an irregular shape and you certainly can't measure a body because there are too many bumps." So he discovered the principle of displacement. So he put the crown in a bucket of water and poured off the overflow and was given the volume of the crown. And since he knew what a cubic weight of gold was, the problem was solved. That was when he yelled out "Eureka!"

"Eureka" was a profoundly accurate statement. Eureka doesn't mean "I did it," but "I found it." The creative breakthrough is usually not a "doing."

How did you develop the concept for the L-shaped desk?

The furniture industry standard had been that a desk consisted of a box, usually with some legs, and the box consisted of two pedestals, which were an integral part of the whole structure. The only dimension you really had to worry about much was the space where one's legs fit under the desk. Because if you had a drawer in here, you had to be pretty much sure you could cross your legs underneath.

Well, we said, that's all very well, it will work for a lot of desks and it will no doubt continue. But a lot of work goes on in offices these days where you've got a secretary or somebody who is working at a typewriter, and we knew that the proper height for a typewriter was somewhat lower than the proper height for a desk. So we said, goodness, if we put the chair on a swivel so that it can be pointed this way to do desk work and telephoning and then can be pointed that way to do all the typing, the secretary can really swing around. And you can put a little storage under the typewriter as well. That was really the ancestor of the modern office workstation.

Once we had broken up the desk into these two components, it followed that we could break it up into all sorts of components. So this was the first step that made all the other steps easier.

[Nelson's concepts often came from technological possibilities. His bubble lamps derived from the technology of mothballing World War II Liberty Ships—spinning cocoons of plastic around them. His Marshmallow Sofa derived from the largest piece of self-skinning foam-plastic then available, though it ultimately had to be produced by hand-tailoring instead.]

Do you draw constantly? Daily?

Yes, designers and architects talk to each other with pencils. Supposedly you're thinking while you are drawing. [In the case of the L-shaped desk drawings, Nelson produced a sketch and turned it over to the drafting room.] And at this point as soon as the guy saw what I had doodled, he saw the difference in height that was needed and said he could do it like that. We had some inordinately talented designers then—Irving Harper, Ron Beckman, and others.

So it is all thinking?

I think so. It is also feeling, which is another kind of thinking, I imagine.

Is designing different from assembling?

Designing is a process by which an idea gets to be a tangible reality. At some point a kid building a sandcastle or some great craftsman building a ravishing cup has an idea as to what the cup or the sandcastle should be. The kid has the pictures in his head. They may not go beyond the next few pailfuls of sand, but he's got them and he knows where to put the next pailful. Whoever does this has a series of thoughts on weight, size, compactness, smoothness of edge, firing times, whatever. The difference between this cup and the greatest porcelain cup ever made is probably a matter of depth and penetration. The artist at some point knows so much that he, maybe, cannot communicate that. He does all sorts of things that are really very precisely conceived, but he just appears to be pushing some pieces of clay around.

How do you consider and apply the design principles and devices?

A designer has all those devices of symmetry and proportion in his mind all the time. They are assimilated. They have to be. You certainly never check off a list whether it is symmetrical or not. It is all done with feel, I think, although you can do it intellectually. But since symmetry and balance go directly back to body reaction, you can practically feel whether this thing should be that way or this way. There is a kind of haptic perception that has to do with your physiological reaction to things: You walk into a place and you see a great big wall made out of masonry and you sort of feel the roughness and smoothness of it just by seeing it. One would think that craftsmen must develop superlative sensibilities of this kind.

How does the consideration of materials affect your concepts?

It depends. If a given room is in an old building full of dirty paneling that is wonderful and that when clean could be very beautiful, you say, "Let's leave it"—at least these days you do. If you're in a place like Portugal, where marble is cheaper than oilcloth and you want to make a bathroom, the cheapest thing you can do is make it out of marble. That is why in Vermont and New York you find a lot of doorsteps made out of marble—it is the scrap left over in the quarries.

[Materials selection was integral to Nelson's concept of the steel-framed chest. Before its invention] there was a strong feeling that, at all costs, the dust must be kept out of a chest of drawers—what my parents called a "chiffonier," which I guess came from a French word that means linen storage. So they closed up the sides and the back. Our general thought was that if you had drawers that were suspended in a frame, you wouldn't really need these sides on the case or the back. All you needed was the frame, which made a lighter, more articulated, interesting little piece of bedroom storage furniture.

There was something inspired about this. Part of it goes back to conditioning, and I don't know how I got to be conditioned. Apparently, it is extremely easy to create a situation in which people will hesitate to challenge, in which everyone is going along and feels "I'd better not get out of step." So you begin to develop patterns of rather timid conformity in the populations of these technological societies. Apparently in Hartford, Connecticut, at the point when I was in high school, it was too backward to create this situation. It's possible that in those naive and disorganized days the kids who enjoyed thinking were not prevented from doing it.

How do different sizes of projects affect your methodology?

Everything depends really on what you have to know. To design a proper spoon, what do you really have to know? There is a list of things that have to do with the material, the manufacturing process, how you decorate it (if at all), where you polish it, how it's got to hold up, how you store it. If, on the other hand, you are designing an urban scheme, say a neighborhood with housing and stores, you are working at a very different information level. Information is probably more complex at the larger scale, although, again, if you boil these things down, it always seems to come to a stupid idea or a bright idea.

I remember a top industrial designer who once had a job with an airline. He showed a group I was in the analysis he had made of how the airline could handle a series of 45-minute flights. And the guy, waving banners of triumph, said on a 45-minute flight maybe you really don't need a toilet. I got a hold of this guy afterwards and said, "I don't understand what you're thinking." And he said, "What do you mean? We did all this research." "But," I said, "is it not possible that, no matter what your research tells you, at some point on some flight somebody will get sick, some old codger gets on with too active a bladder and will have to go to the bathroom before the flight is over? Well then you put in a bathroom. What is all this inquiry about?" He was very put out. And this kind of idiocy prevails in all sorts of areas.

So if you are doing a big thing, I guess you have to know more than if you are doing a little thing. But the knowledge that it takes to design the greatest spoon is probably as profound as any knowledge that you would need for any other scale. So the distinctions between the big and the small scenes have to be handled cautiously, because one is not quite sure what is big and what is little in terms of the complexity you are going to run into.

Is your design procedure different from what you thought it would be when you were a student?

That's an interesting question. Almost everybody who lives long enough to look back at things looks back and frequently worries if he's doing things as well as he did when he was a student. I look back at stuff I wrote in 1955 and wonder why I've gotten so stuffy and stodgy since then. Pietro Belluschi, the architect, who used to do nice fresh watercolors, once said, "You know, as you grow older your command of techniques doesn't necessarily expand or increase as fast as your critical faculties." I think what you learn is not necessarily an advantage, because later you know more about what can go wrong. And that makes you cautious, which then maybe takes the energy out of the thrust that should be very energetic. Young students are innocent and lacking in experience, but they have tremendous energy. This makes them revolutionaries and Nobel Prize winners or whiz kids . . .

They ask questions?

Maybe, or maybe they see answers, which they throw themselves into headlong—because the first answer that comes along is a very thrilling thing.

Mrs. Henry Parish II and Albert Hadley

Parish-Hadley Associates Inc. is one of the most prominent and successful of this country's firms engaged in design and decoration. Its team of twenty-five young designers, decorators, and architects is led by its two principals, Mrs. Henry Parish II and Albert Hadley. The firm's work is mostly in private residences, though a considerable amount is public, including banks, clubs, offices, and institutions. Mrs. Parish redesigned the White House interiors during the Kennedy administration. More recently, Albert Hadley was special consultant to the renovation of Gracie Mansion, the official residence of the mayor of New York City.

Mrs. Henry Parish II, born Dorothy May Kinnicut in Morristown, New Jersey, began her career in 1933, when she opened Mrs. Henry Parish II Inc. in Far Hills, New Jersey. Her success in creating interiors of "com-

fort, luxury, and suitability" was immediate. Without formal training, but with a privileged life that had provided exposure to art and European travel, "Sister"—as she was called by her three brothers and subsequently by most of her friends—opened an office in New York City during World War II. From that headquarters she has practiced for the past forty years.

Albert Hadley, born in Nashville, Tennessee, started his decorating career there with A. Herbert Rogers. After completing a six-week summer course at Parsons School of Design, Hadley was awarded a scholarship for the next year and, upon graduation, taught at Parsons for five years. He later joined McMillen Inc. as a junior designer, and was with that firm until 1962. At that time he began his association with Mrs. Henry Parish II, working closely with her on all aspects of the firm. He became a partner in 1968, and today serves as president of Parish-Hadley.

The two principals work together on some projects and separately on others. They share a respect for the primary importance of architectural background before decoration. Their first consideration is "the skeleton: The basic room or space in question is studied and suggestions are made for necessary architectural improvements, such as altering proportions of windows, doors, moldings, and cabinetwork." Furniture is their next consideration: "the placement of sofas, chairs, tables, and sources of light, with a view toward the intended function of the room." The third consideration is "the selection of schemes: colors, fabrics, rugs, and accessories that determine the ultimate palette and ambiance."

How do your initial concepts first reveal or express themselves? As ideas, or as lines on paper?

Albert Hadley: I like to say that rooms speak and that rooms have personality. Rooms, themselves, give the inspiration for whatever might happen. If a room has personality and has architecture, those are the first clues to what might be done in the space. If a space is without distinction, my first concern is trying to create some sense of balance and scale and architectural integrity. I am really talking about the manipulation of space and volume.

Mrs. Parish: I am not a perfectionist. My approach is to say, well, let's make the best of it. But I assume I have a pretty good eye.

Hadley: [He describes the model room that he designed for a showhouse in the Carnegie Mansion, before it was recycled into the Cooper-Hewitt Museum in New York. The room had been assembled by the Tiffany Studios in the 1890s and had gilded and stenciled leather walls, carved woodwork, a heavy mantlepiece, and built-in bookcases of carved teak.] It was the ugliest room in the house—the upstairs room that is two rooms down the hallway from the staircase. As a design challenge, it is one of the most exciting single-room projects I have done. There was a strong statement because of its quality in design and materials. Since there were no real personalities, I imposed personalities—that is, I developed the room as if the Carnegies had continued living there and had continued to bring the room up to date with the times as they went on. [The idea was, in effect, to invent clients and a program for the room. The first thing Albert Hadley had done was to look at the room; the next thing was to examine the clients.] Yes, those are the two important things—a respect for architecture and a respect for the client.

I found that some of the Carnegies' furniture was stored in the building. There was furniture from the Twenties that had been made in Paris in the idiom of Jean-Michel Frank—a sharkskin-covered writing table, square leather armchairs that were worn soft and cracked, but had a wonderful color. So I thought, "This is the point; these people did progress; they didn't just stop with the Tiffany room; they let the room evolve." So I brought those pieces out; then I added things to bring it further up to date. And they worked well with the intricate carving that was the architecture. The mood had been set and the quality was there, so whatever else was added was the same best quality that we have today.

[A similar direction guided the restoration of the mayor's house in New York City, Gracie Mansion. Albert Hadley was commissioned to redesign the old part of the house, an early nineteenth-century house set in a park overlooking the East River.] The idea was to preserve the identity and authority of the house by carefully selecting backgrounds that would make it a house of today, but with total respect of its own being. The house has no strong architecture, so I thought it should be a bit more sophisticated than its early beginnings. If the Gracies, or whoever the earliest occupants were, had known what we know today and had had access to those things, they would have made the house interesting.

There is a good deal of talk about an "all New York house" and "New York objects," and that is fine. But I don't think any really sophisticated New York family limits itself to one source. As a house grows and as rooms are lived in, places take their place in time. There must be some idiosyncrasies, some spirit, and some strength; otherwise you have stilted rooms that are frozen in time.

Mrs. Parish: My idea is not to have anyone know that any designer has had anything to do with a project, and that the clients have designed it themselves. That's my idea of it. For one of our houses, we were stymied whether they wanted French furniture, Regency furniture, or what they wanted, because they didn't know. They owned nothing in the way of furniture, but they had marvelous books. They were frightfully well educated and successful, but didn't have an idea of what to do. The first thing we said was, "Well, you have to come to New York." I had an image of what I wanted, a big comfortable country house. In my own mind I knew it had to be a mixture, because although the house was basically French, the clients didn't want to live in the manner of stiff Louis XV chairs. They had gotten the idea from reading the magazines that you could have an elegant room without having very delicate French pieces. And that's what they aimed for.

And I said, "You need a big sofa by the fireplace, and you need two chairs opposite. You need something to fill up this gap here. And a coffee table. This is the way the room works—to have twenty-two people sitting down comfortably without moving a chair."

Does that mean that all of your living rooms have a sofa near the fireplace and two chairs opposite?

Mrs. Parish: No, but most of them do.

Do you draw constantly? Daily?

Hadley: My initial concepts always have to be externalized on paper. Usually, all the conceptual process is done totally alone. I sit in bed and think about what I want to do. When I am really into it, I sketch away and can throw out a whole pack of tissue paper in one sitting—going over and over again until I get what I want.

Mrs. Parish: I can't even hold a pencil. Even in the beginning I never knew how to use a ruler. It is easy for me to use a plan in locating the furniture to make it work. But I do that with little lines and shapes to indicate the form and placement.

Hadley: [In his drawing sessions, Hadley usually draws elevations and floor plans, both of which show the arrangement of furniture.] I don't think it is enough to do a floor plan of where the furniture is going to be. Their volumes and their masses are important, so I do elevations in the very beginning. They provide the skyline of a room.

In a room, certain things like sofas, wall pieces, cabinets, and consoles become architectural. They become architecture because they are fixed and are never to move. Other things in a space have a certain flexibility. They have an apparent ease about them in that they can be moved at any moment to punctuate the space with more realistic and human functional ways—without destroying the concept.

How does designing differ from assembling?

Hadley: I think "assemblage" is a good word. I would like to be called an assemblagist instead of a decorator. Everything is design if you're a designer. You cannot put anything on a table without moving it this way or that. You are assembling ideas, you are working with mass and line and volume.

You don't buy from antique shops until you know what you are buying. You know what you are looking for before you go. When a space is finally designed or put together in my mind, I can see that this is what I think it should be and this is the way it should work. And I can see that there is a skyline to the room, that there are volume, movement, and a quality of liveliness. These must be predetermined before anything is selected. The first thing you have to know is what you are trying to achieve, what you are trying to put across, what mood

you are trying to amplify. And if any given object doesn't support that idea, then—out! Design must be a very strict editorial process.

Mrs. Parish: The three most important elements in decorating are quality, suitability, and control. Quality is the use of the finest available materials and workmanship. I have worked with one of our studios for fifty-odd years. We go down to our studios every day to watch our designs being made—sculpted, draped, upholstered. I can't drape anything, but I can work with them and see how it should look. And Albert will work for three hours with a piece of material to drape it and make it right. A lot of designers don't have the craftsmen to do those things. Often we have a muslin mock-up made first, if it is an important piece. The studios produce extraordinary work.

Is there room for happy accidents?

Hadley: That kind of accident is a great advantage, because that is something that can give spice. You may come across something by total accident, but if it works well, then that is terrific, just what we are looking for all the time—the element of surprise.

Original concepts are one thing, but along the line there has to be enough flexibility for play and enjoyment, the spirited quality, those unexpected things that come along. And by those I mean the unexpected color or object—or materials of any kind—that suddenly come in and make the whole concept come to life.

Mrs. Parish: Objects or materials, even of exceptional quality, however, must be selected to suit the given situation. Control and restraint must be exercised if a room is to have style.

Hadley: The untutored eye can run astray, and students should really be wary of that. The clarity of the design is far more important to students than is the idiosyncratic moment of excitement.

Today a designer of interiors cannot afford unhappy accidents. If it is really well thought out and designed, if the journey has been well mapped, well planned, and you know where you are going—you cannot just pack your bags and go—you've got to know where you are going first. That is what designing is all about. You cannot design a motorcar if you are playing around with chairs. You have to know your materials, you have to know your technology and techniques. In order to design you have to know what your goal is. If you are going to the mountains, you cannot just suddenly go to the valley because you are attracted to it along the way. This happens in so many instances: We see design projects that fall short of their marks because somewhere along the line the discipline has not been great enough—the discipline to say, "No, this doesn't work" or, "Yes, it does and we must do this." Discipline is one of the greatest things in all of this process of designing. One of the biggest drawbacks and hazards in design is to lose sight along the way of where you are going.

What is the contribution of clients to this process?

Hadley: I find that most clients are intelligent if they are given reason and the proper presentation. If they have had enough good sense to go to a professional designer, then they come around in the long run to understanding what it is you are trying to do for them. That is, if the designer is working for the client's good rather than working to impose his or her own personality.

There is a difference between personality and taste. My taste, my knowledge, my background must go forward; my personality can be thrown away. It doesn't matter if I like velvet furniture or not. If you as my client want it in a room, then I will buy it and do the best room that I can do. So I don't do anything in spite of my clients' wishes. I work hard for them to understand what it is I am about—after I know what I am about. There is always more than one way to skin a cat. I won't say I have all the answers, ever. I have a great deal of flexibility—and you must have this in a joint project of any kind if something good is going to happen.

Mrs. Parish: Many of our clients are extravagant, they give plenty of time and don't say it must be done tomorrow. That way we can get them interested and some educational exchange can take place.

Hadley: Still, if a client wants something that is not right for the space in consideration, something that is not suitable, I try to demonstrate the more suitable idea as I see it. For example, some friends of mine have a living room with no architectural merit and with ceilings that are very low. It is a big room with a huge bay window that is more horizontal than vertical. Yet the client really wanted to have very elaborate curtains with all kinds of valances. She felt that elaborate curtains would make it a grand room. I was able to convince her that the room would be much more successful and much more exotic if we stayed away from an elaborate window treatment—because that was not really supporting the idea of the space as it should have been. I was able to show her by demonstration that the simpler means of embellishing the bay window was better and, in the long run, would be stronger.

[Mrs. Parish comments frequently on the desirability of "simple draperies" as well as "comfortable and workable rooms that do not have a bad piece of furniture in them."]

How do you consider and apply the design principles and devices?

Mrs. Parish: I do think about them, naturally, because no room works unless it is balanced. No room works unless it is fully used. Most people pile in one end of the room and leave the other end completely naked. And I think any drawing room should be used in any corner.

Hadley: I struggle with proportion by drawing elevations. I think all of that part of a designer's vocabulary is something that must be learned—just like learning to play the piano. You struggle to learn the scales, and with practice you do it automatically, like typing or driving. You don't think that you must put your foot on the brake, you just automatically do it. As a designer, one must automatically take joy and pleasure in having all of the design principles and devices come up at the right time. You sort of toss them around like a cat with a mouse, and out of that consideration comes the final statement.

The design principles and devices are all tools of a designer, the stipulations we must think about. One of the principles that interests me enormously and that I find very important is appropriateness. For instance, if the outside garden looks one way, then the inside has to relate somehow to what is outside. They cannot be totally disjointed. There must be some continuity. If you live in the country and in a rustic house, then there has to be a certain quality of rusticity about it. If you live in town in apartment 19A, you don't expect to find yourself in a French Provincial kitchen with blue tiles and heavy wood beams. It would be inappropriate and out of place.

That kind of interior design is like a stage set, and what we are opposed to is the stage-set concept of our profession. That is exactly where we lose out on a lot of things that could be better today. Students should learn that what they are doing—design—has to do with real people and real situations and should not be overcome by fantasy and fad. Then we will achieve something.

The mental process of a designer is the same no matter what he or she is designing, and no matter what he or she is thinking about. The strongest thing I can say to students, with knowledge and background, with training, work, and passion, is: If you are a designer with sense—and to be a designer you must have sensitivity—you can design anything.

From a regional plan to a spoon, as they believed in the Bauhaus?

Hadley: You have to be knowledgeable. But if you are knowledgeable, a designer can, in fact, apply himself to design anything. The thought process is the same.

Mrs. Parish: I hate the word "decorating."

Hadley: I don't mind at all being called a decorator. Decorating and designing are all part of the same thing. You can decorate a cake, but you still have a design concept as to what your decoration is. So it is all the same thing. If you are decorating something, you are designing. Designing is a frame of mind. Designing really means, "I know what I want something to look like." Designing is knowing what something should look like, knowing how to get it to that point, and producing it that way. That is design. It may involve decoration. There is some design that is decoration in itself; its purity needs no ornamentation. You see, decoration in most people's minds is really only ornamentation. Design is pure; decoration is ornamentation. But they are both design. It is the decorative element of design that heightens or amplifies the design quality of building and interior design.

One who knows the classics is not merely a traditionalist. A classicist knows the background of the culture. And there is no question that I am a classicist, because I respect all that has gone before me. As soon as students recognize that there is a great deal out there that is exciting to learn, they can build on it with security.

Mrs. Parish: But instinct is something you cannot teach. We can learn and look at everything. I was brought up with marvelous luck. I saw every beautiful house there was to see. And one learns. But we can see how to put it all together only if it is born in us.

Is your design process different from what you envisioned it would be when you were a student?

Hadley: The process I work with now is not really different, because I had already been through the hard knocks of working with highly professional designers before I went to school. I knew it was not all glamor, that there is enormous financial responsibility. But today there is much less flight of fantasy and much less flexibility because of the financial responsibility. If there is a lump in the kitchen floor tile or the color is not right or the curtains don't hang properly, it is your responsibility.

Do you have any additional advice to give to students of interior design?

Hadley: Students should not categorize themselves as either decorators, designers, or architects. They should work without demarcations and without pinpointing themselves. This is a creative process. A designer is a designer is a designer. . . . Students should aim just to let it flow.

Paul Rudolph

Paul Rudolph, one of the truly great twentieth-century American architects, is a man of remarkable three-dimensional vision. Also a man of boundless energy, he has exercised his enormous talents at virtually every scale of environmental design—from urban projects to furnishings and detailing. His urbanistic sense of siting and planning, his volumetric vision for massing, his sculptural commitment to spatial variety, and his innovations in textures, materials, furniture, and lighting—all within a dedicated pursuit of a single personal statement—have made him, almost uniquely, the inheritor of Frank Lloyd Wright's role as architectural beacon for America. This is clearly demonstrated in his interior design work.

Born in Kentucky, Paul Rudolph studied architecture at Auburn University in Alabama and then went on to Harvard to study under Walter Gropius. He first practiced architecture as a partner in the firm of Twitchell & Rudolph in Sarasota, Florida, where he made a name for himself as the designer of small houses that used construction systems that were relatively unconventional for residential projects. After the first four years he moved on to work ultimately on a full spectrum of design projects: His 175 commissions, both built and unbuilt over the past thirty-five years, include fifty-eight residential projects—houses, apartment buildings and interiors, additions, and remodelings; twenty educational buildings; seven campus plans; twenty-six master plans for housing and civic projects; twelve office buildings; five religious buildings; four libraries; eight government or civic buildings; an airport; a parking garage; a motor inn; two fraternity houses; a theater; a stadium; exhibitions; parks and recreation facilities; and furniture, lighting, and sculpture. Among the most publicized and acclaimed of these are Boston's Government Services Center; the campus of Southeastern Massachusetts Technological Institute; the New Haven Parking Garage; Yale's Art and Architecture Building; the Endo Laboratories complex on Long Island; the two Tracey Towers apartment buildings in the Bronx; and the master plan for Alabama's Tuskegee Institute, where he also designed several buildings, including the chapel.

For many of these projects, especially the apartment renovations, he has designed a vast quantity of custom-designed products and details—tables and seating, lighting, bathroom fixtures. His commitment to and interest in invention and innovation have led him to create spiral stairs of folded sheet steel, curtains of mirror disks, table-tops of mirror combined with subway grating, and bathroom sinks of transparent Plexiglas. His Modernist dedication to consistent and completely integrated design has led him to design doorways entirely of concrete—without metal door bucks, but instead with concrete jambs as well as concrete sills and heads. Indeed, it has been observed of his Art and Architecture Building at Yale that everything would have been of concrete if he could have made it work, so integrated was the design.

His thirty-five years of experience as a leading architect give him a special craft and approach to conceptualizing and to developing concepts. "I believe that process is a personal thing," Paul Rudolph says, "and what works for one doesn't necessarily work for another." He affirms assertively at the outset that he "cannot personally separate architecture from interiors. It is all one thing." When he says "architecture," therefore, we are to understand that he includes virtually all of design—certainly "interiors."

How do your initial concepts reveal or express themselves? As ideas, or as lines on paper?

It is possible for me, after all these years, to think out very complicated schemes in my head, to go through several schemes before I put a line down to see what the situation is—but only after many years. That did not happen in the beginning. I would insist that all architecture is a matter of thinking—not drawing, but clear thinking.

Of course, in the drawing process one thinks of other things that illuminate the project. Everything starts with the lines. The study sketch is important and essential. But there are two great twentieth-century architects who could not draw—one being Walter Gropius, the other Philip Johnson. Anyone can learn to draw, just as anyone can learn to type. But in my teaching days, talk was not enough. In teaching, less talking and more drawing is important. When I taught, I refused to look at any project unless it was drawn in plan, section, and elevation. There is a difference between those who draw and those who cannot—especially with regard to plasticity. If something is relatively plastic, it probably came from somebody who can draw well.

I conceived my multistory office building in Jakarta as a series of stacked, one-story buildings with roofs like local native roofs in Indonesia. [He recalls arriving at this concept from a consideration of three points: First, the climate of Jakarta, which is hot and sticky and therefore requires, or at least suggests, an air-conditioned building. Second, the local building technology, which does not produce either air-conditioning equipment along American models or double-faced glass to cut down heat loads. And third, the site and regional building traditions.]

I didn't investigate the geometry of the roofs, rather the roofs come from my seeing a village outside Jakarta. [There, the government of Indonesia has built an exhibition village of local building types and constructions, which Rudolph visited on his first trip to Jakarta. The broad and curving eaves of the local roofs, much like the ancient Chinese roof corner, showed him an alternative means of assisting natural air cooling and of circumventing the nonavailability of reflective glass. Rudolph investigated, in his mind, the viability of stacking these roof shapes to screen his tower windows. He designed this all in his mind, he repeats, both in plan and section before he committed the scheme to paper. And he had conceived two other schemes and had investigated them also, before he put a line to paper. "In three weeks I did three schemes in sketch models." However, as he stresses, he learned to think this way only after decades of experience.

["To me," Rudolph continues, "space is the single most important architectural element. How it affects people is of the utmost importance." The drafting room at Rudolph's Yale Art and Architecture Building, when it opened in 1963, was one of the most brilliant and elaborate spaces of the twentieth century. It was a vast, rectangular, two-story interior surrounded by balcony levels that created low and middle-height spaces overlooking and sharing the central space. Steps took one up and down from balcony to balcony, varying the levels further. A flying walkway bridged the space at one end. It was constructed entirely of concrete, yet that concrete was finished in several textures—smooth with board-marks from the forming, and a hitherto-unseen concrete texture of fuzzy ribbing that was to become a model in the next decade for "warming up" natural concrete. Skylights sent shafts of light down through wells that penetrated two floors above. On the way, that light shone over murals in the light wells. Orange carpeting, red-orange plastic laminate drafting tables and dividers, along with other specially designed furniture, enlivened the space. And bare-bulb spotlights provided glittering illumination.

[In addition, found objects such as cargo nets from freighter ships were used as window coverings and prophesied the role of Pop Art in architecture for the next decade. And the walls displayed ornamental plaster casts of historical friezes that prophesied the role of art history in architecture for the next two decades. To visitors, and to those who saw the photographs, the Art and Architecture Building drafting room was one of the most creative and innovative interiors—consistent in planning, structure, detailing, and furnishings, and the most complete integration of all the elements of design that had been seen in two decades.

[Rudolph has always explained the design of the drafting room, indeed the design of the overall Art and Architecture Building, as based on the idea of "turning the corner"—that is, relating the building to the corner site on which it sits. That concept brought about the pinwheel plan of the building with its overlapping corners and multiple levels. At the center of this pinwheel is the great space of the drafting room.]

My Tuskegee Institute Chapel is the opposite idea of space from that demonstrated by such classical spaces as the Pantheon. At Tuskegee Chapel, the idea depends literally on the space being defined in such a way that a series of motions is set up—not around a point, as in the Pantheon—but diagonally. It is the most dynamic space I have ever worked on, and by this I mean that it is simultaneously active and in repose—which is no easy trick. It is a matter of balancing the thrusting and the counterthrusting.

At Tuskegee Chapel the walls catch light and reflect it back into the vessel of the building, so that light and space are constantly changing. The light is coming through the clerestories onto the walls and bouncing back into the space; whereas the space is escaping through the clerestories and connecting you with the sky. The opposing directions of all this light is part of what architecture is all about—it is the essence of the twentieth century—and is purposely set in motion. There are many spaces where you have this thrusting and counterthrusting light and it is not resolved: That is very disconcerting. This is one of the things that makes me tick the most—how to resolve the thrusting and counterthrusting of interior space.

And I can tell you how the concept came about. The original chapel, which had burned, was a place of refuge more than most chapels; the sense of security was of the utmost importance. Religion is a great joy to the people at Tuskegee, and therefore the chapel has a great deal of color and life. I have used joyful color—a clear blue ceiling with the coffers painted red. There are natural brick walls with red and brown-red and a lot of copper.

But how did it come about?

"How do you turn a corner with a wall?" was one of my guiding concepts here [as it was in his Art and Architec-

ture Building]. I chose to offset the corners so that they make a kind of pinwheel. This invites people in. There is a great sense of motion involving the outside court as well as the inside of the chapel.

I made a series of diagrams with arrows to indicate the direction of light. And since the skylights are not parallel with the earth and the level of the eye is constant, and the distance to the skylight changes, the velocity of the space changes as well as the light.

Certain forms intrigue certain peoples. You can say that in the Renaissance they were infatuated with classicism. Why, I don't know. Why did Gothic architects do what they did? They simply adored a particular form or a particular space. I happen to like balanced motion. Why, I can't tell you. These things and how they affect people interest me a great deal: The pinwheel, the conception and plan, the motion of space are most fascinating to me.

Is designing interiors in existing spaces different from creating new spaces?

Of course. You deal with two dimensions in an existing space. You have existing ceilings, and the way natural light has been brought in has already been determined.

[One weekend at Aston Magna, the initial Massachusetts home of the acclaimed original-instruments music organization, Rudolph painted the concrete floor of the living room of investment banker Lee M. Elman to express the concept of a circulation diagram. Wanting to emphasize the possibilities of traffic through the awkward room with its five entry doors, he took a long-handled paint roller and painted stripes on the floor from each door to all the others, as one can cross the space. Then he wound the stripes into three concentric circles—three swirls of gray-blue on the dark blue painted floor. At their centers, as well as at the doorways, Rudolph next dribbled some red-orange paint to say "stop." The swirls seemed to connote old, country-style braided or hooked rugs at the whirlwind centers of stimulating conversation. Around these, Rudolph envisioned locating the furniture.

[To elaborate the rural irony of the hooked rugs further, Rudolph threw out the thought that in this setting, tractor tires as furniture would be the ideal contextual and Pop recall. Graphics designer-hostess Dorothea Elman rounded up tractor tires and airplane tires of several sizes, as suggested. Wondering how to upholster them, she thought of two-way stretch white corset fabric. After finding one that would do, she worked out the construction of the upholstery: Slashes were cut in the tires for webbing; the fabric was drawn together on strings around the tires (like the top of a duffel bag), and smaller airplane tires were bolted onto the tractor tires as vertical backrests.

[From Rudolph's lead, neighboring decorator Priscilla Houston, who helped with these upholstery solutions, suggested making some of the tires into tables by inserting circles of clear acrylic in the donut holes. And so the furnishings were evolved from Rudolph's iconoclastic, irregular, and innovative concept—however uncomfortable they may have been for other than the very supple young.] But that kind of work is only in two dimensions, and it is only when there are three dimensions that I am really interested.

Design has to do with what is possible—possible in terms of materials, technology, site, and context. There is no hocus-pocus. You have to know exactly what you can and cannot do on every level. Mies said about the design of the Seagram Building that he consulted the New York Building Code. That is the sort of thing you have to know. [And knowing that sort of matter-of-fact practical information, basic design craft and background, and, furthermore, having assimilated it are what make the long experience of a practitioner different. That experience makes it possible to telescope or condense the conceptualizing and drawing process in the way Rudolph has described. This is different from the slow, block-by-block buildup of this information in student days.]

One of the problems in the study of architecture and interiors is limitations. Many designers do not want to be circumscribed by the limitations imposed by reality—so they flounder. Limitations in interior design are helpful to students in learning. Only when you know the limitations can you act. In terms of process, one must know exactly what the limitations are.

What are the dimensions that students really know so that they can make comparisons when things are reduced to a drawing? I would insist that students know the dimensions of their bedrooms, or of the street. Perception—this business of making a plan, section, and elevation—is a very difficult thing. I have heard students describe their projects in terms that had nothing to do with what was being presented. Some students who seem intelligent are not talented in three-dimensional design; others who seem less intelligent are very good at conceiving in three dimensions and putting that down graphically. I can only assume that a certain kind of talent exists to deal with such things. In fact, I know that that is true. You cannot teach people to be talented.

How does the consideration of materials affect your concepts, and at what stages?

You start with materials, it doesn't come afterwards. [His statement must be heard in the context of building, of structure and not finishes.] The forms of a bridge are limited by the nature of the span; the materials appropriate for building a bridge are very limited. A cottage, on the other hand, can be built of many materials and can take on many form variations.

Is there one factor that is consistently more critical than the others?

I think the question of human scale is more important in interiors than anything else. And for that reason interiors are often more complicated. People memorize certain dimensions; people can accurately estimate horizontal dimensions, but vertical dimensions are much more difficult. People usually think that vertical dimensions are much taller than they are. When we know the space between familiar places, that space can be reduced to a drawing and we can make comparisons.

I think I have a natural talent for understanding space, and that has nothing to do with intellectual capabilities. One thing that helped me to visualize three-dimensionally was a course I took in architecture school at Auburn, Alabama—called Descriptive Geometry. It was the first time I ever thought three-dimensionally. We had to project the shadow from a curved form upon another curved form, for example. And the idea of projecting through space—what one thing does to another in relationship to two elements—has remained an important part of my interest and my activity. This kind of visualization is a highly mechanical thing that requires complete discipline.

At my Art and Architecture Building for Yale, for instance, there is an imaginary plane between Lou Kahn's building to the south that is reflected on the north side of the A and A Building. So that when you go along York Street, it is as if you are going through a space defined both by Kahn's building and my building. And the horizontals, the heights of Kahn's building, are also carried out into the A and A Building to further the idea of the definition of the invisible volume of space between the two buildings. It is as if the volume of Kahn's building is defined by that, and my building makes a kind of receptive form. It is as if my building is embracing Lou Kahn's building.

The whole idea of an axis as a projection of a plane through space is very much related to Cubism. The projection through space of the visible planes is a part of what Cubism is based on—the whole notion of images projected by various means through space and transformed. For me, the invisible plane is one of the motivating factors in much of what I do.

[Rudolph's discussion may seem a long step from the work of a beginner in interior design, but it is a direct route that any aspiring student will want to travel in reaching for the heights of interior spatial concepts and their development. Interior designers all too frequently have little opportunity to exercise their thinking in this direction. Yet the ability to think in this kind of way will be essential to the broadest and highest caliber of interior design work, as well as when one is working with the most gifted architects on the most advantageous kind of project.

[As with many creative minds, the verbal explanations often give two answers to the same question: In Paul Rudolph's case we remember that everything can be conceived in his mind in advance, to a large degree, after many years of practice and experience. On the other hand, he has also said that everything starts with the line. At the base of all his inspiring examples and explanations, perhaps those two statements should be remembered above all.]

John Saladino

John Saladino is a designer of residential and corporate interiors and architecture. His work is emotional yet disciplined, sometimes romantic and sometimes modern, usually colorful and painterly.

Born in Kansas City, Missouri, he received a B.F.A. in art history at Notre Dame University and an M.F.A. in painting at Yale University, where he studied under Josef Albers and the influence of the Bauhaus. Subsequently he worked with architect Piero Sartogo in Rome. While there he acquired a love of monumentally scaled classical architecture and painterly surfaces.

Saladino started his practice in 1972 and now has a staff of some twenty people. The firm employs a registered architect, four graduate architects, and five designers.

How do your initial concepts first reveal themselves or express themselves? As ideas, or as lines on paper?

The first thing I do is to absorb as much of the program as I can—the client's needs, the size of the site, the scale of the environment, the budget, which way the light comes from, whether the climate is cold or warm, how old the client is, and so on. Each client has his own set of personal needs, and we put these things into lists of "yeses," "noes," and "maybes." When those lists come in, I add my own experience and, psychologically, second-guess the client. I look at the way they dress and take into consideration that different nationalities respond differently to different colors, while also taking into account their education and hobbies.

The process goes from "the specifics" to "the general," and then back to "the specifics." In terms of laying out a space and designing it, we zone things first, allotting a certain space for a certain function, and then we go back again and look at the program. The ability to organize the clients' needs is paramount in establishing a strong foundation for the design.

When you are designing, does your thinking have to be externalized on paper? Do you draw or sketch constantly?

My concepts first jell before they go on paper. Sometimes just while walking home—I walk a lot and think about projects then—and when I drive through the country I do some of my best work. Sometimes in the middle of the night I'll make notes or I'll sketch so an idea doesn't leave me, and then I go back to sleep. I draw every day of my life. Often I will draw instead of write.

When you, the designer, meet the client, you're dealing with the public. When the client leaves, you go into your studio and close the door—that is your trip to the country or your walk back home—and there you turn away from the workaday world and assimilate the client's needs into a new reality. I find that artists are always in competition with "the real world." There is a certain kind of need within artists, a need to reinterpret.

Sketches are personal and represent what I would like to do, if given the freedom. I always find that in the first drawings there is something new and exciting. They are fresh. Good design and good architecture are created through struggle. When design solutions are too refined, they become slick. I don't like any kind of interior or architecture that adheres to rigid doctrines.

After we've conceived a scheme, we sketch it on paper and work out some of the loose ends. One can be designing in his mind, and then later one can also discover things in the actual process of drawing.

Then after a scheme works in terms of traffic flow, zoning space, and other considerations, I make the blanket—the plan. But the blanket is a flat fabric, and it has to become three-dimensional, because you have to move through it. People are going to experience this space on every elevation. So we lift the blanket and make it into a tent. We go from "the specific" to "the general" and back again.

Is there a difference between working on interiors in existing buildings and working on newly created spaces?

I go through the same process with an existing space as with a new space. But existing spaces are much more difficult, because of the constricting problems of working with what is already there. With new work, nothing exists, and the fantasy is surer. The process is more difficult in existing environments. If you tear down walls in your mind and later find that you can't do so, it really slows down the process.

Is there a difference in this process between work for public clients and work for private clients?

Yes. The questions about what goes into a corporate office are much more intensive, since there are many juxtapositions of personalities. We send out questionnaires asking about each person's work habits, such as "Do you go out to lunch?" and so on. All of that takes a long time to work out. Corporate work is like designing a village: You have to find out if the medicine man has to be closer to the midwife or closer to the king. You have to do more homework on corporate jobs.

Residential interiors in my firm are much more flexible than corporate projects because the budget is usually more flexible. In a corporate interior you find yourself using certain materials because you don't have the money to use other materials. So that it doesn't look like an afterthought, you start from the very beginning to use sheetrock, or some such instead of actual plaster. [Budget in relation to materials, he therefore advises, should always be an early consideration for corporate work, at least. In contract work, Saladino observes, the two major concerns are] budget and time. In residential work, you are dealing, first, with emotions.

[Saladino recalls working on a residence that started as "a romantic structure" and that, as it evolved,] became more technological. I started with the core of the house. All the functional needs are in the core. I like to get all the mechanical needs located so that the rest of the house can become staging. Later during the process the painting contractor and I visited the site together and I said, "Stop, just leave the walls alone, as they are now." Our specification for the scheme was different, and would have overkilled it.

Is designing different from assembling? How so?

An object or antique can change the look of a space. An accident can change a design for the better. Discovery is something that can happen at any stage—the planning stage, the drawing stage, or in the process of construction.

How does the selection of materials affect your concepts? And at what stages of the process?

Quite by accident when we were remodeling a barn in Southampton, Long Island, we found a material—a seamless fabric that was 9 feet wide. And we draped this material—banner-like, over oak dowels suspended on fishing nylon—from the 14-foot-high ceiling. Two things happened: When the french doors were open, the material swung gently back and forth so that shadows in the room changed constantly. Without this accidental movement, the room would have been static. We also found that we could backlight the fabric and it was beautiful. We therefore were able also to take a theater idea and miniaturize it. All of this came about from the accidental finding of a wide seamless fabric.

[The purchasing-and-accessorizing phase of interior design has been considered outside the modern sensibility. Saladino believes that it is "another dimension that many designers do not allow." For him the process of ordering everything from catalogues—"predesigned and predetermined—is unimaginative and mechanical." Besides, he adds, in that procedure,] there is no arena for allowing accidents to happen.

After it has all been put down on paper, there is something in me that wants to continue to refine and edit the design. Most of the time I tell clients, "Let's wait until the furniture is delivered," and a few times I have totally turned my back on the furniture arrangement that I had thought was the right one.

[For Saladino, the actuality of the situation provides its own dictates to a design. He compares the design of pathways on university campuses.] They build the buildings first, and wherever the students walk is where they build the walkways. Sometimes that happens in a room. I never read sitting right next to a window, but there are people who will take the best chair and put its back to the window to read.

If you really want to be a restoration architect, you have to make yourself passive to what the building was once, rather than what you would like it to be. If you peel off twelve coats of paint and have them tested and find that the original color was a lime green that you do not like, well, that's what you have it painted.

Where does the client fit into this process?

A client should never feel that he is being given an ultimatum. He should always feel he has an avenue of retreat. There is no one perfect solution, only many good ones.

How do you consider and apply the standard design principles and devices?

Contrast and juxtaposition, for example, are important to me. I like rough with smooth; I like putting an old, faded oriental carpet down on a new silver-paint-rubbed floor. I like to use a Modern table that has a twentieth-century car paint lacquer top and then place a 2,000-year-old piece of sculpture on it. It is an intuitive, romantic instinct in me. And when everything is too perfect and begins to align, I say, let's make that axis so that half the fireplace is seen at the end of the wall and not the whole fireplace. I guard against the expected solution.

Clients come in wanting modern design and I have a hard time getting them also to understand antiques and to buy worn carpets and chairs that are scarred. I like a modern shell with these old things within. I also like the juxtaposition of using outdoor scale indoors. To design an entrance hall as a garden is an incredible injection of stimuli. You don't see the little room anymore, but the bigger scale of an erupting Vesuvius of greenery.

[A distinctive use of color is an unmistakable and acclaimed aspect of Saladino's interior design. He notes three areas of interest in color, without outlining his procedure in color selection with much exactness.]

Color is many things to me; it is such a major part of the whole process. I think it is important to think about how people react to colors. We know that a breakfast nook should have a different ambiance than a cocktail lounge. Most people like to sit in rooms of large scale, but there are exceptions—a bar, for instance.

Why do people like to congregate in tight places? I think deep color helps them to move in closer together. Pale colors isolate us; we become silhouettes against light backgrounds. If you want to snuggle up to a fireplace on a February afternoon, the space preferred has to be dark—a dark wood or a dark color. It has to be a womb.

Designers and architects often use color to establish and reinforce sequential spatial experiences. If you have a dark entrance hall, 6 feet deep, and you paint it a dark color such as aubergine, including the ceiling, and you then walk into a 12-foot-wide living room painted white or a pale color, the juxtaposition of the dark, tunnel-like entrance giving way to the light room will make the latter look—or feel—bigger. North-facing rooms I tend to paint a cool color, and rooms facing south I tend to make warmer. Most people fight nature and do the opposite.

But a client's likes and dislikes have to be acceded to in this area perhaps more than any other, because of the highly subjective and obstinate attachments to color that so many people have. If a client likes red, then he should have red. If a client asked me to use bright colors, I would gag. But then there are beautiful ways of using primary colors, and I would try to do so.

Then there are fashions in colors. For a long time pastel colors were associated with nursery and hospital interiors. Then fashion changed the preference to pastels for the living room and the conference room.

[He discusses the symbolic appropriateness of color. For a cosmetics firm he used peach and white and mauve,] because I thought those colors were appropriate and graphic in describing what the concept of the firm was.

[John Saladino is the only designer among these case studies who has a fine arts background. He describes the effect of that viewpoint on his interior designing.] I am interested in metaphorical design solutions. I like tension; I like ambiguity; and I like what we perceive as "denial." In architecture I like to see three dimensions appear two-dimensional. For instance, many of the buildings in Venice look as if they were designed by pastry chefs. We have no idea whether those façades cover buildings that are 3-feet deep or 300-feet deep. I also like those things in architecture that are tours de force, for instance, the Vatican staircase—the Scala Regia with its forced perspective—which we perceive as half a mile long instead of 40 feet.

The philosophy of this firm is that "reality" is the enemy. We fight against the tyranny of the six-sided box. Most people live in small, undistinguished spaces designed by realtors. As designers we work at making these spaces into Art. We seek an Elysium.

I am by birth a romantic and by choice a classicist. The tension between those two forces makes me elusive. I do not like to be pegged. The shells or backgrounds of the spaces I design come out of my Bauhaus-Minimalist discipline. However, how these spaces are used, and the axial and ceremonial planning of rooms are, I think, influenced by classical and Renaissance ideas.

Lella and Massimo Vignelli

Lella and Massimo Vignelli are designers of such interiors as stores, showrooms, churches, and exhibitions, as well as of graphics and of products for interior use.

Lella Vignelli was born in Udine, Italy; Massimo in Milan. Both studied at the University of Venice in the School of Architecture. They first came to this country in 1957—Massimo on a product design fellowship; Lella as a special student at the Massachusetts Institute of Technology (MIT). The following year Massimo was teaching at Chicago's Institute of Design and Lella was working in the Chicago office of Skidmore, Owings & Merrill. They went back to Milan in 1960 and spent the next five years founding their own design firm, before returning to the United States in 1965.

Among Vignelli designs are the interior of St. Peter's Lutheran Church at Citicorp Center in New York City, and showrooms for E. F. Hauserman, Artimide, and Knoll International. They have designed packaging programs for Bloomingdale's, Saks Fifth Avenue, and Barney's, as well as graphics for American Airlines and for Italy's Lancia automobiles and Ciga Hotels. They also have designed graphics for the Washington, D.C., Metro and for the suburban RER trains around Paris.

Through all the breadth and diversity of their work, Lella Vignelli sees a consistency in the design production of their fifteen-person office. "It is the design approach that we have, which is based on discipline, appropriateness—and a touch of ambiguity," she explains. And of the Vignelli design methodology she says, "It is all the same. The scope or the perspective of one particular work might stress one aspect more than another, but the way you work is much established, as is the sensitivity about certain colors, materials, and finishes. These latter, however, are continuously affected by everything around so there is a continuous dynamic change. At the same time the routine is structured, both the methodology of your thinking and your process as well."

How do your initial concepts first reveal or express themselves? As ideas, or as lines on paper?

Massimo: We first get an idea while walking around thinking about it—sometimes while dressing, sometimes on the way to the office. Often that is when the idea comes, when your mind is free—while you're shaving.

Lella: Yes, in a sense you keep walking. It doesn't come out in one hour. You have a few days in which you start the process. You are affected by a certain thing you have seen and it keeps gnawing at your mind until it finally finds its way to the exit. And the exit might be in the form of a table.

[After that idea becomes clear, they go back to the plan, in the case of an interior design, and discuss what the possible directions of development are. In designing the Los Angeles showroom of the E. F. Hauserman Company,] we wanted to put the emphasis on the wall surface—the office panels, the movable partitions. So we started to think about what we could do, and the very first idea was a series of corridors.

Was all this abstract thinking and talking?

Lella: Well, we already had the plan, which was pretty directional and you couldn't do much to it.

Massimo: In the beginning we had ideas of doing corridors that open up, each one providing a particular experience, all done with products. Then one morning it came to my mind that we had seen, several nights before, an exhibition of artist Dan Flavin's light-work with fluorescent tubes. And he had had to build walls in order to install his work. When that idea came to mind, it was the answer to what we were looking for—something happening in these corridors.

Lella: The answer was to connect our desire to build walls with an art piece. We were looking for something to happen within these corridors—which were to be made of Hauserman walls, obviously—and that is when Dan Flavin's work came back into our minds. Besides, we have always been interested in working with artists to bring back the dimension of ornamentation to design; historically, artists always did the sculpture or the fresco. So we got together with Flavin and talked about it, and he loved the idea.

Is the process the same when you are developing a concept for furniture designs?

Lella: Our Saratoga Sofa design came from the fact that we needed a sofa and then we saw a picture that had a very wide sort of arm. Mind you, at that time 6 inches of arm was very wide, really exaggerated. We started from this hint to design a piece of furniture with a wide ledge that you could put your glass on.

[The Vignellis outline two different ways that projects and their concepts can be initiated.] There are really two kinds of needs: One is the particular assignment, which comes about when we are asked by a corporation or a manufacturer to design something they need. The other is the case of no particular assignment, which comes about when we need a product or a space for ourselves or we have an independent idea about something we would like to design. If we have an idea and we don't have an immediate client, we'll put it in the drawer and use it later.

What is the contribution of clients to this process?

We believe in the process of educating the client, because they come to us for that. We have to give them something that they don't know they want, perhaps, because they cannot express it, but then will recognize that they wanted it all the time. That is the important thing—reaching a point of giving ideas that are yours, but that the client recognizes was what he wanted all along. Sometimes you can give them a crazy idea and they will be willing to experiment with it and be happy. But when you are working with large corporations, you had better try to give them what they need. That is why we say that the more precise the briefing, the easier it is to come up with a concept solution and to do the rest of the work. [Asked about their use of the word "need," the Vignellis explain:] Clients usually don't know what they need. The clients who can express their needs come out with better solutions.

[The interior of St. Peter's Church was designed by the Vignellis after Boston architect Hugh Stubbins, who designed the Citicorp project, had set the shape of the space. The Vignellis designed the interior plan, its platforms, and all furnishings and finishes, including the altar and liturgical appointments.]

Massimo: The church is like two shells with a skylighted opening at the top. The architect's original plan showed the altar parallel to one wall. We thought that was not right, since the altar would have no relation to the shaft of light from the skylight. We felt that the symbolic element wasn't there sufficiently. So we suggested turning the plan around with a series of steps and establishing the main axis along the direction of the skylighted roof. We proposed this to the architect to consider in a very shy way, because it is a very touchy procedure. And he said, "Terrific. It's much better."

Lella: [They envisioned all the furnishings as movable.] We gave the church seven possible plans of arranging the furnishings, and they are using them. They rearrange the church three or four times a week, since they rent it to other groups for concerts and so on.

Massimo: Sometimes you may find out, once you work with a concept, that the idea doesn't work. It is rare that that happens, but it can happen. That is why we have two departments in this office. I am the one who is pushing for concept, regardless; Lella is the one trying to bend the concept into reality. So sometimes she goes too far, and the point is that if you begin to tamper with a concept, you can destroy it to the point that you would be better off starting again from scratch completely. When you see that you really can't make it work, then you have to forget it.

Does bad design occur when one does not start off from scratch again?

Massimo: Right. For example, we always present only one solution to our clients. We may explore different directions, but we always show only one proposal. Otherwise some clients will try to get you to use a piece of this one and a piece of that one.

How do you develop your concepts further?

Lella: After the concept discussion with Dan Flavin [on the Hauserman showroom], we next began to put our thinking on paper. We put it on a plan—

Massimo: which was still basically the one we had already.

Lella: But we have to go back a minute and talk about what the meaning of the showroom was, and what the meaning of showrooms has become lately. They are no longer merely to show products, but now to put the company on the map—communicating on the level of management rather than on the level of salesmen. This new concept of showrooms has been developing for the past couple of years.

So we talked with our client, Bill Hauserman, and said that his firm would be immediately recognized in the Los Angeles area and across the country for having a major installation by a major artist in connection with his products. This cultural event would connect them with the new Museum of Modern Art in L.A. and make them a sort of sponsor. [Hauserman said yes. Next in the development phase, they showed Flavin the plan and said, "If you want to change it, change it." But he just said, "No, my dimensions are 8 feet because the fluorescent tubes are 8 feet, so if you keep it to that, I can do whatever I want." And as he worked he revised the configuration of his light-work, but he changed the plan very little.]

Massimo: First you get the concept and block it out, then you present the drawings or the model to the client. Then when that is done, you go through the usual process of working drawings.

Do you draw constantly? Daily?

Lella: Yes, when we discuss. But not so much as we did years ago; because we are involved personally with these things, talking and talking, we draw and sketch much less. But when we get into the development phase, at that point there is a pile of drawings. And you do a model. We generally work with models. On a showroom for the lighting firm Artimide we went right to models, seven or eight models.

Do you advise students to work with models?

Massimo: I think they should do both.

Lella: We work with a model when we have something like a showroom or something that is in a sense showy. We don't necessarily work with a model when we do the interior of an office, because there is not much that you can do with the space. Then the plan is generally understandable. We find, also, that very few clients can read plans easily and that a sketch-model is more understandable. Certainly, when you design something like a dish or flatware or an object, you cannot draw it; many times there is no way you can draw it. So you have to make a clay or wood model.

How does the consideration of materials affect your concepts?

Lella: Materials affect a concept absolutely, because each material has its own best way of being used. But materials are not the first consideration in a concept.

The first thing is the plan, which is the first thing that you see—what you have in front of you. The given space and what that situation suggests immediately shows you some direction, some possibilities, or some changes that you very strongly want to make. And then you start giving the space your own direction, your own sort of shape, and at the same time you are considering the meaning of that particular project.

When you are through with that, then you start saying, "OK, we want these things all white, or colored," and then you go on to the materials. At least this is our way.

It is easier to talk about the choice of materials in product design and furniture design than in interiors. Someone may start by saying, "I want the room all red," and then the material might be considered first, but generally it's not the way we work. For our Saratoga Sofa, we knew we didn't want it to be upholstered and we didn't want it to be wood, because wood is too directional. So Massimo said, "Marble, black marble" and then we got into lacquer, like a piano.

[For the clergy chair at St. Peter's Church, they needed a ceremonial chair with a high back like a bishop's chair.

But they thought that the clergy should not have to sit on their vestments and crumple them up (see sketch A). "If every chair of this kind is made of granite or solid oak," Massimo continues, "we asked how we could let the vestments fall down freely in the back" (see sketch B). Then they made a mental connection with chair frames of tubular metal and turned the metal cantilever around (see sketch C) so that the vestments could fall between the seat and the back. And they selected thick linen, which is used for suitcases, as the covering of the metal frame, so the linen became a solid-looking chair.]

Lella: But I usually never start on an interior from materials. On a chair, yes, and also on a cup. In interiors the first thing is the space.

Is there a difference between working on interiors in existing buildings and on newly created spaces?

Lella: Interiors are always in existing spaces. Whether the place is new and raw or old with some architectural character, you are always working with existing space. An interior designer can change the plan, but it is always a given.

Massimo: Because we work mostly on public spaces, we always create a space, we always start with a bare plan.

Lella: Yes, but I mean the plan is there. The process is the same. You are always changing it. That is why I don't see the difference between the space as an unfinished space, as it was in the case of Hauserman, or the space only on the drawing board, as it was in the case of St. Peter's. By the time you change it, the process is the same. You are always involved with creating your own, besides something that is existing.

[Asked whether there is a difference between working on public projects and working for private clients, the Vignellis answered that they try not to work for private clients.]

Do different sizes of projects affect the methodology?

Not the creative methodology, but the development yes. [They see the difference in methodology from interior design to product design as rather slight. They see the same sensibility required for both areas of design.]

How do you consider and apply the design principles and devices?

Lella: We check everything, but not in the sense of checking a list. The devices and principles are assimilated, but you keep thinking about where you are, what you are about—generally—and little by little you become more secure about them.

Vignelli Associates. Conceptual development of minister's chair for St. Peter's Lutheran Church. New York City. 1982. *Sketches by Massimo and Lella Vignelli.*

A   B   C

Is one factor consistently more critical than any other?

Lella: Sometimes the budget. I always say to our clients, "Please, if you have a limited budget, let us know from the very beginning."

How does designing differ from assembling?

Lella: Designing is very different from assembling. Assembling is a sort of shopping—and some people are terrific at shopping, which takes patience and knowledge of all the sources. Designing is more sparse and more conceptual.

Is it more intellectual?

Lella: More intellectual in the sense that it never goes into such depth of putting in all the little accessories. Design goes for the big picture.

One of the problems I have with the interiors we do is that to some people they don't look finished because they don't have enough in them. [Some critics consider that this is due to agoraphobia—the fear of blank spaces. Others say that the untrained eye abhors a visual vacuum.] Then I have to send someone out to buy all the accessories and more, because otherwise many clients will put in things that are incompatible with the design concept.

Is your design procedure different from what you envisioned it to be when you were a student?

Massimo: It hasn't really changed. But you must be able to change or take in other influences and strengths. You cannot be mummified in one expression or direction all your life, even though your strongest influence stays with you and creates your personality.

Do you have any additional advice for students of interior design?

Lella: For design students in general, I have the advice of getting a broader and deeper cultural preparation, especially in art history. They need to develop a sensibility about so many things. I believe also that students should be whipped up into working hard and having many projects. They should produce more because they have to learn to draw, to make models, and they have to learn also that they don't have to come out with masterpieces every time, just that they have to come out with a solution. Get it done, then go on to the next one. That is the only way you learn the work—experience.

PART **3**

Interior Design in Twentieth-Century America: A History

Chapter 9

Before 1900: Precursors of the Twentieth-Century Interior

In 1851 the Great Exhibition of the Works of Industry of All Nations spread out, in London's Crystal Palace, the glorious accomplishments of the Industrial Revolution. As the first international exposition, it was a vast array of industry's products, including its decorative and artistic achievements. Some of them were wonderful and beautiful, some bizarre and hideous. For many Victorians it was the first glimpse of the furnishings, appointments, and interior design that could be produced by industry. For nearly everybody it was the first view of the architecture and interiors of metal and glass, which Joseph Paxton (later knighted for his work) demonstrated in the Crystal Palace itself.

The Industrial Revolution

To this day many people believe that the Great Exhibition signifies the beginning of the Industrial Revolution, and therefore the beginning of the modern world. It was not the actual beginning—either of the Industrial Revolution or of Modernism; the Industrial Revolution had already been in effect for at least a hundred years. Mere logic is sufficient documentation of this statement: In order to fill so vast a hall as the Crystal Palace—it was nearly 1,851 feet long—with industrially made objects, there had to have been considerable industrial activity in advance. As with any anthology of literature, the writing must have been produced before the anthology could have been assembled. So too, the many production techniques exhibited at the Crystal Palace had been available before—though many new products were introduced at that time. To the vanguard innovators it was—like most expositions and compendiums—a summary. To the uninitiated it was a revelation of the new.

Above all, the Crystal Palace Exhibition served as a signal and a symbol: It demonstrated that the world had changed. From then on there would be a greater availability and a greater possibility for greater numbers of possessions—regardless of aesthetic quality—by greater numbers of the population than ever before. It also signified the arrival of the masses as a new force in the population, certainly as a new force in design. Now they were wage earners and product buyers.

For that is what the Industrial Revolution meant: not only that machines had arrived; but, more important, that the masses of population now had more possibility to acquire things that would make their lives healthier, happier, safer, and wider-reaching than ever before in the history of humankind.

All this came with more than a few curses, of course. The Industrial Revolution from 1750 onward had brought smoke and pollution, causing the loss of natural daylight behind new manmade clouds. It had brought excesses and abuses of child labor. Long work hours and hazardous conditions brought many accidents and illnesses to workers. Coal-gas poisoning was a common occurrence. The concentration of factory workers had brought urban crowding, to the degree that there was a complete redistribution of population. In England, for example, before 1800, two-thirds of the population lived in rural areas; after 1856 half the population lived in towns and cities.[1]★

The Industrial Revolution also brought an inevitable decrease in handcraft, as more things were made by a greater number of inexperienced people in less time. It brought a greedy and insensitive use of natural materials to the production of manmade objects. Before the arrival of industrial production, true beauty had always "been based on the balance between purpose, process, and the property of the material," as the contemporary metallurgist Cyril Stanley Smith has written.[2] Beauty still means that today, though the effects of the Industrial Revolution and the clouds it produced have been hard to see through. A reform movement was soon to come.[3]

Nevertheless, the Industrial Revolution had brought a whole new world, and the Crystal Palace Exhibition proclaimed that fact for all the world to see. It exhibited the major developments—the precursors—that were leading to modern thinking, modern living, and modern interior design. The exhibition had not brought those developments about. Rather, it announced the possibility that interior design, along with the other advantages of world civilization, was no longer available only to the privileged—to kings and princes, to the aristocracy and successful merchants. Now interior design and furnishings design—the decorative arts and home furnishings—were within the grasp of a broad range of the population. To students of interior design, therefore, the London Crystal Palace Exhibition of 1851 signifies the first possibility for the creation of the modern form of their profession—interior design.

What Led Up to All This?

It had been long in coming—at least four hundred years, if we count Gutenberg's printing of the Bible around 1454. What Gutenberg did was to put together all the basic components of mass production.[4] His first successful use in the West of movable, reusable type for printing contained all the components: (1) mass production of (2) prefabricated (3) multiples that are (4) assembled to (5) form a system

★Notes will be found at the end of each chapter, following the list of books and articles for suggested reading.

for (6) communication, convenience, or comfort. It was a soaring commencement. Prefabrication and assembly made it possible for work to be done by different people. This became known as the division of labor.

Gutenberg's achievement not only initiated mass production; it also led, in due course, to the spread of literacy, literature, and scholarship beyond the confines of the ecclesiastical community.[5] This revolution from script to print led to the founding of many new and great universities in the next century.

From Gutenberg onward, the course of history was set on an unswerving, if occasionally halting, course. Mass production reached its culmination, perhaps, in the machine aesthetic of the Modern movement (see Chapter 12). To that way of thinking the goal of design and production was not only the actuality of machine production, but also the mere image of the machine or the aesthetic suggestion of the machine-made. By 1851 the machine had made its breakthrough and was a pervasive force that affected the life of everyone in the Western world.

Among the factors and developments that contributed to this progress were the increase in population between the fourteenth and eighteenth centuries, the intellectual and scientific revolutions of the seventeenth century, the democratic revolution of the eighteenth century, the technological revolution of the eighteenth and nineteenth centuries, and the development of materials for shelter and protection that the latter brought.

An Increase in Population

Between 1300 and 1350, as the contemporary French historian Fernand Braudel reads the statistics, the population of the world was between 250 and 350 million.[6] By 1780 it had increased to between 836 and 1,380 million. That increase represented a growth of somewhere between 138 percent and 400 percent in 400 years. Whichever remarkable figure is accurate, the population of the entire world, not just Europe, probably doubled during this period. Among the causes of that increase were:

1. Scientific and medical advances against disease, plague, and death. Due to scientific developments in the eighteenth century, disease was markedly brought under control, and the mortality rate—particularly infant mortality—was decreased. As a result, longevity was also increased.

2. Agricultural advances. Due to the migration of populations to newly available arable lands such as the New World, with its more efficient crops of corn and potatoes, the production of food was greatly increased by 1800. Consequently, famine was considerably decreased.

3. Better trade communications. Accompanied by the spread of international banking and credit, which had been established by the Florentines in the fourteenth century, trade between countries began to make necessities more available.

4. A change in moral outlook toward money. In the seventeenth century, production for profit was accepted as an honorable pursuit. No longer was it considered good merely not to waste labor on luxury; now the accumulation of money was also an acceptable goal.

An Intellectual and Scientific Revolution

During the seventeenth century the intellectual revolution, ongoing since the Renaissance, began to free Western thinking from dependence on previous authorities, assumptions, religions, and superstitions.[7] Based on contemporaneous scientific discoveries, it proffered the ultimate reliance on observable fact and on the courageous fusion of data-gathering with deductive theory. This put everyone in the position of being able to question his or her own destiny—and essentially of coming closer to controlling it. Before, one's lot had been generally considered as governed by religion and death, work and taxes, obligation and servitude. The intellectual and scientific revolutions brought the possibility of self-reliance, challenge, and desire.

Among the milestones of that intellectual and scientific progress were (1) René Descartes's examination of Nature and observable fact for proof of reasoning. From that viewpoint he proclaimed in his *Discourse on Method*, "I think, therefore I am" (1637); (2) Isaac Newton's publication of the *Mathematical Principles of Natural Philosophy* (1687); and (3) John Locke's philosophical justification of revolution and independence in his "Letter on Toleration" and "Two Treatises on Government" (1688).

This intellectual revolution led, during the seventeenth century, to Rationalism—including rationalism in design. Rationalism observed, accepted, and applauded the specific functions of each design of nature—each plant, each animal—for its own peculiarities. This was the Age of Reason; its attitudes were the intellectual foundation of functionalism in the twentieth century (see Chapter 11).

A Democratic Revolution

From the third quarter of the seventeenth century onward, revolution by force gradually brought greater political power and greater social independence to the population:[8] (1) beginning with the Glorious Revolution in England (1644); (2) then, notably, in the United States (1776–83); (3) next, in France (1789–92); (4) and again in France, though less successfully, and throughout Europe (1848); and (5) finally, the gradual abolition of slavery throughout this period.

All the democratic revolutions aimed to change the ancient regime that guaranteed position, power, and money by birthright alone. No longer could kings, the nobility, and the clergy rule by divine right. Instead, ever afterward, the democratic revolutions offered, in the battle cry of the French Revolution, a greater degree of liberty, equality, and fraternity to everyone.

A Technological Revolution

Major discoveries and inventions altered the sourses of power, changed machinery, and ultimately produced new materials. The source of power to run machines changed at the end of the eighteenth century. From 1650 to 1800 water and wind had been the primary power sources of the Western world.[9] From 1800 to 1900 steam (produced by burning coal or wood) took precedence as the primary source of power. The availability of coal as opposed to wood was to give a lead to whichever region or country had the most. The discovery of petroleum deposits in northwestern Pennsylvania in 1860 added petroleum to the list of fossil fuels. Then the fossil fuels, coal and oil, became the principal power sources.

The development of the factory system from 1800 onward meant that production no longer had to rely on individual craftsmen working at home from beginning to end. The centralization of work activity and the subdivision of labor into a process, where prefabricated parts or components were assembled, produced widespread mass production. Contributing to this process were the use of iron, as opposed to wood, for the construction of machinery; the transformation of the textile industry; James Watt's invention of the steam engine (1769); Robert Fulton's first steamboat run from New York to Albany (1807); and George Stephenson's first railroad run in England (1825).

The essential fact is that, beginning in the mid-eighteenth century, power-driven machines transformed industry and transportation, trade and communications, and therefore politics and society. People moved to be near the new factory system that used those machines. Thereby numerous new cities were formed, with concomitant disadvantages as well as advantages. This was the Industrial Revolution that was to be proclaimed as a success, however qualified, in the Great Exhibition at the Crystal Palace a hundred years later.

New Materials for Interiors

In the course of these many discoveries, new materials for building and furnishing were developed that made possible our modern interiors. Among them were the building and construction materials of which room envelopes are made, as well as the materials used in the manufacture of furnishings: iron and steel, glass, ceramics and concrete, textiles and carpets. The new materials were outgrowths of basic and ancient industries that go back to the historical origins of our species. But the methods of manufacture and the new uses and applications of these materials became more abundant and more accepted.

Iron and Steel

Iron and steel have made possible our buildings and interiors of metal and glass—from the Crystal Palace to the Seagram Building (see Chapter 15). Yet iron and steel were first considered as "base" and "unfinished" materials that were acceptable only for their practical strength. Only gradually did they become accepted as materials that could be visible and make aesthetic contributions.

The technological possibility was initiated in the fifteenth century, when the blast furnace was first used in the West to produce liquid cast iron. A second major change in this development occurred around 1860, when it became possible to melt large quantities of low-carbon iron and cast it into relatively homogeneous ingots, purifying it of the slag that had previously always been present.[10] This produced steel, which is a simple alloy of iron with carbon. Henry Bessemer's 1856 patent for manufacturing steel from cast iron began this new phase of availability and construction.

In the beginning of this progress, iron was used mainly for fittings, machinery, and equipment, including weapons. Wrought iron or hand-hammered iron art had had an honorable heritage as railings, screens, and ornaments; but pots, pipes, and firebacks were more typical of the thinking of artisans through the seventeenth century about the proper status and use of cast iron.

In the eighteenth century the use of iron increased markedly through the designs of engineers as a purely practical material. The early eighteenth-century architectural uses of iron were for bridges, as Nikolaus Pevsner traces its development.[11] An iron chain bridge was built over the River Tees in the north of England between 1740 and 1742. The earliest all-iron bridge was designed by T. F. Pritchard and built by Abraham Darby at Coalbrookdale, England, in 1775. In America, James Finley built nine iron suspension bridges between 1801 and 1811.

Cast iron was used in the construction of mills in England in 1780. In the same year the Grand Salon of the Louvre was roofed with an iron construction; and that was followed by the iron roof of the Théâtre Français between 1787 and 1790. The first known structure of exposed cast-iron columns and beams was in a flax-spinning factory at Ditherington, Shrewsbury, designed by Benyon, Bage & Marshall in 1796.

Still, in these uses the material was considered for its practical strength alone, essentially, as utilitarian engineering, and therefore concealable or at least not focal. During 1790–92 iron columns in St. Chad's Church, Shrewsbury, by George Steuart, were encased in wood. Then, during 1808–09, Smirke's Covent Garden Theatre in London used iron unconcealed to support the balconies. That was followed by the earliest known example of a metal-and-glass dome—at the Halles au Blé in Paris, designed in 1809 and built in 1811. Shortly thereafter (1815) John Nash designed his renowned all-iron staircase for the Royal Pavilion at Brighton and used iron columns (with copper palm-tree capitals) in the kitchen (1818–21). This was, as Pevsner says, "the first appearance of unmasked iron in connection with royalty"[12] and it signaled the ultimate acceptance of the material.

Iron, then, first appeared on the exterior of buildings for its structural properties, from 1837 on, in cast-iron fronts of commercial buildings in New York City.[13] From 1843 to 1850 Henri Labrouste designed his celebrated Bibliothèque Ste. Geneviève in Paris with iron columns and iron arches, as Pevsner points out, "exposed as frankly as if he were concerned with a factory or a railway station,"[14] in contrast to being concerned, as Labrouste was, with an elegant municipal interior.

Many other buildings followed in a steady succession: the London Coal Exchange, with both its structure and decorations in iron by Bunning (1847 49); cast-iron fronts on warehouses in St. Louis (1850–77); and, bringing us to the first prominent public building almost entirely of metal and glass—Joseph Paxton's Crystal Palace in London (1851). From then on, spurred by the advocacy of, among others, James Bogardus in America—by his building for Harper Bros. in New York of 1854 and especially by his pamphlet "Cast Iron Buildings" of 1856—and by Viollet-le-Duc in France (especially his lectures of 1863–64), the acceptance of iron structures and decorations grew rapidly.

After 1860 construction was further improved by the use of steel, which made possible both wider spans between columns and higher buildings. After the completion of the Brooklyn Bridge (1883) and the Eiffel Tower (1889), no construction could overlook the possibilities and availabilities of iron and steel.

Glass

The ancient craft of glassmaking changed drastically in the late seventeenth century with the development of plate glass. Today, it is plate glass that opens our interiors to daylight and relates them to the openness of outdoor space. Glass is, perhaps, the most dramatic component of the modern interior.

Blown glass had reached a peak of performance in sixteenth-century Venice; but glass for windows and mirrors was not much used until the seventeenth century.[15] Sash windows were invented in Holland in the 1680s, and the first recorded use of sashes in England was in 1685 as replacements in Inigo Jones's Banqueting House at Whitehall Palace (1619–22).[16] Afterwards, sashes rapidly replaced casement windows in all but the smallest houses. Still, when glass was used in them in these early days, it was roundels of blown glass held in by lead cames.

Around 1680 the process for casting glass was invented in France. This new plate glass was developed to achieve perfectly parallel surfaces, and consequently provided almost pure translucency. It was then that larger and clearer panes of glass were used for the orangerie-like windows in the Galerie des Glaces at Versailles and for its inner wall of mirrors. The Galerie des Glaces was therefore something of a technological milestone—as well as one of the truly great rooms of Western civilization—when it was built (1678–84). France led in the production of plate glass for many years afterward.

In the course of the eighteenth century the panes of glass in windows became larger, and the glazing bars or muntins became thinner. This progress shows as New England's 24 panes over 24 panes was reduced to the early nineteenth-century common variety of 6 over 6. But not until the mid-nineteenth century did the ready availability of large panes of sheet glass allow the muntins and transoms to be abandoned—first reducing the number of panes to 2 over 2 (the late-Victorian standard), then reducing that number to a single large pane per sash as the nineteenth century drew to a close.

Using this new plate glass between 1837 and 1840, Joseph Paxton, in his capacity as landscape gardener and horticulturalist to the Duke of Devonshire, built a metal-and-glass conservatory to house the Duke's plants at Chatsworth. In 1845 Decimus Burton and Richard Turner designed the conservatory for Kew Gardens outside London. Other prototypical metal-and-glass buildings accompanied this development.

Then Paxton built the Crystal Palace for the Great Exhibition in London, using 900,000 square feet of sheet glass. The design utilized the largest pane of glass then available, which was 49 inches by 10 inches. Paxton had achieved an astonishing feat of mass production, since all the components of the Crystal Palace were prefabricated in factories and assembled on the building site; and he had brought metal-and-glass construction into the public recognition as a major building system.

From then on an irresistible force moved the glass industry headlong toward the glass-paneled curtain walls of the 1950s and 1960s, and to the twentieth century's glass-pavilion-like houses and interiors with their sliding glass doors, and their (essentially) walls of glass (see Chapters 14 and 15).

Concrete

The third ancient material to be developed further to affect the twentieth-century interior was concrete. Imperial Rome had achieved considerable sophistication in concrete construction, but concrete technology lapsed until its rediscovery in the late eighteenth century.[17] Present-day concrete is a mixture of cement (made from a mixture of limestone and clay), sand, crushed stone (aggregate), and water. This manufactured stone has the supporting or "compressive" strength of natural stone.

The first modern use of concrete was in 1774 for the construction of the Eddystone Lighthouse in England by John Smeaton.[18] Smeaton had used a mixture of lime, clay, sand, and crushed iron-slag. Then, in 1824, Joseph Aspdin produced the first cement that hardened with water. Named for the Isle of Portland, where the limestone was obtained, Aspdin's durable mixture is still called portland cement. A concrete flooring system developed in 1829 used concrete as a filling between iron girders. The first extensive use of concrete occurred in 1867 in the main building of the Paris Exhibition.

Reinforced concrete also was known by the Romans in the form of iron clamps over masonry joints.[19] The method of increasing the strength of concrete by incorporating metal reinforcements in the concrete while it is still wet came about in the 1850s and 1860s in England and France. The first patent for its application was taken out by Joseph Monier for use in making plant pots in 1868; he used a wire network to reinforce his concrete tubs. This was the ancestor of concrete reinforced with steel bars, which made its general appearance by the end of the nineteenth century. Steel reinforcing added the tensile strength of steel to the compressive strength of concrete.

In the 1890s reinforced concrete frame construction for buildings began to be used in America by the Englishman Ernest Leslie Ransome and in France by François Hennebique, who patented a process for it in 1892. In 1894 Anatole de Baudot began work on the first church to have a reinforced concrete skeleton and a thin-walled enclosure—St. Jean de Montmartre, Paris. But it was Auguste Perret at this same time who realized the first complete architecture of reinforced concrete in the design of apartment houses and other buildings in France. Reinforced concrete was to become a key material in the development of twentieth-century building.

Textiles

The textile industry, too, was transformed from the ancient home craft of the distaff side—since the ancients considered it women's work at home—into factory production. In the eighteenth century the methods and equipment for the production of fibers into textiles changed drastically. This was an essential part, if not the spearhead, of the Industrial Revolution. This industry turned out the miles of upholstery, drapery fabrics, and carpets that the Crystal Palace enthroned.

Some of the inventions that aided the development of textile production were the flying shuttle of John Kay (1733); the parallel drawing rollers of Lewis Paul (1738); the spinning jenny of James Hargreaves (1767); the roller spinning frame of Richard Arkwright (1769 and 1775); and the spinning mule of Samuel Crompton (by 1779). Edmund Cartwright's power loom (1785) mechanized weaving; and Eli Whitney's cotton gin (1793) brought America precedence in the production of cotton goods.

The world of textiles was never to be the same. In 1780 nine-tenths of English textile workers labored at home; by 1850 nine-tenths were employed in factories. The factory of Jouy-en-Josas, near Versailles, was started in 1760 and continued to produce *toiles de Jouy*—those cottons printed with designs of landscapes and figures, primarily in monotones of rust, blue, or gray. They remain popular after two centuries. At the same time, English chintzes were having a parallel development from 1760 to 1780.

At Jouy, in 1797, Oberkampf introduced cylinder printing to the factory. He claimed that one machine could do the work of forty hand-block printers. Improving on the perforated-card loom attachments of M. Falcon (1728) and Jacques de Vaucanson (1745), Joseph-Marie Jacquard had, by 1801–05, developed the loom that bears his name. It made possible the machine production of elaborate textures and patterns—tapestries, brocades, and damasks.

Subsequently, the carpet industry underwent a similar transformation as Axminsters and broadlooms were produced on new larger looms in vast quantity. This was made possible after the French Revolution broke up the prohibitive regulations and rules that had been set up by local corporations and guilds. At the Crystal Palace Exhibition all these new carpetings were to be seen, seemingly by the mile. Not until a century later, in the early 1960s, was the carpet industry to see such a marked advance again (see Chapter 16).

In this way the materials for interior construction and finishing were developed. It can be a source of some justifiable pride for interior designers that the development of these interior furnishing materials was often synonymous with the development of the Industrial Revolution itself.

Only two now widely used materials remained to be added to the twentieth-century interior designer's palette: aluminum and plastics. Aluminum was discovered and first demonstrated around 1890. Celluloid, the first acknowledged plastic, was introduced in 1862. The plastics of the twentieth century, including synthetic fibers, were first developed in the 1920s, but only came into widespread usage after World War II (see Chapters 13 and 14).

The Modern Interior

In addition to the effects and new materials made available by the Industrial Revolution, a number of other developments contributed to the twentieth-century interior. From the late seventeenth century and the early eighteenth century—although there were variations in degree from country to country (especially between England and the Continent, which developed differently and somewhat more slowly away from ceremonial hierarchy) and from palace to farmhouse—new types of buildings and new types of interiors came about; privacy and informality increased; comfort and convenience gained new meaning; heating and sanitation were improved; and electric lighting was added.

New Types of Buildings and Rooms

From the late seventeenth century onward, interiors proliferated in many new forms for many new functions. No longer were interiors limited to palace, church, town hall, fortification, and private house. This proliferation accompanied the increase in the new types of buildings that developed to accommodate the daily use of a wide new spectrum of ever more active and independent citizens.[20]

Those new buildings included the hospital and asylum, which were developed in the eighteenth century. In the nineteenth century came public libraries and museums; railway stations; university and school buildings; banks and department stores; hotels and more elaborate hospitals; large theaters and concert halls; and offices for government, municipal, and private or corporate use. What had been perceived as standard plans for some of these buildings since the Middle Ages, and perhaps before, now came to be reanalyzed and reconsidered in light of special functions for new societal changes.[21] This was the beginning of functional interior planning.

In addition, the poverty that had been everywhere and for all peoples, except for the few very rich, gradually began to disappear. Increasing numbers of people had more money to acquire the advantages that were made available by the discoveries, inventions, and advances of the Industrial Revolution.

As a corollary, this ultimately meant that fewer people had less money. There was a decrease in slaves and servants as more people became their own masters, and as industrial production required a more flexible, mobile, and educated working force. This change affected not only modern social conditions, but also the way that interiors could be used or operated—and, consequently, the way they were designed.

Like the traditional Japanese house since the tenth century or earlier, the interiors of the Western world had been operated by uncounted servants. They moved things, arranged things for use, rearranged, and generally transformed interiors at the desires and commands of their employer-masters.[22] They made possible the constant rearranging that was required to turn any palace chamber into a dining room, game room, or, indeed, bathroom. This is the way persons of considerable means operated their houses until the eighteenth century. This is also the way most nonresidential interiors were operated until the end of the eighteenth century.

Specialized Rooms

With the availability of more objects—furniture, furnishings, and all their complement—and with the decreasing availability of servants, rooms became more specialized in the eighteenth century.[23] That is, rooms in residences, as well as in the new public buildings, were designed and furnished specifically for single major functions—distinct from the ceremonial hierarchies they had reflected. No longer did the servants cart in a table and chairs, lay the table, and light the candles in the salon or bedroom. No longer was a single major hall used as a hospital ward along with other hospital functions.

It is hard for us to envision that in the main—in most palaces and houses before the seventeenth century—there were few specialized rooms except for the great halls and kitchens, state bedrooms, and rooms for walking and gaming, like the long galleries in England and France. The long galleries of English Renaissance houses such as Hatfield House, Syon House, Wollaton Hall, and the like were designed specifically for strolling during inclement weather and for playing games such as badminton. In this tradition, also, the gallery of François I was built at Fontainebleau.

Otherwise, most early palaces as well as small houses had multipurpose changeable spaces like those in the houses of ancient Japan. The principal space in any dwelling was designed as a reception room. In it the household also gathered for meals; nearby, as late as the early eighteenth century in Europe, was the heavily curtained bed, which was customarily next to the fireplace.

The eighteenth century changed all that and brought specialized rooms to houses and palaces, and to all the new nonresidential building types. In the eighteenth century a separate room was set aside for dining—permanently set up with a table and chairs—in more and more homes of the new bourgeoisie as well as people of greater means. The bedrooms were set off from the other rooms, usually by moving them upstairs or, in palaces, to other parts of the building.[24] Similarly, specialized interiors were developed for specific nonresidential functions. This specialization continued throughout the nineteenth century, in ever-increasing subcategories. Specialized rooms are a fundamental component of today's interior.

Privacy and Informality

Specialization and the permanent placement of furnishings were not the only results that this idea of separation brought to interior design. It also brought an aspect of life that was virtually an invention of the eighteenth century: privacy.[25] Since living was dependent on servants, one was never alone, never able to go off by oneself. The servants were always there—moving, rearranging, helping, eavesdropping, prying, spying. When the eighteenth century brought separate rooms for separate functions to more residences, it also brought the modern sense of privacy with it.

The development of the corridor in the seventeenth century fundamentally changed the possibility of attaining privacy.[26] Before, most palaces and mansions had been planned as series of interconnected suites of rooms—room joined to room and anteroom in an enfilade without corridors. There was no way to get from one room to another without going through someone else's room—bedrooms included—at any hour of day or night. Servants made the most of this opportunity. The new corridors, however, permitted privacy as well as aiding heating and ventilation. The use of the dumbwaiter made private dining possible. The increasing inclusion of back stairs also led to the separation of servants and masters. This new privacy led to the expression of individualistic behavior.

Informality was a natural result. It gradually supplanted pomp and display, formality and ritual, in daily life in the West. During the eighteenth century the pursuit of happiness for the individual, the acceptance of personal preference and ambition, of desire and challenge, constituted a shift in the system of values to a new set of psychological attitudes. The resultant personal and informal approach to human life and relations was a keynote of the Romantic movement in the early nineteenth century. Privacy and informality are fundamental aspects of the twentieth-century interior.

Comfort and Convenience

In the eighteenth century one additional fundamental component of the twentieth-century interior was established in its present form: the requirement for comfort. Historians have generally claimed that the idea of comfort was born in the eighteenth century;[27] but that may need a bit of modification.

Humankind has generally yearned to make life more comfortable and easy, both at work out in the field and at home back in the cave. This ideal has suffered numerous setbacks, such as the loss of Roman luxuries after the fall of Rome, as well as self-deprivation by monks, and other social standards, including the supremacy of pomp and formality before the eighteenth century. But the emotional need or desire has surely been with the human species from the beginning. In the eighteenth century, however, that quest for comfort as convenience began to seem realizable—possible and available. What was required to produce that comfort, however, began to be more complicated.

Heating   Most important to that sense of comfort was the improvement of heating—and the return of central heating, which had been virtually forgotten since the days of the Romans. Before the eighteenth century, fireplaces and chimneys, which were designed on the medieval model as cooking fireplaces, provided the only heat in some European countries.[28] Coal braziers supplemented them in other rooms—and they caused frequent cases of coal-gas poisoning. Stoves of ceramic tile and, in the late eighteenth century, of iron were used in Northern and Eastern European countries. Until that time, things and people froze—including wine at the king's table in winter. People who could afford to do so wore furs indoors to keep warm.

But, around 1720, that too changed. "The hearth of the chimney was made narrower and deepened," as Fernand Braudel tells us, "the mantel lowered, the chimney shaft curved."[29] The latter prevented it from smoking. With this better chimney construction, there was less heat loss and it became possible to heat domestic-scaled rooms. It was a revolution in heating, and the number of fireplaces and chimneys increased markedly over the next decades—leading to the smoke and pollution problems of the Industrial Revolution as well as to greater comfort. In the nineteenth century, heating systems began to be widely used for necessary industrial and factory production. Today, in cold-winter climates, adequate heating—60 to 65 degrees Fahrenheit—is unquestioned.

Sanitation and Ventilation   Even the eighteenth century, however, did not make much progress in that other component of the twentieth-century interior—sanitation and plumbing.[30] Inside, sanitation was deplorable by our standards, and ventilation primitive in its reliance only on open windows and doors. At the end of the eighteenth century chamber pots were still the norm, despite the fact that the water closet had been invented by Sir John Harrington in 1596. People had not learned from medieval castles, with their privies perched up high in turrets, or from sailing vessels with privies hanging out over their sterns. Far into the nineteenth century chamber pots, sometimes modestly hidden in a *chaise percée*, continued to be dumped out of windows and onto the open sewers of the street.

A separate bathroom was rare in Western Europe until the late eighteenth and early nineteenth centuries. Legendary are the tales about Versailles in the seventeenth century concerning the use of any available interior area for these human functions, even under the Queen's Staircase. But this changed in the eighteenth century. Water and plumbing had become available indoors as water technology developed from 1650 to 1800. Indoor fountains and rainwater cisterns provided water for kitchen use as well as for washing and bathing. But it was expensive and generally unavailable except to the very rich—besides, not all the rich considered these amenities priority items. Personal cleanliness and hygiene were limited at best.

By the early eighteenth century, however, a new attitude of personal cleanliness began to spread throughout the West. It was associated psychologically with the new personal privacy. The body, its wastes, and its odors were to be withdrawn from physical contact with others. Forks, handkerchiefs, and nightdresses came into wider use at this time. Washing the body became the expected norm in upper-class families in the late eighteenth century, when washbasins and portable bathtubs began to be used.[31]

In the nineteenth century, sanitary conditions were improved in the towns. A less expensive water closet had been patented by Joseph Bramah in 1778; the shower bath was invented; and bathtubs replaced the pool-like baths and the portable tubs of the eighteenth century. Benjamin Latrobe is credited with designing the first complete bathroom in America in 1810;[32] but the outhouse lingered in the rural areas until the mid-twentieth century.

American cities did not begin to have water systems until 1820, by which time Philadelphia had acquired reservoirs, pumping stations, and wood water mains. New Orleans, Cincinnati, and New York were to follow before the middle of the nineteenth century.[33] But until the industrial production of steel piping and fittings for such systems, they—along with bathtubs, toilets, kitchen sinks, and laundry tubs—were not common until decades after 1850.

Electric Lighting   One other component of the twentieth-century interior waited until the late nineteenth century to be developed—electric lighting, the "victory over night." Until the sixteenth century most interiors were as dark as caves. Daylight was admitted to residential interiors only through open, wood-shuttered windows—seldom open in winter, probably never at night—or through parchment, oiled paper, or cloth treated with turpentine.[34]

Then, in the early sixteenth century, white glass appeared, still in a form more translucent than transparent. It was never sunny inside, except in streaks. By the late eighteenth century plate glass windows were common in workers' houses in Paris, though less available elsewhere. The new practice of whitewashing ceilings also began to change interior light levels.

Candles had begun to be widespread in the sixteenth century. Oil lamps—with a history of different types of oil that included the increasing use of whale oil—continued to dispel the shades of evening indoors. Around 1808, gas lighting appeared.

But it was the incandescent electric light that made the ultimate and elemental contribution to modern interior lighting. Briefly, the history of electricity in this achievement is as follows:

- 1752: Benjamin Franklin discovers the possibility of channeling electricity.

- 1841: Michael Faraday discovers how to induce an electric current by rotating a wire around a magnet.

- 1844: Samuel F. B. Morse demonstrates his electric telegraph before the U.S. Congress.

- 1878: Thomas Alva Edison develops the first practical electric light.

- 1879: Edison develops the incandescent electric light.
- 1881: Edison helps to build the first public electric-light power plant.

Components of the Twentieth-Century Interior

This, then, is our twentieth-century interior: an interior space composed of walls—in plan either rectangular, circular, elliptical, triangular, or some irregular shape—with a floor and a ceiling as well as windows and doors. To this traditional and ancient assemblage, the eighteenth century added specialized rooms, privacy, and heating as well as comfort of the kind we know today. In the nineteenth century sanitation, plumbing, and ventilation were added along with electric lighting.

These are the fundamental components of the modern interior that had been developed when the twentieth century opened. What succeeding twentieth-century generations have done to vary, alter, transform, improve, elaborate, and minimalize is the subject of the following history of twentieth-century interior design.

In the second half of the nineteenth century, America, with a newfound independence and brilliance, pioneered in construction techniques that permitted interiors to be stacked one on top of the other to unprecedented heights: It was the development of the skyscraper. That building type is rightly acclaimed as the twentieth century's wonder of the world, its Pyramid of Cheops, and more surely as the building achievement of the twentieth century that most captured the modern romantic imagination.

But the skyscraper is not only indicative of our reach for the skies; it is also a compendium of the technologies that were made possible in the second half of the nineteenth century. Then, from 1860 onward, and especially after the great Chicago fire of 1870, when real estate speculation and the growth of large corporations fostered them, skyscrapers put together into one new type of building all the technologies discussed above.

Among them were (1) steel-frame construction; (2) glass; (3) the elevator—made safe by Otis in 1852, and electrified by Siemens in 1880; (4) high-pressured plumbing and sanitation systems; (5) efficient heating systems; and (6) electric lighting and communication systems. These, when combined in a building of ten to fourteen stories, came to be defined as a skyscraper. Among the pioneer skyscrapers were William Le Baron Jenney's Home Insurance Building in Chicago (1884–85); Holabird & Roche's Tacoma Building (1887–88); and Louis Sullivan's achievement of the first expressive skyscraper form in the Wainwright Building in St. Louis (1890).

Interior decorators and designers did not have much involvement in skyscrapers—except in lobby decorations—until the middle of the twentieth century. Before then, office interiors were almost exclusively the province of the office manager and the furniture supplier, except in rare projects by exceptional architects. By the middle of the twentieth century, however, interior designers had developed an expertise that was to make them indispensable in office design in skyscrapers and elsewhere.

Design Education

Design education grew along with other educational institutions. To further the improvement of design in this country, new schools and programs had been initiated throughout the nineteenth century. First came art schools such as the Maryland Institute of Art in Baltimore, founded in 1826, and the Moore College of Art in Philadelphia, founded in 1844; but they did not add design courses or programs until much later.[35] The Massachusetts Institute of Technology (MIT) was the first school of architecture on these shores; founded in 1865, MIT's program was followed by other architecture schools in due course.

Shortly thereafter, specialized design schools began to be established: the Minneapolis College of Art and Design in 1867, the Art Institute of Chicago in 1869, the Columbus College of Art in 1870, the Philadelphia College of Art in 1876. University programs were started at the University of Cincinnati in 1870 and at Syracuse University in 1870, among others. Soon other design schools and programs were initiated: the New York School of Decorative Arts in 1877, the Rhode Island School of Design in 1877, the Cleveland Institute of Art in 1882, the Kansas City Art Institute in 1882, and Pratt Institute in Brooklyn, New York, in 1887.

Most of these design programs seem to have been directed toward art and graphic design and to painted decoration rather than to overall interior design. Education in that broader sphere began in the twentieth century in America. Together, all these factors combined to bring about the existence of educated interior designers as a new and necessary twentieth-century profession.

Suggested Reading

Banham, Reyner. *The Architecture of the Well-Tempered Environment.* London: The Architectural Press, 1969. Chicago: University of Chicago Press, 1969.

Benevolo, Leonardo. *History of Modern Architecture.* Cambridge: MIT Press, 1971 (especially Chapter 7).

Braudel, Fernand. *Afterthoughts on Material Civilization and Capitalism.* Baltimore: Johns Hopkins University Press, 1977.

———. *The Structures of Everyday Life.* New York: Harper & Row, 1981.

Cowan, Henry J. *Design of Reinforced Concrete Structures.* Englewood Cliffs, NJ: Prentice-Hall, 1982.

Eisenberg, Elizabeth. *The Printing Press as an Agent of Change.* Cambridge: Cambridge University Press, 1979.

Fitch, James Marston. *American Building,* Vol. 1: *The Historical Forces That Shaped It.* Boston: Houghton Mifflin Company, 1947, 1966 (see Chapter 4).

Foucault, Michel. *The Birth of the Clinic.* New York: Pantheon Books, 1973.

———. *Discipline and Punish: The Birth of the Prison.* New York: Pantheon Books, 1977.

Giedion, Sigfried. *Mechanization Takes Command.* Oxford: Oxford University Press, 1948. New York: W. W. Norton, 1975.

———. *Space, Time and Architecture.* Cambridge: Harvard University Press, 1941, 1954, 1976.

Girouard, Mark. *Life in the English Country House.* New Haven: Yale University Press, 1978. Baltimore: Penguin Books, 1980.

Hitchcock, Henry-Russell. *Architecture in the Nineteenth and Twentieth Centuries.* Baltimore: Penguin Books, 1958–82.

Kaufmann, Edgar, Jr. "Interior Design: Architecture or Decoration?" *Progressive Architecture.* October 1962, pp. 141–44.

Palmer, Robert R. *Age of Democratic Revolution: A Political History of Europe and America.* Princeton: Princeton University Press, 1970.

———, and Joel Colton. *A History of the Modern World.* New York: Alfred A. Knopf, 1966, 1977.

Pevsner, Nikolaus. *Pioneers of Modern Design.* New York: The Museum of Modern Art, 1949.

———. *An Outline of European Architecture.* Harmondsworth, England: Pelican Books, 1943. Baltimore: Penguin Books, 1972.

Praz, Mario. *The House of Life.* New York: Oxford University Press, 1964.

———. *An Illustrated History of Interior Decoration from Pompeii to Art Nouveau.* New York: Braziller, 1964. New York: Thames and Hudson, 1982.

Pulos, Arthur J. *American Design Ethic: A History of Industrial Design to 1940.* Cambridge: MIT Press, 1983.

Smith, Cyril Stanley. *A Search for Structure*. Cambridge: MIT Press, 1981.

Stone, Lawrence. *The Family, Sex and Marriage in England: 1500–1800*. New York: Harper & Row, 1979.

Thornton, Peter. *Authentic Decor: The Domestic Interior 1620–1920*. New York: Viking, 1984.

Notes

1. Robert R. Palmer and Joel Colton, *A History of the Modern World* (New York: Alfred A. Knopf, 1966), pp. 426f., 563; M. Chambers et al., *The Western Experience* (New York: Alfred A. Knopf, 1979), p. 773.

2. Cyril Stanley Smith, *A Search for Structure* (Cambridge: MIT Press, 1981), p. 308; noting Soetsu Yanagi, *The Unknown Craftsman: A Japanese Insight into Beauty*, ed. and trans. Bernard Leach (Tokyo and Palo Alto: Kodansha, 1972).

3. The Crystal Palace, like most such exhibitions later, was not so much a demonstration of vanguard design vision as it was the sanction of official taste made available to the general public. So appalled by many of the objects were vanguard designers that a sweeping aesthetic reform movement began. See the section "The Arts and Crafts Movement" in Chapter 10.

4. Smith, op. cit., p. 144f.

5. Elizabeth Eisenberg, *The Printing Press as an Agent of Change* (Cambridge: Cambridge University Press, 1979).

6. Fernand Braudel, *The Structures of Everyday Life* (New York: Harper & Row, 1981), p. 41.

7. Palmer and Colton, op. cit.

8. Robert R. Palmer, *Age of Democratic Revolution: A Political History of Europe and America* (Princeton: Princeton University Press, 1970).

9. Braudel, op. cit., pp. 353ff.; see also Palmer and Colton, op. cit.

10. Smith, op. cit., p. 96.

11. Nikolaus Pevsner, *Pioneers of Modern Design* (New York: The Museum of Modern Art, 1949), pp. 70ff.; Nikolaus Pevsner, *An Outline of European Architecture* (Harmondsworth, England: Pelican Books, 1943; Baltimore: Penguin Books, 1972), p. 389.

12. Pevsner, *Pioneers of Modern Design*, p. 74.

13. Ibid., p. 69; Sigfried Giedion, *Space, Time and Architecture* (Cambridge: Harvard University Press, 1941, 1954), p. 200.

14. Pevsner, *Pioneers of Modern Design*, p. 76.

15. Braudel, op. cit., p. 296f.; Leonardo Benevolo, *History of Modern Architecture* (Cambridge: MIT Press, 1971) p. 20.

16. Nikolaus Pevsner, John Fleming, and Hugh Honour. *A Dictionary of Architecture* (Woodstock, NY: The Overlook Press, 1976), p. 545.

17. Henry J. Cowan, *Design of Reinforced Concrete Structures* (Englewood Cliffs, NJ: Prentice-Hall, 1982), pp. 13ff.

18. Ibid., p. 13; Benevolo, op. cit., p. 321f.

19. Cowan, op. cit., p. 17.

20. Pevsner, *An Outline of European Architecture*, p. 382.

21. Ibid., p. 383.

22. Lawrence Stone, *The Family, Sex and Marriage in England: 1500–1800* (New York: Harper & Row, 1979), pp. 169, 245.

23. Braudel, op. cit., p. 307; Mark Girouard, *Life in the English Country House* (New Haven: Yale University Press, 1978. Baltimore: Penguin Books, 1980), pp. 126, 230f.; Mario Praz, *An Illustrated History of Interior Decoration from Pompeii to Art Nouveau* (New York: Braziller, 1964; New York: Thames and Hudson, 1982), p. 152f.

24. Stone, op. cit., p. 246; Braudel, op. cit., p. 308; Girouard, op. cit., pp. 194, 230f.

25. Braudel, op. cit., p. 308; Stone, op. cit., p. 245f.; Girouard, op. cit., pp. 143f., 214ff.

26. Braudel, op. cit., p. 308; Stone, op. cit., pp. 169, 245f.; Girouard, op. cit., pp. 114, 123.

27. Braudel, op. cit., passim; Sherrill Whiton, *Interior Design and Decoration* (New York: J. B. Lippincott, 1937, 1974), p. 156f. Sigfried Giedion, *Mechanization Takes Command* (Oxford: Oxford University Press, 1948; New York: W. W. Norton, 1975), pp. 305–28; Praz, op. cit., pp. 56–59, 152–67.

28. Braudel, op. cit., p. 298f.; James Marston Fitch, *American Building*, Vol. 1: *The Historical Forces That Shaped It* (Boston: Houghton Mifflin Company, 1947, 1966), pp. 15f., 116ff. Girouard, op. cit., p. 263.

29. Braudel, op. cit. p. 299.

30. Ibid., p. 310; Fitch, op. cit., pp. 22, 113f.; Girouard, op. cit., pp. 246ff., 265ff.

31. Stone, op. cit., p. 169; Girouard, op. cit., p. 256.

32. Talbot Hamlin, *Benjamin Henry Latrobe* (New York: Oxford University Press, 1955), p. 342f. Hamlin observes that Latrobe's sketch, dated January 23, 1810, for rearranging the bathroom of the Markoe house in Philadelphia is "perhaps the earliest existing American drawing of a complete bathroom."

33. Benevolo, op. cit., Chapter 7; Fitch, op. cit., p. 113.

34. Braudel, op. cit., pp. 296f., 310; Fitch, op. cit., p. 21.

35. Arthur J. Pulos, *American Design Ethic: A History of Industrial Design to 1940* (Cambridge: MIT Press, 1983), p. 157.

Chapter 10

1900–1910: Pioneers of Twentieth-Century Interior Design

When the twentieth century opened, interior design presented two different directions, or basic approaches, for designers to take. One was the ages-old evolutionary direction that closely followed, built upon, and gradually advanced the historical traditions of the past. This conservative direction led to a concentration on refinements of visual style—to a predominant concern with surface and ornament, color and texture, furnishings and accessories.

The other direction aimed to explore innovation and invention, the future and the new. This more radical approach looked at all aspects of interior design as potential candidates for experiment and improvement. It investigated the shapes of spaces, their structural and construction systems, their functional activity patterns, the use of new materials, new manufacturing processes, and any other aspect of interior design that was of immediate interest. That included walls, ceilings, floors, furniture, and objects. This direction led to an ultimate concern for the integration of all these elements to achieve total design consistency.

The two approaches were distinguished by breadth of concern, scope of interest, and degree of detail. One was concerned more with the way things look; the other was concerned more with the way things work. Their differences may have been matters of emphasis and scope; nevertheless, in the twentieth century their existence led to the division of interior design into two separate professions.

The conservative approach was carried to new prominence in the first decade of the twentieth century by the work of Elsie de Wolfe. She began twentieth-century decorating, both as a style and as a profession. The other direction at that time was epitomized by the work of Frank Lloyd Wright. He brought early Modernism to interior design during that same first decade of the twentieth century. The disparate nature of their approaches and of their activities set the world of interior designers onto two distinct—and often controversial and conflicting—courses for the entire century.

Elsie de Wolfe: The Birth of Professional Decorating

Elsie de Wolfe (1865–1950) called herself America's first woman professional decorator. To a degree, she was justified. Before her there were no independent interior decorators who were considered professionals. It was not that the activity of decorating interiors was new. That had been engaged in at least since prehistoric cave painting. It was new, however, for a woman to practice it as a profession.

The sculptors, architects, and other artisans who had also designed interiors were considered artists or craftsmen. The linen drapers, upholsterers, and painters who traditionally had provided interior furnishings—along with the cabinetmakers-turned-manufacturers of the nineteenth century—were considered shopkeepers. In France these latter were called *ensembliers,* since they assembled all the necessary furnishings for an interior.

Ensembliers and shopkeepers, however, were tradesmen and craftsmen who supplied specific materials. They were not professionals whose primary province was an intellectual or aesthetic discipline. No matter how refined their sensibilities as artists, such firms as Louis Comfort Tiffany's studios, John La Farge's firm, and Herter Brothers were considered among the *ensembliers* that provided services in the craftsman and shopkeeper tradition. Other such firms at this time included William Baumgarten & Company, the Zimmerman Brothers, and the Rambusch Company, all of New York; as well as the Niedecken-Walbridge Company of Milwaukee, Wisconsin. Nevertheless, theirs was not the status of the new professional decorator.

In addition to these purveyors of diverse crafts, antique dealers and art gallery owners plied a similar trade. Knoedler and Duveen Brothers, the most celebrated among them, offered paintings and sculptures by the great Gothic and Renaissance masters along with important furniture from the past. As tastemakers themselves, they recommended interior design schemes and the architects and craftsmen to carry them out. The end of the nineteenth century through the first quarter of the twentieth century was the age of the great collectors.

Elsie de Wolfe, in contrast to this tradition, did not practice as a craftsperson. She was a supervising designer and, consequently, called herself a professional. In so doing she gave an initial stance of independence and social standing to the twentieth-century activity of interior design.

Elsie de Wolfe was born in New York City of parents from Nova Scotia. She was sent off to finishing school in Scotland, and at the age of twenty was presented to Queen Victoria and London society. This event focused her vision of life on elegance, refinement, good living, and good taste. In 1890 she began a fourteen-year career as a professional actress—from the age of twenty-five to thirty-nine. Her reviews were never entirely favorable, but her acting made it economically possible for her to spend summers in France, where she commissioned the clothes that she wore on stage. She first became known for her sense of style in clothes.

During this period she set up housekeeping in New York City with Elisabeth Marbury, who established herself as the foremost theater and literary agent of her day. It was in their house on Irving Place—the house that author Washington Irving had once owned—that Elsie de Wolfe laid the foundation of twentieth-century decorating. She transformed its interiors from those of a dark Victorian dwelling into the prototype of twentieth-century decoration. From it she launched her career as the first American woman professional interior decorator.

The Turn-of-the-Century Interior

Before Elsie de Wolfe made her first foray into the world of interior design, the average American residential interior was almost universally cast in the image of the dark, stuffy, and cluttered late-Victorian art gallery, or as a scrapbook of mementos collected over years of travel. From the homes of the middle class to the monumental interiors of such magnates as the Vanderbilts and J. P. Morgan (see Figure 51), the goal seemed to be to fill rooms with collections—paintings, sculptures, tapestries, manuscripts, and furnishings from the past. Dark, somber rooms were considered evocative of the Gothic age, the Greco-Roman classical inspiration, and the Italian Renaissance summation of both. Antique furnishings were therefore the keystone of this direction.

In average houses, walls—or what could be seen of them beneath their patch-work of gilt-framed paintings, lithographs, and engravings—were papered or

51. McKim, Mead & White. The Pierpont Morgan Library. New York City. 1903–06. *Photograph courtesy The New-York Historical Society, New York City.*

upholstered in heavy, dark patterns. Tables were covered with tapestries, overlaid with embroidery, crewelwork, or handworked linen. Crocheted doilies helped to protect those table coverings from the footprints of countless pictures, bronze statues, vases of china or cloisonné, and whatever bric-a-brac might be acquired in travel or from auction houses. At the windows, multiple layers of shutters, roller shades, lace curtains, and heavy overdraperies helped to sequester this romantic mood. By the late 1890s, however, some exceptions to this general design approach had begun to emerge, and Elsie de Wolfe's house was one of them.

The original interiors of the de Wolfe–Marbury house on Irving Place were typical of the average clutter, stuffiness, and confusion. In the dining room (see Figure 52A) the heavy Victorian moldings, doorjambs, and doors, like the paneled wainscoting and the capitals and bases of two columns flanking the window bay, were all varnished dark brown. A striped wall covering was overlaid with hanging plates, tapestry, and paintings in gilt frames. The chimney breast was layered with a dark panel instead of the striped wall covering; and on top of that panel a collection of plates was hung in a circle around a Rococo gilt-framed mirror. The mantelpiece itself displayed a bowl and four ceramic swans as well as four shaded candlesticks. A grandfather clock stood nearby.

Over the sideboard, which was laden with silver spread out on a cloth runner, was a two-level rack of plates hung in front of a tapestry panel. More plates were hung above this tapestry as well as over the doors to the room. The furniture was dark-finished, the table draped in damask that revealed only the reeded bulbous feet. Above it was a metal chandelier with round glass globes. The chairs, of Chippendale appearance, were upholstered with patterned damask edged with fringe, and had separate fringed back pillows. All this rested on a floor overlaid with oriental carpets and runners with contrasting patterns and colors.

The Elsie de Wolfe Style

Elsie de Wolfe redecorated that dining room in 1898 (see Figure 52B). The striped wall covering remained the same, but the woodwork—wainscoting, doors, ceiling molding, as well as the bases and capitals of the columns—were all painted white. The chandelier, the tapestry, the clock, the easel-mounted portrait, and all the plates were removed. The chairs were replaced with a cane-back Louis XVI model that had a light-colored frame. On the table the same dark damask was lightened by a linen runner, on top of which was a sheet of glass. All the oriental rugs were replaced by a single plain carpet. Over the mantelpiece the dark panel had come down, along with the Rococo mirror and the plates. It was replaced by a single large, paneled gilt mirror that filled the same space. On the mantelpiece the shaded candlesticks remained, but the swans were superseded by a white Louis XVI–vintage bust. Additional wall sconces were mounted against large white-framed mirrors. And at the windows were simple shades and half-curtains of white muslin. The influence of electric lighting on vision was everywhere. It was, in the words of one visitor, "a model of simplicity . . . gold and white."[1]

In the drawing room Elsie de Wolfe wrought a similar transformation. The Turkish cozy corner, which had been hung with fabric, layered with pictures, and piled with pillows covered in a dozen different fabrics, was swept away. Along with it went a mass of chests and tables stacked with brass jardinieres for potted palms, aspidistras, and fronds of pampas grass. In their place she filled the bay window with flowers and let the light come into the room. The heavy furniture was replaced by French pieces. She banished the fabric that had draped the mantelpiece, and stripped away the ornaments and collections of fans, portraits, and bric-a-brac.

In the bedrooms, too, Elsie de Wolfe painted the woodwork and furniture the same shade of ivory. Then she covered the beds, chairs, windows, often the walls,

52A. Elsie de Wolfe. Own dining room, Irving Place. New York City. 1896. *Photograph from The Byron Collection, The Museum of the City of New York.*

52B. Elsie de Wolfe. Own dining room, Irving Place. New York City. After 1898. *Photograph from The Byron Collection, The Museum of the City of New York.*

and even the wastebaskets with a single pattern of chintz (see Figure 53). For a city house, such country simplicity was virtually unheard of.

The entire transformation was, to the eyes of her contemporaries, dazzling. Elsie de Wolfe stripped away the many overlays of *things* that the Industrial Revolution had made possible by 1851. Instead of the dark Renaissance and Queen Anne imagery that had been popular for decades, Elsie de Wolfe had adopted the 1890s preference for Neoclassicism—the elegant eighteenth-century French furniture of Louis XV and of Louis XVI. These she brought back from her summers in Versailles, along with the comfortable chintzes she had seen on visits to English country houses. While Americans were still cherishing their newly rediscovered Colonial interiors and furniture, Elsie de Wolfe offered French eighteenth-century pieces (see Figure 54).

Elsie de Wolfe had begun to redecorate the house on Irving Place sometime between the fall of 1897 and the end of 1898. Elisabeth Marbury's theater and literary connections brought celebrated European visitors to the house such as Sarah Bernhardt, Oscar Wilde, and Beerbohm Tree. New York and Boston society leaders came on invitation to see them—the architect Stanford White, Henry Adams, Isabella Stewart Gardner, William C. Whitney, and Mrs. William K. Astor, the capacity of whose ballroom prompted the epithet "The 400" for the select echelon of New York "society."

To all visitors Elsie de Wolfe's sense of style in decorating was established— just as her sense of style in dressing had first been established on the stage. So she had cards printed, announcing that she was available to supervise the arrangement of other people's houses. Business came in immediately. She had established herself as a professional interior decorator by the turn of the century.

Antecedents of the de Wolfe Style

Elsie de Wolfe was not the first to object to the darkness and clutter of the interiors of her day, nor the first to do something about them. Her protest was part of a quest for "light, air, and comfort,"[2] as she wrote, that became a popular desire

53. Elsie de Wolfe. Elisabeth Marbury's bedroom. New York City. After 1898. *Photograph from Elsie de Wolfe,* The House in Good Taste *(New York: The Century Co., 1913).*

54. Elsie de Wolfe. Own living room, Irving Place. New York City. After 1898. *Photograph from Elsie de Wolfe,* The House in Good Taste *(New York: The Century Co., 1913).*

55. C. F. A. Voysey. Own house, The Orchard. Chorley Wood, Hertfordshire, England. 1900. *Photograph from Karl Mang,* History of Modern Furniture *(New York: Harry N. Abrams, 1979).*

around the turn of the century. All-white rooms had been designed by Boffrand and Gabriel in the eighteenth century, when lightness had also been a goal. After the dark-brown decades of the late-Victorian period, lightness was revived in the 1890s in England by architect C. F. A. Voysey (see Figure 55) and in Scotland by architect Charles Rennie Mackintosh (see Figure 56) and his colleagues, the MacNairs. Their house designs and their restaurant designs had made similarly dramatic effects with light-colored paints and enamels. Their work had influenced the designers of Vienna's Secession movement, including architect Josef Hoffmann and designer Koloman Moser, who also took up the vogue for white.

56. Charles Rennie Mackintosh. Entry hall, Hill House. Helensburgh, Scotland. 1902–03. *Photograph from Karl Mang,* History of Modern Furniture *(New York: Harry N. Abrams, 1979).*

Though she probably knew little of this European work, Elsie de Wolfe adopted the penchant of the 1890s for lightness—beige, ivory, and white. Along with this came the new and brighter electric light that greatly influenced interior design by the turn of the century. She further lightened her schemes with mirrors and glass; the absence of bric-a-brac refreshed and brought air to her work.

Edith Wharton and Ogden Codman   In December 1897 the book *The Decoration of Houses* by Edith Wharton and architect Ogden Codman appeared in America. Edith Wharton, not yet the celebrated novelist she would become, claimed that the book was the only study of house decoration as a branch of architecture that had been published in the past fifty years. *The Decoration of Houses* set out to sweep away the confusion and clutter of "a superficial application of ornament" and to supplant, instead, architectural proportions, harmony of style, and classical European furnishings. Wharton and Codman stressed the importance of "repose and distinction" over the ostentatious display of bric-a-brac. Simplicity, suitability, and, perhaps above all, authenticity were tenets that the book generally established.

The Decoration of Houses is authoritative, enthusiastic, and convincing. Although Elsie de Wolfe never acknowledged her familiarity with it, the evidence strongly suggests that it had influenced her first venture into interior design in her Irving Place house.

Elsie de Wolfe may also have known the interior designs by Ogden Codman, who had opened a Boston office in 1891, one in Newport in 1893, and then another in New York. Among his most important commissions was the decoration of the upstairs bedrooms in Cornelius Vanderbilt's Newport house, The Breakers; they have been restored and stand as a clear example of Codman's work. He had transformed Edith Wharton's Newport house, adding to it "a certain dignity," as she later wrote, and revealing the common "dislike of sumptuary excesses"[3] that led them to collaborate on *The Decoration of Houses*.

Education and Journals   Another source of Elsie de Wolfe's inspiration must have been an article by Mrs. Candace Wheeler, who had been a design partner with Louis Comfort Tiffany in the Associated Artists around 1880 and who had founded the Society of Decorative Art in New York. Mrs. Wheeler's article, "Interior Decoration as a Profession for Women," was published in *The Outlook* magazine in 1895. But her suggested qualifications for women decorators—"much special *training*" and "work in an architect's office"[4]—seem to have given Elsie de Wolfe no hesitation. Besides, such experience was not easy for women to come by in the late nineteenth century.

Education in interior design was not readily available through American schools at this time. Art schools across the country continued to expand their programs in the arts and crafts. Not until after 1904, however, did the New York School of Fine and Applied Arts, which had been established as a school for painting in 1896, begin to offer courses in interior decoration. Those courses were initiated after the arrival of Frank Alvah Parsons, by which time there appeared to be a sufficient number of interested students.

For the general reader *Ladies' Home Journal* (founded in 1883), *House Beautiful* (founded in 1896), and *House & Garden* (founded in 1901) kept readers abreast of the newest developments, including the work of Frank Lloyd Wright. Of the trade journals at this time, *Decorative Furnisher, Arts & Decoration*, and *Good Furniture* were forward-looking; but *The Upholsterer* was published for the audience that indicated the actual early status of the profession.

Stanford White   The real father of the Elsie de Wolfe style and approach was Stanford White (1853–1906). By the 1890s he was the leading American designer of interiors. As a partner in the architecture firm of McKim, Mead & White since 1879, he had gradually begun to change the American interior from one of dark and heavy Victorian dinginess into one that was lighter, more delicate in detail, and more graceful in character.

Buildings were embellished, under his hand, by delicate friezes and moldings in the Florentine style—swirls of vines interspersed with seated griffins and the like. Pale and gilded mosaics, intarsia designs, and carvings further enhanced his schemes. In his country houses a recall of Louis XIII splendor within Adamesque white fluted columns and other trappings of the classical revival created interiors that were, for all their decorative features, lighter and freer than what had gone before (see Figure 57).

In 1905 he effected another change—in both the look of interiors and the profession of interior design—when he secured the commission for Elsie de Wolfe to furnish his new building for the Colony Club. The club was a new women's organization for which he had designed the building at 110 Madison Avenue in New York (now the home of the American Academy of Dramatic Arts). Fortunately for Elsie de Wolfe, Elisabeth Marbury was a founding member along with their new friend Anne Morgan, J. P. Morgan's daughter. Stanford White was to say to the club's planning committee, "Elsie knows more than any of us." Thereafter Elsie de Wolfe had carte blanche for her first big project.

At the Colony Club (1905–07) Elsie de Wolfe adapted the style of her Irving Place interiors to the realm of nonresidential interiors, which were later to become known as "contract interiors." On the entrance floor she lined the rough gray

57. Stanford White. Adamesque living room, C. D. Gibson House. New York City. 1903. *Photograph courtesy The Museum of the City of New York.*

plaster walls and ceiling with green trelliswork and trained ivy to grow up it; there too, she installed a fountain and urns, along with garden furniture that had a Gothic-cottage feeling (see Figure 58). This garden-pavilion scheme had been seen in country houses in Newport and at society balls, but never before in city institutions. In another room she designed there were green-and-white striped walls, white woodwork, dark mahogany furniture, and gold-framed mirrors.

Elsewhere in the Colony Club Elsie de Wolfe installed wallpapers with a chinoiserie feeling; she used chintz both in the bedrooms and in the sitting rooms.

58. Elsie de Wolfe. Trellis Room, Colony Club. New York City. 1905–07. *Photograph from Elsie de Wolfe,* The House in Good Taste *(New York: The Century Co., 1913).*

Bedrooms had simple painted furniture—including a writing table, chaise longue, and chest of drawers with a mirror above it; chintz was used as window coverings and for the bedspreads. She ultimately became known as "the chintz lady." In this way de Wolfe brought light and air—as well as the French style and country chintz—to the nonresidential interiors of her day.

By this activity she made interior design and decorating a professional endeavor, as opposed to an activity of craftsmen, tradesmen, or shopkeepers. She also made interior design and decorating a suitable occupation for a woman. In 1910 she began to recapitulate this achievement in a series of lectures and magazine articles. They promulgated her style and her activity, sponsored her first competitor, and spawned the next generation of American professional interior decorators.

Frank Lloyd Wright: Pioneer of Modern Interiors

What Elsie de Wolfe did to lighten the surfaces and textures of American interiors in the first decade of the twentieth century, Frank Lloyd Wright had already achieved with the core, the plan, and the basic forces of interior spaces.

Frank Lloyd Wright (1867–1959) is generally acknowledged to be the greatest American architectural genius of the twentieth century. His innovative vision helped to transform American interiors, as well as American architecture. His original inventions affected the basic plan, the construction, the spatial character, and the connotative meanings of interiors. He gave his residential interiors a wholly American identity and context. He brought drama and mythic meaning to the hearth and the fireplace, to the great hall and the inglenook. He composed nonresidential interiors of interrelated, interlocking complexity such as had not been created since the Baroque and Rococo churches of Europe. In all his work, space as a single flowing entity was the primary goal on which all materials, technologies, and ornamentation were focused.

The designs of Frank Lloyd Wright are integrated at every level. His planning relates to his siting; his spatial geometry reflects his structural invention; his fenestration and lighting reinforce his spaces; his furnishings reiterate his linear schemes and his construction materials; and his every ornamental detail is integrated with his larger concerns. More than any American designer before him, more than most after him, Frank Lloyd Wright achieved an integrated consistency for the totality of his schemes. He called this integration "organic design."

Frank Lloyd Wright had developed his artistic maturity by 1900. He became the first fully independent American architect—independent of reliance on European traditions. In this regard he surpassed his great predecessors Henry Hobson Richardson (1838–86) and Louis Sullivan (1856–1924), who had begun to develop a truly American architecture. Frank Lloyd Wright developed one around 1900.

The first decade of this century was Wright's golden age, certainly his most active and perhaps the greatest decade of his seventy-year career. During those ten years he designed a half-dozen of his greatest masterpieces. Among them were the Susan Lawrence Dana House in Springfield, Illinois (1903); the Darwin D. Martin House in Buffalo, New York (1904); the Larkin Building in Buffalo (1904); Unity Temple in Oak Park, Illinois (1906); the Avery Coonley House in Riverside, Illinois (1908); and the Robie House in Chicago (1909).

Wright's preparation for his career as an architect followed a direct and virtually single-minded path. He was born in Richland Center, Wisconsin, in 1867, and his mother hoped from the beginning that he would become an architect. During his infancy she introduced him to the process of building through the Froebel kindergarten blocks—a kit of geometric building blocks. To them he later gave credit for his interest in the systematic building up of geometric forms in his concepts, plans, and detailing. His father had played music to him, and from it he recognized the relationship between composition and expression. Another early influence was his summer experience working on his uncle's farm. There he gained his appreciation and respect for the land, for nature, and for natural materials. He recognized that architecture was integrally related to life and to the whole of nature. As historian Edgar Kaufmann, Jr., has written, Wright had "a faith in architecture as the natural link between mankind and the environment."[5]

His technical training was brief. From 1886 to 1887 he took courses in mechanical drawing and basic mathematics at the University of Wisconsin. Then he went off to Chicago—already the center of skyscraper construction—and worked for several months in the architectural office of J. Lyman Silsbee.

Wright's real apprenticeship, however, was in the office of Adler & Sullivan from 1887 to 1893. Louis Sullivan was then the leading innovator in skyscraper development and, with Richardson and Wright, one of the three great American pioneers of twentieth-century design. Dankmar Adler was the engineering genius of his day. Those were the years when the Adler & Sullivan office was working on the Chicago Auditorium, the Wainwright Building in St. Louis, and the Transportation Building for Chicago's World's Columbian Exposition of 1893. What Wright learned from Sullivan about the honest expression of building concepts and about architecture as an expression of the goals of society laid the foundation for his dramatic and innovative career.

In 1893 Wright established his own practice, and spent the next decade developing the Prairie houses that immediately established his independent imagination and his place in the history of interior design and architecture. In his early houses and public buildings during that first decade of the twentieth century, Frank Lloyd Wright revolutionized the design of interiors.

The Prairie Houses

By 1900 Wright had developed a clear relationship between his houses and the context of the prairie region—the region from Ohio to Wisconsin and westward

59. Frank Lloyd Wright. Plan, Darwin D. Martin House. Buffalo, New York. 1904. *Illustration © Frank Lloyd Wright Foundation, 1942.*

to the Rockies. Those states of sweeping flat plains, with "amber waves of grain" divided into vast hectare tracts, provided the contextual imagery of Wright's early houses. To relate them to this terrain in Oak Park and Riverside—suburbs west of Chicago that had until recently been flat farmland on the edge of the prairie— Wright devised long low horizontal forms, long low pyramidal roofs, sweeping cantilevered eaves, and rows of windows overlooking the wide views. The parallel roof lines and extended eaves of the Robie House sum up this direction.

Wright built with narrow brick and roof tiles in tones that echoed the soil. He brought the landscape up to the house in urns and other planters, and extended the house into the landscape by means of projecting walls. He thereby created an interpenetration of interior and exterior space. By these means Wright related his houses specifically to their midwestern terrain—to its landscape, to its recent Chicago-school structural invention, to its local materials—and to early twentieth-century domestic lifestyle. He made his Prairie houses entirely American.

Wright's Prairie House plans were centered on a massive core, usually comprising fireplace—sometimes a double fireplace—and stove chimney, which was also integrated with the heating plant (see Figure 62). This was in the manner of his day, which had been popularized in 1869 by Catherine Beecher's *American Woman's Home*. By the manipulation of adjacent ceiling heights and the inclusion of adjacent benches, Wright often created cozy inglenooks in which people could cluster around the fire. At the same time he augmented the practical value of his fireplaces with perimeter heating systems and clerestory ventilation, which were being used in industrial and commercial buildings at the time. Only by incorporating such central heating systems could Wright liberate the American house from its dependence on multiple fireplaces and stoves and on the servants to keep them burning. Wright later explained that hot-water heating systems and low ceilings had made it possible for him to spread his plans into organic blocks and to open up the windows to light and air. For these plans Frank Lloyd Wright went back to the fireplace as symbol and heart of the house.

Wright specified his fireplaces to be constructed of the same stone or brick as the exteriors of his houses. He left these materials exposed, rather than plastering or paneling them over. The effect was to bring the terrain—the prairie itself—into the center of the house and to give the house an actual as well as symbolic anchor to the soil.

The fireplace in the Robie House in Chicago (1909) was freestanding, central to the principal living spaces, and incorporated with the main stair so that one experienced it as pivotal to the entire house (see Figures 60A and B). The Darwin D. Martin House (1904) in Buffalo had a fireplace that was freestanding between the living room and the entry (see Figure 59), where it originally presented an ornamental gilt panel as a welcome. In the Avery Coonley House in Riverside, Illinois (1908), the brick fireplace had an opening that was low and wide, and the stone lintel was as wide as the chimney breast (see Figure 61). The composition seemed to encompass the whole wall, engulfing, welcoming with outstretched arms the surrounding space and the surrounded family. By all these means Wright reinforced the symbol of the hearth as the heart of the home. It was a dramatization of domesticity, a celebration of the strength of the household and of the American way of life.

Around these cores, and on platforms set on the ground without cellars, Frank Lloyd Wright conceived his houses as composed of blocks of rooms. He based his most innovative plans on this additive "unit" system of composition (the word is Wright's) that recalled his childhood building blocks. The most original of his plans were composed in two ways. In the first way, a living room, dining room, and study were arranged in line and essentially open to each other, with the fireplace on an inside wall backed by service areas. In the second way, living room, dining room, study, and main entry hall were spread out from the core as separate

60A. Frank Lloyd Wright. Plan, Robie House. Chicago, Illinois. 1909. *Illustration © Frank Lloyd Wright Foundation, 1983.*

60B. Frank Lloyd Wright. Dining room, Robie House. Chicago, Illinois. 1909. *Photograph © Frank Lloyd Wright Foundation, 1983.*

61. Frank Lloyd Wright. Living-room fireplace, Avery Coonley House. Riverside, Illinois. 1908. *Photograph by Thomas A. Heinz.*

62. Frank Lloyd Wright. Plan, Ward W. Willits House. Highland Park, Illinois. 1902. *Illustration © Frank Lloyd Wright Foundation, 1983.*

pavilions. The pavilions, expressed as separate units on the exterior also, composed L-, T-, and cross-shaped plans.

The Darwin D. Martin House was the largest of the T-shape plans. It offered a long horizontal interior vista. Of the cruciform plan houses, the Ward W. Willits House in Highland Park, Illinois (1902) (see Figure 62), and the Isabel Roberts House (1908) in River Forest, Illinois, both focused on central fireplaces with the living, dining, and porch/reception areas forming the arms of a cross.

Inside, however, Wright worked to free his spaces from this box-like "unit" derivation. He made the openings between principal spaces wider, though usually separable by portieres, thereby merging and interlocking the adjacent spaces. The effect was that his interiors offered long vistas and seemed to flow outward in horizontal outreaches like the open prairie. He made living rooms two stories high with balconies over the fireplace and inglenook. And he inserted long bands of windows—sometimes as clerestories that inflected the view upward—and created an interpenetration of inside and outside. To reinforce this he extended the supporting walls out beyond his spaces and beyond the roofs. Walls thereby seemed to become independent screens; roofs seemed to hover above the clerestories.

Interior space, though defined for different functions by specific furnishings, appeared not as enclosed, but as a single flowing entity. He stepped floors and ceilings so that there were different areas within a single room and spatial variety was achieved, yet openness was not impeded. Corners were often designed as if open. Other openings were semitransparent through ornamental leaded-glass panels. Wright often called these devices "breaking the box."

Wright's plans interrelated one space with another, bringing about an interpenetration of the one with the whole. With his variations on openness, he created the free-flowing space. In this, perhaps influenced by his admiration for the traditional Japanese interior, Wright returned somewhat to the multipurpose interior concept that preceded the eighteenth century's separation of specialized rooms. Such plans were virtually unknown before Wright's work, though there had been some intimations or probings in the area of open planning by the preceding generation of Shingle Style architects in New England. Other forward-looking architects in the Chicago area who shared similar aims came to be called the Prairie

School. None was so dedicated to advancing spatial expression as Frank Lloyd Wright. His free-flowing space, in fact, was the progenitor of the "free plan" of the later Modern movement. This was all part of Wright's consistent view of architecture and the site, of architecture and human life as integral and organic. It was also part of his view of the turn-of-the-century American lifestyle as assertively informal and democratic.

Wright's genius reinforced the fundamental functions and underlying meanings and symbolism of a house. He expressed, afresh for our century, elemental statements about "house" that evoked our ancient myths of shelter, that related to our subconscious connotations of nest and fortress. For this and for his respect of the land and its materials, as well as for the informal strength of his house plans, Frank Lloyd Wright is considered the quintessential American architect.

The Larkin Building

The Larkin Company Administration Building (1904) in Buffalo, New York, was the first monumental scheme of Frank Lloyd Wright to be constructed (see Figures 63A and B). An office building for the Larkin mail-order firm, the rectangular-plan building (demolished 1949–50) had a five-story-high skylighted central atrium (see Figure 64) surrounded by tiers of balconies. Brick was used consistently inside as well as on the exterior, although the exterior was of red brick and the interior of cream-colored brick.

On the top level was an employee restaurant and rest area; the other levels were, in the main, open office space—a concept that had recently begun to be

63A. Frank Lloyd Wright. First-floor plan, Larkin Building. Buffalo, New York. 1904. *Illustration © Frank Lloyd Wright Foundation, 1985.*

63B. Frank Lloyd Wright. Section, Larkin Building. Buffalo, New York. 1904. *Illustration © Frank Lloyd Wright Foundation, 1985.*

adopted by American businesses. This included open space for executives on the ground level. It was, again, democratic and American. All levels opened onto and therefore shared the large space of the atrium. Mechanical systems such as conditioned air and fire stairs were housed in windowless corner piers. The cubic forms, therefore, stretched out the interior space both horizontally and vertically. Each element clearly expressed its function. It was a major achievement.

The interiors of the Larkin Building demonstrate Wright's skill and subtlety in building up units. He used them to compose his interior elevations as well as his plans. Inside the perimeter walls (see Figure 65) rectangular blocks of built-in file cabinets (in variable and versatile grids) were beneath rectangular windows. On the atrium elevations, rectangular brick balustrades formed a grid with the rectangular openings to the atrium; on the workspace side the balustrade was composed of a long bank of built-in file drawers. His alternation of rectangles of different dimensions, and of horizontal and vertical ones, and his formation of grids—articulated by the exposed brick piers—showed his mastery of the principle of repetition. It created great rhythm in the Larkin interiors and produced a working space of power, strength, and dignity.

Furnishings and Objects

For all of his projects Wright designed as much of the required furnishings as his clients were prepared to pay for. He designed sofas and chairs, tables and bookcases—piano cases, even. He designed lamp fixtures and stained glass, carpets and textiles, desk appointments, metal urns and vases, andirons and fire tools, china and glassware, and other objects and equipment. In his office, Wright was assisted in his furniture designs by the architects Marion Mahony and her husband Walter Burley Griffin.

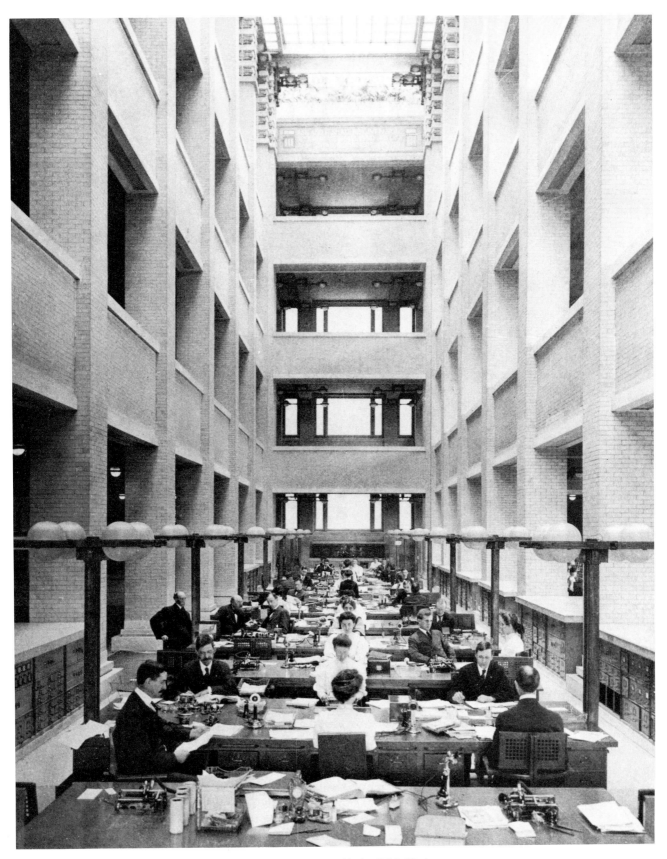

64. Frank Lloyd Wright. Atrium, Larkin Building. Buffalo, New York. 1904. *Photograph from the Buffalo and Erie County Historical Society.*

65. Frank Lloyd Wright. Perimeter wall, Larkin Building. Buffalo, New York. 1904. *Photograph from the Buffalo and Erie County Historical Society.*

For the Larkin Building he designed all the furniture and appointments, making a number of innovations. It was the first metal furniture of the century to express its material and construction so honestly. Manufactured by the Van Dorn Iron Works Company of Cleveland, Ohio, the Larkin desks and three chairs were among the earliest metal office furniture.

The desk chair (see Figure 65) was on a cantilevered metal arm; when the seat back was folded down onto the seat, the arm automatically returned the seat to the knee-space under the desk to facilitate floor cleaning. The two executive armchairs were framed with tubular metal, prefiguring the tubular chairs of two decades later. One version had a swivel seat on a four-legged base, which was elevated on casters. The adjustable back panels of these two armchairs were made as double-layered boxes of metal; for air circulation and visual detail the back panels were perforated in a gridded square pattern. This grid pattern was similar to the detailing of Charles Rennie Mackintosh in Scotland and of Josef Hoffmann in Vienna about this same time. The furnishings of the Larkin Building were innovative and also achieved a degree of consistency that was a model of "total design."

Ultimately, Frank Lloyd Wright's monumental achievement was his consistency, his unity of design. His interiors were inextricably integrated with the massing and structural systems of his buildings. In his interior elevations he made a

66. Frank Lloyd Wright. Armchair, Larkin Building. Buffalo, New York. 1904. *Photograph by Thomas A. Heinz.*

constant effort to relate walls to ceilings, windows to doors, benches to lowered soffits and clerestory windows. Oak-banded panels in ceilings reiterated the rectangular forms of windows and doors. Rectilinear clerestory windows were balanced, were almost symmetrical with long benches beneath them. His furnishings and appointments were unified with his interior spaces, and furniture functions—regardless of their varying success at providing comfort—were integrated with each other: Sofas were combined with occasional tables; electric lighting or candle stands were joined to dining-table corners. Yet, for all that doubling up or inter-relating of functions, Wright's furniture designs retained a simplicity of purpose and of line. "Simplicity and repose," Wright wrote, "are the qualities that measure the true value of any work of art."[6]

Unity Temple

The supreme example of Wright's achievement of those values is Unity Temple (see color plate 1), the sanctuary building of the Unitarian Universalist Church complex, which Wright designed and built in Oak Park (1906). It was his first exposed reinforced-concrete public monument, and perhaps his best-integrated, most organic early work. The temple has a square plan with stairs rising in blank corner piers (see Figure 67A). The remaining cruciform interior space has two tiers of balconies on three sides. On the focal fourth side is the pulpit, with the organ behind it. Over the central square of the cruciform, a coffered roof is skylighted at the top with clear glass. Clerestories of amber glass atop the balcony walls further lighten the roof and make it appear almost weightless. The floor of the temple is higher in the central square than in the surrounding passageways under the balconies, producing a more complex section than one anticipates (see Figure 67B).

67A. Frank Lloyd Wright. Plan at auditorium level, Unity Temple. Oak Park, Illinois. 1906. *Illustration © Frank Lloyd Wright Foundation, 1983.*

67B. Frank Lloyd Wright. Section, Unity Temple. Oak Park, Illinois. 1906. *Illustration © Frank Lloyd Wright Foundation, 1985.*

The space flows in, over, and under the balconies, around the great square piers supporting them, and around pendant light fixtures. The eye is led through this constantly flowing space by linear ornament of oak trim banding. That banding merges the two-dimensional with the three-dimensional elements and sends the eye along its raceways to discover the interlocking space and, at the same time, it coalesces the space, bringing it all back together to the center. That center is the acceleration or concentration of oak battens screening the organ box above the speaker's rostrum. The entire composition is a masterly interweaving of major space and circulation passageways with structure, lighting, furnishings, and ornamentation.

In Unity Temple the integration of all elements is unified to a degree unparalleled in American interior design—perhaps from that day to our own. Wall and window are one; ceiling and skylight are one; furniture is part of the walls; ornament is wall. Only the lighting fixtures stand apart as separate sculptural elements. Yet even they are treated in the linear vocabulary of the total design. As a metaphor of the temple itself, as well as a culmination of Frank Lloyd Wright's work to that date, the unity of this design is absolute. And if ever in twentieth-century interior design one can be elevated to transports of the sublime, it is in Unity Temple.

In 1910 the decade was recapitulated by Wright in the pair of portfolios of his work published in Berlin by Ernst Wasmuth. Wright had spent more than a year in Europe preparing the one hundred large lithographs of his projects. The Wasmuth Portfolios and the companion paperbound volume of illustrations and plans were avidly read by the European progenitors of the Modern style in architecture and interior design, including Berlage, Gropius, Mies, and Le Corbusier. The publications established Wright as the American pioneer of the Modern movement for the next two decades.

The Arts and Crafts Movement

Wright had not been alone of his generation to seek the goals of simplicity, total design, and an American way. Simplicity had been gaining adherents throughout the nineteenth century, and Wright was the direct heir of its tradition. A reform movement against the excesses and disadvantages of the Industrial Revolution (see Chapter 9) was spearheaded in England by the mid-1800s. With Ralph Waldo Emerson and Walt Whitman as inspiration, these reformers railed against these excesses—the evils of the machine and the morally "dishonest" ornamentation it produced when used to imitate handcraft. The development of the Modern movement can be seen as the battle for and against the machine. From the early nineteenth-century reformers until the birth of the Modern movement in the second decade of the twentieth century, pioneer after pioneer, and designer after philosopher, contributed to a shifting statement and sentiment—first against the machine, then accepting it, and finally celebrating it.

The recommended paths to improvement were different for each reformer. A. W. N. Pugin (1812–52) believed in the superiority of the Middle Gothic age. John Ruskin (1819–1900) praised the ideals and models of North Italian and Venetian Gothic. William Morris (1834–96) advocated a medieval model. All equated handcraft with regenerative good and with moral honesty in design. William Morris was the first to return to such a handcraft activity, banning the machine and designing and producing handmade furnishings on a communal basis in a simplified medieval style. The furnishings of Morris & Company were the basis of inspiration for much of the Arts and Crafts furniture that followed.

By the 1890s the Arts and Crafts movement had been spread in America through the writings of Charles Locke Eastlake (1836–1906). Eastlake's *Hints on*

Household Taste of 1868 advocated stripping away heavy Victorian trappings and returning to the simple lines of Tudor England. He acclaimed honest construction "without sham or pretense"; he felt, as previous reformers had, that machine carving should not look like hand carving. Simplicity was the keynote. The lecture tour of Oscar Wilde throughout America in 1882–83 helped spread the movement, and in 1888 the Arts and Crafts Exhibition Society was founded in London, marking the first use of the term. Throughout the 1890s numerous arts and crafts societies, workshops, and salesrooms were founded in Chicago and throughout America.

In 1901 Frank Lloyd Wright had delivered his provocative and influential lecture "The Art and Craft of the Machine" at Chicago's Hull House. From 1901 to 1916 designer Gustav Stickley (1857–1942) published his *Craftsman* magazine, which was the chief platform for Craftsman designers and a strong influence on the public. *House Beautiful*, which was initiated in 1896, also gave space to craftsmen and the Craftsman tradition; as did *Ladies' Home Journal*, which published the work of Frank Lloyd Wright at the beginning of the century. Other publicizers of the movement included a number of professional publications about architecture and building.

The first sixteen years of the twentieth century were the years of the Craftsman movement. The decorative arts—furniture, glass, and art pottery—were produced in a new handcraft idiom; and a whole generation of designers established a sturdy, straightforward, simple style of furnishings, objects, and ornamentation. Theirs was a dedication to quality of design and craftsmanship in every aspect of life. This approach was the correspondent of the wholesome, strenuous, and back-to-nature life that the Craftsmen believed in. For many of them Theodore Roosevelt was the public symbol. They believed that original, handcrafted, honest designs would bring a new social utopia. That search for a spiritual and physical utopia pervaded the first two decades of the twentieth century.

Among the most prominent of the Craftsmen designers was Gustav Stickley, who designed and produced hefty, foursquare oak furniture in his Craftsman Workshops in Eastwood, a suburb of Syracuse, New York, between 1900 and 1916 (see Figure 68A). Two of his brothers, Leopold and J. George Stickley, produced similar furniture in nearby Fayetteville, New York. Elbert Hubbard (1856–1915) worked in this reform tradition at his Roycroft Shops in East Aurora, near Buffalo, New York, from 1901 until his death. He also published his furniture designs, which were among the best in the Arts and Crafts tradition—simple and heavy, of oak and mahogany (see Figure 68B). And George Niedecken of Milwaukee, who had made some of Frank Lloyd Wright's furniture for his houses, went on to design and produce Craftsman designs of his own.

This furniture came to be popularly known in America as Mission Style. Usually of simple, sturdy golden oak and fumed oak, it was the popular version of the prototype furniture that Frank Lloyd Wright designed for his Prairie houses. When his clients could not afford complete furnishings of his own design, Wright encouraged them to purchase harmonious pieces from the Stickleys.

Wright's furniture designs, like his architecture and interior spaces, were a summation of this reform tradition. His designs gave the authority of genius to the movement, and a whole Prairie School of design—based on the Arts and Crafts tradition—sprang up on this basis in Chicago, Minneapolis, Detroit, Cleveland, and St. Louis. Most of these midwestern cities had art schools that offered programs in arts and crafts. There, too, architects and interior designers emphasized "the unity of interior and exterior, the desire for simplicity, a respect for natural materials, an interest in Japanese art, and a geometric rectilinear style,"[7] as the movement has been summarized.

68A. Gustav Stickley. Reclining armchair, white quarter-sawn oak with leather spring seat and cushion, by Craftsman Workshops. Eastwood, New York. Circa 1909. *Photograph courtesy Jordan–Volpe Gallery, New York City.*

68B. Elbert Hubbard. Drop-front desk, white quarter-sawn oak with copper hardware, by Roycroft. East Aurora, New York. Circa 1910. *Photograph by H. Peter Curran, courtesy Jordan–Volpe Gallery, New York City.*

69A. Greene & Greene. Dining room, David B. Gamble House, Pasadena, California. 1908. *Photograph by Marvin Rand.*

Wright himself had first gone to Japan in 1905 but, like the rest of his contemporaries, he had long admired Japanese art. It had been a totem of his era since at least the 1880s, when Gilbert and Sullivan parodied the penchant for "things Japanese." For Wright, Japanese art and architecture had set an exemplar for his dictum, "Bring out the nature of materials, let this nature intimately into your scheme."

Other Prairie School practitioners produced interior design work that followed this precept. Harvey Ellis (1852–1904), in the last year of his life, produced some of the best designs in Gustav Stickley's catalogue, giving the Stickley operation a fresh lift and perhaps its best designs. George Grant Elmslie (1871–1952), like Wright, worked with Adler & Sullivan before starting his own architecture practice; a number of his Prairie-style interior furnishings show the influence of Sullivan's ornament. Will Bradley (1868–1962) designed Arts and Crafts furniture and interiors in the idiom associated with Charles Rennie Mackintosh in Scotland and its development in Vienna.

Contemporary with Wright in California were Greene & Greene—brothers Charles Sumner Greene (1868–1954) and Henry Mather Greene (1870–1957)—whose work combined the Arts and Crafts tradition with Shingle-Style architecture and Japanese detailing and decoration. They redefined and refined the bungalow for its California setting and thereby ultimately influenced popular taste for the

69B. Greene & Greene. Plan, David B. Gamble House. Pasadena, California. 1908. *Illustration from Esther McCoy,* Five California Architects *(New York: Reinhold, 1960).*

next decade. Their masterpieces, built between 1907 and 1909, were the Robert R. Blacker House and the David B. Gamble House (see Figure 69B), both in Pasadena; the Charles M. Pratt House in Ojai; and the William R. Thorsen House in Berkeley. The craftsmanship of Greene & Greene's interiors and furnishings is consummate (see Figure 69A). Bernard Maybeck, Irving Gill, and Julia Morgan, who was the first woman architect registered in California, also worked in this tradition during this time. Lucia and Arthur F. Matthews provided many designs and executed furnishings in the Craftsman idiom for their California contemporaries.

Also influential in this vein was Wallace Nutting, a furniture collector and dealer who focused on seventeenth- and early eighteenth-century unpainted wood pieces. As historian Edgar Kaufmann, Jr., has written, Nutting's was "a brusquer attitude . . . and to him, more than anyone, the tradesmen of the United States owe the sempiternal vogue for 'Early American maple.'"[8]

European Directions

Art Nouveau

Fashionable as Art Nouveau was in Brussels and in Nancy, and fascinating as it has been to mid- and late-twentieth-century observers, it had little stylistic effect on American interior design. Art Nouveau held the design stage of Europe from the early 1880s until around 1900, then was popularized by numerous commercial examples. Largely curvilinear with whiplash curves and flower-and-plant-derived decoration, it was the first stylistic development since Gothic that was not directly imitative of previous historical styles. But it was almost purely a design approach that focused on ornamental effects in interior design. Its influence spread to Italy, where it was called the Stile Floreale and the Stile Liberty—after the fabrics and metalwork sponsored by the Liberty of London store. In Germany and Austria it came to be known as Jugendstile.

Among the rare American Art Nouveau contributions are the glass and metal work of Louis Comfort Tiffany; the book illustrations and posters of Will Bradley; the furniture of Charles Rohlfs; and some of the decorative details of Harvey Ellis, which are in the tradition of Mackintosh. The Arts and Crafts reform movement was in direct opposition to design approaches that focused on surface finish, visual effects, and ornamentation. It was, therefore, in direct opposition to the fantasy ornamentation of Art Nouveau, however antihistorical the aims of that late-nineteenth-century movement.

The early popularity of the Arts and Crafts tradition in America was, perhaps, responsible for the lack of success and the paucity of American practitioners in the Art Nouveau idiom. Art Nouveau did, however, have a profound effect on the ideologies that shaped the Modern movement in providing the other foundation of that movement along with the belief in the machine. That foundation was that contemporary work should be of the day, for the times, and therefore nonhistorical.

The Wiener Werkstaette

At the turn of the century the reformers were joined, in Vienna, by Josef Hoffmann, Adolf Loos, and the Wiener Werkstaette. Inspired by England's Guild of Handicraft, the Wiener Werkstaette (Vienna Workshop) was founded in Vienna in 1903 by Josef Hoffmann (1870–1956) and Koloman Moser to make handcrafted utilitarian objects that would be as aesthetically significant as the work of fine artists. The goals of the Werkstaette were to produce—by handcraftsmanship and the proper treatment of materials—total works of functional art and a "style of today."

The Werkstaette "Work Programme" of 1905 again lashed out against the machine: "The boundless evil, caused by shoddy mass-produced goods and by the uncritical imitation of earlier styles, is like a tidal wave sweeping across the world." Instead, the Werkstaette Programme proclaimed, "We wish to create an inner relationship linking public, designer, and worker, and we want to produce good and simple articles of everyday use. Our guiding principle is function, utility our first condition, and our strength must lie in good proportions and the proper treatment of material."[9]

From 1905 to 1911 Josef Hoffmann, who was Wright's exact contemporary, was engaged in the design and furnishing of the Palais Stoclet (see Figure 70) in Brussels, to which the major members of the Werkstaette contributed objects, decorative paintings and mosaics, and furnishings. It was the unique Viennese total work of art. Although the Wiener Werkstaette had no widespread stylistic effect on American interior design until after its shop was opened in New York in 1911, the Werkstaette was continuing to build the foundations of the Modern design movement.[10]

The Ecole des Beaux-Arts

All the moral integrity of the nineteenth-century reform tradition had focused on the honest use of the machine and of natural materials, and had reinforced structural honesty in design. That last goal reflected the long tradition of rationalist design theory. The Craftsman tradition was, therefore, also in opposition to the prevailing classical revival—or academic classicism—that was promulgated by the Ecole des Beaux-Arts in Paris.

The Ecole des Beaux-Arts not only fostered a style based on historical models, but also established a working method for architectural design that remained a foundation for that profession for many decades. The Beaux-Arts method of composition focused on the importance of the plan, minimal expression of interior on exterior, the progressional aspects of passage through a series of spaces, and the *parti*—the concept that denoted the specific function and character of the building. The predominant style fostered by the Ecole des Beaux-Arts from the last third of

70. Josef Hoffmann. Dining room, Palais Stoclet. Brussels, Belgium. 1905–11. *Photograph from Karl Mang*, History of Modern Furniture *(New York: Harry N. Abrams, 1979).*

the nineteenth century—and taken up by most of its American students—consisted of axial plans, façades broken up into separate pavilion-like blocks, and a vocabulary of ornaments and of elements such as mansard roofs. Among the ornaments were carved swags, trophies, and cartouches; cove moldings around windows and doors; and other French Renaissance and later seventeenth- and eighteenth-century details that ultimately gave the style the name Beaux-Arts Baroque.

Many American architects and designers still flocked to the Ecole des Beaux-Arts for their training. Among them had been Charles Follen McKim, a partner of Stanford White in McKim, Mead & White. This Beaux-Arts classical overlay had been widely popularized in America by the World's Columbian Exposition in Chicago of 1893 with its "White City" of buildings decorated in classical ornament. Four of its pavilions had been designed by McKim, Mead & White. Their work, along with that of such architects as Carrere & Hastings (see Figure 71), can be considered a pinnacle of the Neoclassical Beaux-Arts tradition in America at that time. In twentieth-century America the Beaux-Arts influence lingered through stylistic changes—from the nineteenth century's eclectic French Second Empire to an increasingly refined expression of the classicism of the Ancients.

As the foremost practitioner of these principles in interior design in America, Elsie de Wolfe proffered a similar vein of surface ornament. From the time of the 1893 Columbian Exposition in Chicago, the Beaux-Arts approach had increasingly become the prevailing mode of American architecture and design. Of that exposition, Louis Sullivan had said that it would set back the cause of Modern, organic architecture and design in America for at least fifty years.

Organic = Integrated

The term "organic" had been invoked in early nineteenth-century German philosophy. By the time of the Crystal Palace Exhibition, it seemed to signify a return

71. Carrere & Hastings. Marble foyer, New York Public Library, New York City. 1898–1911. *Photograph © Peter Aaron/ESTO, 1984.*

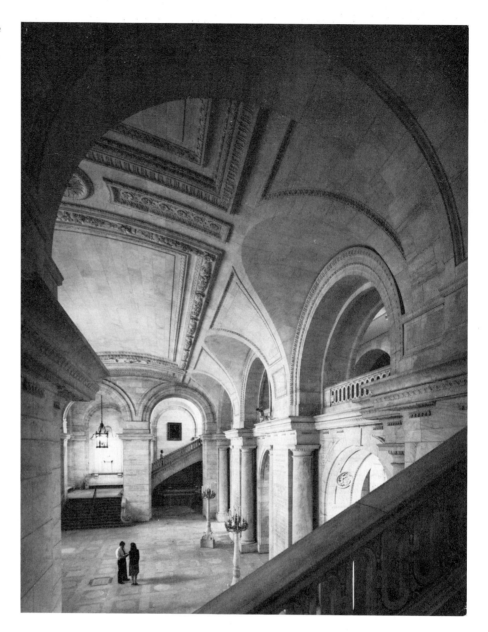

in design to the principles of intrinsic growth in nature. There, that principle was manifest in leaf-covered ceramic wares and other plant-form decoration. Later, Louis Sullivan developed the term "organic" to mean that the structure of a building should be expressed on the exterior, as if structural system and exterior elevations were part of a single, growing organism. Sullivan's dictum "form follows function" is in the design-theory tradition of Rationalist structural honesty. Later, this idea was developed to mean that the form or shape of a design should follow the structural function of its construction technique, and this was to be called functionalism.

Frank Lloyd Wright's goal was to extend Sullivan's concept of the organic throughout the entire building. He used the term to mean complete consistency of design, unity of all elements from planning through construction, and ultimate integration and interrelationship of process and product, exterior and interior, large-scale elements and smallest details. He aimed for spatial continuity and an integration of plan, structure, and ornamentation.

It was from this vision of integrated design that he developed his goal of the interpenetration of interior and exterior space. For Wright, organic meant integrated and consistent. He wrote, "Integration as entity is [the] first essential."[11] In this he represented the mid- to late-nineteenth-century European quest for the "total work of art"—the *Gesamtkunstwerk*—also epitomized in the music-dramas of Richard Wagner.[12] In America Greene & Greene also held and achieved this ideal; and in Austria the founders of the Wiener Werkstaette also aspired to it. No one in his day was more successful in achieving this goal of unity—and in sustaining it over seventy years of monumental production—than Frank Lloyd Wright.

Suggested Reading

Banham, Reyner. *The Architecture of the Well-Tempered Environment*. London: The Architectural Press, 1969. Chicago: University of Chicago Press, 1969.

Behrman, S. N. *Duveen*. Boston: Little, Brown, 1972.

Brooks, H. Allen. *Contemporary Architects*, ed. Muriel Emanuel. New York: St. Martin's Press, 1980.

———, ed. *Prairie School Architecture*. New York: Van Nostrand Reinhold, 1983.

Clark, Robert Judson, ed. *The Arts and Crafts Movement in America: 1876–1916*, exhibition catalogue. Princeton: Princeton University Press, 1972.

de Wolfe, Elsie. *The House in Good Taste*. New York: The Century Co., 1913.

Fowler, John, and John Cornforth. *English Decoration in the 18th Century*. London: Barrie & Jenkins Ltd., 1983.

Giedion, Sigfried. *Mechanization Takes Command*. Oxford: Oxford University Press, 1948. New York: W. W. Norton, 1975.

Hamm, Margherita Arline. *Eminent Actors in Their Homes*. New York: James Pott & Co., 1902.

Hanks, David A. *The Decorative Designs of Frank Lloyd Wright*. New York: E. P. Dutton, 1979.

Heinz, Thomas A. *Frank Lloyd Wright*. New York: St. Martin's Press, 1982.

———. *Inside Frank Lloyd Wright: Furniture, Glass Decorative Arts*. New York: Harry N. Abrams, 1985.

Hitchcock, Henry-Russell. *In the Nature of Materials: The Buildings of Frank Lloyd Wright, 1887–1941*. New York: Da Capo Press, 1973.

———. *Architecture in the Nineteenth and Twentieth Centuries*. Baltimore: Penguin Books, 1958–82 (especially "Wright and His California Contemporaries").

———. "Frank Lloyd Wright," *Encyclopedia of Modern Architecture*, ed. Gerd Hatje. New York: Harry N. Abrams, 1964.

Hoffmann, Donald. "Frank Lloyd Wright," *Who's Who in Architecture*, ed. J. M. Richards. New York: Holt, Rinehart and Winston, 1977.

Jacobus, John M., Jr. "USA," *Encyclopedia of Modern Architecture*. ed. Gerd Hatje. New York: Harry N. Abrams, 1964.

Kaufmann, Edgar, Jr. "Interior Design: Architecture or Decoration?" *Progressive Architecture*. October 1962, pp. 141–44.

———. "Frank Lloyd Wright," *Macmillan Encyclopedia of Architects*. New York: The Free Press, a division of Macmillan Publishing Company and Collier Macmillan Publishing, 1982.

Koch, Robert. *Louis C. Tiffany: Rebel in Glass*. New York: Crown, 1964.

Lambourne, Lionel. *Utopian Craftsmen*. Salt Lake City: Peregrine Smith, 1980.

McCoy, Esther. *Five California Architects*. New York: Reinhold, 1960. (Paperback New York: Frederick A. Praeger, 1975.)

Manson, Grant C. *Frank Lloyd Wright to 1910*. New York: Reinhold, 1958.

Roth, Leland M. *McKim, Mead & White, Architects*. New York: Harper & Row, 1983.

Scully, Vincent J. *Frank Lloyd Wright*. New York: Braziller, 1960.

Smith, Jane S. *Elsie de Wolfe*. New York: Atheneum, 1982.

Smith, Mary Ann. *Gustav Stickley: The Craftsman*. Syracuse: Syracuse University Press, 1983.

Spencer, Brian A., ed. *The Prairie School radition*. New York: Whitney Library of Design, 1979.

Wharton, Edith, and Ogden Codman. *The Decoration of Houses*. New York: Charles Scribner's Sons, 1897.

Wheeler, Candace. "Interior Decoration as a Profession for a Woman," *The Outlook*. April 6 and 20, 1895, pp. 559f., 649f., respectively.

Notes

1. Margherita Arline Hamm, *Eminent Actors in Their Homes* (New York: James Pott & Co., 1902), p. 60.

2. Elsie de Wolfe, quoted from the first known history of the profession of interior design—Edgar Kaufmann, Jr., "Interior Design: Architecture or Decoration?" *Progressive Architecture* (October 1962), p. 143.

3. Quoted from Edith Wharton's autobiography, *A Backward Glance* (New York: Charles Scribner's Sons, 1933, 1964), p. 106f.

4. Candace Wheeler, "Interior Decoration as a Profession for Women," *The Outlook* (April 6 and 20, 1895), pp. 559f., 649f., respectively.

5. Edgar Kaufmann, Jr., "Frank Lloyd Wright," *Macmillan Encyclopedia of Architects* (New York: The Free Press, a division of Macmillan Publishing Company and Collier Macmillan Publishing, 1982), p. 447.

6. Frank Lloyd Wright, "In the Cause of Architecture," *Architectural Record* (March 1908); reprinted in *The Work of Frank Lloyd Wright* (New York: Horizon Press, 1965), p. 10. This is the reprint of the Wendingen edition of 1925, which was one of Wright's favorite books.

7. David A. Hanks, "Chicago and the Midwest," *The Arts and Crafts Movement in America: 1876–1916*, exhibition catalogue, ed. Robert Judson Clark (Princeton: Princeton University Press, 1972), p. 59.

8. Kaufmann, "Interior Design: Architecture or Decoration?" loc. cit.

9. Work Program of the Wiener Werkstaette, quoted from *Vienna Moderne: 1898–1918*, exhibition catalogue (University of Houston: Sarah Campbell Blaffer Gallery; New York: Cooper-Hewitt Museum, 1978), p. 87f. Reprinted there with permission from *Architecture and Design: An International Anthology of Original Articles*, ed. Timothy and Charlotte Benton, with Dennis Sharp (London: Granada Publishing, Ltd., 1975).

    Christopher Wilk points out, in a letter to C. Ray Smith dated August 1985, that the anti-machine outlook of the Wiener Werkstaette should not be overstated. He cites the first article on the Werkstaette published in the German magazine *Deutsche Kunst-und-Dekoration* (Vol. 8, No. 15, October 1904) by Joseph Lux, who wrote: "Amid the clangour of machinery the art craftsman's quieter and more inspired manual work makes its appearance here, even though machines are by no means absent. On the contrary, the Wiener Werkstaette is excellently equipped with all the technical innovations which can assist the work in hand. Here, however, the machine is not a ruler and a tyrant, but a willing servant and assistant." Many of their designs were soon made for machine production, such as furniture and perforated metal objects. Essentially, like other reformers of the day, the Werkstaette members were vehemently opposed to the "mindless imitations of old styles."

10. The influence of the Wiener Werkstaette on American design in this period seems, at this writing, not to have been widespread. But a number of designers were influenced by the group early on. Wilk points out that our view is conditioned by the fact that this period has been little researched up to now.

11. Frank Lloyd Wright, *The Natural House* (New York: Horizon Press, 1954; New York: New American Library, 1970), p. 22.

12. In recent years, a number of scholars have begun to challenge the identification of Richard Wagner with the *Gesamtkunstwerk*. See such works as *Wagnerism in European Culture and Politics*, ed. David C. Large and William Weber. (Ithaca, NY: Cornell University Press, 1984).

Chapter **11**

1910–1920: The Birth of the Modern Movement

There are two choices in most human situations, it appears—two sides to every coin, as the maxim goes. There is inside and outside, male and female, positive and negative, action and reaction, reason and emotion, intellect and heart, subjective and objective, and so on. Sometimes it seems as if the world were divided between good and bad, happy and sad. But, of course, it is not so simple—so black and white—as that. Instead, the graduated areas of gray—where two sides meet in a nonexclusive blend—make them difficult to distinguish.

The years from 1910 to 1920 offered a paradigm of this dual, polarized aspect of life. The decade was divided—ruptured—between a peaceful first half and the ravages of war in Europe. World War I completely consumed Western culture for the second half of the decade. The decade was also divided, in the art movements of Europe, between the peaceful reason of the classical intellect and the unbridled emotion of the romantic spirit. The intellectual direction led toward the pursuit of ever greater abstraction, whereas the emotional direction led to a storm and drama of expressionist movements. The second decade of the twentieth century, therefore, offered two choices to American designers: the choice between Europe and America.

Also, from the beginning of the second decade of the twentieth century, there was a new and important cross-fertilization of design ideas between Europe and America. Whereas European ideas continued to influence American designers, the influence of Frank Lloyd Wright on Europe securely put American design on an equal footing with its European counterpart. In design as well as in politics, America gave up its isolationism.

American Design: A Dichotomy

American interior design exhibited a pluralism of choices. America was a generally agrarian society in 1910, although it was changing as the cities grew rapidly. Class structure was changing with the economy, as usual. The suffragette movement to gain the vote for women was at the height of its campaigning. In the area of industrial technology, conveyor-belt assembly was begun in 1913 by Henry Ford, whose Model-T Ford had been introduced in 1908. By 1915 Ford had produced his millionth auto.

In interior technology, electricity increasingly pervaded lifestyle. New mechanical conveniences, as historian Sigfried Giedion has pioneered in explaining, included the electric refrigerator, first on the market in 1913, and electric vacuum cleaners, which were offered in mail-order catalogues in 1917 (although these large and clumsy machines were used mostly in hotels and mansions).

American interior design and architecture were, in general, more conservative at this period than were their European counterparts. The spirit of innovation, which had reached such peaks in Chicago after the fire of 1870, had given way to historical revivalism. The Neoclassical idiom promulgated by the Chicago Exposition of 1893 prevailed as the establishment style, with Elsie de Wolfe as the most prominent exemplar in the interior design field. The Arts and Crafts movement and the Prairie tradition, with Frank Lloyd Wright as the supreme proponent, was pitted against this Neoclassical Revival. By about 1915 the Arts and Crafts movement began to die out.[1]

In the interiors of the very rich, the great antiques collectors were still amassing treasures from the cathedrals, cloisters, and country houses of Europe. Funding was abundant; clients were spending freely; design factories were facile and efficient. Decorating at this time meant antiques, almost exclusively. Historical splendor and theatrical completeness were the aspirations. A client who ordered a Tudor room expected the designers to complete it with Tudor furnishings. The plunder of the periods was seemingly unconfined. Gothic and Renaissance works were the prized treasures, following the lead of art historian Bernard Berenson and art dealer Joseph Duveen. But Tudor, Jacobean, Georgian, and French periods began to supply the needs of the less rich.

The search went on in Europe to find sufficient pieces to fill a room. Architects as well as decorators joined in the search to find objects for the clubs, residences, and chapels of clients striving to create a myth of tradition. Gothic furnishings and fragments, stained-glass panels and sculptured columns, Italian and Spanish Renaissance treasures, English baronial imagery—Tudor and Jacobean furniture—as well as Hepplewhite, Queen Anne, and Chippendale pieces, and oriental carpets—all were collected with piratical greed. Interiors were rich with carved oak and ivories, cut velvet and tooled leather, Italian brocade and French marquetry. Historian Richard Pommer has noted that it looked as if the American children were dressing up in their European parents' clothing. However, during this time Americans also began collecting furnishings from their own newly rediscovered Colonial houses.

The Arts and Crafts style had been popularized for more modest homes by 1910, as *Ladies' Home Journal* indicates. Frank Lloyd Wright's message that the fireplace was the center of the home had been promulgated, and his designs for dining tables with integral candle stands or electric lighting were broadly interpreted by others. The golden oak of the Mission Style had become the popular fashion. Among the mainstream American dreams were cottages—especially the California bungalow inspired by the original work of Greene & Greene—along with their sleeping porches, which were a sign of the integrated life of art and health that the Craftsmen advocated.

72. Bernard Maybeck. Christian Science Church. Berkeley, California. 1910. *Photograph by Julius Shulman.*

But editorial and critical counsels were beginning to be offered against Mission, which had begun to be diluted with vaguely Edwardian decoration. Craftsman interiors and Mission furniture began to be elaborated as "Flanders" and "Holland Dutch" furniture. The simplicity of the Arts and Crafts movement was beginning to wane. Black oak and black walnut were offered as the substitute for golden oak. In favor of something "trimmer and better proportioned," the *Ladies' Home Journal* in 1910 advocated "simpler furniture of older times." Colonial and Queen Anne Revival in rustic Shingle-Style form seemed to be the answer, along with trimly upholstered furniture that was vaguely Cromwellian. It was apparent that the effects of the Chicago Exposition of 1893 were continuing to spread down the generations and across the country. The Arts and Crafts style had run its course by the time America entered World War I.

Academic Classicism, or the Neoclassic Revival

In contrast to Wright's pioneering effort toward Modernism, the tradition of classicism—elaborated and redeveloped in the nineteenth century and given fresh impetus in America by the Chicago Exposition of 1893—continued to grow stronger in the first two decades of the twentieth century.

In California the Arts and Crafts approach began to fade even in the work of Bernard Maybeck and Greene & Greene. Bernard Maybeck (1862–1957), who was five years older than Frank Lloyd Wright, combined the honest Arts and Crafts approach with a decorative and historical Beaux-Arts overlay. Maybeck designed his celebrated Christian Science Church in Berkeley (1910) with Gothic detailing set amid simple factory-produced elements such as cement-asbestos wall panels and metal factory-sash windows. The interior (see Figure 72) has a singularly rich romanticism despite the paradoxically straightforward construction system. But in his Palace of Fine Arts, built for San Francisco's Panama Pacific International Exposition of 1915, Maybeck adopted the increasingly popular vein of classicism.

Greene & Greene ceased to practice around 1916. In their place the buildings designed by Bertram Goodhue (1869–1924) for the San Diego World's Fair of 1915 initiated a new interest in the Spanish Colonial/Churrigueresque style at its most ornate. Instead of a regional style based in the land, Goodhue imposed a romantic imagination on the historical context of California.

Irving Gill (1870–1936) designed his Dodge House in Los Angeles in 1916. In its entry hall (see Figure 73) he forcefully demonstrated the early minimalism for which he later became celebrated. His Wilson Acton Hotel in La Jolla, California (1908), is contemporaneous with the pared-down forms of Adolf Loos in Vienna (see Figure 74). With no formal architectural training, Gill had worked for Louis Sullivan in Chicago before practicing as an architect in California. From Sullivan, perhaps, he gained his respect for the integrated whole; yet he also maintained a romantic regard for the past. In line with the Arts and Crafts movement, he admired early California missions. It was the simple adobe forms of these missions that he used as inspiration for a stripped, purified architecture and interior design.

Gill's interiors and exteriors, therefore, exhibit a mixture of historicism and Modernism, and the moving back and forth between them that was the choice of

73. Irving Gill. Entry hall, Dodge House. Los Angeles, California. 1916. *Photograph by Julius Shulman.*

74. Adolf Loos. Shop for Knize. Vienna, Austria. 1898. *Photograph from Nikolaus Pevsner, Pioneers of Modern Design (New York: The Museum of Modern Art, 1949).*

the decade. His work looks like the severest kind of Modern functionalism. Yet, in terms of inspiration, the derivation of Gill's work from the California missions makes it historically oriented—if with regional validity—and puts it within the classical tradition of the day.

On the East Coast at this time, where little vanguard investigation was in progress, architects were at a peak of reinterpreting academic eclectic period styles. The Neoclassical idiom prevailed. In New York Warren & Wetmore designed their celebrated French Classical Revival Grand Central Station (1912–13). Cass Gilbert designed the Woolworth Building in Gothic style (1911–13). Perhaps the prime example of this Neoclassicism was architect Henry Bacon's 1914 design for the Lincoln Memorial in Washington, D.C. (completed 1917).

On the domestic scale of Fifth Avenue mansions, architect Horace Trumbauer designed the sumptuous foyer and reception rooms of the Louis XVI Revival Duke House in 1912. Architects Carrere & Hastings designed the classical atrium and period rooms (with the English architect-decorator Sir Charles Allom) of the house (1913–14) for the coal-and-steel millionaire Henry Clay Frick. (It is now the Frick Collection.) Both houses were recreations of late-eighteenth-century Parisian *hôtels*.

During the same period (1914–17) architect George Howe's firm, Mellor, Meigs & Howe, designed and built High Hollow for Howe himself at Chestnut Hill, Pennsylvania. It was designed as an Italian farmhouse in local stone and red brick with fifteenth-century Norman roofs. There, without borrowed ornament, but with a new sense of sculptural massing, a variation on late-nineteenth-century English "Banker's Tudor" houses came about. Howe's approach can be compared with the work of Irving Gill at this time, not only in the similarly stripped window treatments of the Dodge House and High Hollow, but also in their attempts to move beyond the customary correct historical orientation.

In this general reverence for historical models, the image of the adopted model was borrowed to bestow significance on the building or interior under question. As a determinant of the design, no consideration was given to the local context or to the regional area in which the room or building was located. Regionalism and contextualism—which aim to respect and reflect the location or site in which a building or interior is built—were not considerations of the day, much less of the Neoclassical tradition.

Furthermore, the Neoclassical tradition continued the battle of handcraft and ornamentation versus the machine and functionalism. Despite the sneering contempt—or obliviousness—of this historical tradition on the part of the growing number of modernists, the tradition continued—diminishing in numbers and in visibility perhaps, diminishing in scope and elaborateness of design, but ineradicable, it seems, from the consciousnesses and desires of designers.

The Elsie de Wolfe Tradition

As the most prominent exemplar of this Neoclassical tradition in American interior decorating, Elsie de Wolfe's position as society figure and international interior decorator continued to grow. She designed houses for the William Crockers near San Francisco, for the Ogden Armours at Lake Forest, for the Weyerhaeusers in Minneapolis, for Ethel Barrymore in New York, and for Mrs. George Beckwith in Wayzata, Minnesota, as well as a dormitory for Barnard College in New York.

It was the decade of Elsie de Wolfe's prime. She was a success as an arbiter of decorating taste and as a shrewd businesswoman. As part of her promotional performance, she turned herself into an eccentric personality—doing headstands in demonstration of her fitness and tinting her hair blue (it was said that she was the first to do so). She had defined the new profession and started it on the way toward professionalism.

In 1910 Elsie de Wolfe organized a series of lectures on art, architecture, and decoration at the Colony Club. Through such efforts more people became aware of the possibilities of taste and style—and of having designed interiors. Elsie de Wolfe also began designing a new house for Elisabeth Marbury and herself at 123 East 55th Street in Manhattan. Recreating the architectural improvements that had been made the year before to a brownstone house on East 71st Street, which she had designed as a showcase of ideas in collaboration with Ogden Codman (see Chapter 10), she elaborated on her stylistic mixture of French antiques and upholstered pieces, on attractive yet comfortable furnishings, on pale colors and light, on simplicity and Neoclassical proportions.

Committed as they both were to Neoclassical tradition, Codman and de Wolfe had removed the traditional nineteenth-century New York stoop and had put the entry to the showcase house at ground level through a flagstone courtyard. Codman had taken out the original stair along the party wall and had substituted a curving stair between the two parlors so as to increase the width of the rooms. Elsie de Wolfe repeated these improvements in the new Marbury–de Wolfe house. In the entry hall, checkerboard black-and-white marble flooring (see Figure 75A), a fountain with plants, and a copy of an eighteenth-century architect's table set the "country house" tone that was to become the essence of the de Wolfe style (see Figure 75B).

Her color scheme was again white, pale gray, and beige. (So much did she favor beige that when she first saw the Parthenon she exclaimed, "It's beige—just my color!") She used mirrors throughout the house—mirror-lined dressing rooms, mirrors inside the doors of her rose-chintz canopied Breton bed, sliding mirrored panels to close off the dining room windows, gilt-framed mirrors that were hung like paintings in the drawing room, and stair landings sheathed in squares of mirrors attached with gilt rosettes—as at Versailles.

To ensure that her influence continued to grow, Elsie de Wolfe began turning her Colony Club lectures into a series of articles. They were published in the women's magazine *The Delineator* during 1911. In the next year she reworked these articles, along with articles on her work that were published in *Ladies' Home Journal*, and in 1913 they were published in book form as *The House in Good Taste*. The book concentrated on tidying up and prettifying—unlike Catherine Beecher and Harriet Beecher Stowe's *The American Woman's Home*, which had been a mainstay of American house planning, heating, and management since it was published in 1869 (it influenced Frank Lloyd Wright's Prairie House designs). But the de Wolfe book was also unlike Wharton and Codman's *The Decoration of Houses*, in that it was clearly useful for average, as opposed to palatial, houses.

The de Wolfe book offered suggestions about painting decorations on simple furniture; about doubling the use of bedrooms as libraries/studies (and thereby recreating the eighteenth century's multiple-use spaces); about the substitution for garish colors of the pale and light palette—ivory, light gray, white, beige, rose, and pale blue. Black and white were recommended for drama, leaf green for accent. She advocated the elimination of collections of objects, including those that were treasured for their personal associations. The association with Versailles was enough for her, and reproductions were calmly admitted. Family matters did not enter Elsie de Wolfe's sphere of concern. For her, the design of houses was a matter of tidiness and order, of style and fashion.

Still, a sufficient balance or alternation was achieved in the book between middle-class economy and priceless-class patrons to make *The House in Good Taste* not only successful, but helpful. By the end of the decade it had proved popular enough to sell out several editions. Elsie de Wolfe thereby added to her successes the status of an authority/author on the subject of decorating. Despite the stylistic changes of the past half century, the tradition that Elsie de Wolfe established in

75A. Elsie de Wolfe. A typical entrance hall. New York City. Circa 1910. *Photograph from Elsie de Wolfe*, The House in Good Taste *(New York: The Century Co., 1913).*

75B. Elsie de Wolfe. Living room, own house on 55th Street. New York City. 1910. *Photograph from Elsie de Wolfe*, The House in Good Taste *(New York: The Century Co., 1913).*

both her work and her writing about it persists as the foundation of American interior decorating in the late twentieth century.

In 1913 Henry Clay Frick, who (following the death of J. P. Morgan that year) had suddenly become the most important American art collector, hired Elsie de Wolfe to design some private family rooms on the second floor of his Fifth Avenue mansion. The principal main-floor rooms were decorated by the English architect Sir Charles Allom, who had been recommended to Frick by both his art dealer Joseph Duveen and his architect Thomas Hastings. According to tradition,

Elsie de Wolfe became rich on the commission she received for counseling Mr. Frick on the purchase of fine French furniture. She had assumed the position of an international dealer in art and antiques.

The Growth of Professional Decorating

The public espousal of decorating as a factor in modern living was on the rise. The New York School of Interior Design was founded in 1916 by Sherrill Whiton. The growth of the profession of interior decorating had spread beyond the personal practice of Elsie de Wolfe. Among the other women decorators who rose to prominence in the Teens were Elsie Cobb Wilson (see Figure 76), Nancy McClelland, Ruby Ross Goodnow Wood, and Mrs. Cushing in New York; Katherine Parker in Pittsburgh; Lee Porter of Wingate & Son in Boston; Mrs. Katy Tyson in Palm Beach and New York; and Mrs. Edgar de Wolfe, who in California traded on her sister-in-law's fame.

A number of other women decorators formed the Decorators Club of New York in 1914. At the end of the decade, the Decorators Club drew up incorporation papers and the club registered about a hundred members. Prominent early members were Mrs. Mary Linton Ackerman, Miss Mary Coggeshall, Mrs. Emmott Buel, and Mrs. Gertrude Gheen Robinson (the name of her firm was "Miss Gheen"), who had been an associate of Elsie de Wolfe in London.

Elsie Cobb Wilson Elsie Cobb Wilson began practicing in New York City before World War I and decorated many houses in Palm Beach, in New York, and on Long Island. She continued working until 1936, when her firm was reorganized as Smyth, Urquhart & Marckwald. During those years she gave Eleanor McMillen Brown (see Chapter 12) her first job.

Nancy McClelland In 1913 Nancy McClelland established the first known decorating department in a department store. Called Au Quatrième, it was opened at Wanamaker's department store in New York and offered advice on the purchase of interior furnishings as well as antique furniture—in the Teens and 1920s "decorating" meant "antiques." Nancy McClelland went on to become one of the most respected interior designers of the next four decades. She was known for formal interiors in correct period styles. Among her favorite styles were the eighteenth-century French periods; she was soon to add English Regency, Colonial, and Duncan Phyfe (see Figure 77).

Born in Poughkeepsie, New York, Nancy Vincent McClelland (1876–1959) graduated from Vassar College in 1897. She first worked with the Philadelphia Press for four years, then joined the advertising staff of Wanamaker's in Philadelphia from 1901 to 1907. For the next six years she lived in Paris, where she took courses in art history. Then she joined Wanamaker's New York store to create and direct Au Quatrième. It was an immediate success. She was to open her own firm in the 1920s.

Ruby Ross Wood Elsie de Wolfe's assistant on her editorial projects, actually her ghostwriter for *The House in Good Taste*, was a young journalist named Ruby Ross Goodnow. After her marriage to Chalmers Wood in the 1920s, she became celebrated as Ruby Ross Wood. She was Elsie de Wolfe's first disciple—and her major competitor.

Ruby Ross Goodnow Wood, née Pope (1880–1950), was born in Monticello, Georgia. She first worked as a reporter for a Georgia newspaper, and then edited a farm journal for William Randolph Hearst. She contributed Sunday features to other newspapers, along with personality pieces for *The Delineator*, which was

76. Elsie Cobb Wilson. Living room. Long Island, New York. Circa 1914. *Photograph from Nancy McClelland,* The Practical Book of Decorative Wall Treatments *(Philadelphia: J. B. Lippincott, 1926).*

77. Nancy McClelland. Dining room, Iselin residence. New York. Circa 1914. *Photograph from Nancy McClelland,* The Practical Book of Decorative Wall Treatments *(Philadelphia: J. B. Lippincott, 1926).*

edited by Theodore Dreiser. In 1911 Dreiser chose her to write the articles that he was to publish by Elsie de Wolfe. The next year, Ruby Ross Goodnow contracted to write a second series of articles by Elsie de Wolfe for *Ladies' Home Journal.* She answered the voluminous mail that followed these publications and quickly learned about the de Wolfe style and approach. Soon she was interested enough to go into the decorating field herself.

In 1914 she wrote her own book, *The Honest House,* in collaboration with Rayne Adams. The book is more about the planning of houses and about lifestyle than about furnishing and decoration. Its chapters include "The Quest of the Ideal House," "Good Taste and Common Sense," and "A Plea for the Hearth." They indicate the direction of the time: "Ideal" here means historical romanticism; "common sense" indicates the sensible matter-of-factness of the day; and the hearth chapter shows the influence of Frank Lloyd Wright's work. "Suitability is the first and most important law of good taste," she wrote. Among other precepts offered were "absence of unnecessary ornament"; "finer, cleaner, and more beautiful"; and "honest white paint."

Included in *The Honest House* are descriptions and photographs of the house in Forest Hills Gardens, Long Island, where Ruby Ross Goodnow and her first husband then lived. She treated the hall, living room, and dining room (see Figure 78) as a single unit. Against deep-gray walls, she set a deep-orange velvet couch,

78. Ruby Ross Goodnow Wood. Living room, Goodnow House. Forest Hills Gardens, Long Island. Circa 1913. *Photograph from Ruby Ross Goodnow and Rayne Adams,* The Honest House *(New York: The Century Co., 1914).*

large pillows in the same orange velvet, and a small black-painted table; lighting fixtures were of pewter and creamy-white pottery, with an orange-colored shade. In the dining room, oak furniture waxed warm brown rested on a red and dark-blue rug; the curtains were natural linen. The furniture, a mixture of Jacobean and Cromwellian turned pieces, demonstrated the serious consideration of historical periods.

Her upstairs sitting room featured a figured wallpaper of peacocks "perched on flowery boughs" in soft tones of dull blues and greens and gray-mauves on a dark-gray ground. The woodwork was painted the blue-green of the peacock tails, and the ceiling was silver. She also chose curtains of blue, green, and silver Japanese chintz; the daybed cover of a deep sulphur-yellow velvet; and had a rug dyed black to set it all off. For her other bedrooms, she specified cream-color woodwork and ceilings, with Japanese figured papers. Her approach was in the mainstream direction of period rooms, with the inclusion of personal preferences for color, daylight, and freshness.

In 1914 she joined the staff of Wanamaker's in Philadelphia. In 1918 she was asked to direct Au Quatrième at the New York store.

Frances Elkins   In 1918 Frances Elkins, sister of the Chicago residential architect David Adler, bought an 1824 adobe house in Monterey, California. She made the house, Casa Amesti, one of the showplaces of the state, and it began her professional career. Frances Elkins has been called one of the most creative of American decorators.

Born in Milwaukee, Wisconsin, Frances Adler Elkins (1888–1953) traveled in Europe while her brother was at the Ecole des Beaux-Arts in Paris. She studied in France, Italy, and Switzerland. By 1918 she had married socialite Felton Elkins, had bought Casa Amesti, one of the most important adobe buildings in California (now occupied by the Old Capital Club), and had had an early divorce. It was often said of these first-generation women decorators that a woman either had a happy marriage or was a decorator.

Frances Elkins's choice of an adobe house was inspired, perhaps, by the recent San Diego Exposition, which popularized Spanish Colonial architecture; certainly her choice was part of the national romanticism and search for an American tradition that occurred in the Teens. Her decorating transformed the house: She added antique English and French furniture and Chinese appointments (see Figure 79). During the decoration of Casa Amesti over the next several years, friends began asking Frances Elkins to share her decorating talents. She went on to become a prominent California traditional designer for the next two decades, and also designed interiors throughout the country.

"The ladies," as this first generation of American decorators came to be called, brought discipline and order along with style and taste to the upper-middle-class home as well as to the less rich. They continued the academic historical revival of recreating complete period rooms seriously, if somewhat inaccurately according to later scholarship and taste. In this they were passionate, if somewhat primitive. Innovation was restricted to upholstery and drapery patterns and colors, to overall color schemes, and to the discovery of interesting pieces of antique furniture.

Frank Lloyd Wright

Amid all this traditionalism the work of Frank Lloyd Wright continued to be anti-historical, innovative, and consistent. During the Teens Wright's practice expanded nationally and internationally—to California and Florida, to Canada and Japan. His commissions grew from middle-class mansions to include public and semi-

79. Frances Elkins. Casa Amesti. Monterey, California. 1918–24. *Photograph © Fred Lyon, 1983.*

80. Frank Lloyd Wright. Taliesen. Spring Green, Wisconsin. 1911. *Photograph © Ezra Stoller/ESTO, 1945.*

public buildings of large size. But at home his pioneering example and his twenty-year-old style were generally disregarded and overlooked.

In 1911 Wright began work on his own house outside Spring Green, Wisconsin. Called Taliesin, the house was designed as a residence, a studio, a farm, and eventually as a school for his apprentices. Sited around the crest of a knoll, Taliesin both encompasses and is dug into the rise of the land; it produces an interior courtyard and embraces the landscape. Loggias and carports help to merge the massing with the site. Floating flat roofs are intermixed with low, hovering, pyramidal gables that seem to echo the lines of the terrain. Inside, there is rusticity as well as simplicity (see Figure 80). Plain-lined built-in furnishings include drawers and bookcases, lattices and grilles, wood banding and long horizontal shelves. The latter were enriched by oriental porcelains and screens, by plants and fur throws.

Wright's house for the Francis W. Littles, at Lake Minnetonka near Wayzata, Minnesota, was designed in 1912 and begun the following year. It was not completed until after Wright's return from Japan in the early 1920s, and the design was complicated by the demands of the clients. The design is pavilion-like, constructed of traditional brick masonry, and is long, horizontal, and large. Henry-Russell Hitchcock considered the living room to be "the most spacious domestic interior Wright had ever designed"[2] up to that time. It is 49 feet 9 1/2 inches long, and symmetrically designed with 40-foot runs of windows on each side. By the time of the Little House in Wayzata, Wright had achieved the chief qualities that identify his work, as historian Edgar Kaufmann, Jr., has summarized: "the command of space as an individualized portion of a continuous whole; a rare skill in asymmetric composition; a sensitivity to materials; miscellaneous requirements of use harmonized in masterful unity in key with the environment." As an example of these qualities, Kaufmann considers the Little House living room, as it has been reconstructed in the Metropolitan Museum as "basically presentable, with a Wrightian aura, not brilliant but clear"[3] (see Figures 81A and B).

Midway Gardens In 1914 Wright completed his monumental and lavishly decorated Midway Gardens project on Chicago's South Side. Midway Gardens was conceived by the client as an open-air restaurant along the model of the beergardens in Europe. Designed as a quadrangle, with a taller wing enclosing the Winter Garden restaurant at the entry side, the open central area was flanked by raised and covered "terraces" for dining on each side; each terrace was open to and faced a covered bandshell on the far side of the table-filled quadrangle (see Figures 82A and B).

Midway Gardens did not attract the anticipated following, and subsequently declined. It succumbed to the anti-German sentiment during World War I, was eventually closed by Prohibition, and, regrettably for us today, was demolished in 1929. Of all Wright's public buildings, we may most miss this example of his artistic genius at its prime. It had an atmosphere of festivity, joyousness, and ebullience that was generally lacking in the honest, foursquare work of the Arts and Crafts movement. At Midway Gardens there was an openness that was a breath of fresh air; the architectural elements gave a sense of floating, flying wings. From the cantilevered entry marquees upward through the stepped horizontals of the ascending roof planes to the open-work rectangles—which were extended finials reaching skyward—there was an Isadora Duncan-like exultation of the healthy, happy, and full life—the life that Wright saw as integral and organic with architecture.

As Henry-Russell Hitchcock has written,

> Nowhere was interior and exterior space more elaborately interwoven and freely composed, while the ornamental effects are of endless variety and novelty. . . . Sculpture and wall paintings designed by Wright parallel the most advanced forms of European painters, barely known at this time in America through the Armory Show. And the open frames of the tower tops, a sort of linear sculpture of space, reach forward to aesthetic concepts hardly imagined abroad at this date.[4]

81A. Frank Lloyd Wright. Plan, Francis Little House. Lake Minnetonka, Minnesota. 1913–22. *Illustration © Frank Lloyd Wright Foundation, 1942.*

81B. Frank Lloyd Wright. Living room, Francis Little House. 1913–22. As installed at the Metropolitan Museum of Art. *Photograph from The Metropolitan Museum of Art, New York City.*

82A. Frank Lloyd Wright. Midway Gardens. Chicago, Illinois. 1913. *Photograph courtesy Frank Lloyd Wright Foundation.*

82B. Frank Lloyd Wright. Section, Midway Gardens. Chicago, Illinois. 1913. *Illustration © Frank Lloyd Wright Foundation, 1957.*

Inside the enclosed Winter Garden restaurant, balconies surrounded a tall central space (see Figure 83). In his customary manner, Wright juxtaposed the tall space with low-ceilinged spaces. Wright, himself 5 feet 8 1/2 inches tall, preferred low spaces (6 feet 4 inches to 7 feet 2 inches) and tall ones, but did not like medium-height spaces (8 feet 6 inches to 10 feet).

Wright took the opportunity to design a full range of furniture and appointments for Midway Gardens, some of which, such as the table lamps, were produced. He drew up metal-wire furniture (based on the ever-present soda-fountain wire chair); lighting; table appointments (including ceramic dinnerware); as well as murals, art glass windows, and sculptures. The sculptures were a joint effort by Wright and sculptors Alfonso Iannelli and Richard Bock.

The Imperial Hotel   The decade was as divided for Frank Lloyd Wright personally as it was for the political world, with its juxtaposition of peace and war. In 1914 Wright suffered a tragedy when a houseman went berserk and killed seven

83. Frank Lloyd Wright. Winter Garden restaurant, Midway Gardens. Chicago, Illinois. 1913. *Photograph from Thomas A. Heinz.*

members of his household and burned Taliesin to the ground. So it was a godsend that his fame had already brought him the commission to design the Imperial Hotel in Tokyo. For the next six years, until the hotel was completed, Wright worked primarily in Japan.

Long interested in the art and design of Japan, Wright had first visited Japan in 1905 and was an avid collector of Japanese prints. He greatly admired the traditional Japanese house. Now he was called to take his synthesis of that simplified style back to Japan.

The Imperial Hotel scheme was an enlarged development of Midway Gardens and had lavishly scaled and lavishly ornamented public spaces (see Figure 84) and spare, simple guest rooms, which were "Zen-inspired," as Edgar Kaufmann, Jr., has written.[5] For the Imperial Hotel, Wright designed a full range of ornamental windows and sculpture and completely new furniture, lighting fixtures, carpeting, and dinnerware.

Wright's technical genius (in collaboration with Paul Mueller, who had been an engineer in Adler & Sullivan's office) devised a structural system that floated the hotel on multiple-pile foundations, and provided new plumbing and heating safeguards, as well as reflecting pools in the courtyards that additionally served as water supply for firefighting. The results brought the architect worldwide acclaim when the hotel survived the serious earthquake of 1923. (That acclaim did not rescue the hotel, however—it was demolished by the wrecker's ball in 1963.) The solidity of this earthquake-proof structure contrasted with the vast public spaces—restaurants, theater, ballroom, and private-function rooms—which were enlivened by carved and painted decorations, lighting columns, and patterned carpeting that reinforced the overall integrity. It was a total work of art.

European Design: The Case For and Against the Machine

In Europe, architecture took new impetus from Frank Lloyd Wright's work. The 1910 and 1911 Wasmuth publications of his plans and photographs and his lecture "The Art and Craft of the Machine" influenced the next generation of modern pioneers.

At the same time, several new and revolutionary art movements and design-related developments arose. They became the ultimate catalysts for the development of Modern design. The art movements focused on Cubism and Futurism in Paris. The design developments focused on the founding in Germany of the Deutscher Werkbund and the continuing development of Expressionism through groups like Die Bruecke and Der Blaue Reiter. At the end of the decade the Dutch school of De Stijl served as the catalyst to meld these directions together into the Modern idiom that was to follow. Together they led to an abstractionist architecture and design movement.

The "moral integrity" of the nineteenth-century reform movement had established the concepts of honesty of construction, honesty to materials, and simplicity. Honesty of construction meant honesty of production; in reform terms, that meant handcraft. Soon to be resolved was the case for and against the machine—versus handcraft—which continued to seesaw along with the conflict between ornamentation versus stripped functionalism. In the second decade of the twentieth century, honesty of production came to mean accepting machine production; honesty

84. Frank Lloyd Wright. Lobby, Imperial Hotel. Tokyo, Japan, 1914–22. *Photograph from Thomas A. Heinz.*

to "our own time" was adapted to mean the materials of the day—metal and glass—and no-nonsense directness.

Modern design was born in this second decade of the twentieth century. Developed first in Germany and given final synthesis by De Stijl in the Netherlands, the Modern movement was based on the final acceptance, indeed total endorsement and celebration of the machine—not only for production, but also as the aesthetic idiom and visual ideal.

Cubism and Abstraction

Around 1910, in the fine arts of painting and sculpture, a direction toward increasing abstraction was leading to Cubism, which indirectly influenced the case for the machine. That acceptance was made possible by abstraction, which was developed by the Cubists.

In 1907 Pablo Picasso and Georges Braque simultaneously yet independently began investigations that led to Cubism. They were inspired by a Paris retrospective exhibition of the work of Paul Cézanne, who had died the year before, and who had explored the breaking up of the landscape and the painterly field into rectangular segments. Cézanne had said that natural objects can be reduced to the forms of the cylinder, the sphere, and the cone. Separately, Picasso and Braque recognized that they had been similarly investigating the imposition onto nature of systems of analytically derived geometric forms. Picasso's seminal painting *Les Demoiselles d'Avignon* (1907) is considered the beginning of Cubism and therefore the first Modern painting. It demonstrates a play of flat planes and angles that depict human figures conceived in terms of African primitive art. This was one step away from natural representation and toward abstraction.

The decisive year was 1911, when Picasso painted his *Portrait of D. H. Kahnweiler* and Braque painted *Les Portugais*. In these two works the detachment from representation, through the dissolution or decomposition of the representational forms, is complete. This is the development by Cubism of semirepresentation. Later painters carried this further into totally nonrepresentational abstraction.

Abstraction, then, is the drawing out or separating of one thing from another, whether by physical or mental distillation. Abstract painting concerns itself with detaching, breaking up, and fragmenting its natural or physical subject matter into an analyzed pattern of rather more geometric shapes. Or, seen another way, it is the separating out of an analyzed or distilled geometric pattern from its basic physical subject matter. In either case, abstract artists reject the basic value of traditional representation. Natural appearances are merely the theme on which they work their variations. Their invention is concentrated on the arrangement of patterns, shapes, textures, and colors. Modern designers and architects developed this as overall surfaces and volumes composed of rectangles and squares.

From 1907 to 1914 in Paris, Cubism was developed by Picasso, Braque, and Juan Gris. By 1912 Gris was experimenting with structural grids in his paintings. These were later to become keystones of Modern design. Also in 1912 the Cubists began to experiment with collage—the tearing or cutting of pieces of paper—and, more important to Modern design, the assembly of these pre-torn (prefabricated) elements into a composition.

In sculpture the Cubists developed volumes with voids or open holes in the surface, which suggested the interpenetration of several planes and the existence of other sides and surfaces not in view. For the Cubist concept of space was an interplay between plane and depth. The Cubists therefore investigated sculptural forms that were overlapping, interlocking, and interpenetrating. At this time, physicists such as Albert Einstein were formulating new concepts of space-time and of relativity. The Cubist aesthetic correspondence—multiple focus or multiple visual viewpoints—suggested seeing from many points of view rather than entirely from a single viewpoint, in order to express the total image. This juxtaposition of fragments presented a vision, first, of discontinuity and, second, of simultaneity. These became the fundamental goals of the Modern precept of space.

There were no direct connections between the pioneer Cubist artists and the contemporaneous vanguard ideas in architecture; however, this general cultural movement toward abstraction corresponded with current developments in design and architecture. In addition, the combination of Cubism with other art movements of the day had direct influence on Modern design in the 1920s. Among those other movements were Futurism (see below) and the work of the Russian abstractionists—the Suprematism of Kasimir Malevich (1878–1935) and the Constructivism of Vladimir Tatlin (1885–1953). All these movements were coalesced by the De Stijl movement in the Netherlands (see below). Later Modern architecture incorporated into its structure the Cubists' simultaneous experience of outer and inner space.

During the early Teens Marcel Duchamp began to exhibit his "ready-made" artworks, which were prefabricated machine-made artifacts. His seminal *Coffee Mill* (1912) was followed by *Bicycle Wheel and Kitchen Stool* (1913). Both were constructed of items previously produced by machine fabrication and intended for everyday utilitarian activities. Duchamp's ready-made *Fountain* of 1915—a urinal— so scandalized people that they failed to see the aesthetic advance made by declaring that a machine-made object had aesthetic value.

The new Cubist vision, then, first presented this method of seeing the world as detached from nature, as fragmentary and geometric. Cubism thereby prepared the way for the Modern aesthetic system of prefabricated geometric elements assembled into patterns of flat planes. In so doing, Cubism also prepared the way for the acceptance of an abstraction from the human spirit, from the human hand, toward an endorsement of the anonymity and homogeneity of the machine.

Futurism

Simultaneously with Cubism, from 1909 to 1914, a movement toward Futurism in art was promulgated in Milan, Paris, London, and elsewhere in Europe by the poet and dramatist Filippo Tommaso Marinetti and others. The Milan exhibition of the "Città Nuova" (New City) by Antonio Sant'Elia and Mario Chiattone was followed by the "Manifesto dell'Architettura Futurista" (Futurist Manifesto), written by Sant'Elia, Marinetti, painter Umberto Boccioni, and others. The manifesto aimed to change the world, proclaiming that "everything must be revolutionized. Architecture is breaking loose from tradition. It is forcibly starting from scratch again." Marinetti declared that Venice should be taken down and paved over, started over.

Extreme as this wholesale acclamation of the new was, the Futurists dealt the deathblow to traditionalism and historicism in vanguard art. The Futurist manifesto acclaimed "what is light, practical, ephemeral, and swift"—ocean liners, trains, airplanes, zeppelins, and, above all, electric light. These were to be the preferences of Modern designers for the next half century. In painting, Futurist Boccioni showed a plasticity and an interpenetrating quality in his fragmentation that gave a sense of motion unforeseen by his Cubist contemporaries. In this space-time demonstration, Boccioni's paintings directly influenced Duchamp and all of Modern design.

The Futurist movement, however, was largely a verbal and pictorial activity. No Futurist buildings were built, and no interior schemes are known. But the Futurist drawings of Sant'Elia around 1912 to 1914 inspired the vision of city planners, architects, and those concerned with Modernism for the next several generations.

Americans were introduced to the new movements in European art at the 1913 Armory Show in New York City, and later in Chicago. The sensation of the show was Marcel Duchamp's *Nude Descending a Staircase*—not because it showed a nude figure, but because it was a revelation of the Cubist-Futurist depiction of motion. At this time, American interest in Modern art began.

The Deutscher Werkbund

In design, contemporaneously with these art movements, the Deutscher Werkbund was founded in 1907 at Dresden by critic and educator Hermann Muthesius, among others.[6] Most of the major German architects and designers were members, including Peter Behrens, Richard Riemerschmid, and Walter Gropius. The aims of the Werkbund, as set forth by Muthesius, were to unite creative designers and industrial production into what today we would call an industrial design society. Designers of both handcraft and machine production were brought together, and as a group they were brought to the attention of industry and commerce. In that same year Peter Behrens began his work for the electrical corporation AEG; Bruno Taut also began to work for industry; and Bruno Paul began developing a line of furniture for mass production. Richard Riemerschmid had pioneered in developing lines of furniture for mass production even earlier.[7]

Muthesius aspired to the creation of a contemporary style. In endorsing machine production he was both renouncing Art Nouveau and going beyond the contributions of the Arts and Crafts movement to unite excellence of workmanship in modern materials with the machine. Whereas the Wiener Werkstaette had hesitatingly admitted, "We . . . are aware that, under certain circumstances, an acceptable article can be made by mechanical means, provided that it bears the stamp of manufacture," they had added, "but it is not our purpose to pursue that aspect yet."[8] The Deutscher Werkbund, going further, explicitly aimed to integrate the machine style with the ideals of Arts and Crafts. It was a major step in the development of the Modern movement.

The next year, 1908, in Vienna, Adolf Loos proclaimed that "Ornament is a crime." He was reiterating what was then a sixty-year-old argument against dishonest machine ornamentation, but his slogan was taken up as a battle cry for the acceptance of the machine. Fundamental to the outlook of the German and Austrian designers of the decade was the spirit of directness, straightforwardness, or matter-of-factness *(Sachlichkeit)*, which gave birth to an art movement by that name. It has correspondence in Adolf Loos's Steiner House in Vienna (1910), with its plain and stripped garden façade, which has been so much admired by Modernists; perhaps more telling is the less-publicized arched-roof street elevation, which is a matter-of-fact solution to a zoning requirement for building height.

In 1911 and 1912 U.S. museums mounted an exhibition on the Deutscher Werkbund. It began the American public's recognition of Werkbund goals and accomplishments.

Expressionism

Many of the members of the Deutscher Werkbund were adherents of the fundamental twentieth-century design idiom based on rational, structural principles—principles derived from logical or rational construction techniques, and therefore based on the structural grid. Their forms were most often crystalline. Others of the group were more individualistic, however, aiming for what was called, at the time, "untramelled artistic creation." Their designs appeared personal and capricious, tending either to fluid, free-form, organic forms or to irregular crystalline configurations. In this latter group, known first by the self-explanatory term "The Individualists," were some of the most inventive designers of their day: Max Berg, Hans Poelzig, Bruno Taut, and others. The post–World War I work of Erich Mendelsohn was in this idiom, especially his dynamic drawings of 1914–17 and his subsequent Einstein Tower in Potsdam (1919–21). Underlying all their work was a search for a spiritual and social utopia; this search pervaded the work of the immediate World War I period.

The term Expressionism was first applied to the work of painters during this time—Emil Nolde, Oskar Kokoschka, and James Ensor—who exaggerated their forms, distorted their outlines, and applied strong colors, with the goal of expressing the moods and sensations of the mind, the imagination, and the subconscious. They were responding to Sigmund Freud's formulation of psychoanalysis and to his writings of the previous decade. Expressionist painters aimed to reveal this world of emotion, its hidden drives and mysterious motivations underlying human behavior. No such goals were contemplated by the architects and designers of interiors of the time, yet Expressionist has become the term by which the Individualist German designers are known.

Of the interiors designed in this context, Max Berg's Jahrhundertshalle in Breslau (1913)—a giant dome of reinforced concrete—was an isolated work of genius that prefigured the work of Pier Luigi Nervi in the 1950s. Hans Poelzig's Grosses Schauspielhaus in Berlin (1919) showed a Modern direction that movie house interiors could have gone.

The Birth of Modern Design

From the other school of Werkbund designers—those who followed Rationalist structural principles in composing their rectilinear designs—came what is justifiably considered the first Modern building: the Fagus Factory at Alfeld, Germany, completed in 1913 by Walter Gropius and Adolf Meyer. This was the first time a building's façade was conceived in glass, according to architecture historian Nikolaus Pevsner.[9] The south elevation is composed of glass curtain wall set between brick-faced piers, and thereby achieves the complete interpenetration of a multistory interior and exterior, the first entirely unhistorical and antitraditional use of the Modernists' materials—metal and glass—and the first use of the machine aesthetic that was to prevail for the next six decades.

The next year, 1914, at the Cologne Exhibition, Gropius and Meyer built their celebrated Werkbund Pavilion, with its glass-enclosed helical corner stair towers and wraparound glass corridor. On the other elevations the pavilion owed a great deal to the pavilion schemes and formal symmetry of Frank Lloyd Wright. But the use of glass and metal was a pioneering achievement.

Bruno Taut's Glass Industry Pavilion also opened in Cologne at the same exhibition (see Figure 85). It is a far more individualistic or expressionistic composition, having a sixteen-sided lower level, in which stairs have glass treads and risers ascending between walls of glass bricks; but the upper level is a remarkable pointed lattice or faceted dome of metal and colored-glass panels. In that year novelist Paul Scheebart's *Glasarchitektur* advocated a Futurist time when whole walls of colored glass would liberate and enhance our environments. Bruno Taut achieved that romantic image in this primary example of the emerging ideas of Expressionism. In 1917 a glass curtain-wall façade was designed by architect Willis Polk for the Halliday Building in San Francisco.

85. Bruno Taut. Glass Industry Pavilion. Cologne, Germany. 1914. *Photographs courtesy Parsons School of Design, New York City.*

With these structures the Modern style had been achieved. As a sign of the times Peter Behrens, in 1914, designed the cover of a book entitled *Arte für Alles— Art for All.* The ideological inference was inescapable: On the way was good design for everyone, art for the masses—everything for everyman. William Morris had proffered that art is valuable only "if all can share it." Mass production was the only way to make this possible; therefore machine art for the masses would be the goal from then onward. The pioneering mass production by Gutenberg had been extended to architectural design and construction. The Modern movement not only accepted the machine for the potentials of its production and distribution, but also celebrated it by adopting the machine as its visual vocabulary and idiom. So it was that the machine and factory aesthetic of the Modern movement developed.

The Impact of World War I

From the time the decade was divided by World War I (1914–18), this design progress was interrupted. Wartime depression was pervasive in most fields, with the exception of technological development. American troops entered the action in November 1917. Millions died in the trenches; flu epidemics added thousands to those numbers. In 1917 the October Revolution in Russia and the abduction of the Czar's family dramatically demonstrated the people's revolution. T. S. Eliot elegized the malaise and pervasive depression in his poem "The Love Song of J. Alfred Prufrock."

World War I was a dividing line between the old world and the new—between the old world of aristocracy and handcraft and the new world of democracy and the machine. Then the people's revolution had made a common group of humankind—a community of democracy or socialism. Whether in the emerging Modern movement or in the growing field of decorating, more and more people were to find good design available to them. Then, nineteenth-century life ended, and the modern world was irrevocably predominant.

De Stijl

Only one European country that had taken part in the development of Modern design remained neutral during World War I—the Netherlands. There, during the war, architects and designers continued to advance design and design theory. In 1917 Theo Van Doesburg began publication of the magazine *De Stijl*. Piet Mondrian, the painter, and architect-furniture designer Gerrit Rietveld were among the group endorsing Van Doesburg's ideas.

De Stijl, both the magazine and the movement, realized the ideas of the prewar years. Among them were the extreme and pure abstraction of Piet Mondrian, whose rectangular grids and primary colors provided the ultimate refinement of the model for Modernism. Gerrit Rietveld's Red and Blue Chair (1918[10]) was another De Stijl paradigm of Modernism (see Figure 86). Rietveld's Schröder House (1924) in Utrecht later provided De Stijl's major interior design (see Chapter 12). In espousing abstraction, Rational rectangular construction, and machine production, the De Stijl group coalesced all the strains that had been leading toward the Modern movement, gave them focus and refinement, and fixed the path of design for the next decade.

86. Gerrit Rietveld. Red and Blue Chair. 1918. *Photograph from The Museum of Modern Art, New York City.*

World War I ended in 1918. That year, a new design direction in favor of lightness and purism was announced: Le Corbusier and Amédée Ozenfant wrote their manifesto on Purism, "Après le Cubisme," which was given a limited circulation (see the discussion in Chapter 12). In 1919 the sculptor Constantin Brancusi created his soaring bronze *Bird in Space*, which was to become a symbol of lightness and flight in the years to come.

Also in 1919, Walter Gropius was confirmed as the director of the Bauhaus, in Weimar, where he was to establish the design school that subsequently directed the way of the Modern movement in architecture, interior, product, and graphic design. That same year, Mies van der Rohe produced his first scheme for an all-glass-and-metal curtain-wall apartment building. These end-of-decade events were to shape interiors for the next five decades.

Orientalism: The Ballet Style

Modernism was by no means pervasive or popularized in Europe during the Teens. Instead, the oriental style popularized by the Diaghilev ballet and the stage settings of Leon Bakst were the rage. In 1911 fashion designer Paul Poiret opened his decorating firm Maison Martine based on this style. Furniture became lower and smaller—deeper seating pieces, small dining chairs, low beds—and built-in cupboards came into use. The oriental style also featured textiles with elaborate patterns and vivid colors, cushions with long silk tassels, and other elements of Scheherazade imagery. This was to remain the fashionable style for interiors in France through the first half of the 1920s.

Suggested Reading

Banham, Reyner. *Theory and Design in the First Machine Age.* Cambridge: MIT Press, 1960, 1981.

Barr, Alfred H., Jr. *Cubism and Abstract Art.* New York: The Museum of Modern Art, 1936.

de Wolfe, Elsie. *The House in Good Taste.* New York: The Century Co., 1913.

Giedion, Sigfried. *Mechanization Takes Command.* Oxford: Oxford University Press, 1948. New York: W. W. Norton, 1975.

Goodnow, Ruby Ross, and Rayne Adams. *The Honest House.* New York: The Century Co., 1914.

Hanks, David A. *The Decorative Designs of Frank Lloyd Wright.* New York: E. P. Dutton, 1979.

Hitchcock, Henry-Russell. *In the Nature of Materials: The Buildings of Frank Lloyd Wright, 1887–1941.* New York: Da Capo Press, 1973.

———. *Architecture in the Nineteenth and Twentieth Centuries.* Baltimore: Penguin Books, 1958–82 (especially "Wright and His California Contemporaries").

Jaffe, Hans L. C., et al. *De Stijl: Visions of Utopia,* ed. Mildred Friedman. New York: Abbeville Press, 1982.

Jeanneret, Charles-Edouard. *Le Corbusier: 1910–65.* Zurich: Les Editions d'Architecture Zurich, 1967.

Kaufmann, Edgar, Jr. "Interior Design: Architecture or Decoration?" *Progressive Architecture.* October 1962, pp. 141–44.

McCoy, Esther. *Five California Architects.* New York: Reinhold, 1960. (Paperback New York: Frederick A. Praeger, 1975.)

Pratt, Richard. *David Adler: The Architect and His Work.* New York: M. Evans & Company, 1970.

Sharp, Dennis. *Modern Architecture and Expressionism.* New York: Braziller, 1966.

Smith, Jane S. *Elsie de Wolfe.* New York: Atheneum, 1982.

Notes

1. Although vanguard designers began to leave the Arts and Crafts movement behind by mid-decade, all across the country for the next two decades furniture and interiors continued to be designed and produced in the Arts and Crafts tradition.

2. Henry-Russell Hitchcock, *In the Nature of Materials: The Buildings of Frank Lloyd Wright, 1887–1941* (New York: Da Capo Press, 1973), caption to Figure 200.

3. Edgar Kaufmann, Jr., "Wright at the Met," *Skyline*, The Architecture and Design Review, New York (January 1983), p. 25.

4. Hitchcock, op. cit., caption to Figure 192.

5. Edgar Kaufmann, Jr., "Frank Lloyd Wright," *Macmillan Encyclopedia of Architects* (New York: The Free Press, a division of Macmillan Publishing Company and Collier Macmillan Publishing, 1982), p. 439.

6. Muthesius, although director and most prominent, was not alone in founding the Deutscher Werkbund. See Joan Campbell, *The German Werkbund: The Politics of Reform in the Applied Arts* (Princeton: Princeton University Press, 1977).

7. The 1899 chair designed by Richard Riemerschmid has become one of the pioneering classics of Modernism.

8. Work Program of the Wiener Werkstaette, quoted from *Vienna Moderne: 1898–1918*, exhibition catalogue (University of Houston: Sarah Campbell Blaffer Gallery; New York: Cooper-Hewitt Museum, 1978), p. 89. Reprinted there with permission from *Architecture and Design: An International Anthology of Original Articles*, ed. Timothy and Charlotte Benton, with Dennis Sharp (London: Granada Publishing, Ltd., 1975).

9. Nikolaus Pevsner, *Pioneers of Modern Design*. New York: The Museum of Modern Art, 1949), p. 131.

10. There is some disagreement about the date of Rietveld's Red and Blue Chair: Some say 1917–19; Wilk gives 1917–18. See Christopher Wilk, *Marcel Breuer: Furniture and Interiors* (New York: The Museum of Modern Art, 1981).

Chapter **12**

1920–1930:
The First Generation

If the Teens presented a dilemma for American interior designers—a choice between America and Europe—the 1920s presented the more specific option of choosing between the design idioms of Art Deco classicism and the new Modernism of the machine. Modern design was being promulgated in Germany by the Bauhaus and in France by Le Corbusier and several of his contemporaries. Art Deco was popularly demonstrated in Paris by the Exposition Internationale des Arts Décoratifs et Industriels Modernes. In America's mainstream design, Art Deco first took the lead. For America's vanguard designers, the new Modernism was only beginning to be the revered ideal.

In the 1920s the American interior design profession began to grow in numbers of practitioners and of marketable outlets. Many of the traditional residential designers who were to become the luminaries of the profession for the next forty to fifty years arrived on the scene at this time. Later in the decade the profession of industrial design began in the United States. That is, designers for industry began to win significant commissions, and they identified themselves as an independent profession. Soon they were to develop their own style. But at the beginning of the decade, despite all these contributors to American interior design, the lead of Frank Lloyd Wright was forgotten and Europe was again the undisputed mentor.

Paris was the undisputed magnetic center of art and style to which Americans flocked for inspiration. There, during the 1920s, settled a host of expatriate artists and writers—Gertrude Stein, F. Scott Fitzgerald, Ernest Hemingway, and others. Josephine Baker's appearances at the Folies Bergère personified the popular interest in Africa and primitive art. Women of style, like Elsie de Wolfe, still sailed to Paris for their clothes.

Art Deco from France

In the summer of 1925 the Exposition Internationale des Arts Décoratifs et Industriels Modernes opened in Paris. It is sometimes believed by students that Art Deco was a style initiated at the 1925 Paris exhibition. But, as the analogy with anthologies previously mentioned in relation to the Great Exhibition at the Crystal Palace in 1851 clearly indicates, a style must already exist in order to be exhibited in many examples. Like other exhibitions the 1925 display was a summation of French design of the past fifteen years, allowing for the interruption of World War I. (The exhibition had, in fact, originally been planned for 1914.)

As much as the word "industry" in the title of the 1925 exposition may have signified the machine, greater prominence was given to handcrafted decorative arts. Art Deco as a style was in the French tradition of Art Nouveau, but it was less tortuous, more geometric, and in lower relief.

The sources of Art Deco included the art movements of the preceding years— Fauvism, Cubism, Futurism, and Expressionism. Art Deco adopted the wild, hot colors of the Fauve painters (dubbed "wild beasts" for their bold use of color) of 1905 and after. Following the success of Leon Bakst's designs for the Ballets Russes of Diaghilev in 1909, French style had been influenced by oriental and Russian traditions (see Figure 87).

87. Maison Martine (Paul Poiret). Bedroom. Paris, France. 1924. *Photograph from* Art et Décoration *(February 1924).*

In the 1920s Art Deco was updated. It transformed the classical vocabulary of forms and symbols derived from the classical education at the Ecole des Beaux-Arts. Art Deco motifs, therefore, were drawn from classical, or at least ancient, civilizations—sometimes combining ancient Egyptian, archaic Greek, and Mayan Mexican elements in a romantic, if anachronistic, synthesis. The tomb of Tutankhamen was opened in 1922; and its treasures were inspirational images to designers for at least the next fifteen years. From that inspiration developed the late–Art Deco classicism that combined Egyptian and Greek motifs—notably highly stylized figures in bas relief, dancing maidens holding amphoras, urns, and swags of drapery.

Other Art Deco motifs, often in gilt stucco, included conventionalized garlands and baskets of flowers—often derived from the Mackintosh rose—octagonal panels, elongated ovals, bold lines, fountains, and other Neoclassical motifs. Geometric patterns figured largely in late–Art Deco design—sunbursts, lightning bolts, electrical currents, and radio waves, which were both popularized machine-age imagery and "toned down" Cubism. It was a tentative French approach to making a modern style in the 1920s.

Metal and glass were fundamental to the Art Deco vocabulary. Exotic woods such as macassar ebony, amboyna, amaranth, rosewood, olivewood, lemonwood, and zebrawood were inlaid with ivory, amethyst, and mother-of-pearl. Furniture was elaborately lacquered or covered in snakeskin, shagreen (sharkskin), tortoiseshell, or leather. Mirror, glass, and chrome were sanded and etched in patterns. Wrought iron and aluminum were worked by highly creative metal artisans. Colors during the 1920s became lighter.

The leading interior designers of Art Deco were French. They included Emile-Jacques Ruhlmann, André Groult, Paul Iribe, Louis Sue, and André Mare, who had previously worked in the Art Nouveau idiom. Also among the highest achievements of Art Deco in France were the glass of René Lalique and Daum, the silver of Jean Puiforcat, the clothes of Paul Poiret, and the costume designs of Erté.

88. Emile-Jacques Ruhlmann. Desk, chair, and file cabinet of amboyna wood and ivory. 1918–19. *Photograph from The Metropolitan Museum of Art, New York City, Bequest of Collis P. Huntington, 1973.*

Other major French achievements of the period include the metal-and-lacquer work of Jean Dunand, the metal work of Edgar Brandt, the sculpture of Armand-Albert Rateau, and the fabrics of Sonia Delaunay. With them, but never achieving wide recognition until rediscovered in later decades, were Pierre Legrain, who was inspired by African primitive art, as the Cubists had been; and Eileen Gray, an English designer working in Paris with luxurious lacquers.

Emile-Jacques Ruhlmann

Emile-Jacques Ruhlmann (1869–1933), born in Paris, was the premier furniture designer of his day, and he also created complete interiors. His work was among the best at the 1925 exposition—a combination of refined design, luxurious and rare materials, and exquisite craftsmanship. Applied to delicately formed pieces of furniture were precious veneers inlaid with ivory, coral, shagreen, or the finest leather (see Figure 88). From 1919 to 1933 he worked only for the wealthy, because he wanted to design only the most precious and elegant furniture. His highest achievements were in the best traditions of the French cabinetmakers of the eighteenth century.

The Bauhaus: 1919–1933

In 1919 the Bauhaus school of design had opened in Weimar, Germany, under the direction of Walter Gropius (1883–1969). He had combined two previous schools—the Grand-Ducal Saxon Academy of Pictorial Art and the Grand-Ducal Saxon School of Arts and Crafts—to achieve a union and an equality of the fine and applied arts. It was a realization of the goal of the Arts and Crafts movement and of the Wiener Werkstaette.

The program of the Bauhaus in April 1919 stated: "The Bauhaus strives to bring together all creative effort into one whole, to reunify all the disciplines of practical art—sculpture, painting, handicrafts, and the crafts—as inseparable components of a new architecture. The ultimate, if distant, aim of the Bauhaus is the unified work of art—the great structure—in which there is no distinction between monumental and decorative art."[1] In this Bauhaus aim, the turn-of-the-century objective of putting the decorative arts and crafts on an equal footing with the fine arts and the ultimate goal of the *Gesamtkunstwerk*—the total, integral, consistent design—became an official educational program. Bauhaus education was to influence designers for the next sixty-five years.

However, the fundamental belief of Walter Gropius, expressed in the first sentence of the Bauhaus program, was that "The ultimate aim of all visual arts is the complete building!" Despite the statement in the same Bauhaus program that there would be no distinctions between the structural or monumental and the decorative arts, this attitude that architecture was queen over all the other arts was to persist. This hierarchy of the arts also led to the separation of the other arts from architecture and widened the rift between architectural design and interior design for almost the rest of the century. Despite the proclaimed goals of the Bauhaus, the other arts were used merely as additive applications. Ironically, this meant the ultimate banishment of decoration and ornamentation from all architecture, interior design, and furniture design—all but machine-inspired ornamentation.

Bauhaus instruction opened with a preliminary course of half a year, which was devoted to problems of form—observation of nature and materials, studies of composition, and analyses of paintings by old masters. After passing this preliminary course, students were admitted to the second part of the instructional program, which consisted of working for three years with a specific material in one of the crafts studios—stone in the sculpture workshop, wood in the carpentry workshop, metal in the metal workshop, clay in the pottery workshop, glass in the stained-glass workshop, color in the wall-painting workshop, or textiles in the weaving workshop. Each workshop was taught by two masters—a craftsman and an artist—to overcome "the disastrous secession of art from the workaday life of the people," as Gropius wrote. Johannes Itten taught the preliminary course. Over the years, the other teachers were Lyonel Feininger, Gerhard Marcks, Adolf Meyer, George Muche, Paul Klee, Oskar Schlemmer, Wassily Kandinsky, Marcel Breuer, Laszlo Moholy-Nagy, Josef and Anni Albers, and Herbert Bayer.[2]

In 1923 the first Bauhaus exhibition presented students' designs of furniture and furnishings, along with two seminal interiors. One interior was the office of the director, Walter Gropius; the other was an experimental one-family house— the Haus Am Horn—built and furnished by Bauhaus students on the grounds of the school.

Gropius's office (see Figure 89B) was arranged with a cubic volume for seating and conferences in one corner and the desk and bookshelves surrounding it on two sides (see Figure 89A). Horizontality—a major design emphasis of the Bauhaus— was expressed in the arms of the seating units as well as in the bookshelf design. To define the conference-area cube, the ceiling above was painted as a blue square. Above the desk, a light fixture of exposed incandescent tubes showed the influence

89A. Walter Gropius. Axonometric drawing, Director's office, Bauhaus. Weimar, Germany. 1923. *Illustration by Herbert Bayer.*

89B. Walter Gropius. Director's office, Bauhaus. Weimar, Germany. 1923. *Photograph courtesy The Museum of Modern Art, New York City.*

of the De Stijl movement (see Chapter 11) and of Theo van Doesburg, who not only had taught at the Bauhaus in 1922, but had previously designed a similar fixture. Indeed, Rietveld's Schröder House, which was being constructed at this time in Utrecht, was perhaps the last flowering of the planar De Stijl style that we associate with the paintings of Piet Mondrian. On its upper floor (which was a collaboration with the client, Mrs. Truus Schröder-Schräder) sliding partitions made possible both a large open space and a series of smaller spaces. It was an example of simultaneity of time and space (see Figures 90A and B). Pursuing that imagery, wiring for the lighting in Gropius's office was carried through thin aluminum tubes, which were repeated to reinforce the linear motif.

For this same exhibition the Haus Am Horn, designed by George Muche and Adolf Meyer, had a square plan with, at the center of the main floor, a square two-story living room that was lighted by the lantern-like second story. The living room, somewhat like an atrium, was surrounded by separate and enclosed spaces (except for the study, which was open to the central space)—dining room, kitchen, bedrooms, and bath. Furnishings were designed by students, including Marcel Breuer (see Figures 91A, B, and C).

90A. Gerrit Rietveld and Mrs. Truus Schröder-Schräder. Plan of second floor with partitions open (left) and closed (right), Schröder House. Utrecht, Netherlands. 1924.

90B. Gerrit Rietveld and Mrs. Truus Schröder-Schräder. Upper level, Schröder House. Utrecht, Netherlands. 1924. *Photograph by E. A. van Blitzen Zoon, 1925, from Gemeentelikje Archiefdienst Utrecht.*

91A. Marcel Breuer. Furniture for ladies' chamber, Haus am Horn. Weimar, Germany. 1923. *Albert Langer Verlag, Munich:* Neue Arbeiten der Bauhaus Werkstaetten *(Bauhausbuecher 7). Photograph from Karl Mang,* History of Modern Furniture *(New York: Harry N. Abrams, 1979).*

91B. Marcel Breuer. Bed for Haus am Horn. Weimar, Germany. 1923. *Bauhaus-Archiv Berlin. Photograph from Karl Mang,* History of Modern Furniture *(New York: Harry N. Abrams, 1979).*

Gropius had stated the theme of this exhibition as "Art and Technics, a New Unity" but it was only after the Bauhaus moved to Dessau in 1925 that the school placed emphasis on the technology of the machine. The curriculum was changed at that time to reflect the fact that each teacher had become, through Bauhaus training, combination creative artist, craftsman, and industrial designer. In the Dessau studios the goal was to achieve designs that could be submitted to industry for production.[3] In due course, designs for furniture, lamps, textiles, metal, and glassware were produced by manufacturers with royalties for the student designers, as well as to the school and the teacher. Design for industry had moved to the world of education.

The new style that this approach created was efficient and functional. The matter-of-fact reduction to necessity was economical, simplified, and pure—to the point of being clinically clean. Shiny metal, richly veined stone, and nubby fabric were among the natural materials used to enrich the spare, functional designs. But structural rationalism—which posited structural logic as the basis of design—along with clarity of parts and meticulous alignment was the fundamental principle as well as the aesthetic effect of the new machine-based Modernism.

With this new emphasis, after nearly a century of debate over the machine versus handcraft and of moves for reform, the Bauhaus was able to coalesce the goals of Arts and Crafts and the Wiener Werkstaette with those of the Deutscher Werkbund and the Futurists into a modern theory of design and industry. It was a celebration of the machine, an aesthetic imagery of machine-made production. The Bauhaus, thereby, first acclaimed Machine-Age art.

It meant the coming together of the goals of Modernism—geometric simplicity, the use of machine production, the imagery of machine production, and functional (meaning structural) appropriateness. Function, materials, and the process of manufacture were the goals. Along with these came two taboos: There shall be no historicism, and there shall be no applied ornamentation.

91C. Wilhelm Wagenfeld and Karl J. Jucker. Table Lamp, glass and chrome-plated metal, globe 17″ high, 8″ diameter. 1923–24. *Collection, The Museum of Modern Art, New York City. Gift of Philip C. Johnson.*

Gropius wrote of the Bauhaus concept:

> Architecture during the last few generations has become weakly sentimental, aesthetic, and decorative. Its chief concern has been with ornamentation, with the formalistic use of motifs, ornaments, and mouldings on the exterior . . . —not as part of a living organism. . . . This kind of architecture we disown. We want to create a clear, organic architecture, whose inner logic will be radiant and naked, unencumbered by lying façades and trickeries; we want an architecture adapted to our world of machines, radios, and fast motor cars, an architecture whose function is clearly recognizable in the relation of its forms. . . . modern materials—steel, concrete, glass. . . . The old method of building is giving way to a new lightness and airiness. A new aesthetic of the Horizontal is beginning to develop . . . a new conception of equilibrium, which transmutes this dead symmetry of similar parts into an asymmetrical but rhythmical balance.[4]

These were the Futurist goals toward which the Bauhaus worked—a timely style and a ready availability through mass production by machines. Art for all—everything for everyman—had arrived.

This was the decade of the classic furniture designs of the Modern movement—those by Marcel Breuer, Mies van der Rohe, and others. As usual, technology was not as advanced as design vision. Many early Bauhaus furniture designs, like many later building systems, which were designed to be made by machine and to look as if they had been made by machine, had to be constructed by hand.

The "assembly of prefabricated and standardized parts" was the aspiration of the Bauhaus, and not to achieve it was considered a betrayal of Bauhaus principles. However, one cannot criticize technology because it is not yet advanced enough and available. Marcel Breuer's Wassily Chair (1925), designed for the house of painter and colleague Wassily Kandinsky, has a tubular metal frame inspired by bicycle production; "iron-cloth" canvas or leather bands constitute the straight-forward (*sachlich*) seat, back, and armrests. But it had to be hand-welded and hand-sewn rather than machine-made. So too did Mies's cantilevered, tubular MR Chair (1927) (see Figure 92A), and the handwork required for the X-joint of the Barcelona furniture (1929) (see Figure 92B) has been much discussed by historians. But in 1928 Breuer designed the tubular metal, cantilevered Cesca Chair with seat and back pads of cane woven on wood frames, and it could be made entirely by machine production at that time. Technology was catching up.[5]

Walter Gropius

Born in Berlin, Walter Gropius (1883–1969), the first Bauhaus director, had studied architecture at the universities of Berlin and Munich and from 1908 to 1910 was chief assistant to Peter Behrens. During that time both Mies van der Rohe and Le Corbusier worked in the Behrens office. In his next years of private practice, Gropius designed the two first truly Modern buildings in collaboration with Adolph Meyer—the Fagus Factory at Alfeld (1913), and the Deutscher Werkbund Pavilion at the Cologne Exhibition of 1914 (see Chapter 11). After service in World War I, Gropius was called to Weimar to become director of the Bauhaus on the recommendation of his predecessor at the Grand-Ducal schools, the Belgian architect Henry van de Velde.

In 1925, on the move of the Bauhaus to Dessau, Gropius designed the new building occupied by the school. It is one of the most influential structures of Modern architecture. Composed of three blocks—one for classroom-studios, one for administration, and one for living quarters—Gropius's Bauhaus building in Dessau exhibits the Bauhaus design directions: horizontals—in the flat roofs, the bridge-like administration wing, and emphasis of linear windows and floor slabs;

92A. Ludwig Mies van der Rohe. MR Chair. 1927. *Photograph courtesy Knoll International.*

92B. Ludwig Mies van der Rohe. Barcelona Chair. 1929. *Photograph courtesy Knoll International.*

asymmetry—in the plan and vertical massing; and expression of functions—in the fenestration as well as the massing. In 1928 Gropius retired as director of the Bauhaus, and Hannes Meyer was appointed his successor.

Ludwig Mies van der Rohe

In 1930, following Hannes Meyer's resignation, the Berlin architect Ludwig Mies van der Rohe (1886–1969) was appointed director of the Bauhaus. Mies had been born in Aachen (Aix-la-Chapelle), Germany; he worked first with his father as a stonemason, and apprenticed in the offices of Bruno Paul and then Peter Behrens, while Gropius and Le Corbusier were there. His early architecture was inspired by the classicism of the nineteenth-century German architect Karl Friedrich Schinkel and by the Expressionists and the De Stijl movement. From 1921 to 1923 Mies designed his first steel-framed and glass curtain-wall tower schemes; they had expressionistic free-form plans. In 1927 he was director of the Deutscher Werkbund exposition at Stuttgart—the Weissenhof Housing Settlement or community

93A. Ludwig Mies van der Rohe. Plan, German Pavilion. International Exposition, Barcelona, Spain. 1929. *Illustration from Philip Johnson,* Mies van der Rohe *(New York: The Museum of Modern Art, 1978).*

93B. Ludwig Mies van der Rohe. Interior, German Pavilion. International Exposition, Barcelona, Spain. 1929. *Photograph courtesy Mies van der Rohe Archive, The Museum of Modern Art, New York City.*

94A. Ludwig Mies van der Rohe. Study and living room, Tugendhat House. Brno, Czechoslovakia. 1930. *Reprinted by Hedrich-Blessing.*

94B. Ludwig Mies van der Rohe. Plan, Tugendhat House, Brno, Czechoslovakia. 1930. *Illustration from Henry-Russell Hitchcock and Philip Johnson,* The International Style: Architecture Since 1922 *(New York: W. W. Norton, 1966).*

94C. Ludwig Mies van der Rohe. Dining room, Tugendhat House. Brno, Czechoslovakia. 1930. *Reprinted by Hedrich-Blessing.*

housing project. There he demonstrated the great social goal of early Modernism—to provide low-cost housing for everyone.

In 1929 Mies designed the German Pavilion for the International Exposition in Barcelona, Spain (see Figure 93B). The pavilion crystallized all the thinking of the first generation of modernists—machine imagery, ornamentation only through the textures of natural materials, and, most important, free-flowing space unimpeded by structural walls. Inspired by Frank Lloyd Wright, Mies developed his vision of dissolving wall planes. Mies "broke with the conception of the wall as a continuous plane surrounding the plan," wrote Hitchcock and Johnson, "and built up his composition of sections of intersecting planes."[6] The plan (see Figure 93A) clearly showed the influence of De Stijl and of Mies's own previous work in that vein. It was Mies's supreme example of reducing design to its most elemental essentials. "Less is more" was his slogan.

For the Barcelona Pavilion, Mies designed the furniture—chair, stool, and table—that became the ultimate achievements (and later the ultimate status symbols) in furniture design of this Machine Age. Revered as the Barcelona Pavilion has become, it is imperative to note that it was more of a fine-art work of architecture than an applied-art creation for a function of occupancy. It was a walk-through, unenclosed, demonstration space, not a residence or office designed to facilitate continual and habitual daily activities.

In 1930 Mies completed his Tugendhat House in Brno, Czechoslovakia (see Figures 94A, B, and C). There, in an actual house, a free-flowing interior space of monumental proportions is similarly subdivided by freestanding screens—a flat one made of Malaga onyx, which divides the study from the living room, and a semicircular partition made of macassar ebony, which surrounds the dining area. The partitions stood independent of the building structure, which was expressed as freestanding columns sheathed in cruciform-plan polished stainless steel. These were offset on a floor of white linoleum (first marketed that year in Darmstadt by Rohm & Haas). Walls were flat and untrimmed planes.

All furnishings were designed by Mies, including lighting fixtures, and located with the most meticulous care in relation to his plan and luxurious materials. Raw-silk draperies were hung at the windows, which had alternate panes that descended into the floor at the push of a button, opening the interior to the exterior without physical barrier. In the living area was a natural wool rug on which sat Mies's Tugendhat Chair, designed for the house, and the Barcelona furniture. The upholsteries were pale-green cowhide, tan glove leather, and white vellum. In the study stood a credenza of white wood and translucent dark-green glass panels; at the table-desk were MR chairs. And the dining table was surrounded by Brno chairs with tubular frames. In his interior design he was assisted by Lilly Reich.

Although he designed at every scale—from large urban-planning projects to small lighting fixtures—Mies, more than any architect since Frank Lloyd Wright, demonstrated his attention to detail. "God is in the details," he was to say later. He also showed a remarkable ability to create a total design. The decade closed, therefore, with the creation by Mies of one of the pinnacles of early Modern design—which remains one of the supreme total design works of the century—and with Mies's appointment as director of the Bauhaus. He was first vice president of the Deutscher Werkbund when he was called to the Bauhaus in 1930.

Machine-Age Furniture by Marcel Breuer

Born in Hungary, Marcel Breuer (1902–82) joined the Bauhaus as a student in 1920. He became a master or teacher in 1925 on the move from Weimar to Dessau, where he took over the carpentry workshop. Soon he was designing some of the most expressive furniture in the new machine style. In 1925 he designed the Wassily Chair for the house of his colleague Wassily Kandinsky. In that same year he designed the Laccio Table/Stool of tubular steel;[7] and in 1928 came his design of the Cesca Chair. Later in his career he became an internationally respected architect. When Gropius left the Bauhaus, Breuer also left, moving to the office he already had in Berlin.[8]

Art Moderne

Contemporaneous with the development of the Bauhaus was a new movement in France. After 1925 many French designers, perhaps already bored by Art Deco, began to turn to the new Modernism, which they had seen exhibited at the same exhibition—in Le Corbusier's Pavillon de L'Esprit Nouveau, in the Tourism Tower pavilion by Robert Mallet-Stevens, and in the Lyons-Saint-Etienne pavilion by Tony Garnier. They were also attracted to Swedish Modern design, which offered pale-toned color schemes and the look of simple provincial but graceful handcraft and machine craft. These helped to inspire a new French Modernism, which is distinguished from Art Deco by the term Art Moderne.

Stylistically, Art Deco is classical, traditional, and representational, even when geometric. Art Moderne is machine-inspired, more abstract, and more consistently rectilinear, or at least more geometrically formal. The two styles are distinguished physically, as they are verbally, by ornament and decoration versus machine-inspired abstraction. Art Moderne rejected the classicism of Art Deco and adopted, instead, the imagery of Futurism and of the machine. It proffered rectilinear forms, parallel lines, and the modern materials, such as glass, mirror, and metals. But French Modernism, except for the work of Le Corbusier, was less rigid than the purgative, ascetic approach of the Bauhaus.

The French architects and designers who led the way along this Art Moderne path were the Formalists Tony Garnier, Robert Mallet-Stevens, Djo-Bourgeois, François Jourdain, and René Herbst. Eileen Gray and Pierre Chareau, who earlier had worked in a highly refined Art Deco style, also began to work in the Moderne idiom. They were to be joined in the 1930s by Jean-Michel Frank. Le Corbusier was the supreme genius among these designers. All of them adopted Machine-Age Modernism, in varying degrees and with varied success. Also at this time, new furniture of metal and leather—some of it made by the French branch of Thonet, the makers of bentwood furniture—also began to appear in France.

From 1928 to 1932 in Paris, Chareau and the Dutch architect Bernard Bijvoet designed and built the Maison de Verre (see Figure 95), which expressed the goals of Machine-Age Moderne in its exposed steel structure and walls of lens-like glass block; it has black metal bookcases, a ladder, and industrial rubber flooring among its furnishings in the two-story living room; upholsteries on Chareau-designed sofas were tapestries by the painter Jean Lurçat.

The mechanical system in the Maison de Verre is integrated into the structural system: grilles along perimeter platforms supply ducted warm air. Electrical and telephone wiring is conveyed along the steel columns, with clustered control panels for both switches and outlets. Up lights at the upper level reflect ambient lighting from the ceiling.

The Purism of Le Corbusier

The pioneer of this French Modernism was Charles-Edouard Jeanneret (1887–1965), the Swiss-born architect who later called himself Le Corbusier, because of his crow-like affectation of tight black suits and round black eyeglasses that emphasized his

95. Chareau & Bijvoet. Living room, Maison de Verre. Paris, France. 1929–31. *Photograph by Evelyn Hofer, New York City, 1982.*

crow-like profile. Born in La Chaux-de-Fonds, Switzerland, Le Corbusier was trained in art school in his home town. During travel to Italy and the Mediterranean he developed a lifelong admiration for vernacular white stucco structures. He then worked briefly for Josef Hoffmann; for Auguste Perret, from whom he learned about reinforced concrete; and for Peter Behrens, before setting off again for a year-long tour of Mediterranean countries—including his favorite island, Mykonos.

In 1914–15 Le Corbusier had devised his elemental structural system, le Domino, which reduced necessary building structure to a grid of freestanding columns supporting three slabs that were joined by a stair (see Figure 96). This innovative reduction of structure to its barest essentials allowed all interior walls to be located

96. Le Corbusier. Drawing of le Domino. 1915. *Illustration from Charles-Edouard Jeanneret,* Le Corbusier: 1910–65 *(Zurich: Les Editions d'Architecture Zurich, 1967).*

independent of the structural grid and at random, therefore making possible the freeflowing space that became the ideal of the Modern movement. In the 1920s Le Corbusier began to demonstrate the potential of this system. It was this concept of space that Mies van der Rohe was to express so elegantly in his Barcelona Pavilion and in his Tugendhat House.

In 1918, with the painter Amédée Ozenfant, Le Corbusier published his manifesto on Purism—"Après le Cubisme." It proclaimed a new art era based on sweeping away the past, starting clean with a new slate of whitewash and with mathematically geometric pure forms of severe simplicity and economic elegance. "The purism of whitewash," it came to be called. The Purists felt that natural selection and economy through the ages had perfected the cylinder, the cube, the cone, and other such elemental forms. They felt similarly about the bottle, the classical column, and the violin. These were universal forms, impersonal and therefore heroic; they were used in both Purist paintings and architecture at the time. The doctrine was another expression of refinement and reduction with a goal of universal understanding.

Le Corbusier also eagerly endorsed the Futurist ideals of industry and the machine, of speed and lightness. The imagery of grain silos and factories, the speed of airplanes and automobiles, and the fully mechanized life aboard sleek ocean liners fascinated him. From ocean liners he drew his early Purist motif of parallel tubular railings and his interest in ladders, compartment-like tight spaces, and roofs as sports decks. He later wrote in "Vers une Architecture" that steamships manifest the virtues of discipline, harmony, and a calm vital beauty.[9] He said that they present a pure, neat, clear, clean, and healthy architecture. Except for the last adjective, these became the catchwords of later Modernism.

In 1920, by which time he had permanently settled in France, Le Corbusier began publishing the magazine *L'Esprit Nouveau,* also with Ozenfant; it lasted twenty-seven issues. His 1923 manifesto on Modern architecture, "Vers une Architecture," was first published in the magazine as "Manuel de l'Habitation." There he first stated his maxim that a house was "a machine for habitation." It expressed his espousal of the Futurist vision of the Machine Age.

From the name of the publication came the Pavillon de l'Esprit Nouveau at the 1925 Art Deco exhibition. There, he built one living unit of an apartment block that he envisioned composed of stacked multiples of that unit. It had a two-story living room overlooked by a balcony space and flowing into a dining space beyond an elevated cabinet (see Figure 97). This looked out onto a two-story terrace and garden. But it was the simple furniture, including the 1900 Thonet bentwood chairs that Le Corbusier chose—saying that there was no other good contemporary furniture to use—that further astonished exhibition-goers. Le Corbusier's manifesto-like description was, as was his custom, abrasive and eye-opening:

> The program: to reject decorative art. To affirm that architecture extends from the smallest furnishing to the house, to the street, to the city, and beyond. To show that industry creates pure objects by selection (by means of the standardized series). . . . To show that an apartment can be standardized to satisfy the needs of a "seriesman." The practical, habitable cell, comfortable and beautiful, a veritable machine for habitation. . . . A new term has replaced the word furnishing . . . the equipment of a house. . . . In replacing the innumerable furnishings of all shapes and sizes, standard cabinets are incorporated in the walls or set against the walls, so located within the apartment as to best serve its exact daily function . . . they are constructed not of wood, but of metal, in the shops where office furniture is fabricated. The cabinets constitute, in themselves, the sole furnishing for the house, thus leaving a maximum amount of available space within each room.[10]

It was the public beginning of "the poor man's style."

97. Le Corbusier. Pavillon de l'Esprit Nouveau, Paris Exhibition. Paris, France. 1925. *Photograph from Karl Mang,* History of Modern Furniture *(New York: Harry N. Abrams, 1979).*

For the Deutscher Werkbund exposition in Stuttgart in 1927, Le Corbusier designed two houses of the prophetic Weissenhof Housing Project. One of the houses revealed his interest in small, or rather minimal, dimensions: The size of the corridor was that of a railway compartment. Le Corbusier described it as "a house resembling a car, planned and fitted like a bus or ship's cabin. . . . A house must be thought of as a living-machine or a tool." The interior was conceived as a single large living area divided at night into compartments by means of partitions that slid into position, revealing beds that had been concealed during the day. Understanding critics agreed that this was "a new conception of living."[11]

Le Corbusier's Villa Stein at Garches (1927) clearly expresses this new doctrine and imagery. Also in 1927, with his brother Pierre Jeanneret and with his cousin Charlotte Perriand, he designed the celebrated serpentine-profile chaise longue of tubular chromium-plated steel resting on a black lacquered-steel base. Like his furniture of 1928—the Basculant/Sling Chair, the Cube Chair, also called Grand Confort (see Figure 98), and the LC5 Sofa—it was furniture for the Machine Age. When upholstered in black leather, it was similar to the furniture of Breuer and Mies at this time; but when upholstered in black-and-white pony skin, it reflected the French spirit of the 1920s.

From 1929 to 1931 Le Corbusier worked on his early-Modern masterpiece, the Villa Savoye at Poissy, outside Paris. An all-white, ship-like machine for living, the Villa Savoye demonstrates the five principles or points that Le Corbusier endorsed:

98. Le Corbusier. Cube Chair and Sofa (Grand Confort). *Photograph courtesy Atelier International, Ltd.*

First, the concrete skeleton construction of the Domino format, which permits a structure to be raised up above the ground on columns—called *pilotis*—so that the ground is free for use by automobiles and people. Second, this cantilevered slab construction also makes "free" or independent façades possible, since the walls no longer have a load-bearing function. Third, the free façades make possible the use of ribbon windows, which ideally can be horizontal in the new Modern vision. Fourth, the Domino construction permits an open, free-form interior plan—the Modern concept of space. Fifth, the building can, and should, have a sculptural playground and garden on its flat roof.

On the ground floor of the Villa Savoye, a semicircular glass entranceway laid out between the columns instantly proclaims its independence and freedom from the grid of cylindrical concrete columns of the structural system. A long straight ramp running from ground to roof, which is adjacent to a floating spiral stair (see Figure 99A), further shows the separation of space and structure; it also expresses the interpenetration of vertical spaces.

On the main floor (see Figure 99B) the interpenetration of interior and exterior is re-emphasized by the inclusion of both the enclosed spaces and two outdoor spaces within the square plan and its perimeter wall. Most demonstrably, the ribbon windows of the living room are repeated along the open-air terrace. The cylindrical columns are straightforwardly left freestanding and unornamented in the living room. Tables are cantilevered from columns; the bathroom has a tiled chaise longue with the S-profile of the chaise longue of 1927 (see Figure 99C); but it is integrated with the adjacent bathtub, like the monolithic sculptures that were to occupy Le Corbusier later. Throughout the white Villa Savoye, occasional wall panels are painted ochre, light red, and other colors from Le Corbusier's own Purist paintings. So the decade closed in Europe with an early masterpiece by Le Corbusier, as it closed with an early masterpiece by Mies.

99A. Le Corbusier. Plan, Villa Savoye. Poissy, France. 1929–30. *Illustration courtesy The Museum of Modern Art, New York City.*

99B. Le Corbusier. Living room and terrace, Villa Savoye. Poissy, France. 1929–30. *Photograph courtesy The Museum of Modern Art, New York City.*

99C. Le Corbusier. Bath chaise, Villa Savoye. Poissy, France. 1929–31. *Photograph courtesy Parsons School of Design, New York City.*

Design in America

Few American designers picked up on any of these European advances until after the mid-1920s. A number of immigrants, however, who had arrived during and just after World War I, began to make the new directions known.

From the beginning of the decade America was on the move and in the midst of a postwar economic boom. It produced an atmosphere of euphoria and buoyancy that earned the epithet "The Roaring Twenties." In 1920 American women were at last able to vote, and the prohibition of alcoholic drinks was introduced across the country. The ensuing days of being daringly naughty in the speakeasies were epitomized by the flapper girls and by the new dance crazes—the Charleston, the Black Bottom, and the Turkey Trot. The Argentine tango was popularized by Rudolph Valentino. The saxophone, the raccoon coat, egret feathers in headbands, and Stutz Bearcat cars were the rage. Daily radio broadcasting began in 1922, the year that Albert Einstein published *The Meaning of Relativity*. In 1926 television was invented by J. L. Baird (it was successfully transmitted in 1928, but did not become generally available until after World War II). In 1926 the first rocket-powered missiles were built. Walt Disney introduced Mickey Mouse in 1928. It was a decade of relativity and choice.

Postwar prosperity fostered a building boom and produced the second great wave of skyscraper construction. By 1920 more than half the population of the United States lived in cities. Department stores increased in number and size, as shopping became a pastime for the many women who had been liberated from household chores by technological (mainly electrical) advances. More department stores added decorating services, which still connoted the use of antique furniture. In the 1920s using antiques still implied complete and accurate—"correct"—period rooms.

The contemporary furniture industry, which had been essentially a cottage industry of artist-craftsmen and small manufacturers, began to develop large manufacturing centers such as Grand Rapids, Michigan. For buyers on the installment plan, Grand Rapids and the Southern states produced pastiches of period furniture, which was derisively called "Borax"—reportedly after the cleanser that was sometimes offered as a premium with purchase. In its watered-down way, mass-produced furniture continued the nineteenth-century tradition of revival styles.

Professional Design Education

The 1920s brought a surge of new interest and attention to design education. The National Association for Decorative Arts and Industries recognized the need for new training. Only eighteen schools offered design education. The curator of industrial art at the Metropolitan Museum of Art in New York, Richard F. Bach, led an influential campaign for better design education, which he felt should be aimed at product design directors for industry. From 1917 to 1931 he directed a series of annual exhibitions at the museum to display American industrial art. His 1932 and 1934 exhibitions had great impact. Many other exhibitions and model room displays brought new design to professional and public attention alike.

In 1923 the Finnish architect Eliel Saarinen settled in the United States and, within a decade, made the Cranbrook School of Design in Bloomfield Hills, Michigan, one of the frontrunners in American design education. During the 1930s Cranbrook was to produce many of the designers who became leaders in the 1950s and 1960s.

At the New York School of Fine and Applied Arts, Frank Alvah Parsons continued his program of interior architecture and decoration; and Grace Fakes, Hamilton Preston, and Mildred Irby taught architectural detailing. The antiques expert William Odom headed the school's summer extension program in Paris. In the mid-1920s Hope L. Foote began to teach in the interior design program of the University of Washington in Seattle. All these educators broadly influenced the traditional approach of young interior designers in the next several decades.

To recreate the tone of American design education in the 1920s, the director of New York's Museum of Modern Art Alfred H. Barr, Jr., wrote,

> Some of the younger of us had just left colleges where courses in modern art began with Rubens and ended with a few superficial and often hostile remarks about Van Gogh and Matisse; where the last word in imitation Gothic dormitories had windows with one carefully cracked pane to each picturesque casement. Others of us, in architectural schools, were beginning our courses with gigantic renderings of Doric capitals, or ending them with elaborate projects for colonial gymnasiums and Romanesque skyscrapers.[12]

American Architecture

Most architects and interior designers in America during the 1920s were still exploring the academic Beaux-Arts formula of eclectic historicism. The interiors of houses, churches, and other buildings were designed in such popular styles as Gothic, Tudor, Georgian, and Spanish. The Renaissance palazzo was still a model for many banks, such as those by York & Sawyer. Palladian-Georgian was a current mode for the thriving businesses of William Delano, David Adler, and John Russell Pope. Tudor/Gothic was the specialty of James Gamble Rogers, who had begun designing buildings in this style at Yale University in 1917 and continued throughout the 1920s.

Spanish styles became popular during the 1920s owing to the work in Santa Barbara, California, of George Washington Smith, James Osborne Craig, and William Mooser. The Spanish background of Palm Beach, Florida, was created by Addison Mizner. Mizner also acted as interior decorator on his projects, collecting and fabricating antique-style furnishings to sell to clients. Among the other fashionable residential architects of the decade with whom interior designers worked were Aymar Embury II, Harrie T. Lindeburgh, Mott B. Schmidt, and Rosario Candela.

Bertram Goodhue at this time began to work in a stripped, almost bald classical idiom that resulted in his Nebraska state capital building (1920–32). Sculpture sprouted out of the structural stonework like the faces that seem to grow integrally from Mount Rushmore. It was an early historical minimalism, of which the architect Paul Cret was perhaps the ultimate master, as demonstrated by his Folger Shakespeare Library in Washington, D.C. (1928–32).

Along with all this high-style historicism, the American public was also being treated to a popular fantasy of interiors by the movie industry. Hundreds, perhaps thousands, of movie palaces were created across the country for Warner Bros., Paramount, Fox, and Loews. The great cinema impresarios and their architects concocted a compendium of historical styles—Baghdad-Alhambra-Neuschwanstein-Versailles-Parthenon—to mesmerize a romantic and wide-eyed public. Gilded plasterwork, mythological murals, fantasy sculptures, baroque metalwork railings, and magical lighting fixtures were all created by such craftsmen as the Rambusch Studios and Caldwell Lighting in New York; Dapratto Inc. in Chicago; and D' Assenzo Studios in Philadelphia. Built in 1927, the Roxy in New York City was a 6,214-seat gilded Florentine fantasy; designed by architect Walter W. Ahlschlager, it was the most lavish of all.

Skyscrapers What most captured the aspirations of professional designers and the public alike were the skyscrapers that raced for the clouds from 1922 to 1932 in the midst of the economic boom. The most optimistic towers were blazoned across the sky at that time, showing American optimism, ingenuity, and daring. They became the great achievement of twentieth-century building, as well as the romantic icon of the decade.

In the parade of 1920s skyscrapers, we see the gradual transition from historicism toward the new Modernism. This was the second wave of skyscraper construction, following the first generation of skyscrapers that originated in Chicago in the 1870s and ended with the construction of the Woolworth Building in 1913. After the interruption of World War I, this second wave of skyscrapers was initiated by the international competition in 1922 for the design of the Chicago Tribune Tower. That competition was won by John Mead Howells and Raymond Hood with a Perpendicular Gothic–inspired scheme. Many early-1920s skyscrapers were in this historical tradition, and were ornamented with Gothic detailing, such as Raymond Hood's American Standard Building (1924). Such schemes came to be known as American Perpendicular.

By the end of the decade Hood, like other architects, had adopted Art Deco and early Streamlining motifs to the basic classical tower form. The culmination of this decade of skyscraper construction were the Art Deco–Streamline Chrysler Building (1930) by William van Alen; and the blander Art Deco Empire State Building (1930–32) by Shreve, Lamb & Harmon. Vanguard critics considered all these stylish designs either with contempt or as if they did not exist. They pejoratively called even the later 1920s skyscraper style "modernistic."

As an example of a battle of styles within a single building, the interiors of the skyscraper Waldorf Astoria Hotel in New York by Schultze & Weaver (1930) were symptomatic of the decade: The public spaces were originally Art Deco (they were Neo-Georgianized in the mid-1960s, just when the hotel owners should have known better); but the private guest rooms for the hotel's affluent clients were originally furnished with quasi-Georgian interior detailing and furnishings. The Colonial and Federal revivals were the establishment styles; Art Deco and Art Moderne were styles only for the wealthy that were depicted in movies.

Interior designers did not get to do much work inside these towers during the 1920s. But the romantic imagery of the step-topped setback skyscraper, enhanced by the soft-focus drawings of Hugh Ferriss, was soon adopted in interior design and decoration for furnishings (see Figure 100), appliances, and decorative objects.

100. Paul T. Frankl. Skyscraper Furniture. Circa 1930. *Photograph from Paul T. Frankl,* New Dimensions *(New York: Payson & Clarke, 1928).*

American Residential Interior Design

The 1920s saw a consumer buying spree. Designers continued to scour Europe for its apparently unending supply of antique furniture and old textiles—velvets, damasks, and brocades—which had been kept in the cupboards of churches and houses. Dark, heavily carved furnishings of Spanish or Italian origin were still eagerly sought after, along with heavy dark tapestries, and red velvet hangings and upholsteries. An antique church vestment was a prize in many houses. Splendor was the goal.

A number of clients began to recreate American traditions. The newly redis-covered Colonial houses of America set the aspirations of a vast segment of the population, and a Colonial Revival soon swept the nation. "Early American" became a new vogue. The open fireplace hung with antique utensils, the corner cupboard, the spinning wheel, and the cobbler's-bench coffee table were the dreams of count-less homemakers.

The number of professional interior decorators increased rapidly in the 1920s. However, since the most celebrated and successful of the new women decorators had begun as society figures who decorated for their friends, they were often slightingly referred to as "the ladies." They had, to many minds, merely turned the daily pastime of shopping into a form of profit. Architects and the large dec-orating firms still gained most of the commissions to design interiors for major houses. However, architectural interests during the 1920s often gave short shrift to residential furnishings. Consultations with the *ensembliers* or with major art dealers, such as Duveen, Knoedler, or French & Company, were sometimes left until after the house was built. But change was in the air.

Among the new decorators to appear in America was a new wave of the old guard: Eleanor McMillen Brown of McMillen Inc.; Mrs. Truman Handy (Charlotte Chalmers) of Thedlow Inc.; Dorothy Draper; and Rose Cumming. Among those already working, Elsie de Wolfe continued her designing, her eccentric self-pro-motion, and her lucrative business; Elsie Cobb Wilson continued her restrained period decorating (see Figure 101) and offered a job to Eleanor McMillen Brown. Dianne Tate and Marian Hall became known for their Directoire interiors; they later redecorated Sherry's Restaurant in the former Metropolitan Opera House. Other prominent decorators in the 1920s were Mrs. Frances Lenygon, who for-warded the concept of restoration; Mrs. Polly Jessup, who continues to work in Palm Beach, Florida; Agnes Foster Wright, who was the wife of *House & Garden* editor Richardson Wright; Miss Gheen; Bertha Schaefer; Pierre Dutel; Sarah Hunter Kelly; and Dan Cooper, who was among the first to show Swedish Modern in his showroom.

Nancy McClelland   In 1922 Nancy McClelland left Wanamaker's Au Quatrième decorating department and opened her own firm, Nancy McClelland Inc., in New York. It specialized in antique furnishings, including fine French hand-painted antique wallpapers, and interior design and decorating. The interiors designed by Nancy McClelland were rather correct and formal (see Figure 102). She worked in the French periods, in Regency, and with Colonial furnishings. Among her clients were the Webbs and the Havermeyers. In 1924 she wrote an authoritative book, *Historic Wallpapers*, which was considered the first complete treatment of the subject. She followed that with *The Practical Book of Decorative Wall Treatments* (1925) and *The Young Decorator* (1927). Her writing put her in the forefront of the profession, and revealed the stylistic interests of the decade.

Ruby Ross Wood   In the 1920s, Ruby Ross Goodnow, who had married the investment banker Chalmers Wood, opened her own interior design firm, Ruby Ross Wood Inc. She designed comfortable, informal, English-style rooms. Her

101. Elsie Cobb Wilson. Living room, residence of Mrs. Cornelius N. Bliss. New York. Circa 1925. *Photograph from Nancy McClelland,* The Practical Book of Decorative Wall Treatments *(Philadelphia: J. B. Lippincott, 1926).*

102. Nancy McClelland. Hallway, residence of Mrs. Edward S. Moore. Roslyn, Long Island. Circa 1925. *Photograph from Nancy McClelland,* The Practical Book of Decorative Wall Treatments *(Philadelphia: J. B. Lippincott, 1926).*

motto was, "Decorating is the art of arranging beautiful things comfortably." She was a sophisticated colorist and liked fresh colors in fabrics and wallpapers. She knew the art of gracious living, and taught it to many of her clients through her designs.

In 1928 Ruby Wood was asked by Mrs. Emily Inman of Atlanta to design the interiors of Swan House, which was to be designed by the architect Philip Schultze. Ruby Wood's interiors—with black-and-white checkerboard floors in the hallway, hand-painted floral wallpaper in the dining room (see Figure 103), and comfortable antique furniture—was typical of the taste of the 1920s, but it also showed Ruby Wood's personal color sense. The house was later given intact to the Atlanta Historical Society and remains an example of decorating in the 1920s.

In 1928 the work of Ruby Ross Wood began to be published by *House & Garden*. The following year she and her husband moved into their house in Syosset, Long Island, which was designed by architect William Adams Delano. The living room was spacious, comfortable, and filled with both antique furniture and comfortable upholstered pieces all in almond greens, with a Savonnerie carpet of muted yellow-greens accented with orangey coral. In the white Adamesque dining room hung blue-and-white damask draperies with a pattern of swans—a popular motif of the 1920s. The dining table was Irish Chippendale—a style variant that was to become a tradition of Ruby Wood's design descendants. High-backed, black leather

103. Ruby Ross Wood. Dining room, Swan House. Atlanta, Georgia. 1928. *Photograph courtesy Atlanta Historical Society.*

104. Rose Cumming. Living room. New York City. Late 1920s. *Photograph courtesy Rose Cumming, Inc.*

armchairs were provided at every place. Her own bedroom had pale-green walls with panels outlined in molding; against them stood a black-painted four-poster Sheraton bed hung with oyster-white silk. Louis XV chairs, an Italian Directoire floor pattern, and shaded sconces at the chimney breast proclaimed the 1920s ideal of the refreshed English country house.

Rose Cumming When the editor of *Vanity Fair,* Frank Crowninshield, suggested decorating as her profession, Rose Cumming said, "First tell me what it is." Her intuitive sense brought something new to it.

Born in a small village near Sydney, Australia, Rose Stuart Cumming (1887–1968) had been caught by World War I in New York on her way to England. She began decorating by working at Wanamaker's Au Quatrième boutique, briefly, then worked with Mrs. Emmet Buel. In 1921 she opened her own shop for decorating and antiques, which she ran for over forty-five years.

Her work was eclectic and eccentric, unlike the more correct period decorating of the other "ladies." It did not matter to Rose Cumming whether the period was correct, so long as the furnishings were old and beautiful, romantic and lush, exotic and original (see Figure 104). She liked good antique furniture, but she was passionate and flamboyant in her taste as well as in her behavior. It was called "flair." She wore big hats and dyed her hair violet, one-upping Elsie de Wolfe's blue tint. Once, for a customer who insisted on seeing a fabric's colors by daylight, she rolled out a bolt of chintz across Madison Avenue, then announced that there would be no sale to *that* customer.

She made a name for herself with her intuitive use of strong deep colors, such as bright pink with lavender, orchid, and deep blue. She had silks dyed and chintzes printed in her own colorations, which she sold exclusively and at exorbitant prices. Billowing draperies, sometimes puffed and gathered, hung under elaborately cut-out valances of gilt or of layered mirrors. Bedcovers were sometimes swagged up to reveal carved and gilded bed legs, creating a surprising yet lavish effect. The fabrics themselves were rich silk taffetas or Baroque-patterned damasks shimmering with silver thread. It was said that she could drape fabrics more inventively than any of her compeers, and they recognized "a glow" in her decorating.

Rose Cumming also espoused smoked mirrors, bare but highly polished parquet floors, and silver-blue foil wallpapers. Among her clients were the Potter Palmers of Chicago, Marlene Dietrich, Mary Pickford, and Norma Shearer. Among the designers who served apprenticeships with her were George Stacey, John Robert Moore, Richard Hare, Harrison Coultra, and Georgina Fairholme.

She believed that "In real decorating, there are no precedents." Rose Cumming's methodology was to "pull and drag everything back and forth, trying objects here and there, until one finds the exact place in the room where this or that piece looks best." She added, "and there it stays forever." She had been in her own house for a quarter of a century and claimed that she had "never moved one stick of furniture."[13] Her living room, therefore, was a preserved example of 1920s decorating. It was a historical eighteenth-century room with uncarpeted parquet floors on which sat Louis XV pieces, most of which were signed. The walls had early-eighteenth-century Chinese hand-painted wallpaper panels, and above hung an eighteenth-century Chinese chandelier made, unexpectedly, of papier-mâché. It was all historically possible, but the combination showed that Rose Cumming, by the end of the 1920s, was beginning to expand the boundaries of historical accuracy.

McMillen Inc.   In 1924 Eleanor McMillen (she became Mrs. Archibald Brown in 1934) opened what she called "the first professional full-service interior decorating firm in America." Professional is the operative word. "When I decided to go into business, I went to business and secretarial school as well," she has said. "I thought that if I were going to do it at all, I'd better do it professionally. I wasn't one of the ladies."[14] She therefore called her firm McMillen Inc. rather than "Eleanor McMillen." Her ability as a level-headed and methodical businessperson was certainly a strong reason why McMillen Inc. continued in business as a leading decorating firm for the next fifty years. In this regard McMillen made a step forward in professionalizing the decorating field.

Born Eleanor Stockstrom in St. Louis, Missouri, Mrs. Brown (1890–) was brought up among considerable affluence. She attended finishing school in Briarcliff, New York. In 1914 she married engineer Drury McMillen and began ten years of travel related to his business. Between trips she took the three-year design course at the New York School of Fine and Applied Arts. She subsequently studied at the school's branch in Paris under William Odom's tutelage, visiting many of the great houses and museums of France and Italy. She thought so highly of this training that, for the first forty years—with one exception—McMillen Inc. hired only graduates from that school. Among McMillen's early commissions were a house for H. H. Rogers of Standard Oil and a house for Arthur Houghton of Corning Glass.

Eleanor Brown's style was based on French classicism, the prevailing taste in American society that had been established by Elsie de Wolfe twenty years before. But she added Directoire and English Regency to her repertoire and used these periods intermixed, since she cared for the background of the room—its interior architecture—and wanted it to set off the furnishings to best advantage.

Her taste was more disciplined than that of many of her contemporaries, however. She preferred to use flowered chintzes only in country houses, and then sparingly. Important rooms had painted walls within classical pilasters and niches. Always she was concerned with good scale and good proportions. She used wall-papers only in more private areas. With minor stylistic variation and with the inclusion of Art Deco–derived Modern, this was her style for the next fifty years— and it looked as fresh in 1950 and it did in 1930. In fact, the undatable quality of McMillen interiors, no matter which partner or associate was in charge, is one of the hallmarks of the firm's work.

The apartment that Mrs. Brown designed for herself in 1928, although modified slightly over the years, is an example of her work from that period. Mrs. Brown and her new associate, Grace Fakes (who taught at the New York School of Fine and Applied Arts), gave the living room (see Figure 105A) definition and symmetry by closing off one window and articulating the wall planes with white-painted pilasters and moldings. This flat and thin architectural detailing, including a pedimented door, is in the late-1920s Greek Revival or modified Directoire style. The walls were first canvas-lined then painted yellow; a black marble mantelpiece of a type advocated by William Odom had a classical revival mirror above it. On the floor was an Aubusson rug; and the furniture was a collection of Louis XVI pieces, both gilt and painted, and upholstered in yellow fabrics and leather. Two layers of tie-back draperies hung at the windows.

105A. Eleanor McMillen Brown. Living room, own apartment. New York City. 1928. *Photograph by Drix Duryea, courtesy McMillen Inc.*

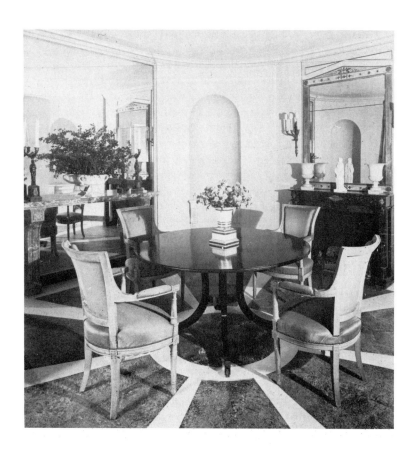

105B. Eleanor McMillen Brown. Dining room, own apartment. New York City. 1928. *Photograph courtesy McMillen Inc.*

Mrs. Brown shaped the dining room (see Figure 105B) into a flattened oval with four niches, which originally remained bare. A large, framed, floor-to-ceiling mirror, which had a marble console and black-bronze Directoire candelabra on it, faced the doorway. Another pedimented mirror was above a fireplace. The floor was marbled in a sunburst pattern of green and white. At the table, a round Directoire table of dark wood, were painted Directoire chairs. Both rooms have been modified slightly in the intervening years—consoles, unifying of the furniture periods, enlarging of the mirrors into wall panels, simplification of the draperies, and, of course, changes in light levels—but the early scheme shows the late–Art Deco classical Greek decorating of the 1920s.

Thedlow Inc.   Another design firm, which maintained a major residential practice for the next forty years, was established in 1919. Thedlow Inc. was founded by the three Chalmers sisters, who formed the acronym Thedlow from letters of their first names—Theresa, Edna, and Charlotte. Charlotte Chalmers, later Mrs. Truman Handy, headed the firm. Charlotte Chalmers Handy (1892–) was born in New York, attended the Brearley School, and later was schooled in Indiana. Lyman Martin, a graduate of the New York School of Fine and Applied Arts, was to become a mainstay of the firm, which primarily designed residences for the affluent, until it closed in 1970.

Frances Elkins   Frances Elkins attracted attention in California in the early 1920s after she restored her 1824 adobe house Casa Amesti in Monterey. She soon became one of California's leading interior designers. At Casa Amesti, within the envelope of rough plaster walls, rough-planked floors, and exposed-beam ceilings, Frances Elkins placed a large English partners' desk in the center of the living room and surrounded it with several conversation groups. The seating pieces were a mixture of French, English, and Italian periods—usually pairs, but placed separately in an informal mix. She later added Chinese carpets, paintings, and porcelains. The colors were yellow, blue, and white. The room offers a rich mix of uses—both entertainment and work, both solitary and for company.

Owing to the acclaim she received for this work, in the mid-1920s Elkins began to decorate houses for friends, such as the Griffins in Pebble Beach, as well as friends in Monterey and Santa Barbara. In 1927 she opened offices in the Robert Louis Stevenson house in Monterey. At that time her work was fairly typical of 1920s period rooms. She later became known for more eclectic mixtures of periods and countries, and for juxtapositions of textures and colors—Spanish Colonial architecture with French and Italian palace furniture, the rough with the polished, the poor with the grand. Billy Baldwin was later to call her "perhaps the most creative decorator we ever had."

Syrie Maugham   One of the most prominent interior designers who practiced in the 1920s was Syrie Maugham. Born Gwendoline Maud Syrie Barnardo in London, Syrie Maugham (1879–1955) was married to author Somerset Maugham. In 1920 she had asked Elsie de Wolfe if she should open up shop as a decorator in London. Elsie de Wolfe had said no, that the field was already too crowded. Undaunted, Syrie Maugham opened her shop in 1922 and was a great success with furniture that was either pickled or decorated with painted floral designs. Her success was so immediate that, beginning in 1926, she opened shops in the United States in New York, Chicago, Los Angeles, and Palm Beach.

In her own house on the north coast of France in 1926, Syrie Maugham finished the living room entirely in tones of beige enlivened with peach silk draperies; moldings had been stripped; the concrete floor was covered in sheepskins sewn together to make a carpet; the wood furniture was stripped and pickled; and all upholstery was beige. The dining room was virtually all white: Walls were paneled in untreated waxed pine and had rock-crystal appliques around them; stripped oak chairs were covered in white leather; the dining table, also of stripped oak, was set with white porcelain-handled knives and forks, which were reproductions of early-eighteenth-century Meissen models; white silk draperies had a design in sapphire blue. Throughout, closets were papered with hand-printed Italian book endpapers.

For her London house, completed in 1927, Syrie Maugham designed a living room with white walls, white satin curtains, white-painted Louis XV bergères and wing chairs, white chair covers with flower patterns, white velvet lampshades, two large camellia bushes with white porcelain flowers, arrangements of white lilies, and mirrors (see Figure 106). An Italian bureau-bookcase was papered with engravings on a white ground and then lacquered. The dining room paneling was pickled and waxed to a honey color and offset with white brocade draperies. White-and-gold painted chairs were set at an oval table set with white porcelain. She also popularized the design of bathrooms all of mirror, and made all-white a popular vogue.

The vogue for white was not only a return to 1890s schemes of the Mackintoshes, the MacNairs, and of Elsie de Wolfe for lightening late-Victorian stuffiness. It also corresponded with the white architecture of the 1920s, and it was a direct reversal on the vogue for the black rooms that grew up early in the 1920s; and as a refinement on silver rooms, which had been papered in tea-chest paper. Both had been adopted as suitable backgrounds for lacquered furniture, which had become popular with the recalls of Egyptian, Greek, and Chinese furnishings. Syrie Maugham brought an extreme all-white lightness to these schemes.

Elsie de Wolfe   During the 1920s Elsie de Wolfe updated her style in line with the times. At her house in Versailles, called the Villa Trianon, she began to use

106. Syrie Maugham. Own living room. London, England. 1927. *Photograph from* The Studio *(February 1933).*

leopard-skin chintzes to cover eighteenth-century stools and cushions. Fur throws replaced blanket covers on beds. Silk cushions were embroidered with mottoes that were humorous, sentimental, or cute—"Never complain, never explain" was one of them. Elsie de Wolfe again offered not innovation, but the image of nightclub society as the definition of fashionable design. She seemed to reflect the giddy flapperdom of life and the surrealism of the 1920s. In 1926, at the age of sixty-one, Elsie de Wolfe married Sir Charles Mendl, British press attaché in Paris. From then on she preferred to be known as Lady Mendl.

Dorothy Draper   Dorothy Draper was the first American woman decorator to concentrate on nonresidential design. Her commissions from the 1920s through the 1950s, during which she became one of the most publicized personalities in the design world, included lobbies, hotels, clubs, restaurants, shops, and hospitals.

Born Dorothy Tuckerman in Tuxedo Park, New York, Dorothy Draper (1889–1969) attended the Brearley School in New York, and in 1912 married Dr. George Draper. After three children, they were divorced in 1930. Before that, with the backing of her family social and diplomatic connections, she opened a firm in New York called the Architectural Clearing House and began by designing apartment house lobbies. In 1925 she founded Dorothy Draper & Company, which was soon an established success.

By 1930 Dorothy Draper had designed lobbies for New York's then new Carlyle Hotel, and for the apartment house at 770 Park Avenue. Both were in the prevailing classical late–Art Deco, Greek–Egyptian idiom. The lobby of 770 Park Avenue, still virtually unchanged, has flooring of black marble with white-and-gray banding, dead-white walls, and doors in black enamel with white moldings (see Figure 107). A niche, then painted blue, features a female figure. Greek-revival sofas, then covered in terra-cotta brick red, are flanked by tables with classical motifs. The Carlyle Hotel lobbies show the same flooring scheme and classical late–Art Deco detailing, though the furnishings and colors have largely been changed. At this time, Dorothy Draper had not yet developed her Neo-Baroque style of the 1930s.

The Impact of Art Deco on America

When the Art Deco exposition of 1925 was being planned, the United States declined the invitation to exhibit its modern decorative and industrial art on the grounds that the country had no modern or industrial arts worth exhibiting. The design professions of America were galvanized by this decision: Designers were determined to sail to Paris to see what really was new and to show that America did indeed have contributions of merit in those fields.

Those who went to see the 1925 exposition, including buyers for American department stores, brought a popularizing impetus. Among the department stores, Macy's, Lord & Taylor, B. Altman, Wanamaker's, Franklin Simon, Marshall Field, and others displayed room vignettes in the new styles.

107. Dorothy Draper. Lobby, 770 Park Avenue. New York City. 1930. *Photograph from* Architecture and Building, *1931.*

108. Joseph Urban. Own house. Yonkers, New York. Before 1926. *Photograph from Nancy McClelland,* The Practical Book of Decorative Wall Treatments *(Philadelphia: J. B. Lippincott, 1926).*

109. Rudolph M. Schindler. Living room, Lovell beach house. Newport Beach, California. 1926. *Photograph from UCSB Art Museum, University of California at Santa Barbara.*

The Spread of Modernism

The new European Modernism was first brought to the United States by a number of immigrants who began to explore new directions in America early in the 1920s. They brought the varying waves of Modernism to active production in this country.

Joseph Urban (see Figure 108) had come from Austria in 1911 to set up the Wiener Werkstaette shop in New York. He created interiors for the Ziegfeld Theater, of which he was also the architect; the Casino in the Park; the Persian Room in the Plaza Hotel; the St. Regis Roof; and the auditorium of the New School.

Rena Rosenthal opened what was considered the first contemporary shop in the United States, where the work of European designers and craftsmen was available, including the ceramics of Wally Wieselthier and Russel Wright (see below).

Paul T. Frankl emigrated from Austria in 1914. He spent the 1920s in New York, designing his attention-getting skyscraper furniture and establishing what was considered one of the first Modern furniture firms.

After the war, architects Rudolph M. Schindler and Richard Neutra came from Vienna; and, early in the 1920s, architect William Lescaze arrived from Switzerland. Rudolph Schindler designed his house on Kings Road in Hollywood (1921–22), and his beach house for the Lovells in Newport Beach, California (see Figure 109). Richard Neutra began his series of influential houses with the Lovell House in Los Angeles (1929) (see Figure 110). The latter is considered the earliest masterpiece in the International Style to be constructed in America, and the only

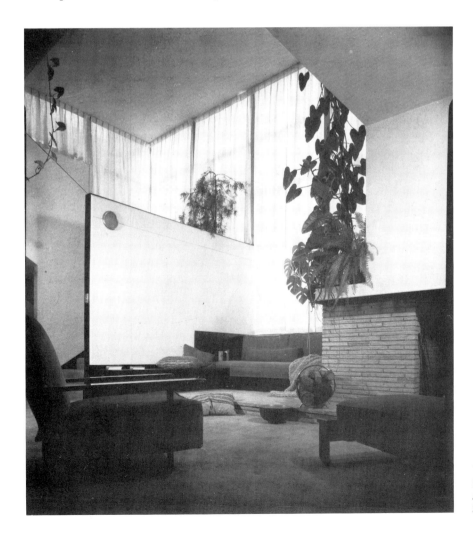

110. Richard Neutra. Living room, Lovell House. Los Angeles, California. 1929. *Photograph by Julius Shulman.*

111A. Frank Lloyd Wright. Detail, Hollyhock House. Los Angeles, California. 1920. *Photograph by Thomas A. Heinz.*

one of its period to be in the class with Le Corbusier's Villa Savoye and Mies's Tugendhat House.

During the 1920s the pioneering influence of Frank Lloyd Wright was in eclipse. His practice had dwindled while he was in Japan, but his previously designed Hollyhock House in Los Angeles for Aline Barnsdall was completed in 1920 under the supervision of his then assistant, Rudolph Schindler. The house is called the Hollyhock House because of the stylized geometric design based on the hollyhock flower that is consistently used throughout the house (see Figure 111A). The hollyhock design appears on the ornamentation of the heavy, somewhat Mayan massing of the exterior, through the interior and into the design of chairs, leaded windows, and other furnishings (see Figure 111B). Most of the original furniture, except the dining table and chairs, was designed by Schindler.

In 1923 Wright designed a house for Mrs. George Madison Millard in Pasadena, California, with textured and ornamented concrete blocks. He called them "textile blocks" because they were held together by a network of steel rods. Used inside and outside the Millard House, these textile blocks provide richly textured decoration; since some of the blocks are glass-filled, they streak the interior with pinpoints of light. Split-level in section, the house has a bedroom balcony overlooking the living room; this section produces a larger space than might be expected in the small house and, with the textile-block patterning, the house provides a rich and atmospheric setting for the Renaissance furnishings that Mrs. Millard collected and sold.

The Impact of the Bauhaus on America

"It is hard to recall when and how we in America first began to hear of the Bauhaus," the director of the Museum of Modern Art in New York, Alfred Barr, Jr., wrote in 1938.

> In the years just after World War I we thought of German art in terms of Expressionism, of Mendelsohn's streamlined Einstein tower, Toller's "Masse Mensch," Wiene's "Cabinet of Dr. Caligari." It may not have been until after the great Bauhaus exhibition of 1923 that reports reached America of a new kind of art school in Germany. . . . A little later we began to use some of the Bauhaus books, notably Schlemmer's amazing volume on the theater and Moholy-Nagy's *Malerei, Photographie, Film.* . . . A few American pilgrims had visited Dessau before Gropius left in 1928; in the five years thereafter, many went to stay as students. During this time, Bauhaus material, typography, paintings, prints, theater art, architecture, and industrial objects had been included in American exhibitions. . . .[15]

In addition, the build-up of American interest in the factory aesthetic of the Teens was seen in the paintings of Stuart Davis, Charles Sheeler, and Charles Demuth. But the direct and widespread transportation of Modern design and of Bauhaus principles and methodology to the United States had to wait until the next decade.

Industrial Design in America

Modern design from Europe strongly influenced the newly emerging designers who came to be known as industrial designers. In the decade of the 1920s, the American profession of industrial design began. It was the first American flowering of the long-brewing marriage of design and industry, and the first recognition of the potential of combining machine production with good design.

The pioneer industrial designers and their followers were to have an enormous effect on interior design through the design of furnishings, appliances, and countless other products used in houses and offices, in educational facilities and hospi-

111B. Frank Lloyd Wright. Living room, Hollyhock House. Los Angeles, California. 1920. *Photograph © Ezra Stoller/ ESTO, 1954.*

tals. Soon, industrial designers took on the design of entire interiors, first for the transportation industry—ocean liners, trains, airplanes, and automobiles—and then for every other type of interior for which they could gain a commission.

Designing for industrial production was by no means an entirely new activity, of course. Witness the Deutscher Werkbund's success in the Teens. Even earlier in the Industrial Revolution, all the textiles that were woven by the new machines were designed by designers for industry. Some of these designers were architects working in their offices; others were craftsmen working at their looms. In the mid- and late eighteenth century, Jacquard and other designers of the revolutionary machinery for textile production were designers for industry. And it should be remembered that Josiah Wedgwood, of the celebrated English porcelain works, designed a number of elegant "useful" wares for the kitchen, among his designs for his industrial production. In the early and late nineteenth century also, the Shakers turned their handcraft furniture production into a machine industry. And Michael Thonet's nineteenth-century process for bending wood sparked one of the most widely recognized and popular furniture industries of the past hundred years.

In the mid-nineteenth century, as historian Edgar Kaufmann, Jr., has written:

> A few books mention that Pugin himself, the sculptor Alfred Stevens, and Henry Cole (Prince Albert's right arm in the Crystal Palace exhibition venture and thereafter) were early designers-for-industry with sizable, systematic practices. It is less clearly recognized that they had an ample following in succeeding generations. Side by side with the Arts and Crafts Movement, there were men who had no illusions about a return to the Middle Ages, who worked for machine productions, and who tried to better the prevailing standards of marketable wares. The best of them, following the lead of James A. McN. Whistler and his friend Edwin William Godwin were keenly aware of the lessons of Japanese design, first displayed to Europe's gaze at the 1862 international exhibition in London, a result of Matthew Perry's mission. Notable among these men, who became known under the tag of "the Aesthetic Movement" were Christopher Dresser, Lewis F. Day, and C. F. A. Voysey.[16]

Among the American industrial designers of the 1920s were several who had recently emigrated from Europe, where they were in the direct tradition of the Deutscher Werkbund, the Bauhaus, and the long-abuilding designers-for-industry tradition. First came Kem Weber, who was caught in America by World War I; in 1919 Raymond Loewy came from France and John Vassos came from Greece. In the mid-1920s Peter Muller-Munk came from Germany.

Some of the first Americans to call themselves industrial designers were Laurelle Guild, Egmont Arens, Ernest Elmo Calkins, and Harley Earl. The pioneer industrial designers in America who became most famous were Norman Bel Geddes, Henry Dreyfuss, Walter Dorwin Teague, Raymond Loewy, Donald Deskey, and Russel Wright. In the 1930s they created a school of industrial production and a style for their time.

Norman Bel Geddes   Norman Bel Geddes (1893–1958) began his career as a stage designer in Los Angeles and New York in 1916. Born in Michigan, he spent six months studying at the Cleveland School of Art and Chicago Art Institute before he began in the theater. He first designed settings for Max Reinhardt's production of *The Miracle*, where he turned the entire theater auditorium into a Gothic church, using wood benches as audience seating. He continued as a theater producer throughout his career.

From the 1920s onward, his reputation brought him product-design commissions. He designed automobiles for the Graham Paige Motor Company in 1927, and gas stoves for the Standard Gas Equipment Company around 1929. Bel Geddes went on to become one of the most prominent and successful of all American industrial designers. Throughout his career he was a visionary, inventing forms and techniques that would suit the futuristic spirit of the times.

Henry Dreyfuss   Another industrial design pioneer who started in the theater was Henry Dreyfuss (1904–72). Born in New York City, Dreyfuss began his design career working for Norman Bel Geddes on scenery and costumes for Max Reinhardt's *The Miracle*. He later was art director of scenery, costumes, and lighting for the Strand Theatre in New York City, where he designed over 250 weekly shows. He went on to design settings for numerous other productions, then to design theater interiors, and subsequently to design industrial products. In 1928 he opened his own office for industrial design.

In 1929 American Telegraph & Telephone Company (AT&T) asked him to do some sketches for the redesign of telephones. Dreyfuss replied that sketches were no thorough way to design such important products, and he expanded the commission to a complete design analysis and thorough solution. His continuing association with AT&T for the next fifty years produced some of his most influential industrial designs.

Dreyfuss went on to design transportation interiors, building interiors, household and consumer products, and farm and industrial products. His later independent work in cataloguing human measurements and the tolerances for human activities led to the establishment of the field of human factors engineering. It was said that Dreyfuss was dedicated to proving that people were more important than products. In the 1930s, he was to design interiors as well.

Walter Dorwin Teague   Walter Dorwin Teague (1883–1960) began his career as an illustrator and worked in advertising before opening his own advertising agency. In the mid-1920s he went to Paris to see what was happening in the new Art Moderne. On his return he designed packages, sketched a line of automobiles, and designed some grand pianos. Around 1927 he began an association with Eastman Kodak that ultimately led to his lifetime contract as design consultant to Kodak. In the 1930s he, too, began to design interiors.

Raymond Loewy   In 1919 Raymond Loewy (1893–) came to the United States from Paris. He started his career in New York as a fashion illustrator, advertising designer, and costume designer (for Florenz Ziegfeld). His first product design assignment was for the Gestetner Duplicator in 1929. From the 1930s through the 1960s he headed one of the largest, most successful, and best-known industrial design firms in the world. He designed offices and other commercial interiors, residences, automobiles, and numerous interior furnishings products.

Donald Deskey   Donald Deskey (1894–) worked in advertising in Chicago and New York in the early 1920s, and soon founded his own art agency. He went to Paris for a year, returned to teach in the art department at Juniata College in Pennsylvania, then went back to Paris to see the 1925 exhibition. On his second return to New York he began to produce furnishings that were sought after by architects and stage-set designers. In 1927 he was at work on a candy-vending machine. At the end of the 1920s Deskey was designing furniture and interiors for the Radio City Music Hall in Rockefeller Center (see Chapter 13).

Russel Wright   Russel Wright was one of the pioneer industrial designers; but, even more, he was an artist-craftsman devoted to the design of household objects, furnishings, and interiors. Born in Lebanon, Ohio, Russel Wright (1904–76) enrolled in art classes at the Cincinnati Academy of Art and at the Art Students' League in New York in 1920, where he studied painting and sculpture. He then went to Princeton University, where he worked with the Triangle Club, directing and designing sets. In the summers he continued to work in the theater, including a stint with Norman Bel Geddes designing for *The Miracle*. At the Maverick Festival theater in Woodstock, New York, he met and later married sculptor-designer Mary Small Einstein.

Following his theater years he began designing life-size caricature masks of celebrities. They were executed in new materials—plastic with spun glass, mirror, and marshmallows—which prefigured his inventive use of materials throughout his career. Soon miniature plaster animals were added to his designs, along with others made of aluminum and chromium-plated metal. From this investigation he moved on to produce, at the end of the 1920s, a set of spun-pewter bar accessories and then spun-aluminum table accessories and serving pieces. They were the beginning of his industrial design career in household objects—especially ceramic dinnerware, for which he became most widely known.

In this way the profession of industrial design emerged in the United States as a direct response to competition with European industry and in the direct tradition of the goals of incorporating machine production and "design for the times" into a new style for its day. The new industrial designers were to develop a new style in the 1930s.

By these means the Modern movement came to America. But in 1929, the year that the Museum of Modern Art was founded in New York, there occurred that cataclysmic event that was to affect the entire world—the Wall Street crash of October 29, 1929. Its repercussions on every field of life and design around the world lasted throughout the next decade.

Suggested Reading

Battersby, Martin. *The Decorative Twenties*. New York: Walker & Company, 1971.

Bayer, Herbert, Walter Gropius, and Ise Gropius, eds. *Bauhaus: 1919–1928*. New York: The Museum of Modern Art, 1938.

Brown, Erica. *Sixty Years of Interior Design: The World of McMillen*. New York: Viking Press, 1982.

Caplan, Ralph. *By Design*. New York: McGraw-Hill, 1984.

Fisher, Richard B. *Syrie Maugham*. London: Duckworth, 1978.

Hanks, David A. *Donald Deskey*. New York: E. P. Dutton, 1985.

Hennessey, William J. *Russel Wright*. Cambridge: MIT Press, 1983.

Hillier, Bevis. *Art Deco*. Minneapolis: Minneapolis Institute of the Arts, 1971.

Hitchcock, Henry-Russell, and Philip Johnson. *The International Style: Architecture Since 1922*. New York: W. W. Norton, 1932, 1966.

Jacobus, John M., Jr. "Architecture, American Style: 1920–45," *American Art*. New York: Prentice-Hall, Harry N. Abrams, 1979.

Jeanneret, Charles-Edouard. *Le Corbusier: 1910–65*. Zurich: Les Editions d'Architecture Zurich, 1967.

Johnson, Philip C. *Mies van der Rohe*. New York: The Museum of Modern Art, 1947, 1978.

Kaufmann, Edgar, Jr. "Interior Design: Architecture or Decoration?" *Progressive Architecture*. October 1962, pp. 141–44.

Lesieutre, Alain. *The Spirit and Splendour of Art Deco*. New York: Paddington Press Ltd., 1974.

Maxtone-Graham, John. *The Only Way to Cross*. New York: Macmillan, 1972.

McFadden, David Revere, ed. *Scandinavian Modern Design: 1880–1980*, a Cooper-Hewitt Museum exhibition. New York: Harry N. Abrams, 1982.

Meickle, Jeffrey L. *Twentieth Century Limited: Industrial Design in America, 1925–39*. Philadelphia: Temple University Press, 1979.

Pool, Mary Jane, ed. *20th Century Decorating, Architecture, and Gardens*. New York: Holt, Rinehart and Winston, 1980.

Pulos, Arthur J. *American Design Ethic: A History of Industrial Design to 1940*. Cambridge: MIT Press, 1983.

Robinson, Cervin, and Rosemarie Haag Bletter. *Skyscraper Style, Art Deco New York*. New York: Oxford University Press, 1975.

Tweed, Katharine, ed. *The Finest Rooms by America's Great Decorators*. New York: Viking Press, 1964.

Wilk, Christopher. *Marcel Breuer: Furniture and Interiors*. New York: The Museum of Modern Art, 1981.

Notes

1. Work Program of the Staatlichen Bauhauses Weimar, quoted from *Vienna Moderne: 1898–1918*, exhibition catalogue (University of Houston: Sarah Campbell Blaffer Gallery; New York: Cooper-Hewitt Museum, 1978), p. 90f. Reprinted there with permission from *Architecture and Design: An International Anthology of Original Articles*, ed. Timothy and Charlotte Benton, with Dennis Sharp (London: Granada Publishing, Ltd., 1975).

2. At the time of the 1923 exhibition, Breuer and Bayer, for example, were still students.

3. This goal was adopted as early as 1922 or 1923, but was reinforced after the move to Dessau.

4. Walter Gropius, *Idee und Aufbau des Staatlichen Bauhauses Weimar* (Munich: Bauhausverlag, 1923); translated in *Bauhaus: 1919–1928*, ed. Herbert Bayer, Walter Gropius, and Ise Gropius (New York: The Museum of Modern Art, 1938), p. 27f.

5. Christopher Wilk, *Marcel Breuer: Furniture and Interiors* (New York: The Museum of Modern Art, 1981), notes that the name "Wassily" was given to the Breuer Chair only in 1960, when it was put into production; in the 1920s and 1930s, it was known simply as "Model B3, club armchair." Also it was not made with leather until that time. Similarly, the Cesca Chair was so named (for Breuer's daughter, who was not yet born during the Bauhaus years) only in 1960.

6. Henry-Russell Hitchcock and Philip Johnson, *The International Style: Architecture Since 1922.* (New York: W. W. Norton, 1932, 1966), p. 33.

7. Wilk, op. cit., points out that Laccio was not a name of the period but was adopted when Knoll and Stendig began producing the designs. Wilk also notes that some of the pieces made under this name were not original designs, but rather adaptations of the design. The stool was original; but an extended version was not.

8. Wilk, op. cit. Breuer already had an apartment in Berlin and a furniture business, designing for Standard-Mobel.

9. Le Corbusier, *Towards a New Architecture* (London: The Architectural Press, 1949; New York: Frederick A. Praeger, 1949), p. 96.

10. Charles-Edouard Jeanneret, *Le Corbusier: 1910–65* (Zurich: Les Editions d'Architecture Zurich, 1967), p. 28.

11. Ibid., p. 50.

12. Alfred Barr, Jr., Preface to *Bauhaus: 1919–1928*, ed. Herbert Bayer, Walter Gropius, and Ise Gropius (New York: The Museum of Modern Art, 1938), p. 5.

13. Rose Cumming, quoted from *The Finest Rooms by America's Great Decorators*, ed. Katharine Tweed (New York: Viking Press, 1964), p. 51.

14. Eleanor McMillen Brown, quoted from Erica Brown, *Sixty Years of Interior Design: The World of McMillen* (New York: Viking Press, 1982), p. 15.

15. Barr, loc. cit.

16. Edgar Kaufmann, Jr., "Interior Design: Architecture or Decoration?" *Progressive Architecture* (October 1962), p. 142.

Chapter 13

1930–1940: Modernism Comes to America

In the 1930s the Modern design movement reached the United States. It was increasingly seen in the American work of the postwar immigrants and in the work of a number of American designers who had gone to Europe in the second half of the 1920s to learn what was new.

In interior design the influential new directions were several strains from the 1920s: the Art Deco of the traditionalists that had been exhibited at the 1925 Paris exposition; the Art Moderne and Swedish Modern of the formalists that had been seen at the same exhibition; and the De Stijl–based international Modern of the functionalists that was being promulgated by the Bauhaus and by Le Corbusier (see Chapter 12). A skirmish ensued as these three new directions began to be transplanted into the home soil of Beaux-Arts academic historicism.

As a consequence, the decade of the 1930s witnessed a battle between the Futurists' look toward Tomorrow and the historicists' view of traditional American designers back to Yesterday. Designers were split into opposing camps and proclaimed rival ethics, morality, and social virtues—of historical tradition versus modern progress, of the old versus the new, of ornamentation versus purgation, and of verticality versus horizontality. Yet the use of the same modern materials by both camps, and the ability of designers to work in opposing styles at the same time, made for similarities and crossovers that make distinctions and categorization difficult, but perhaps more necessary now than ever.

In the 1930s the Modernist outlook gained a strong impetus when it became a political and economic goal as well as an artistic one. The political goal was to get the American economy and the country on the go again following the Great

Depression. The Depression that began in 1929 was an economic disaster unparalleled in modern times. More than five hundred banks failed. As the effects spread, the number of unemployed throughout the industrialized nations was estimated at 30 million in 1932; in Germany alone more than 6 million were unemployed. In the United States 9 million people were unemployed; that represented 25 percent of the work force. Unemployment spread insidiously across professions, classes, and countries until 1936 and 1937. Mortgage foreclosures and breadlines were daily concerns. The natural disaster of the Dust Bowl drought exacerbated the hopelessness of the situation.

The reach for tomorrow, therefore, was America's offer of hope; it also made the country, for the first time, a leader in the design fields. Optimism about the future was a campaign fought by President Franklin D. Roosevelt's New Deal; new jobs were created by the Works Progress Administration (WPA) from 1933 onward—including programs to support artists. Roads and transportation were improved and rural electrification spread. The Century of Progress exhibition in Chicago in 1933 was the first public design front; victory was proclaimed by the World of Tomorrow World's Fair in New York in 1939.

New Materials

A parade of new materials came before the public during the 1930s to point the way toward a cleaner, more functionally efficient, and healthier world of tomorrow. The plastics industry got its launch into major production in 1932. Celluloid had been invented in 1870 and Bakelite in 1907; but they were not adaptable to products that were durable, hygienic, colorful, and virtually unbreakable. In 1930 Plexiglas (Lucite) was invented and vinyl coating was manufactured. In 1932 a premium give-away cereal bowl for General Mills' Wheaties was made of a urea formaldehyde thermosetting plastic produced primarily by American Cyanamid; it was so popular that over 5 million were distributed. Nylon was invented in 1937. The Age of Plastics had begun.

Of other materials, glass—especially glass block—along with chromium-plated brass, Monel metal, and stainless steel, found their ways into interiors. Better linoleum, asphalt and rubber tiles, and acoustical tiles were produced. Plywood and Flexwood panels and sheets of plastic laminate spliced with chrome strips came into general use. As a poor stepchild of the Great Depression, knotty pine became the wall surfacing that bespoke the first years of the decade. In 1938 the Lumiline incandescent tube was announced by Westinghouse and General Electric. Fluorescent lighting was demonstrated widely at the New York World's Fair of 1939; and neon, introduced before 1930, became increasingly popular.

The Streamline Style

As the 1930s unfolded in America, the newly emerged profession of industrial design began to develop, or to be prominently recognized for developing, a new style for a futuristic tomorrow—Streamline Modern. Practitioners designing in this vein were pursuing a middle path between Modernism and Traditionalism, and between the Art Deco skyscraper style of the late 1920s and the Modernism and Purism of vanguard architecture. Specifically, they combined the Futurist-Expressionist interest in speed and motion into an aesthetic image. Whereas Art Moderne rejected historicism and adopted a geometric basis, Streamlining, which also rejected historicism, adopted Expressionism. But both avoided the ideological warfare over Modern versus traditional and concentrated on designing and styling. This put them at odds with design moralists on both sides.

The Streamline Decade, as those concentrating on this aspect of the 1930s have called it, based its stylistic idiom on the Futurists' love of speed and motion and on the Expressionists' sleek lines. Another inspiration was the early drawings of Erich Mendelsohn. The justification of Streamlining was speed and efficiency—including such miracles of modern technology as the pop-up toast robot in the kitchen. So Streamlining adapted aerodynamics and its most efficient form—the teardrop—which had been shown to increase speed by decreasing air resistance. Airflow designs as disparate as factory products, business equipment, household appliances, furnishings, and interiors began to come from the design offices of the new industrial designers.

Norman Bel Geddes, Henry Dreyfuss, Walter Dorwin Teague, and Raymond Loewy were the foremost of these industrial designers throughout the 1930s. Donald Deskey and Russel Wright made important contributions; Buckminster Fuller was the most visionary of these contemporaries. Most of their work was in the design of household appliances, business machines, and transportation. For this latter industry—and for museum and department store exhibitions—industrial designers got their first commissions to design interiors. Early on, industrial designers got to design some of the airplanes, ocean liners, and railroad trains that had inspired their imagistic style. Gasoline service stations, touring service centers, and other commercial interiors followed.

The airplane was the primary influence on and objective of the industrial designers. Plane exteriors developed from their angular, strut-supported, geometric wings to smooth airstream forms. Inside the first clipper seaplanes of 1931, the cabins were tubular-looking spaces lined with Flexwood and joined with wood-grained splines; decorative features such as donut life preservers recalled the sailing-yacht-like quality of seaplanes. In 1934 the Douglas DC-2 interior was designed as more stripped, functional, and mechanical-looking.

Ocean-liner interiors were a different matter because of their size and established clientele. The French *Normandie*, launched in 1932, was the last compendium of French Art Deco, with interior decorations by Jean Dunand, René Lalique, Jean Dupas, Raymond Subes, and Emile-Jacques Ruhlmann. Art Deco and Art Moderne were mixed in the interiors of the *Queen Mary*, which was designed by British designers and launched in 1934. It was called "ocean-liner modern."

No ship was produced in as visionary a Streamline style as Norman Bel Geddes's project, published in 1932 in his book *Horizons*; it was a fully enclosed water-going vessel that looked almost rocket-like. But from 1933 to 1936 Raymond Loewy designed the *Princess Anne* ferry that crossed the Chesapeake Bay from Cape Charles to Norfolk, Virginia, in as sleek a realization of this style as was achieved in ships.

From 1936 to 1938 Loewy designed the interiors of the *Panama* and other ships. Machine-art ideals and fireproof technology inspired simple industrial furnishings. Stainless-steel doors, metal tables with plastic laminate tops, metal-tube-framed chairs, and tubular lighting composed a spare, institutional, club-like atmosphere. Rounded corners and geometric motifs fixed the style as Streamline Modern. However, there were also concessions to popular taste in applied decorations, and a color scheme of coral, beige, and apple green; peach-colored mirrors, a totem of the decade, softened the scheme.

Streamline Trains

Railroad trains were the supreme realization of the Streamline ideal. The public was introduced to this new style by way of the first streamliner trains, which were exhibited by the Union Pacific and Burlington railroads at the Century of Progress Chicago World's Fair's second year, 1934. First came the Union Pacific Railroad's

City of Salina, which was made by the Pullman Car and Manufacturing Company. It had a trim interior of blue-banded walls progressing upward from dark to light blue, each band separated by an aluminum strip, and topped by a white coved or vaulted ceiling. Tubular aluminum seats were upholstered in a gold-brown tapestry.

Second of the streamliners was the Burlington *Pioneer Zephyr*, designed by architect Paul Cret with E. G. Budd and built by the Budd Manufacturing Company. It had an exterior with unpainted stainless-steel side panels that were corrugated for extra strength, but that also expressed the horizontal direction of the airstream, however much the corrugations may have impeded that stream. On the interior Cret specified bright colors accented with chrome or stainless-steel moldings. A striped linoleum floor and coved ceilings that incorporated air-conditioning and indirect strip lighting were used in the lounge and observation cars, which were furnished with tubular metal furniture and metal-based tables with plastic laminate tops. Flexwood and Masonite were also used.

112A. Henry Dreyfuss. Observation car on the *20th Century Limited*. 1938. *Penn Central Transportation Company Photograph. From Arthur J. Pulos,* American Design Ethic: A History of Industrial Design to 1940 *(Cambridge: MIT Press, 1983).*

The New York Central's *Mercury*, designed by Henry Dreyfuss in 1936, was conceived as a total design—integrating everything from the locomotive exterior to the table china inside. But it was Dreyfuss's design of the New York Central's *20th Century Limited* (1938) that was the high point of streamliner design.

Also a total design, the *20th Century Limited* was conceived in a kind of stately minimal vein that Dreyfuss called "cleanlining." The observation-car interior (see Figure 112A) had, at each end, a photo mural above an arc-shaped banquette and a round table; the effect was to make the interior plan bullet-nosed, like the ends of the train exterior. Sleek lozenge-plan gun-gray columns along the sides of the train car apparently supported a soffit and a shallow coved ceiling. Narrow horizontal bands atop the columns suggested capitals and continued the horizontal airflow motif of the ribbed-metal lampshades and the venetian blinds at the windows. In the *20th Century Limited* this airflow motif was more abstracted than in other train car design. Between built-in seating units upholstered in blue leather

112B. Henry Dreyfuss. Dining car on the *20th Century Limited*. 1938. *Penn Central Transportation Company Photograph. From Arthur J. Pulos,* American Design Ethic: A History of Industrial Design to 1940 *(Cambridge: Mit Press, 1983).*

were tables with integral lamps that had polished-metal shades. Gray carpeting and gray leather walls reiterated the brushed-metal finishes. The entire car had a unity that no other train car design achieved. The mirror-ended dining car (see Figure 112B) continued this theme of stripped elegance; metallic finishes in blue, gray, and rust-brown were used along with the new materials—Flexwood, cork paneling, and plastic laminates. Dreyfuss also designed the train's tableware and matchbook covers.

These early streamliners were custom-made (see Figure 113). By the end of the decade, mass production—of complete diesel locomotives by General Motors and of standard train cars by other companies—ironically signaled the end of the heyday of design innovation for streamliners.

Other Streamlined Interiors

Raymond Loewy and stage designer–author Lee Simonson created a model office and studio for an industrial designer for the Metropolitan Museum's 1934 exhi-

113. Raymond Loewy. Bar car on the *Broadway Limited*. 1938. *Raymond Loewy/William Snaith, Inc. Photograph. From Arthur J. Pulos,* American Design Ethic: A History of Industrial Design to 1940 (Cambridge: MIT Press, 1983).

bition Contemporary American Industrial Art (see Figure 114). The room had rounded corners of ivory plastic laminate paneling, round-ended horizontal windows, half-round metal trim, and three parallel horizontal bands—the latter a motif that became a trademark of the Streamline style. The flooring was blue linoleum; gunmetal blue metal tubular furniture had yellow leather upholstery. Desk-tables were supported on up-light verticals, suggesting a knowledge of Le Corbusier's combinations of table and column at the Villa Savoye. The up-light urn was prominent; tubular lighting was exposed. It was the epitome of the Streamline interior.

Norman Bel Geddes's House of Tomorrow (1931) combined the ideas of European Modernism with minimalist elements and Streamlining. Geddes's Elbow Room Restaurant in New York (1938), later renamed the Barberry Room, had many of the elements of Streamlining—curved walls, mirrored walls, strip lighting, horizontal emphasis—but it was an early example of the institutional style that continued in restaurants into the 1980s.

Donald Deskey The interiors of that pinnacle of movie houses, Radio City Music Hall in Rockefeller Center (completed in 1932), are a compendium of the Deco-

114. Raymond Loewy and Lee Simonson. Model office and studio for an industrial designer. 1934. *Raymond Loewy/William Snaith, Inc. Photograph. From Arthur J. Pulos,* American Design Ethic: A History of Industrial Design to 1940 *(Cambridge: MIT Press, 1983).*

Streamline style. It was designed by an association of architects with Edward Durell Stone as project architect and with interiors and furnishings by Donald Deskey.

Deskey designed fifty rooms in the Music Hall, including furniture, lamps, fabrics, and wallpapers. The associated architects orchestrated an assembly of artworks to show the period's attention to integrating the arts into architecture and interior design. Some of those artworks include the vast lobby mural painted by Ezra Winter, sculpture by William Zorach, and sculpted bronze panels by René Chambellan depicting jazz in different countries. The main lobby (on which Deskey did not work) conjures up the ballroom of an ocean liner of the day: Oval-ended and high-ceilinged, the vast space is overlooked by balconies, sheathed in mirror, hung with vertical chandeliers, and features a monumental staircase of colossal effect (see Figure 115). Crystal spheres articulate bronze balusters. Ruth Reeves designed the geometric carpet.

In Deskey's lounges and smoking rooms (see Figure 116), metal-based furniture with black plastic laminate tops, murals based on social themes, wallpapers in harmony with those themes, and dark-toned brown, burgundy, and blue color schemes combined to make Radio City Music Hall a landmark of Deco-Streamline design.

During the decade Deskey also designed cane furniture that was produced by the Ypsilanti Reed Furniture Company and designed rooms with the most up-to-date Bauhaus imagery, using Mies van der Rohe's MR Chair.

115. Associated architects and Edward Durell Stone. Grand foyer, Radio City Music Hall. New York City. 1932. *Photograph by Anne C. Brown, © The Rockfeller Group, Inc., 1985.*

Critics of Streamlining

Functional as some airflow design was on the exterior, it was arbitrary decoration on most interior products. To Rationalists, who believed that all design should be based on structure, the exterior design of Streamlined trains and cars had little relation to inner structure or function. "Modernistic" was the pejorative appellation such designs encountered. Streamlining offered the aesthetic of industrial production in its linear, extruded elements, but more generally it offered the image of flying speed, if not the actuality of it. However, this was not unlike the early designs of the Modernists that offered the image of the machine without the actuality of it. But the Modernists ultimately attained their goal of structural honesty; Streamlining did not.

Styling such as Streamlining also offered the manufacturers of industrial products the newly acclaimed advantage of obsolescence, based on changing styles. In the early days of the Depression this apparent guarantee of future sales seemed like a lifesaver. If products could be restyled with new advances, greater efficiency, and more up-to-date appearances, sales would increase. If sales increased, not only would the financial status of individual manufacturers improve, but the national economy would get a boost. The nation got behind this idea; Streamlining was adopted as a political and economic goal. To the Streamline designers, this was a means of forwarding their version of Modernism. To crusading Modernists, who believed that theirs was a style without change, for all times and all peoples, the

116. Donald Deskey. Ladies' lounge, Radio City Music Hall. New York City. 1933. *Photograph by Anne C. Brown, © The Rockefeller Group Inc., 1985.*

concept of purposely built-in and designed-in obsolescence was anathema—second only to historicism and ornamentation, of course.

Beyond Streamlining: Interior and Industrial Design

Russel Wright and Buckminster Fuller are notable among those designers who did not go in the direction of Streamlining. Although they worked in disparate styles, both would have an impact on American design.

Russel Wright   Russel Wright was less concerned with Streamlining, and was perhaps more influential than other industrial designers on interior design during the 1930s. He displayed a dedication to American nationalism and the American way of life in the household objects and interiors that he specialized in designing.

Early in the decade he and his wife Mary developed a line of spun-aluminum serving pieces that accommodated the new servantless, and therefore less formal, way of dining and entertaining that came with the decade. Wright invented the concept of "stove-to-table ware." He went on to expand his aluminum line, to design modestly priced flatware and chromium-plated table accessories, and furniture.

His designs were derived both from Streamlining and from the Bauhaus, yet had their own distinctive look that was associated with modern informal living. The chair he designed in 1932 for his own use (see Figure 117) was somewhere between late–Art Deco–archaic and the Peasant style. Constructed of primavera wood, it had a leather sling back and a pony-skin seat.

In 1934 Wright designed a sixty-piece line of coordinated furniture for the Heywood-Wakefield Company. The line introduced a new concept—the sectional sofa, which was to become a staple of furniture designers. One copper standing up light in particular was something of a classic.

In 1935 he designed his widely successful Modern Living line of furniture for the Conant Ball Company. Reminiscent of Swedish Modern in its bentwood arm construction, the furniture was available in a reddish maple tone and in blonde wood. The latter was especially appealing to 1930s taste. Constructed of native woods, the Modern Living line offered an American flavor with something of a Craftsman recall. It was the first total design room furnishing to be made available as mass-market home furnishing. The association of his name with the furniture in advertising made Russel Wright known nationwide.

In 1937 Wright designed his ceramic American Modern Dinnerware, which was first produced in Steubenville, Ohio, in 1939. It was his biggest commercial and artistic success. Its forms were reminiscent of the undulating lines of Hans Arp and the amoeboid motif (see Figure 141). The dinnerware was produced in plain muted colors—Seafoam Blue, Granite Grey, Chartreuse Curry, and Bean Brown. It was the first dinnerware intended to be used in mixed rather than matched sets.

Among their residential interiors, Russel and Mary Wright's own duplex on Park Avenue (1938) was lined, beneath the balcony, with large squares of flat wood paneling, which were rotated to emphasize the decorative qualities of the grain. The ceiling was covered with a pattern of squares and lattices. Draperies at the large-gridded windows hung from the high ceiling to the floor.

Although Russel Wright belonged to the first generation of American industrial designers, he always was more of a craftsman-designer than a businessman-consultant. As idealistic as his American nationalism was, it was not universally admired in a decade that still looked to Paris as the art center of the world.

Buckminster Fuller   As independently original an inventor-engineer-architect as Richard Buckminster Fuller (1895–1983) was, his commitment to production by industry links his first proposals with industrial design. His circular metal-

118. Buckminster Fuller. Dymaxion bath. 1927. *Illustration from Donald J. Bush,* The Streamlined Decade *(New York: Braziller, 1975).*

117. Russel Wright. Armchair with pony-skin seat. 1932. *Photograph from George Arents Research Library for Special Collections, Syracuse University.*

skinned Dymaxion House concept (1927) had adapted airplane construction techniques to the housing industry. His Dymaxion bathroom designed in 1927—produced as a prototype in 1930, of which about two dozen were produced in 1936, and the design patented in 1938 (see Figure 118)—was of sheet metal composing two compartments. One was the tub-shower compartment; the other was the sink-toilet compartment. The idea had to wait until the 1960s before production in plastic made such bathrooms commonly available.

Industrial Design Education

Educational programs in industrial design were slow to be established. The first degree-granting program in industrial design was offered in 1935 at the Carnegie Institute of Technology (now Carnegie-Mellon) in Pittsburgh. Other programs were at Pratt Institute in Brooklyn, at New York University, and at Columbia University. In 1935 the WPA provided a grant to establish the Design Laboratory school in New York, with Gilbert Rohde as director; but it was underfunded and short-lived.

Professional organizations for industrial designers began in 1938 with the American Designers Institute, founded in Chicago. Although its original members were mostly concerned with home furnishings, the organization was the precursor of the Industrial Designers Institute.

The Spread of Modernism in America

California had already welcomed the first architectural examples of European Modernism produced in this country. They were two houses: one by Schindler and the other by Neutra.

The Viennese architect Rudolph Schindler (1887–1953), who had worked as Frank Lloyd Wright's assistant during the Imperial Hotel days, designed the earliest American masterpiece in the new international Modern style—the Lovell House at Newport Beach (1925–26). It hovers over the beach on an exposed, open, and plug-in concrete structural frame; one end of the two-story living room has a floor-to-ceiling glass wall with detailing that we would associate with Wright's work at that time; at the other end is a surprisingly spare tall-backed banquette adjacent to a frameless two-sided fireplace. The combination is European–American Modern.

In 1929 another Viennese architect, Richard Neutra (1892–1970), built the Lovells' Los Angeles house, which is recognized as the only American design that can be considered to approach the quality of the Tugendhat House and the Villa Savoye of the same period. This design is a multilevel steel-frame house built on a hillside, with an exterior that reflects the combined Futurist-factory aesthetic in its large grids of glass and horizontal bands of white wall. The interior began to set the pattern for Neutra's later light and open metal-and-glass houses in California in the 1930s and 1940s.

Paul T. Frankl continued to design in the Modern idiom, getting more and more spartan after his skyscraper furniture of 1930. Joseph Urban (1872–1933), the Viennese architect and theater designer, also decorated in the Art Moderne style. Just before he died Urban designed an apartment in New York for Katherine Brush (see Figure 119). He used sleek-lined mantelpieces, banquette sofas with built-in bookcases along the backs, white leather upholstery, zebra-skin cushions, round mirrors, and Wiener Werkstaette appointments by Josef Hoffmann and Dagobert Peche. The color scheme was a bold white, black, and red.

Two Banking Halls: Irving Trust and PSFS

No better example of the rise of Modernism over lingering Art Deco can be found than two banking halls in two skyscrapers of 1932: the banking/reception hall of the Wall Street headquarters of the Irving Trust Company, designed by architect Ralph Walker of Voorhees, Gmelin & Walker (1932); and the Philadelphia Saving Fund Society.

   In the tall, lozenge-shaped space of Irving Trust (see Figure 120), flaming

120. Ralph Walker. Banking hall, Irving Trust Company. New York City. 1932. *Photograph by Nyholm Lincoln, courtesy Haines Lundberg Waehler, Architects/Engineers/Planners, the successor firm to Voorhees, Gmelin & Walker.*

mosaics—graduated from red to orange—created a brilliant room. It represented the last effects of Art Deco in America.

The banking hall of the Philadelphia Saving Fund Society (PSFS) (1931–32), by George Howe and the Swiss architect William Lescaze, was a rugged and dynamic combination of De Stijl, Constructivist, and Expressionist directions (see Figure 121A). The PSFS exterior was the first International Style skyscraper produced in America, and it remained the most progressively Modern skyscraper until Mies's work after 1951.

In the main banking room (see Figure 121B), which was elevated on the second floor to permit the ground level to be occupied by street-enhancing shops, the tall

121A. Howe & Lescaze. Plan, banking hall, PSFS. Philadelphia, Pennsylvania. 1931–32. *Illustration from Henry-Russell Hitchcock and Philip Johnson,* The International Style: Architecture Since 1922 *(New York: W. W. Norton, 1966).*

121B. Howe & Lescaze. Banking hall, PSFS. Philadelphia, Pennsylvania. 1931–32. *Photograph by Richard T. Dooner.*

freestanding columns and broad expanses of window wall were in deep contrast with the classicized Beaux-Arts buildings visible across the street. The radius-corner plan of the central tellers' counters and of the corner mezzanines reflected the rounded exterior corner of the base of the building. Black, gray, and white marble were used to finish the columns, floor, and counter fronts. Chromium-plated metal furniture upholstered in blue leather was designed by the architects to complete this first-generation Modern interior in America.

Elsewhere in the PSFS building, sleek, glossy, linoleum floors and lacquered columns were lighted by strips of fluorescent tubes to compose interiors of sparkling severity. Howe had decided his interiors would be based on "the elimination of meaningless mouldings."[1] More attention was given to such technological innovations as air-conditioning (PSFS was the second completely air-conditioned American skyscraper, following the 1928 Milam Building in San Antonio); acoustical ceiling tiles on a metal spline system were another innovation. In the executive offices on the 32nd floor, luxurious wood partitions were exploded by natural light effects both above the partitions and in the free-flowing spaces beyond.

The interior design of general offices in skyscrapers, except in rare instances, was still largely the purview of the client's office manager. This was a situation that did not change materially until the 1950s. Rare, then, were the Larkin Building of 1904 and, in the 1930s, PSFS and Frank Lloyd Wright's S. C. Johnson & Son Administration Building (see below).

The Cranbrook Academy of Art

Modern design education in America also received a new impetus at this time from the Cranbrook Academy of Art, which opened in 1932 in Bloomfield Hills, Michigan, outside Detroit. It was sponsored by the philanthropist George G. Booth and designed and directed by the Finnish architect Eliel Saarinen, who designed the campus buildings and their interiors (see Figure 122).

Many of the major designers and craftsmen of the next decade were associated with Cranbrook—either as family, faculty, or students. They included Eliel Saarinen, sculptor Carl Milles, ceramic designer Maja Grotell, and textile designer Marianne Strengell. Many of the designers who became the design leaders of the next decade studied at Cranbrook: Charles Eames, his wife Ray Kaiser Eames, Harry Bertoia, Benjamin Baldwin, Harry Weese, Edmund Bacon, Jack Lenor Larsen, Ralph Rapson, Pipsan Saarinen Swanson, and David Rowland. Florence Schust Knoll, who attended Cranbrook's Kingswood School for Girls, was a protégée of the Saarinen family. After terms as graduate students, many of these students went on to teach on the Cranbrook faculty. Cranbrook students in the 1940s included Don Knorr, David Rowland, and Niels Diffrient, all of whom became leading designers of furniture and other products.

Cranbrook Academy did not hold regular classes. Modeled on the American Academy in Rome, it offered graduate studio work in consultation with faculty artists-in-residence. The academy proposed no specific style or approach; its goal was the studio process rather than the designed product. Its influence was seminal.

The Promulgation of the International Style

In the first half of the decade the Modern movement as defined by the Bauhaus was spread to the American public. Alfred Barr of New York's Museum of Modern Art recalled that by 1930 there had been "a few pilgrims, a few students, and a few exhibited pieces, plus several books." Then, at the 1930 Paris exhibition of the Salon des Artistes Décorateurs, "the whole German section was arranged under

122. Eliel Saarinen. Dining room, President's House, Cranbrook Academy. Bloomfield Hills, Michigan. 1928–30. *Photograph from The Metropolitan Museum of Art, courtesy Cranbrook Archives.*

the direction of Gropius. Consistent in program, brilliant in installation, it stood like an island of integrity, in a mélange of chaotic modernistic caprice, demonstrating (what was not generally recognized at that time) that German industrial design, thanks largely to the Bauhaus, was years ahead of the rest of the world."[2] Next, Bauhaus lighting fixtures and chairs began to be imported into America privately, and American students at the Bauhaus began to return. Meanwhile, progressive architects in America were creating works in the idiom—Neutra, Schindler, Howe & Lescaze, and a few others.

The most widespread promulgator of the Bauhaus in the 1930s was undoubtedly the new Museum of Modern Art, which opened in New York in 1931. Its exhibitions of art, design, and furnishings were to influence the public for the next forty years. In 1930 Philip C. Johnson, then the twenty-three-year-old director of the department of architecture at the Museum of Modern Art, produced his first exhibition of Modern furniture and decorative arts.

In 1932 Henry-Russell Hitchcock and Philip Johnson organized their celebrated International Exhibition of Modern Architecture. It traveled for twenty months to eleven cities and was followed by a more portable version that traveled for six years. At the same time, Hitchcock and Johnson produced their seminal book, *The International Style: Architecture Since 1922*, which explained and defended the style, detailed its principles and taboos, and suggested how it might be adapted for American use.

The exhibition and book did not announce anything previously unheard of to the leading edge of the design professionals in America who were already working in the idiom; still, the book and exhibition together produced another of those anthologies or compendium expositions that further spurred on that vanguard of the profession to newer things. The exhibition and the book summed up the European achievement, gave it a name, and spearheaded the establishment of the Modern style in the minds of the public—and future clients— in the United States. The term International Style became a symbol of the American crusade for Modernism throughout the next quarter of a century (see Figure 123).

International-Style Principles

Hitchcock and Johnson defined the canon of the International Style:

> There is, first, a new conception of architecture as volume rather than as mass. Secondly, regularity rather than axial symmetry serves as the chief means of ordering design. These two principles, with the third proscribing arbitrary applied decoration, mark the productions of the international style.[3]

The authors did not list articulation of structure as a principle, nor clarity and alignment, which became essential in later International-Style work in America. And in their effort to distinguish a new art-historical style and give it historical credence, they proclaimed its formalist virtues over any functionalist aspirations.

This division had already created a rift among practitioners in Europe. It had caused Alfred Barr to name the new style "Post-Functionalism." In addition, in an effort to remove all political overtones of Marxist communism, the authors negated the social goals of the European movement, which had aimed to create good design for everyman. "This architecture will actively raise the general standard of living," the Russian Constructivist El Lissitizky had written in his mani-

123. Lilly Reich. Bedroom, Berlin Building Exposition. Berlin, Germany. 1931. *Photograph from Henry-Russell Hitchcock and Philip Johnson,* The International Style: Architecture Since 1922 *(New York: W. W. Norton, 1932).*

festo of 1929. In so doing, Hitchcock and Johnson would later be accused of making Modernism into an aesthetic system without a social calling.

In *The International Style* Hitchcock and Johnson distinguished three concepts of interior space:

> first, the inside of the volume of the building, consisting of the entire content of the building or of a considerable part of it; second, interiors which open up into one another without definite circumscribing partitions; and finally, the ordinary enclosed room. . . .
>
> The second sort of interiors is the particular invention of the international style. In contrast to the completely enclosed rooms of the past [the International-Style designers] stress the unity and continuity of the whole volume inside a building. The independence of the dividing screens and their variation in size and placing contrast with the regularity of the [independently] isolated [structural] supports. The flow of function and the relation of one function to another can be clearly expressed. The different screens serving different purposes may well be of different materials provided always their thinness and freedom from structural duty is stressed. While the visible supports give an underlying rhythm, the variety of the screens produce, as it were, a melody which may be restrained or lyric as the architect wishes.
>
> The development of free planning, particularly with the use of curved and oblique screens, has been carried furthest in constructions of definitely architectural character. It gives to modern interiors a new kind of abstract space design unknown in the architecture of the past. But it is one of the elements of modern architecture which is easily abused, both practically and aesthetically. . . .
>
> Enclosed rooms of ordinary size, the third sort of interior, seldom have definite architectural character. They depend for their interest on their proportions and on their contents.[4]

Two years later, in 1934, the Museum of Modern Art produced its Machine Art Exhibition under the direction of Philip Johnson. It was a celebration of the goals and achievements of the Bauhaus in this regard, but it also reached out to include some of the work of American industrial designers, which was being exhibited simultaneously by the Metropolitan Museum of Art's Richard F. Bach. The basic tenets of machine art were defined at the time as geometry (the square, the circle, and the triangle—or, more accurately, despite Gropius's assertion—the cube, the cylinder, and the cone); precision; simplicity; and economy. The machine-art philosophy was shared by both the International Style and the Streamlining of the industrial designers. Similarly shared were the use of slick machine surfaces, chromium, and primary colors.

As Edgar Kaufmann, Jr., has written, "The Bauhaus believed architecture was the governess of the arts and acknowledged its ancestor-worship of the Arts and Crafts. . . . Nothing did more to confirm the architect's belief in his supremacy as universal designer and in his art as the ruling authority for design."[5] So the split in the professions was continued.

But in 1933, when Hitler had become Chancellor of Germany and the persecution of Jews began, the National Socialist (Nazi) government had closed the Bauhaus—as if Modern furniture, flat-roofed architecture, and abstract painting were degenerate and an attack on the state. The best designers of Germany and Austria began to be scattered around the world.

Finally, as a contributor to the promulgation of the Modern movement in America, the settings of Hollywood movies had, from 1930 onward, begun to feature International-Style design (see Figure 124). Those settings were surely as convincing—and probably more immediate and wide-reaching—in etching an image of Modern design into the minds of the general American public. All these factors contributed to the promulgation of the International Style in America.

124. Cedric Gibbons. Movie set for MGM's *The Easiest Way.* 1931. *Photograph from The Museum of Modern Art/Film Stills Archive, New York City.*

The Resurgence of Frank Lloyd Wright

During this period Frank Lloyd Wright, long considered passé and already in his sixties, completely rejuvenated himself and his style of work. He designed two masterpieces in the 1930s that place him among the most daring of American designers for all of this century—Fallingwater, and the S. C. Johnson & Son Administration Building.

Fallingwater

Fallingwater (see color plate 2) at Bear Run, Pennsylvania, near Pittsburgh, was designed in 1934 and completed in 1936. It was a luxurious weekend house for Edgar Kaufmann, the Pittsburgh department-store owner. His son, Edgar Kaufmann, Jr., who later became a brilliant architecture and design curator, an influential critic, historian, and teacher, had been a fellow at Taliesin and it was he who recommended Frank Lloyd Wright to his parents. At Fallingwater Wright eschewed all regional or historical recalls—of Roman villas, as in the Prairie houses, and of Mayan Mexico, as in his California houses of the 1920s. Instead, he combined his vision of organic architecture—expressed as natural fieldstone masonry growing out of the rugged, rocky site—with daring cantilevers of concrete over the waterfall. The cantilevers proclaimed the horizontal "white architecture" of the 1920s more dramatically and with more clarity than even Le Corbusier or Mies had done in Europe—despite Wright's vehement denunciations of European Modernism; and the combination with the indigenous rocky site showed his continuing dedication to the organic continuity of architecture and nature.

Inside (see Figure 125A), the main floor of Fallingwater consists almost entirely of a single space spreading out into subordinate spaces—including the terraces, which are connected to the water below by a seemingly suspended staircase. The entry side, where the masonry of the house is anchored to counterbalance the cantilevers, is solid and enclosed; the water side is open through walls of glass and red-painted metal to the views of the wooded landscape and to the sounds and rainbows of the waterfall. The structural achievement is of unparalleled daring and virtuosity for its time. Upstairs were family bedrooms, each of which opened onto one of the cantilevered terraces.

In the living room (Figure 125B), the fireplace is sited just behind the rock on which the family used to have picnic outings before the house was built; and that rock is left exposed, rising gently out of the concrete floor as the central origin and heart of the house. The rock masonry walls inside are more rugged and rough than the rectangular masonry forms of the exterior. Banquettes and wardrobes are built-in throughout the house to reinforce the rectangular slab motif on which the concept is based, and even the design of the freestanding furniture reiterates the cantilever motif.

North Carolina walnut and walnut veneer are used throughout the house, with the graining run horizontally instead of the more typical vertical runs; the intent was to reduce warping from the moisture of the waterfall, but, clearly, it had to do with contemporary design thinking as well. The heating system is run through built-in seating, tables, and bookshelves, which were made by the Gillen Woodworking Company of Milwaukee with some of the craftsmen who had made furniture for the earlier Prairie houses. The lighting in the upstairs bedrooms is incorporated into the wardrobes as indirect fluorescent up lights. The warm wood tones meld with the rock and the sand-color concrete so that the red window framing seems the only color in the house. Yet nature provides its tapestries beyond.

Justifiably published in every major book on Modern building design, Fallingwater is Wright's quintessential realization of organic integration: of site and natural materials with building; of natural and handcraft imagery with the industrial and Modern aesthetic of the twentieth century. It is a total work of art at its most complex juxtaposition of two seemingly disparate elements—handcraft and nature along with the machine. Now open to the public, Fallingwater is a milestone for all designers.

The S. C. Johnson & Son Administration Building

At the S. C. Johnson & Son Administration Building in Racine, Wisconsin (1936–39), Wright showed that he could also work in the Streamline style yet broaden its impact to achieve a kind of timelessness and innovative genius that far surpassed others working in that vein (see color plate 3). In the large (128 feet by 228 feet by 20 feet high) main bullpen office space which updated the Larkin Building's skylighted and clerestoried atrium, tall slim lily-pad-topped columns are a structural tour de force; the enclosed, air-conditioned, indirectly lighted environment is the stuff of Futurists' dreams; and the furniture—of wood on metal tubing in a rich rust color to blend with the brick of the building—was the world of tomorrow (see Figure 126).

125A. Frank Lloyd Wright. Plan, Fallingwater. Bear Run, Pennsylvania. 1934–36. *Illustration © Frank Lloyd Wright Foundation, 1942.*

125B. Frank Lloyd Wright. Living room, Fallingwater. Bear Run, Pennsylvania. 1934–36. *Photograph © Ezra Stoller/ ESTO, 1963.*

126. Frank Lloyd Wright. Metal office furniture, S. C. Johnson & Son Administration Building. Racine, Wisconsin. 1936–39. *Photograph courtesy Johnson Wax Company.*

The furniture again showed Wright's devotion to the smallest detail of every project—and to the concept of total design. Composed of the circular motifs used throughout the building, the vocabulary of the furniture reveals how significantly Wright had rejuvenated himself since his work on the more rigidly rectangular Larkin Building. Desks were constructed by Steelcase Inc. of tubular steel with triple-decked walnut tops that have round ends. Tubular steel composes the sides of the desks, reiterating the tubular glass and other horizontal motifs throughout the building; drawers are semicircular in plan and swing in on pivots to be closer to the desk user. The semicircular desk-top ends are cantilevered beyond the ends of the vertical supports. An integral wastebasket is hung up on the ladder support to facilitate floor cleaning. Chairs, both executive and secretarial, are designed on the same tubular ladder principle, but with semicircular ladders. The backs tilt on pivots with changing seating positions. Secretarial chairs were designed with only three legs. The concept was futuristic and innovative, but the good posture demanded of the user—keeping both feet on the floor for balance—was not universally attainable, and many of the chairs have been converted to four legs.

Partitions, clerestory windows, and interior domes are constructed of Pyrex glass tubing, again showing Wright's futuristic use of glass. On the exterior, the virtuosic use of glass tubing laid up as bands between brick masonry creates the most continuous horizontal windows imaginable. And the lighting effect on the outside at night brilliantly demonstrates Wright's design imagination. In the next decade he was to add a tower to this complex that was an even more extraordinary feat of cantilevering and of innovative glass-wall design.

At this same time, also, in his Wingspread House for Herbert F. Johnson north of Racine, Wisconsin (1937), and in his Sunbelt studio Taliesin West in Scottsdale, Arizona (1938), Wright continued to show his inventiveness and daringly visionary interiors and furnishings. He was over seventy at the end of the decade—and he had twenty years more of productive work to go.

Design in France

A refined and reductive style appeared in Paris in the 1930s. It was somewhere between the work of traditional decorators working in the late–Art Deco vein—such as Jules Leleu, André Groult, and Emile-Jacques Ruhlmann—and the work of the Formalists, who were contributing to the development of Art Moderne—such as Pierre Chareau, François Jourdain, Eileen Gray, and Le Corbusier. The leading French designer in this direction was Jean-Michel Frank. His influence on American interior designers was enormous.

Jean-Michel Frank

Born in Paris and educated in law, Jean-Michel Frank (1895–1941) had traveled extensively before he became interested in eighteenth-century styles around 1927; in 1929 he began to work with decorator Adolphe Chanaux on an apartment for himself. A darling of society, his work attracted the attention of clients and patrons, including the Vicomte and Vicomtesse de Noailles, fashion designers Elsa Schiaparelli and Lucien Lelong, as well as Nelson Rockefeller in New York and Templeton Crocker in San Francisco. For these and many others he designed interiors.

In 1932 Frank and Chanaux opened a shop in Paris for the sale of their furniture designs and as headquarters for their interior decorating. From the first year of operation, their furnishings were eagerly bought by designers such as Elsie de Wolfe, Syrie Maugham, Frances Elkins, and Eleanor Brown for use in American interiors. Chanaux had studied at the Ecole des Beaux-Arts and had worked with decorator André Groult and with Ruhlmann before beginning his association with Jean-Michel Frank.

Rare among decorators, Jean-Michel Frank designed complete and "total" interiors—room architecture as well as furniture and appointments. Also, in the tradition of the *ensembliers*, Frank and Chanaux assembled a collaborative of other artists and designers with whose decorative arts they could furnish their interior design concepts; these included stage designer Christian Berard, architect-decorator-furniture designer Emilio Terry, and Swiss sculptor Alberto Giacometti and his brother Diego. Frank worked with the Giacometti brothers on sculptures and on sculpted furnishings beginning in 1934—notably a series of bronze lamps and white plaster lamps, sconces, and sculptural up-light urns. Carpets were designed by Christian Berard, or after his drawings. The assemblage by so many different designers was in the direct tradition of the eighteenth century, if now reminiscent of some newly personalized Wiener Werkstaette creation.

The Frank Style The style of Frank and Chanaux was based on refined simplicity and chaste purity, on proportion and balance, and on sensitivity to textures and materials. Frank's concepts depended on form and line, and on juxtapositions and contrasts of fullness with emptiness. He avoided superfluous objects and ornamentation. Moldings and valances were stripped away. Rooms were left bare and box-like. The lines of furniture were straight and unornamented—simplified to a functional minimum. He preferred not to hang pictures in his interiors, only to exhibit sculpture. The beige-white palette of the 1930s was his arena. Still, since Frank's designs were not based on the machine aesthetic, they were neither clinical enough nor vanguard enough to be accepted by the Modernists from the Bauhaus or Purism.

The Jean-Michel Frank style was reductive rather than additive and elaborate; it was abstracted, refined, stripped, and minimal. It was also rather classical, in that it made references to simplified Louis XVI and primitive art and to archaic

Greece and ancient Egypt. The tomb of Tutankhamen, opened in 1922, was still an inspirational image of late–Art Deco classicism.

Frank's fundamental belief was that an apartment could be furnished by unfurnishing it.[6] Sometimes he called his finished rooms "unfurnished" because they were so comparatively bare. Some rooms were "empty" except for a solitary piece of furniture, a Grecian bust, or an Egyptian fragment. An oft-repeated joke was that in an apartment by Jean-Michel Frank you had to go through three bare foyers before finding the lady of the house seated at a plain table on which was only the nose of a statue. "Ah, but the nose was from Alexandria," went the joke. Jean Cocteau said, on seeing one of Jean-Michel Frank's interiors, "Pity the burglars got everything."[7]

Frank's Materials What Frank eliminated from the forms of his interiors was made up for by sumptuous materials. The materials used by Frank and Chanaux were among the most recherché, rare, and luxurious that they could imagine: Walls were covered in rare woods, varnished straw marquetry, sanded white lacquer, or parchment (also called vellum or sheepskin). Frank's rare woods included macassar ebony, Brazilian rosewood, okoume from Gabon, adze-finished oak, black pearwood, as well as sand-jetted woods. Furniture finishes included bleached split-straw marquetry, veneers of glittering gypsum mica, white shagreen marquetry, gilded wood, and white lacquer. Some furniture was inlaid with ivory, embossed with bronze or silver. White plaster lamps or lamps with quartz crystal or bronze bases had vellum lampshades. Upholsteries were cowhide, lambskin or golden lambskin, lambswool or saddle-sewn leather, fawn leather, champagne-colored satin, and white leather. Among Jean-Michel Frank's combinations of wood and upholstery were sycamore wood with golden lambskin; varnished oak with white leather; ebonized pearwood with wool tweed; sycamore wood and champagne satin; oak and wicker, ebonized beech and tweed.

With his rare and unusual materials, Frank made unexpected contrasts: He had Louis XVI armchairs stripped and recovered them in cowhide or men's suiting cloth. He offset his elaborately sheathed furniture with the simplest canvas-covered director's chair—albeit a hand-carved director's chair. He also used straw, cane, and plain white plaster. In his work, he seemed to combine the monumental and the palatial with the simple Peasant style.

Some of Jean-Michel Frank's interiors were like small jewel boxes. In the drawing room of his own apartment, the walls were covered in straw marquetry, chairs and a low screen were upholstered in white leather, and low occasional tables were finished in mica squares. The library had walls upholstered in natural leather, chairs and sofa upholstered in pale-colored leather, a mantelpiece of travertine, low tables of sanded oak, and nesting tables covered in parchment. In the bedroom the bed was a thin mattress atop a wide low platform. At the same time his partner Adolphe Chanaux designed a similar platform bedroom that was all sparse primitiveness.

In the townhouse mansion of Vicomte and Vicomtesse Charles and Marie-Laure de Noailles, Frank created the two most important rooms of his career, beginning in 1932. In the grand salon, or main drawing room (see Figure 127), he lined the walls with squares of tawny parchment, which made the rooms look as if they were constructed of blocks of stone; he hung draperies of heavy beige silk; he laid *parquet de Versailles* on the floor, over which was a *tête-de-nègre* carpet. He offset this pale envelope with monumental double doors of burnished bronze. A mantelpiece was finished in small squares of glistening mica.

Rounded puffy sofas and chairs were upholstered in white leather (in 1936 the upholstered furniture was replaced by a more boxy, rectilinear group, again in white). Small screens at the end of the sofa as well as a small two-door cabinet and

127. Jean-Michel Frank. Living room, townhouse of Vicomte and Vicomtesse de Noailles. Paris, France. 1932. *Photograph from Leopold Diego Sanchez and Andree Putman,* Jean-Michel Frank *(Paris: Editions du Regard, 1980).*

a library table were finished in fan-patterned straw marquetry. Other low tables were finished in shagreen or bronze, and on them sat lamps with bases of crystal or ivory and with silk shades. One lamp was shaded by sheaves of thick split ivory set into a bronze base. Other materials were beige velvet, pale-beige leather, oyster-white plush. The effect was of timeless, ethereal monumentality. This interior was as grand and imposing, as monumental and rich as some pharaoh's treasure-laden tomb. But the Noailleses hung their important collection of paintings in this room against Frank's wishes, and that created a rift between client and designer.

Less typical was Jean-Michel Frank's work in New York in the apartment of Nelson Rockefeller (1937). There (see color plate 4) he provided the furniture, carpets, and lighting fixtures in a living room designed by architect Wallace K. Harrison. The walls were sheathed in polished oak from floor to ceiling, with a minimal molding making the connection/transition. Windows and valances as well as the surround of the fireplaces at each end of the room were framed by undulating, semi-Rococo, semi–Art Nouveau lines, and in one fireplace surround was a mural executed by Henri Matisse; Fernand Léger painted a fresco surrounding the other fireplace.

Seating pieces were all overstuffed units with the same lines, and stubby legs of Louis XV inspiration. Flanking the Matisse fireplace were gilt armchairs adapted from Louis XVIII models. Tables included straight-lined pieces as well as gilded consoles, lamps, and firedogs by the Giacometti brothers. The console was a semicircular, gilded wood piece with surrealistic legs. An Aubusson carpet of leaves floating on a solid ground was designed by Christian Berard. Paintings by Picasso from the family collection hung on the walls. The room and furnishings were to be recast in the 1980s (see Chapter 18).

Jean-Michel Frank's work in South America at the end of the decade, and in San Francisco for Templeton Crocker, was also less sparse than the work in France for which he is most admired; but it was rich in imagination. The Templeton

Crocker apartment had a dining room and a breakfast room entirely in lacquer by Dunand, a black marble and crystal fountain from St. Gobain in the party room, and two splendid bathrooms. One was in black Belgian marble and hammered glass; the other was in Swedish green marble and etched glass. The living room was somewhere between ocean-liner Modern and a prefiguring of 1950s Modernism. The bedroom had one of Frank's platform beds that prefigured 1970s Minimalism.

Perhaps more than any other French designer of the 1930s, Jean-Michel Frank influenced American residential design—due largely to his influence and exposure to American interior designers at the Paris program of the New York School of Fine and Applied Arts, where he served as a critic. Much of his idiom has been carried down to our own day by the older, established American decorating firms—who espoused his French Modern as their model. It is from his designs that the later, popular Parsons table was derived.

Surrealism

Surrealism began to have a recognizable influence on interior design in the late 1920s in Europe. In 1924 André Breton had issued the First Surrealist Manifesto, "Surrealism," which applied Freud's theories to art and took imagery off (literally) to another world, a dreamworld. Sigmund Freud's turn-of-the-century theories had begun to have general currency beyond Vienna; his influence had become pervasive. Carl Jung had published *Psychological Types* in 1920; psychology had become the new twentieth-century science. Apparently inconsistent with reality, Surrealism was above and beyond reality. It was in the cyclic twentieth-century tradition that, along with Abstraction and musical Dissonance, has been called Irrationalism.

Surrealism espoused weightless inversions, random influences and content; all devised to change perception, and ultimately to change the world. Surrealism was thought of as revolution, a system of radical change. It quickly confused these political goals with artistic goals. Among the Surrealists, who passed through several stylistic periods, were Hans Arp, Paul Klee, Pablo Picasso, Man Ray, and Joan Miró; Max Ernst stayed with Surrealism for the longest run; Salvador Dali and René Magritte mocked the merely functional from the 1930s through the 1950s. But the strongest impact of Surrealism on interior design was to be seen in the 1930s.

Surrealism was the new spirit of the decade—a mannered inversion of the expected, paradoxical, ironic, sardonic, perverse, and whimsical. It was popularized as that brand of humor called "camp." Surrealism was manifest in the work of Jean-Michel Frank and his collaborators, as well as in the work of other French and English designers. Soon, Surrealism became an influence on American design and display.

Dada and Surrealism had been investigated by the painters Salvador Dali, René Magritte, Giorgio de Chirico, and Man Ray, and by filmmaker Luis Buñuel since before the 1930s. Buñuel's film *Le Chien Andalou*, sponsored by Charles de Noailles, had been privately shown in 1929 and 1930. Salvador Dali's painting *The Persistence of Memory* dates from 1931. Meret Oppenheim's *Object (Déjeuner en fourrure)*—the fur-lined teacup—was done in 1936. It was artists' interpretation of Freud's interpretation of dreams, which began to be more popularly known in the 1920s and 1930s. In interior design this Surrealism was demonstrated by a kind of discontinuous, dissociated, manic humor, by dreamlike fantasy, the baroquely bizarre and perverse.

In Jean-Michel Frank's work the Surrealist element was displayed as a combination of human forms and foliage inspired by Matisse and Picasso, but inter-

128.   Jean-Michel Frank. Cinema-ballroom for Baron Roland de l'Espée; with sofa by Salvador Dali inspired by Mae West's lips. Paris, France. Circa 1936. *Photograph from Leopold Diego Sanchez and Andree Putman,* Jean-Michel Frank *(Paris: Editions du Regard, 1980).*

jected into functional furnishings such as tables and lamps, vases and sconces. Draperies of molded plaster of Paris, or of real fabric oddly draped over windows and stair rails, appeared in the fashion salons of Lucien Lelong and of Elsa Schiaparelli. A cinema-ballroom for Baron Roland de l'Espée (see Figure 128), which showed the influence of Jean Cocteau and of Salvador Dali, had each wall a different color—pink, pale blue, sea-green, and straw-yellow—a carpet of Pompeian red, and stage-set theater boxes in the corners draped in purple velvet. Between the boxes was a lip-shaped red satin sofa modeled on Dali's lips of Mae West. Frank also designed interiors for Guerlain perfumes with stage-set trompe l'oeil by Christian Berard; the influence of ballet, theater, and Picasso's harlequins was rampant.

Elsewhere, Surrealist tables and stools were designed with human legs and feet as table legs and feet; life-size hands held sconces or vases; feet and legs made other appearances in furniture of the period. Frank also used the tables designed by Emilio Terry with white plaster bases of large-scale palm leaves, scallop shells, and other neo-Baroque and neo-Rococo imagery, such as the white plaster palm-tree torchères that figured largely in this period and later.

Le Corbusier also became involved with the Surrealist theme in the mid-1930s. The Surrealist influence on his architecture has since been analyzed, though he would not have admitted or perhaps recognized it. For the Paris apartment of the Mexican art patron Carlos de Bestigui, Le Corbusier created a Futurist "machine for entertaining" in 1931. The spaces he designed for de Bestigui were stark, austere, high-ceilinged white boxes with large expanses of floor-to-ceiling sliding glass. At the touch of buttons, walls disappeared or reappeared, windows slid into walls, and chandeliers moved along recessed tracks in the ceiling to permit movies to be projected without interference.

But the furnishings were a different theme altogether: By the time the architecture of the apartment was finished, de Bestigui had become interested in Surrealism, and the furnishings were designed in that idiom by de Bestigui or—one

129A. Le Corbusier and de Bestigui. Living room, de Bestigui apartment. Paris, France. Circa 1936. *Photograph from Martin Battersby,* The Decorative Thirties *(New York: Walker & Company, 1971).*

is tempted to suspect—by Emilio Terry. Terry, the architect-decorator who designed the white neo-Baroque scrollwork furnishings for Jean-Michel Frank, was the Paris-born scion of a wealthy Cuban family. In the living room (see Figure 129A) the fireplace was jammed uncomfortably in a corner and appointed with a nineteenth-century gilt-framed mirror and prismed girandoles. An ornate Venetian chandelier hung in the middle of the room over an opulent, puffy ottoman with a scalloped base and fringe. Overstuffed sofas and chairs in a Victorian mode had the same upholstered treatment. Hung at the windows were ice-blue velvet floor-to-ceiling draperies bordered with a Second Empire design. A life-size blackamoor figure in porcelain was a blown-up version of eighteenth-century figurines; the blackamoor became a component of many interior schemes by different designers in these years. Here, the scale and the sense of period were bizarre. Electricity may have moved walls in this apartment, but the nighttime lighting was solely from candles. Such was Surrealistic fantasy.

In the movie room (see Figure 129B) heavy gold-and-white Second Empire furniture, looking only slightly better than merry-go-round appointments, surrounded a carpet with a coat-of-arms medallion surrounded by fleurs-de-lys. Le Corbusier's spiral ribbon-balustraded stair looked unclimbable. The movie projectors were concealed behind gilt-framed mirrors that had ormolu candle brackets superimposed on them—the dismembered-hand motif of Surrealism.

The outdoor terrace joined in this Surrealistic exercise by becoming an outdoor room—literally (see Figure 129C). Carpeted with grass and daisies, the sky-blue walled space with its sky-ceiling was furnished with a marble Baroque commode sporting a birdcage and mechanical bird; the space also had a Baroque marble fireplace appointed with clock and candlesticks. Above the mantelpiece a circular frame offered a view to the Arc de Triomphe and Paris rooftops. Hedges in boxes slid away electrically to reveal other views. Le Corbusier may have created the spaces for this apartment, but Carlos de Bestigui clearly directed the bizarre Surrealist decor.[8]

1. Frank Lloyd Wright. Unity Temple. Oak Park, Illinois. 1906. *Photograph by Thomas A. Heinz.*

2. Frank Lloyd Wright. Fallingwater. Bear Run, Pennsylvania. 1936. *Photographs © Ezra Stoller/ESTO, 1963.*

3. Frank Lloyd Wright. S. C. Johnson & Son Administration Building. Racine, Wisconsin. 1936–39. *Photograph © Ezra Stoller/ESTO, 1963, courtesy Johnson Wax Company.*

4. Jean-Michel Frank and Wallace Harrison. Living room for Nelson Rockefeller. New York City. 1937. *Photograph © Ezra Stoller/ESTO, 1963, courtesy The Rockefeller Group, Inc.*

5. Le Corbusier. Notre-Dame-du-Haut, Ronchamp, France. 1950–54. *Photograph © Ezra Stoller/ESTO, 1955.*

6. Luis Barragan. Chapel at Tlalpan. Tlalpan, Mexico. 1952–55. *Photograph by Armando Salas-Portugal.*

7. Fabric designs. Circa 1950. Left: Alexander Girard. *Courtesy Herman Miller Inc.* Top right: Jack Lenor Larsen *Courtesy Jack Lenor Larsen Inc.* Bottom right: Dorothy Liebes. Fabric design "High Mass," 1946. Handwoven studio production: cotton, rayon, silk, cellophane, metallic, strung beading; combination of 1/3 (filling face) twill and plain weave. *Photograph by Ferdinand Boesch for the American Craft Museum, of the American Craft Council, New York.*

8. Philip Johnson Associates. The Four Seasons Restaurant. New York City. 1959. *Photograph © Ezra Stoller/ESTO, 1960.*

9. McMillen Inc. Residence for Gregory B. Smith. New York City. 1962. *Photograph courtesy McMillen Inc.*

10. Billy Baldwin. Own apartment. New York City. 1963. *Photograph by Horst.*

12. Moore, Lyndon, Turnbull, Whitaker, with Lawrence Halprin and Barbara Stauffacher. Supergraphic stripes and mailboxes as lockers, Athletic Club Number One. Sea Ranch, California. 1967. *Photograph by Morley Baer.*

13. Moore, Lyndon, Turnbull, Whitaker. Faculty Club. University of California at Santa Barbara. 1967–68. *Photograph by Morley Baer.*

14. Benjamin Baldwin. Own house. East Hampton, Long Island. *Circa 1978. Photograph by Jon Naar.*

15. Michael Graves. Sunar showroom. Chicago, Illinois. 1979. *Photograph at left by Idalia, 1982.*
Photograph at right by Sadin/Karant, courtesy Sunar Inc.

129B. Le Corbusier and de Bestigui. Movie room, de Bestigui apartment. Paris, France. Circa 1936. *Photograph from Martin Battersby,* The Decorative Thirties *(New York: Walker & Company, 1971).*

129C. Le Corbusier and de Bestigui. Terrace, de Bestigui apartment. Paris, France. Circa 1936. *Photograph from Martin Battersby,* The Decorative Thirties *(New York: Walker & Company, 1971).*

The Peasant Vernacular

More typical of Le Corbusier's interiors at this time was vernacular, provincial architecture and peasant-style furniture. Spare and minimal, rustic and simple, this primitive style suggests the influence of Picasso's studio and of modern Primitivism. Beginning with the Errazuris House in Chile (1930) and the de Mandrot

130. Le Corbusier. Own bedroom. Paris, France. Before 1935. *Photograph from Martin Battersby,* The Decorative Thirties *(New York: Walker & Company, 1971).*

House (1931), he used local stone walls along with the stucco and glass of International Style. In the de Mandrot House, the ceiling was of natural plywood and the floor of local tiles. Simple wood furniture accompanied metal tubular furniture designed by René Herbst and Hélène de Mandrot.

Similar was Le Corbusier's design for a weekend house outside Paris. Le Corbusier explained that because the house was to be as little visible as possible, its "height was reduced to 8 ft."[9] That was a notable statement. The roof was flat, but the interior ceilings were reinforced barrel vaults, giving the interior a cosiness and richness as well as more height than expected. Some of the interior walls were of local stone; glass blocks constituted other walls. Flooring was of white ceramic tile, fireplace and mantel of exposed brick. The furnishings were, again, a mixture of rustic, provincial pieces. Le Corbusier was already moving beyond the Machine-Age Modern of the 1920s and working also in a more poetic, simple regional idiom.

Most of Le Corbusier's work of this decade, however, was directed toward urban-planning projects of a large nature, and his publications did not emphasize interior design. From 1936 to 1945 he designed the Ministry of Education Building for Rio de Janeiro in Brazil with Oscar Niemeyer, Lucio Costa, and other Brazilian architects on the team. The sunscreens surrounding the building provided a new word in architecture—*brises-soleils*—and a lesson about the need to shield glass curtain walls from the sun that was not well heeded by later architects. This slab-like building, which was the impetus for the United Nations Secretariat building in New York, became the model for numerous other office buildings for the next thirty years.

Design in England

One of the more prominent English decorators of the 1930s, Sibyl Colefax, started her business in 1933. She specialized in Regency schemes and was later joined by

John Fowler, a restoration specialist who had great knowledge about the history of draperies and also was gifted with a special color sense. Other prominent English designers of interiors and furnishings in the 1930s included decorator and fabrics designer Arundell Clarke; architect Raymond McGrath; Oswald P. Milne; Oliver Hill; Humphrey Deane; Ronald Fleming; and Oliver Bernard, who designed the glass, mirror, and lightning-streaked interiors of the Strand Hotel in London. Ambrose Heal and Gordon Russell were the major English furniture designers at the time. Photographer Cecil Beaton and stage designer Oliver Messel also began influencing and designing interiors at this time.

Unlike the American traditional decorators who were generally concerned with correct period rooms through the 1920s, those in England were more casual about their historicism. This surprised American designers who visited England; it also reinforced the early American concern for proper period restoration of American interiors.

The English continuation of romantic historicism was accompanied by fancifully decorative painted panels and murals—shepherdesses and harlequins, pastoral and aerial scenes, along with trompe l'oeil. English artists who became popular in this work included Rex Whistler, Duncan Grant, Etienne Drian, Allan Walton, and Eugene Berman.

Syrie Maugham   Although the Depression forced the closing of her shops in America, Syrie Maugham continued to decorate in Europe and America throughout the 1930s. She worked in the pale-toned color range, but white became her trademark and on it she made her reputation. She specified white for mirror frames, rugs, and satin draperies; she had furniture painted, often white; she used white china figurines of birds, white bamboo, white plaster palm-tree table bases. Many of her white pieces of furniture came from the shop of Frank and Chanaux in Paris. These latter designs were attributed to both Serge Roche and Emilio Terry (see Figure 131). Syrie Maugham also used Giacometti's white plaster urn up lights.

131.   Syrie Maugham. Dining room, own country house, The Pavilion. Weddesdon, Bucks., England. 1935. *Photograph by Millar & Harris, London.*

White camellias and white lilies were her trademarks, and calla lilies became a symbol of the time.

Syrie Maugham extended the white motif by using mirrors and glass—for table pedestals, lamp bases, and folding screens. It all seemed the ultimate blizzard of white. But white was not her only approach. Although fairly casual about historical elements, as most of her English contemporaries were, she sometimes left original woodwork and lightened rooms with her mirrors, white, and fresh pale colors.

One of her most influential interiors was a bedroom in Mrs. Tobin Clark's David Adler–designed house in San Mateo, California (1930). All the furnishings were white, including wood tables, upholstered chairs, draperies and venetian blinds, a four-poster bed, and a zigzag-sculpted white carpet by Marian Dorn. The Swedish white linen walls had an overall scroll pattern in two tones of green that created a fresh trellis around the room. Syrie Maugham's design for Mrs. Clark's bedroom (see Figure 132) was much imitated and recreated during the next several decades.

American Decorating

During the Great Depression much of the design world had to turn inward to behind-the-creative-scenes activities that continued to support the field—and to federal arts projects. Professional interior design societies in America were consol-

132. Syrie Maugham. Bedroom for Mrs. Tobin Clark. San Mateo, California. 1930. *Photograph courtesy Jerome Zerbe.*

idated by the founding in 1931 of the American Institute of Interior Decorators (now the American Society of Interior Designers). New York already had its Decorators Club for women only, and a Society of Interior Decorators for men only; Chicago had sponsored the Woman Decorators' Association; and there was an Interior Decorators Club of Philadelphia.

The American Institute of Interior Decorators, organized in Grand Rapids, Michigan, was to provide a focus and a podium for all of the young profession as well as a meeting ground with the furniture industry with which it was so closely associated. The first president was Chicago decorator William R. Moore. In 1936 the headquarters of the new professional organization was moved to New York and its name and initials changed to American Institute of Decorators (AID). It was to be renamed the American Society of Interior Designers (ASID) in the 1970s.

Grand Rapids and Southern furniture plants continued to produce cheap furniture. "Early American Maple" furniture poorly pretended to recreate the image of the Colonial revival of the 1920s, which was given popular impetus by the opening of Colonial Williamsburg in 1932. The search for new historical periods led to the rediscovery of mid-nineteenth-century balloon-back Louix XV Revival chairs and loveseats, which came to be labeled "Victorian furniture"; and there was some degree of interest shown in Art Deco styling by the use of blue mirrors and rose-beige mirrors. But a new sense of the importance of historical accuracy and a new knowledge of antique furniture was growing in Grand Rapids. It was to be seen in the furniture designs of Gilbert Rohde and Edward Wormley (see below). That conscience also included an awareness of the rich clients of interior decorators.

At this time, too, new professional magazines appeared to spark communication (and advertising) in the field. *Home Furnishings Daily* had begun publication in 1929. In 1932 *The Decorator's Digest* was founded; it was renamed *Interior Design and Decoration* in 1937 and, by the early 1950s became simply *Interior Design*. In 1934 *The Upholsterer*, which had been published since 1888, was renamed *The Interior Decorator*; it became *Interiors* in 1940. These publications assumed that the profession had a broadening base, that the model set by the "great collectors" of the previous decades was gradually shifting to include more of the population. The new young profession was coming of age.

While in architectural interiors the battle raged on between "warm" handcraft and the "cold" machine, between romantic historicism and vanguard Modernism, in residential decorating it was a much more one-sided approach. Many more decorators continued to practice in the tradition of Elsie de Wolfe's "good taste." This was not surprising in view of the educational commitment to French historicism, but it is ironic in view of the potential exposure to concurrent French modernism on the part of students in Paris.

Still, American residential designers did demonstrate a few definite moves in the direction of simplification and Modernism. Among them were the essays in Art Moderne and in the late–Art Deco idiom that combined simplified classical motifs from both Egypt and Greece. After the Depression American decorating began to express the spirit of Parisian Surrealism in small yet notable areas. The mannered twists of Surrealism were somewhat responsible for the loosening up of correct period styles. Designers looked for new themes, such as all-white rooms or outdoor rooms that were inside, and vice versa. Relieved from the Depression, inspired by the new wave of synthetic materials, American designers were riding high on a wave of daring and inventiveness. It led to a new American eclecticism that began in the 1930s.

Among the prominent American designers of the 1930s was the first generation of women decorators—Elsie de Wolfe, Ruby Ross Wood, Rose Cumming, and Nancy McClelland—along with the second generation—McMillen Inc., Thedlow Inc., Dorothy Draper Inc., Smyth Urquhart & Marckwald, and in Chicago Mabel Schamberg, Lorraine Yerkes, and Irene Sidley. In California, Frances Elkins was at the peak of her career. Among the designers who began their practices in this decade were Mrs. Henry Parish II and Melanie Kahane, as well as a new generation of male designers including William Pahlmann, Edward Wormley, George Stacey, Pierre Dutel, T. H. Robsjohn-Gibbings, and Billy Baldwin. In Chicago Samuel Marx decorated the Pump Room. Joseph B. Platt brought his interior design influence to bear on the public with his settings for the movies, among them *Dinner at Eight*, *Rebecca*, and *Gone With the Wind*.

McMillen Inc.

As the Depression hit McMillen, the early years of the 1930s were spent designing and making miniature rooms for benefits and for exhibitions, such as Chicago's 1933 Century of Progress World's Fair. When things picked up after the Depression, McMillen showed that American designers could work in the latest Art Moderne style. The entry foyer of the Cosmopolitan Club in New York (1933) stressed classical balance and a black, white, and gray-banded flooring pattern along with Deco-Moderne detailing of the stair railing. In 1934 McMillen designed a store for Steuben Glass on Fifth Avenue that also revealed classicized Art Moderne design and simplicity, as well as glass furniture (appropriate for the client). Glass spheres supported the upper tier of a metal, mirror, and glass display table.

As head of McMillen, Mrs. Brown constantly sought out new artists, and her eagerness to accept new art forms within the traditional context kept the work of the firm fresh and continually evolving. The list of McMillen's residential clients in the next years reads like a Social Register: Cravath, Lorillard, Porter, Rogers, Bliss, Choate, Busch, Goelet, Mosely, Lambert, Smith, Paley, Duke, Post, Ford, Guest, Kress, Field, Chase, Hennessey, Vanderbilt, Winthrop, Topping, Stevenson, Mellon, Burden, Hutton, Cowles, Houghton, and so on.

Ruby Ross Wood

From behind her pink-tinted round tortoiseshell glasses, Ruby Ross Wood was working in her casual, comfortable English style. She used English and French eighteenth-century furniture, as well as Directoire furniture, but always with comfortable overstuffed seating pieces.

In the mid-1930s Ruby Wood explored the all-white, no-color direction of the decade. For her own New York living room she used white-lacquered floors, brown-and-white Moroccan rugs, a white-painted table 12 feet long that was piled with magazines and personal photographs, and large dark-blue porcelain lamps with white paper shades. These latter, as opposed to the then fashionable silk lampshade, came to be a tradition of high-style decorating. In this room Ruby Ross Wood also used blue-and-white-striped bed ticking for all upholstery and drapery. Many designers later claimed credit for the first use of ticking as a decorative fabric. This uncommon use of a common material was, perhaps, in the general spirit of the Peasant style (see page 361f.) as well as in the spirit of the mannered twists of style that recurred throughout the decade.

In 1936 Ruby Wood designed the interiors of the Palm Beach, Florida, house of the Woolcott Blairs, whose architect was David Adler. The living room had walls of pale buff with white trim and floors of parchment-colored Cuban marble, which was bordered in bleached oak. In the center of the room she placed a Louis XV frame table with a honey-brown leather slipcover-top, scalloped on the edge and banded in white carpet tape. Such tape also became a tradition. Chairs were covered in matching fabrics; sofa covers and curtains were of a beige cotton from Sweden; and occasional chairs were covered in Elsie de Wolfe's trademark leopard chintz.

Included were a pair of Adam cabinets of pale, stripped pine and carved wood palm-tree-shaped torchères. This interior, also, was in the no-color and white tradition of the 1930s.

Ruby Ross Wood gained a new influence in 1935, when she hired Billy Baldwin as her assistant. He was to work with her until she died in 1950. She also contributed to *Vogue* as a columnist on decoration from the late 1930s into the 1940s.

Nancy McClelland

Nancy McClelland continued to operate her 57th Street shop for the sale of fine wallpapers and as the headquarters of her decorating business. During the 1930s her writings indicated the decade's changing interests in stylistic periods: *Furnishing the Colonial and Federal House* (1936) and *Duncan Phyfe and the English Regency* (1939).

Her great interest became the restoration of interiors in historic American buildings. She worked on museum restorations such as Shelburne Village and Williamsburg, and did interior restoration work on Blair House in Washington, D.C.; on the Jumel Mansion in New York; on George Washington's home, Mount Vernon; on General Lee's headquarters in Fredericksburg, Virginia; and on the Henry Wadsworth Longfellow House in Portland, Maine. Mary Dunn, Inez Croom, and Michael Greer came to serve their apprenticeships with Nancy McClelland Inc. (Nancy McClelland and Mary Dunn subsequently became presidents of the American Institute of Interior Designers; McClelland's term was from 1941 to 1943.)

Rose Cumming

During the 1930s Rose Cumming continued to design residences and operate her shop for antiques and colorful chintzes. In this decade she extended her flamboyant, daring, and eclectic approach. Like Elsie de Wolfe, who capitalized on her own flamboyant personality, Rose Cumming wore big hats, and fastened swatches of fabric samples as jewelry on her black dress; with her hair dyed violet, she made an imposing impression. When there was no work, she unhesitatingly added cut fresh flowers (and a waterfall) to her shop's wares. She also demonstrated her taste for Chinese monkeys, frogs, mice, and snakes. These were all combined into occasionally Venetian fantasies of taffeta-swagged beds, and Chinese silver-and-flowered wallpaper fiestas.

One of her interior designs in the 1930s had soft yellow antique Chinese wallpaper with flame-colored taffeta draperies. Another had honey-colored walls and draperies trimmed in apple green. One bedroom she designed had walls gleaming with blue-mauve metallic foil paper, an eighteenth-century Chinese carpet "of the 1,000 vases" on the parquet floor, and an iron sixteenth-century Portuguese bed hung with silver-and-blue lamé. At the windows was cloth of silver sari silk hung under elaborately patterned mirror valances. Around the bed were silver-plated Moorish tables and stools believed to have belonged to Catherine the Great. An eighteenth-century Persian child's bed served as a low table; a gilt wood and tôle (painted tin) chandelier was seventeenth-century Italian; one Louis XV chair had a pink silk upholstered seat. It was a fantasy of imagination.

Dorothy Draper

In the 1930s Dorothy Draper increased her influence on the design of hotels, restaurants, and offices by ridding them of stuffiness and by introducing strong, overscaled elements and vivid colors. Large, bold, and strong were her catchwords.

133.   Rose Cumming. Bedroom for her mother. New York City. Circa 1934. *Photograph by Harold Haliday Costain, courtesy Rose Cumming Inc.*

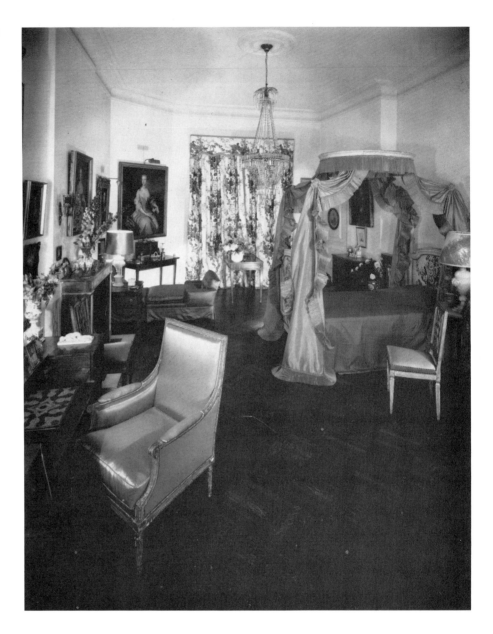

Her favorite periods during this decade, as Lester Grundy joined the firm, became Italian and English Baroque, but she was not concerned with historical accuracy. Instead, she adapted the designs of William Kent and Grinling Gibbons to late Art Deco. She became known for bold white plaster appliques—and consoles, frames, and accessories—with overscaled scroll motifs of leaves, feathers, and cockleshells. She used these plaster-white elements strikingly against dark-green or dark-burgundy walls.

Draper made most of her decorative elements overscaled. She doubled the proportions of the traditional checkerboard floor pattern. She also used wallpaper with wide pink-and-white stripes; wall coverings with glossy black patent leather finishes; elaborately swagged drapery; puffy chenille upholstery; and chintzes with large-scale clusters of cabbage roses in bold lipstick reds and emerald greens. These became her trademarks, and soon became the basis of widespread neo-Baroque in the 1930s. Though Dorothy Draper might not have understood the analogy, her designs also showed the influence of Surrealism.

In the early 1930s Dorothy Draper designed the interiors of the River Club in New York and of the Gideon Putnam Hotel in Saratoga Springs, New York. Her work also extended to real estate consulting: She styled the exteriors of New York's Sutton Place row of brownstones—the façades were painted black with white trim, each front door was painted a different color, and the fire escapes were dressed with scrollwork.

In the mid-1930s Dorothy Draper designed a formal octagonal entrance hall in the style of her 1920s work, but with new materials and with her new large-scale elements. The foyer had a flooring pattern of black with a white border, but the material was the new linoleum. The walls were gray, the ceiling white; but to lower the ceiling, she had a black band painted at the ceiling cove and divided the wainscoting into two bands, one of black and one of white. In this severe scheme, which had a large-scale white plaster clock above the fireplace, the chimney breast was painted a clear yellow.

In 1935 she designed the interiors of the Arrowhead Springs Hotel in Southern California. It had all her trademarks: overscaled lamps, overscaled sofas, overscaled chenille upholstery, and overscaled neo-Baroque white plaster appliques. At Arrowhead, also, she used geometric carpets, cabbage-rose chintz, and white-painted furniture against dark walls.

In 1937 Dorothy Draper completed one of her largest commissions, the thirty-seven-story Hampshire House apartment-hotel on Central Park South in New York (see Figure 134). There she designed everything from the interior architecture and

134. Dorothy Draper. Hampshire House. New York City. 1937. *Photograph by Hans van Nes, courtesy Carleton Varney.*

furniture down to the buttons on the bellboys' liveries, the toothpicks, and the stationery. Her goal was to design rooms that would have an English country-house atmosphere rather than the customary hotel look. In the lobbies, her customary black-and-white marble floors took shape as bold-scaled checkerboards; doors were mahogany with egg-and-dart carvings and bolection moldings of mirror. These were flanked by metal trees in espaliered form.

The lobby to the second-floor banquet and function rooms was designed as an outdoor space—garden furniture stood outside a bow-windowed Georgian building exterior. Called The Cottage, it became one of the most popular rooms in New York for deb parties in the next years. The dining room was designed as two spaces in one, separated only by columns. One half was a patio garden, with bold checkerboard flooring, wire-like wrought-iron chairs with cockleshell-shaped backs, and ceiling-height metal-leafed trees. The other half was a formal interior dining room with a wood-burning fireplace, high-back chairs covered in red velvet (they were slipcovered in rose chintz for summer), and a vast crystal chandelier in the shape of a wedding cake. This space looked out through a paneled glass wall to a real garden decked with urns, with flowers and plantings, and with a vast neo-Baroque, scrollwork-and-fishscale-patterned fountain. It all showed the mannered inversions for the sake of theatricality that Surrealism inspired. There, in Hampshire House, Dorothy Draper lived—with a contract for maintaining the hotel—and there she finished her first book, *Decorating Is Fun!*

Frances Elkins

During the 1930s Frances Elkins's practice spread nationwide as she began to collaborate with her Chicago-based architect-brother David Adler. From 1931 to 1935 she designed the interiors of four houses designed by him that are indicative of her 1930s approach, and she also designed the interiors of the Cypress Point Club in Pebble Beach.

For the house of Mrs. Evelyn Marshall Field, in Syosset, Long Island, George I paneling was installed in the library. There Frances Elkins assembled Queen Anne and Georgian pieces along with comfortable upholstered furniture. The living room had floral-patterned chintz upholstery, Georgian wood furniture, and a Chinese screen.

For the house of Mrs. Kersey Coates Reed, in Lake Forest, Illinois, also in 1931, Frances Elkins created a silver-and-white guest bedroom that had silver foil walls, a four-poster bed with ivory posts ornamented with silver; a japanned Queen Anne *secrétaire* and a bombé chest of drawers complemented the otherwise pale scheme. The same house had a mirrored powder room with silver-leaf moldings and fireplace surround all enriched with wainscoting that was lacquered yellow. Here, Frances Elkins installed Georgian seating pieces with elaborate scalloped aprons.

Also indicative of 1930s interior design, Frances Elkins's interiors for Mrs. J. Ogden Armor, in Lake Forest, Illinois (1934–35), had Georgian furniture with a Chinese carpet in the living room, shieldback Hepplewhite chairs and a Sheraton sideboard in the dining room.

But, that same year, a new influence was to be seen. Frances Elkins had begun to import furnishings from the Paris shop of Jean-Michel Frank in 1932, and she used his lamps for many clients, whose interiors began to reveal a Paris-inspired sensibility.

In the house of Mr. and Mrs. Leslie Wheeler, also in Lake Forest, Illinois, the paneled library (see Figure 135) with round-pedimented bookstacks had zebra-skin rugs on the floor, and the living room sported a carpet in a bold Chinese key design. In the dining room, Queen Anne chairs—all side chairs at the breakfast table bay; all armchairs at the main dining table—flanked pedestal tables in the

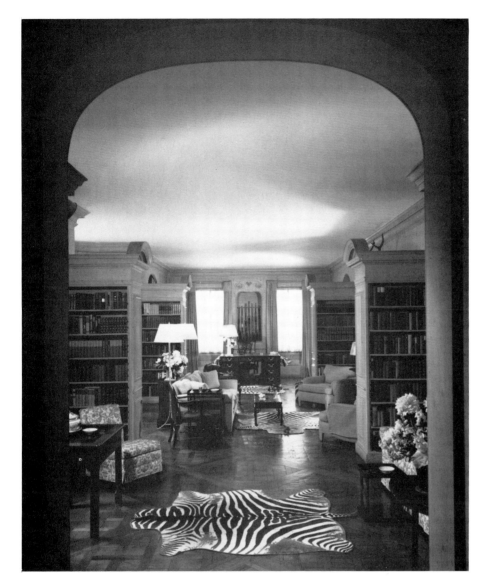

135. Frances Elkins with David Adler. Library for Mr. and Mrs. J. Leslie Wheeler. Lake Forest, Illinois. 1934–35. *Photograph © Ezra Stoller/ESTO, 1966.*

Duncan Phyfe idiom. Elaborate, almost Baroque window valances were used in both living and dining rooms.

The bar and cardroom she designed in 1938 for the Zellerbach residence (see Figure 136) in San Francisco not only showed the influence of this new Parisian outlook, but also revealed the complete formation of her own eclectic American style. In that project Elkins mixed her modification of Portuguese Chippendale–inspired banquette and chairs with a Jean-Michel Frank metal cocktail table and wall sconces, and a Hollywood-looking mirror-framed mirror. It was her own brand of international eclecticism, and it was in the vanguard of the special American eclecticism of the 1930s. By the end of the decade she was producing neo-Baroque interiors in public buildings as well—including the interiors of the Royal Hawaiian Hotel in Honolulu, the Santa Anita Turf Club, and the interiors of the Pebble Beach Club and the Women's Pavilion at the San Francisco World's Fair of 1938.

Mrs. Henry Parish II

In 1933 Mrs. Henry Parish II began her interior design practice in Far Hills, New Jersey. She continued to work prominently for the next fifty years and was one of

136. Frances Elkins. Hallway, Zellerbach residence. San Francisco, California. 1938–39. *Photograph © Fred Lyon, 1983.*

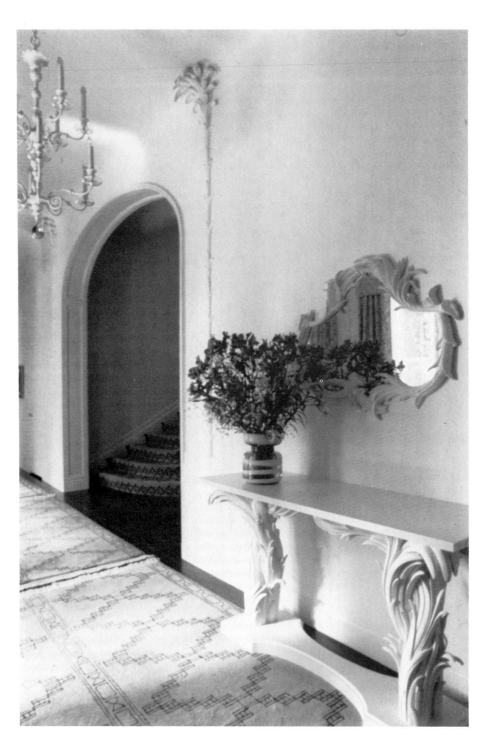

the most celebrated residential designers from the 1960s to 1980s. She became known for her casual, comfortable "undecorated" English country-house look.

Born in Morristown, New Jersey, Dorothy May Kinnicut (1910–)—called "Sister" by her family and friends—had no formal training in design, but she had traveled extensively, had visited great houses, and to that experience she attributes her educated eye. To the lack of such experience she also attributes the uneducated eyes of others. Her association with the decorating world began when she married: Her mother asked Eleanor McMillen to decorate and furnish the new bride's Gracie Square house in New York. At the low point of the Depression, Mrs. Parish began decorating for friends and soon built up a residential clientele.

T. H. Robsjohn-Gibbings

Close in spirit to the work of Jean-Michel Frank was the work of T. H. Robsjohn-Gibbings, who came to New York from London. In 1936 the thirty-year decorating career of Robsjohn-Gibbings began when he opened a showroom on Madison Avenue.

Born in England, Terence Harold Robsjohn-Gibbings (1909–73) studied architecture at the University of Liverpool and then worked as a designer in London and as art director for British International Pictures at Elstree before being brought to the United States by Charles Duveen, the antique-furniture dealer and brother of art dealer Sir Joseph Duveen. After the Depression "Gibby," as he was nicknamed, opened his own firm.

The showroom carried the late–Art Deco idiom of archaic classicism farther by recreating ancient Greece (see Figures 137A and B). It had broad expanses of

137A. T. H. Robsjohn-Gibbings. Own showroom with Klismos Chair. New York City. 1936. *Photograph by Richard Garrison.*

137B. T. H. Robsjohn-Gibbings. Klismos Chair. Circa 1936. *Photograph © Ezra Stoller/ESTO, 1963.*

plain wall with a double-banded baseboard and a textured cornice; a mosaic of Greek dancing maidens formed the floor; and Klismos chairs, which Robsjohn-Gibbings had recreated from originals in Greece, sat serenely like thrones among other Greek-modeled furnishings.

His clients in the next years were Mrs. Otto Khan, Mrs. Myron C. Taylor, Elizabeth Arden, Antoine, the hat designers John Fredericks and Lily Daché, Thelma Chrysler Foy, Doris Duke, Conrad Hilton, Neiman-Marcus, and the River Club.

Robsjohn-Gibbings designed furniture in a refined, minimalist vein, notably a simple table desk (1937) with solid side panels as supports that had its drawer space not hung beneath the apron, but elevated above it like a writing desk. His most popular chair design—so popular that it became known as "The Robsjohn-Gibbings Chair"—was a simple pale walnut armchair (1938) with linen-upholstered, buttoned cushions that were supported on leather strapping. The influence of Swedish Modern was apparent.

In 1939, for the California showroom of jeweler Paul Flato, Robsjohn-Gibbings designed a set of paneled doors of birch that were paneled with superimposed tiers of flat squares mitered to look pyramidal. The simplicity and monumentality of the concept were much emulated. Furnished with chairs of strapped leather, reminiscent of Alvar Aalto's slightly earlier designs, the effect was so refined that it seemed as if, within traditional decorating, a move toward reductiveness, simplicity, and purification had begun to reflect the tendencies of Modern design. This similarity to academic Modernism was curious, especially since Robsjohn-Gibbings wrote so vehemently, in the next decade, against Bauhaus design.

Edward Wormley

Among the influential American interior designers who started their careers in the 1930s, Edward Wormley sustained the longest continuity as a furniture designer. From 1931 until 1968, a period of thirty-seven years, he designed 150 pieces of furniture a year for the Dunbar Furniture Company of Berne, Indiana. It was a model of sustained productivity, infused inspiration, and professional perseverance.

Born in Oswego, Illinois, Edward Wormley (1907–) attended art school at the Art Institute of Chicago for a year when he was nineteen, then joined the design department of Marshall Field in Chicago from 1927 to 1930. There he designed residences for the department store's customers, advised on furnishings, and in the last year he was there began designing a line of furniture that was to be produced for the store by the Berkey & Gay Company. That project led to a brief employment with Berkey & Gay, after which he went to Dunbar.

Early production samples of Wormley's designs for Dunbar were immediately bought by the newly opened Mechandise Mart in Chicago—and immediately sold. The Merchandise Mart's showrooms and semi-annual markets for the trade were to become a basic influence on mainstream taste in succeeding decades. Soon, market reaction convinced Dunbar to put Wormley's sample designs into production. Each year, he produced a traditional line and a contemporary line (see Figure 138). His sources of inspiration became wide-reaching over cultures and eras. Combinations of Hitchcock benches as seen through Japanese simplicity were highpoints of his refined eye. Wormley's work, therefore, became a new resource of contemporary American-made furniture for the interior design field.

William Pahlmann

Acclaimed in the mid-1930s for his showstopping displays and model rooms at Lord & Taylor in New York, William Pahlmann was influential in loosening the

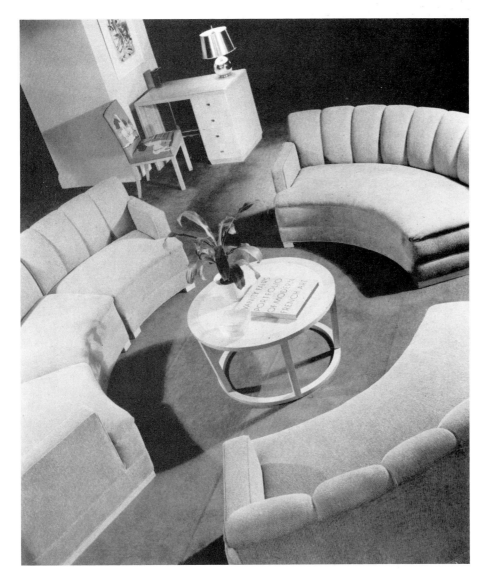

138. Edward Wormley. Sectional furniture for Dunbar. 1935. *Photograph by Frank Willming, courtesy Edward Wormley.*

grip of correct period rooms on the work of American interior designers and in fostering the new interior design eclecticism of the 1930s. His eye was good enough to combine and mix centuries, cultures, and contrasts in a daredevil manner, yet make them seem to work. In the 1940s and 1950s he went on to become one of the most successful interior designers of the century.

Born in Pleasant Mound, Illinois, William Carroll Pahlmann (1900–) moved with his parents to San Antonio, Texas, at the age of nine, and went to school there. As he grew to 6 feet 1 inch tall, he took on the Texan image with its large, expansive, and outgoing manner. After a series of construction and traveling salesman jobs, he took a correspondence course with *Arts and Decoration* magazine; and in his mid-twenties he determined to be a designer. In 1927 he enrolled in the New York School of Fine and Applied Arts, where he drew well and put himself through school as a song-and-dance man in Broadway musicals. Pahlmann continued in the school's Paris program, and got the grand tour of Europe, where he met his first important clients.

Back in America in 1931, he designed residences for them—the Seton Henrys at Pen Ryn, Delaware; then for Mrs. William Paley on Beekman Place in New

York; and for Mrs. Pauline Rogers at Southampton, Long Island. He also worked briefly for the B. Altman department store.

In 1936 Pahlmann joined Lord & Taylor to do interior display in the home furnishings division. His merchandise displays attracted great crowds, gained much publicity, and brought him immediate professional recognition. What was unique about his model rooms was his theatrical sense and eclectic style. The Lord & Taylor displays always had a theme that related to store merchandise (see Figure 139A) or to the merchandise and crafts of specific countries, such as Swedish Modern (see Figure 139B). His displays, which included a Swedish dining room with painted furniture and a family room with a rug of irregular stripes, established his color sense. The most celebrated of these promotions was "Pahlmann Peruvian" (see Figure 163) for which he brought back Peruvian handcrafted fabrics, fringes, and objects, as well as paintings, silver, and Inca treasures. Crowds were estimated at between 20,000 and 30,000 per month. It was the beginning of the prominence of theatrical model rooms in the merchandising campaigns of American department stores.

In those room displays, Pahlmann was acclaimed for his color schemes, and some of those combinations became associated with him at the time. He lists some of them in his 1955 book, *The Pahlmann Book of Interior Decorating:* in 1938— "cinnamon, tan, and sage green"; also "pistachio green, grape, and white"; and also "sky blue, elephant gray, and pink." This latter became widely popular in the next several years. In 1939 he combined "black, white, cerulean, and orange." In 1940 he presented "Harlem pink, Regency green, and white"; "sulphur yellow, olive green, and rosy red"; and "brick, bottle green, rawhide, and bleached cypress." Pahlmann Peruvian in 1941 featured "Cuzco blue, lime, fuschia, deep blue, and whitewash"; another of his Peruvian combinations was "avocado, lime, plum, tan, orange, and white." Pahlmann's color schemes demonstrated the American eclecticism of the 1930s.

139A.   William Pahlmann. Model room for Lord & Taylor's "Dramatic Rooms" promotion. New York City. 1938. *Photograph by Van Nes–De Vos, courtesy William Pahlmann.*

139B. William Pahlmann. Model room for Lord & Taylor's "Swedish Modern" promotion. New York City. 1938. *Photograph courtesy William Pahlmann.*

139C. William Pahlmann. Model room for Lord & Taylor's "Excitement in Summer Decor" promotion. New York City. 1939. *Photograph courtesy William Pahlmann.*

Billy Baldwin

In 1935 Billy Baldwin became an assistant in Ruby Ross Wood's firm and began to make a name for himself. Born in Roland Park, Maryland, William Baldwin (1903–84) studied for two years at Princeton University and by the end of the 1920s had built up a decorating clientele in the Baltimore area. He met Ruby Ross Wood in 1930 and moved to New York to work for her five years later. His design of his own office at Mrs. Wood's established what became one of his trademarks— the glossy dark-brown wall, which he used for the next four decades.

For Ruby Ross Wood, in 1935, he worked on the interiors of the Woolcott Blair House in Palm Beach, Florida, and in 1938 designed the interiors of a house in Montego Bay, Jamaica. There the influence of Surrealism was to be seen. The scheme that he and Mrs. Wood decided upon was to be "in the spirit of a ballet, whimsical, light, and sketchy."[10] In the living room, the sofa was upholstered in bright yellow, the chairs in white with yellow-stenciled orchids. Two metal commodes were painted with trompe l'oeil drapery by Joseph B. Platt. A dining area had wire-like wrought-iron chairs painted the color of bougainvillea, a wire-based table with an apron of large-scale white fringe, and a cantilevered console-sideboard with the same fringe decoration. The theatrical whimsy of it all was indicative of the new eclectic, perhaps Surrealist spirit of 1930s design.

Europe and America: The Threat of War

In 1934 Hitler was appointed Chancellor of Germany. Only two years later Mussolini annexed Abyssinia as part of Italy. Then, too, began the Spanish Civil War; Picasso's mural *Guernica* shrieked in anguish at this event in 1937. In 1938 Germany mobilized its armed forces, and the Anschluss of Austria began; it was soon followed by the fall of Czechoslovakia and France and by the London blitz.

After the Bauhaus was closed in 1933, the first of the Bauhaus faculty to flee from this onslaught and come to the United States were Anni and Josef Albers; in 1933 they began teaching at Black Mountain College in North Carolina. Walter Gropius and Marcel Breuer came in 1937, after interim sojourns in London. Gropius came to head the Graduate School of Design at Harvard University, where he remained until 1953, and Breuer came to teach in Gropius's program. Walter Baermann settled at the California Institute of Technology. Also in 1937, Laszlo Moholy-Nagy, who had gone to England when Gropius did, came to Chicago to head the New Bauhaus, which was renamed the School of Design in the following year.

In 1937, too, Mies van der Rohe made his first trip to the United States. In 1938 Mies settled in Chicago, where from 1938 to 1958 he was Director of Architecture at Armour Institute (renamed the Illinois Institute of Technology in 1940); and where, from 1938 to 1969, he maintained an architecture practice. Bauhaus faculty member Herbert Bayer came to the United States in 1938 to work with Walter and Ise Gropius on the Museum of Modern Art's retrospective exhibition "Bauhaus, 1919–1928." The influence of these immigrants from the Bauhaus, however indirect their connections were with American industry, was to become the foundation of American design education for the next two decades.

The World of Tomorrow

The New York World's Fair of 1938–39, like the simultaneous World's Fair in San Francisco, was politically both the victory celebration over the end of the Depression and a futile hope that what was happening in Europe would not come to a showdown. For industrial designers and architects, the New York World's

Fair was as close to a realization of tomorrow's world of Streamlining as they were to get.

Norman Bel Geddes and architect Albert Kahn created the pavilion for General Motors, with its popular "Futurama"—a scale model of the future American city and countryside as viewed from a moving train of two-person wingchairs with audio speakers in the wings. The city and the countryside were seen in daylight and by night, in fair weather and in foul. The recreation of this stratospheric inspection tour of Sant'Elia's Futurist metropolis was eye-opening and magical. Henry Dreyfuss's "Democracity" presentation inside the Perisphere seemed anti-climactic by comparison.

Walter Dorwin Teague created the Ford Motor Company Pavilion, with its rooftop speedway test-drive or ride in a new bright-colored Ford. Inside the Ford Pavilion Teague also designed a lounge that was free of the stylistic motifs of either Deco's radiowaves of Streamlining's airstreams. A chandelier of vertically run, indirectly reflected fluorescent tubes hung over a sofa-and-endtable group that was designed as a single unit (see Figure 140). Lamps with cylindrical brass shades were built into the endtables. The overall group was tied together visually by a white stripe, like large-scale welting. It prefigured the furnishings in the railroad observation cars of the next decade.

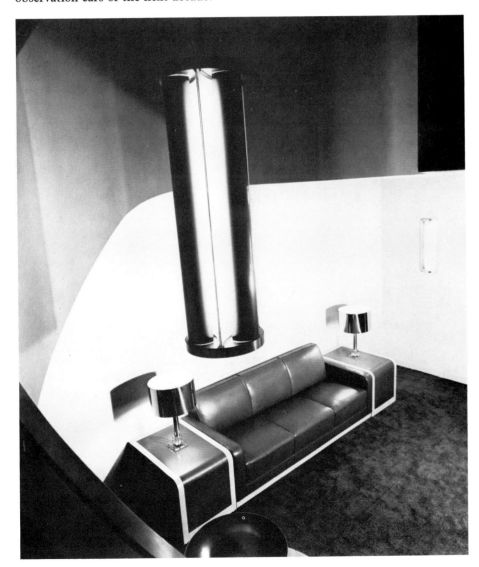

140. Walter Dorwin Teague. Lounge, Ford Pavilion. New York World's Fair. 1939. *Photograph courtesy Walter Dorwin Teague Associates, Inc.*

141. Russel Wright. American Modern dinnerware. Designed 1937, produced 1939–59. *Photograph by Courtney Frisse, courtesy The Smithsonian Institution.*

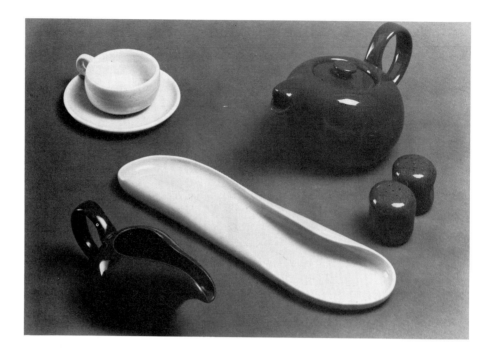

Russel Wright (see Figure 141) also designed exhibitions at the fair, the largest of which was for Focal Foods; it was similar to his showroom for the International Handkerchief Company of the same year. At the Focal Foods display, visitors walked through dimly lit halls subdivided by large geometric and biomorphic sculptural units. Amoeboid show windows revealed symbolic and realistic elements of food; dioramas depicted food production and distribution. For these Wright designed Surrealistic displays—a field that smiled, a group of flying lobsters. It was at this time that Salvador Dali designed his jewelry group in which a garnet heart thumped and pulsated. Surrealism pervaded.

Other architects and designers whose work was exhibited at this World's Fair were Donald Deskey, Gilbert Rohde, Morris Lapidus, Egmont Arens, William Lescaze, Oscar Niemeyer, and Alvar Aalto.

Alvar Aalto

A star of the New York World's Fair show, in terms of interior design, was the Finnish Pavilion designed by Alvar Aalto. The vast undulating ceiling of wood strips that Aalto designed brought attention to that Modern master from Finland, and created curiosity about his other works (see Figure 142). The Scandinavian Modern idiom had been popular since 1925, and in the 1930s Americans began to have access to the furniture designs of Bruno Mathsson, Borge Mogenson, Kaare Klint, and Magnus Stephensen.

Born in Kuortane, Finland, Alvar Aalto (1898–1976) studied architecture at the Technical University of Helsinki. He was first recognized internationally for his design of the Tuberculosis Sanatorium at Paimio, Finland, completed in 1933. His major early interiors had included the Viipuri Library, completed in 1935, with its undulating wood lecture room ceiling (see Figure 143), which was determined by acoustical considerations, and its daylighting domes over the two-level reading room. Aalto's concern for lighting and acoustics inspired new considerations for the Modern movement.

In the Paimio and Viipuri buildings Aalto used chairs, stools (shown in Figure 143), tables, and children's furniture that he had designed for factory production

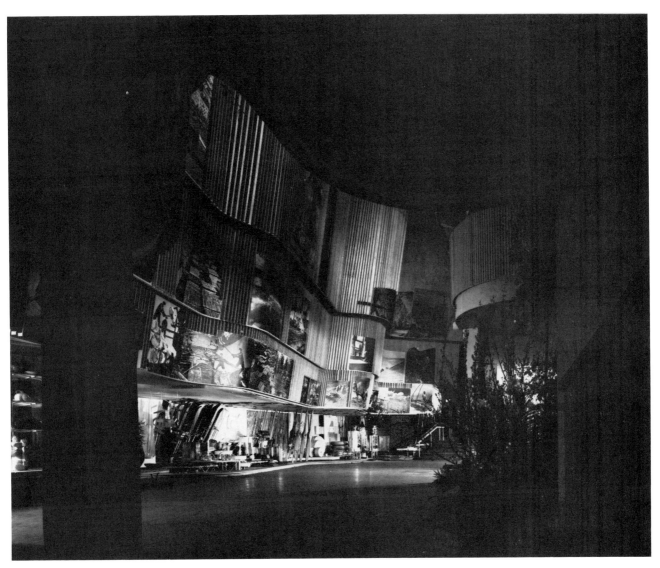

142. Alvar Aalto. Finnish Pavilion, New York World's Fair. 1939. *Photograph © Ezra Stoller/ESTO, 1940.*

143. Alvar Aalto. Lecture hall in the library. Viipuri, Finland. 1930–35. *Photograph by Artek Oy AB, Helsinki. From Karl Mang,* History of Modern Furniture *(New York: Harry N. Abrams, 1979).*

144. Alvar Aalto. Villa Mairea.
Noormarkku, Finland. 1937–39.
*Photograph © Ezra Stoller/
ESTO, 1960.*

using new techniques of laminating and bending birch plywood; this furniture had been put into production by Artek of Finland during 1932–33. It had the lightness and simplicity that imbued all his work, and it soon became internationally known after being exhibited in the Paris Exhibition of 1937 and the New York World's Fair of 1939. Besides, in expressing the cantilevered chair forms of other Modern designers in fresh, pale, light wood, instead of in shiny, machine-made tubular metal, Aalto provided another alternative as well as opposition to the (equally) machine-made imagery of the German school of Modernism.

From 1938 to 1939 Aalto had worked on his Villa Mairea, in Noormarkku, Finland, for his lifelong patron Maire Gullichsen, with its sensitive integration of an L-shaped plan into the landscape and with its plan and section influenced by De Stijl—especially Rietveld's Schröder House of 1924. Inside, Aalto displayed his delicate if perplexingly ambiguous manipulation of the Modern concept of free-flowing space. The Villa Mairea interior offered multiple levels and multiple vistas (see Figure 144); it had double-functioning elements such as the undulating entry wall that both separated the foyer from the dining room and also inflected or directed circulation into the house. Within this sophisticatedly complex envelope, simple though elegant provincial-idiom wood furnishings were combined with crisp Machine-Age objects such as lighting fixtures. In his interior designs Aalto was assisted by his wife, Aino Marsio Aalto, who was an architect as well as his partner. She died in 1949.

By the time of the 1939 World's Fair, Aalto had clearly established his position as one of the principal masters of International Style. He was unique among them in bringing an atmosphere of warmth and sensitivity, thoughtfulness, grace, and charm to the stark, Machine-Age, structurally oriented style. And his furniture, which was widely imported for use in American interiors during the 1930s, had established his reputation here as a designer before his influence as an architect was seen.

The New York and the San Francisco World's Fairs of 1939 were the last creative steps forward for Streamlining, and they were also the last bubble of the effervescent, perhaps desperate, optimism of the 1930s. It was a victory short-lived. For Americans, it was a blind optimism that corresponded to the manic Surrealism of the Europeans. World War II lasted from 1939 to 1945. During that time 35 million died in warfare and 10 million more died in Nazi concentration camps. During the winter of 1939–40, among those fleeing the holocaust, Jean-Michel Frank left France for South America and soon came to the United States on the invitation of several former clients, including Templeton Crocker, and at the urging of former students and friends of his from the Paris program of the New York School of Fine and Applied Arts, including Eleanor McMillen Brown. Frank's depression over the war, however, led to his suicide in 1941, when he jumped out of a New York building. For interior designers, too, the war had hit home.

Suggested Reading

Albrecht, Donald. *Designing Dreams: Modern Architecture in the Movies.* New York: Harper & Row, 1985.

Alvar Aalto. New York: Rizzoli, 1978.

Baldwin, Billy. *Billy Baldwin Remembers.* New York: Harcourt Brace Jovanovich, 1974.

Battersby, Martin. *The Decorative Thirties.* New York: Walker & Company, 1969, 1971.

Bayer, Herbert, Walter Gropius, and Ise Gropius, eds. *Bauhaus: 1919–1928.* New York: The Museum of Modern Art, 1938.

Brown, Erica. *Sixty Years of Interior Design: The World of McMillen.* New York: Viking Press, 1982.

Bush, Donald J. *The Streamlined Decade.* New York: Braziller, 1975.

Design in America: The Cranbrook Vision, 1925–1950. New York: Harry N. Abrams, 1983.

Draper, Dorothy. *Decorating Is Fun!* New York: Art & Decoration Book Society, 1939.

Fisher, Richard B. *Syrie Maugham.* London: Duckworth, 1978.

Frankl, Paul T. *New Dimensions.* New York: Payson & Clarke, 1928.

————. *Form and Re-Form.* New York: Harper & Row, 1930.

Giedion, Sigfried, ed. *A Decade of Contemporary Architecture.* New York: Wittenborn, 1954.

Hanks, David A. *The Decorative Designs of Frank Lloyd Wright.* New York: E. P. Dutton, 1979.

————. *Donald Deskey.* New York: E. P. Dutton, 1985.

Hennessey, William J. *Russel Wright.* Cambridge: MIT Press, 1983.

Hitchcock, Henry-Russell, and Philip Johnson. *The International Style: Architecture Since 1922.* New York: W. W. Norton, 1932, 1966.

Jacobus, John M., Jr. "Architecture, American Style: 1920–45," *American Art.* New York: Prentice-Hall, Harry N. Abrams, 1979.

Jeanneret, Charles-Edouard. *Le Corbusier: 1910–65.* Zurich: Les Editions d'Architecture Zurich, 1967.

Johnson, Philip C. *Mies van der Rohe.* New York: The Museum of Modern Art, 1947, 1978.

Kaufmann, Edgar, Jr. "Interior Design: Architecture or Decoration?" *Progressive Architecture.* October 1962, pp. 141–44.

McCallum, Ian. *Architecture USA*. New York: Reinhold, 1959.

McCoy, Esther. *Five California Architects*. New York: Reinhold, 1960. (Paperback New York: Frederick A. Praeger, 1975.)

———. *The Second Generation*. Layton, Utah: Gibbs M. Smith, 1984.

Meickle, Jeffrey L. *Twentieth Century Limited: Industrial Design in America, 1925–39*. Philadelphia: Temple University Press, 1979.

Pahlmann, William. *The Pahlmann Book of Interior Decorating*. New York: Thomas Y. Crowell, 1955.

Pool, Mary Jane, ed. *20th Century Decorating, Architecture, and Gardens*. New York: Holt, Rinehart and Winston, 1980.

Pratt, Richard. *David Adler: The Architect and His Work*. New York: M. Evans & Company, 1970.

Progressive Architecture. February 1982. Special issue on International Style commemorating the fiftieth anniversary of the Museum of Modern Art Exhibition.

Pulos, Arthur J. *American Design Ethic: A History of Industrial Design to 1940*. Cambridge: MIT Press, 1983.

Sanchez, Leopold Diego, and Andree Putman. *Jean-Michel Frank*. Paris: Editions du Regard, 1980.

Stern, Robert A. M. *George Howe*. New Haven: Yale University Press, 1975.

Tweed, Katharine, ed. *The Finest Rooms by America's Great Decorators*. New York: Viking Press, 1964.

Notes

1. Robert A. M. Stern, *George Howe* (New Haven: Yale University Press, 1975), p. 62.

2. Alfred Barr, Jr., Preface to *Bauhaus: 1919–1928*, ed. Herbert Bayer, Walter Gropius, and Ise Gropius (New York: The Museum of Modern Art, 1938), p. 5.

3. Henry-Russell Hitchcock and Philip Johnson, *The International Style: Architecture Since 1922* (New York: W. W. Norton, 1932, 1966), p. 20.

4. Ibid., pp. 86ff.

5. Edgar Kaufmann, Jr., "Interior Design: Architecture or Decoration?" *Progressive Architecture* (October 1962), p. 144.

6. Leopold Diego Sanchez and Andree Putman, *Jean-Michel Frank* (Paris: Editions du Regard, 1980), p. 14.

7. Ibid.

8. Christopher Hemphill believes, after interviewing the nephew of Carlos de Bestigui (sometimes spelled Bestiguy) and the nephew of Emilio Terry, when neither made claims or suggestions regarding the involvement of Terry in the design of the furnishings for this apartment, that it was de Bestigui and not Terry who directed the decoration.

9. Charles-Edouard Jeanneret, *Le Corbusier: 1910–65* (Zurich: Les Editions d'Architecture Zurich, 1967), p. 67.

10. Billy Baldwin, *Billy Baldwin Remembers* (New York: Harcourt Brace Jovanovich, 1974), p. 70.

Chapter 14

1940–1950:
The Second Generation

Once again a decade was divided by war into an active and an inactive period for designers of interiors. But the order of those periods was reversed in the 1940s—the war and inactivity came first, and the reactions that followed were markedly different.

When the 1940s began, World War II had been in progress in Europe for a year, devastating the populations, resources, treasures, and emotions of Western Europe and North Africa. But the United States was not yet actively fighting. Here, wartime efforts were directed toward whatever technological inventions might bring the war to quick conclusion.

For civilians, installing blackout curtains and drilling for blackouts and air raids were the order of the day, along with rationing food and gasoline and salvaging aluminum and other metals for reuse. Progress in interior design was curtailed while many interior design professionals made their contributions to the armed forces, notably in camouflage work. But none of those precautions and deprivations prepared Americans for the Sunday morning surprise attack on Pearl Harbor on December 7, 1941.

The shortage of materials led to wartime make-do: The old elegant materials that Modernists had relied on to provide natural texture and ornamentation were not available; the new materials were common materials that were used in uncommon ways. Exaggeratedly rough natural textures had been used by German architects, including Mies and Breuer, during the 1930s and were more widely seen as used by the Slavs and Balts at the 1938 Paris Exhibition; wartime shortages made them a necessity in the 1940s. Burlap and jute fabrics were lauded as wall coverings and drapery materials; sisal carpeting provided pattern and texture; interwoven strips of webbing were hung like hammocks within chair frames to supplant upholstery. Cardboard egg crates were used to texturize some ceilings. This was the first mass adoption of the Dada-Surreal concept of found objects.

Stylistically, the motif of the early 1940s was the bulbous curve and the amoeba form with its undulating, biomorphic outline. It was derived both from camouflage shapes and from the work of painters Pablo Picasso and Joan Miró and sculptors Hans Arp and Alexander Calder. It was a free-form shape like a painter's palette. Americans had been introduced to this undulation as an interior motif by Alvar Aalto's glass vase (1936–37), by his Finnish Pavilion at the New York World's Fair (1939) (see Figure 142), and also by the Brazilian Pavilion at that same fair. In Brazil the parabola forms of Oscar Niemeyer and others presented a conga line of undulation. In New York biomorphic furniture was designed by Frederick Kiesler in 1938 and was exhibited at Peggy Guggenheim's Art of This Century Gallery beginning in 1942.

Among interior furnishings the Hardoy or Butterfly Chair (1938) (see Figure 145), designed by Antonio Bonet, Juan Kurchan, and Jorge Ferrari-Hardoy, was

145. Antonio Bonet, Juan Kurchan, and Jorge Ferrari-Hardoy. Butterfly Chair, metal rod and leather, 35″ high. *Collection, The Museum of Modern Art, New York City, Edgar Kaufmann, Jr., Fund.*

146. Isamu Noguchi. Free-form coffee table for Herman Miller Inc. 1944. *Photograph courtesy Herman Miller Inc.*

147. Charles Eames and Ray Eames. Folding, undulating molded plywood screen. 1946. *Photograph courtesy Herman Miller Inc.*

the popular epitome of this form. Isamu Noguchi's free-form coffee table for Herman Miller Inc. is another evocation (see Figure 146). The undulations of Charles Eames's folding screen (1946) reiterated the motif (see Figure 147). The cutleaf philodendron, the indoor plant that most approximated the amoeba form, was adopted as the plant of the decade. The use of plants was canonized both as the principal means of providing decorative sculpture and as the means of bringing nature indoors. The use of indoor plants sought to create the interpenetration of inside and outside that Frank Lloyd Wright had been proclaiming since 1900. In the 1940s this shape became a mass fashion in interior design; by the 1950s it resulted in the kidney-shaped swimming pool.

In the fine arts the spare, gaunt wartime realism of Edward Hopper and others would be displaced by Abstract Expressionism in 1947 and 1948. Other motifs that found their way from the fine arts to interior design in the 1940s were the "cheese holes" of sculptors Jean Lurçat, Henry Moore, and Barbara Hepworth. Notably, these holes were adapted to the design of seatbacks.

Alexander Girard

One American designer who began to make a name for himself toward the end of the war was Alexander Girard, who designed houses and commercial interiors in the Detroit area. Although an architect, he has devoted his career to the design of interiors, exhibitions, and textiles.

Born in New York City, Alexander H. Girard (1907–) was raised in Florence, Italy, studied at the Royal Institute of British Architects in London, at the Royal School of Architecture in Rome, and at New York University. He worked in architects' offices in Florence, Rome, London, and Paris, before opening his own practice in New York in 1932. In 1937 Girard moved to Detroit, where he designed interiors for the Ford Motor Company (1943) and Lincoln Motors (1946). He designed several houses, as well as the influential exhibition "Design for Living" for the Detroit Institute of Arts in 1949. Girard and his wife Susan began collecting folk art and primitive art around 1939; it was to influence much of his later work. Girard later became renowned for exhibition design as well as interior and fabric design.

In 1943 Girard designed a cafeteria to seat 1,400 employees of the International Detrola Corporation in Detroit. It was a preview of the restaurant designs he was to become acclaimed for in the 1950s. The space was a long rectangular industrial-loft space with a grid of structural columns that Girard made efforts to disguise rather than express (see Figure 148). He introduced an entry foyer, with a bulbous curving plan, and established a diagonal orientation to the cafeteria with a bulb-ended, free-form serving and kitchen area. He furred out the interior columns as canted or rotated rectangles and ellipses, and furred out the perimeter columns to reinforce the diagonal orientation. This inflection was the keynote of the circulation plan. He located three executive dining rooms behind the serving-kitchen area and turned one of the central columns into a large circular divider that incorporated storage and a stage for company presentations and speeches. The cafeteria tables were also rotated along the diagonal axis, even at the perimeter. All of this was topped by a suspended ceiling with recessed lighting troffers. It was one of the early suspended ceilings.

He used simple materials, typical of the availabilities of the day: Natural woods—mostly white pine and red cedar siding—were used for wall surfaces; asphalt tile surfaced the floor, part of it in a striped pattern; columns were faced with bent plywood strips. Window recesses were filled with undraped venetian

148. Alexander Girard. Plan, employee cafeteria, Detrola Corporation. Detroit, Michigan. 1943. *Illustration from* Architectural Forum *(October 1944).*

blinds. Tables had metal column bases; chairs were molded plywood from Artek of Finland. The color scheme was gray-green, beige, and red.

During 1946–47 Girard designed an office-showroom in Detroit for his practice—in an old hamburger stand. This and other renovations were early examples of the recycling that was to become a major direction of future decades. Girard's search for new textures was typical of the decade: vertically striated plywood in its natural pale yellow-tan color was used for wall surfacing; asbestos cement was painted gray-blue; natural jute and burlap fabrics were used on the walls; the fiberboard ceilings were painted black; and tan carpeting was used on the floors. A glass partition separated one room from another; lighting was from exposed spotlights and ellipsoidal can lights. Most telling of the 1940s search for natural textures was the large-scale stainless-steel mesh covering of the front door.

Shortly thereafter, Girard moved his office and showroom to Grosse Pointe, Michigan, where he painted the interior structural and mechanical elements in a gray and off-white scheme: Exposed steel beams were painted dull black, steel columns painted blue-white, ducts were enameled white; and exposed nuts and bolts were painted orange-vermilion. This textured color-coding was indicative of the 1940s and its respect for natural materials. Split-bamboo screen, natural plywood, and hung cabinets, along with a vertically striated divider and shelves hung on vertical wall-attached strips, demonstrated the end-of-the-decade interest in the linear string-and-wire motif.

In 1948 Girard designed a new, modest, board-and-batten house for himself and his family. Planned as blocks of rectangles, the interior boxes were broken up by inflected diagonals and corner doorways (see Figure 149A). The 20- by 30-foot living room was subdivided—into areas for entryway, study, and three different seating groups—by room dividers. One divider was a freestanding fireplace; the other was a boomerang-plan banquette and screen (see Figure 149B). On the living room side of the screen, which was made of plywood painted gray, hung a display of the Girards' collection of paintings, masks, and folk art. On the work-study side of the screen were pin-up boards as well as shelf on shelf of repeated jars, crocks, bottles, cups, and boxes for equipment, along with toys and other objects.

149A. Alexander Girard. Plan, own house. Grosse Pointe, Michigan. 1948. *Illustration from* Architectural Review *(April 1950).*

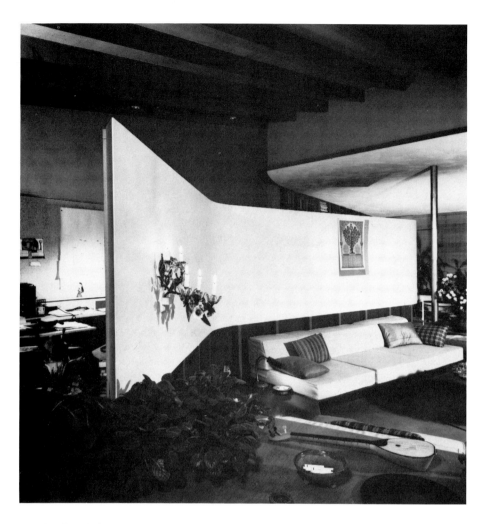

In the dining room of this same house was a boomerang-plan serving bar that hovered on attenuated pipe legs. In the kitchen a triangular island counter with chamfered corners separated the L-plan cooking area from the family dining table. The bedrooms established Girard's minimized bedroom concept, which set a model for hotel bedrooms for the next two decades. Throughout the house indirect cove lighting and spotlighting were used, as well as new materials and furniture such as black plastic laminate tabletops and countertops, natural fir plywood, wire-based chairs, and chairs by Saarinen and Eames as well as the popular Butterfly Chair. Colors used in the house were orange, yellow, magenta, blue, and purple. Throughout the house were Peruvian rugs, collections of Mexican figurines, Chinese paper kites, nativity scenes, birdcages, and other folk art. The Girards' collection of folk art from South America and of Victorian artifacts had already been started. In this house Alexander Girard began to show the flair for assembly and display technique he would refine and elaborate in the coming years. That technique was to make him one of the most respected exhibition designers of the next two decades.

The Scandinavian Influence

Throughout the decade the influence of Scandinavian design on American interiors was prevalent. It had been introduced in the 1930s as Swedish Modern, and continued to make the 1940s known, logically, as the Scandinavian Decade in America. The foremost Swedish furniture designer in the United States during the 1940s was Bruno Mathsson (1907–), whose pale, cool designs included a trend-setting armchair of bent plywood and fiber webbing in 1940; it had followed a reclining chair with a similar bent-plywood frame designed in 1935. Mathsson's work had become a mainstay of Swedish Modern in the mid-1930s, when he developed his split-top leg for tables and beds.

In 1941 the Danish designer Jens Risom, who had designed furniture for the Knoll Furniture Company, opened his own firm in New York, devoted mainly to furniture design, and helped to popularize Danish Modern during the decade. By the end of the 1940s Danish and Finnish designs were somewhat more popular in the United States than the Swedish Modern idiom. In 1949 the Dane Hans Wegner (1914–) designed his classic chair with its exposed sculptured frame of oak or teak, and with a cane seat and cane-wrapped back. It became so popular that it was known for the next decade simply as "The Chair" (see Figure 150). Many people felt that The Chair was reminiscent of ancient Chinese tradition. The sinuous furniture designed by Finn Juhl (1912–) was introduced to the States in the same year. Other popular Danish designers were Borge Mogenson (1914–72); Magnus Stephensen (1903–); and Mogens Koch, whose classic folding chair (1938) was among the earliest popular Danish designs.

Among the Finns Paavo Tynell's pinpoint-pierced brass lamps with their snowflake-like umbrellas of flower petals charmed Americans after 1947; and Ilmari Tapiovaara (1914–) pioneered in knock-down furniture designs. In 1947 Alvar Aalto designed his acclaimed coffee table of birch and glass, and from 1947 to 1949 he worked on the design of Baker House, a dormitory for the Massachusetts Insti-

150. Hans Wegner. The Chair. 1949. *Photograph courtesy Knoll International.*

tute of Technology in Cambridge, Massachusetts, with an undulating plan, which was his first architectural work in the States since the Finnish Pavilion at the 1939 New York World's Fair. The Scandinavian designers offered a pale palette of natural woods that was acceptable to several segments of the population: those accustomed to 1930s colors; those who preferred a homey, easy, somewhat provincial style, such as those nostalgic for Arts and Crafts simplicity and those who admired the Peasant style of Picasso; those young people whose budgets permitted only the simplest of good design; and, in addition, the confirmed Modernists, who were dedicated to the texture and honesty of natural materials.

After World War II

The impact of postwar economic and social changes in America was enormous. Postwar victoriousness and optimism brought about prosperity and a widespread and freewheeling building boom that was forwarded by wartime technological advances. Technological innovation was the aspiration of the day. The return of the armed forces brought both a baby boom and manageable FHA home mortgages for veterans. The annual number of new-home construction starts grew from 200,000 in 1945 to 1,154,000 in 1950.

This contributed to the building boom and began the suburbanization of America. It was the beginning of the end of servants; no servants at home meant do-it-yourself for everyman. At this time, too, television and the family room became regular components of American interiors. The number of television sets produced in America mushroomed from zero in 1945 to 7.5 million by 1950.[1] They produced a new spider's web of antennas over the cities of the land. For interior designers, what had been a comfortable practice for a few mushroomed into big businesses for a great many. Not only residential and club interiors were their commissions, but transportation and many more commercial projects were on the horizon.

The epochal explosion of the atomic bomb at Hiroshima and Nagasaki in 1945 had opened the Atomic Age. The horror and awesomeness of the event, however, were of less concern to the general American population than the potential of atomic fission. The concept caught the imaginations of designers. A popular inspiration and motif were atomic and molecular shapes made of metal rods with small disks or spheres attached at the tips (see Figure 151). This atomic-molecular motif was often expressed with wire or string, especially in the cat's-cradle structures of tables and chairs, and, architecturally, of staircases, which were aimed at dematerialization. It was a symbol of the new exposure to atomic power as well as the feeling of discontinuity that the revelation of atomic fission produced.

An Expanded Availability of Furnishings

New materials, new furnishings, new technologies, and new availabilities were abundant. Among the newly available technologies was plastics, which began to influence design in the 1940s. Americans had begun to get used to the quickening of travel and communications before the war. Air travel had begun to increase in frequency and distance. Long-distance telephoning and radio reception became expected components of living.

Americans began to travel widely, and a new generation discovered Europe. Americans were liberated and began to take a new look. The desire for everything from everywhere and the availability of imports and inspirations from all countries and all periods began to be expected as well. Hawaiian and Brazilian motifs—large tropical leaves and bamboo, as well as Carmen Miranda—were incorporated into North American imagery. Eclecticism was rampant. It brought with it broad-reaching romanticism, exuberance and excitement, and flamboyance. It also brought incompatibilities of forms, lines, colors, textures, periods, and cultures.

As Edgar Kaufmann, Jr., wrote of the 1940s,

> America assumed a new position as a source of design creativity. Her product designers had overcome their original brashness, had looked long and intelligently at the ideals upheld by their critics, had absorbed a second generation of practitioners, and were maturing successfully. American architects, who had enjoyed something of a world reputation for several generations, also moved ahead, incorporating many influences and emerging with a new commercial style that swept across the metropolitan centers of the world. Architectural firms had no hesitation in adding [interior design] departments for the purpose. Some of the freest modern furnishings found their best utilization through such intermediaries.[2]

Postwar Designers

New industrial designers, such as Gilbert Rohde and Edward J Wormley, filled the gap in demand for new interior furnishings along with the established industrial designers from the 1930s. Among the new furniture designers was a group who had studied at the Cranbrook Academy in Michigan. Others included Paul Frankl and Paul Laszlo in California; the sculptor Isamu Noguchi; furniture designers Wharton Esherick and George Nakashima; and a host of others. The California design team of Van Keppel and Green began at this time also. Paul McCobb designed furniture—both chairs and case pieces—and, later on, furniture systems for Modernage, Raymor, and his own firm. Among the best new fabrics designers were Dorothy Liebes, Boris Kroll, Vera Neumann, and Arundell Clark, who had moved here from London, as had carpet designer Marian Dorn. The V'Soske family also experimented with carpet textures and designs, and the introduction of brilliantly colored silks from Thailand was made at this time by Jim Thompson's firm, Thaibok.

Dorothy Liebes   Most influential among the new fabric designers was Dorothy Liebes. Born in California, Dorothy Wright Liebes (1899–1972) studied at the

University of California at Berkeley and Columbia University in New York City. She had operated a studio in San Francisco specializing in custom-handwoven work for architects and decorators since 1930. Her handweaving was notable for its bright colors in unusual combinations—orange and sage, fuschia and chartreuse—and for its unconventional yarns and other materials.

She first became involved in larger-scale production in 1940, when she was engaged by Goodall Fabrics in Sanford, Maine. In 1948 she moved her design studio to New York City. She was to go on, in the next decade, to initiate a revolution in machine-weaving techniques based on her handweaving, and to become a leader in the color revolution.

Cranbrook Academy   Among the new furniture designers of the 1940s was the group that had studied and taught at the Cranbrook Academy in the 1930s (see Chapter 13). They included Charles Eames, Eero Saarinen, Florence Schust Knoll, Benjamin Baldwin, Harry Bertoia, Harry Weese, and Ralph Rapson. These designers and architects were to become leaders of the second generation of Modern design.

For the Cranbrook designers of the 1930s, the decade began with the award to Charles Eames and Eero Saarinen of two first prizes in New York's Museum of Modern Art's "Organic Design in Home Furnishings" competition of 1938–41, which was directed by Eliot Noyes, then a recent graduate of Walter Gropius's program at Harvard. Their award-winning designs were a chair of molded sheet plywood with a sculpted outline, and a series of gangable cabinets, drawer units, and coffee tables.

The technical innovation of the chair was that its plywood components were bent in two directions, making it more complex than either the bentwood furniture of Belter or Thonet or the plywood chairs of Aalto and Breuer. That chair was revolutionary; it became the inspiration for chair designs after the war by Eames and Saarinen separately—Eames for the Herman Miller furniture company and Saarinen for Knoll Associates, both in 1946. It then became the inspiration for the world of interior and furniture designers.

Eero Saarinen   The son of Cranbrook's president, the Finnish architect Eliel Saarinen, and his weaver wife Loja, Eero Saarinen (1910–61) was born in Kirkkonummi, Finland, and was brought by his family to the United States when he was thirteen. He first intended to be a sculptor, but decided to become an architect and studied at Yale University.

After travel in Europe Eero Saarinen joined his father's architecture office from 1936 to 1941. It was in that period that he worked with Charles Eames on the "Organic Design" competition (see Figure 152). During the war he worked in Washington for the Office of Strategic Studies from 1942 to 1945, then returned to practice with his father until the latter's death in 1950. In 1948 Eero Saarinen gained international recognition for his competition-winning design for the Gateway Arch in St. Louis, Missouri. From that point on he became, for the next decade, the most promising American architect.

Charles Eames   Charles Eames was one of the major interior and furniture design innovators of the twentieth century. His award-winning furniture designs with Eero Saarinen pioneered a new approach that changed the course of twentieth-century furniture.

Born in St. Louis, Missouri, Charles Eames (1907–78) studied architecture at Washington University in St. Louis, and began to practice architecture in 1930. After studying at Cranbrook on a fellowship offered him by Eliel Saarinen in 1938, he headed the Department of Experimental Design at Cranbrook Academy, where

152. Charles Eames and Eero Saarinen. Conversation Chair, competition drawing, colored pencil, wood veneer, and paper cutouts on white poster board, 20″ × 30″. Organic Design competition winner. 1940. *Collection, the Museum of Modern Art, New York City.*

he met his future wife and partner, Ray Kaiser Eames. In 1942, when the Eameses had moved to California, they were commissioned by the Navy Department to develop splints, stretchers, and glider shells out of molded plywood. Their technical findings advanced the design of their subsequent plywood furniture.

Eames began to design furniture for the Herman Miller company in 1946 (see Figure 153). His chairs of molded plywood were cut from plywood sheeting, which had been made since the early 1930s, but had only recently become available for uses other than doors, drawer bottoms, and automobile running boards. The chairs, which won immediate acclaim both for their structural ingenuity and for their

153. Charles Eames and Ray Eames. Molded plywood chair. 1946. *Photograph courtesy Herman Miller Inc.*

sculptural affinity with the amoeba-form of Hans Arp, were sometimes dubbed "potato-chip chairs."

To the serious direction in Modern design, Eames brought a touch of whimsy and sculptural lightness with these forms; but his design was backed up by meticulous analysis, technological invention, and innovative genius. Eames has been called the most original American furniture designer since Duncan Phyfe, and the designer of three major chairs of the twentieth century.[3] He and Ray Eames went on to design other furniture, furniture systems, exhibitions, and buildings, and to make major advances in movie production for the next thirty years.

Florence Schust Knoll Another Cranbrook affiliate, Florence Schust Knoll (1917–) also began to leave a mark on the interior design world in the 1940s. Born in Michigan, she studied at Cranbrook's Kingswood School for Girls and became a protégée of Eliel Saarinen and his family. She continued her education at the Architectural Association in London, and graduated from Mies van der Rohe's architecture program at Armour Institute (now the Illinois Institute of Technology). She worked briefly as an architect for Breuer, Gropius, and Herbert Bayer before becoming involved with the new Modern furniture of the 1940s—specifically, the Knoll Furniture Company (see below).

The New Modern Furniture Manufacturers

The availability of Modern, practical, and durable new furniture expanded greatly during the 1940s, owing to the founding of two major new furniture firms—the Herman Miller company and the Knoll Furniture Company.

Knoll Furniture Company

Knoll Furniture was founded by Hans Knoll (1914–55), who had come from Germany and established the Hans G. Knoll Furniture Company in 1938. Emigrés from the Bauhaus had found a receptive ground for their buildings, but appropriate furniture was not available in the United States. Other Modernists who searched for suitable furniture were Florence Schust, recently from Cranbrook. She met Hans Knoll, formed a business with him in 1943, and in 1946 they founded the Knoll Planning Unit for the design of interiors—offices, residences, and college dormitories. In 1946, the year they were married, the name of their firm was changed to Knoll Associates. Hans Knoll was killed in an auto accident in 1955; but in slightly more than a decade he and Florence Knoll had initiated some of the significant second-generation Modern furniture designs and had established what became known as the "Knoll look."

Among the first furniture they produced were designs by Eero Saarinen, whose first designs for Knoll in 1943 were chairs of cut-out laminated wood frames with seats and backs of woven canvas strips. Other early designers of furniture for Knoll were Pierre Jeanneret from France; Jens Risom from Denmark; Ralph Rapson, who had been at Cranbrook; and George Nakashima, who had recently forsaken architecture for furniture crafting (see below). In 1948 Knoll produced Saarinen's Womb Chair design, making it the first known molded fiberglass-reinforced plastic shell to be mass produced. It was the precursor of a series of office chairs that Saarinen designed that came to be known as "the chair with the hole in the back" (see Figure 154).

154. Eero Saarinen. Womb Chair (left); chair with hole in the back (right). 1948. *Photograph courtesy Knoll International.*

In 1948 Knoll Associates began producing Mies's Barcelona chairs and stools and Mies's Tugendhat coffee table. The act made them seem promulgators of the Bauhaus ideal.[4] The same year Knoll began producing textiles designed by Marianne Strengell, who had headed the weaving studio at Cranbrook. Knoll was among the principal creators of Modern interiors of the succeeding decades.

Herman Miller Inc.

The Herman Miller company of Zeeland, Michigan, was another of the Modern furniture firms that came to prominence in the 1940s. From the mid-1930s the Herman Miller company, headed by D. J. DePree, had been producing Modern furniture designed by the industrial designer Gilbert Rohde. Other early furniture designers whose works were produced by Herman Miller in the 1940s were Paul Laszlo and the sculptor Isamu Noguchi.

Born in 1904 in Los Angeles and trained in Japan, Noguchi studied sculpture with Constantin Brancusi and later, in addition to his sculpture, also designed furniture for both Herman Miller and Knoll. In 1944 he introduced a palette-shaped or free-form table for Herman Miller that became a symbol of organic furniture for the decade. His paper lanterns for Knoll (1948) reinterpreted the traditional Japanese concept in a new guise.

George Nelson

After Gilbert Rohde died in 1944, D. J. De Pree turned to George Nelson as his new design consultant. Nelson, with Henry Wright, had become known for the Storagewall concept, introduced in 1945, which was developed into a prefabricated closet-like piece of case goods with flexible shelving that could also be used as a room divider. It was the first of Nelson's series of provocative and innovative concepts for the furniture industry.

Born in Hartford, Connecticut, George Nelson (1908–) graduated from Yale College and, in 1931, from the Yale School of Fine Arts. He went on to study architecture at Catholic University in Washington, D.C., winning a Prix de Rome that allowed him two years of travel and study in Europe.

Back in Depression-ridden New York in 1934, he first worked as an editor of *Architectural Forum* magazine, eventually becoming its co-managing editor with Henry Wright. During this time he worked both as architect and author, collaborating with Henry Wright on the book *Tomorrow's House* (1945). There, they put forward the concept of Storagewall, which provided storage space in increased wall depth. The next year Nelson began to design furniture for Herman Miller, and soon became the firm's director of design.

In 1947 he left magazine work and established George Nelson & Company, industrial designers. He designed furniture, graphics, promotion, and showrooms for the firm. Under his auspices Herman Miller was guided to a position as one of the two foremost producers of Modern furnishings in the United States. In the late 1940s George Nelson persuaded Herman Miller to produce Charles Eames's furniture designs, and he negotiated the firm's association with Alexander Girard in the early 1950s. By the 1960s Herman Miller had become the design laboratory for the American furniture industry.

Among Nelson's design innovations were the slat bench (1948), the headboard with adjustable backrests (1948), and the L-shaped desk (1949) (see Figure 155). He continued to invent for the furniture industry for the next three decades. George Nelson has demonstrated the extraordinary talent of conceptualizing environments with a freewheeling and unfettered vision that sees past traditions, customs, and barriers to arrive at innovations of virtually poetic imagination (see page 198ff.).

His concepts more than his formal detailing make him one of the geniuses of twentieth-century design, which he considers to be principally a matter of clear thinking and hard work.

155. George Nelson. The L-shaped desk from Executive Office Group. 1949–50. *Photograph courtesy Herman Miller Inc.*

The Eames Chairs

In 1946 the Herman Miller company introduced the first of Charles Eames's chair designs. For Eames, the century-long goal of industrial mass production—and mass distribution—was immediately realized.

The chair, a version of the earlier potato-chip chair, was made in two heights— for dining and for lounging—with steel rods (5/8-inch-diameter legs, 7/8-inch back stile) forming the frame. Molded plywood panels (5-ply, 5/16-inch thick) are attached to the steel-rod frame with rubber shock mounts. Leg pads were originally rubber, later nylon. The overall composition has both technical innovation and the look of technology, a light and delicate air despite structural strength and durability, and it captured something of the sculptural imagery of Alexander Calder's mobiles of that decade. It became one of the classic chairs of the twentieth century. The earlier version of the Eames Chair had bent plywood legs, making it perhaps more 1940s in appearance and more integral in materials. But the steel-framed chair was the progenitor for the 1950s.

Eames continued to experiment with molded plywood until 1948. During that time he produced his folding, molded, undulating plywood screen, and a series of other pieces that were produced by Herman Miller.

Harvard under Gropius

The 1940s were the prime years of Walter Gropius's influence in bringing the Bauhaus educational program to America as director of the Harvard Graduate

School of Design (1937–53). From 1937 to 1946, Marcel Breuer also taught there. Their exposition of Bauhaus teaching, which proclaimed an ideal faith in social betterment, was revered at the time in architecture and education circles across the country. From that program came a dozen of the foremost architects, who were also designers of major interiors in the next decades: Edward Larrabee Barnes; John Johansen; Philip Johnson; I. M. Pei, and his partners Henry N. Cobb and Araldo Cossutta; Paul Rudolph; Ulrich Franzen; and Victor Lundy. They were to become leaders of the second generation of Modern design.

Gropius's program emphasized functional planning and expression, clarity and simplicity, and visual interest and texture. Walter and Ise Gropius's own house of 1938 in Lincoln, Massachusetts, indicated the kind of simplicity intended. Its living space was dividable by sliding fabric partitions; its hallway was sheathed in vertically scored siding to reflect the regionalism of New England clapboard construction; and its exterior was textured by horizontal windows, glass block, and a slat-trellised terrace. This more relaxed International-Style house along with other similar houses by Marcel Breuer, which had local fieldstone fireplaces or bases, was proclaimed as the idiom of the new American everyman. It was a non-style for all time, and it continued to affect American interior design for the next three or four decades.

The Spread of the Miesian Idiom

Philip Johnson

Philip Johnson was the most prominent advocate of the work of Mies van der Rohe, and he was also the most active disciple in demonstrating the potential of the Miesian idiom.

Born in Cleveland, Ohio, Philip Cortelyou Johnson (1906–) graduated from Harvard University in 1930, where he studied philosophy and the classics. From 1932 to 1934 he was director of the department of architecture at the Museum of Modern Art in New York, and in 1932, at the age of twenty-five, he mounted the exhibition "The International Style: Architecture 1922–1932" and co-authored with Henry-Russell Hitchcock the catalog of that exhibition (see Chapter 13).

In 1940 he returned to Harvard to study architecture under Gropius and Breuer, graduating in 1943. In 1942, while he was an architecture student, Johnson designed a house for himself in Cambridge, Massachusetts, that was modeled on the courtyard-house concepts of Mies in the 1930s. Johnson finished these Miesian interiors with the furniture by Mies that he had acquired in the 1930s.

Johnson resumed his position at the Museum of Modern Art in 1946, and in 1949 directed the construction in the museum garden of a modern house by Marcel Breuer. In 1955 he established his own design office. During that time he designed another house for himself in the Miesian idiom. That Glass House in New Canaan, Connecticut, made him—and that idiom—famous to a general public.

Glass Houses

Mies's glass-and-steel house for Dr. Edith Farnsworth in Plano, Illinois (near Fox River, Illinois), had been initiated as a design in 1946; but was not completed until 1951. During this time Johnson had completed his own celebrated Glass House. The Farnsworth House and the Glass House (as well as the Irwin Miller House by Saarinen and Girard discussed on page 438f.) raised consciousness for the potential of Modern glass architecture in creating timeless elegance and classic simplicity. These glass houses were unabashedly honest about structure; they were models of clarity and alignment, and models of the use of sumptuous natural materials. Their Machine-Age directness achieved unparalleled Modern richness through the juxtaposition of the purest Machine-Age refinement against the rich variety and color of the living natural landscape.

Mies's Farnsworth House   The Farnsworth House (see Figure 156A) of white-painted, wide-flange steel columns and all-glass walls elevates a single space floored in travertine above a terrace entry—and, in fact, above the ground, over which it hovers. In a new way appropriate to its age, the Farnsworth House makes architecture one and the same with interior design. The interior space, 54 by 28 feet, has no divisions except for a core of utilities running along one of the long sides in the form of a rectangle with projecting fins at the outer corners (see Figure 156B). That core incorporates all the mechanical and service systems for the house: At the center are the furnace, heating ducts, and water heater; a bathroom is at each end of the core; on the back side of the core is a galley kitchen—two refrigerators and two ranges are beneath the single counter, which also contains dishwasher and sink; on the other side of the core are a fireplace and a paneled storagewall overhang that shelter the firewood and create the semblance of an inglenook.

156A. Ludwig Mies van der Rohe. Plan, Farnsworth House. Plano, Illinois. 1946–51. *Illustration from Mary Jane Pool, ed.,* 20th Century Decorating, Architecture, and Gardens *(New York: Holt, Rinehart and Winston, 1980).*

156B. Ludwig Mies van der Rohe. Entry, Farnsworth House. Plano, Illinois. 1946–51. *Photograph by Bill Hedrich, Hedrich-Blessing.*

156C. Ludwig Mies van der Rohe. Living room, Farnsworth House. Plano, Illinois. 1946–51. *Photograph by Bill Hedrich, Hedrich-Blessing.*

Dr. Farnsworth's furnishings (see Figure 156C) were Scandinavian Modern instead of Mies's own designs, and for that reason the house was not widely published as an epitome of the Machine-Age idiom. But as a minimal, atticless, basementless, suspended industrial object—an object that is ineffably serene, precisely conceived, and meticulous in detail—the house is an archetypal image of the plug-in unit that spurred the design imaginations of the next two decades. "Architecture is the will of an epoch translated into space," Mies wrote.[5]

Johnson's Glass House   In 1949 Philip Johnson completed his Glass House in New Canaan, Connecticut (see Figure 157B). Designed for his own use in 1947, the Glass House was widely published immediately and brought an eye-opening new image of lightness, transparency, freedom, and the end of the Victorian era of hideaway window draperies.

Not only are interior and architecture of the Glass House one and the same, but the exterior landscape became the wall decoration of historical tradition. Set

157A. Philip Johnson. Plan, Glass House. New Canaan, Connecticut. 1949. *Illustration from* Selected Writings of Philip Johnson *(Japan: ADA Edita Tokyo, 1979).*

157B. Philip Johnson. Living room, Glass House. New Canaan, Connecticut. 1949. *Photograph courtesy Philip Johnson, Architect.*

off by its machine-image black-steel structural frame, this transparency seemed the ultimate realization of the glass-architecture aesthetic as well as of Frank Lloyd Wright's early interpenetration of interior and exterior.

Inside, the single space—56 by 32 by 10 feet 6 inches high, which is set on a concrete slab on grade—contains living and dining areas, kitchen, and bedroom; each is set off from the other by walnut storage-cabinet dividers. The "room divider" became a motif of the next several years. Only the bath is separate and enclosed, being incorporated into a brick cylinder along with a fireplace. Heating is provided by radiant electrical heating in both the floor and the ceiling.

The original furnishings (see Figure 157B) were a compendium of the classic designs of Mies and Breuer from the 1920s—Barcelona and Brno chairs in natural pigskin, and the Mies couch and bolster in black nylon, which Johnson had acquired in 1930, sitting on a white-wool carpeted island on the highly waxed dark brick floor itself. The glass walls were shielded, when required, by sliding panels of fabric, which were hung in flat sections of natural-color pandanus cloth reminiscent of Japanese shoji screens. To enrich these furnishings, Johnson displayed a sculpture of two female figures by Elie Nadelman and a painting attributed to Poussin. A tall wrought-iron candelabrum, designed by Johnson, originally stood near the fireplace cylinder to add a further touch of the patina that was so much desired during the late 1940s.

In the bedroom area the bed was covered in a quilt of bottle-green raw silk; the desk top was covered in black leather; the tubular Brno Chair in natural calf-skin; and Breuer's Laccio Stool in black leather. Johnson spoke much of the historical background of the house, and these historical overtones contributed to a large part of what were seen as the timelessness and accessibility of the house for non-Modernists.

Mies's Lakeshore Drive Apartments   From 1949 to 1951 Mies was working on his first pair of curtain-wall apartment towers in Chicago on Lakeshore Drive. These were the first realizations of his high-rise curtain-wall schemes of 1921–22, and they were, essentially, stacked versions of the Farnsworth House in different configurations. Except for the planning of the apartments and the finishing of the lobby spaces, those apartment interiors were little known compared with his exterior architecture, until the 1970s, when apartments began to be recreated faithfully to the Miesian idiom. Meanwhile, other disciples were reinterpreting Miesian architecture for corporate towers.

Skidmore, Owings & Merrill

The architectural firm of Skidmore, Owings & Merrill (SOM), which had been initiated in 1936, began to develop its design department in 1945 for the interiors of Cincinnati's Terrace Plaza Hotel. It was the beginning of new interior design departments in large architectural offices; this development was brought about by the desire to have an integrated approach—total design—in the Modern idiom.

Benjamin Baldwin was in charge of the hotel's interior design; with him were Natalie DeBlois and Davis Allen, who later directed interior design in SOM's New York office. The department designed everything that went into the hotel—furniture, fabrics, china, match folders, and uniforms. The hotel was Modern—though not yet in the full Miesian idiom that SOM was to develop in the 1950s.

The Terrace Plaza Hotel was also one of the first public buildings in America to follow the Bauhaus aim of incorporating the work of fine artists as well as interior craftsmen. The design included murals by Joan Miró and Saul Steinberg, a mobile sculpture by Alexander Calder, as well as furniture by Benjamin Baldwin and Davis Allen, fabrics by Cranbrook's Marianne Strengell, and metal lighting fixtures by Ward Bennett. The subsequent work of SOM was to make the Miesian idiom prominent throughout the world—both for its handling of exterior planning, massing, and structural elements, and for its interior design and finishing.

The Eames House

One other house of the late 1940s confirmed the machine imagery of the Modern idiom. The Eames House (1949) in Pacific Palisades, California, by Charles and his wife Ray Eames, was another metal-and-glass house; but it incorporated aspects of California informality and found objects in the Dada-Surrealism vein (see Figure 158).

The Eameses constructed their house of standard items from manufacturers' catalogues—steel columns, open-web metal joists, windows, and metal siding, as well as transparent and translucent glass. They assembled these components into a Mondrianesque image of differently colored and textured rectangles that had straightforward sophistication and a light gridded rhythm reminiscent of traditional Japanese houses. The Eames house design was a rare example of architects making architecture and interiors out of specified rather than designed components—selecting and arranging, rather than redesigning every element. It was a model for future architecture, but it was not the principal model that architects of the day elected to emulate.

The interior of the Eames house was furnished with their own plywood chair and case-piece designs. The shelving units manipulated the spidery-wire aesthetic of the late 1940s by exploiting the tensile qualities of lightweight steel wire as bracing. Filled with plants and collections of objects (some of them South Amer-

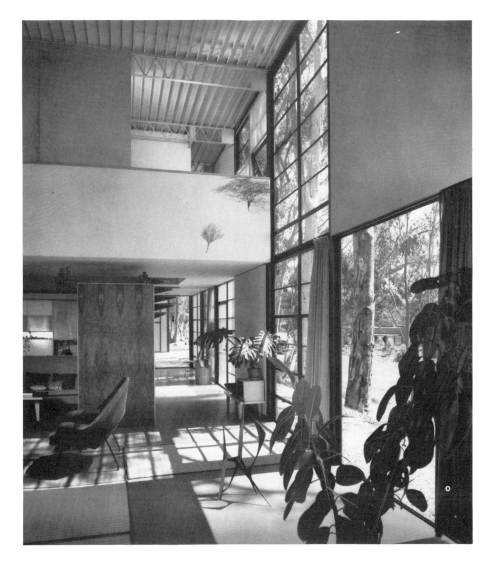

ican), Eames's furniture, and Noguchi's paper-lantern lighting, the Eames House interior became another prototypical image of Miesian design. Along with the Case Study house for John Etenza by Eames and Saarinen, it was a less rigid and formal image than that of Mies or Johnson.

The Bay Region Style

In California at this time there also emerged a local idiom based on the earlier houses of Bernard Maybeck and Greene & Greene (see Chapter 11) called the Bay Region style. It vied with the formalism of International Modern by offering informal living and patios. The houses of architects William B. Wurster, Harwell Hamilton Harris, Gregory Ain, J. R. Davidson, and Rafael Soriano made them leaders of this movement, which featured relaxed planning and natural wood textures that were a West Coast equivalent to the contemporaneous houses of Gropius and Breuer. Richard Neutra and Rudolph Schindler (see Chapters 12 and 13) continued their more structurally crisp California houses, finishing their interiors in exposed plywood sheeting, built-in storage units, and the new 1940s furniture.

Paul T. Frankl, from Vienna, and Paul Laszlo, who had come from Hungary in the 1930s, also worked in this California Modern idiom. Boxy square furnishings

159. Paul T. Frankl. Residence in California. 1940s. *Photograph by Julius Shulman.*

of reeded or dowel-paneled wood reiterated the bamboo motif in Modern terms (see Figure 159). The California industrial designer Kem Weber also designed reeded walls and modernistic furnishings, such as for the Bismarck Hotel (1944). Some of the forms of these designs had the lingering air of Streamlining, but the aim was to follow the Modern tenet of accepting, as the only ornamentation, the textures of natural materials.

Concurrently, two furniture makers on the East Coast formed a link with this Bay Region style through their continuation of the California Arts and Crafts tradition of the earlier part of the century. George Nakashima and Wharton Esherick made furniture by hand; both worked in a sculptural, somewhat rustic aesthetic that recalled their own native regions and backgrounds.

Wharton Esherick (1887–1974) was born in Philadelphia and studied at the School of Industrial Art there and at the Pennsylvania Academy of Fine Art. From the 1920s onward he continued the Arts and Crafts tradition, operating a crafts shop at Paoli, Pennsylvania. His work suggested a combination of Windsor, William Morris, and Early American spindleback chairs. Esherick developed a sinuous, sublimely refined line that gained him the reputation of "dean of twentieth-century American woodworkers."

George Nakashima (1905–), born in Spokane, Washington, studied architecture at the University of Washington and at the Massachusetts Institute of Technology. He first worked in the architecture firm of Antonin Raymond in Tokyo and India. From the mid-1940s he designed chairs and other furniture in New Hope, Pennsylvania, working in an idiom that suggested an Early American heritage as well as traditional Japanese forms. He also designed furniture for Herman Miller Inc.

The furniture of both designers was eagerly sought-after as an alternative to clinical machine-imagery Modern furniture. Their delicate lines and graceful intensification of the graining of natural woods enhanced interiors for the next several decades.

"Traditional" versus "Contemporary"

World War II affected American decorating along with the rest of life. Many of the new generation of male decorators went off to serve in the armed forces. William Pahlmann directed a camouflage school for the Air Force; also in attendance were theater designers Jo Mielziner, Donald Oenslager, and display designer Tom Lee, who would later become a prominent designer of hotel interiors and exhibitions. The effect of theater, display, and camouflage on American interior design has not yet been adequately explored.

At home, during the war, Mrs. Henry Parish II moved into an apartment in New York City and, with several colleagues, formed the Budget Decorators. Eleanor McMillen Brown organized exhibitions of antique furniture; after the war she exhibited contemporary French furniture.

The prominent American decorators of the decade were George Stacey, McMillen Inc., Mrs. Henry Parish II, William Pahlmann, Edward Wormley, Valerian Rybar, Bertha Schaefer, Eleanor LeMaire, Elizabeth Draper, Sarah Hunter Kelly, Joseph B. Platt, Joseph Mullen, and Billy Baldwin. Mabel Schamberg practiced in Chicago; and in California, Frances Elkins worked toward a California regionalism. Other prominent interior designers in the 1940s were Paul Laszlo, Paul T. Frankl, Robsjohn-Gibbings, and James Amster.

The spread of Modernism in the United States did not bring the end of historicism. Decorators working in the historical and period-room tradition continued to explore different periods and combinations to renew their direction. Diane Tate and Marian Hall recreated rooms in the Robert Adam idiom and also designed ship interiors. McMillen Inc. explored earlier eighteenth-century English decoration furnished with Sheraton and Hepplewhite pieces.

The beginning of a Regency revival was apparent. A Victorian revival was also witnessed, perhaps inspired by the film version of *Gone With the Wind*—the settings of which had been furnished by Joseph B. Platt, who also wielded influence as decoration consultant to *House & Garden*.

Rooms with dark-green walls—forest green—became a popular scheme during the 1940s. Green walls were a trademark of Elsie de Wolfe, who also continued her use of leopard-patterned chintz and a white chintz with green fern fronds. Among many others who adopted deep greens were Thedlow, Dorothy Draper, and Billy Baldwin.

A rich new array of fabrics, wallpapers, and furniture became available. Colonel Roger and Mrs. Zelina Brunschwig became mainstays of interior designers. The search for the new meant not espousing the Modern idiom, but trying the untried—previously not-revived historical periods, innovative directions, uncommon color combinations, and different textures. Surrealism enjoyed another wave of popularity after the war: disembodied hands went public as sconces; the disembodied eye was taken up by the vanguard, Dali included. Billy Baldwin wrote of the second half of the 1940s, "Decorating in America was just about as emotional an art as it ever has been."[6]

Design Education

A new educational influence on interior designers came about with Hope Foote, who was appointed chairman of the department of interior design at the University of Washington. She brought a new vitality to the Pacific Northwest, which had not been prominent in interior design circles before.

In 1940 the New York School of Applied and Fine Arts was renamed the Parsons School of Design, after its past president, Frank Alvah Parsons. Van Day Truex was appointed president of Parsons, bringing a new fame to the school that had been the principal educator of New York traditional decorators since the early part of the century. Truex had been a painter and knew the art world. As a teacher and editor of taste, he brought the life of creative people to his students and directed them to travel, look, feel, and try the new. He emphasized historical accuracy, drawing, and experimentation, and set the direction for a whole generation of designers.

During those years, shop window design became a major activity—some of the windows were considered art-form tableaux. They greatly influenced other designers as well as the public. Among the windows that people flocked to see every time they were changed were those at the shops of Rose Cumming, Greeff Fabrics, James Pendleton, Roslyn Rosier, and Jarvis House. Henry Callahan continued the tradition at Lord & Taylor. It was almost a necessary opening-night activity to see these new ideas.

Influential Designers

Dorothy Draper

At the height of her career in the 1940s, Dorothy Draper was in the tradition of "lady decorators," but her work was primarily in commercial buildings, especially stores and hotels. Her design of the public rooms Camellia House for the Drake Hotel in Chicago (1940–41) demonstrated her flamboyant neo-Baroque trademarks: large-scale, deeply sculpted, white plaster ornaments—volutes and scroll moldings, cartouches, and borders composed of such motifs as leaves, feathers, and shells.

Her restaurants often featured these overscaled decorations—including mirrors, chandeliers, and borders for doors and windows—against dark-green or burgundy walls. Here was English–French Baroque decoration blown up to an even larger scale, remaining ungilded and all white, like some Surrealist negative (though she would not have thought so), yet somehow immediately accessible to the public as well as to designers. It was a distinctive innovation.

Dorothy Draper's influence was popularized through her position as design consultant for the *Good Housekeeping* magazine studio from 1939 to 1946. John B. Wisner was her assistant from 1941 to 1946. During that time (1943–44) she designed the 46th Street Theater in New York and the Mayflower Hotel in Washington, D.C. In planning the guest rooms for the Mayflower Hotel, Dorothy Draper's goal—as it had been with slightly earlier hotel projects of hers—was to change the appearance of the conventional twin-bedded room of the day. Instead, she made them look more like sitting rooms.

To achieve the sitting-room effect, Draper placed standard twin beds away from the walls, like conventional facing sofas. Boxsprings and mattresses were fitted with a backrest, one armrest, and bolsters; the entire unit was covered in upholstery fabric rather than customary bedspread material. Sometimes these upholstered beds were hinged at the front edge of the armrest so that they could be swung out to facilitate making up of the beds. Lacquered cabinets served as end tables and also provided for pillow storage. These were among the early convertible sofa-beds. The innovation became standard in hotel design during World War II, when the shortage of hotel rooms for meetings and business appointments made the use of guest rooms as meeting rooms necessary.

Almost all of Dorothy Draper's innovative ideas were related to her belief that decoration was an important factor in the promotion of the hotel or property under consideration. That was perhaps what made her work so well suited to public spaces. At one hotel she convinced the management to put the unusually high cost of maintaining elaborate muslin casement curtains into the advertising budget.

Dorothy Draper also began to use wall stencils to increase the potential of her overscaled decorative elements. These were developed to match her large plaster elements, since no large-patterned wallpapers were then available. Floral patterns, connecting ribbons or scrolls, or overall damask-like patterns were stenciled on canvas-covered walls that had been painted white. In this way she influenced the market style and marketing.

Her interiors for the Quitandinha Hotel in Petropolis, outside Rio, Brazil (1946), continued this tradition (see Figure 160) with what seemed like even larger-scale checkerboard marble floors; heavy white moldings on black doors; bold white consoles, sconces, and chandeliers; cabbage-rose chintz; and red and green combinations. When people said the latter looked like Christmas, Draper replied that she wanted rooms to look bright and happy. In 1947, when the Greenbrier resort hotel in White Sulphur Springs, West Virginia, was reclaimed from its wartime use as a government hospital, Draper redecorated it with her trademark motifs, in an overall scheme of white and green. It seemed at the time like the springtime after the war. For this project Glenn Boyles, teacher and illustrator, was her chief designer.

160. Dorothy Draper. Quitandinha Hotel. Petropolis, Brazil, 1946. *Photograph by Studio Rembrandt, courtesy John B. Wisner.*

Frances Elkins

In California, mostly for houses in Pebble Beach and San Francisco, Frances Elkins continued to develop a mixture of unlikely and wide-ranging periods and furnishings. In her own adobe house in Monterey, with its ceiling of rough white-painted boards, Frances Elkins, in 1945, had her brother, David Adler, install a Georgian fireplace and cornice. She added these to her Louis XIII chairs, Sheraton consoles, Regency stools, contemporary sofas, Chinese carpets, and Venetian prints.

In the bedroom, French provincial furniture was covered with red and white *toile de Jouy*. Biedermeier pieces were used in the foyer; Directoire wallpaper by Zuber was used in the upstairs hallway; and elsewhere, sculpted white-plaster shell-like forms were used as up lights. Prominent colors were yellow with turquoise; and white with pink, red, and gray. Her sophisticated and international mix of periods brought freshness, originality, and flamboyance to the historical correctness of previous decades.

During the 1940s Frances Elkins worked with California craftspeople to develop an appropriate style for Northern California. Leaning toward Mexico for inspiration, she used Marian Dorn's heavy handwoven rugs, hand-tooled leather, and pottery instead of porcelain. She worked with Dorothy Liebes on coarse-woven fabrics shot with shimmering metal threads to texturize her spaces. She commissioned Tony Duquette to design his first console of antlers. She had chairs carved in Queen Anne style, but finished in bleached oak. She had terrazzo-topped coffee tables made. And she played with pattern-on-pattern (see Figure 161), which may have inspired Billy Baldwin's admiration. It was another approach toward regionalism, corresponding to the West Coast's Bay Region style.

161. Frances Elkins. Winslow residence. Pebble Beach, California. 1949–50. *Photograph by Julius Shulman.*

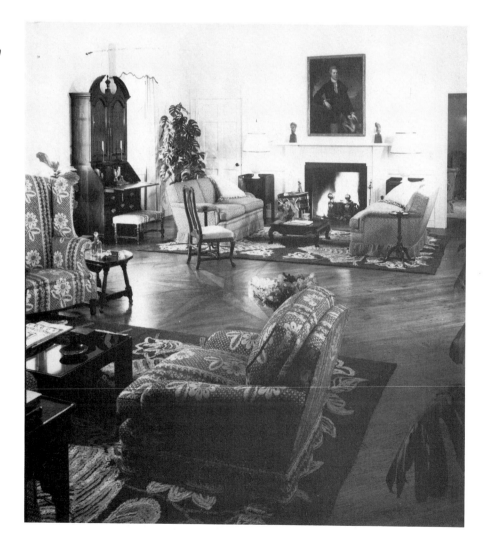

Hers was a personal anthology of periods that was freer than the strict historical recreations of many of her contemporaries. This eclecticism became the mainstream direction of decorating in the next decade.

Ruby Ross Wood

The living room that Ruby Ross Wood designed for herself and her husband in the 1940s was "an entirely red room," as Billy Baldwin described it. Floors were "carpeted wall to wall in a dark damson color"; walls were strié, the color of "rich red currant"; curtains were "ruby-red satin"; tufted Victorian furniture was upholstered in "the color of a Harvard-red carnation"; and objects "ran the whole spectrum of red, with bright punctuations of scarlet."[7] It was not the first red room, but its pervasive color scheme established a tradition in many designers' minds for the next several decades.

Billy Baldwin

Just after World War II the first published credits for "William Baldwin of Ruby Ross Wood" began to appear. Billy Baldwin had become an assistant in Ruby Ross Wood's decorating firm in 1935. In the early 1940s he served in the U.S. Army. When he returned to Ruby Ross Wood, he began his series of residential interiors for the theater producer Gilbert Miller and his wife Kitty Bache Miller. The design of his own apartment (see Figure 162) in 1946 featured dark, glossy green walls—

162. Billy Baldwin. Own living room. New York City. 1946. *Photograph by Danny Wann, courtesy Condé-Nast Publications Inc.*

the color of a wet gardenia leaf, he wrote—with curtains of emerald-green silk, and furniture slipcovered in darker-green textured silk.

Billy Baldwin was also associated with the combination of dark-brown walls and furniture, enlivened by large black-and-white drawings on the walls and green accents—occasional tables and lamp bases. Another of his combinations featured pink walls, white woodwork, and a bold black-and-white runner on a black floor.

"Transitional Modern" and "Contemporary"

In the 1940s the decorating field began to veer toward Modern design without full commitment or espousal of the purgative, machine-based idiom. It produced an interest in a wider range and mixture of historical periods, broadening the more strict adherence of older decorators to single periods or styles for each room. It also admitted the value of Scandinavian Modern and, later in the decade, of Italian Modern to soften the German-French Machine-Age idiom.

This leaning also produced some new American furniture designs with more varied eclecticism, both somewhat pared down and calling on period styles beyond the eighteenth-century canon. This furniture was a compromise to make the Modern idiom acceptable to a broader public, and it came to be called Contemporary. Among the designers whose work was in this middle ground were William Pahlmann, Edward Wormley, T. H. Robsjohn-Gibbings, and Russel Wright.

William Pahlmann

For the first two years of the decade William Pahlmann continued his series of flamboyant display rooms at Lord & Taylor in New York (see Figure 163). After serving in the U.S. Air Force from 1942 to 1946 as director of a camouflage school, Pahlmann opened his own design firm in New York. He went on to design department stores and boutiques, restaurants and nightclubs, country clubs and hotels,

163. William Pahlmann. Model room for Lord & Taylor's "Pahlmann Peruvian" promotion. New York City. 1942. *Photograph courtesy William Pahlmann.*

showrooms and offices, hospitals and apartment-house lobbies, as well as residential projects. Bonwit Teller's president, Walter Hoving, was a regular client, for whom he designed six or seven stores.

Pahlmann's expressed aims were to blend modern living with tradition. He designed a house for himself that combined a 200-year-old Chinese table, a recent Charles Eames chair, a brass Moorish brazier, and a Louis XVI armchair upholstered in sky-blue leather. He was extravagant, sometimes outrageous in this eclecticism, but he was influential in opening the doors and relaxing the rules of preceding decades. It was typical of the expansion of influences in the 1940s.

During the 1940s William Pahlmann continued to gain attention for his use of color. He was influenced by the colors of Dorothy Liebes and was credited with using the first of her window blinds in New York. He especially used a blue-green that came to be called "Pahlmann blue"; he was always opposed to dead-white and used off-white instead. In 1940 he presented Harlem pink, Regency green, and white; sulphur yellow, olive green, and rosy red; and brick, bottle green, rawhide, and bleached cypress. Pahlmann Peruvian in 1941 featured Cuzco blue, lime, fuschia, deep blue, and whitewash; another of his Peruvian combinations was avocado, lime, plum, tan orange, and white. Such color names led to the term "decorator colors." After the war he was associated with medium cerulean, lime, magenta pink, and white, as well as deep sage, ripe persimmon, and French blue. Each of these color combinations was for a single room. Together, they indicate both the Pahlmann palette and the progression of the decade. Pahlmann served as president of the New York chapter of AID from 1948 to 1950.

Edward Wormley

Another prominent transitional designer—the term is his—was Edward Wormley. He continued to design interiors—ranging from residences to showrooms and

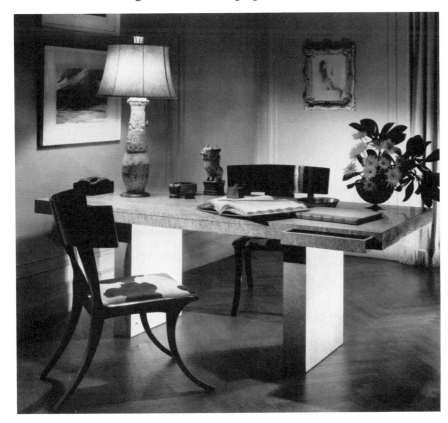

164. Edward Wormley. Own office. New York City. 1945. The Klismos Chair is Dunbar's reproduction in 1939 of Jean-Michel Frank's reconstruction of a chair measured from a bas relief at the Acropolis. *Photograph by F. M. Demarest, courtesy Edward Wormley.*

offices (see Figure 164)—but made his major contribution designing furniture for Dunbar.

During the war he headed the Furniture Unit of the Office of Price Administration in Washington, and in 1944 he opened his own firm in New York City. There he continued to design furniture for Dunbar and Drexel and lighting for Lightolier. His showroom for Lightolier at the end of the decade had a mahogany wall that was detailed as masonry-like blocks that decreased in size as they rose to the ceiling. This forced perspective was designed to inflect the viewer's attention to the ceiling-hung fixtures on display; it was a device that presaged the interior techniques of the 1970s.

Wormley aimed to combine traditional forms with Modern ones, especially with Scandinavian Modern, and produced what became known as Contemporary furniture designed to appeal to a widely divergent buying public. He called this "transitional design." His designs were directed to mass-production techniques and changing markets. He was notable for producing line after line of new pieces year after year—for thirty-seven years. Few other designers of the period demonstrated this kind of professional perseverance, endurance, and productivity.

T. H. Robsjohn-Gibbings

During the war the individualist designer T. H. Robsjohn-Gibbings participated in camouflage experiments at Columbia University, and was vehement in expressing his views on design: *Goodbye, Mr. Chippendale* and *Mona Lisa's Mustache* (see Suggested Reading) were among his best-selling books. He could not easily be categorized as a decorator in the American tradition of historicism, because his work was so vanguard.

165. T. H. Robsjohn-Gibbings. Chest with clapboard-like drawer pulls. 1941. *Photograph from* Interior Design *(May 1961).*

In 1941 he designed store interiors for Neiman-Marcus. In 1942 he designed a living room with shadow-blue walls against which sat a dark-gray upholstered sofa with fuschia cushions; these were flanked by Louis XV chairs covered in violet fabric. That color scheme was to influence designers for a decade. A coffee table he designed in 1942 had a free-form glass top in the then typical mode—standing on three legs with their stretcher running along the floor. It was another of the amoeboid designs that epitomized the early part of the decade. A living room he designed in 1944 with a stripped and molding-less envelope had bare floors and red-lacquered bamboo-framed furniture covered in a printed fabric with a large-scale tropical leaf design. The Hawaii-Rio motif was thereby established.

Robsjohn-Gibbings designed his first mass-produced furniture for the Widdicomb Furniture Company in 1946. His designs included bleached-oak desks and chairs. The desks had glass tops; the chairs were slung with ash-gray leather. Other pieces were of pale walnut; some case pieces had flush doors; others had handle-less drawers designed like overlapping clapboards for the drawer pulls (see Figure 165). His coffee-table designs were of comparatively distended length. There was always a strength of severity and elegance about his work.

Russel Wright

Another individualist designer, Russel Wright, could not be easily categorized as either an industrial designer, decorator, or Modernist. He worked to bring Modern design to the American public. Exempted from armed service in the 1940s because of age and poor eyesight, Russel Wright, with his designer-wife Mary, continued to design interiors, furnishings, and industrial products.

In the spirit of Modernism's goal of social improvement, though stylistically opposed to the Bauhaus, Wright conceived a complete line of home furnishings designed and produced by a cooperative of sixty-five artists, craftsmen, and manufacturers, and accessible to middle-income families. It was called the American Way. It never attained either high quality of design or, despite considerable press coverage, popular success. The war killed it.

Among the Wrights' interiors in the 1940s were a redesigned floor for Saks' 34th Street store, their own house in New York, and their country house, Dragon Rock. They designed kitchen appliances, glassware, table linens, aluminum and pewter serving pieces for the dinner table, plastic trays and colanders, and a line of free-form "art" ceramics. In addition, they designed a line of stainless flatware with plastic handles, four lines of furniture, numerous lighting fixtures, and ceramic dinnerware. Their stackable Iroquois Casual China of 1946 was produced in colors that were typical of the decade—ice blue, forest green, avocado, and lemon yellow; it was strongly resistant to breakage and became widely popular until 1959.

At the end of the 1940s Russel Wright's Meladur melamine plastic dinnerware was put into production. It was a popular American symbol throughout the decade, showing the importance of new materials and the importance of industrial designers.

The Low-Cost Furniture Competition

In 1948, because of the continuing need for less expensive, well-designed, and well-made furnishings after the war, the Museum of Modern Art in New York exhibited the results of the "International Competition for Low-Cost Furniture Design," directed by Edgar Kaufmann, Jr. First prize went to Don R. Knorr of San Francisco and Georg Leowald of Berlin-Frohnau. Knorr's chair, made by Knoll Associates, was a truncated cone of sheet metal on wire legs. Leowald's seating design had a molded plastic back sliding in metal grooves. Charles Eames shared second prize for a molded fiberglass chair, made by Herman Miller; it was

166. Charles Eames and Ray Eames. Molded plastic armchair for Herman Miller Inc. 1949. *Photograph courtesy The Metropolitan Museum of Art, New York City. Lent by I. Wistar Morris, III.*

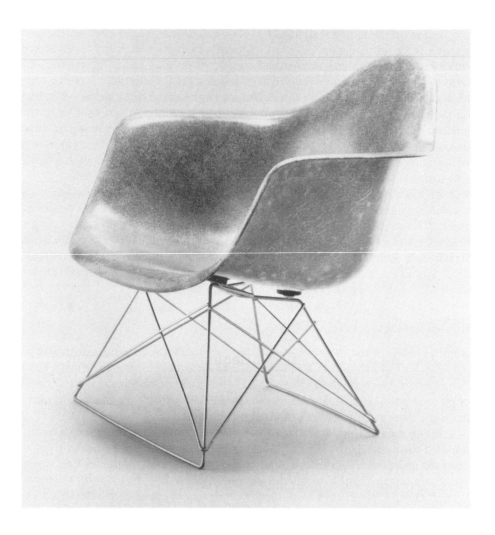

a development of the 1940 competition winner with Saarinen (see Figure 166). British designers Robin Day, Clive Latimer, and Ernest Race also won awards and mentions.

The Italian Influence

At the end of the decade a new wave of interior design and furnishings began to come from Italy. Those designs had a spare, sculptural quality that was soon to force out the heavy square look of the early part of the decade. This furniture, along with other Italian industrial designs and a new vogue of filmmaking, brought glamor and admiration back to Italy once again, making Italy a deeply ingrained influence on the design world for the next four decades.[8]

Italian craftsmanship was revived by a number of collective studios of artisans in Milan and Rome, aided by a cooperation among big business, small workshops, and progressive designers and spread by triennial exhibitions in Milan. The design of Olivetti typewriters by Marcello Nizzoli (1948–49) was an inspiration for designers of furnishings. Modern furnishings were based on craftsmanship with wood in natural finishes and with sometimes sinuous, spidery, and relaxed lines. Structural elements of steel exploited the potential thinness and distendedness.

This new Italian design approach indicated a clear formal logic, yet it had a sculptural freedom that was spontaneous-looking, playfully witty, and light-hearted.

Wire-hung stairs and bookcases by Franco Albini, and wire-like bases for tables and desks made of slim metal rods or bars, expressed the discontinuity and the atomic-molecular idiom of the decade. Sculptural reflector lighting was often attached to poles in a manner that was more reminiscent of display and exhibition techniques than of traditional interior design. Paintings and drawings, too, were hung or mounted this way in residential and commercial interiors in Italy.

Most influential on Americans was the use of Modern furnishings alongside Baroque sculptures with antique patina, or the combination of handcraft with machine-craft; even Renaissance and Baroque paintings were supported on exposed metal standards, some with construction-like scale and texture. In this latter direction, the poetic juxtapositions of Carlo Scarpa (1902–78) in restoring museums and in museum installation design became the supreme inspiration. Prominent Italian designers at this time also included Gio Ponti and the firm of BBPR (Banfi, Belgiojoso, Peressutti, Rogers)—all of whom were architects. Furniture by other Italian designers, such as Tempestini, Parisi, Peretti, and Carlo Mollino, whose furniture designs aimed to be fantastic, captured the attention of American interior designers. Italian sculptors of this period, such as Agenore Fabbri, also influenced American interior designers. Italian design could not be ignored for the next three decades.

The End of an Era and a New Beginning

The Last of "The Ladies"

The year 1950 saw the death of three influential designers: Sybil Colefax, Ruby Ross Wood, and Lady Mendl—Elsie de Wolfe. Sir Charles and Lady Mendl had moved to Los Angeles during World War II. There she pursued her Louis XV and Louis XVI adaptations, often in collaboration with Los Angeles artist Tony Duquette, adding such personal touches as a drapery-framed mirror over a fireplace, along with contemporary fabrics and carpets. Their house in Beverly Hills had one room tented with green-and-white-striped awnings, another room with a lattice-work ceiling; and she used black floors, wrought-iron furniture painted white, and leopard-skin chintz upholstery. In 1950, at the age of eighty-five, Elsie de Wolfe died.

Frances Elkins would die in 1953. Syrie Maugham continued her exploitation of white, but enriched it with antique wallpapers and furniture of high quality, adding tufted Victorian loveseats and chairs to her trademarks; she was to die in 1955. Nancy McClelland died in 1959. It was the end of the first generation of "lady decorators."

The Arrival of Air Conditioning

A new technological age was about to dawn. General use of air conditioning was to begin around 1950 with the designs in New York for the United Nations headquarters and Lever House, the headquarters office building of Lever Brothers. Residential use became widespread at this same time, after the development of a sufficiently small air-conditioning unit.

Air conditioning had been developing since the turn of the century. The inventor of air conditioning, Willis Havilland Carrier, patented "dew-point control" in 1906. This permitted the control of atmospheric humidity by raising or lowering temperature. Carrier devised his method by observing fog. First developed to provide fresh air in factory and industrial environments, some form of air conditioning had been installed in Frank Lloyd Wright's Larkin Building (1904) and in the New York Stock Exchange (1904). Shortly thereafter, air-conditioning systems were developed for hotel dining rooms and ballrooms, and, in the 1920s, Pullman cars and theaters began to be air-conditioned. Graumann's Metropolitan Theater in Los Angeles was air-conditioned in 1922 by Willis Havilland Carrier. So it was the movies that first introduced the public to air conditioning for comfort, as opposed to industrial efficiency.

The first office buildings to be air-conditioned were the Milam Building (1928) in San Antonio, Texas, by architect George Willis and engineer M. D. Diver; and the PSFS building in Philadelphia (1932–34) by Howe & Lescaze (see Chapter 13). At that time Radio City Music Hall was also air-conditioned. By 1936 lounge, dining, and sleeping cars on major long-distance trains had already been air-conditioned; and by the end of the 1930s department stores and shops across the country began to be air-cooled. The availability of fluorescent lighting at the end of the 1930s made lower heat loads possible, and therefore lowered the cost of air conditioning. So all was ready for the development of general air conditioning by the end of the 1940s.

Residential interiors also had to wait until around 1950 for a compact air-conditioning unit to be developed. Experiments with residential air conditioning had been going on since 1929, when General Electric installed a room cooler in Carrier's own house. Other isolated experiments in residential air conditioning were made in the Chicago area in the early 1930s. In 1932 Carrier's Atmospheric Cabinet was marketed, but it was cumbersome and expensive and designed to be installed in the cellar. It took until 1946 to 1948 for smaller through-wall air-conditioning units to be developed by the McQuay Company and General Electric. Air conditioning did not reach New York office buildings until 1947.

By the 1950s, air conditioning was readily available for all interiors. A new kind of interior comfort had arrived for the rest of the twentieth century—and also another technological and design challenge for the designers of interiors. When the next decade opened, the full range of the Modern dream—Futurist, Expressionist, and Bauhaus—was available to Modern American designers of interiors.

Suggested Reading

Baldwin, Billy. *Billy Baldwin Remembers*. New York: Harcourt Brace Jovanovich, 1974.

Banham, Reyner. *The Architecture of the Well-Tempered Environment*. London: The Architectural Press, 1969. Chicago: University of Chicago Press, 1969.

Darling, Sharon. *Chicago Furniture: Art, Craft, and Industry 1833–1983*. New York: W. W. Norton, 1983.

Design in America: The Cranbrook Vision, 1925–1950. New York: Harry N. Abrams, 1983.

Design Quarterly. "Nelson/Eames/Girard/Propst, The Design Process at Herman Miller." Minneapolis: Walker Art Center, 1975.

Drexler, Arthur. *Charles Eames*. New York: The Museum of Modern Art, 1973.

Emery, Sherman, ed. 50th Anniversary Issue, *Interior Design*, April 1982.

Gueft, Olga. "Two Decades of Interiors: 1940–1960," *Interiors*. November 1960.

Hennessey, William J. *Russel Wright*. Cambridge: MIT Press, 1983.

Herdeg, Klaus. *The Decorated Diagram: Harvard Architecture and the Failure of the Bauhaus Legacy*. Cambridge: MIT Press, 1983.

Hiesinger, Kathryn B., and George H. Marcus, eds. *Design Since 1945*. Philadelphia: The Philadelphia Museum of Art, 1983.

Hillier, Bevis. *The Decorative Arts of the Forties and Fifties Austerity Binge*. New York: Clarkson N. Potter, 1975.

Jacobus, John M., Jr. "Architecture, American Style, 1920–45," *American Art*. New York: Prentice-Hall, Harry N. Abrams, 1979.

———. "Postwar Architecture, 1945–60," loc. cit.

Kaufmann, Edgar, Jr., "Interior Design: Architecture or Decoration?" *Progressive Architecture*. October 1962, pp. 141–44.

Mang, Karl. *History of Modern Furniture*. New York: Harry N. Abrams, 1979.

McCoy, Esther. *The Second Generation*. Layton, Utah: Gibbs M. Smith, 1984.

Meadmore, Clement. *The Modern Chair*. New York: Van Nostrand Reinhold, 1975.

Rae, Christine. *Knoll au Louvre*. New York: Knoll International, 1971.

Robsjohn-Gibbings, T. H. *Goodbye, Mr. Chippendale*. New York: Alfred A. Knopf, 1944.

———. *Mona Lisa's Mustache: A Dissection of Modern Art*. New York: Alfred A. Knopf, 1947.

The Architecture of Skidmore, Owings & Merrill, 1950–1962. New York: Frederick A. Praeger, 1963.

Notes

1. Arthur J. Pulos, *American Design Ethic: A History of Industrial Design to 1940* (Cambridge: MIT Press, 1983), p. 422. In the prewar period, hundreds of RCA television kits had been produced as early as 1928. The war halted production.

2. Edgar Kaufmann, Jr., "Interior Design: Architecture or Decoration?" *Progressive Architecture* (October 1962), p. 144.

3. Arthur Drexler, of the Museum of Modern Art in New York, made this statement without considering such late-nineteenth-century furniture designers as Henry Belter, George Hunzinger, or other inventors of ingenious multipurpose furniture.

4. Knoll's production of furniture designs from the Bauhaus period was of the most expensive custom variety. As such, it had nothing to do with the Bauhaus ideal of producing furniture for everyman at prices everyman could afford. The Barcelona furniture, of course, had nothing to do with the Bauhaus, except that Mies was to become its director shortly after the designs were completed.

5. Ludwig Mies van der Rohe, *Aphorisms on Architecture and Form* (1923); quoted in Philip Johnson, *Mies van der Rohe* (New York: The Museum of Modern Art, 1978), p. 188.

6. Billy Baldwin, quoted in *20th Century Decorating, Architecture, and Gardens*, ed. Mary Jane Pool (New York: Holt, Rinehart and Winston, 1980), p. 10.

7. Billy Baldwin, *Billy Baldwin Remembers* (New York: Harcourt Brace Jovanovich, 1974), p. 39f.

8. The first opportunity for most Americans to see the new Italian design was at a traveling exhibition titled "Italy at Work," which began its American tour at the Brooklyn Museum.

Chapter 15

1950–1960: The Triumph of Modernism in America

For American designers of interiors, confident of America's design leadership at last, it was, as the press said, "the fabulous fifties." The capital of the art world had shifted from Paris to New York. In politics the Iron Curtain had fallen across postwar Europe, creating a threatening and edgy coexistence; nevertheless, it was a decade of comparative peace. Economically—for Americans, at least—it was a decade of enormous prosperity. That prosperity fostered the largest building boom in American history—one that was to last twenty years. Together, these factors produced an ebullient optimism.

The boom was upward and outward. More Americans attended college than ever before, owing to the G.I. Bill of Rights; more Americans traveled to Europe than ever before, owing to new jet air travel that began in 1952. And more Americans built houses—the suburbanization of America continued uncontrolled. The baby boom that began in the late 1940s produced the coming need for more high schools; by the end of the 1950s schools could not be built fast enough.

In that building boom, at the beginning of the 1950s, the dreams of the first-generation Modernists came to fruition in the new wave of International-Style skyscrapers. In 1951 Mies at last built his thirty-year-old vision of a structural frame sheathed with a glass curtain wall in his 860 Lake Shore Drive Apartments in Chicago. Its lobbies were furnished with his Barcelona furniture of the late 1920s, which Knoll Associates had reintroduced in 1948.

Le Corbusier had built the first of the slab-like towers that had been fundamental to his garden-city vision: the Ministry of Education in Rio de Janeiro (1945). His second slab tower was the United Nations Secretariat, completed in 1950 in

New York, designed by a committee of international architects—including Sweden's Sven Markelius and Brazil's Oscar Niemeyer—with Le Corbusier as its recognized design progenitor, and Wallace K. Harrison as its director of planning and design committee chairman. By 1952 Le Corbusier had also realized his concrete apartment slab, the Unité d'Habitation in Marseilles, in which the apartment interiors reflected his 1920s admiration for ocean-liner compartments. It was in the 1950s that interior designers—rather than office managers, as had previously been the case—became involved in office interiors in skyscrapers.

Technological Advances in Interior Design

The technological advances resulting from the war set the nation on a dedicated technological path. Among the technical advances that most influenced interior design were the public availability of television, the further development and widespread use of synthetic materials, and the development of the suspended ceiling.

Plastics

By the mid-1950s synthetic fibers and permanent forming or shaping had brought a whole new world of manmade materials. Among them were plastic sheeting and panels, vinyl upholsteries and drapery fabrics, new artificial leathers and other coated textiles, and synthetic carpets by the mile. Plastics were used more and more broadly for chair frames, tables, and other furniture, and for every conceivable household equipment, utensil, furnishing, bibelot, and toy.

The situation raised a serious question that the plastics industry fumbled for a long time to answer: What was the inherent nature of plastic? Manufacturers seemed unable to accept the solid-colored, untextured nature of natural plastic, saying it had "no intrinsic nature." Instead, they used the new artificial material, largely, in imitation of natural materials—vinyl wood, vinyl stone or ceramic tile, vinyl tortoiseshell and suede, and so on.

For those brought up on the philosophy of honesty of materials, it was a painful time. Seemingly, only when plastic was used to approximate glass did the two approaches come together. Otherwise, there was imitation—or, what began to seem worse, the ubiquitous use of flecked, spotted, spattered, and otherwise patterned plastic panels and sheeting. In the popular sector flecked and speckled freeform patterns—amoebas, snowflakes, and boomerangs—appeared in plastics, fabrics, and objects. Plastic of all patterns had gold and silver flecks blown into it, as if it were mica. With the alleged purpose of "not showing dirt," these patterns were designed for those who could not bear the visual vacuum of plain blank walls in the International Style.

The 1950s became known as the Plastic Decade, a decade of exuberance to the point of silliness. It was an age that appreciated cuteness in objects and design, objects that were considered kitsch by many. Disneyland opened in California in 1955; and during the decade the excessive hotel designs in Miami Beach, such as the Fontainebleau by architect Morris Lapidus, were opened. Two-tone cars, clothes, and houses appeared. All these, however, were designed to appeal to the status symbolism of the popular market. The "Good Design" shows at New York's Museum of Modern Art, which were planned to counteract this unrefined vision, represented the attitudes of the decade's vanguard and its mania for modernity.

The Suspended Ceiling

Another widely influential innovation in interior design during the 1950s was the development of the suspended ceiling, which aided the building boom materially.

The suspended ceiling—now an accepted part of our vocabulary for commercial and institutional buildings—permitted the integration, for the first time, of mechanical systems and lighting systems into a finished ceiling surface. Like other developments, the suspended ceiling had not come about entirely without precedent. It derived from isolated attempts at concealing air-conditioning ducts on the one hand, and at concealing lighting fixtures on the other.

Early examples of concealed air conditioning began with the installation in the Kuhn Loeb Bank in New York (1906), where air-conditioning was concealed behind a glass-skylight-like ceiling. When Willis and Diver's Milam Building went up in San Antonio in 1928, with its air-conditioning ducts running in furred-down spaces above the corridors and conditioned air supplied through louvers over the office doors, something like a prototypal suspended ceiling had been achieved. But lighting was not yet a part of these schemes.

The concealment of lighting fixtures in ceilings and wall units had also been seen since the first decade of the century. Recessed lighting had been pioneered by Frank Lloyd Wright as early as the Robie House (1909). Drawing on this tradition in the mid-1920s, Rudolf Schindler's beach house for the Lovells (1926) incorporated lighting into vertical fin-like structures with alternating rectangles of light and opaque panels that historian Reyner Banham called "light-towers" and "light-ladders." Richard Neutra's Lovell House in Los Angeles of 1927 had a long, rectangular lighting unit suspended from the ceiling on thin cables; but its form, as a linear fixture running nearly 50 feet over bookcases and reading locations, also put it into the new tradition of lighting troffers.

During 1927–28 the Arizona Biltmore Hotel by Albert Chase McArthur, with Frank Lloyd Wright's influence and consultation, offered integrated and recessed lighting in glass-block-like units, similar to Wright's work and to Schindler's Lovell House light-towers. From 1924 to 1927 Erich Mendelsohn had designed indirect lighting concealed in open, linear coves along ceilings and walls; sometimes the coves were repeated continuously to achieve a linear, parallel-lined effect like Streamlining. In 1936 Frank Lloyd Wright used indirect lighting on the backlit, glass-tubed ceiling of the main office space of the S. C. Johnson & Son Administration Building.

None of these installations of air-conditioning or lighting, however, were yet integrated together into ceilings. The next development came in that still under-acclaimed pioneer among Modern skyscrapers—Howe & Lescaze's PSFS building in Philadelphia (1932). There, in the lobby areas, air-conditioning ducts were run in furred-down spaces in the ceilings, and conditioned air was supplied through ring-diffusers surrounding recessed lighting fixtures. It was the first step in combining air-conditioning outlets and lighting fixtures that became standard in the developed suspended ceiling.

Still one further element in the development of the suspended ceiling was the design of the ceiling surface itself. First came several systems of using the space between floor slab and bottom of open-web steel joists—either running ductwork and electrical lines through the space, or using the overall space as a plenum, in which the entire open area, without being ducted, is used to distribute conditioned air. By 1936 there were ceiling systems of perforated tiles to form the ceiling surface as a continuous diffusing outlet. These were the first suspended ceiling surfaces that permitted the integration of all these mechanical elements. Meanwhile, the black-painted ceiling with exposed but painted-out mechanical systems was the standard during the 1940s. In 1947 came the louvered or egg-crate suspended ceiling.

Around 1950 several versions of the fully integrated suspended ceiling appeared. The General Motors (GM) Technical Center by Saarinen, Saarinen & Associates opened in Warren, Michigan, in 1950, when Willis Carrier finished air-conditioning the United Nations Secretariat building in New York. Both buildings have overall suspended ceilings in the fully developed manner that became the standard for the next several decades. The GM Technical Center ceiling offers a highly flexible overall grid, the squares sometimes filled entirely by lighting louvers, sometimes by rectangular troffer-like lighting fixtures and opaque ceiling panels. At the United Nations Secretariat building, rectangular lighting troffers are set between square air-conditioning diffusers, both of which are recessed in a plain, white-tile ceiling surface. The variations and the refinements occupied designers of interiors for decades.

The development of the suspended ceiling led to increasingly comfortable year-round environments. It also led to a new design concentration for interior designers. Integrated suspended ceilings opened the door to the design of systems of partitions and furniture that were integrated with that ceiling and with the rest of the building. Such systems were to become the whetstone of the late-Miesian idiom. Based on clarity and articulation of individual parts and on alignment of each element with the overall building, partitioning systems became the new wheel— to be reinvented by the designers of architectural interiors for the next two decades. The goals of clarity and alignment, and the imagery of the grid, were, thenceforward, to be served as never before.

Formalism versus Functionalism   Here, in the development of the suspended ceiling, we see once again the battle between formalism and functionalism, which had divided the Bauhaus thirty years before. The honest functionalist exposure of mechanical systems, such as was demonstrated at the United Nations General Assembly building in its lobby (see Figure 167) and in its Trusteeship Council Chamber by Finn Juhl (1952–53), was in contradistinction to the concealment of all these functions behind a suspended ceiling, as in the United Nations Secretariat building. To the formalists these ceilings increased the possibility of a "clean"— the byword of the decade—aligned, and consistent interior. No other development at this time more clearly illustrates the different potentials of formalism versus functionalism. Again, for designers, there was a choice to be made between the two directions. In America in the 1950s, the formalists won out.

Functionalism was given lip service by the adoption of a single, universal formal system developed by Mies. "Form follows function" was the commandment of the decade. But it was variously interpreted—not only as "form should be derived from function," but also as "form merely comes after function." And the discussion lasted more than a decade. In fact, the forms and formalism of Mies, under the banner of functionalism, were adopted as the mainstream of mid-century Modernism. Formalism, which had been rejected, in principle, by the mainstream of early Modernism, came to be, in actuality, the first cause and crusade of the second generation of Modern designers.

The International Style: Triumph of the Modern Crusade

In the 1950s in America, the International Style was finally accepted by a wide spectrum of the population, becoming the adopted style of commerce and proclaiming the victory of Modernism over historicism/traditionalism. This mid-century Modernism focused on function, technology, and economy, with innovation and refinement in design as the means of improving the quality of people's lives. The pristine, purgative clean-lined Miesian aesthetic formed the mainstream of the decade. That idiom relied on overall, pervasive structure as the keystone, emphasizing clarity, regularity, and alignment more than the earlier International Style's irregular and dynamic features. The repetition of the square module was the standard form of both unification and visual pattern.

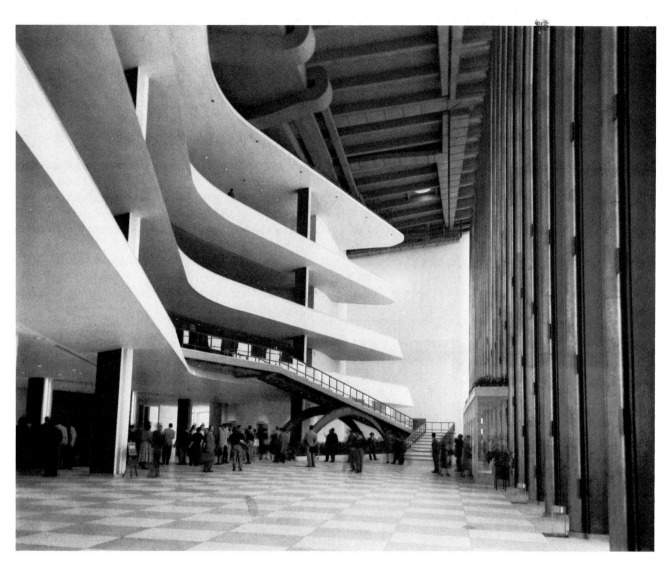

167. Le Corbusier, Wallace K. Harrison, Sven Markelius, and Oscar Niemeyer. Lobby, United Nations General Assembly building. New York City. 1952. *Photograph courtesy UNATIONS.*

The International Style of the 1950s varied, however, especially in its social goals, from the goals of the 1920s and 1930s. Earlier Internationalism had aimed to provide mass housing and better work environments for everyman. Mid-century American Internationalism was seen as creating palaces for the giants of commerce; and in the 1960s and 1970s this was considered a debasement of first-generation Modernism—despite the fact that better work environments had been provided for an entire generation. But the differences were also stylistic. The change had been evident immediately at the GM Technical Center, where a brighter range of colors and of ornamental detail was apparent.

In the office-building boom of the 1950s, which created the third generation of American skyscrapers, the new patrons were the rich giants of corporate enterprise. The building boom meant that new headquarters offices sprang up everywhere, creating a great demand for interior design services. Surprisingly, despite the example of Frank Lloyd Wright's Larkin Building and his S. C. Johnson & Son Administration Building, the design of general offices had been, through the 1940s, primarily the province of office managers. From the 1950s onward, as Edgar Kaufmann, Jr., wrote, "the day of the *retardataire* client was past, even among corporations. . . . Eventually industry and business became the most courageous of all commission-givers."[1]

Saarinen's General Motors Technical Center

Among the first of these new corporate structures was Eero Saarinen's complex of buildings for the GM Technical Center at Warren, Michigan (1946–50). The rural location was evidence of the flight to the suburbs that was taking place by businesses as well as by home owners.

The planning and furnishing were in the forefront of the decade's updated International Style. The center was planned on a pervasive 5-foot module, but colors and textures were richer than earlier Miesian work, especially colored exterior panels. The suspended ceilings in the lobby of the Research Administration Building were square wood panels molded with a circular motif that was alternately cut out to receive down lights. Trim rectilinear Saarinen-designed furnishings, a variation on Le Corbusier's Grand Confort furniture, reiterated the modular approach. In this lobby, also, the decade's theme of discontinuity or alienation was reflected in a lightweight wire-tensioned spiral stair (see Figure 168), which became a symbol of dematerialization for the next two decades; its design is attributed to Kevin Roche. Furnishings in the luxurious executive offices and elsewhere in the complex were drawn mainly from those produced by Knoll Associates. The No. 71 and 72 Chair—the chair "with the hole in the back," as it became known—was first used at the GM Technical Center.

168. Saarinen, Saarinen, and Associates. Lobby staircase, General Motors Technical Center. Warren, Michigan. 1950. *Photograph © Ezra Stoller/ ESTO, 1955.*

Skidmore, Owings & Merrill

The most prominent of the new large Modern design firms was the architecture firm of Skidmore, Owings & Merrill (SOM). SOM became almost synonymous with the building boom of the 1950s and with corporate design, and did perhaps more than any other design firm to establish the Miesian idiom as the mainstream of Modern architecture.

Begun in 1936 in New York (see Chapter 13), SOM later operated offices simultaneously in Chicago and San Francisco, and in Portland, Oregon (after 1955). In the next two decades the firm expanded further. SOM developed a team or group practice, a method of organizing separate teams to provide comprehensive design services for each project. Their work included planning, architecture, engineering, and interior design for large and small projects—commercial, industrial, and educational buildings; hotels, hospitals, airports; recreational, religious, and residential facilities.

The teams were also responsible for urban planning projects and central business district redevelopment. Among SOM's works are some of the best major office towers and rural office headquarters buildings in this country.

Gordon Bunshaft   The chief of design in the New York office of SOM was partner Gordon Bunshaft, who was a major influence on office interiors from the 1950s to the 1970s. Born in Buffalo, New York, Gordon Bunshaft (1909–) studied architecture at the Massachusetts Institute of Technology (MIT), and first worked for architect Edward Durell Stone and for industrial designer Raymond Loewy. He joined SOM in 1937, spent the war years from 1942 to 1946 in the Army Corps of Engineers, and returned to SOM in 1946, first in Chicago, then in New York. He was made a partner of the firm in 1949, and from that time on was the formidably outspoken chief design partner of the New York office, designing or overseeing virtually everything that was designed there.

With Mies as the model, SOM produced several dozen buildings that made good architecture seem like explications of the Miesian gospel. Although this culminated in the Seagram Building (1954–58) in New York by Mies van der Rohe and Philip Johnson, it was largely because of SOM and Gordon Bunshaft that the Miesian idiom became pervasive as the mainstream idiom and technology at mid-century.

Among Bunshaft's works was the early masterpiece Lever House in New York (1952), which followed closely on the completion of the United Nations Secretariat building. Lever House set the new archetypal model for the third generation of skyscrapers, including SOM's other New York landmarks: the Pepsi Cola Building (1960), the Chase Manhattan Bank headquarters (1961), and the Union Carbide Building (1961).

For the interiors of Lever House, Bunshaft developed a suspended ceiling system wherein the lighting troffers were recessed into an acoustical-tile surface with square air-conditioning diffusers between the troffers rather than at their long ends. The partitioning system at Lever House was comprised of wood-veneered panels between thin metal posts. The glass curtain walls were screened by a new mesh fabric called a casement, which was designed by Jack Lenor Larsen (his first major commission). Here was the beginning, not only of a new phase of skyscraper construction, but of a new look for open offices—long lines of rectangular desks cleanly placed in relation to the building, to sources of light, and to circulation corridors—a strength through repetition.

Another work by SOM in which Bunshaft influenced interior design was the Manufacturers Hanover Trust Company branch bank (1954) at Fifth Avenue and 43rd Street in New York. There, Bunshaft applied Miesian idiom to banking, completely transforming the former idiom of granite-and-bronze temple-fortress into one of pristine, crystalline, unprotected glass.

Behind the glass on the street level, Bunshaft located the vault, with its huge door of burnished stainless steel designed by Henry Dreyfuss. He placed the main banking floor on the second level, drawing customers all the way across the first floor, which was for quick-stop customer service, and up an escalator. The main banking floor was entirely consistent with the exterior—all clarity and alignment. A grid of suspended ceiling—luminous panels between unequal strips of metal, the wider of which incorporated air conditioning and down lights—and a grid of terrazzo were aligned with the columns and the tellers' counters, which were stripped of their traditional grille-work cages. "Open" was the keynote of mid-century Modernism. Behind one leg of the tellers' counter stood a 70-foot-long screen of bronze panels created by Harry Bertoia. For this interior SOM consulted with the firm of Eleanor Le Maire on the selection of furniture and fabrics.

SOM and the Knoll Planning Unit From 1954 to 1957 SOM and Bunshaft designed the rural headquarters for Connecticut General Life Insurance Company in Bloomfield, Connecticut, five miles from the insurance city of Hartford. The interiors were designed in consultation with the Knoll Planning Unit headed by Florence Schust Knoll (see below). It was in this project that the American International Style interior reached its first peak. Florence Knoll's Planning Unit pioneered in studies to determine how work procedures affect office layouts and furniture.[2] Clean, crisp, serene, efficient, and businesslike, interiors by SOM and the Knoll Planning Unit were the models for Modern designers for the next ten years.

At Connecticut General the 6-foot module of the building was reiterated throughout the interior as well as the exterior. Terrazzo flooring was divided into 6-foot squares. The suspended ceiling was composed of 2- by 3-foot modules, which were rectangles of interlocking fins of perforated sheet metal with exposed fluorescent tubes within them. The depth of the fins prevented the bare-bulb effect in perspective. The partitioning system (see Figure 169) at Connecticut General

169. Skidmore, Owings & Merrill and the Knoll Planning Unit. Office module, Connecticut General Life Insurance Company. Bloomfield, Connecticut. 1957. *Photograph © Ezra Stoller/ESTO, 1957.*

170.   Skidmore, Owings & Merrill. Inland Steel Company Building. Chicago, Illinois. 1958. *Photograph © Ezra Stoller.*

was designed to be movable, and was composed of metal posts that plugged into the ceiling grid and held 6-foot-square panels of glass or solid clear colors. It was at Connecticut General that the full integration of interior and exterior design based on a modular dimension began to take over the profession's focus on rectilinear total design.

Davis Allen   Davis Allen headed SOM's interior design department for thirty years. Born in Ames, Iowa, Davis Allen (1916–) was raised in Chicago and attended Brown University and the Yale School of Architecture. He first worked in the early Knoll Planning Unit with Florence Knoll. After this he spent nearly two years with Harrison & Abramovitz, Architects, doing design work on the United Nations General Assembly building interiors; he then worked six months with Raymond Loewy. Allen joined SOM in 1950 and worked on the Istanbul Hilton Hotel, the Inland Steel building in Chicago, and on the Crown Zellerbach building in San Francisco.

The Chicago office of SOM designed the headquarters of Inland Steel Company in Chicago (1956–58). In its interior the building was based on a 5-foot-2-inch module so as to integrate a ceiling system that used an exposed 60-inch fluorescent tube as well as sound, heat, and air conditioning. With offices of 10-foot squares, smaller desks than the then standard 72-inch desk had to be designed (see Figure 170). Davis Allen, as senior interior designer at SOM Chicago at the time, designed a new 60-by-30-inch desk for the Inland Steel interiors that later was put on the general market by Steelcase and the G. F. Furniture Company.

Davis Allen moved to the SOM New York office to design the interiors for the Chase Manhattan Bank headquarters (1958–61). Allen also supervised SOM's furniture designs. Ward Bennett was engaged by Chase Manhattan as a consultant to provide small artworks, antiques, and objects to accessorize the interior. This

171. Skidmore, Owings & Merrill. Union Carbide Building. New York City. 1960. *Photograph © Ezra Stoller/ESTO, 1960.*

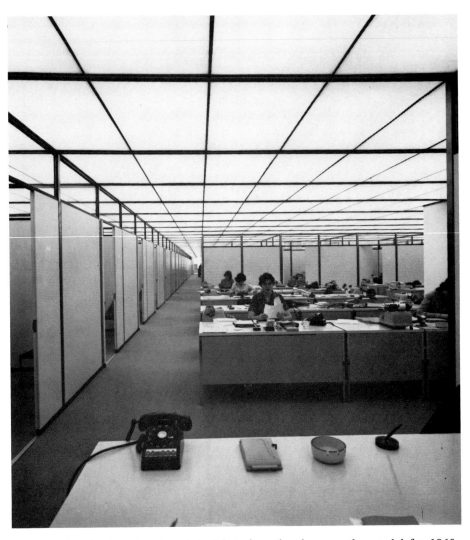

team produced refined and enriched interiors that became the model for 1960s Modernism.

Throughout the next three decades SOM, with Bunshaft as chief of design and with Davis Allen as head of the interior design department, worked a series of variations and refinements on all these interior elements—for the Reynolds Metal Company in Richmond, Virginia, in 1958; for Pepsi Cola in New York City in 1960; and for Union Carbide (see Figure 171) in New York in 1961. The Chicago office of SOM, at this same time, varied and refined interior systems and furnishings for the U.S. Air Force Academy in Colorado (1954–62) and the Harris Trust and Savings Bank in Chicago (1957–60).

Also notable among SOM's interiors in the 1950s were the Crown Zellerbach building in San Francisco (1957–59), on which Davis Allen worked; the First City National Bank in Houston (1959–61); and the Upjohn Company building in Kalamazoo, Michigan (1959–61). These developments are a monument to the flowering of the Miesian idiom at mid-century—and they are SOM's monumental achievement in modular regularity, integration, innovation, and total design.

The Knoll Planning Unit

For two decades following the mid-1940s the Knoll Planning Unit was the leading independent modern interior design firm in America. Under the direction of Florence Knoll as interior designer, the Knoll Planning Unit designed interiors for offices, banks, hotels, embassies, universities, and hospitals.

In 1951 the Knoll Planning Unit designed a new showroom for Knoll, at 575 Madison Avenue in New York City, that demonstrated what came to be called "the Knoll look" (see Figure 172). The showroom featured a black metal grid that hid the building's architectural irregularities with infill panels of primary colors in the De Stijl manner. The showroom was adopted as a model of the new wave of International Style planar, rectilinear interiors.

The San Francisco showroom that Knoll Planning Unit designed in 1957 took advantage of the high loft space to include two levels set off by a white-painted structure and ceiling of closely spaced fins. This was offset by brightly colored panels of an even clearer and stronger palette, which Knoll offered as its contribution to the new rich colors at the end of the decade (see below).

The Planning Unit's corporate office designs—for CBS (beginning in 1954); for the H. J. Heinz Company in Pittsburgh (1958); and for Cowles Magazines (completed in 1961)—were among the most sumptuous and refined in America. Florence Knoll's work demonstrated an impeccable sense of clean detail, a deft manipulation of domestic scale for institutional spaces, a precise juxtaposition of pure forms, and a crisp yet rich orchestration of textures. She truly believed that the world could become a better place through Good Design.

172. Florence Knoll. Knoll showroom. New York City. 1951. *Photograph courtesy Knoll International.*

The "Good Design" Shows

Continuing to spread the gospel of Modernism, the Museum of Modern Art, from 1949 to 1955, mounted a series of annual "Good Design" exhibitions directed by Edgar Kaufmann, Jr. They showed how meticulous discrimination could fill every interior with clean and sparkling machine beauty, readily available in the marketplace. Kaufmann, who later wrote that Elsie de Wolfe had added the "good" to the all-too-prevalent taste of her day, similarly added the "good" to the too widely expanding design activity of the 1950s. "Good design" became a widely adopted concept in America at this time, through the exhibitions by museums and marketing centers. A design center was opened in London in 1956. Industry, business, and governments seemed to be convinced at last that good design was at least good public relations.

The first Good Design show, mounted in New York in 1949, traveled, like successive others, to the Merchandise Mart in Chicago six months later.[3] Designed by Charles and Ray Eames, the first of these exhibitions included Russel Wright's American Modern Dinnerware and folding chair for Samsonite, as well as nine designs by Edward Wormley for Dunbar. The 1950 show was designed by Finn Juhl; the 1952 exhibition was designed by the young architect Paul Rudolph; and the 1953 and 1954 exhibitions were designed by Alexander Girard. For these five years every major American and European designer was represented in these Good Design shows, the influence of which was enormous.

In its continuing promulgation of Modernism, the Museum of Modern Art built complete Modern houses for exhibition in its garden. Marcel Breuer had designed one in 1949; California's Gregory Ain designed another in 1950. Thousands of people toured these houses, and many gained their first views of what Modern architecture and Modern design could be.

The New Space Planners

With the construction of offices booming in major American cities, a number of urban interior designers seized this opportunity and applied themselves almost exclusively to the area of office design. They proclaimed a new wing of the profession under the name "space planners," although planning spaces had always been a major concern of both architects and residential decorators.

In the 1950s virtually all designers of interiors were still called "decorators." But, by mid-decade, designers of nonresidential spaces were moving toward use of the term "interior designer." The founding of the National Society of Interior Designers in 1957 helped to forward the use of this term. Still, few architect-trained graduates were interested in working for an interior design firm.

So polarized had the distinction between interior design and interior decorating become that they did not think of interior design as a wing of architecture, but as being of lesser interest. The majority of architecture firms involved in designing the big new buildings had become so specialized that their design procedures codified the division. Architects were accused of not giving adequate attention to the details of planning and finishing interiors. Design education, in addition, reinforced this separation. Architecture students were not taught much about the design of interiors, and interior design students were not taught much about architectural directions. Nor were there yet any degree programs in interior design. This situation would change at the end of the decade; but it had created the opening for the new space planners.

The situation also revealed the need for step-by-step analysis of human functions and activities. Average human measurements, dimensional tables, and graphic standards were drawn up, notably those by Henry Dreyfuss in his *Designing for*

People and *The Measure of Man*. Thereby the new discipline of "human factors" was established, and it put the design of commercial, institutional, and educational spaces on a considerably more scientific basis.

Among the new space planning or office design firms were Designs for Business with Gerald Luss as chief designer; Saphier-Lerner-Schindler; the Space Design Group; and ISD (see page 193ff.). Others were Maria Bergson Associates and Eleanor LeMaire Associates. Designs for Business won considerable acclaim for a more woodsy style of modular and movable partitioning systems and furnishings. Among the selling points of Designs for Business were analysis and flexible systems that would permit rearrangement, expansion, and relocation of offices without massive construction procedures or costs. Their major commissions included offices for Tower Fabrics in 1954, offices for C. J. La Roche & Company in 1958, and fourteen floors of offices for Time-Life Inc. in New York City, in 1959.

Industrial designers also figured in the new space planning and design of offices and other interiors. Henry Dreyfuss, besides continuing to design products and ocean liners, such as the *Independence* (finished in 1951), also designed offices. Raymond Loewy worked on products, packaging, kitchen equipment and cabinets, and offered space planning for offices, stores, and virtually any other type of interior. Loewy was at the peak of his career, both as a designer and as a celebrity. His "design factory" was one of the largest and provided apprenticeship for countless young designers and architects.

Walter Dorwin Teague did space planning for the offices of Reichold Chemicals and many other companies. Space planning for office interiors was also offered by the firms of Donald Deskey, Lippincott & Margolies, and other industrial designers. It was at this time that the new efficiency experts called "systems analysts" began to affect the profession of office design. Industrial design had become pervasive throughout the furnishings industry, but it had acquired a sleek, sometimes glib overlay that made it unrelated to the honest functionalism of Modern design.

European Influences

Italian Modern

In the 1950s the attenuated look that exploited the tensile qualities of steel was further explored by Italian designers. They created wire bases and frames for tables and chairs; spindly, spidery lighting fixtures—among the most prominent of which was the three-branch swivel standing fixture with conical shades (1949), designed by Barbieri and manufactured by Arteluce of Milan. This "wire look" was a continuation of "le Style Atomique," as the French had called it.

In 1952 Gio Ponti designed his version of the Chiavari chair; it became a staple of inexpensive elegance. In addition, furniture by Carlo Mollino and Parisi continued their sculptural vein with gazelle-like animal forms. Painted screens and ceramic dinnerware by Arnoldo Fornasetti—some of it with a Surrealist motif of disengaged eyes—became popular at this time. Highly original were the designs for furniture and interiors by the Castiglioni brothers.

Danish Modern

New in the 1950s was the ascendancy of Danish Modern over other Scandinavian expressions. Although Finland's Alvar Aalto put forward his fan-shaped joint between legs and tops of stools and tables in 1954, Danish Modern offered a sensuous expressiveness that was based in handcraft rather than the machine, and therefore produced an atmosphere of a softer elegance. "Warm" was the common praise of the decade, in opposition to the "coldness" of machine-image Modern.

The Danish designer Finn Juhl created the Trusteeship Council Chamber of the United Nations headquarters in New York (1952) with its walls of undulating battens, derived from Alvar Aalto's vocabulary. Hans Wegner continued to produce sculptural wood chairs with richly exposed graining and gracefully refined forms. Poul Kjaerholm began to be recognized for furniture with combinations of brushed stainless steel and pale ash butcher-block-like wood construction. Kjaerholm's armless chair (1956) had a brushed stainless-steel frame covered in raffia.

The fabrics of Unika-Vaev splashed onto the market with geometric patterns and vibrant colors. The sublimely sinuous silver serving dishes of Henning Koeppel seemed to typify the decade, and were among its peaks of achievement. At the end of the decade Vernor Panton's chair—a single piece of plastic cantilevered for base, seat, and back (1959–60)—achieved what Rietveld had set out to do with his Zigzag Chair (1934) and Eero Saarinen had aimed for with his Pedestal Chair—to unite structure and seat with a continuous seamless material.

The Growth of American Modern Furniture

More Modern furniture began to be produced by the U.S. furniture industry in the 1950s. The leaders in this activity were Knoll Associates and Herman Miller Inc.

Knoll Associates

At Knoll the designs of Finn Juhl, Jens Risom, and Mies were joined by the designs of Franco Albini, Pierre Jeanneret, Ralph Rapson, and Marcel Breuer. In 1952 Harry Bertoia designed his series of wire chairs, culminating in the Diamond Chair, which was produced by Knoll in two sizes (see Figure 173A). Saarinen's Pedestal Furniture (1955–56) was intended to reduce the number of furniture legs in a room

173A. Harry Bertoia. Diamond Chairs. 1952. *Photograph courtesy Knoll International.*

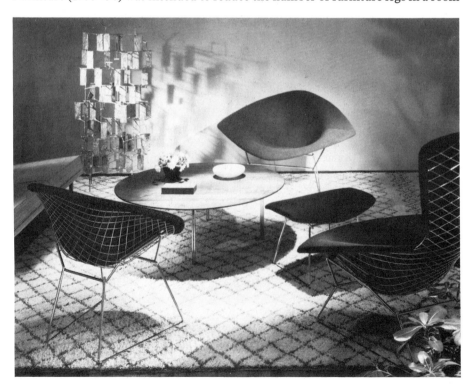

(see Figure 173B). Anni Albers, who had taught fabric design at the Bauhaus, began to design fabrics for Knoll in 1959.

Florence Knoll also contributed designs to the firm's line. They were usually what she called "fill-in pieces" that were not otherwise available: seating units—chairs and sofas—and case pieces that were based on a modular, square concept, furthering the idiom of De Stijl and the popularity of Mondrian (see Figure 173C). Her furniture looked more serenely classic with each design. Florence Knoll's furniture designs proffered Miesian steel bases and luxurious and luscious marbles, which were sometimes white as cakes of snow glistening in the spotlights. Florence

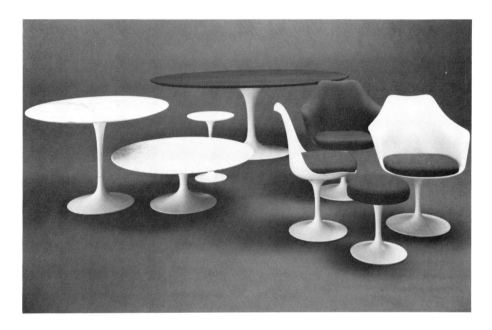

173B. Eero Saarinen. Pedestal Furniture. 1955–56. *Photograph courtesy Knoll International.*

173C. Florence Knoll. Lounge chairs, table, sofa. 1950s, 1960s. *Photograph courtesy The Metropolitan Museum of Art, New York City, Collection CBS, Inc.*

Knoll said they looked like "sugar cubes." She also conceived the boat-shaped conference table that made narrower conference spaces negotiable. Planned originally for office use, the Knoll furniture was soon adopted for residential use as well.

In 1958, when she was among the most influential designers of both furniture and interiors, Florence Knoll married Harry Hood Bassett. She sold her interest in Knoll to Art Metal in 1959 and retired from the presidency the following year, remaining as a consultant. In 1965 she withdrew from all connections with Knoll to work as an independent designer.

Herman Miller Inc.

Herman Miller continued in the 1950s to produce innovative and straightforward furniture by Charles and Ray Eames and by George Nelson. Nelson also negotiated the association of Alexander Girard with the firm in 1952 to design textiles.

Plastic shell chairs were designed by the Eameses in 1950 on spidery metal-rod legs. Their all-wire chairs were produced in 1951; their plastic-shell stacking chairs in 1954. The large bent-plywood leather-cushioned chair and ottoman were produced in 1956 (see Figure 174A). Aluminum-framed pieces began to appear from their design boards in 1958; the first had pre-molded vinyl upholstery slings. It was a corpus of work that established Eames as the most innovative designer of the decade and changed the look of interiors throughout the country.

George Nelson also continued to produce innovations in furniture design in astonishing numbers. During the 1950s his designs included the first metal case pieces hung within a structural frame (1954) in the manner of architectural construction. These pieces had recessed tracks in the drawers, which slid on the horizontal members of the frames.

174A. Charles Eames and Ray Eames. Chair and ottoman. 1956. *Photograph courtesy Herman Miller Inc.*

At that time, Nelson designed his pole-and-shelf bookcase systems that reversed the customary wall-mounted support systems. In preceding designs metal runners mounted on the wall served as tracks for cantilevered brackets that supported shelves. In Nelson's version the Comprehensive Storage System poles (1956) were freestanding out from the wall, and the brackets were cantilevered toward the wall so that the shelves stood between the poles and the wall. The system was therefore independent of built-in construction. Designed concurrently with, but independently of, related shelf systems for store display, Nelson's Comprehensive Storage System prefigured architectural developments that placed structural supports outside the curtain wall.

An example of the dematerialization or discontinuity of the decade was George Nelson's Marshmallow Sofa (1956) (see Figure 174B). The sofa derived, conceptually, from the idea of using self-skinning foam plastic—as in automobile armrests—instead of stitched upholstery. In execution, however, each cushion had to be upholstered separately.

One other chair was widely acclaimed and popular in this decade—the three-legged chair, designed in 1952 by Katavolos-Littell-Kelley and produced by Laverne Inc., with a leather sling supported by a T-shaped back member. The Lavernes also produced a mammoth-scale wall covering that was a reinterpretation of endpapers for books.

Residential and Technical Advances

Lighting

The contribution of artificial lighting to interior design continued to become more crucial in the 1950s, and it received both greater attention and greater sensitivity.

Lighting designer Richard Kelly began to demonstrate the need and value of the lighting consultant. Most apparent was the effect of the new suspended ceiling on interior lighting, as well as on the urban scene at night. Especially striking was the emphasized image of horizontality—that goal of the early International Style—which lighted suspended ceilings brought to the black-and-white striping of buildings. Kelly's all-over illuminated ceiling at the Seagram Building was the most eye-opening of all these demonstrations.

Throughout the decade the lamp—conceived of as a shaded candle—was anathema to Modernists. Instead, geometric cans, which pointed unidirectional light, or pull-down shaded lighting fixtures became the accepted models. Folded paper shades from Denmark made by Le Klint, along with the pinpoint-pierced brass shades of Finland's Paavo Tynell and lamps from Italy, gave a more playful facet to the bullet- and cone-shaped reflectors of the 1940s.

Isamu Noguchi's Akari lamps—paper bubbles and assemblages of other geometric forms made of paper, in the construction technique of traditional Japanese lanterns—were introduced by the Bonniers shop, which had been designed by Warner-Leeds. (One partner, Harold Leeds, went on to become the chairman of Pratt Institute's department of interior design.)

George Nelson lighted three showrooms for Herman Miller with adjustable lamps clipped onto Bulldog Trol-E-Ducts that were attached to a grid of white-metal pipes as an open suspended ceiling. Greta von Nessen continued the Bauhaus tradition of lighting inherited from her husband. Paul Laszlo and others took up the leaning wire standard-lamp concept, perhaps derived from the firm Stilnovo in Italy. And the luminous, varicolored glass shades of Italy's Paolo Venini became social symbols of equal prominence with the copper-shingled "artichoke" chandelier of Denmark's Poul Henningsen.

New Products

Drywall construction—using gypsum-board panels instead of troweled, wet plaster—began after the war in the suburban housing boom, owing to rising costs of plaster work caused by the declining plaster trade. Drywall was to move into office design in the 1960s, and to make the plaster trade almost obsolete in the 1970s.

Television and high-fidelity sound systems became widely available around 1950. Antennas could be seen sprouting from virtually every roof. The 1953 coronation of Great Britain's Queen Elizabeth II was the first internationally televised event that captured a wide audience. From then onward the TV set became the twentieth-century fireplace—sometimes it was even designed to look like a fireplace. It was hidden inside cabinets, set into small-screen units, and then wide-screen sets on splayed-legged units appeared. Decorators continued to hide them for decades, continuing the battle between functionalism and formalism.

Alexander Girard

The J. Irwin Miller House

Eero Saarinen's and Alexander Girard's house for J. Irwin Miller, in Columbus, Indiana (1952), was among the significant residential designs of the decade. It was a model of the forthcoming reinterpretation of or move beyond the Miesian idiom.

Inside a 100-foot-long and 80-foot-wide rectangular pavilion that had wide expanses of glass shaded by a wide overhanging flat roof, the interior featured a skylighted living room with the first sofa-deep square conversation pit (see Figure 175). The pit was fully carpeted and upholstered, entered down padauk-wood

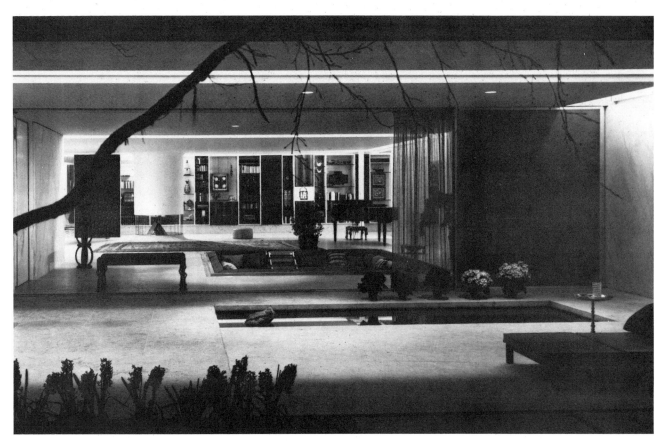

175. Eero Saarinen and Alexander Girard. J. Irwin Miller House, Columbus, Indiana. 1952. *Photograph © Ezra Stoller/ESTO, 1958.*

rubber-laminated steps, and lined with multipatterned and multicolored pillows in fabrics designed by Girard and fabrics found by him in Morocco, Tunisia, Indonesia, and India.

Along one 50-foot-long wall of the living area was a floor-to-ceiling-height wall of book and display cases, storage cases, and a patchwork quilt of objects from around the world that expressed both the decade's "one world" and "global village" awareness as well as Alexander Girard's singular new vision of display. Among the objects were a Chinese birdcage and a Peruvian figure-pageant; antique Italian, Greek, and Chinese objects; an English antique brass box; a Victorian flower montage; a French Provincial clock; Hopi Indian figures; Latin American religious figures; Venetian glass birds; an Early American toy; an eighteenth-century Austrian chest; East Indian gouaches and bronzes; a Balinese carving; a New Mexican crucifix; Mexican candelabra; an oriental lute; and a William Blake engraving. Interspersed were books, decorative backings of fabric and paper, and storage for camera equipment and television.

Among the innovations in this interior was the exploration of the vertical dimension of space in this room and the interplay of heights. The floor was pierced, recessed as a conversation pit; above, at the standard height, was a grand piano; the display-storage wall rose from floor to ceiling; and in between, suspended in air, were both a ceiling-hung cylindrical fireplace screened by a bead-chain firescreen and a Kashmir shawl hung as a flat panel at the main entrance. The stretching up and down for space; the reaching across the world and across time for texture, pattern, color, culture, and inspiration; and the combination within a serene pavilion seemed, at the time, like the ultimate enrichment of the Machine-Age idiom—and without the representational motifs of previous decades.

Girard's Santa Fe House

In 1953, after he established his association with the Herman Miller company as fabrics designer (see below), Girard and his family moved to Santa Fe, New Mexico, to live and work in an old adobe house that he remodeled (see Figure 176A). Adopting the culture of the old Southwest, the Girards designed not a temple to Modernism but, with tradition-shattering innovation, established a link between Modernism and the old tradition of interior design *ensembliers* (see Chapter 10).

Somehow, he managed to appease both traditions. The adobe, some of it 200 years old, was refurbished or built anew and painted white, like the bare rafters (see Figure 176B). Doorways were left frameless and doorless; other square and rectangular openings were cut from room to room to serve as picture frames. An adobe support for cushions constituted a sofa—prefiguring the work of the Minimalists two decades later; an adobe table and stool, an adobe chaise and display platforms also stood in the living room. Floors were a dark reddish stone, laid fairly unevenly; and this was offered as the rationale for suspending the pine-board dining table on stainless-steel cables tensioned from ceiling to floor. Reported as stable, but admittedly wiggly at times, the table was nevertheless in the tradition of the atomic-molecular style and the wire idiom of the late 1940s. Perhaps as a contrast, a French butcher's table of metal rods and brass mounts stood prominently silhouetted in the hallway. The few other movable pieces of furniture were chairs by Eames and Saarinen, and bubble lighting by Nelson.

One living room wall displayed the Girards' steadily increasing collection of folk art and other handcrafted objects: kachina figures by the Hopi of Arizona, a Tibetan devil trap, East Indian puppets, Peruvian ceramics, Mexican painted chests, and other paintings from South America. Behind a serving-and-display shelf in the dining room was an irregularly striped mural painted by Girard in pinks, reds, and blues. Among the objects displayed against that mural were Guatemalan chests, a Sicilian cart, and Bohemian glass candle sconces. There was a brass Moroccan coffee table, an Indian spread, and objects from other places and times.

It was a house of delicate, intricate things to be examined at close range. Like Alexander Girard's other work, it had the pattern, texture, and color that the purgative Modern movement had caused people to starve for. His house and his work were warm and human. And Girard offered all that with the sensitivity of a

176A. Alexander Girard. Plan, own house. Santa Fe, New Mexico. 1953. *Illustration courtesy of the architect.*

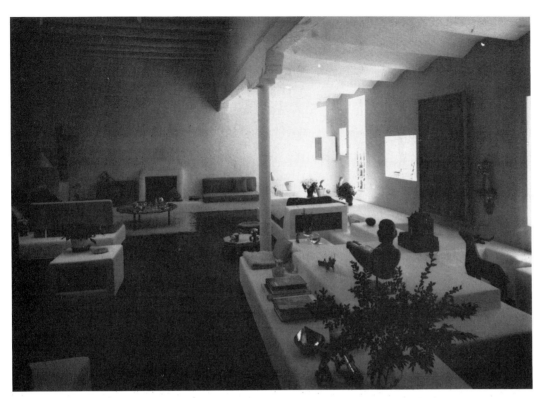

176B. Alexander Girard. Own house. Santa Fe, New Mexico. 1953. *Photograph by Julius Shulman.*

fresh and original mind, with spareness and elegance. He brought the joy of collecting folk art and internationalism to the sober monumentality of Modernism.

Girard's Other Commissions

Girard was approaching the peak of his career in the 1950s. He designed residences as well as showrooms for Herman Miller; served as consultant to I. M. Pei on the interiors of the Denver Hotel; designed an apartment in Los Angeles for movie director Billy Wilder; and designed offices for Irwin Miller in Columbus, Indiana. In the Miller offices, Girard's interpretation of a doorstop as a recessed hemisphere to receive the doorknob showed the sublime wit that—at rare intervals—elevates interior design to an art form. The socket in the wall seemed so natural that one wondered why it was not used before. Of this kind of vision, Dr. Samuel Johnson in the eighteenth century had written, "The first effect is sudden astonishment, and the second rational admiration."

For Herman Miller's 1958 San Francisco showroom, which was in a 1907 music hall (a notable early example of the recycling of buildings that was to become widespread in the 1960s), Girard emphasized the existing decor to produce an updated multicolored carnival midway of the Gay Nineties. To him we owe the subsequent wide use of lines of marquee-like lightbulbs in interior work. Fabrics were displayed as flat or folded panels on wire-hung brass poles to subdivide the space. Mirrors, beading, and brilliant colors added to the carnival midway effect.

Girard also continued his series of spectacular exhibition designs. Among them were two Good Design shows for the Museum of Modern Art (1953 and 1954), and "Textiles and Ornamental Arts of India" (1955), also for the Museum of Modern Art. That Indian exhibition remains one of the most dazzling displays within living memory. Throughout his work Alexander Girard brought a new canon of decoration in a witty and whimsical idiom, with spontaneity, and with pure sensual pleasure and joy.

Individualist Designers

Several others who designed interiors in the 1950s demonstrated similarly icono-clastic and individualistic approaches—moving beyond the Miesian doctrine that was, at that very time, becoming publicly accepted. Among them were Bruce Goff and Russel Wright.

Bruce Goff

Architect Bruce Goff, who worked out of Oklahoma, made a strong statement about interior design in the 1950s. Viewed by doctrinaire Modernists as eccentric and irrelevant, Goff's designs presented such a multitude of approaches, influences, techniques, and materials that his work defied categorization—other than to call him individualistic, expressionistic, and pluralistic.

An exact contemporary of Russel Wright, Bruce Alonzo Goff (1904–82) was born in Alton, Kansas, and was educated in public school in Tulsa. Apprenticed to the architecture firm of Rush, Endacott & Rush at the age of twelve (he worked there from 1916 to 1930), Goff had designed major buildings before he left high school and at the age of twenty-two designed a church in Tulsa that brought him international attention. In the 1930s he worked for the industrial products design firm of Alfonso Iannelli in Chicago, was in private practice as an architect, and became director of design for the VitroLite Division of Libbey-Owens-Ford Glass Company. He served in the U.S. Navy Construction Batallion from 1942 to 1945, and settled to teach at, and later to head, the school of architecture at the University of Oklahoma from 1948 to 1955. He was in private practice in Oklahoma, Kansas City, and Texas from then until his death in 1982 at the age of seventy-eight.

Two of Goff's house designs alone qualify him for a place in the history of twentieth-century interior design: the Bavinger House in Norman, Oklahoma (1950), and the Price House in Bartlesville, Oklahoma (1956). The Bavinger House has a spiral plan of saucer-like spaces suspended by tension cables from a steel mast centered within a fieldstone wall that spirals inward like a nautilus shell. This was Goff's first full realization of free-flowing space that had been pioneered in the Teens and 1920s and that he himself had explored since the 1940s. Inside, suspended from the steel mast, are five living areas in the form of carpeted saucers, each stepped up 3 feet above the preceding one, each one with a cylindrical satellite closet sheathed in copper, and separable from the overall space only by fishnets or by opaque draperies. The wire-suspended stair that gives access to these spaces rises over a pool, a conversation pit, and a plant-filled, skylighted, conservatory-like world in which the flying saucers float.

The Price House, which immediately reveals the influence of Frank Lloyd Wright, contains Goff's most innovative and refined interior. Based on a triangular 3-foot module in both plan and section, the house was planned as a large triangle with its sides extended beyond the angles. Outside, the sloping walls and roof are covered with gold-anodized aluminum; hard coal and large chunks of rough blue glass are used for the masonry walls.

Inside the triangulated space (see Figure 177) the walls slope outward to become a backrest for reclining. The living room has a hexagonal conversation pit with a mosaic-topped cocktail table. Thick white nylon carpet covers the floor, banquettes, and lower part of walls; part of the floor is surfaced in white vinyl sheeting to provide a dance floor.

Goff's furnishings and finishes display an array of "found" or "ad hoc" mate-rials—anthracite coal, sequins, mosaics, chunks of colored glass; they offer fantasy with abandon. Part of the ceiling above the conversation pit is covered with goose down. Gold-colored plastic rain—the plastic tinsel used by display studios—hangs

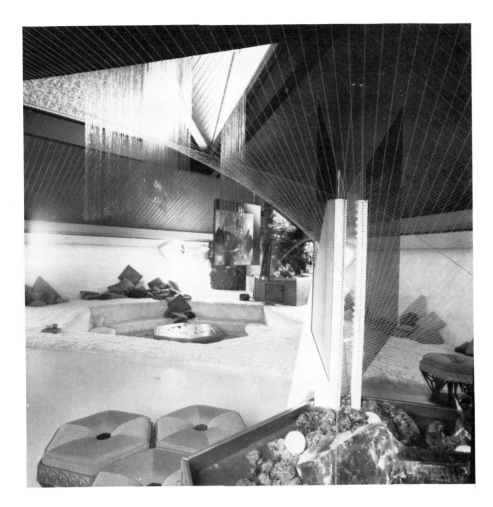

177. Bruce Goff. Joe D. Price House. Bartlesville, Oklahoma. 1956. *Photograph by Joe D. Price, courtesy Bruce Goff Archive.*

as a chandelier above the conversation pit; light-reflecting and air-mobilized, the plastic rain is a startling reinterpretation of the traditional beaded curtain. Lighting is provided from indirect coves that are of stamped gold-anodized aluminum, and from behind the blue glass chunks. Critic Jeffrey Cook has written of Goff's work that it "simultaneously epitomizes the vagaries of the century and some of its most creative variants."[4] The 1950s were called "funky" as well as "fabulous," and any number of critics made an analogy between 1950s design and the concurrent Theater of the Absurd.

Russel Wright

During the 1950s Russel Wright was at the peak of his recognition and productivity. He continued his search for an appropriate expression of American living in the post–World War II era. His province was the middle America that was becoming more design conscious, of necessity tending toward a more casual, servantless lifestyle than was previously known. His concepts were "easier living," "informal hospitality," and "stove-to-table ware." As evidence of his recognition, Russel Wright's designs were included in numerous exhibitions, including the "Good Design" shows at the Museum of Modern Art. In 1952 he was elected president of the American Society of Industrial Designers.

Among his 1950s design commissions for table and household objects were appliances for dining room and kitchen, American Modern glassware, aluminum and pewter table pieces and cutlery, American Modern flatware, and ceramic dinnerware. He continued to design the Melamine plastic dinnerware, for which he became celebrated—Meladur (1949), Residential (1953), and Flair (1959). He also designed plastic tablecloths and mats, other table linens, and paper plates and cups.

Russel Wright's designs for interior furnishings in the 1950s included carpets, drapery fabrics, upholstery fabrics, vinyl upholstery colors, floor tiles, and lamps. He also designed folding metal "patio" chairs and tables for Samsonite in 1950; his colors were aqua, coral, chartreuse, and green. That same year he also designed a group of fifty pieces for Stratton Furniture Company's Easier Living line; it was sold exclusively by Modernage, New York, a prominent popularizer of postwar Modern furniture.

The Easier Living line was a model of inventive ideas for functional use: One side panel of the lounge chair folded up to provide a writing surface; the other side folded out to produce a magazine rack; a coffee-table top slid open to expose a water- and alcohol-proof porcelain tray; bed headboards tilted to expose storage space and to provide comfortable backs for reading in bed. A nightstand had pullout shelves to hold books or trays. Slipcovers snapped on and off. It was as homey American in concept as the American ideals of Frank Lloyd Wright (they were not related). Like him, Russel Wright's personal style was soon rejected in favor of the European import—Machine-Age Modern—which more crisply, glitteringly, and soon richly outshone his soft curves and muddy pastels.

In 1955 Russel Wright designed a line of school furniture for Samsonite in steel tubing with plywood and plastic writing surfaces. To the burgeoning school-design field, Russel Wright brought a new line of brighter colors—brighter than the gunmetal gray and "eye-ease green" that had preceded, but not so vibrant as the colors of Dorothy Liebes or Alexander Girard. Wright's colors were yellow-ochre, light red, gray-blue, and gray-green. Even in his color sense, Russel Wright was a transitional "Contemporary" designer. But by 1953, he felt, "contemporary began to be defeated."[5]

Among his interior designs in the 1950s were a showroom for Stratton Furniture Company and a house in Croton-on-Hudson, New York. But it was his own house—Dragon Rock, in Garrison, New York—that was his interior design preoccupation, and to which he increasingly withdrew as the stylistic winds blew in a direction different from his own. His house, now called Manitoga, was completed between 1956 and 1961. Perched above a water-filled quarry, Dragon Rock was divided into public and private wings, each with views of the romantic "improved" natural landscape.

In the interior Russel Wright aimed to find a harmony between the natural and the manmade, a harmony of both continuity and contrast. One bathtub had its own rocky waterfall. He mixed real and natural materials with synthetic and artificial ones. Styrofoam insulation was exposed between natural wood beams of the living-room ceiling (see Figure 178); kitchen and bathroom partitions, like the transparent Melamine dinnerware, were of plastic in which real wild flowers from the surrounding woods were cast.

He used materials that were beyond the consideration of most serious designers. Textures and colors of draperies, upholsteries, rugs, and accessories—even cabinet doors on double hinges—were varied with the seasons. With his fascination for labor-saving devices, a counterbalanced kitchen storage shelf could be raised to the ceiling; drawers for silver opened into both the kitchen and the dining area. It was, perhaps, a final step to integrate the world of industry with the world of the artist and nature, and it was a tentative, faltering step toward the coexistence of the natural and the manmade that was to be proclaimed in the next decade.

Russel Wright, as William J. Hennessey has written, "ranks with this nation's most original, inventive, and influential designers. . . . His . . . work opened the

178. Russel Wright. Dragon Rock. Garrison, New York. 1956–61. *Photograph by Louis Reens.*

eyes of millions of ordinary Americans to the aesthetic possibilities of everyday life."[6] He was to create one additional masterwork in the 1960s (see Chapter 16) before his career came to an end.

Other Influential Designers

Paul Rudolph

During this decade the work in Florida of the young architect Paul Rudolph came to attention for its delicate textural effects—using filigree screens, fishnet casement draperies, string-tied hammocks, fabric throws, and lacy tree ferns—which offset dramatic structural expressions. Born in Elkton, Kentucky, Rudolph (1918–) studied architecture at Alabama Polytechnic Institute (now Auburn University) and at Harvard's Graduate School of Design under Gropius. The war interrupted his studies and he spent three years in the Navy in ship construction at the Brooklyn Navy Yard.

After returning to Harvard to complete his master's degree, he joined Ralph Twitchell in an architectural partnership—Twitchell & Rudolph—in Sarasota, Florida. There, he began to make a name for himself for small houses that utilized relatively unconventional structural systems and elements for residential buildings. Furnishings for these houses were spare, square, and largely built-in. Movable pieces were usually slim-legged metal pieces with something of the wire look— Eames and Bertoia wire chairs, string-strung chairs, and the like—along with wood-framed seating pieces and platform sofas that were upholstered in white. Rust-colored cushions and natural leather reiterated the wood tones of the furniture frames. They were simple furnishings, selected to meet the criteria of Modernism from the few available designs.

Benjamin Baldwin

Benjamin Baldwin, who became a leader of Minimal interior design in the mid-1960s and 1970s, and a prominent designer of furniture later in his career, began to become a prominent designer in the 1950s. Born in Montgomery, Alabama, Benjamin James Baldwin (1913–) studied painting with Hans Hofmann and architecture under Jean Labatut at Princeton (he received his M.F.A. in 1938) and under Eliel Saarinen at Cranbrook Academy (1938–39). He subsequently worked in Eliel and Eero Saarinen's architecture office (1939–40).

Just before the war (1940–41) Baldwin was in architectural partnership in Chicago with Harry Weese, who later became his brother-in-law. Together they entered designs and won top prize for outdoor furniture and honorable mentions for living room furniture, bedroom furniture, and lighting in the Museum of Modern Art's 1940–41 "Organic Design Competition."

Baldwin served in the Navy during the war and afterward worked with Skidmore, Owings & Merrill in New York (1945–47), helping to establish the firm's interior design function. During that time he was in charge of interior design for

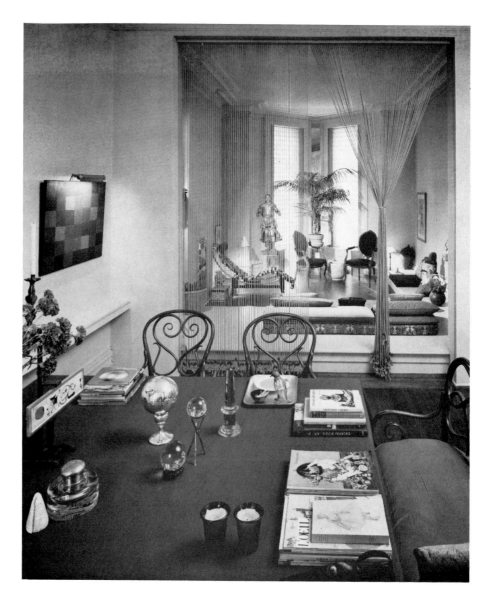

179. Benjamin Baldwin. Own house from dining room to living room. Chicago, Illinois. 1957–58. *Photograph by Idaka.*

the Terrace Plaza Hotel in Cincinnati. He then established his own practice in New York and later formed a partnership with William Machado for the design of interiors and textiles, first in New York, then in Montgomery, Alabama (1948–55), and later in Chicago (1956–63). It was there that he began to receive significant commissions for the design of furniture, textiles, industrial design, and residential and office interiors, including offices for the Solo Cup Company in 1958.

Baldwin's own Chicago house (1957–58) showed the spare-rich approach with which he later became associated. In a late-nineteenth-century townhouse with adjacent living room and dining room open to each other, Benjamin Baldwin elevated part of the living area on an L-shaped platform; floors and windows were bare; cushion seating was on the platform. In addition, there was a collection of chairs and objects that, though few, reached out across all centuries and cultures— Venetian Louis XV chairs, a Le Corbusier chaise in zebra skin, a gilt Baroque figure, and Modern, oriental, and ancient artworks and objects.

The dining room (see Figure 179), separated by an open curtain of heavy jute packing cord weighted by plumber's washers, had a glass-fronted fireplace that was elevated to the height of the large dining-reading-work table; dado-height narrow shelves held artworks and objects; the chairs were curlicue-bentwood by Thonet. The house was spare and clearly in a Modern sensibility, but it was also reaching out beyond Miesian purity to encompass the rich historical traditions, textures, and colors of our cultural heritage.

From 1963 to 1973 Benjamin Baldwin practiced in New York. He then moved his independent practice to East Hampton, Long Island, and Sarasota, Florida, between which locations he divides the year.

Ward Bennett

Another designer of interiors who was to become a major influence in the next several decades was Ward Bennett, who began to turn to the design of interiors and furnishings in the 1950s. Born in New York City, Ward Bennett (1917–) first worked in display and design for fashion designer Hattie Carnegie, and helped Carnegie on a house she was having refurnished by Syrie Maugham in Redbank, New Jersey. Bennett also worked in theater design on Broadway. He studied painting with Hans Hofmann and came under the influence of sculptor Constantin Brancusi. He began working on sculpture and jewelry, sharing a studio with Louise Nevelson.

In the 1940s he had begun to design furnishings, including the lighting he worked on for SOM's Terrace Plaza Hotel in Cincinnati at the invitation of Benjamin Baldwin.

In the 1950s he began designing interiors and was thrust into international prominence by his appointment, at the end of the decade, as design consultant to David Rockefeller on the interior furnishings and art collection for the headquarters of the Chase Manhattan Bank, the interiors of which were being designed by Davis Allen of SOM. For that project Bennett acquired, selected, and placed small artworks, antiques, and appointments throughout the building. Many of his furniture designs, which were being produced by Lehigh Furniture Company at that time, were used by SOM for the Chase project.

In the late 1950s Ward Bennett designed a living room around that device of the decade: a conversation pit with fireplace.[7] It was a room based on platforms, an idea that gained considerable popularity in the next two decades. Wide, low platforms were built around the perimeter of the room, leaving a rectangular conversation pit, which was lighted from beneath the platforms. Tufted and quilted mattress-like pads were used as the seating; one had bolster-cushions as the backrest, the other was a version of Mies's sofa with cylindrical bolster. In one corner was a lighting fixture composed of an up light that was reflected from a shallow, conical metal disk hung from the ceiling on wire. It was a discontinuous lighting fixture.

As the decade came to a close, Ward Bennett and Benjamin Baldwin led in a search for the ultimate purity of the International Style. With them and a few others, that style reached its final refinement as the Minimal style or Minimalism. They developed a sparse elemental look, a museum-like placement of objects in space, and a visual richness within that rarefied atmosphere.

Luis Barragan

The influence for this new Minimalism, in addition to the development at this same time of Minimal sculpture, was the work in Mexico of Luis Barragan. A poet of solitude and of meditative space, Luis Barragan (1902–) was born near Maza-mitla in the state of Jalisco, Mexico. In the 1920s he moved to Mexico City, was trained as an engineer, and traveled to Europe, where—in Spain—he became fascinated by the terraces, patios, and water gardens of Moslem architecture.

From 1927 to 1936 he worked as an architect in Guadalajara, designing houses and a park playground that prefigured his later landscapes. His work in that period combined the Moslem architecture he had seen in Spain with the indigenous architecture of Mexico.

From 1936, he designed houses and an apartment building in Mexico City in the idiom of the "white architecture" of the early International Style; and in 1945 he began planning the subdivision El Pedregal; there, on a landscape filled with volcanic boulders, he juxtaposed crisp, spare, white houses and phosphorescent red metal entry gates and car turnarounds. After a visit to North Africa in 1951, his work began to achieve the sublime, poetic, sculptural abstraction that made him increasingly influential.

Barragan's own house in Mexico City, designed in 1947, became the touch-stone of the early Minimal movement in interior design in the 1950s (see Figures 180A and B).[9] Focused on interior, on garden and patio, and on roof terrace, the house is elemental in its use of planes and materials, making it like a primal myth of a house. It echoes the continuity of uninterrupted Vernacular tradition. Planar walls intersect strongly and starkly and are occasionally finished with the joyous decoration of sumptuous and vibrant colors, sometimes on the exterior as well—pink, lemon, magenta, fuschia, and coral. In this regard, Barragan's work has given a new life to the planar idiom of De Stijl.

The view from the library toward the garden looks over a series of interior partitions of varying heights and through the reception room to a window with cruciform mullions. It is both a three-dimensional homage to the square, like Josef Albers's paintings, and a religious confirmation. The stair of seemingly folded wood cantilevered from the wall of the library rises to a wood door that is, so the legend goes, always closed (see Figure 180B). It is a stair steeped in the surreal, as is the roof terrace, which has been increasingly enclosed by Barragan over the years, more colorful, and abstract, with only the Mexican sky for its changing ceiling. Here, at the boundary between architecture and nature, Barragan has created his most magical and mystical spaces.

Luis Barragan's chapel (see color plate 6) and garden at Tlalpan for the Capuchinas Sacramentarias del Purismo Corazon de Maria (1952–55) was his other masterwork interior in this decade. The chapel is set back behind a garden and was planned with a patio between it and the convent (see Figure 181). In the chapel Barragan employed rough-textured concrete in flat unbordered planes, but it is painted a glowing yellow. A triptych reredos designed by the sculptor Mathias

180A. Luis Barragan. Plan, own house. Mexico City, Mexico. 1947. *Illustration from Emilio Ambasz,* The Architecture of Luis Barragan *(New York: The Museum of Modern Art, 1976).*

180B. Luis Barragan. Library and stair, own house. Mexico City, Mexico. 1947. *Photograph © René Burri, Magnum.*

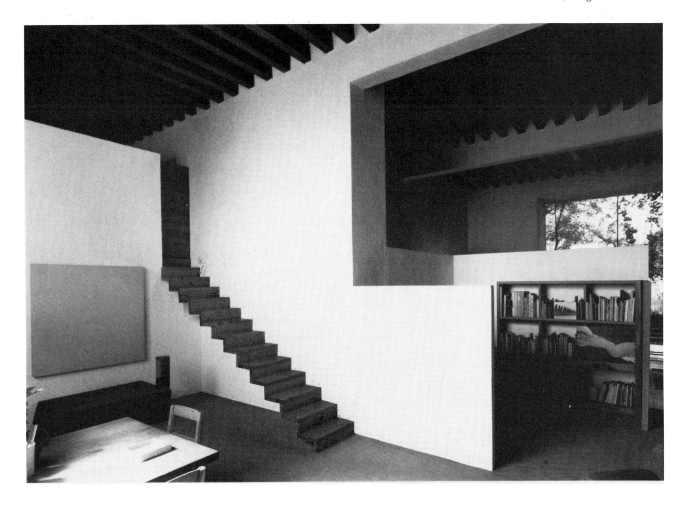

181. Luis Barragan. Plan, Chapel at Tlalpan. Tlalpan, Mexico. 1952–55. *Illustration from Emilio Ambasz,* The Architecture of Luis Barragan *(New York: The Museum of Modern Art, 1976).*

Goeritz is plain and unornamented except by its gridwork pattern of gold leaf. Both the simple and unadorned standing cross, which is lighted by a gold glass window also designed by Mathias Goeritz, and the simple wood benches recall those at Le Corbusier's Chapel at Ronchamp (see below).

Between the chapel and an adjacent smaller chapel, which is for confession and meditation, Barragan designed a lattice screen of wood that is lighted from above to produce a semi-wall of mystical lightness. Outside in the patio is another lattice screen, this one of concrete that is painted pale yellow on the outside and brighter yellow on the inside.

At Tlalpan there is throughout an atmosphere of golden mystery, an ineffable serenity that is also somewhat surreal—not the bizarre, desperate Surrealism of 1930s interiors, but that of de Chirico's empty outdoor spaces. Barragan's Surrealism evokes the eternal peace of religious meditation. The chapel at Tlalpan became a pivotal icon for designers.

The Resistance to Modernism

It would be completely misleading to suggest that the triumph of Modernism in the 1950s was an unresisted coup. Many professional designers and the general public alike were vehement in their opposition to the spread of the European import. Anti-Modernism was an entrenched camp from 1913 to 1960, and certainly afterward. Historical revivalists dug in their heels. Understandably, those trained in one style or generation cannot change overnight to another craft or approach. The triumph of Modernism was more dependent on the growth of the new, young generation than it was dependent on a change of sympathies. However, in their search for the new, which appealed to both designers and their clients, the well of historical styles had begun to run rather dry, and the compromise of the Transitional-Contemporary style was something of a mediator.

Traditionalism and Historicism

The scope of interior work for traditional designers expanded in the 1950s beyond the work for the affluent that had been their mainstay since the beginning of the century—houses and country clubs, yachts and executive offices. Now there were not only more of those projects, but also work for a greater number of private clients with smaller incomes. Countless semiprofessional and amateur decorators appeared to help out. In addition, there was now a great deal more corporate work for traditionalists as well as for Modernists—executive offices, suites, and floors of offices; hotel suites; and entire hotels.

Now too there were more commissions from industry, including airplanes and products for interior design use. The goal of the Deutscher Werkbund and of the Bauhaus to unite artist/designers with industry had been achieved. Only the criterion of quality remained to be raised.

Because of the increase in interior design work, it was more important than ever to distinguish works of quality and innovation from mere rehashes with better-produced (but still Borax) furnishings. The French eighteenth-century styles were now produced in all degrees of quality and accuracy.

Still, there was a yearning for the new—patterns and materials, shapes and other cultures—to the point of excess: trompe l'oeil and marbleizing (especially in imitation of malachite and lapis lazuli) were the rage. Country-house decorating fostered interiors that were essentially theatrical stage settings with little relationship to either function or contemporary life. Fantasy and romantic association or aspiration seemed to lead both designers and clients of these creations. The bywords of these sentiments were "comfortable" and "warm." In the search for patina, as large parts of our environmental heritage were being swept away by the building boom and urban renewal, antique or reproduction antique furniture and objects prevailed in this sector of the profession.

French Provincial Unpainted French Provincial pieces, which were sometimes distressed—beaten, battered, and chained—and aged in an effort to antique them, were a romantic symbol of the decade. Was it, in fact, a revival, a rediscovery, or a new invention? Even more suspect in provenance was the "Mediterranean" furniture that became popular with the middle market during the 1950s. It was based on an arch detail in walnut and other dark-toned woods, which were given a rough finish. To vanguard designers it was the Borax of the day.

Victorian Revival The revival of interest in Victorian art and design gained new impetus during the 1950s, sparked no doubt by the hundredth anniversary of the Crystal Palace Exhibition. In England, scholarly studies about the Victorian age appeared, including Henry-Russell Hitchcock's *Early Victorian Architecture* in 1954.[9] In America, the Brooklyn Museum opened its corridor of Victorian period rooms in 1953. They were widely published and drew great crowds. And in 1960 the Brooklyn Museum held the first major exhibition of Victorian decorative arts in this country; it was called "Victoriana."

The Residential Designers

Among the established decorating firms that were at the peak of their popularity with the affluent were McMillen Inc., Thedlow Inc., and Mrs. Henry Parish II, in New York; and 1930s revivalist Michael Taylor, the idiosyncratic John Dickinson, and the Neoclassicist Anthony Hale in San Francisco.

Always concerned with new art forms, Mrs. Archibald McMillen Brown felt that there were so many new ideas coming from France that, in 1952, she exhibited French Modern furniture, pictures, and art objects by twenty-six Parisian artists, designers, and craftsmen in the rooms of McMillen's brownstone offices. For McMillen's efforts in promoting French contemporary design, Mrs. Brown was awarded the Légion d'Honneur. French Contemporary/Moderne was, thereafter, a staple of the firm's designs.

Mrs. Henry Parish II (see Figure 182), by the end of the decade, had worked for then Senator and Mrs. John F. Kennedy, as well as for the Vincent Astors at Rhinebeck, New York, and for the Charles Engelhards in South Africa.

Michael Greer, who had first worked with Nancy McClelland, became interested in Napoleonic steel furniture and in Directoire style. It had made him something of an authority, and he created a number of stylish and truly refined if precious interiors in that style. Among them were his own apartment of 1954 and the restaurant Le Directoire in New York City.

French decorating firms also began to establish a secure clientele among this new international traveler set. They included Stephane Boudin of Jansen, the firm of Alavoine, and designers Jean Royere and Pierre Scapulla, the latter of whom created some of the most acclaimed historical restorations of the decade. The young American designer Charles E. Sevigny stayed in Paris after his education at the Parsons program there and designed interiors for the U.S. Foreign Buildings Operation. For them he showed a way to combine the new American International-Style furnishings with French antiques.

English designers also began to make an impact on American interior design, especially the recently prominent David Hicks, who was to bring a new look to floors with his checked and gridded carpet designs and his bathrooms with tubs centered in the room. Stage designers Oliver Messel and Cecil Beaton continued to design interiors and printed fabrics.

Dorothy Draper continued her practice in commercial interiors, including renovations of San Francisco's Fairmont Hotel and Mark Hopkins Hotel; New York's Park Lane Hotel and Barclay Hotel; and hospitals, retail stores, and automobile interiors for Detroit. She also wrote a newspaper column, beginning in 1959, that was syndicated to seventy papers. It made her one of the most popular names in interior design. Dorothy Draper was gradually to stop working in the next decade, when her firm was acquired by Carleton Varney. Although Mrs. Draper died in 1969, the firm bearing her name continues to design commercial interiors to this day.

182. Mrs. Henry Parish II. Own living room. New York City. Circa 1955. *Photograph from Katharine Tweed, ed.,* The Finest Rooms by America's Great Decorators *(New York: Viking Press, 1964).*

Among other designers doing commercial work were Maria Bergson & Associates, Emily Malino, Melanie Kahane, Elizabeth Draper, and Ellen Lehmann McCluskey, as well as the new group that called themselves space planners.

T. H. Robsjohn-Gibbings

T. H. Robsjohn-Gibbings continued in his spare, classically derived idiom based on natural materials such as marble, on solid colors, and on squares as in over-scaled ottomans, square lampshades, and frameless fireplaces. In 1951 he designed a bathroom for *Look* magazine with wall-to-wall and floor-to-ceiling heavily veined white marble and with walnut furniture that had all the sleekness of later Minimalism—without moldings or reveals.

He designed a display living room for the National Homefurnishings Show the next year with the same floor and wall surfacing; with exaggeratedly long and low fireplace, mantelpiece, and furniture; and with a leopard-skin rug. A walnut chair carved in simulated bamboo was a Robsjohn-Gibbings design of 1954, and screens with varying patterns ornamented his interiors for the rest of the decade.

Among the most extravagant of his interior designs was a dining room in the Graf House in Dallas by Edward Durell Stone in which the dining group floated

183. Edward Durell Stone and T. H. Robsjohn-Gibbings. Dining room, Bruno K. Graf House. Dallas, Texas. 1958. *Photograph © Ezra Stoller/ESTO, 1958.*

on a circular island in a pool flanked by one of Stone's pierced screens (see Figure 183). Robsjohn-Gibbings's table was a truncated fluted column of walnut.

His furniture designs of this decade, many produced by the Widdicomb Furniture Company of Grand Rapids, also included an amoeba-shaped cocktail table with two additional tiers of smaller amoebas, and case pieces that dispensed with visible drawer pulls by using clapboard-like overlapping drawers. His continuing interest in classicism also offered round arched panels and fluted columns.

Billy Baldwin

Following the death of Ruby Ross Wood in 1950, Billy Baldwin reorganized the firm with Edward Martin in 1952 and continued designing as Baldwin & Martin. He adapted the square, cane-wrapped side chair that Jean-Michel Frank had designed in the 1930s. He began to work with pattern-on-pattern, which became one of his trademarks, and often hung all the walls of a room with printed fabrics shirred on poles (see Figure 184). He liked simple, inexpensive furnishings—Indian prints

184. Billy Baldwin. Fabric-draped living room. New York City. Circa 1955. *Photograph by Horst.*

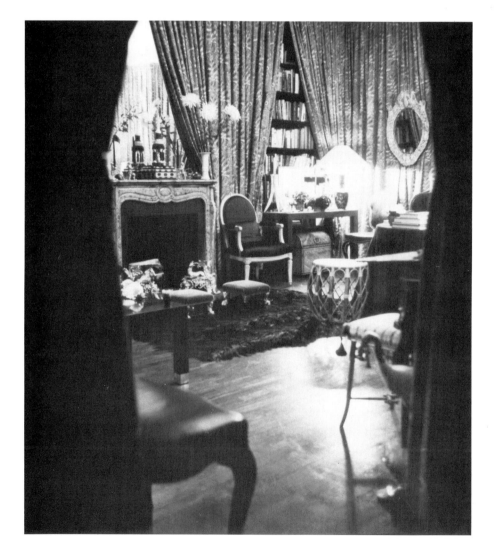

and rush matting—but used them with surprising elegance. He liked fabric-draped tables, wicker furniture, and chintz slipcovers. An admirer of Matisse, he filled his rooms splashily with fresh bright blues, pinks, and greens, with flower patterns, and white furniture. It was an Americanized country-house look.

Early in the decade Billy Baldwin transformed his own living room from its dark-green scheme (see Chapter 14) to one of white-painted walls with yellow silk curtains, for which he used imported Thaibok dress material for the first time, and vivid yellow satin upholsteries.

In 1955 Baldwin refinished his living room again. Without changing the furniture plan, he recovered walls, sofa, and windows with a white-on-white French linen-and-rayon brocade; with it he added apricot cut-velvet upholstery, brown-and-cream basketweave-patterned cut-velvet, and brown satin on a draped table. The transformations revealed how he stayed ahead of his time. In the same year he designed an apartment for Cole Porter in New York. The walls were covered in tortoiseshell vinyl, against which he designed tubular brass bookcases. He filled the rooms with a mixture of Cole Porter's French antiques and contemporary pieces.

During the decade he designed stage settings for producer Gilbert Miller, as well as a dining room for the Gilbert Millers' residence that had walls the color of strawberry sherbet and a Bessarabian carpet with a black background and medallions of pink and red flowers. He covered one floor with saddle-leather pieces studded with brass, an idea that was to be widely imitated.

As the 1950s continued, Baldwin & Martin decorated a house on Long Island by painting the principal rooms white glossy enamel—including the floor of one sitting room—and using a single brightly multicolored, boldly patterned floral chintz on the large upholstered pieces in each room. Most other furniture was also finished in white—lacquer tables, upholstered furniture, a white rug in one sitting room, and white-lacquered carved Victorian Louis XV Revival armchairs. (The concept has been credited to Edward Martin.)

Billy Baldwin's spare, meticulously chosen appointments and table vignettes completed his trademark. Those vignettes were composed assemblies of objects—two Japanese lacquer bowls, two turtle backs, one brass turtle from Morocco; or he combined bamboo, brass bamboo, a plant in a cloisonné jardiniere, a silver cigarette box, and a small oil painting; he also used watercolors, bronzes, cachepots, porcelains, pre-Columbian sculptures mounted on Plexiglas, and a wide range of small, textured, folk art and museum-like objects, and unusual objects from around the world. The vignettes were composed as carefully as still-life paintings, and showed Billy Baldwin's eye for texture, scale, juxtaposition, and detail.

Michael Taylor

In the 1950s the designs of Michael Taylor came to national prominence. Born in Modesto, California, Michael Taylor (1927–) grew up in Santa Rosa and began his career at Jackson's furniture store and with the decorator Mrs. Kasper in San Francisco. In 1952 he formed a partnership with Frances Mihailoff and began to design his off-white rooms with tall doors and other large-scale pieces. He formed his independent practice in San Francisco in 1957.

Taylor liked to use color, but not many colors in a single space, feeling that "a good room should be predominantly one color." He also liked to use a single pattern throughout a room. He used semitropical plants extravagantly, since it was possible to maintain them well in the California climate. "Plants have a way of preventing a room from appearing overdecorated; they also soften the light," he said.[10] Michael Taylor's style is a special unorthodoxy that at its best is alive with freshness.

Taylor was strongly influenced by Syrie Maugham. When Frances Elkins died, he bought much of her business property, including lamp molds and other furniture designs that Mrs. Elkins had acquired from Syrie Maugham.

Taylor then began to revive and reinterpret the all-white room schemes of Syrie Maugham. In one California bedroom (1957), Taylor reinterpreted Syrie Maugham's celebrated bedroom for Mrs. Tobin Clark in San Mateo, California (see Chapter 13). In Taylor's reinterpretation all the walls, ceiling, carpet, and furniture were white, including an English chinoiserie four-poster bed (he did another bedroom in this scheme with two four-posters), benches, and lamps. He draped the beds and side tables in white patterned brocade. Mantelpiece, andirons, occasional tables, and accessories were also white. Two small armchairs copied from the Syrie Maugham collection, as were the beds and benches, were upholstered in white but accented with green tufting buttons and green ribbons; the bench pads were covered in green, in a patterned fabric like the bed drapery. Tree ferns and other green plants brought the crisp fresh scheme to life, while a tall ornate Venetian mirror of fine quality and one multicolor painting gave the room sparkle and accent.

John Dickinson

In California, John Dickinson began to come to attention. Born in Redlands, California, John Dickinson (1920–82) studied at the Parsons School of Design in the 1940s and returned to Redlands to do his apprenticeship in a furniture store. He later moved to San Francisco to begin his career with E. Coleman Dick, and soon began to be recognized for his idiosyncratic approach. His style matured in the next several decades, which were cut short after too-few completed projects in the 1970s (see Chapter 17).

Albert Hadley

Among the new designers of the decade was Albert Hadley, teacher and residential designer who was to become one of the leading residential designers of the next three decades. Born in Nashville, Tennessee, Hadley (1920–) began his design career by working for A. Herbert Rogers in Nashville. But with his eyes set on New York, he went in 1946 determined to meet Eleanor McMillen Brown, Billy Baldwin, George Stacey, William Pahlmann, and other important designers of the time.

After Mrs. Brown asked if he had been to Parsons, he learned that she hired only Parsons graduates. He enrolled in the Parsons six-week summer course and was awarded the Elsie de Wolfe scholarship to study in Paris. He graduated from Parsons in 1949.

He next worked for Roslyn Rosier, one of the most inventive antique dealers in New York, and then was asked by Van Day Truex to teach at Parsons in New York and Europe. Among his students in the next five years were Joseph Braswell, David Whitcomb, Carrie Donovan, Jay Hyde Crawford, Thomas Morrow, A. T. Hammet, and Albino Cimonetti.

After that five-year teaching period, Hadley was in independent practice for a period and in 1956 joined McMillen Inc. as a staff decorator. Among his first acclaimed interiors was a bedroom in New York for theater director Joshua Logan, who wanted the room to complement his paintings. Hadley's design was conceived to be like a Vuillard painting—all pattern on pattern, in the new wave of the decade—and something of what the designer considered "a fantasy." His own apartment, always in transformation, featured carved wood white palm-tree torchères that had been acquired from Elsie de Wolfe and are believed to have been designed by Emilio Terry (see Figure 185). They started a revival. From then on Albert Hadley began to be known for his fresh imagination and thorough historical background. He was to join Mrs. Henry Parish II in 1961 (see page 201ff.).

185. Albert Hadley. Own apartment. New York City. Late 1950s. *Photograph by Richard Jeffery.*

Other Residential Designers

Other prominent residential designers in the 1950s were James Amster, Yale R. Burge, David Whitcomb, and Braswell-Cook. The firm of Tom Lee Ltd., which combined traditional and Modern design for exhibition and hotel spaces, also came to the forefront of interior design at this time. The model rooms designed by Barbara D'Arcy for Bloomingdale's began to attract crowds and publicity from

1957 on. As much as any other designer, Barbara D'Arcy made the public aware of the varieties of style that the decade offered—both historicism and Modernism, as well as eclectic and imaginative mixtures of substyles and periods. That leavening helped the public to understand Modernism's honesty and discretion in design (see page 177ff.).

The Transitional–Contemporary Designers

William Pahlmann

In the 1950s William Pahlmann was at the height of his career, designing hotels and offices, residences and apartment lobbies, exhibitions and showrooms, department stores and shops, as well as interior design products. Among his clients were Henry Morgan & Company, John Wanamaker and Bonwit Teller stores, and hotels in Miami, Atlanta, and Atlantic City. In 1950 he served as president of the New York chapter of the American Institute of Decorators. He wrote *The Pahlmann Book of Interior Design* in 1955. He also wrote a syndicated newspaper column called "A Matter of Taste."

Pahlmann and his associates—who included Daren Pierce, George Thiel, James Hendrix, and Jack Conner—designed rooms as striped tents, and mixed antiques and contemporary pieces. Throughout the 1950s William Pahlmann Associates also designed fabrics, wallpapers and other wall coverings, carpets and floor tiles, lighting and lighting fixtures. In 1952 the firm designed a line of furniture with oversize castors—chairs, tables, and even a credenza that had twin beds in it. The castors made the pieces more easily mobile to swing around to face the television; it was called the Momentum Line (see Figure 186). They used that line along with wall-hung exposed bookshelves, Moroccan carpets, and antiques covered in glossy tortoiseshell leather. It was a highly patterned and textured decade.

186. William Pahlmann. "Momentum" Furniture. 1952. *Photograph courtesy William Pahlmann.*

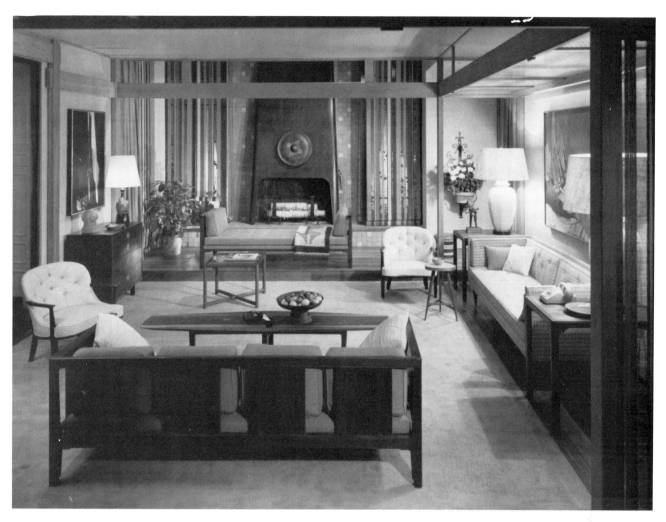

187. Edward Wormley. Model living room for Dunbar's Janus Collection. Chicago, Illinois. 1957. *Photograph courtesy Edward Wormley.*

Pahlmann was also in the forefront of the new color richness that swept the end of the decade (see below). Among the color combinations he was proud of introducing were *tête de nègre*, green, orange, and deep cerulean blue for the lounge of the Columbus Hotel in Miami (1953); driftwood, lime, orange, and white (1954); Siamese pink, sandalwood, ivory, and pink (1955); and Venetian red, Florentine green, Carrara white, and vulcan brown (1956).

During the decade he was design consultant to Restaurant Associates, for whom he designed The Forum of the Twelve Caesars, The Brasserie, La Trattoria, Charlie Brown's, and the Zum-Zum chain. He also served as consultant to Restaurant Associates on Philip Johnson's Four Seasons Restaurant (see Chapter 16).

Edward Wormley

Throughout the decade Edward Wormley continued to produce line after line of furniture designs—150 pieces a year for the Dunbar Furniture Company. Nine of his designs were chosen for the Museum of Modern Art's Good Design show of 1951. His A Chair of 1959 with its wood frame of compass-shaped rear legs and caned back was among the most popular. Dunbar's advertising campaign of furniture photographed outdoors—on the plains of the Midwest or Africa—captured public attention.

Wormley also produced numerous showrooms (see Figure 187) and interiors. Among them was his own apartment design in Manhattan, which was a laboratory of his ideas. One of his designs with Bertha Schaefer in 1955 was for an L-shaped living room in which the L was used as a bedroom with a three-cushion sofa; walls and ceiling were covered in a blue strié paper; blue-gray taffeta draperies were hung at the windows; the carpet was of blue chenille; furnishings were Wormley's designs for Dunbar.

Other American Furniture Designers

Swelling the ranks of designers to meet the demand for interior furnishings were Tommi Parzinger, who continued to produce lacquer and brass furniture in the lingering Wiener Werkstaette idiom, and who opened a showroom in 1954; Paul McCobb, who designed rational Machine-Age pieces and storage walls; and Harvey Probber, Paul Laszlo, and Hoffman & Hedrich.

Professional Organizations

In 1957 the National Society of Interior Designers (NSID) was founded, making two rival, competitive, and redundant professional organizations. It was a situation that lasted until 1975. But the very name of the new organization furthered the move away from the term "decorator." It was not without some resistance that this happened—Billy Baldwin, for example, refused to be called an interior designer—and to this day many of the traditionalists prefer to call themselves decorators. In 1961 the American Institute of Decorators changed its name, but not its acronym (AID), to American Institute of Interior Designers. The new twentieth-century profession was at last mature.

Renewal versus Heritage

The Federal Urban Renewal program was passed by Congress as part of the Housing Act of 1954. Since the 1930s the "elimination of slums" had been a goal. In the 1950s a "slum" seemed to mean any building over thirty years old. At this time the federal highway program began to cut swathes around and through American cities. These highways usually were planned to run through slum areas, stripping them away. Stripped away along with the "slums" were superb old buildings, treasuries of our culture, architecture and interiors of all descriptions. It was all in the goal of stripping away that taboo of Modernism—history. It was also with the aim of creating the city beautiful, the *ville radieuse* concept of Le Corbusier, the city filled with gardens and sunshine—the triumph of Modern urban planning. In this decade construction of cultural centers and performing arts centers was initiated, and many much-needed new housing developments were created. But often, to make them, the continuity of cities was shattered.

This fitted in with the decade's viewpoint on quality: If a thing was good enough in isolation, then it could stand next to anything else also good. It was the attitude of Good Design. But it disregarded stylistic and other incompatibilities, disregarded context and continuity. So it was that isolated towers—detached on podiums or plazas, devoid of commercial shops with urban vitality, and discontinuous with pedestrian traffic—gradually replaced what was old in our downtowns.

The Search for Texture and Patina

At the same time a counterdirection showed an innate human need for salvaging the old, for the patina of centuries. Bereft of ornament and decoration due to the International Style's taboo against historicism and applied decoration, designers wriggled in desperation to find some substitute for this culturally established need.

Objects such as carriage lights, balancing scales, and old equipment and tools—optimally of brass or bronze—were sought after and collected by the score as decorative pieces that offset the new, crisp Modern interiors. Even in the realm of architecture the newly developed steel COR-10—which weathers to develop its own rusted finish as a protective surface—was adopted. The balance of two directions and textural effects was continued.

A New Free-Form Expressionism

Even within the Modern movement after the middle of the 1950s, former disciples of Mies and Gropius began to invert their theories—or to expand their theories in order to enrich the idiom. The impetus of this was not only their own search to enrich the Modern idiom as the second generation of Modernists, but also the example of Le Corbusier, who completely rejuvenated his own work—as well as that of all other designers from then on—with the design of his Chapel at Ronchamp.

The Chapel at Ronchamp

The culmination of this search for something beyond the machine-image rectilinear Modernism of Mies was Le Corbusier's masterpiece of architectural sculpture, the Chapelle Notre-Dame-du-Haut (see color plate 5) at Ronchamp in the south of France (1950–54). A free-form sculpture unparalleled among all previous buildings, Ronchamp was initially considered both expressionistic and irrational, on the one hand, and a compendium of religious symbolism on the other. Its symbolism was hauntingly evocative, if mannered and elusive. Le Corbusier called it "ineffable space."

In terms of form-giving, Ronchamp was the apotheosis of free-form. It was epochal in the design of architecture and interiors, and brilliantly if disturbingly presented a new alternative of organic plasticity. It changed the potential of architecture and interiors at mid-century by offering this totally new option. Its free-form vocabulary was emphasized by being contrasted with rectilinear elements to create both tension and balance.

At Ronchamp Le Corbusier inscribed a center axis in the flooring, and rectangular window and door openings, along with rectangular furniture and altar elements to reinforce the contrast. But the plan and section were a free and unprecedented assemblage of undulating curvilinear forms (see Figure 188A).

The interior (see Figure 188B) is essentially a single major space with ancillary spaces formed by the apparent folding or curving of concrete wall surfaces to enclose three chapels. Rough-textured walls of white-painted concrete, which was sprayed over masonry, are sloping—both toward the top and progressively thicker in plan. The floor slopes down to the altar on the natural grade. The curving, upturned gray ceiling floats above the walls on pins and on a spacer, which is sometimes translucent. Benches are grouped into a trapezoidal block. Windows, rectangular and square, are of varied sizes and in random pattern, with glass that is both clear and colored, but always transparent; they create truly mystical pinpoints of light away from the outerworld.

The chapels, one of which is painted an intense red, are lighted by half-domes with glass on one side. The wall leading to the sacristy is painted violet. This nebulous, flowing world is mysterious and mystical, supremely evocative of religious atmosphere—though personally, willfully, and iconoclastically so, in view of traditional ecclesiastical architecture. For both religious interiors and for form-making, Ronchamp was epochal.

Le Corbusier showed at Ronchamp—as he had showed at the Unité d'Habitation apartment house in Marseilles (1947–52) and at his later Jaoul houses at

188A. Le Corbusier. Perspective axonometric diagram, for Chapel at Ronchamp. Ronchamp, France. 1950–54. *Illustration from Duane and Sarah Preble,* Artforms *(New York: Harper & Row, 1985).*

188B. Le Corbusier. Notre-Dame-du-Haut. Ronchamp, France. 1950–54. *Photograph © Ezra Stoller/ESTO, 1955.*

Neuilly-sur-Seine (1955–57) and at the Convent of La Tourette near Lyons (1957–60)—how rough strength could be as powerful an achievement as refined sophistication. The free-form plasticity achieved at Ronchamp opened a new avenue for the world of design.

Due largely to Le Corbusier's work at this time, concrete came to be thought of almost as a superscale modeling clay; by analogy, it took the clay of the potter's wheel and threw it now at the scale of buildings. No one could make a claim that the history of concrete—or indeed the production and use of it—was directly descended from the production or use of ceramics. Yet the mixture of earth and water, of molds and forms, and of curing processes seemed—after Ronchamp provided its leap of vision—sufficiently similar to make the analogy with the larger-scale, and thereafter ever more pliable and potentially sculptural, building industry.

European Parallels

Ronchamp was the beginning of a new era in design. There had been a few precedents—in the work of the German Expressionists, in the work of Erich Mendelsohn, and elsewhere. Another forerunner of Ronchamp's sculptural quality was Frederick Kiesler's Endless House project, which had been frequently revised from 1923 to 1960. The Endless House was an egg-shaped sculptural dwelling with continuously curvilinear walls and no distinctions between floors, walls, and ceilings. Never built, it was widely influential through publications.

In Europe the search for such texture and sculptural character was expressed by England's New Brutalism, which gave rugged functionalism the lead over smooth formalism. It was epitomized in the work of Peter and Alison Smithson and in the work of James Stirling. In addition, Alvar Aalto's Town Hall at Saynatsalo, Finland (1951), along with his church at Vuoksenniska, Imatra (1957–59), continued his personal free-form Expressionism. More sculpturally expressionistic was the Opera House for Sydney, Australia, designed by Denmark's Bjorn Utzon (1958–68), with its roof of sail-like structures at the edge of the Sydney harbor.

This direction was strongly reflected in interior work by Arne Jacobsen's new kind of Expressionism in his SAS Royal Hotel in Copenhagen, where the Egg and Swan chairs that Jacobsen had designed in 1959 gave sculptural life to the International Style surroundings.

The Decade of the Parabola

In South America the work of Oscar Niemeyer at the new capital city of Brasilia reiterated these sculptural directions. Neo-Baroque parabolas and inverted parabolas were to be seen on Oscar Niemeyer's new buildings in Brasilia—the Presidential Palace (1958) and the government parliamentary buildings, which were completed the next year.

From the United States came some elaborately convoluted sculpturing—all under the name of concrete technology. These structural gymnastics aimed to proclaim an independence from the Miesian rectangle. Other structural gymnastics, such pyramidal forms called hyperbolic-paraboloids, were added to this search to go beyond the square and the rectangle. This direction gained the epithet "the new sensualism."

It was all part of the search by the second generation of Modernists to go beyond the tenets of their predecessors and teachers. They aimed not to imitate the teaching of Mies or Gropius, but, as Paul Rudolph said, to bounce off those satellites to aim at a new direction. The new generation began to explore plasticity, classicizing elements, decorative and historical motifs, and vernacular and contextual approaches. They based their thinking on the functional diagram, but aimed to enrich it with visual interest. That plastic direction included Minoru Yamasaki's vaulted St. Louis Airport (1956), Philip Johnson's open-air church in New Harmony, Indiana (1960), and Saarinen's TWA Terminal (see Chapter 16). This search for new form also led to Saarinen's Pedestal Furniture (1955) and to the new rich colors in fabric design (see below).

In this vein, in the mid-1950s, Eero Saarinen's chapel for the Massachusetts Institute of Technology (MIT) in 1955 had a mystical interior, intended to be daylighted by reflections from a moat through floor-height arched windows, and a glittering reredos of gilt-bronze confetti-like screen by Harry Bertoia. Saarinen's John Deere Building in Moline, Illinois (1958–62), which was the first to use the new weathering COR-10 steel, had offices of especial elegance and richness beyond the work of his contemporaries.

At its most common, the automobile tail fins introduced by Detroit in 1956 reiterated this new sculptural direction of the decade. Stylistically, it was the age of the two-tone design—cars, jackets, and upholstery. And between the freest free-form sculpture of Ronchamp and the sleekness of rectilinear machine-image International Style, the polished bronze sculpture of Constantin Brancusi's *Bird in Flight* became a mediating symbol.

The Interiors of Louis Kahn

After the early 1950s the work of Louis Kahn began to influence architecture and interior design with another approach to sculptural effects. Following the opening of his Yale Art Gallery (1951–53), Kahn was on his way to becoming the reigning American architect, as he certainly was after the death of Eero Saarinen in 1961.

Born on the Island of Saarama, Estonia (now USSR), Louis I. Kahn (1901–74) was brought to Philadelphia by his parents in 1905. He studied art at the Pennsylvania Academy of Fine Arts in Philadelphia; he studied architecture at the University of Pennsylvania till 1924. He worked for other architects through the Depression and for the WPA, and formed partnerships with George Howe and Oscar Stonorov primarily designing housing until the late 1940s. Then he began to teach at Yale. It was not until after his Yale Art Gallery building was in progress, when he was over fifty, that he began to become known beyond Philadelphia.

Louis Kahn's Yale Art Gallery spaces offered universal loft space with a degree of flexibility for changing exhibitions owing to some demountable, though heavy, partitions. But it was the clarity of his design and the ornamental quality of his tetrahedral concrete ceiling that showed the way to the new richness in architecture and interiors.

Louis Kahn's interiors, following on the raw concrete work Le Corbusier planned for the Indian capital of Chandigarh, added a superscale dimension of similar motifs along with the grace and refinement of concrete and brickwork that made him a poet of materials. His Richards Medical Center in Philadelphia proclaimed him the most influential architect of his day when the drawings were shown in the late 1950s (see Chapter 16). Kahn's First Unitarian Church in Rochester, New York (1959–67), was an interior of major significance. Its monumental skylit monitors or lanterns admitted ever-changing light onto the sanctuary and onto its Jack Lenor Larsen–designed tapestry hanging.

The Filigree Screen

Among the ornamental devices that architects and designers adopted in the 1950s were openwork, patterned screens. They were a 1950s device to provide texture as well as ornament for the new Modernism that forbade other than integral orna-mentation. Even then, it was only under the guise of a sunscreening device or some other lighting or privacy function that such screens could be accepted. Louis Kahn's Art Gallery ceiling was prototypical in this direction of patterning to coun-teract the ubiquitous planar surfaces of Modern design (though it was closer to the space-frames of Buckminster Fuller than to other openwork screens, and by no means a direct influence on interior designers).

At the same time the young architect Paul Rudolph designed a curve-plan screen made of folded cardboard between wood strips for his entry to the Museum of Modern Art's Good Design show of 1952. The California architects Campbell & Wong installed cut-and-pierced lattice Japanese screens in several interiors they designed. But it was the work of Edward Durell Stone, who devised an openwork structural concrete block that when stacked formed a filigree screen, that brought this concept to popularity and ultimate overuse. Stone's American Embassy in New Delhi (completed in 1954)—along with his U.S. Pavilion for the Brussels World's Fair (1958), his house for Mr. and Mrs. Bruno K. Graf in Dallas (1958), and his own townhouse on Manhattan's East 64th Street (1959)—catapulted both the architect and the filigree screen into international prominence.

In this same vein, though usually constructed of aluminum, were the large-scale screens used to shield the sun—as well as to provide integral ornamentation to buildings—by Minoru Yamasaki. His McGregor Conference Center for Wayne State University in Detroit (1958) and his Reynolds Metal Office Building in South-field, Michigan (1959), were immediate popularizers of this new Decorated Modern style, which his theme arches for the Seattle World's Fair (1962) capitalized.

In interiors, then, it was the decade of filigree screens. They offered layering and semitransparency as well as pattern and texture. Moroccan panels and mesh casements were other variations on this concept. Harry Bertoia's sculptural metal screens were a vanguard of this direction. One of the most popular versions was the sinuous interweaving openwork screen designed by Erwin Hauer. Some called this the reaction against and rejection of Modernism; others called it the search for pattern, texture, and decoration to fill the gap that Modernism had created with its taboos against these fundamental elements of design.

The New Color Richness

Midway in the 1950s, Bauhaus principles were enriched by the sensuous colors of the color-field school of Abstract Expressionism. In the art world Abstract Expres-sionism was making New York the new art capital. The color-field painters aimed to make statements with abstract fields of large colored areas. The romantic colors of the color-field painters—Bernard Newman, Mark Rothko, Robert Motherwell, Adolph Gottlieb, Clyfford Still, and Ad Reinhardt—though sometimes dark and somber, were far more sensuous than the primary colors that had been the staple of De Stijl–Bauhaus ideology. They opened a new color freedom in the design world of the 1950s.

In fabrics the romantic colors—sometimes deep and mysterious, sometimes vibrant and pulsating—of Dorothy Liebes, Alexander Girard, Jack Lenor Larsen (see color plate 7), Jim Thompson, and Boris Kroll—revolutionized the color sense of the 1950s and helped to make more palatable to more people the spare designs derived from Miesian principles. The rich Siamese silks imported by Jim Thomp-son's firm Thaibok and the fabrics produced by Franco Scalamandre and Greeff Fabrics also continued this direction, which *House Beautiful* deemed "the return to elegance."

Dorothy Liebes

Dorothy Liebes (see Chapter 14) was the pioneer in this new color richness in fabrics for the general public (see color plate 7) as her commissions for large-scale work came from du Pont in 1955 and Bigelow-Sanford in 1957. For them she adapted the unusual materials and color combinations of her handweaving to machine-weaving techniques. Among her combinations were leather, rayon, silk, and metal thread; or bamboo splits, wood dowels, rayon, cotton, chenille, and metallics such as Lurex. She also used plastics, sequins, grass, and ticker tape in her weaving. Typical placemats and, later, roll-up window blinds might have flat bamboo strips, matchstick bamboo dowels, and ribbons of narrow purple grosgrain and wide purple satin.

Boris Kroll

During the 1950s weaver-designer Boris Kroll established the colors and textures that became his signature. Born in Buffalo, New York, Kroll (1913–) began working in his brother's Modern furniture factory in New York at the age of seventeen and recognized that there were only a few good traditional weaves available. He has spent the rest of his life remedying that situation.

He opened his first showroom in 1934, and in 1936 established his first collection of handwoven imported fabrics. At this time he also taught himself to weave, and became dedicated to the jacquard loom. During the 1930s he provided fabrics for Robsjohn-Gibbings's Weber House, for Raymond Loewy's exhibition room at the Metropolitan Museum of Art, for the Neiman-Marcus and J. L. Hudson department stores, and for several ocean liners. At the end of the 1930s he switched from handweaving to power production. He spent the war in armed service stationed in the Pacific, and in 1946 began to open his string of showrooms across the country.

In the 1950s his signature weaves and colors were hot and vibrant. His Caribbean collection of 1952, Mediterranean collection of 1955, and Etruscan collection of 1956 established him as a colorist and were major contributions to "the return to elegance." In 1953 he won thirteen awards in the Museum of Modern Art's Good Design show.

Jack Lenor Larsen

Fresh in the world of fabric design (see color plate 7), Jack Lenor Larsen made his debut with the fabrics commissioned for Lever House in 1952 (see above) and continued as one of the most imaginative designers of textiles for the next three decades. Born in Seattle, Washington, to Danish-Canadian parents, Larsen (1927–) studied architecture at the University of Washington in Seattle, then studied furniture design, but settled on weaving. He attended Cranbrook Academy from 1950 to 1951, and opened his New York studio later that year. At that time he demonstrated the direction for which he has become recognized—weaving on power looms with handspun yarns and random repeats to create a handwoven look.

Larsen has concentrated on the structure of fabrics more than on printed applied patterns, although he was first to introduce printed velvet upholstery in 1959, the first stretch upholstery in 1961, and the development of warp-knit casements such as the Saran monofilament Interplay (1960). Among his commissions have been fabrics for Pan Am and Braniff; large-scale theater curtains for Wolf Trap Farm Park performing arts center in Virginia and for the Phoenix Civic Plaza concert hall; quilted silk banners for the Sears bank in Chicago's Sears Tower (1974); and numerous other commissions and collections of fabrics.

Alexander Girard

In the Modern movement's concentration on structure, only one designer triumphed in the realm of printed pattern—Alexander Girard. He was color consultant to the GM Research Center from 1951 to 1952, and in 1951 began to design fabrics for Herman Miller.

Girard's fabrics (see color plate 7) reclaimed the province of two-dimensional applied pattern that was initiated by the fabric designs of C. F. A. Voysey at the end of the nineteenth century, and they were also part of this color revolution. He acclaimed "simple geometric patterns and brilliant primary color ranges."[11] His fabrics were riots of color—one design of 1/4-inch stripes alternates purple, green, orange, blue, and magenta to produce a spontaneous, fun-filled revelation. Dismissing representational pattern because of the distortions created when draped and folded, Girard adopted stripes and checks, and repeated geometric forms such as circles and hexagons.

Simplicity and a planar effect are fundamental to his designs. "His endless variations on related stripes, checks, and solids primarily within the confines of one weave, one yarn, and one density prove his innovative prowess," Jack Lenor Larsen has written.[12] Girard continued to design fabrics for the next two decades.

A New Elegance in Furniture

In the area of furniture design Eero Saarinen's Pedestal Furniture of 1955, produced by Knoll, signaled not only the arrival of the plastic chair in an elegant form, but also its adoption for use in living rooms and board rooms. In 1958, therefore, when Saarinen's Expressionistic TWA Terminal design was beginning to capture people's fancies, the Museum of Contemporary Crafts in New York mounted an exhibition of the glass and metal work of Louis Comfort Tiffany. The design world was prepared to accept whiplash curves and sensuous colors as a bold new direction.

Frank Lloyd Wright

The H. C. Price Company Tower

In the early 1950s Frank Lloyd Wright also built his first, and only, freestanding skyscraper—the H. C. Price Company Tower (1953–56) in Bartlesville, Oklahoma. He had added a tower to the S. C. Johnson & Son Administration Building, but the smaller Price Tower was his only freestanding high-rise project.

Based on a 1929 proposal, the Price Tower is a residential and studio complex with double height and mezzanine spaces based on an interlocking plan of triangles and trapezoids and sheathed in copper panels, copper louvers, and glass. In the 1940s Wright had begun to investigate designing buildings as single geometric forms, such as triangle and arc; subsequently, he composed projects from repeated modular units such as triangle, hexagon, and circle. Price Tower was in this vein.

The furniture Wright designed for these spaces—in line with his goal of consistent, integrated, total design—was of cast aluminum in forms that reiterated the elements of the plan. The design of this furniture seemed at the time rather bizarre and unrealistically futuristic; yet it was to prefigure or, perhaps, serve as the basis for countless movies and television productions about outer-space travel twenty and thirty years later. His designs for other furniture, fabrics, and wallpapers were mass-marketed during the 1950s, but it was an homage rather than a financial venture.

The Guggenheim Museum

The decade closed with the death of Frank Lloyd Wright in April 1959, two months before his ninety-second birthday. His Guggenheim Museum (1943–60) was in construction and nearly finished, giving New York City a major building by Wright. A total design based on the circle inside and out, the poured-in-place concrete Guggenheim Museum has a breathtaking interior space (see Figure 189) that is one of the masterpieces of twentieth-century design—Philip Johnson called it one of the greatest rooms of the twentieth century.

The museum interior combines formalism and functionalism in its expanding spiral ramp, which is a single, continuous circular route along which artworks are displayed on the perimeter wall. Regardless of the controversial nature of the ramp as a way of seeing paintings and sculptures—and there are vehement opinions on both sides—the ramp is dynamic enough a line for the space to require no further ornamentation. A skylight-dome 92 feet above ground level relates the space to

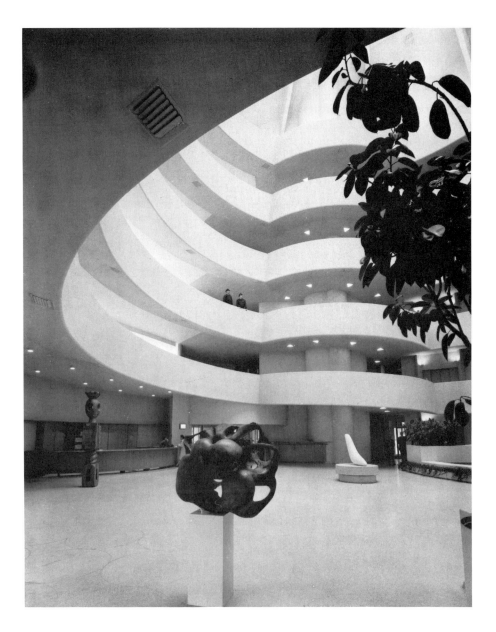

189. Frank Lloyd Wright. Guggenheim Museum. New York City. 1943–60. *Photograph by Julius Shulman.*

outdoor nature and light; though one can regret the pattern of the supporting ribs that the building code dictated, instead of Wright's proposed design of glass tubes, like those at the S. C. Johnson & Son Administration Building tower. Still, it is a major monument to the life and work of America's greatest architect, who lived long enough to see the triumph of Modern design, in a form different from what he envisioned yet of which he himself had been the American pioneer.

Suggested Reading

Ambasz, Emilio. *The Architecture of Luis Barragan.* New York: The Museum of Modern Art, 1976.

Baldwin, Billy. *Billy Baldwin Remembers.* New York: Harcourt Brace Jovanovich, 1974.

Banham, Reyner. *The Architecture of the Well-Tempered Environment.* London: The Architectural Press, 1969. Chicago: University of Chicago Press, 1969.

Bony, Anne. *Les Années 50.* Paris: Editions du Regard, 1982.

Brown, Erica. *Sixty Years of Interior Design: The World of McMillen.* New York: Viking Press, 1982.

Cook, Jeffrey. *The Architecture of Bruce Goff.* New York: Harper & Row, 1978.

Darling, Sharon. *Chicago Furniture: Art, Craft, and Industry 1833–1983.* New York: W. W. Norton, 1983.

DeLong, David. *The Architecture of Bruce Goff: Buildings and Projects 1916–1974.* London and New York, 1977.

Design Quarterly. "Nelson/Eames/Girard/Propst: The Design Process at Herman Miller." Minneapolis: Walker Art Center, 1975.

Dixon, John Morris. "Goff on Goff." *Progressive Architecture.* December 1962.

Drexler, Arthur. *Charles Eames.* New York: The Museum of Modern Art, 1973.

Dreyfuss, Henry. *Designing for People: Human Factors in Design.* New York: Simon & Schuster, 1955.

Emery, Sherman, ed. 50th Anniversary Issue, *Interior Design.* April 1982.

Futagawa, Yukio. *Bruce Goff: Bavinger House and Price House.* Tokyo: ADA Edita Tokyo, 1975.

Gueft, Olga. "Two Decades of Interiors: 1940–1960," *Interiors.* November 1960.

Hennessey, William J. *Russel Wright: American Designer.* Cambridge: MIT Press, 1983.

Herdeg, Klaus. *The Decorated Diagram: Harvard Architecture and the Failure of the Bauhaus Legacy.* Cambridge: MIT Press, 1983.

Hiesinger, Kathryn B., and George H. Marcus, eds. *Design Since 1945.* Philadelphia: The Philadelphia Museum of Art, 1983.

Il Design Italiano Degli Anni '50. Editore: IGIS Spa, 1981.

Jacobus, John M., Jr. "Postwar Architecture, 1945–60," *American Art.* New York: Prentice-Hall, Harry N. Abrams, 1979.

Jeanneret, Charles-Edouard. *Le Corbusier: 1910–65.* Zurich: Les Editions d'Architecture Zurich, 1967.

Mang, Karl. *History of Modern Furniture.* New York: Harry N. Abrams, 1979.

McCoy, Esther. *The Second Generation.* Layton, Utah: Gibbs M. Smith, 1984.

Meadmore, Clement. *The Modern Chair.* New York: Van Nostrand Reinhold, 1975.

Pinkham, Roger, ed. *Oliver Messel,* catalogue of an exhibition. London: Victoria and Albert Museum, 1983.

Rae, Christine. *Knoll au Louvre.* New York: Knoll International, 1971.

Robsjohn-Gibbings, T. H. *Homes of the Brave.* New York: Alfred A. Knopf, 1954.

Robsjohn-Gibbings, T. H., with Carlton W. Pullin. *The Furniture of Classical Greece.* New York: Alfred A. Knopf, 1963.

Smith, C. Ray. "Model of Office Planning," *Progressive Architecture*. March 1962, pp. 151ff. Executive Offices, Cowles Magazines, Inc., by Knoll Planning Unit.

———. "Offices for Irwin Miller in Columbus, Indiana, by Alexander Girard," *Progressive Architecture*. October 1962.

The Architecture of Skidmore, Owings & Merrill, 1950–1962. New York: Frederick A. Praeger, 1963.

Notes

1. Edgar Kaufmann, Jr., "Interior Design: Architecture or Decoration?" *Progressive Architecture* (October 1962), p. 144.

2. C. Ray Smith, "Model of Office Planning," *Progressive Architecture* (March 1962), pp. 151ff.

3. Since the Good Design shows were seen not only for six months at the Museum of Modern Art but also for six months subsequently at the Merchandise Mart in Chicago, they had considerable influence on the store buyers and professional designers who visited the Mart and its showrooms.

4. Jeffrey Cook's critical appraisal of Bruce Goff's work in the encyclopedia *Contemporary Architects* (New York: St. Martin's Press, 1980), p. 292.

5. Russel Wright, in a 1976 speech to the Society of Industrial Designers, quoted by William J. Hennessey in his illuminating exhibition catalogue *Russel Wright: American Designer* (Cambridge: MIT Press, 1983), p. 65.

6. Ibid., p. 86.

7. The conversation pit, used by many designers during the 1950s (see p. 439), became a motif of the decade.

8. Not many designers knew about Barragan during the 1950s. However, Benjamin Baldwin, Ward Bennett, and several others of their generation and older generations did become influenced by his work because they wintered in Mexico.

9. In England, scholarly studies about the Victorian age included John Steegman's *Consort of Taste* in 1950, Sir Nikolaus Pevsner's *High Victorian Design* in 1951, H. S. Goodhart-Rendel's Slade Lectures in 1953, and Henry-Russell Hitchcock's *Early Victorian Architecture*, which was published first in England in 1954. The Victorian Society was founded in England in 1958, and was followed later by a sister organization in America.

10. Michael Taylor, quoted from *The Finest Rooms by America's Great Decorators*, ed. Katharine Tweed (New York: Viking Press, 1964), p. 158.

11. Alexander Girard, quoted in textile designer Jack Lenor Larsen's splendid appraisal of Girard's work in "Nelson/Eames/Girard/Propst: The Design Process at Herman Miller," *Design Quarterly* 98/99 (Minneapolis: Walker Art Center, 1975), p. 31.

12. Larsen, loc. cit.

Chapter 16

1960–1970:
The Third Generation

In the 1960s the interior design field grew almost explosively. Along with a continuing building boom, adequate design work was available to support hundreds, perhaps thousands of professional and semiprofessional designers, of all degrees of creativity, in both residential and nonresidential design projects. Nonresidential design came to be known as contract design. Among the technical advances, synthetic fibers and permanent forming or shaping of manmade textiles continued to influence interior designers, both in the direction of simplicity and in the direction of excess.

Stylistically, a few vanguard Modern interior designers further refined and simplified the International Style into what became known as Minimal design. At the same time, the mainstream of interior designers and decorators who could see the possibilities of new business began to accept and adopt the Modern idiom. Also at the same time, however, a group of vanguard architects began to rebel against established Modern aesthetics and started a new—a perverse and contradictory—design approach. It was a complex and multidirectional decade.

The Architectural Establishment

For mainstream Modern designers at the beginning of the 1960s, total design was the objective for buildings and interiors. The Seagram Building by Mies van der Rohe and Philip Johnson (1958) had been recognized as the pinnacle of International-Style achievement in America.

The Four Seasons Restaurant

The Four Seasons Restaurant (see color plate 8), which had opened on the ground floor of the Seagram Building in 1959, was the most accessibly beautiful interior of the High Modern/International Style idiom. Designed by Philip Johnson with a team of consultants—including decorator William Pahlmann, lighting designer Richard Kelly, industrial designer Garth Huxtable, landscape architect Karl Linn, and graphic designer Emil Antonucci—the Four Seasons reached a balance of machine-made and living objects, of rectangular and free-form design that gave it relaxation and repose, movement and stability all at the same time.

The restaurant is planned as two principal rooms (see Figure 190A)—the main dining room and the bar—in the low block at the base of the tower; the two rooms are connected by a glass-enclosed passageway off the rear of the building lobby. There, art collector Philip Johnson hung a stage curtain painted by Picasso. The main dining room is walled on two sides by the bronze and glass curtain wall of the building, on a third side by rosewood paneling, and on the fourth by panels of rawhide—a cream-colored leather with a pale onyx-like texture. In the center of the space is a raised and gently circulating 20-foot-square pool sheathed in white marble; at the corners of the pool huge ficus trees spread their canopies. At each window module a planter basket is suspended on piano wire at head height to give the room a further sense of enclosure and focus.

The Bar and Grill room, however, is the real pinnacle of late-Miesian elegance (see Figure 190B). One enters up a carpeted stair to a grand space; it has a luxurious square bar to the right of the stair, a seating and planted seating area to the left, and tables with Brno chairs straight ahead. Beyond the table area is a raised mezzanine or gallery for more tables that gives the room multilevels of activity. Walls are of rosewood paneling; the ceiling is a gridded system that incorporates the heating, ventilating, and air-conditioning system as well as lighting designed by Richard Kelly. A discontinuous sculpture of narrow brass rods and steel wires by Richard Lippold is suspended over the bar.

At the curtain-wall windows small strands of aluminum chain, which are anodyzed brass and copper fabricated by Marie Nichols, are swagged to create large-scale Austrian shades of chainmail. Thoroughly consistent with the concept of the Seagram Building, the window covering also offers the unexpected effect of movement: The heating in winter activates the chains in a rippling movement from the bottom of the windows to the top; in summer the air-conditioning moves the chains from top to bottom.

Furniture made by Knoll Associates includes Mies's Brno and Barcelona chairs, and adaptations of Saarinen's Pedestal Furniture. All appointments were custom-designed by Johnson and his team of consultants. Johnson had taken the Miesian idiom to a new level of decorative elaboration. It was masterfully elegant and luxurious; it was third-generation Modern design.

Skidmore, Owings & Merrill and Davis Allen

Throughout the 1960s Skidmore, Owings & Merrill (SOM) continued to design interiors of the greatest refinement. Davis Allen had moved from SOM's Chicago office to become senior interior designer in SOM's New York office after his designs for the Inland Steel Building.

In the New York office he was responsible for the design of interiors for the Chase Manhattan Bank headquarters (see Figure 191), which in 1961 set the standard for corporate interiors for the decade; and for the interiors of the Beinecke Rare Book Library (1963) at Yale University; the Marine Midland Bank Building (1967) in New York; and the Texas Bank & Trust Company Building (1969) in Dallas. His interiors for the Mauna Kae Beach Hotel (1965) in Hawaii created a new model for oriental regionalism with its combination of Modernism and country-style furnishings of willow and cane.

Beyond Mies: Girard's Colors and Crafts

In the early 1960s other Modernists developed approaches to Modern interior design beyond the Miesian idiom, but with a continuing goal of total design. In 1960 Alexander Girard, at perhaps the height of his career as an architect specializing in interior design and fabric design, designed La Fonda del Sol, a restaurant in the Rockefeller Center complex that offered South American cuisine.

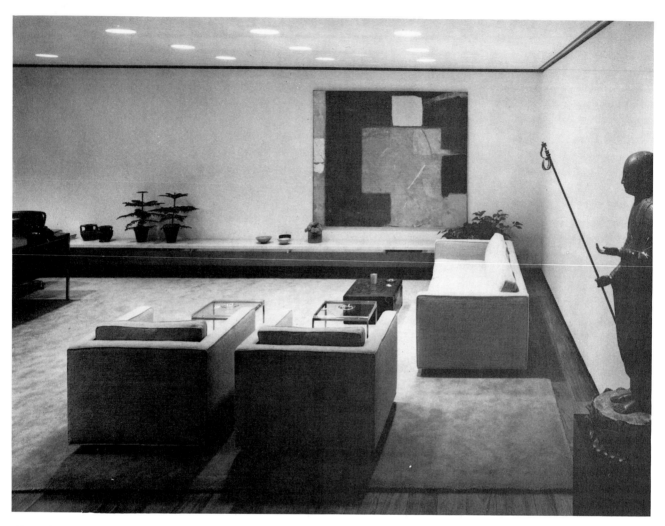

191. Skidmore, Owings & Merrill. Chase Manhattan Bank headquarters. New York City. 1958–61. *Photograph by Alexandre Georges.*

Within the space, he created a bar in the form of an adobe building; it had a random pattern of windows, reminiscent of Le Corbusier's Chapel at Ronchamp, that were used as vitrines to display the folk-craft objects that Girard was collecting. The passage to the main dining room was through a cafeteria-like space with open-pit cooking tiled in vibrating patterns of tile and graphics that echoed the busyness of the cooking activities taking place there. In the main dining room diners were presented with a plan composed of arc-shaped alcoves—in the manner of Mies's Tugendhat House dining room—clustered around a central space; each alcove was upholstered in a different vibrantly colored or patterned fabric, and the chairs at the round tables were similarly multicolored with upholstery on their white plastic shells. The world of Op Art had come to interior design.

In 1961 Girard created the Textiles and Objects shop as a retail outlet in Manhattan for the Herman Miller furniture company. All white and glistening, with high-gloss enameled walls and ceiling, onto which specially designed silver-bowl lamp bulbs reflected light, the shop's plan (see Figure 192) offered free-flowing space in the manner of the Barcelona Pavilion, though at much tighter scale. Girard achieved that plan by suspending flat panels of his fabric designs from the ceiling in a maze effect (see Figure 193); the panels did not touch the white tile floor. Within the white envelope, the textiles—of brilliant and vibrating colors and of sheer transparent virtuosity—along with the objects—multicolored or shimmering metal folk handcraft from South America, India, and elsewhere—created a sensational expansion of the Miesian idiom. The imagery of folk crafts had been joined to industry.

In 1965, when Girard's corporate design program for Braniff International Airlines (see color plate 11) was introduced, it should have been no surprise to find all these elements combined into one package for a public commercial enterprise. But it was. Girard designed not only the airplane interiors with his blend of vibrating fabrics—each seat in a different pattern—but also the plane exteriors, which were each painted a brilliant solid color—yellow, purple, red, orange, or apple green. Girard also designed Braniff's ticketing offices and posters; and he coordinated a team of consultants who designed coordinated uniforms, plateware, and everything that customers identified with Braniff—even the baggage-pickup trucks on the field.

It was total environmental and graphic design—and significantly for industry and transportation—and it added multicolor, a folk-craft decorative theme, Op Art effects, and true elegance. This was a considerable achievement in view of the average thin theatricality of most commercial and industrial design of the day. In the early 1980s Alexander and Susan Girard gave their 100,000-piece folk-art collection to establish the Girard Wing of the Museum of International Folk Art in Santa Fe, New Mexico. Alexander Girard designed the wing and the exhibition of the collection.

Russel Wright's Shun Lee Dynasty Restaurant

Not entirely dissimilar in its remarkable combination of influences, the Shun Lee Dynasty Restaurant designed by Russel Wright opened in New York in 1966. It was Wright's last major commercial interior. The midtown Chinese restaurant, now demolished, was a dedicated Modernist's reinterpretation of Chinese tinsel glitter and flamboyant color. Chinese cultural elements were expressed in industrial materials as well as in common, unexpected Chinese artifacts.

Columns were covered in candy-apple vinyls, each side a different color—magenta pink, hot orange, royal blue, torrid purple, bright green, soft light blue, and chartreuse. Hot colors were on the entrance faces; cool colors led toward the exit. Inch-wide strips of gold vinyl tinsel composed curtains to divide alcoves for large tables. And an overhead wind chime, which also served as a focal chandelier, was composed of kappa shell, steel, and hundreds of Chinese toy animals, birds, dolls, fans, pom-poms, feather dusters, and coins of gold vinyl. All of this spun

192. Alexander Girard. Plan, Textiles and Objects Shop for Herman Miller Inc. New York City. 1961. *Illustration courtesy Herman Miller Inc.*

193.   Alexander Girard. Textiles and Objects Shop for Herman Miller Inc. New York City. 1961. *Photograph by Todd Webb, courtesy Herman Miller Inc.*

around, swiveled, and tinkled in the air conditioning along with the gold-tinsel dividers and other elements. In addition, Russel Wright incorporated Chinese paper cutout animals and figures on window panels.

As might be expected from his career in designing dinnerware, Wright designed all the serving equipment and china. Black plates were provided for appetizers, turquoise for soups, burnt orange for entrees, and hot pink for desserts. Linen was gold- or lime-colored.

It all created a bright, shimmering, tinkling, Modern Chinese environment, a remarkable combination of modern materials and Chinese culture. As much as it expressed Russel Wright's interest in Chinese culture, it also spoke for the decade's reach for enrichment and for a greater humanistic regionalism beyond the machine aesthetic.

Saarinen's TWA Terminal

In 1962 Eero Saarinen's long-awaited sculptural TWA Terminal at JFK International Airport (then Idlewild Airport) in New York was finished (see Figure 194). Saarinen himself had died suddenly the year before. Cesar Pelli was the project designer for the terminal.

Sculptural furniture elements grow organically out of the floor. No distinction exists between architecture, interior design, and decoration. Only circulation graphics and other announcements stand as separate elements. Integral with the structure are signposts, seating units, counters, desks, and vertical units that integrate air-conditioning, heating, and lighting; all are both decorative and functional. Saarinen aimed for "the same integral character throughout the entire building so that all of the curvatures, all of the spaces, and all of the elements would have one consistent character." Sculptural forms synthesize the swift curves that were adopted "to catch the excitement of the trip."[1] Since more than two of these elements are seldom prominent from any single point, the overall space remains serene, as air flight at its ideal best.

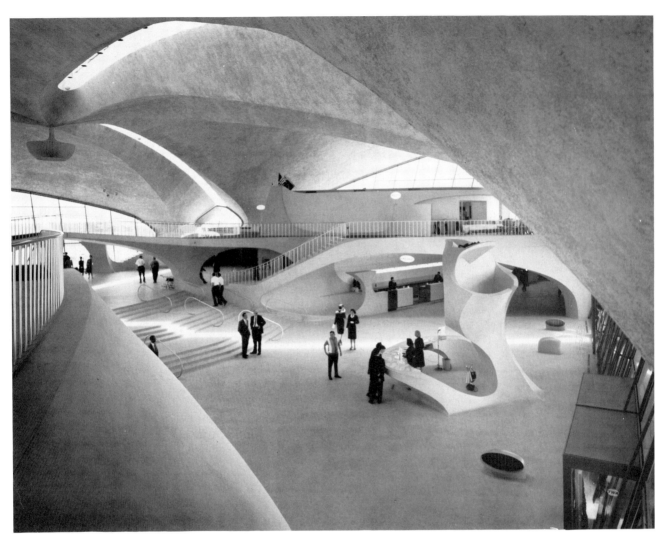

194. Eero Saarinen & Associates. TWA Terminal, JFK International Airport. New York. 1962. *Photograph by Ezra Stoller Associates, courtesy TWA.*

Part of this effect in the TWA Terminal is due to the use of scale, part to a manipulation of color. The seemingly huge main space is 51 feet at its highest points, but this height is divided between two levels. A bridge bisects the main area and distinguishes the entrance lobby from the waiting room on the field side. Each space seems to have human scale, despite the vastness of the sculptural ceiling vaults. Color in the terminal, seemingly only off-white and charcoal, is withheld until, as one mounts the broad stair toward the field, a conversation-pit waiting lounge is gradually revealed—carpeted and upholstered in a rich red. The red seems to draw the pit-lounge together so that it coalesces, providing a calm and cozy oasis for travelers.

Furnishings in the terminal are composed of concrete, which was formed on the site, and of the same dime-size, white-with-gray-flecks ceramic tile finish that is used as the flooring. The functions of the furniture are, in some cases, multiple: Seating forms partitioning for some of the minor spaces, and it is used also to establish and control traffic patterns. The stairways from the mezzanine, for example, sweep down in flowing curves that double back to form the edges of a broader stair that leads down from the main waiting area. These same curves continue up the edges of lighting standards at the entrance to the baggage-claim area and the ticket lobby.

Counters and strip lighting emanate from the far side of the standards. The strip lighting (Stanley McCandless was the lighting consultant), which extends the length of the ticket lobbies, hangs free on wires above the counters. Both the standards and the bases of the counters are faced with the pervasive tile. Seating pieces are based on Saarinen's earlier Womb Chair and Sofa designs—upholstered pads rest in contoured niches. Everything bears witness to Saarinen's desire to have each element belong to "the same form-world."

Other Total Design Interiors

In 1964 Alvar Aalto completed his second project in the United States—the Edgar Kaufmann, Jr., Conference Rooms (see Figures 195A and B) at the Institute of International Education in New York City. There Aalto created a diagonally oriented small auditorium with adjacent conference rooms in the white birch–snowy forest imagery for which he had become renowned. He included a number of his other trademark motifs, notably the undulating ceiling, the vertically tiled walls, and the sculptural evocation of the Finnish woodland. Had he been headquartered in New York or Philadelphia, visibly and verbally more accessible to American designers, instead of being so distant in Helsinki, he might have been acclaimed as the most influential architect of the 1960s.

In 1965 Florence Knoll designed the executive offices in the CBS Building in the elegant Modern idiom she had so brilliantly refined with the Knoll Planning Unit. But here, for the board and waiting rooms, she included reproduction Louis XVI chairs in bleached wood and dark-brown leather. The rigid rules were being stretched.

Yet Modernism was being ever more broadly marketed to the general public—and with wide acceptance. Such stores as Design Research, which were design-directed by architect Benjamin Thompson, offered "good design" at reasonable prices—and with some invention. There the fabrics of Finland's Marimekko, with their bold superscale and bright flat colors, were introduced to the public. Design Research stores spread across the country, to be followed by other inexpensive

195A. Alvar Aalto. Plan, Edgar Kaufmann, Jr., Conference Rooms. New York City. 1964. *Illustration from* Progressive Architecture *(February 1965).*

195B. Alvar Aalto. Edgar Kaufmann, Jr., Conference Rooms. New York City. 1964. *Photograph by Louis Reens, courtesy Institute of International Education.*

"good design" outlets such as Azuma and the Pottery Barn. It was all another evidence of the acceptance of Modernism.

Rudolph's Art and Architecture Interiors

Another total design structure had opened amid great fanfare in 1963—the Yale University Art and Architecture Building designed by Paul Rudolph. It was to become the most controversial building of the next twenty years.

Art and Architecture was a monumental building with great scale and powerful sculptural massing, constructed entirely of poured concrete that was finished with a rich, hitherto unseen ribbed texture, which was used consistently on both interior and exterior. Inside was an astonishing series of spatial varieties—changing levels, juxtaposed ceiling heights, small nooks adjacent to soaring spaces. The main drafting room for the architecture department (see Figure 196) was a vast two-story hall bridged by flying walkways, surrounded by balconies, providing low and middle-height spaces overlooking the central two-story hall. Skylighted wells rose two stories above, through the upper floors. The heating system fulfilled architects' dreams of integrating mechanical elements with structure—the main ducts were the hollow spaces in the four central piers at the corners of the drafting room.

Specially designed furniture, finished in brilliant orange, rested on flaming orange carpeting. Bare-bulb spotlights provided glittering illumination. Walls displayed ornamental details—plaster casts of Sullivan ornament and Assyrian friezes, of Greece and Rome—that prophesied the role of art in architecture for the next decade and the role of art history in architecture for the next two decades, at least. Such found Pop-like objects as cargo nets were used as window coverings. Murals, sculptures, and such poured-concrete details as the Modulor of Le Corbusier and feet-and-inch dimensions were integrated into the building. The detailing of the concrete revealed door bucks that were, instead of the common metal bucks, poured integrally into the structure.

It was one of the most creative and innovative structures—consistent in planning, structure, and detail, with the most complete integration of all the elements

196. Paul Rudolph. Architecture school drafting room, Yale University Art and Architecture Building. New Haven, Connecticut. 1963. *Photograph by Julius Shulman.*

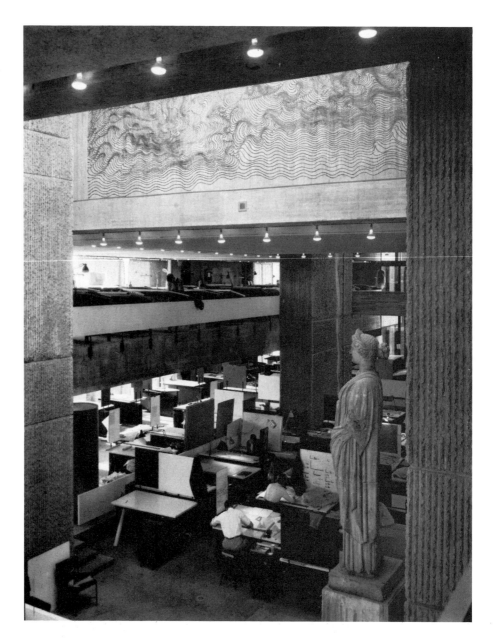

of architecture that had been seen in two decades, perhaps the most innovative and truly consistent building since Mies's Tugendhat House or Frank Lloyd Wright's Larkin Building. Mechanical systems, spaces, finishes, furnishings, and art program all proclaimed the Art and Architecture Building, to many observers, as most carefully designed and brilliantly inventive at every stage of the process and in every area of the building. It fulfilled a dream of the Modern movement as the total design building of its era. To some architects and designers it seemed like the second coming.

To the faculty and students who were using the building, however, it was another story—a failure, a nightmare, and a disaster. Several painters had moved out immediately, saying they could not work in the building; for them it had neither the traditionally desired illumination, nor a large freight elevator to move paintings up and down. Sculptors, moreover, were in the second basement under 7-foot ceilings and could not work on large vertical pieces; they too had no hoist to raise and lower their large and heavy materials. The print department, in the first basement, had no exhaust fans for their acid-reeking equipment; and the photography enlarger was in so low a space that it had to be laid horizontally and operated contrary to design.

Near the ground-floor entry to the Art and Architecture Building, a nautilus shell, cut in half with its delicate pinwheel of fins exposed, was embedded into the poured concrete, set into the monumental wall of massive concrete that rose crushingly eight stories above it. Observers dazzled by the virtuosity needed to preserve the delicate object throughout the process of pouring and curing the concrete may have also seen the feat as symbolic of the vanity of human wishes—fragility daringly exposed in the midst of irresistible force, the segment of pearly perfection innocently laid bare in the face of a rough and stony mass. Some of the faculty and students seemed to see the shell as a symbol of naive foolhardiness, inappropriateness, and something inevitably to be crushed—literally.

Within three years the interior was virtually unrecognizable—students had built squatter-like shacks as mini-environments—filled with cardboard, hanging bedsheets, and found objects, and covered with graffiti. In 1969 a mysterious, if not suspicious, fire tragically destroyed three upper floors of the building; and this was followed, even more tragically many felt, by an extensive rebuilding program, on which the original architect was never consulted.

A decade after the opening (1974–75), medical findings that asbestos was cancer-inducing caused a new scandal. The exposed asbestos ceilings, which had been installed throughout the building in the customary manner of the early 1960s, were torn out and new "improvements" made in what was, in effect, the third building program for Art and Architecture for a total of $1.5 million in slightly more than a decade. In this rebuilding, Rudolph's interior design concept was almost totally demolished.

Questioning the Modern Movement

Around 1963, then, the Modern movement began to be questioned. It was questioned not only by the general public, whose resistance to functional innovation and machine-made "coldness" had continued, but by professional designers as well. The Art and Architecture Building was not the only structure with problems. Louis Kahn's first great public acclaim from his Richards Medical Center laboratories in Philadelphia was simultaneously tarnished by the functional failures of its laboratories. Those failures were due to what the researchers considered small and inflexible spaces as well as to unshaded windows that, as in the Art and Architecture Building, caused "unbearable" glare and heat to build up. The High Modern movement began to seem suspect. Just as the public was coming to grips with Modern design, and the crusade for Modernism had been won, a professional segment began to question the very validity of the Modern movement. Indeed, from this time, we can date the beginning of what was ultimately seen as the failure of Modernism.

Integration of structural and mechanical systems, the consistent design of exterior and interior, along with the multiple and overlapping functions of these and other elements, were often achieved at the expense of efficient use and customary activity. Too often form followed only *design* function, not user function or activity function, and rarely psychological function. Innovation was more important to total designers than the cultural habits, traditions, and expectations of users or occupants of interiors and buildings. Brilliant as the best total design of the early 1960s was, the time had come to refocus design attention.

The Ford Foundation Building

Kevin Roche and John Dinkeloo completed the Ford Foundation Building in 1967, and Warren Platner achieved a new elegance in the design of its interiors (see

197. Roche, Dinkeloo Associates with Warren Platner. Executive office, Ford Foundation Building. New York City. 1967. *Photograph © Ezra Stoller/ESTO, 1967.*

Figure 197). At the center of the building is the celebrated 10-story landscaped atrium. In the surrounding offices, Platner designed elegant mahogany and bronze furniture, beige accordian-fold shades for the windows overlooking the atrium, and appointments of meticulous care and refinement. Even there, however, the level of elegance, the vast expenditure, and the degree of detail raised the question of conspicuous consumption, as Thorstein Veblen had earlier called such lavish spending.

Minimalism and Elegance

Earlier in the 1960s a group of vanguard designers of interiors developed a further refinement on the reductive or minimalistic approach of the International Style. Corresponding to a contemporaneous movement in sculpture by such Minimal sculptors as Sol LeWitt and Donald Judd, and influenced by the inspirational interiors of Mexican architect Luis Barragan, this new direction was to become a strong and widely accepted idiom in the 1970s. It was called Minimalism, or the Minimal school. Among the leaders were Benjamin Baldwin, Ward Bennett, and Nicos Zographos.

Their approach was to refine the Bauhaus principle "less is more" to its ultimate. For the Minimalists, "nothing was all." The Minimal approach could go almost unnoticed—especially by clients—since it looked effortless. Yet it was an elaborate undertaking, a kind of acrobatic prestidigital manipulation to conceal all elements into the smoothest, geometric forms that proclaimed the supremacy of technology and intellectual discipline. Whereas Bauhaus and 1930s designers ostensibly eliminated ornamentation, actually they had only simplified it. The Miesian idiom had restricted ornamentation to structural articulation. As one young student-architect said, "Even Mies had excess extrusions."

The Minimal style eliminated ornamentation even of this kind; it stripped nonessentials; minimized, miniaturized, or eliminated everything that might possibly be considered visually extraneous—joints, mechanical and electrical elements, reveals, moldings—and elements with duplicate functions. It produced simple white plaster boxes with broad expanses of plain surfaces—including bare floors, ceilings, and walls. Door and window openings were flush, frameless, and trimless—sliced severely into the planes. Window coverings were spare and ascetic.

These pure, "clean" envelopes depended on meticulous detailing to conceal functioning supportive systems. They were enriched only by natural-grown textures in deep wools, burl woods, veined marbles, and crisp Machine-Age furnishings that contrasted the natural-made with the products of industry. If there was an unrecognized antecedent of all this, it was the rarefied work of Jean-Michel Frank in the 1930s. The avowed aim was to focus on what is most variable in our environments: that is, on portable changeable objects, such as paintings, artworks, plants (often reduced to a single flower), and (ostensibly) people.

Ward Bennett

In 1961 Ward Bennett designed a suite of offices for L. J. Glickman in New York (see Figure 198). Bennett simplified the structure—furring out jogs in the walls and dropping the ceiling to conceal beams; he then unified the space with white walls and ceiling (including a white baseboard), buff-colored tile flooring, off-white draperies over a transparent interior partition, and white vertical blinds over

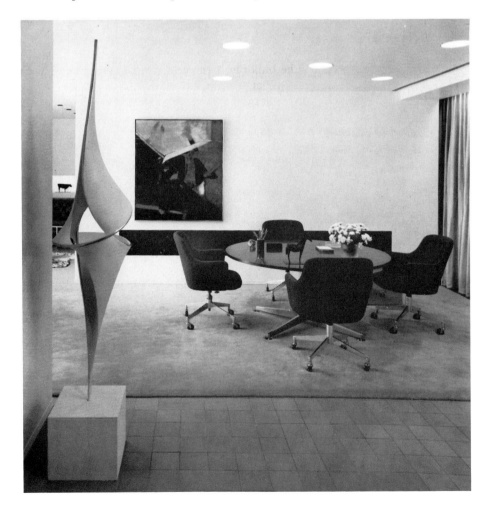

198. Ward Bennett. L. J. Glickman offices. New York City. 1961. *Photograph by Louis Reens.*

the window that afforded a view of the New York Public Library and its surrounding greenery. A sand-colored carpet was laid over the central work area, which also served as a dining area; it distinguished the functions of these areas from the entranceway and from a banquetted alcove for more relaxed conferences.

Within this background Bennett placed stainless-steel and richly grained elm-burl tables and cabinetwork of his own design. He lined the alcove with banquettes upholstered in natural glove leather, and at the desk and trestle table placed his Column-X chairs, upholstered in the clear blue that, Bennett felt, Braque often used. Notable was the unabashed inclusion of stainless-steel units for communication and controls of lighting and draperies; these Machine-Age units amid the more luxurious furnishings prefigured the contradictory juxtapositions of later Minimalism. Most of the furnishings were designed by Bennett, from built-ins and furniture to doorknobs, drawer pulls, and accessories.

The total effect was spare and cool, but it was the orchestration of the design within this minimal palette that was notable at the time: soft, warm textures against smooth, shiny surfaces; strong bright colors against a monochromatic beige-and-white background; patterns against plain materials; and the severe, machine-art statement of the communications and control equipment against the individualistic, romantic expressions of the artworks, which Bennett inspired the client to choose. The office was refined and graceful, yet patently masculine, owing to its spare—minimal—approach. From then on Ward Bennett produced a continually expanding line of chairs and tables of considerable elegance that soon became staples of twentieth-century interior design.

Benjamin Baldwin

Benjamin Baldwin was a leader in this idiom, with designs of rarefied simplicity yet uncommon humanism. Working virtually on his own, he was almost oriental in his purity and his connoisseur's discrimination. His combination of the Minimal approach with a sophisticated casualness produced utmost serenity. These qualities

199.   Benjamin Baldwin. Own apartment. New York City. 1964. *Photograph by Louis Reens.*

made him sought-after as a collaborator by such architects as Edward Larrabee Barnes, for the Cowles residence in Wayzata, Minnesota (1964); I. M. Pei, for the Charles and Ann Tandy residence in Fort Worth, Texas (1970); and Louis Kahn, for the library at Philips Exeter Academy (1967–72) and subsequently for the Mellon Center for British Art at Yale University (1969–74).

In a Minimal apartment (see Figure 199) Benjamin Baldwin designed for his own use in New York City in 1964, the interplay of rectangular wall planes with paintings was the strong yet subtle design force. Broad, ceiling-height doors pivoted back against storage cores like unnoticeable walls; planes met without reveals; nearly invisible narrow-slatted, undraped venetian blinds served as the only window coverings; the sofa was a frameless, built-in nook, carpeted and filled with loose pillows. The alignment of the linear elements was meticulous, and furniture was kept to a minimum—yet as he changed it, the furniture could reflect eons of world culture in its eclectic sparseness.

His own house and garden in East Hampton, Long Island (1967), became a mecca for Minimalist designers (see Chapter 17). "My work in interior design expresses my opposition to the chaotic world man creates," he wrote. "It is a constant search for the calm tranquility one finds in nature. . . . In nature I find a sense of order—logical and lyrical—which I would like my work to express."[2]

Nicos Zographos

Also in the Minimal idiom, Nicos Zographos—a designer of both furniture and interiors—designed an office for the New York advertising agency Papert, Koenig, Lois (1966) that retained some functionalist structural articulation, but that distilled and refined it to an almost surreal essence.

Even the most luxurious executive spaces had no overlay of so-called elegance—no carpets, no draperies. In the office of partner George Lois (see Figure 200), bare wood floors, windows bare except for venetian blinds, and a column-mounted marble desk were enlivened by the sculptural effects of Marcel Breuer's Wassily chairs, cube occasional tables, and—seen through a floor-to-ceiling frameless smoked-glass partition—a tree next to the cylindrical plaster balustrade of a stair to the floor below. Zographos commented that "this design is romantic in its way: It is a throwback to the early days of the Bauhaus, but brought up to date."[3] These offices were startling for their evocation of 1920s Bauhaus imagery.

The Paradox of Minimalist Simplicity

That such opulence could be created from simplicity and that simplicity could be achieved by complex detailing are the paradoxes of the Miesian and Minimal idioms. As the boldest illustration of this effort, the invisible use of marble as the baseboard in SOM's Banque Lambert penthouse of 1965 in Brussels is the most elaborately minimal detail.

Designed by Jack Dunbar of SOM's New York office in 1965, white plaster walls appear to come down to the travertine floor line. But since a plaster base would be impractical for cleaning, the baseboard was actually white marble—white marble painted white to match the plaster wall. If the white paint chipped, went the thinking, then the white marble underneath would still appear continuous with the plaster walls until repainting. One further point about the baseboard demonstrated the difference between Miesian and Minimalist detailing: No reveal or scored line was used between plaster and marble to denote a change of materials; no spacer or recess connects baseboard to floor. It had been time for a change, at least for this refinement. SOM's chief New York designer, architect Gordon Bunshaft, said, "Maybe in the past we used to have too many notches."[4]

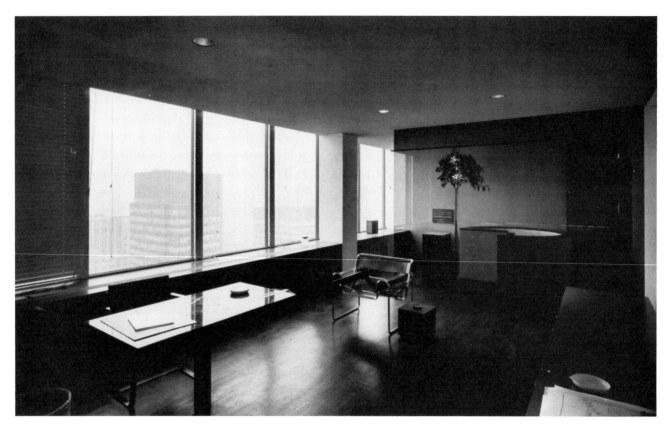

200. Nicos Zographos. Offices of Papert, Koenig, Lois, Inc. New York City. 1966. *Photograph by Carl Fischer.*

The purgative austerity of the post-Beaux-Arts period produced the Minimalist idiom, whose keynote word was "simplicity." What Minimalist designers aimed to provide was purer, clearer, cleaner visual scenes for our Athenian delectation. What they designed were simple geometric forms, "similar glass cages for dissimilar uses,"[5] isolated each from each, surrounded by as much space as possible, increasingly flatter, cleaner, textureless of elevation, accented only by some token artwork. This was the Minimalist refinement of Bauhaus goals—and perhaps the highest realization of them—in the 1960s.

The Residential Designers

For traditional interior designers, also, the scope of work increased during the 1960s. It encompassed corporate planning, the design of large office complexes, whole chains of hotels, and important public buildings as well as residential work in America and abroad for the very affluent. Many of these firms organized separate departments to do contract work—including McMillen Inc.

Decorators by and large continued the tradition of historicism and the application of printed and painted ornament—as the last vestige of the Beaux-Arts. At its most refined, decorating in America offered continuing elegance. Among many others, McMillen Inc. (see color plate 9) and Thedlow Inc. in New York City, and Michael Taylor and John Dickinson in California, worked a widely appealing kind of magic.

During the early 1960s Mrs. Henry Parish II was at work on refurbishing the White House (see Figure 201) for President and Mrs. Kennedy in a style far more appropriate than the mansion had seen for decades. Based on the idea of historical restoration, her scheme envisioned assembling American pieces to make the White House a museum-worthy display of late-eighteenth- and early-nineteenth-century

201. Mrs. Henry Parish II. Oval Room, the White House. Washington, D.C. 1962. *Photograph by Henry S. Fullerton.*

American interior design—the period when the house was built. About this time Albert Hadley joined her as partner to form Parish-Hadley.

Billy Baldwin

Billy Baldwin was at the peak of his career in the 1960s, designing houses and apartments, hotel suites, the Round Hill Club in Greenwich, Connecticut, and a hair salon for Mr. Kenneth in New York.

In 1963, for his own apartment (see color plate 10) Baldwin used high-gloss brown lacquered walls, a bare wood floor, and dark-brown raw-silk roman shades. A Korean lacquer screen was the background for cream-colored raw-silk upholstery, fur throws, feather arrangements in vases, and appointments of brass and bone, tortoiseshell and bamboo. The textural orchestration was rich and warming, refined and elegant; the apartment became a touchstone of the elegance of the decade. In another decade he would lighten the scheme further, in the use of both colors and textures.

Billy Baldwin had popularized Indian paisley walls, plaid rugs and upholstery, Matisse-inspired fabrics and wallpapers (see Figure 202), and pattern on pattern. He had decorated residences for Billy Rose, Mary Wells Lawrence, the Paul Mellons, Mollie Parnis, and Diana Vreeland. It was the last decade of his active career—he retired in 1972—but his influence was considerable.

Barbara D'Arcy

Barbara D'Arcy (see page 177ff.) was jamming traffic with her model rooms, in every conceivable style, at Bloomingdale's. Not since William Pahlmann's model rooms in the 1930s and 1940s at Lord & Taylor had the public been so drawn.

Barbara D'Arcy's model rooms established a new popularity and merchandising viability for furniture and interior design. Detached from live-in clients, since they are residences without residents, her model room designs nevertheless opened the eyes of the public to the potential variety in interior design. They were regularly considered news by the daily papers, both for their commercial aspects and for the

202. Billy Baldwin. Living room with chintz pattern taken from a Matisse drawing; manufactured by Woodson Fabrics. New York City. Circa 1965. *Photograph by Horst from Billy Baldwin*, Billy Baldwin Decorates *(New York: Holt, Rinehart and Winston, 1972).*

stylistic flair that Barbara D'Arcy brought to them—sometimes Mediterranean in flavor with simulated hand-hewn beams; sometimes glitzy silver mylar spaceship imagery; sometimes pure Williamsburg historical tradition. D'Arcy presented a compendium of interior styles to reach out and appeal to as broad a market as possible.

The New Young Decorators

Other prominent American decorators of the decade included Ellen Lehman McCluskey, Melanie Kahane, Tom Lee, Joseph Braswell, and Inman Cook. In addition to those established decorators, a younger group of decorators began to be noticed. Among them were Edward Zajac, Richard Callahan, Angelo Donghia, Tom Britt, Robert Denning, and Vincent Fourcade. These new decorators, in their reduplicated historicism, seemed to echo the outrageousness of the decade— but with a sense of opulence and, even, magnificence.

Zajac & Callahan   Edward Zajac and Richard Callahan formed Zajac & Callahan in 1964 and began to demonstrate their eclectic and multilayered style. Edward Zajac (1932–) was born in Camden, New Jersey, and completed his design studies at the Parsons School in 1956. He first worked for McMillen Inc. for two years, then for Baldwin & Martin for seven years. Richard Callahan (1936–) was born in Manhasset, Long Island, and completed his design studies at the Parsons School in 1956, in the same class with Zajac. Callahan first worked with Jansen Inc. for three years and then with Valerian Rybar for four years.

During the 1960s, in addition to residences in New York and Dallas, they designed shops across the country for Splendiferous; Bendel's Fancy at Henri Bendel in New York; and apartments for the Albert Nippons, Mike Nichols, and Mr. and Mrs. Claude Giroux in Paris.

Angelo Donghia   Zajac & Callahan's Parsons classmate Angelo Donghia (1935–85), who had apprenticed with Yale Burge, won immediate acclaim for a model room with deep-blue gloss walls and white upholstered furniture. Donghia was to go on to become one of the prominent interior designers and furnishings designers of the next two decades (see page 180ff.).

Denning & Fourcade The firm formed by Robert Denning and Vincent Fourcade also began to attract attention in the early 1960s. Robert Denning had worked with fashion and furnishings photographer Edgar D'Evia; Vincent Fourcade had moved from Paris to New York in the 1950s. Together they began an extraordinary new imagery: It was multilayered, multipatterned, becarpeted, and oversized, and appointed with clusters of bronzes and large oriental porcelains (see Figure 203). Their own offices were covered in oriental carpets—on floors and tables and as upholstery. They were to go on to do museum-quality work for some of the most affluent private clients in the next decade.

Other Designers Other decorators began to catch up with the crusade of the Modern movement. They recognized the value of the increasing quantities of furniture in the Modern idiom and got into the mainstream of the age's office design—banishing ornamentation along with the clean sweep of the Modern idiom. They could do so because general merchandising had also begun to feature Modern design across the board. And "good design" shops such as Design Research, the Pottery Barn, and others were spreading industrial design and Modern design throughout the country. New furniture from Italy—including the designs of Carlo Scarpa, the Castiglione brothers, and others—was also beginning to have a profound influence on the vision of interior designers.

But just as this was happening, a small group of vanguard Modern architects was beginning to espouse decoration, ornamentation, and history. Once again, just when the two fields were veering toward a meeting of minds and directions, architecture and decorating went off in opposite directions. It seemed a frustrating if understandable event in light of the complex and contradictory expansions and investigations throughout the world during this decade.

203. Denning & Fourcade. Apartment for Vincent Fourcade. New York City. Circa 1960. *Photograph courtesy Denning & Fourcade.*

Design: Expansion and Revolution

An Expansion of Design Services

Throughout the 1960s, expansion was in the air—in the interior design field as well as in outer-space exploration. For interior designers this meant expansion of practice, expansion of contract work, and expansion in the use of materials and technology. The subcategorization of the design process accompanied an expansion in the number of consultant specialists available to interior design projects—lighting designers, acoustical designers, systems analysts, and many more. This expansion also included the closer alliance of interior design educators with the activities of the profession; the Interior Design Educators Council (IDEC) was founded in 1962 to achieve this goal. IDEC led to the creation of the Foundation for Interior Design Education Research (FIDER), which evaluates educational programs in interior design.

A Stylistic Revolution

The decade's expansionism soon led to a stylistic revolution as well. That change was generational and ideological before it was stylistic. Activism and involvement were the new passions, as well as the new passwords. Youth, now the majority of the population, assertively took part in the decisions and actions of the day. Social and political issues captured their concern—areas unrelated to formal or even nonformal design. Activism centered on the antiwar movement, on drugs and rock music, and on "doing your own thing."

The result was a design approach and a style based on the vision of the eighteen- to twenty-five-year-old age group. Economics made this possible, and the marketplace took advantage of, or played to, this new audience opportunity. All this led to a diversity of approaches in the design professions.

In the design fields this decade's revolution was initiated by architects and architecture students. Since many of these design revolutionaries were of a new generation with young practices, their innovations were demonstrated most strongly in interior designs. The 1960s design revolution was not an even, consistent movement with a single thrust—any more than any other twentieth-century design movement, since individuals of leadership and genius make up movements. Nor was there a unified view of style and technology. Architects and designers who were concerned about matters of form and style were usually not equally concerned about expansion of practice, about process as much as product, or about technology and materials. Nevertheless, the fundamental direction of growth and expansion was consistent in those concerned with practice and those concerned with vision.

Perhaps behind it all was the expansion of acceptable possibility and the expansion of scale that the decade's space exploration program brought about—or at least directly influenced. Space exploration was reaching for the moon, and throughout the decade youngsters especially believed that virtually anything was possible. The spokesmen and the leaders—Robert Venturi, Charles Moore, Philip Johnson, and Paul Rudolph—were as much as a decade older; but the newness of their rebellion and the adventuresomeness of their frontier gave it all a consistently youthful outlook and appearance.

This third generation of Modern architects and interior designers, who reflected these new attitudes in their theory and formal designs, was a new breed that rebelled against "the uptight formality of the past," which they believed had produced the uninspired, copybook curtain-wall towers. This new generation reacted against the unrelated nature of such freestanding buildings, since they stood on isolating podiums and plazas. They rebelled against static and fixed furniture and against refined preciousness—against the "design gestapo" regimentation of many established designers. Instead, vanguard designers in the 1960s showed greater interest in furniture systems that involved users and were adaptable to the psychological as well as the physical requirements of an environment and of activities.

The new designers rejected the uptight, packaged formality of the past—the Minimalist purity that had created monotonous, sterilized, easy-to-copy-badly pigeon crates and that seemed to negate the sumptuous and exquisite monuments produced in the idiom. They rebelled against the pure, clean, off-white and beige rectilinear designs that had been the established tradition for over a decade. To the designers of that tradition, tidy "tastefulness" had been the goal. To the new designer of the 1960s, tastefulness was a dirty word. Their new approach was an irreverent rebellion against the design establishment.

Paradoxically, then, around 1962—just when increasing numbers of traditional designers of residences and offices were adopting the Modern movement and espousing its taboos against historicism and decoration—along came a whole new school of vanguard architects who, in the rebellion of their generation to find something new for themselves, began to reject Modernism and overthrow its taboos. They espoused both historicism and ornamentation once again.

Supermannerism Formally and stylistically, this rebellious vanguard presented a wider range of visual experience as candidates for our design vocabulary—it included more effects by which design could arrest our accustomed and habitually unseeing eyes. Also included, once again, were historical traditions such as decoration, applied pattern, and ornament. This revolution thereby aggressively adopted and espoused the very sacred taboos of the International Style. Areas previously considered undesigned and unworthy of designers' attentions, such as the influence of our commercial and roadside environments, were also part of this revolution. Among its new attitudes were permissiveness and chaos; whimsy and humor; synthetic and commercial allusions; ambiguity and invisibility; superscale, supergraphics, and superimposition. The relationships between this approach and Existentialism and the Theater of the Absurd are only beginning to be explored. During 1961–62, the two protagonists of this vanguard movement in architecture, Robert Venturi and Charles W. Moore, each designed houses that became the manifestos of their credo.

Robert Venturi

Born in Philadelphia, Robert Venturi (1925–) studied architecture at Princeton University, where he received his master's degree in architecture in 1950. Subsequently, he worked for Eero Saarinen and then for Louis Kahn. In 1958 he opened his own practice, first with partner William Short, and in 1964 with John Rauch; the firm became known as Venturi, Rauch & Scott-Brown when planner Denise Scott-Brown (Mrs. Venturi) became a partner.

The foremost design theorist of his generation, Robert Venturi made his thinking generally available with the publication of his book *Complexity and Contradiction in Architecture* by New York's Museum of Modern Art in 1966. He proclaimed in his opening chapter—"A Gentle Manifesto"—"I welcome the problems and exploit the uncertainties. By embracing contradiction as well as complexity, I aim for vitality as well as validity."[6]

Venturi also aimed to include in formal design a number of attitudes that he insisted prevailed in contemporary life, especially ambiguity and duality. He included contradictions as potentials of architecture, and acclaimed the inclusive dualities of "both/and" rather than "either/or," which had been the attitude of High Modernism. In his interior renovation of New York University's Institute of Fine Art, which is located in the Duke House of 1912, designed in the Louis XVI style by by Horace Trumbauer, Venturi included industrially produced, non-high-style-design metal bookshelves juxtaposed to the Louis XVI woodwork. The metal shelving included "the undesigned," as Venturi deemed it, into his concept; and the juxtaposition with the classical detailing created a complex contradiction of "both/and" that was fundamental to Venturi's new vision of design.

The Chestnut Hill House   In 1962 Venturi designed a house in Chestnut Hill, Pennsylvania, outside Philadelphia for his mother. The house is a simple-looking building on a suburban lot. Its overall form is that of a gabled and chimneyed cottage, but Venturi twisted it around in plan and put the entrance on the gable side. Whimsically, the Palladian hallmark—the arched window—is alluded to by a broken arch of tacked-on wood trim. This and other details are historical allusions—typical of the allusions to Mannerist architecture that Venturi espoused—and they were used by Venturi ironically, sardonically, and perhaps perversely.

Inside the Chestnut Hill House the rectangular plan (see Figure 204A) is spiked with diagonals—at the entry, into other rooms, and at the fireplace and stair plans. The entry funnels circulation into the dining area, straightforwardly past the kitchen, and past the adjacent stair to the second floor. The stair and kitchen walls are inflected, to use Venturi's term, like directional signals to lead occupants and to accommodate their movement. In section, the dining room ceiling is a half barrel vault, echoing the arch motif above the main entry. Light streams in through oddly, distinctively placed monitors. Moldings are used decoratively; yet they are chopped off in a way that seems strange, but in fact recalls the sliced moldings of seventeenth- and eighteenth-century Mannerist and Baroque architecture. Above the bookcases in the living room (see Figure 204B), a valance of flat arches does not spring from the vertical supports of the bookcase.

Finally, the furnishings indicated a new attitude on the part of Modernists: Old furniture previously owned by the client was accepted—recycled—into the radical new design, was accommodated by the new design. In this way Venturi showed his intention to accept both the historical continuity and the activity patterns and desires of his client. Formerly, in the High Modern mode, the reuse of such furniture would have been considered an unfortunate allocation of the budget. Only new, consistent Modern furniture would have been acceptable to that total-design approach. Venturi expressed a new attitude—historical continuity; accommodation of the actual uses and desires of occupants; inconsistency as a fact of real life; and acceptance of common, undesigned items within a designed framework.

204A.   Venturi & Rauch. Plan, Venturi House. Chestnut Hill, Pennsylvania. 1962. *Illustration from* Progressive Architecture *(May 1965).*

204B. Venturi & Rauch. Entry and living room, Venturi House. Chestnut Hill, Pennsylvania. 1962. *Photograph by Rollin R. La France.*

This recognition and acceptance of the contradictions in architecture led to his new and complex view of how the design professions could be more in step with the realities of actual use by people. But non-use by people was also demonstrated in a stair that led nowhere, in illustration of our alienation and frustration and, perhaps, of our continual reaching for the stars.

Charles W. Moore

One of the most facile and productive designers of his generation, Charles W. Moore (1925–) was born in Benton Harbor, Michigan. He received a bachelor's degree in architecture at the University of Michigan in 1947, and taught for two years before going to Korea with the U.S. Army Corps of Engineers. Thereafter he studied at Princeton University with Louis Kahn, taking a master's degree in 1956 and a doctorate in 1957. From 1957 to 1959 he taught at Princeton, and from 1960 to 1965 he taught at the University of California at Berkeley and practiced in the partnership Moore, Lyndon, Turnbull, Whitaker, which included two of his former students as partners. In 1965 he assumed the chairmanship of the Department of Architecture at Yale University, following Paul Rudolph.

He moved his practice to New Haven, Connecticut, and continued (with various partners and colleagues in San Francisco and Connecticut) to design and build over a hundred houses and numerous other structures in the next decade. In the activity of his fertile design facility and in his teaching, he brought a witty, colorful, and informal atmosphere to the complex attitudes of his generation. More than all the others, perhaps, Moore jangled the establishment by espousing the taboo that Modern design most vehemently rejected—decoration.

Moore's Orinda House   In 1962 Charles Moore designed and built a house for himself in Orinda, California, that became another exemplar of the new design movement (see Figure 205A). The house has a simple rectangular plan and plain white wood siding; its roof is pyramidal, with a monitor or skylight running along the long ridge.

The outside is simple, although the enclosing walls are hung in sections on barn-door tracks so that they can be slid along to open up the house to the outside.

205A. Moore, Lyndon, Turnbull, Whitaker. Perspective section, Moore House. Orinda, California. 1962.

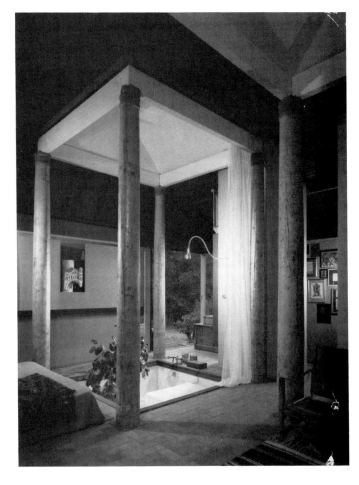

205B. Moore, Lyndon, Turnbull, Whitaker. Interior domed bathing area. Moore House. Orinda, California. 1962. *Photograph by Morley Baer.*

On this square structure no two façades are identical, yet it is so foursquare that found-object molds for waterworks equipment, used as exterior sculptures, seem almost free-form by contrast.

Inside, however, Moore's Orinda house was another story. Within the single large space, which was painted pale hospital green or "eye-ease green," are two pyramidal domes, each resting on four 10-foot-high Tuscan columns that were salvaged and recycled from a San Francisco demolition. They define two square areas—a living area or conversation pit under the larger dome and a sunken tub and shower under the smaller (see Figure 205B). Because these two areas are off-center and nonaligned, the smaller dome leans in toward the middle to reach into the rectangular skylight; the larger dome leans toward one end of the skylight. The domes are asymmetrical statements of the roof form. Like inverted funnels, they pull light down onto the areas they define. They and their supporting columns also compose rooms-within-rooms.

Around and between the domes, the space is open. During the day, sunlight moves across the space, picking up the ceiling, the mauve and magenta paint on the column capitals, the vibrant blue fascia, the soft putty-green walls, and the dark floor.

The furnishings were casual, found, undesigned, accommodating pieces—items collected on Moore's personal travels—Mexican pottery, Indian brass candlesticks, Peruvian rugs—and director's chairs, lamps with shades, ordinary found objects. These things had association and meaning for him (and they also had a quality of visual excellence because of his designer's eye)—things that Elsie de Wolfe and the Modernists alike had banished from residential design.

206A. Hugh Hardy and Tiziana Hardy. Supergraphic cone, Hardy apartment. New York City. 1966. *Photograph by Louis Reens.*

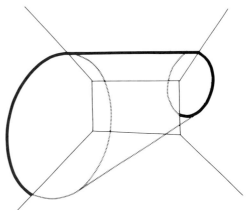

206B. Hugh Hardy and Tiziana Hardy. Conceptual sketch, supergraphic cone for Hardy apartment. New York City. 1966. *Illustration courtesy Tiziana Hardy, from C. Ray Smith, Supermannerism (New York: E. P. Dutton, 1977).*

This was the inclusive and accommodating view of this new generation of design revolutionaries. Besides bringing design closer in line with the understanding and desires of ordinary people—in a rejection of design for designers' sakes—the attitude was permissive, witty, and flagrantly flaunting historical allusion and ornamentation, the taboos of Modernism.

Other Designers

Hugh Hardy Another young architect, Hugh Hardy, demonstrated this more inclusive view with the recycling of a number of old buildings for new functions. Among them were some new theaters that had new kinds of audience-performer relationships—irregular, faceted, and unequal groupings of audience seating that offered what Hardy viewed as the corresponding vision of the day—random viewing, like television and the movies. It was a view of the live theater that aimed for the kind of overlaid vision, multiple vantage points, and all-around interaction that we see in flashbacks, crosscuts, and other film techniques.

Hardy's residential interiors (see Figures 206A and B) also showed a use of multiple vision and overlaid decoration; for example, mirrors overlaid with stripes, laissez-faire acceptance of reality (exposed electrical cables), painted and applied decoration, and other pranksterish tricks. Among the alleged "spatial investigations" were a number of fragments of geometric forms—circles and cones, predominantly—that Hardy and his partners in Hardy Holzman Pfeiffer Associates painted onto wall and ceiling surfaces. They were large-scale decorative stripes, which thumbed the nose at the taboo of Modernism against decoration. But as abstract painted fragments—which the best of them were—the viewer completed them mentally to make an even larger element. At their best, these decorations produced the effect of two simultaneously different visions for the viewer—one at human perspective, the other looking down from the skies. These came to be known as supergraphics, which were popularized in the last years of the 1960s.

207. Philip Johnson. Foyer, New York State Theater. New York City. 1964. *Photograph by Louis Reens.*

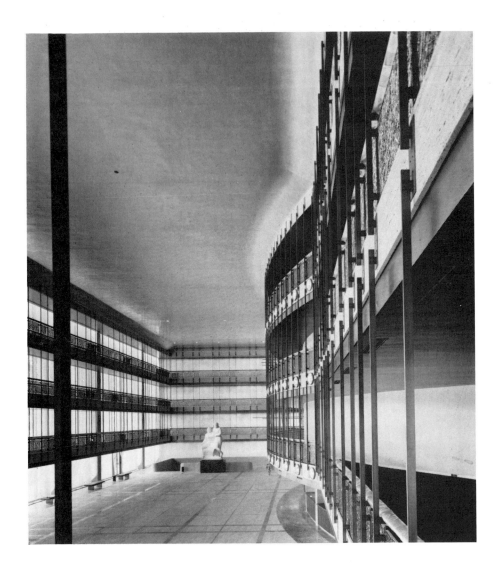

Barbara Stauffacher   Among the most flamboyant of these supergraphics were the painted stripes designed in 1967 by Barbara Stauffacher for Athletic Club Number One (see color plate 12), which was designed by Moore, Lyndon, Turnbull, Whitaker at Sea Ranch, in California. Part roadside caution stripes, part circulation graphics, part scale investigation, and all a decorative scheme to salvage a cut budget, these paintings were recognized as the ultimate overthrow of the Modernist taboo against decoration.

Philip Johnson

Philip Johnson had been prominent in the move away from the High Modern idiom. In 1964 he completed the New York State Theater at Lincoln Center—a design he intended to be the first monumental interior in the Pop Art idiom. Its auditorium was a reinterpretation of the nineteenth-century horseshoe auditorium—but in Pop materials—perforated metal, superscale lights, and Harry Bertoia–inspired metal lattice work. The foyer of the New York State Theater (see Figure 207) is one of the grandest and most handsome rooms in this idiom of breaking away from the Modern movement. Its surrounding balconies reminded some people of a jail, to which Johnson replied, "Yes, I saw it in a jail, and I liked it." Mies would not have understood the joke.

In 1966, with the wryest laugh of all, Johnson designed another handsome, classic room in the Miesian idiom, but sent it sky high. At first glance, the Founders Room (see Figure 208) atop Johnson's annex to the Museum of Modern Art in New York appears to be merely a domed version of the Miesian idiom that Johnson mastered so well. An exposed I-beam structure of modular bays apparently supports plaster Gothic vaults lighted with strips of exposed, unfrosted incandescent lamps. The immediate effect is a combination of Mies, Gothic, and a carnival midway of the Gay Nineties. But as the eye follows the steelwork downward, we see that the structure simply stops—a foot-and-a-half above the floor. It is, quite literally, a Miesian take-off—or lift-off. It gets off the ground because it has inverted the Miesian idiom by bringing it indoors and using it frankly as decoration. It was camp Mies.

A Diversity of Directions

By the mid-1960s, therefore, the Minimalist, purgative, exclusivist approach that had been the mainstream of the International Style was challenged by a counter-movement—one that waggishly, rebelliously raised an elaborately ornamented head—a decidedly un-minimal head. That movement was expansive, inclusive, and highly mannered. With cries of "shame," "ghastly chaos," and "trivial fad" ringing through the design establishment, a new breed of designer began to appear.

Their new approach espoused new attitudes toward design and living. It aimed to include speed and motion as well as monumental stillness; to include the boring as well as the interesting; nudity, profanity, and scandal as well as the polite and the decorous. The new approach also accepted additional formal devices: the diagonal as well as the rectangle and the square; and the influence of our often anonymous commercial environment on our designed environment. Just as early Modern designers discovered industrial factory buildings as a source of inspiration, designers in the 1960s spent time studying "roadside America," as Robert Venturi called it.

208. Philip Johnson. Founders Room, The Museum of Modern Art. New York City. 1967. *Photograph by Louis Reens.*

The diversity of directions—also called inclusiveness and pluralism—was indicated not only by these stylistic inclusions and expansions; it was also seen in the interest in structural process and construction technology—in prefabricated boxes to be used as housing units. The foremost example of this was Habitat, a hill-like town composed of prefabricated concrete boxes designed by Moshe Safdie for the Montreal Expo 67. These structural and architectural solutions, however, led to no advances in interior design.

Among expanded design services, financing was included, making the designer part of the client-entrepreneurial team. John Portman in 1967 completed the Hyatt Regency hotel in Atlanta, Georgia—not only as its architect, but as part-owner of the scheme, which he initiated. The "people-space" of the multistory, glass-enclosed atrium that was the center of the hotel scheme set a new vision for hotel design for the next two decades.

The interest in historicism on the part of this new generation of architects was also seen in the concurrent development of the preservation movement, which fought back against the demolition of our urban heritage by "urban renewal." That had destroyed countless treasures in the name of providing a clean sweep for Modern glass-and-metal towers surrounded by open plazas. As a consequence, the preservation movement encouraged an interest in restoration and recycling, that is, redesigning old buildings for other uses than the original use. In San Francisco the old Ghirardelli chocolate factory was preserved instead of being demolished. It was structurally restored and recycled into a new kind of urban shopping center that incorporated the history of the city into its merchandising program.

Recycling created some odd contradictions: Churches were turned into houses or discotheques, railroad stations became libraries, and the 1928 RKO Paramount movie house in Brooklyn, New York—perhaps the oddest example of recycling—became the gilded Baroque auditorium of Long Island University's basketball court and gymnasium. Soon it was recognized that the economies of preservation were more beneficial than had been thought, and the rationale of the preservation movement was established on financial bedrock.

By 1967 this new design movement based on diversity had recognized other Princeton architecture colleagues of Venturi, Moore, and Hardy. Along with their political activism, students also evidenced a new spirit of design activism—designing their own rooms, apartments, and houses as inventive experiments in the new attitudes that the movement proffered, and also building them, and getting them published well before they got out of design school.

In 1968 and 1969 this rebellion had been publicized enough so that it was reinterpreted in a popularized form that came to be known as Psychedelic. That version espoused the whiplash curve of the popularly rediscovered Art Nouveau, but expressed it in phosphorescent colors called Day-Glo. The vanguard of this rebellion was more interested in new attitudes such as the inclusion of Pop Art and of commercial and roadside imagery into the vision of academic architecture; in inversions of Modernist theories and approaches; in mannered manipulations of Bauhaus principles; and in tricks of scale and optical effects. This latter corresponded to the contemporaneous interest in Op Art. The rebellion was also interested in permissiveness, laissez-faire design, spontaneity, ambiguity, and chaos.

Office Landscape

In the field of office design, one significant development during the 1960s corresponded to the interests of this design revolution. That was the office design system called "office landscape," which seemed to exhibit many of the attitudes of the

209A. Conventional partitioned office layout proposed for du Pont's Freon Division. Wilmington, Delaware. 1966. *Illustration from* Progressive Architecture *(May 1968).*

209B. Quickborner Team. Office landscape plan, du Pont's Freon Division. Wilmington, Delaware. 1967. *Illustration from* Progressive Architecture *(May 1968).*

rebellious vanguard and also appealed to a wide range of differently oriented mainstream interior designers.

Office landscape was adopted by a number of office designers who called themselves space planners. The assertion of the term was that office spaces would be planned rather than decorated, but the implication that no one had planned spaces before was embarrassing. Just as vanguard architects were opening up their design vocabulary, so too office landscape, a system of free-form furniture arrangement based on traffic, work flow, and communication, opened up the rigid rectangularity of previous office layout and design. To many the system looked like visual chaos (see Figures 209A and B).

Imported from Germany, where it was conceived by Eberhard and Wolfgang Schnelle, office landscape was adopted by major office planners and architects amid great controversy around the mid-1960s; it became the prevailing direction of office design for the next decade.

Office landscape was based on the idea of free-flowing communication and traffic between departments and working groups. It therefore eliminated barriers, such as the rigid rectangular-plan partitioning systems that had become so fixed a part of office design in the late 1950s and early 1960s—perhaps best achieved in the integrated partitioning and suspended-ceiling system designed by Skidmore, Owings & Merrill (SOM) for the Union Carbide Building (later Manufacturers Hanover Trust Building) (1961–62) on Park Avenue in New York. In office landscape planning, aisles became integrated with working spaces; major traffic flow was also merged with work areas to a degree to utilize workspace more intensively— thereby appealing to economy-minded clients. The large, open—that is, partitionless—bullpen office concept that had been the prevailing mode from the beginning of the century and earlier—the typing-factory image—was revived. But this time it had a scatter-pattern plan—and square-footage studies documented its economic advantages.

To compensate for the acoustical disadvantages of open offices, carpeting was assumed as an integral component. Carpeting had for centuries been a handmade craft and treasured artifact. But in the early 1960s, due to larger high-speed looms and to the tufting process, it became an economically available finishing material for virtually everywhere. It spread from the living room to the kitchen and bath. It was spread, almost like paint, in schools and playgrounds—which gave the carpet industry its new impetus. It became "wall-to-wall" everywhere. It even climbed the walls of many interiors, as in the foyer of Philip Johnson's New York State Theater and Saarinen and Mielziner's Beaumont Theater, both at Lincoln Center. Carpet was suddenly available, therefore, for banks, elevators, and offices.

Also to modulate the acoustics of open office landscape, large expanses of flat ceilings were lowered and hung with fins to break up reverberation; reflective-glass windows were hung with fabric curtains; and even the few remaining low and movable partitions that were required as divisions between work teams and for visual privacy—reaching to a maximum of 6 feet high and often arc-shaped in plan—were upholstered with fabric or carpeting so as not to be sound-reflective. Plantings also were adopted to aid in acoustical diffusion—as well as to provide a sculptural and alive quality. Finally, acoustical perfume, or white sound, could be added to diffuse any lingering acoustical annoyances.

It was a new functional order, this office landscape; but it was achieved physically—in planning terms, "formally"—with visual disorder. Its irregular arrangements looked like primitive, outrageous, free-form chaos. The controversy that greeted its use was vehement for the first several years, from 1965 to 1967. Historian Edgar Kaufmann, Jr., explained, however, that "Clustering is the pattern of human life; regularity is the pattern of theory."[7] To designers who espoused this new chaos, the results of office landscape were justified by the fact that the actual uses by people were the true and proper determinants of its organized—or disorganized—design.

Office landscape, like the approach of the third generation of Modern designers, justified itself on psychological grounds. This was something of a breakthrough at the time, although designers had been discussing the additional benefits of better environments and had been decrying the fact that adequate research had not been done in this area for some years. Office landscape justified its visual chaos and its chaos of movement by saying that when faces and movement are constantly visible, there is no distraction through single actions. The idea was that when everything is distracting, then nothing is more distracting than anything else. It was a psychological justification.

Among the design firms that advocated and adapted the office landscape system to American use was the Quickborner Team, which was the unit sent by the German originators to promote their work in this country. They designed the first installation of the system in this country for the du Pont Company's Freon Division (see Figure 210) in Wilmington, Delaware, in 1967; and in 1968 they followed that office landscape design with others for John Hancock Mutual Life Insurance Company in Boston, for Eastman Kodak in Rochester, and for the New York Port Authority at the World Trade Center in Manhattan. American designers who adapted the system included the Research and Design Institute (REDE) in Providence, Rhode Island; and the Space Design Group and Saphier Lerner Schindler in New York City—the principals of which firms were ardent public advocates for the system; as well as Designs for Business, ISD Inc., Duffy Inc., and others.

Manufacturers were not long in following their lead. Herman Miller, Robert Propst, along with George Nelson Associates, designed the first of the new-generation furniture along the lines of these psychological needs of workers. Called

Action Office, Propst's furniture line provided options for workers in the ways they could work—standing as well as seated, on high stools as well as on low soft chairs, at multi-tables instead of at single-unit desks.

Subsequently, the desk was superseded by the work station—which included desk, filing storage, bookshelves, pin-up boards, closets, and the like—as the unit that could be varied and expanded or contracted to suit the individual needs of each worker. Lighting, too, was incorporated into these units and, in the next decade, became a major focus of furniture designers and manufacturers.

Overall, the development of office design was indicative of three things: First, it demonstrated the greater interest in interiors that involve the user and are adaptable to both the physical and the psychological requirements of users. Second, it demonstrated the messy vitality—or energetic messiness—that was a keynote of the 1960s. Third, it demonstrated the growth of the interior design field in nonresidential areas, which became known as contract design. Like the term space planner, this was a questionable if not silly term, more indicative of a field in transition than of an actuality. Residential design had been commissioned by contracts at least since the early days of Elsie de Wolfe's and Frank Lloyd Wright's practices; so the distinction of nonresidential design from residential design by its business arrangements was not very distinct. Still, it did indicate that a greater segment of the interior design profession was beginning to be involved in nonresidential as well as residential design.

210. Quickborner Team. Office landscape, du Pont's Freon Division. Wilmington, Delaware. 1967. *Photograph by Louis Reens.*

This expansion of practice was accompanied by the overthrow of the Modern movement. Le Corbusier had died in 1965, Gropius and Mies in 1969. The door had been opened for a stylistic revolution—for anything-goes in design. Instead of the pure and the geometrical, the new generation proclaimed the fragmented and the layered; instead of total design the new generation now proclaimed the inconsistent, the ad hoc and spontaneous, the irregular and the incomplete. It was a new vision for the 1970s.

Suggested Reading

Baldwin, Billy. *Billy Baldwin Decorates*. New York: Holt, Rinehart and Winston, 1972.

———. *Billy Baldwin Remembers*. New York: Harcourt Brace Jovanovich, 1974.

Dreyfuss, Henry. *The Measure of Man*. New York: Whitney Library of Design, 1960.

Herdeg, Klaus. *The Decorated Diagram: Harvard Architecture and the Failure of the Bauhaus Legacy*. Cambridge: MIT Press, 1983.

Hicks, David. *David Hicks Living with Design*. New York: William Morrow, 1979.

Hiesinger, Kathryn B., and George H. Marcus, eds. *Design Since 1945*. Philadelphia: The Philadelphia Museum of Art, 1983.

Platner, Warren. *Ten by Platner*. New York: McGraw-Hill, 1975.

Scully, Vincent. *American Architecture and Urbanism*. New York: Frederick A. Praeger, 1969.

Smith, C. Ray. "Guest Apartment for Hallmark Cards by Alexander Girard," *Progressive Architecture*. February 1963.

———. *Supermannerism: New Attitudes in Post-Modern Architecture*. New York: E. P. Dutton, 1977.

Stern, Robert A. M. *New Directions in American Architecture*. New York: Braziller, 1969, 1974.

The Architecture of Skidmore, Owings & Merrill, 1963–73. New York: Architectural Book Publishing Company, 1974.

Tweed, Katharine, ed. *The Finest Rooms by America's Great Decorators*. New York: Viking Press, 1964.

Venturi, Robert. *Complexity and Contradiction in Architecture*. New York: The Museum of Modern Art, 1966.

Notes

1. Eero Saarinen, quoted from C. Ray Smith, "One Family of Forms," *Progressive Architecture* (October 1962), p. 158.

2. Benjamin Baldwin, quoted from an interview with C. Ray Smith, as recorded in "Minimal Interiors," *Progressive Architecture* (March 1967), p. 154.

3. Nicos Zographos, quoted from an interview with Smith, op. cit., p. 150.

4. Gordon Bunshaft, quoted from an interview with C. Ray Smith, as recorded in "SOM Details for the Minimal Age" *Progressive Architecture* (September 1967), p. 138.

5. Gordon Bunshaft, quoted in C. Ray Smith, *Supermannerism: New Attitudes in Post-Modern Architecture* (New York: E. P. Dutton, 1977), p. 68.

6. Robert Venturi, *Complexity and Contradiction in Architecture* (New York: The Museum of Modern Art, 1966), p. 22. This book has been generally recognized, as critic-historian Vincent Scully asserted at the time of its first publication, as the most important theoretical book on architecture since Le Corbusier's "Vers une Architecture" in 1923.

7. Edgar Kaufmann, Jr., speaking at a symposium on office landscape held at La Fonda del Sol restaurant in New York circa 1967. Quoted in Smith, *Supermannerism*, p. 125.

Chapter **17**

1970–1980:
The Fourth Generation

After the vast space expansion of the 1960s, nothing, apparently, could get any bigger or more outgoing. The cyclic result was that the design professions, like so much of humanity, turned inward once again to smaller scale, to local and personal concerns and visions. Politically, the 1970s brought the end of American involvement in the Vietnam War, the reopening of China to the West, the emergence of Japan as a major industrial power, scandals in the White House, and the erosion of American primacy as international leader and police force. The reasons for this were both the ideological and humanistic goals of the decade and the general economic retrenchment.

Economically, the United States witnessed several periods of serious recession in the 1970s, bringing high unemployment and an end to the twenty-year-long building boom. Instead of vast urban schemes, the prevalent activity was piecemeal restoration and the refitting of new and old building elements together into a blend of new-old tradition and continuity. For many designers whose services were not fully engaged, it was a period of theorizing and of drawing. Yet the 1970s was also one of the worst periods of inflation in the country's history; it led to widespread real estate speculation. As a consequence, although there was less building construction than before, there was a great deal of interior design work in residences, apartments, lofts, and offices.

The oil embargo of 1974 began a series of energy crises that also shook the country's confidence. Energy costs for interiors rose sharply, bringing energy-conscious design to the forefront of design considerations throughout the decade. Because of this groundswell of concern for conservation—of energy resources, of endangered wildlife species—and for pollution—of the air and water, and of the landscape by solid wastes—the 1970s became known as the Environmental Decade. Environmental designers—as many called themselves—shared these concerns, focusing on underground and bermed buildings, on solar energy, heat loss, and a new technology to deal with this new concern. Preservation and recycling, with energy-consciousness, were therefore mainstay activities for designers of interiors.

Design Pluralism

The 1970s were characterized by a multiplicity of design approaches: The inclusiveness of the 1960s was more widespread than ever, and was called Pluralism. The single approach of the Modern crusade was rejected in favor of a multiplicity of approaches, possibilities, and directions. No longer was there a concerted design crusade even within the architecture community. The "failure" of Modernism was proclaimed by critics of widely different ages (see Blake, 1977; Jencks, 1977). The new appeals were to accustomed function, to a respectful humanism, and to the continuity of historical context.

The decade showed convincingly that each generation has singled out idiosyncratic incidents and elements from the work of the preceding generation and has developed it into major features. The diagonals, inflections, and violin curves of the 1920s and 1930s that had begun to be explored in the 1960s were adopted as pivotal motifs of the 1970s. The tentative interests that were new in the 1950s—historicism, classicism, decoration, and the vernacular—had grown beyond platforms of rebellion, which they had been in the 1960s, to become, in the 1970s, the general interests of the profession. It was not surprising that a popular revival of the 1940s and 1950s began at this time. Other directions, adopted primarily by architects, were Structuralism, Constructivism, and Italian Rationalism and neo-Rationalism. Although they did not have much broad visible influence on the design of interiors, except for those interiors in the buildings designed by the architects who espoused such directions, it could be expected that Structuralism, Constructivism, and Rationalism would be stronger in the 1980s.

A New Humanism

The focus on designing for the needs of people, which was expressed so frequently during the 1960s, gained even more sharpness in the 1970s. Some of it was real; some was mere lip service. But it was clearly on the minds of many designers. At mid-decade Charles Moore, Donlyn Lyndon, and Gerald Allen proclaimed this new humanism in "The Order of Dreams"—a chapter in their *The Place of Houses*. They wrote:

> The dreams which accompany all human actions should be nurtured by the places in which people live. . . . The Order of Dreams demands that you . . . open up the full range of your own responses to the world, your own concerns. It demands that you acknowledge and display the pretenses which you habor . . . that you imagine your house in the ways your daydreams and memories suggest, and that you envision the special places that might correspond to them. . . .[1]

It was a new kind of proclamation for the humanism and the plurality of the times.

Historicism

At the beginning of the 1970s, for a brief moment, it seemed as if the divergent paths of the different interior design professions were beginning to come together in the explorations of vanguard designers. Historicism, of one kind or another, was a common thread, albeit adopted for different ideologies. A wide array of historical influences, design work, and personalities came to attention. In the continuing rediscovery of Art Deco, the work of Eileen Gray from the 1920s and 1930s came to greater recognition than during her lifetime. The preservation movement, with recycling and renovation as its most prevalent activities, was a pervasive aspect of historicism.

The Return to Ornamentation

A new generation of architects, in their continuing rebellion against mid-century International Style, rejected Modernism's taboo against historicism and applied ornament. They brashly adopted, headlong, a new kind of flattened, silhouetted, outlined ornamentation. First brightly painted on in multiple colors, this ornamentation soon sported simplified three-dimensional classical motifs. This new generation of architecture began to call itself Post-Modern around 1974. Traditional decorators, still using the highly molded forms of classicism, may have wondered what was new about all this, but they nevertheless began to share a common ground with architects who were designing such interiors.

Contextualism

Along with historicism came a renewed commitment to and respect for the context, location, and adjacencies of one building to another, one space to another. Architects called it contextualism (see Figure 211). They said it restored "meaning" to urbanism and to architecture, which had been lost during the purgative clean-up of Modernism's taboos. Indeed, both contextualism and the historicism that designers were adopting ever more eagerly at this time were also first justified as "returning lost meanings."

Minimalism

Other designers of interiors continued to explore the Minimal approach. Their work also showed a tendency toward enrichment. It was found sometimes through a return to natural rustic materials and sometimes to the Modern furniture classics of the 1920s. By 1970 the use of a chair design from 1920 was, for the young generation, a historical recall.

Industrial Pop

The straightforward expression of all building elements, which had been the goal of the functionalists since the 1920s, was popularized in the 1970s. Designers exposed structural systems, air-conditioning ducts, sprinkler systems, lighting troffers, alarm systems—whatever existed—as honest, expressible design elements. Often each subsystem was differently polished or painted—sometimes differently color-coded for clarity of expression and for decorative effect. By the end of the decade the mirror-polished duct and the mirror-polished steel round column were literal glosses on this imagery.

In this direction, the firm of Hardy Holzman Pfeiffer Associates led daringly in the design of public interiors such as Orchestra Hall in Minneapolis (1974),

211. Susana Torre. Reception room, Old Pension Building. Washington, D.C. 1978. *Photograph by Norman McGrath.*

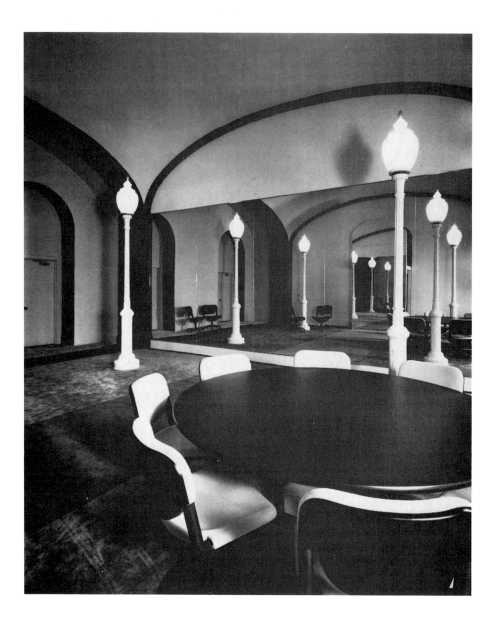

Boettcher Concert Hall in Denver (1979), and the Columbus Occupational Health Center (1973) (see Figure 212).

The Pompidou Center in Paris, completed in 1977, raised this long-established direction to international attention. Designed by architects Piano & Rogers, the Pompidou Center was an ultimate expression of this kind of functionalism in that it put the structural and mechanical systems on the exterior as a kind of superscale, tinker-toy decoration.

Some of the new generation of Minimalists also pursued this approach, using high-gloss and highly polished ducts and other building elements. Also popular were pipes and wire shelving, lighting with coiled electrical cables, and other items originally made for commercial, industrial, or construction uses. They were used in offices, restaurants, and residences. They were adopted as a last stylistic symbol of the Industrial Revolution, of High Modernism, and of their final acceptance in the chic living room of everyman, it was said. A campaign of serious intent since before World War I, these components became high-style fashion and were journalistically categorized as High-Tech.

212. Hardy Holzman Pfeiffer Associates. Columbus Occupational Health Center. Columbus, Indiana. 1973. *Photograph by Norman McGrath.*

Country Vernacular

The 1970s also saw widespread interest in Country Vernacular and in Arts and Crafts and Mission style furniture. It was something of a resurgence of the Peasant Vernacular of the 1930s, but Americanized. Residential subdivisions and shopping malls were designed as farm-like, barn-like spaces, with exposed wood beams and trusses, woodsy textures, and nostalgic cracker-barrel imagery (see Figure 213). It was a popularization of the California Vernacular idiom pioneered in the 1960s by the recycling of San Francisco's Ghirardelli Square and by architects Moore, Venturi, and Hardy. It also owed something to a 1940s revival of natural materials and to the perennial yearning for the country, the primitive, the provincial, and the peasant look.

More people began to collect old and new patchwork quilts, wicker and willow woven baskets, old farm implements, dried flowers and herbs, and other country items. For architects it was another approach to contextualism. For designers of all ideologies, it was a popular field from which to assemble decorative objects to give patina and texture to interiors.

213. Haines Lundberg Waehler. Offices of Haines Lundberg Waehler, Architects/Engineers/Planners. Basking Ridge, New Jersey. 1979. *Photograph by Ashod Kassabian, courtesy Haines Lundberg Waehler.*

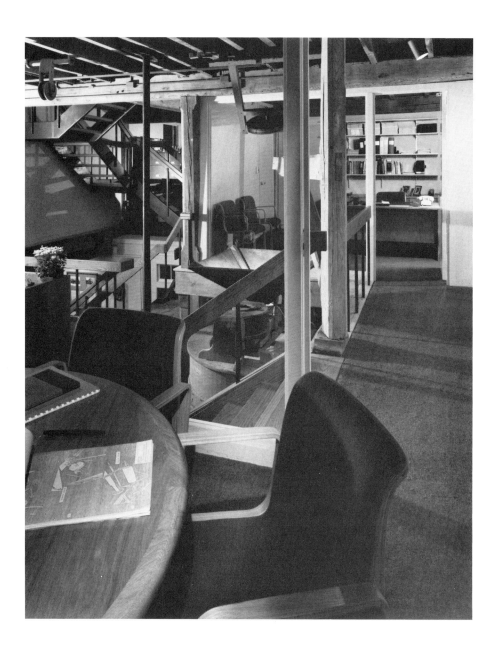

Late Modern

Still, the common language or mainstream of corporate and commercial interior design continued to be the modular, clean-lined internationalism that had developed around 1960 (see Figure 214). Some observers called it Late Modern.

Throughout the 1970s all these directions were not only explored simultaneously, but accepted as part of the pluralism (recognized also as confusion) of the design fields. There was an air of rather dilettantish excitement—as at a scholars' convention—yet the designs were sophisticated and refined, elegantly formed and colored. It was, perhaps, the Rococo of the Modern movement.

Restoration and Recycling

Historical preservation of buildings and interiors became a mainstream design activity in the 1970s. Changes in federal tax laws allowed greater tax credits and

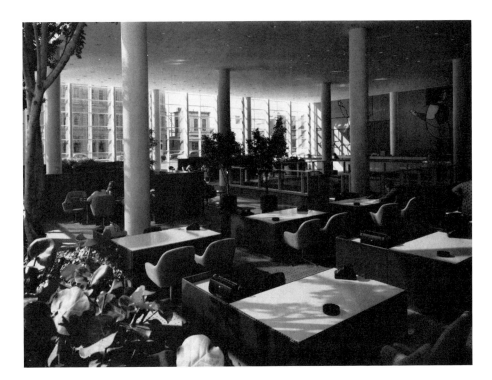

214. Skidmore, Owings & Merrill. First Bank of Wisconsin. Madison, Wisconsin. 1974. *Photograph © Ezra Stoller/ESTO, 1974.*

accelerated depreciation for commercial preservation and restoration. Because of the economic recessions and inflation, as construction costs and interest rates soared during the 1970s, restoration was recognized as a sometimes more economical approach than building anew.

Preserved, restored, or recycled were such interiors as the original Senate Chamber in the U.S. Capitol; Frank Furness's Pennsylvania Academy of the Fine Arts in Philadelphia; the Cooper Union in New York; the Oak Room at the Plaza Hotel in New York; the 1931 Timothy Pfleuger–designed Paramount Theater of the Arts in Oakland, California; the recycling of the Andrew Carnegie mansion into the Cooper-Hewitt Museum; the recycling of McKim, Mead & White's Villard houses into the Helmsley Palace Hotel in New York; as well as the Chicago Public Library, the Minnesota State Capitol, and countless more across the country. Crucial to this work was the discovery of available craftsmen such as the Rambusch Studios and the muralist Richard Haas, who helped in different ways to solve the problems posed by restoration.

One paradox in this seemingly enlightened new opinion came to light, however; many people began to adopt a respect for the old as a wholesale axiom. For them, "old" came to mean "good." It was again necessary, if treacherous, to distinguish the age of an old building or interior from its quality.

Hotel Design

The design of new hotels with large central atrium spaces—larger than the skylighted palm courts of the older hotels by being almost the full height of the building—continued to be one of the major goals of hotel design in the 1970s. Beginning with the Atlanta Hyatt Regency Hotel in the late 1960s, architect John Portman produced a series of hotels with atriums: Among them was the Hyatt Regency Hotel in San Francisco (1973), with its pyramidal ziggurat effect, its vast sculpture, hanging plants, and exposed glass-walled and midway-lighted elevators that ran up and down in the atrium like space capsules.

215. Johnson/Burgee Architects. Guest room, Marquette Inn, IDS Center. Minneapolis, Minnesota. 1974. *Photograph by Phillip MacMillan James & Associates.*

The atrium as an indoor room was recalled to modern usage. Its earlier incarnation had been during the 1880s and 1890s in department stores. In the 1960s Kevin Roche's Ford Foundation Building in New York offered a garden atrium amenity for the surrounding offices. Cesar Pelli's town-square atrium for Columbus, Indiana, during this time also showed the value of large indoor rooms to urban life. As much as any other interior spaces, these glassed atriums indicated the new humanism, the new concern for occupants and passersby. They offered places to sit and chat, places where people could look at splashing water and colorful flowers, or could watch people and the activity of the constantly moving elevators.

Architects Philip Johnson and John Burgee showed how the atrium could be an effective town square with their Crystal Court at IDS Center in Minneapolis, Minnesota, and at Pennzoil Place in Houston, Texas. As part of IDS Center, Johnson/Burgee designed the interiors of a new hotel, the Marquette Inn (1974) (they worked with an associate firm of architects on the overall building). The interiors were unique among hotel designs by being in the Modern idiom. Not only were the public spaces stylish, original, and comfortable, but they were beautifully detailed within a commercial budget. The zigzag lighted corridors alone made the hotel innovative, but the uncompromisingly modern guest rooms (see Figure 215) were a distinctive mixture of Pop and Minimalism. There was something of this same mixture in the New York restaurant Genghiz Khan's Bicycle, designed by Gamal El Zoghby with plastic laminate and vinyl furniture that was integrated with the overall interior.

Store Design and Display

Designers were more and more active in department-store and boutique design during the 1970s. Display design had another surge of inspiration in the cartoon-like tableaux that were created with mannequins in store windows. Robert Currie drew crowds with his theater-like scenes in the windows of Henri Bendel and elsewhere. He was followed by Candy Praz at Bloomingdale's and by others across the country. All owed a debt to the long tradition of Gene Moore's windows for Tiffany & Co. and for other firms. This new store and window display seemed like a new concern for human response.

Product Design

The involvement of interior designers as designers of products for furnishing was markedly increased in the 1970s. In addition to specialist product designers, many prominent designers of interiors found their ways into designing products for what had been called "the home furnishings industry." It was a great improvement over the "decorator colors" slogan of the previous decades. In the tradition of "designer name" labels for wearing apparel, interior designers attached their names to furniture and fabrics, sheets and towels, carpeting and rugs, and a broad spectrum of products for interiors.

Corporate Office Design

The mainstream of commercial interior design—office planning—continued to provide business and design opportunities for a wide range of design professionals. The marketing of design services was organized by large space-planning firms as a structured and separately staffed program. A quick marketing growth brought the California firm of Gensler Associates to the position of largest interior design firm in the country. Stylistically, offices were invested with a wide range of options, from supergraphic murals and photomontages to Post-Modernist historical allusions and the full pluralism of the decade.

Workstations

Workstations and their new lighting requirements became a major technical concern. It had been only thirty years since all mechanical systems had been incor-

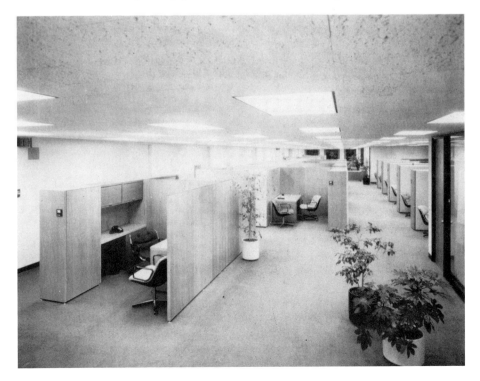

216. ISD Inc. Stephens Plus System workstations by Knoll International, installed in offices of Atlantic Richfield. Philadelphia, Pennsylvania. 1975. *Photograph courtesy Knoll International.*

porated into suspended ceilings. By the mid-1970s, after office-landscape systems had liberated the furniture plan from the regimentation of the building grid, those same office-landscape systems began to let lighting break out of the ceiling grid and become more related to movable work tasks. The new goal was for task lighting that was in balance with ambient lighting.

First had come the redefinition of the office as a workstation—a low-partitioned (58 to 74 inches high) enclosure that was, ostensibly, easily movable and that incorporated desk/table surfaces and drawer/shelf storage, usually hung from the partitions. By the mid-1970s furniture manufacturers were producing more and more of these systems (see Figure 216).

The separation of these open-plan mini-rooms from the overall ambience revealed the need for a separation in the way the two were lighted. Task lighting needed to be brighter than the lighting in ambient corridors. The new lighting, although it took many different forms—fixtures, optics, and lamps—consisted of indirect up lighting for general illumination and direct down lighting for work activities. Both were being incorporated into the design of the workstation itself. The economic advantages were the elimination of the modular illuminated ceiling and virtually all ceiling troffers, along with a consequent saving in electricity as well as savings in taxes for building elements versus movable furniture. Once again in the 1970s, adaptability to change and a concentration on people and their activities were the humanistic goals.

Lighting design at last reached a recognized position among design professions. More and more lighting designers not only practiced, but were consulted by the designers of interiors. The first textbook for architects and interior designers on the subject of interior lighting was written in this period by James L. Nuckolls (see Suggested Reading).

The New York Five

The prominent leaders of the decade's fourth generation of Modern designers were a group of young architects who became known as the New York Five: Richard Meier, Charles Gwathmey, Michael Graves, Peter Eisenman, and John Hejduk. Their work became known through the publication in 1972 of the book *Five Architects*. The first three became influential on interior design in the 1970s; the latter two were more concerned with conceptual architecture, structuralism, and teaching. Fundamental to their early work was the influence of and inspiration from the white architecture of the 1920s, especially Le Corbusier's Purism. Le Corbusier's investigations provided their model—the language that they continued to develop. In this regard, the work of the Five was the most prominent example of the decade's new historicism.

Richard Meier

Meier began to be known in professional circles in the mid-1960s for his Smith House in Rowayton, Connecticut (1964), and for his Salzman House in East Hampton, Long Island (1969); but his work was neither publicly prominent nor influential on interior design until the 1970s. Then his explosions of the Corbusian idiom, including ever larger and more complicated violin curves and ocean-liner railings, became broadly influential on the decade's design direction.

Richard Meier (1934–) was born in Newark, New Jersey, and studied architecture at Cornell University. He began his career working for Frank Grad Architects in New Jersey; for Davis, Brody & Wisniewski in New York; then for Skidmore, Owings & Merrill and Marcel Breuer. He opened his own practice in 1963

217. Richard Meier. Salzman House. East Hampton, Long Island. 1969. *Photograph © Ezra Stoller/ESTO, 1969.*

in New York and since then has designed numerous houses and housing units, shops, health and educational facilities, clubs, galleries, and other buildings.

Meier's Salzman House (see Figure 217) had built-in furniture (albeit uphol-stered in tiger-skin plush by the clients) and Mies- and Corbusier-inspired fur-nishings, with crisp tables in plastic laminate and glass tops, with white-lacquered cabinets for the music system and bar storage. But except for furniture essentials, paintings, and animal-skin upholstery, the architecture of the house—its structural columns, bridges, and ocean-liner railings—was the only decoration used.

Late in the 1970s Meier designed a library reading room within Frank Lloyd Wright's Guggenheim Museum. It was a model of respect for the context of the room, and presented new furniture designs by Meier as well. This led to the production of his furniture designs by Knoll International.

Charles Gwathmey

From the beginning of his career Charles Gwathmey extended the Corbusian idiom of large-scale cylinders, angles, and the open-free plan by, at first, sheathing those forms in shingles. Architecture historian Vincent Scully acclaimed this work as adapting the International Style of Le Corbusier to the New England context.

Charles Gwathmey (1938–) was born in Charlotte, North Carolina. He stud-ied architecture at the University of Pennsylvania under Louis Kahn and Robert

218. Gwathmey Siegel & Associates, Architects. Shezan Restaurant. New York City. 1976. *Photograph by Norman McGrath.*

Venturi and then at Yale University under Paul Rudolph and James Stirling. He began his architecture practice in New York in partnership with Richard Henderson and, since 1971, has been in partnership with Robert Siegel. The firm has designed numerous residences, educational and commercial buildings, and interiors of many kinds. By the end of the decade, Gwathmey was designing furnishings for major production.

Along with his partners, Gwathmey designed a number of interiors—for houses, apartments, and galleries—that reflected the Corbusian influence in the sculptural modeling of white plaster, in ship railings, and in direct quotations of Le Corbusier's work. In an apartment for actress Faye Dunaway in New York (1970), Gwathmey's firm reinterpreted a bathroom in Le Corbusier's Villa Savoye of 1929–31 (see Chapter 12). Later in the decade Gwathmey and his partner, Robert Siegel, began to be represented by furniture and carpet designs that further reiterated Corbusian themes and motifs.

His reconstruction after a fire at Whig Hall at Princeton University in 1972 brilliantly demonstrated the inclusion of the Corbusian free-plan Domino and large-scale Corbusian forms within a nineteenth-century Greek revival temple. His design of Pearl's Restaurant (1974) and Shezan Restaurant (1976) (see Figure 218), both in New York City, demonstrated how the materials of Internationalism—glass block, polished metal acoustical ceiling tiles, travertine, and oak—could be manipulated to achieve an unexpected elegance within commercial spaces.

Michael Graves

Of the Five, it was Michael Graves who was to contribute the most to interior design in the 1970s. His influence was first through a symbolic use of colors that aimed to give "meanings"; and later through his mannered classical ornamentation, delicate pastel colors, and furniture designs.

Michael Graves (1934–) was born in Indianapolis, Indiana, and studied architecture at the University of Cincinnati and at Harvard University. Then, at the

American Academy in Rome, he became especially interested in the work of Borromini and spent days drawing everything by Borromini that he could. It was then that his celebrated drawing technique was developed. In 1962 he settled in Princeton, New Jersey, where he has practiced architecture and taught at Princeton University ever since.

By the end of the 1970s his designs included a dozen or more houses and house additions, half a dozen museums and galleries, several medical facilities, offices for an investment group, and the beginning of a series of showrooms for Sunar (see color plate 15) that would provide direct exposure to his work for a vast number of young designers and of potential clients. In all of these projects, his use of color and ornament was liberal and remarkable.

The principal feature of Michael Graves's work is an art-historical approach—especially a Cubist simultaneity of images, meanings, and inspirations or derivations. He is concerned with multiple layers of space, of structure, and of symbolism. The relationships of his interiors and architecture to their physical sites and cultural backgrounds—questions of contextual continuity—are primary concerns for Graves. His is architectural storytelling. He relates base, wall, and ceiling to ground, horizon, and sky or to foot, body, and head. His is anthropomorphic symbolism rather than machine symbolism. It rejects abstraction in favor of the representational, the humanistic, the communicative.[2]

In the 1970s Michael Graves assumed the mantle as the leading young philosopher-theorist-aesthetician of the day. His designs and drawings, the latter of which became among the most celebrated by architects in our time, showed classical manipulations and Mannerist inventions, along with delicacy of colors and original juxtapositions of scale and texture, of form and structural reference. All these factors made him one of the leading influences on and inspirations for young designers in the 1970s (see Figure 219).

By the end of the decade Graves was attacking the very precept of twentieth-century space. Along with other Post-Modernists, he maintained:

219. Michael Graves. Gunwyn Ventures Office. Princeton, New Jersey. 1972. *Photograph by Norman McGrath.*

[In the open-free plan, Modernism] lost the divisions that gave us privacy, that gave us hierarchy of rooms. If you look at the Tugendhat house you see a De Stijl–like arrangement without hierarchy. I don't think that is our culture's rule system. I think it is wrong and inappropriate for all of us all of the time to make a homogeneous world of space. Rooms are all we have; space is within the room. Without the room we have no walls, and without walls you don't need architects or designers.[3]

It was the Post-Modernists' indictment of Modernism, but it did not preclude their historical reverence for and revival of the white architecture of the 1920s.

Early in the 1970s Graves experimented with a system of colors used for symbolic content. He called it color metaphor. Graves's use of color was an example of the influence of French and Russian Structuralism on 1970s design. Structuralism in design was an analogy with Structuralism in linguistics, which had sought meanings in the underlying nature of language and its fundamental structure. Graves, along with Peter Eisenman early in the 1970s, was concerned with meanings expressed by forms arranged as an architectural language. Graves's experiments and his correlations with nature were part of this investigation.

His color use—in additions to houses, in offices, and in the medical offices for Ear, Nose, and Throat Associates (see Figure 220) in Fort Wayne, Indiana (1971)—aimed for a "metaphorical landscape." That is, colors themselves offered connotations or "cultural references": Blue symbolized sky or water; yellow signified sunlight; green connoted the leaves of plant life; and Etruscan red meant "wall."

Graves's design for the ENT interiors followed this analogy: Sunlight streaks in by means of the low yellow partitions of the central nurses' station; overhead, the green-painted air-conditioning ducts suggest a canopy of leaves; above them is a track from which spotlights are hung—painted blue to suggest a halo of sky. In each treatment room at ENT Graves himself painted a cubistic mural of the surrounding landscape that reiterates these color analogies.

It was, in fact, the compounding of these multiple images, metaphors, and meanings that gave Graves's work its depth and richness, both intellectually and

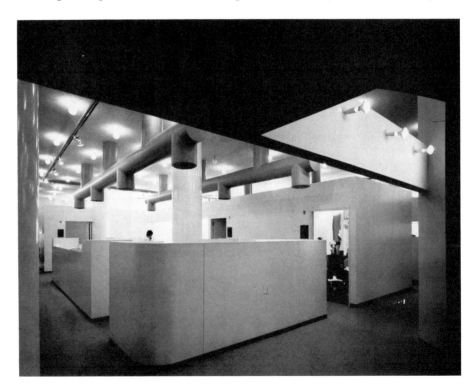

220. Michael Graves. Nurses' station in medical offices for Ear, Nose, and Throat Associates. Fort Wayne, Indiana. 1971. *Photograph by Balthazar Korab.*

visually. The expression of this full imagination of aesthetic metaphors, connotations, and multiple meanings made his interior designs and his architecture vital and stimulating in the early 1970s and brought him to international stature. Later, he moved away from color reference and changed his way of conceiving space.

The Post-Modernists

Around 1973 or 1974 a small vanguard group of architects adopted the term Post-Modern to explain their work. For them, it meant manipulating and applying the tradition of history—especially classical architecture and classical decoration, but also including any other historical reference that attracted them at the moment. Historical allusion and mannered classicism were the keystones of what they called Post-Modernism. What all this led to was a rage of classical recalls and motifs that was as mannered as the mannerism of the 1960s had been. The Post-Modernists claimed that this direction provided multiple levels of meaning for people who had been deprived of humanistic content by the Modern movement. In this approach, they were reaching out beyond the abstraction of the Modern movement toward a representational architecture with more communicational content.

The term Post-Modern had long been used by the art world to designate the change of sensibilities that occurred around 1950, when Abstract Expressionism and the second generation of Modern designers had led the rebellion against the rigid abstraction of Modernism. The Post-Modernists of the 1970s used the term more specifically to denote their particular brand of historical inclusion and manipulation of historical elements.

The third generation of Modernists, who had begun to shake the foundations of Modernism in the 1960s—such as Robert Venturi and Charles Moore—continued their allusions and quotations from architecture history. Although they resisted the term, they had to accept being called Post-Modernists. Philip Johnson dared direct imitation—or "quotation"—in his design of New York University's Bobst Library floor, which repeated, identically, the marble flooring pattern in the sanctuary of Palladio's church of San Giorgio Maggiore in Venice (see Figure 221). Years before, Johnson had maintained, "You cannot not know history."

In the late 1970s, even more publicly, he gained the spotlight in this activity for his design, with partner John Burgee, of the AT&T building in New York with its broken-pediment roofscape. That histrionic motif scandalized many observers from all classes of understanding. It came to be called "a Chippendale broken pediment," though the broken pediment had had a longer lineage in the history of ideas—certainly before Chippendale, most obviously in the work of Inigo Jones and Grinling Gibbons. To the public, Chippendale was the most known. It was an age that took travesty seriously.

A younger generation of Post-Modernists also investigated historical allusion. The most prominent and vociferous spokesmen for this generation and for this direction from about 1974 onward were Robert A. M. Stern and the writer-architect Charles Jencks. They led the campaign for the term Post-Modern to denote the sleuthing out of new historical models.

Among the periods and architects that the Post-Modernists revived for adaptation were Sir Edwin Lutyens, Georgian periods, Alvar Aalto, Paul Cret, Josef Hoffmann, the lattices and grids of the Wiener Werkstaette and the Shingle Style, along with other sources. The forms and ornamentation of these designers and periods were adapted to a system of classical ornamentation for our day.

It therefore became a popular, elegant half-joke to design classicized furniture. Also influential to architects and to Minimalist designers of interiors was Post-Metabolism (the Japanese correspondent of Post-Modernism) in Japan led by Arata Isozaki, Kisho Kurokawa, and Fumihiko Maki, as well as a younger generation.

221. Philip Johnson and Richard Foster. Palladio-inspired marble floor pattern, Elmer Holmes Bobst Library, New York University. New York City. 1973. *Photograph courtesy Philip Johnson & Richard Foster, Architects.*

Robert A. M. Stern

His activities as critic, architect, and historian; his single-minded dedication to work; and his perseverance of the Post-Modernist ideal made Robert A. M. Stern one of the prominent spokesmen and advocates for the movement. Born in New York City, Robert A. M. Stern (1938–) studied history at Columbia University, then architecture at Yale University, where he came under the influence of Philip Johnson, Vincent Scully, Robert Venturi, and Paul Rudolph. He began working in New York as organizer of programs for the Architectural League. He worked in the office of Richard Meier for a few months, then with the New York City Housing and Development Administration; and in 1969 established his own architecture practice with his Yale classmate John S. Hagmann. In 1977 the partnership was dissolved and Stern formed Robert A. M. Stern, Architects. During those years he designed apartment renovations, showrooms, educational facilities, and houses—the latter numbering twenty major renovations and complete new works in that decade.

His work in the 1970s demonstrated his advocacy of Post-Modernism. He created spaces that were explosions of shapes—twists, literally, on the images of Le Corbusier, Robert Venturi, and Art Deco. His spaces were formed of flat paneled walls, curving walls, diagonals, layers of screens—and they were illumi-

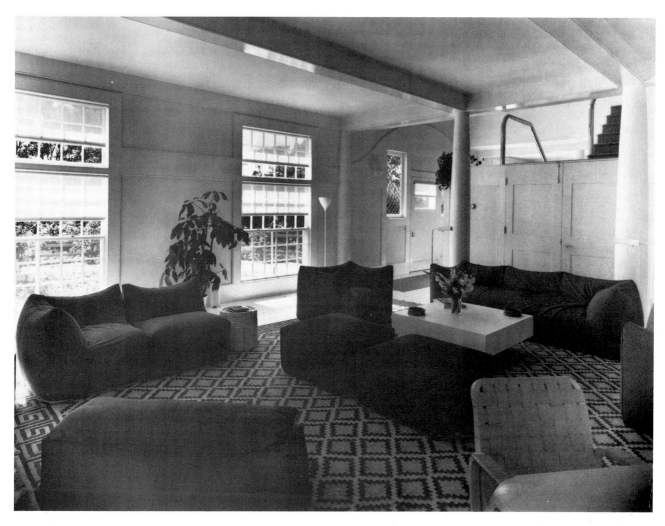

222. Robert A. M. Stern. Living room. East Hampton, Long Island. 1976–77. *Photograph by Ed Stoecklein, courtesy Robert A. M. Stern, Architects.*

nated by Aalto-esque skylights over fireplaces, over unexpected setbacks of ceiling, and from side ports.

As a proponent of applied ornament and historicism, he decorated with architectural elements in a wide range of historical styles—with Palladian pilasters and arched windows, with Gothic string courses, and Georgian paneling. He included Shingle-Style inglenooks, Art Deco cabinetwork, parallel lines, and indirect lighting coves. Like his lounge at Columbia University Law School, one of Stern's houses in East Hampton, Long Island, gained white pilasters, wide borders to achieve paneling, small-paned windows, and cream-colored walls (see Figure 222). Both decorative schemes returned the interiors to the vintage of their original structures. With other contemporary Post-Modernists, he felt that such interior treatments could, unlike the abstract industrialism of Modernism, communicate to people once again.

The Italian Influence

Throughout the 1970s the influence of Italian designers was stronger than it had been since around 1950. Furniture designs from Milan continued to electrify professionals and laymen alike. In 1972 New York's Museum of Modern Art produced a lavish exhibition and catalogue by Emilio Ambasz, "Italy: The New Domestic Landscape." From Italy also came the influence of neo-Rationalism and neo-Pur-

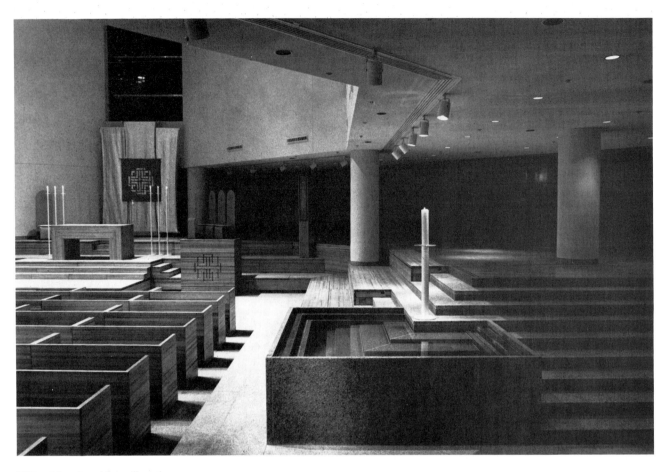

223. Massimo Vignelli and Lella Vignelli. St. Peter's Lutheran Church. New York City. 1977. *Photograph by George Cserna.*

ism, which were led by Aldo Rossi, Massimo Scolari, and Mario Botta. Their work gave a new direction to Surrealism—or was it Existentialism? There was also a revival of interest in the work of the 1920s Italian Modernist-Rationalist Giuseppe Terragni. Among the most prominent of the Italian furniture designers were Mario Bellini, Ettore Sottsass, Jr., and the Castiglione brothers.

Meanwhile, since the mid-1960s, the Italian design team of Massimo and Lella Vignelli had maintained an outpost of Italian design in New York (see page 212ff.). They continued to expand beyond their graphic designs into product and interior designs. Among their designs were furnishings and household objects—including popular tableware in multicolored plastic—and the interior of St. Peter's Lutheran Church in New York (see Figure 223).

Emilio Ambasz

Emilio Ambasz developed a design practice in the United States and in Italy. Born in Argentina, architect Emilio Ambasz (1943–) studied architecture at Princeton University and subsequently taught there as well as at Carnegie-Mellon University in Pittsburgh and in Ulm, Germany, before being appointed curator of design at the Museum of Modern Art in 1969. He left the museum to form his own practice in 1977.

In Italy, with Giancarlo Piretti, he designed a series of chairs that automatically adjusted to a variety of seating systems while providing proper orthopedic and posture support. This Vertebra Seating System was produced in America by Kreuger.

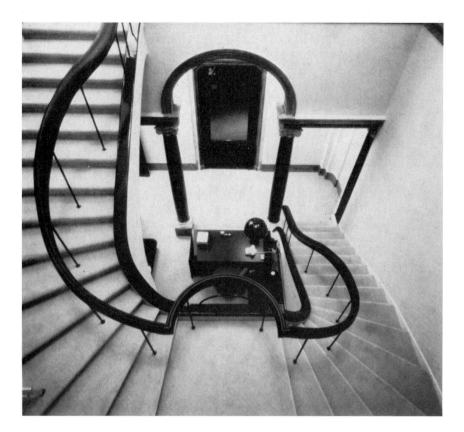

224. Emilio Ambasz. Banque Bruxelles Lambert. Milan, Italy. 1979. *Photograph by Santi Caleca.*

At the end of the decade Ambasz and Piretti completed a branch bank in Milan for the Banque Bruxelles Lambert (see Figure 224). It combined preservation with Post-Modern inclusions and the tradition of decorating craftsmanship—a multicoated paint schedule, varied furniture specification and coloring, and decorative detailing. The paint scheme for the walls began with a layer of heliotrope color, was next sprayed with clouds of white paint, and finally a light spray of gray and brown speckles. The effect was deep, like traditional lacquers, and yet overall creamy white. The carpet also achieved this delicate multicolored effect with yarn dyed lilac at the base and light beige at the carpet surface. The bank interior is poetic and inventive, especially in its imaginatively inventive stair railing, which not only turns from a vertical rail to a horizontal one at mid-stair level, but also meanders from the stair edge into the stair tread area.

The Late Modernists

Among those mainstream designers who continued to refine the Miesian idiom from the 1960s were the interior design departments of the large architecture firms, the large space-planning firms, and many independent architects and interior designers. Several designers became newly prominent during the 1970s for their work in this area.

Skidmore, Owings & Merrill (SOM), across the country and now around the world, continued to produce new and fresh variations on corporate and institutional interior design. In SOM's Chicago office Bruce Graham, with senior interior designer George Larson, brought a new image to banking with his red-lacquered workstations—the system Davis Allen designed for G. F. Business Equipment—at the First Bank of Wisconsin in 1975 (see Figure 214).

225. Skidmore, Owings & Merrill/Davis Allen. Conference/dining room of Alexander & Alexander. New York City. 1978. *Photograph by Jaime Ardiles-Arce.*

Davis Allen

In 1974, after nearly twenty-five years of designing interiors and custom furniture designs for SOM projects, New York senior interior designer Davis Allen was finally permitted by SOM to have his name assigned to a line of furniture he had designed that was to be mass-marketed. Called the Davis Allen Collection by G. F. Business Equipment, the furniture, through its publicity, began to bring the recognition that should have been accorded to Davis Allen for the past fifteen years. Allen had been the chief interior designer at SOM's New York office since the late 1950s. He had been the interior designer of the Chase Manhattan Bank Headquarters, and it had been due to him that the interiors by SOM in project after project steadily grew in refinement, sophistication of systems, appeal of textural juxtaposition, and range of artworks.

Among his major projects during the 1970s were a suite of offices for Gianni Agnelli in Paris (completed in 1975); the headquarters of a major grain company in New York (completed in 1976); and the headquarters of Alexander & Alexander in New York (completed in 1978) (see Figure 225). All were interiors projects with vast budgets, costly materials, ingenious artworks programs, and palatial planning and detailing. In the evolution of Modernism and in the revolutions against it, the interiors of SOM were less in the forefront than they had been in the 1960s, when such work was the mainstream center of interior design; but it was, in the 1970s, a corpus of work that showed continual refinement, invention, and elegance. Davis Allen was the virtually unknown hero of this operation.

Powell/Kleinschmidt

From the Chicago office of SOM in 1976 sprang the new interior design firm of Powell/Kleinschmidt in Chicago. Donald D. Powell (1933–) was born in North Dakota and studied architecture at the University of Minnesota, where he received his B.Arch. in 1956. He joined SOM's Chicago office in 1962 as a senior designer of interiors and became an associate partner in 1968. His knowledge of virtually every dimension of Mies's furniture designs and other details of the Miesian canon was impressive.

Robert D. Kleinschmidt (1939–) was born in Chicago and studied architecture at the University of Illinois, receiving his B.Arch. in 1963, and at Columbia University, earning his M.Sc. in architecture in 1964. He joined SOM's Chicago office in 1964 and became an associate partner in 1973.

From 1966 to 1976 Donald D. Powell and Robert D. Kleinschmidt had been interior designers in the Chicago office of SOM. There, their work on SOM's Sears Bank and Trust Company in Chicago (1974) brought a golden richness to bank offices.

Their work for SOM's Banco di Roma in Chicago of the same year showed their ability to take the SOM idiom into permissiveness, ambiguity, and reflection. Based on the building's rotated square columns, the bank design manipulates rotated squares and diagonals along with mirror surfaces and rich colors of burgundy, plum, rust, and eggplant.

By the end of the decade their independent work included banking facilities, educational and cultural institutions, residential units, restoration work, showrooms, banks, and office complexes. In this they showed a meticulous and colorful approach—influenced by color-field painting—and humanized in the direction of the decade. Basic to their approach was the goal of total design—the consideration of all the elements that comprise the total environment. They aimed to challenge manufacturers to respond with new technology.

Charles Pfister

From the San Francisco office of Skidmore, Owings & Merrill, the designs of Charles Pfister began to be noticed in the early 1970s. Born in Santa Rosa, California, Charles Pfister (1939–) studied architecture at the University of California at Berkeley and worked independently in San Francisco for a brief period before joining SOM's San Francisco office in 1965. He became an associate partner of that firm in 1974 and continued as director of interior design in the San Francisco office until 1981. In that year he formed his own practice.

Pfister was first recognized for the interior design of SOM's headquarters for the Weyerhaeuser Corporation in Tacoma, Washington, in 1971. There, with SOM design partner Edward C. Bassett, he designed 300,000 square feet of office landscape—the largest installation of the concept in this country at that time. The entire five-level building was planned and furnished as an open landscape (see Figure 226), including the office of the president. Islands of rectilinear workstation groups, rather than totally free-form arrangements, composed the plan.

Pfister also designed the furniture system, which was the first new landscape system produced in this country. This oak panel system was produced by Knoll as the Stephens System, because SOM designers were then not permitted to have their names on their furniture designs. Acoustically, the open space was modulated by an acoustical-tile ceiling with gray sound added for privacy and by partitions that were acoustically treated on both sides. Carpeted throughout—one floor each planned as blue, gray, amethyst, and camel—and filled with Colombian upholstery fabrics by Jack Lenor Larsen, the interiors were richly warm in contrast to the rugged landscape visible everywhere through expansive glass walls. It was for this project that Pfister designed his first seating pieces, also produced by Knoll, a sofa and lounge group modified from a tuxedo sofa and made modular—a single lounge chair, a settee, or a three-cushion (or longer) sofa.

In the mid-1970s Pfister designed a tubular metal chair for the offices of the fashion designer Halston; it was produced by Metropolitan Furniture. In addition

226. Skidmore, Owings & Merrill/Charles Pfister. Weyerhaeuser headquarters. Tacoma, Washington. 1971. *Photograph © Ezra Stoller/ESTO, 1971.*

to his continuing series of interior designs for SOM, Pfister designed a line of radius corner tables for Knoll; and by 1980 he was designing the executive offices of Swid/Cogan in New York.

Warren Platner

Throughout the 1970s Warren Platner produced elegant designs in the Late-Modern idiom that were also expansive and flamboyant. His Grill restaurant in the TWA Terminal at Kennedy Airport in New York, completed in 1970 with Kevin Roche, John Dinkeloo & Associates, was an enrichment of the building's sculptural forms with heady colors and textures.

His American Restaurant in Kansas City, Missouri, completed in 1974 in Edward Larrabee Barnes's building, combined window walls that were covered with floor-to-ceiling louvered shutters—a kind of New Orleans effect—with Perpendicular Gothic fan vaultings lighted with midway lights in each fan (see Figure 227). Superscale mirror-brass lighting fixtures—a scaled-down version of the Castiglione brothers' Arco Lamp of 1965—arched over banquettes to provide downlight on tables. It showed the historical pluralism of the decade.

In 1976 the Windows on the World restaurant atop the World Trade Center in New York was opened with interiors by Warren Platner. There, Platner produced a design both modern enough to be sympathetic with the building and intricate enough to be competitive with the view from the 110th floor. Terraced floors made the view uninterrupted from the inner levels. Highly polished, large-scale brass railings and lighting fixtures gave glitter to the elaborately textured spaces with their carpeted ceiling-high nooks and banquettes and other elaborations.

Platner's designs for offices, educational institutions, clubs, and residences at this time were less flamboyant, and all displayed balanced full-range orchestration of textures, a blown-up scale, and inventive if multitudinous detailing.

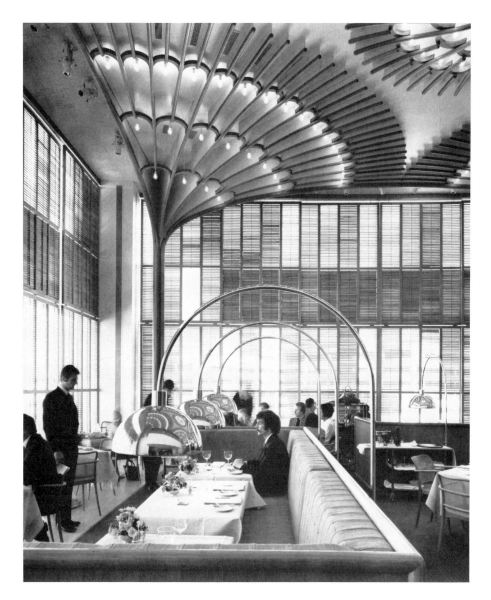

227. Warren Platner Associates. American Restaurant. Kansas City, Missouri. 1974. *Photograph by Alexandre Georges, courtesy Warren Platner Associates.*

Paul Rudolph

During the 1970s Paul Rudolph maintained a lower profile than he had during the previous two decades, but he regularly continued to design large and small projects with his usual invention and detail in interiors. He demonstrated his fertile imagination and his zeal for innovation at every scale of total design, from siting and materials to furnishings and inventive detail. His chapel for Tuskegee Institute in Alabama (see Figure 228) at the end of the 1960s was a continuation of these themes and an exploration of the motifs of Ronchamp in flat rather than molded planes and with imaginative lighting and integral coloring (see page 205ff.).

Among his significant interiors during the 1970s were the lobby of the Borroughs Wellcome building in Durham, North Carolina (1972), which integrated the horizontal effect of 1920s architecture with diagonals; an unpublished house in Fort Worth, Texas (1979); and several churches and chapels. The chapel in Boston's Health Services Center (see Figure 229) is a poured-in-place concrete sculpture within a much larger complex that utilizes the corrugated concrete texture Rudolph had devised a decade before. A totality in its consistency of forms and details, the chapel is one of the high points of Rudolph's interior work.

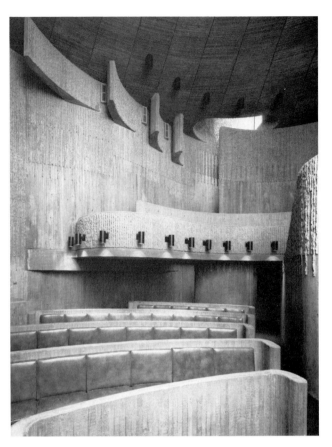

228. Paul Rudolph. Chapel, Tuskegee Institute. Tuskegee, Alabama. 1969. *Photograph © Ezra Stoller/ESTO, 1969.*

229. Paul Rudolph. Chapel, Health Services Center. Boston, Massachusetts. 1971. *Photograph by Robert Perron.*

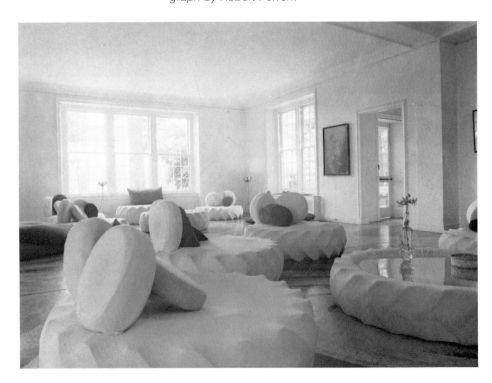

230. Paul Rudolph. Living room, Elman residence. Great Barrington, Massachusetts. 1975. *Photograph by Robert Perron.*

231. Louis Kahn. Mellon Center for British Art, Yale University. New Haven, Connecticut. Circa 1976. *Photograph by R. D. Smith, courtesy Center for British Art.*

In addition to these major works and numerous residential projects during the 1970s, Rudolph also made one of the great jokes on the dream of the Industrial Revolution and on Industrial Pop: In the living room of the Elman residence in Great Barrington, Massachusetts (1974), Rudolph the functionalist painted the concrete floor as a colorful circulation diagram to emphasize the possibilities of the awkward five-door room (see Figure 230). His colors were pale-blue stripes winding into swirls of concentration, symbolically, at the whirlwind centers of conversation. On top of those swirls he located what was the most superscale Pop furniture of its day—tractor tires covered in stretch fabric with upright cushion backs to serve as seating and with glass tops to serve as tables. It was Pop Country Vernacular as well as Industrial Pop—and it was also one of the most forceful demonstrations of the battle between innovation and tradition.

Louis Kahn

Among the other established masters of the 1970s, Louis Kahn completed his library for the Exeter school in New Hampshire in 1972 with furniture designed and specified by Benjamin Baldwin. Like the Mellon Center for British Art at Yale (completed after Kahn's death in 1974), interior walls and paneling were in a rich warm wood that contrasted ingeniously with the exposed concrete (see Figure 231). Furnishings, again, were specified by Benjamin Baldwin, who, by this time, had become interiors consultant to some of the most renowned American architects. These interiors, along with those of Kahn's Kimball Art Museum in Fort Worth, Texas, showed that raw concrete, natural wood, and superb detailing could create as finished and elegant an interior as any lacquered space.

The Minimalists

The Minimalism of the 1960s came to general public attention in the 1970s. Prominent was the work of the older generation of Minimalists: Benjamin Baldwin,

Ward Bennett (see page 172ff.), and William Machado with Norman Diekman. In addition, the work of a number of architects was more commonly recognized as sharing this Minimalist intent: Edward Larrabee Barnes; I. M. Pei & Partners; Skidmore, Owings & Merrill; Kevin Roche; Cesar Pelli; and Hugh Stubbins. They were joined by a new younger generation of Minimalist designers.

Among the purest of the older generation's work was I. M. Pei & Partners' National Airlines Terminal, a design from the 1960s that was completed at Kennedy Airport in New York in 1970. Robert Lym was Pei's director of interior design in charge of this and other Minimalist designs by Pei & Partners.

Benjamin Baldwin

Benjamin Baldwin's work in the 1970s, which included interiors for architects Louis Kahn, I. M. Pei, and Edward Larrabee Barnes, also included furniture designs produced by Larsen Furniture. Beginning with the chair Baldwin had designed for the Ritz Bar in Boston in 1967, he went on to create a line of new designs.

During the 1970s designers traveled to see the house and garden Baldwin had built for himself in East Hampton, Long Island, in the late 1960s and which he was constantly refining. It showed his Minimal detailing and his sensitivity to juxtapositions of scale, of texture, and of house to garden. In addition, his inclusion of a somewhat Japanese refined rusticity pointed a new direction for the decade.

The house (see Figure 232 and color plate 14) is a small and modest Long Island barn-like structure perched above the brick foundations of a former house; the foundations have been turned into a garden. Inside the house an exposed wood structure—reminiscent of both barn construction and traditional Japanese houses—divides the two floors into three bays. In the middle is a living area with glass doors opening onto gardens on both sides of the house. The two end bays, which are windowless, are open to this central interior space, separated from it only by

232. Benjamin Baldwin. Own house. East Hampton, Long Island. Circa 1978. *Photograph by Jon Naar.*

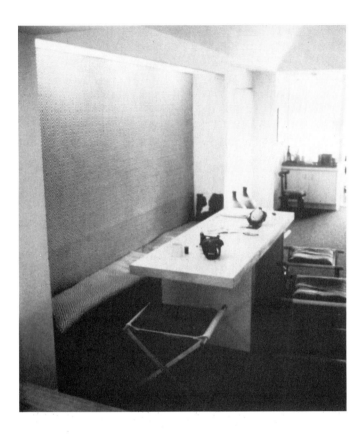

233. Benjamin Baldwin. Dining room, own house. Sarasota, Florida. 1979. *Photograph by C. Ray Smith.*

the exposed wood columns and by pull-up bamboo-strip roller blinds. In one end bay is a kitchen, which is surrounded by white floor-to-ceiling doors to storage cabinets and in the center of which is a 6-foot-square island counter topped in 4-inch-thick butcher block. It is luxuriously spacious and appropriately rustic in juxtaposition to the kitchen equipment. The other end bay was originally a lounge area with a central platform covered in dark-gray industrial carpeting, with a fireplace at the center of the end wall, and with gold-and-black eighteenth-century Japanese screens at each side of the room.

Originally, the middle living-room bay contained a choice selection of furnishings—a Venetian Louis XV chair, a nickel-steel footrest, a small stainless-steel and glass table, and a standing lamp by Giacometti. It was a tour of cultures and ages through four furnishings, as he had in Chicago in the 1950s. Subsequently, these furnishings were changed to reflect the decade's interest in low, sculptural, modular seating; still later, that seating was moved into the end bay in front of the fireplace, and the middle bay acquired a sumptuously spacious, superscale library table and chairs; they doubled for conversation, reading, and dining.

Baldwin's East Hampton house typified his ideal of interior design as "tranquil, calm, and serene." It was echoed by his winter house in Sarasota, Florida, designed in the 1970s. There, the banquetted dining nook (see Figure 233) and the plaster details combined Minimal sculpture with calm rusticity.

Ward Bennett

During the same period, Ward Bennett designed a house for himself at Springs, Long Island, in 1973. It combined Minimal Purism as a Miesian pavilion with country and Japanese overtones. The square wood house has a central skylighted space that is surrounded by modular bays, some open to and some separate from the central living space (see Figure 234). An exposed structure of wood is juxta-

234. Ward Bennett. Own house. Springs, Long Island. 1973. *Photograph © Peter Aaron/ESTO, 1978.*

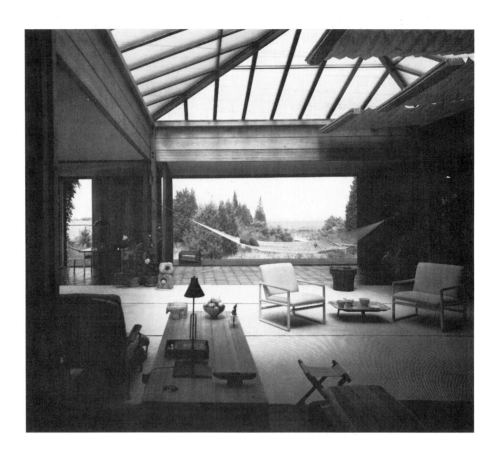

posed with glass walls, huge plants, an industrially carpeted fireplace inglenook of Miesian character, a Mexican white-string hammock, and a collection of Ward Bennett's elegant furniture designs. The house has a high pitch of refinement, even within the rustic structural system, and the combination of the two is superbly orchestrated.

A New Generation of Minimalists

Among the younger designers who espoused and continued the direction of Minimalism in the 1970s were Joseph D'Urso, Bray-Schaible, Scott Bromley and Robin Jacobsen, Peter Andes, Michael Kalil, James Maguire, Dennis Jenkins, Juan Montoya, and a number of others. They were inspired by the work of Luis Barragan (see Chapter 15), which was publicized by the Museum of Modern Art's 1972 exhibition directed by Emilio Ambasz and by Ambasz's book (see Suggested Reading).

So widely publicized was the use of industrial and industrial-looking products—in interiors, out of normal context—by this younger generation that it became known, in some circles, as "High-Tech" design. After seventy years industrial mass production had become popularized to the widest possible audience. In other circles the work of this generation of Minimalists was categorized as "the platform school."

A few corporate-office interiors of the 1970s were designed in the Minimal idiom. Notable were the offices designed for RCA Corporate Headquarters in New York by Ford & Earl's New York office, headed by James P. Maguire with a team of Marlys Hann and Ziva Gruber. Sleek, flat, trimless planes of white, red, and charcoal-brown were enlivened by polished-metal frames of the plug-in furniture system. But it was the residential work in this idiom that drew the most attention.

Joseph Paul D'Urso Combining a spartan Minimal envelope with industrial furnishings and materials, Joseph Paul D'Urso achieved a rich style in which chairs from the early Modern industrial period served as silhouetted sculptures.

Born in Newark, New Jersey, Joseph Paul D'Urso (1943–) got his B.F.A. in interior design at Pratt Institute and won a New York chapter AID scholarship award on his graduation in 1965. He then traveled and spent two years studying in England—first at the Royal College of Art in London, then as a fellow at the Manchester College of Art and Design, where he earned a master's degree in art from the Manchester Polytechnic Institute. In 1968 he began his independent practice in New York for the design, first, of residential interiors, and then of furnishings and larger interior projects. Since 1968 he has taught at Pratt Institute. His work was highly influential during the 1970s (see page 184ff.). His interiors were radically stripped—stark white walls, offset by platforms and steps often covered in dark-gray industrial carpeting, furnished with industrially produced chairs, tables, doors, track lighting, and vertical blinds. With this limited palette, D'Urso created interiors that nevertheless had a strong and expansive sense of scale, a crisp sculptural disposition of furnishings, and true richness and elegance. Punctuated by a single red flower, his uncompromising interiors often achieved an air of refined magic.

At mid-decade D'Urso designed an apartment for shoe designer Reed Evins in an undistinguished New York apartment building. He accepted the givens—low ceilings, wide rooms—without attempting to hide them or create something that was not there. He then opened the space further by painting walls and ceiling glossy white, and by installing integral platforms—a continuous one (6 feet 6 inches wide by 11 inches high) for seating along the 28-foot window wall and two 5-inch-high platforms stacked at one end of the first platform as a bed base. The sleeping area was defined by pull-back vertical venetian blinds, as was the 28-foot-long window wall. Gray industrial carpeting, track lighting, and a hospital door to the kitchen completed the minimal envelope. At the long platform stood a 10-foot-6-inch-long three-pedestal-base table with a glossy black rubber top banded in polished stainless steel. Complementing this spare and ascetic environment was a

235. Joseph Paul D'Urso. Calvin Klein Menswear showroom. New York City. 1979. *Photograph courtesy D'Urso Designs Inc.*

chaise designed by Le Corbusier—the only conventional furniture except for the mattress; it also served as a sculpture. Paintings and flowers, along with the lights of the city, provided the only color. The apartment was similar to one that D'Urso designed at this time for couturier Calvin Klein.

About the same time, D'Urso also designed a showroom for Calvin Klein Accessories, for women, that had bare high-gloss white walls, gridded windows of glass block, dark-gray industrial carpeting, lines of exposed fluorescent tube lighting between the beams, exposed white-enameled air-conditioning ducts, and polished-metal pipe fixtures for fabric display. White plastic-laminate-topped black-based pedestal tables and black chairs completed his severe industrial image, in which the colorful handbags and belts, and an occasional bright-red door and flowers, enlivened the space. It was a summation of Industrial Pop and what came to be called High-Tech.

Bray-Schaible The partnership of Robert Bray and Michael Schaible has produced interiors that have all the spartan purity of Minimalism, but also incorporate a decorative, less rigorous and doctrinaire approach.

Robert Bray (1942–) was born in Ardmore, Oklahoma, and studied architectural engineering at Oklahoma State University. Michael Schaible (1940–) was born in Oakley, Kansas. He received a B.F.A. from the University of Colorado and attended the Università di Firenze per Stranieri. They were classmates at the Parsons School of Design and began their careers working for the large space-planning firms of Ford & Earl Design Associates and Saphier, Lerner, Schindler Environetics, where most of their experience was in corporate work.

The work of Bray and Schaible is cool, clean, and elegant with an impression of spaciousness. This effect is produced by long, unbroken lines—by broad, open, and uncluttered planes—wide platforms and broad table surfaces set off against clearly defined floor areas and an almost seamless and uninterrupted background.

That seamless background is the signature of Bray-Schaible's craft: smoothed to the bone, cleared of all intruding blemishes—such as trim and baseboards, handles and knobs, light switches and electric outlets, air conditioning and light tracks (see Figure 236). Their interiors are usually pale, often vanilla-colored envelopes composed of eggshell-enameled walls, bleached wood floors or beige carpeting, off-white accordian-pleated window shades, and pale-toned stone used as flooring, fireplaces, tabletops, and serving credenzas. These envelopes are crisp, spare, and ascetic. They would be almost slick and cold if the designers did not enrich them sumptuously, as they do, differently for each client. In the 1970s they investigated rooms-within-rooms, layering, and historical allusions and quotations. Plushes and velvets, suedes and natural glove leathers, needlepoint carpets, and museum-quality artworks and objects embellished and personalized their concepts.[4]

Bray and Schaible opened their practice in 1969 with the design of a flower shop that was all glossy black enamel, aluminum shelving, glass shelves, mirrors, and spotlights on the flowers. The flower lighting became a restaurant tradition by the end of the next decade. In 1974 they designed the interiors of the First National Bank of Hialeah, Florida (see Figure 237), rigorously carrying through on the inside the planar horizontality of the speculative building exterior. Each plane meets the next at a sharp edge: Floors butt directly against walls, partitions, and counters; walls butt directly against ceilings and soffits—like a fine line drawing. It was a model of hidden details that achieve simplicity. The planar effect and the horizontality again recall the white architecture of the 1920s. The tellers' counter has a half-round metal lighting troffer hung above head level from airplane cables mounted in the 60-foot-high, atrium-like ceiling. Other work of Bray-Schaible has included residential interiors, corporate installations, and complete house designs that include both planning and architecture.

236. Bray-Schaible. Dina Cerruti Schmidt apartment. New York City. 1978. *Photograph © Wulf Brackrock for* Jahres Zeiten Verlag.

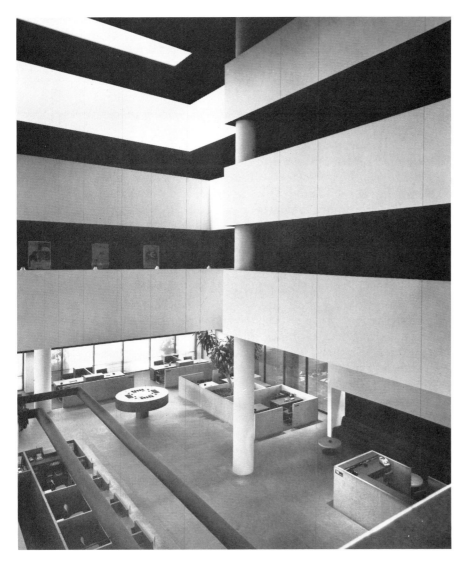

237. Bray-Schaible. First National Bank, Hialeah, Florida. 1974. *Photograph by Norman McGrath.*

Peter Andes Peter Andes was among those who pushed Minimalism to its barest, most reductive limits. Born in Lancaster, Pennsylvania, Andes (1935–) studied architecture at Yale University under Paul Rudolph's chairmanship. In the 1960s he worked in New York for Florence Knoll's Planning Unit, for which he was a project designer of interiors in New York—he worked on the CBS Building executive offices—and abroad, in Japan and Australia, where he designed the offices of the Bank of New South Wales; and in Mexico City, where he designed the interiors of the Camino Real Hotel. There he came to know Luis Barragan and Mathias Goeritz, who changed his vision.

Returning to New York in the 1970s, Andes pursued the most elemental interiors he could produce—furniture was eliminated wherever possible; platforms served as benches, banquettes, and bedsteads. All floor-related built-ins were covered in dark-gray industrial carpeting; walls were painted white or off-white; window coverings were aluminum venetian blinds. Mirrors and plants were additions to this palette to reinforce the element of repetition. His approach to elimination of detail included leaving existing room defects or moldings in place, accepting them as part of the recycling process. For one New York apartment (see Figure 238) he employed this vocabulary with tricks of enormous scale: The bed platform was 36 inches high; the venetian blinds covered the entire window wall. It was difficult to determine how large things in the apartment were.

For another apartment Andes repeated this black-and-white vocabulary, enriching it with glossy white trim and flat off-white walls. He furnished it with thirty 3-foot-square stacking cushions and 2-foot-square throw pillows, all in dark-gray suiting cloth with Turkish corners; these made up the portable, flexible, and Minimal seating. The scale trick of the larger-than-normal cushions was disorienting. Stacking white plastic tables, stacking ashtrays—and, in the dining room, stacking chairs, plateware, and glasses—completed the system of multiple function and repetition.

These appointments emphasized the extreme effects that the repetition of a minimal number of elements can produce—this work has been called "The Emperor's New Furniture."[5] By the late 1970s Andes was devoting himself to recycling lofts for residential use, doing the actual construction with his partner to learn more about the craft of this interior sculpture and the potential of minimalizing it further.

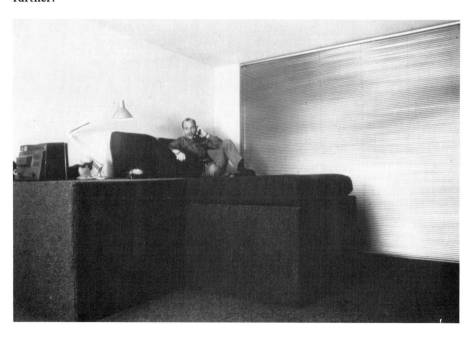

238. Peter Andes. Own apartment. New York City. Circa 1970. *Photograph by Jon Naar.*

The Residential Designers

More and more contract work was being done by traditional decorating firms. Billy Baldwin retired in 1972, leaving his firm to his partner, Arthur Smith. In his book *Billy Baldwin Remembers* he wrote about the interiors and people he most remembered. He spent the last decade of his life on Nantucket island, off Massachusetts, and died in 1984. William Pahlmann, after completing a large commission for Texas A&M University in 1976, retired to live in Mexico. Then in the 1970s, a new group of residential designers came to prominence.

David Hicks

From England to America, in 1968, had come the designs of David Hicks—carpets and fabrics patterned with all-over squares, plaids, and other small-scale geometric shapes. Billy Baldwin wrote that Hicks had "revolutionized the floors of the world with his small patterned and striped carpeting."[6]

Hicks had begun his career as an interior designer in London in 1955, and in 1960 his first carpet designs were produced. Fabric designs followed in 1964. They were immediately popular with American designers. Hicks's bathroom designs with tubs set in the center also influenced American designers in the 1970s. He had liked the straightforwardness with which Americans hung large contemporary paintings unframed, and began using English contemporary abstracts unframed, in rooms filled with eighteenth-century furniture. It was a fresh liberation of the sometimes stiff approach to formality taken in English interior design up to that time. The French liked it and called it "Le Style Anglais." By 1979 Hicks had published seven books about his design approach.

Albert Hadley

In the 1970s Parish-Hadley redesigned the Southampton, Long Island, summer house that William Paley of CBS had bought from Eleanor McMillen Brown, bringing another circle of connections between McMillen and Parish-Hadley. Hadley also designed and completed in three weeks, as originally required, a library-study for Mrs. Vincent Astor in New York that showed his inventiveness.

The herringbone-pattern flooring, which was scraped and restained in alternating zigzags three floorboards wide of dark and light, began a revival of stained and painted floor patterns. The wall paneling of this room was marbleized on a cream-color ground. The frames of some of the eighteenth-century French furniture were lightened and painted; upholsteries were in tones of yellows and creams. A silk fabric with an irregular black-and-white stripe, designed by Hammet & Morrow, reinforced the flooring pattern. One calfskin upholstery was stenciled to look like leopard. Draperies were of a crewel pattern. The entire composition was a personal mixture of disparate elements with a variety of scales and textures, yet complete unity.

About the same time, Albert Hadley designed a larger, more formal library for Mrs. Vincent Astor in New York that won praise. Paneled in red-lacquered wood with polished-brass trim for delineation, the library had a Bessarabian rug of red medallions with cream-and-brown flowers resting on *parquet de Versailles*. A red-and-green chintz striped with dark brown was the upholstery for the overstuffed seating. One bergère was painted white and upholstered in natural suede. An antique ikat silk was draped over one table; a coffee table was of brown lacquer. Billy Baldwin wrote, "Albert Hadley has made Mrs. Vincent Astor's red lacquer library a timeless triumph. He is a decorator with inspired ideas and great knowledge of the past."[7]

Michael Taylor

In San Francisco, the 1970s saw Michael Taylor at a peak of his career with combinations of the sophisticated and the rustic. His long use of wicker furniture, quarry-tile flooring, desert plants, and desert colors was extended by a series of furniture designed of large-scale logs—stripped and bleached but with branch stubs and knot holes retained. It was an updating of late-nineteenth-century Adirondack furniture at superscale and in 1940s California imagery—somewhere between adobe construction and cowboy bunkhouse. These pieces were made by Mimi London and Dixie Marquis, who later went on to design their own line in this idiom.

A penthouse apartment by Taylor for writer Pat Montandon in San Francisco at the end of the 1970s was spectacular at the start because of its view through 25-foot-high floor-to-ceiling glass walls. Michael Taylor transformed it into a floating white-looking aerie that was nevertheless warm and rich. He floored the space with travertine, installed a French sandstone mantelpiece, and mirrored the chimney breast and the wall opposite the windows. He then filled the space with ceiling-high ficus trees, retained the Belgian tapestry that was already there, and furnished his space with Taylor-designed cast-stone seating units that were piled with pale-beige cotton basketweave pillows. He added bleached Régence chairs upholstered in yellow-beige and tables of cast-stone that he designed, as well as rattan and stone, shell, and large-scale sculptural objects.

John Dickinson

The designs of San Francisco's John Dickinson were acclaimed for their oddly spare, peculiarly selective historical references, and the distinctive manner in which these inspirations were assembled. In his own San Francisco house, he had assembled a wide assortment of primarily nineteenth-century objects and recreations within a framework of white that was outlined or punctuated with black and softened by natural wood tones.

His living room had a bare floor, white tongue-and-groove siding on the walls, and a white ceiling; nineteenth-century iron furniture was upholstered in white. One wall displayed a collection of ironstone platters hung above a Dickinson-designed console that looked like a stripped late-nineteenth-century country table that had been cut in half. Brass kerosene lamps, Art Nouveau bronze tree-trunk lamps, and opaline globes that recalled barbershop poles served as the quasi-nostalgic lighting. Decorative elements included a group of farm tools—a scythe, a rake, two hoes—that had been enameled white, along with an armoire painted in trompe l'oeil to look like an 1870s townhouse. In the bedroom Dickinson recreated an 1870–90s look with a bamboo-turned four-poster bed that was undraped, like the windows, which were framed in dark wood tones like the tongue-and-groove wainscoting. All these rested on leopard-skin-patterned carpeting. The updated and America-inspired historicism were symptomatic of the decade.

At mid-decade, Dickinson designed a virtually all-white entertainment room in a San Francisco house by architect Julia Morgan. Beyond the dark redwood-paneled woodwork of Julia Morgan's design, Dickinson painted matte-white walls with glossy white woodwork and moldings of pearl gray, pale apricot, and chamois color. A thick white wool rug of octagonal shape rests on a dark-stained wood floor. White Belgian cotton canvas is used for Roman shades and upholsteries—even those on backless benches, the frames of which are covered in natural linen velvet. Pull-up chairs have white epoxy-lacquer finishes. The juxtaposition of the all-white scheme with rustic coffee tables designed by Dickinson to look like packing crates was evocative of both Syrie Maugham and the 1940s.

In 1979 John Dickinson designed a San Francisco residence in a renovated 1930s building with contextual respect for its surroundings. Dickinson designed all the furnishings, including the occasional tables that suggested African animal legs. Minimalism was the overall effect because of the pale, monochromatic scheme, but there was an echo of Robsjohn-Gibbings in the long banquettes and large-scale chairs.

John Dickinson demonstrated a special flair for mixing then-undiscovered periods of late-nineteenth-century style with furniture of his own design and inspiration. His range of white-on-white combined with tawny "unfinished" wood textures showed a notable sensitivity to the orchestration of both textures and colors. His untimely death in 1982 deprived the world of interior design of a master of style who had just come into his own.

Zajac & Callahan

In the 1970s Zajac & Callahan designed interiors ranging from Paris and London to Dallas and San Francisco. They continued to design virtually every element of their interiors—all newly made furniture except for the fabrics—upholstered pieces, tables, desks, lamps, mirrors, and screens. They often sculpted models of elements such as moldings to serve as prototypes. Other pieces were either antiques or signed by artist-craftsmen. They were intrigued by uncommon styles—Swedish Louis XV and Irish Chippendale, which was in direct descent from Ruby Ross Wood— as well as textures from other cultures, Japanese lacquers especially.

One New York apartment living room by Zajac & Callahan was richly expressive of the decade's multidirectional historicism (see Figure 239). Within a multi-

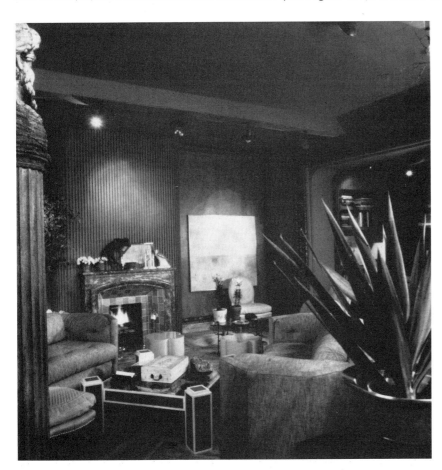

239. Zajac & Callahan. Apartment. New York City. 1975. *Photograph by Alexandre Georges.*

textured terracotta-red envelope was a gray-and-gold subscheme. Walls were striped with battens, were given twig-moldings like Adirondack furniture, and were strié-lacquered in four coats of rust-red. Windows were covered with Madagascar-inspired lattice screens lacquered the same terracotta-red. To compose the gold-and-gray secondary colors, floors were painted the pattern of Chopin's house in Warsaw—pale-beige graining and small blue-gray squares; a tobacco-gold Louis XV marble mantelpiece was lined with beige and gray tiles. Bleached pigskin Louis XVI chairs with trapunto cushions and tufted backs along with tables of cream-colored plastic laminate and lacquer inlaid with cane continued the gray-and-gold subscheme. A coffee table was by Giacometti.

Lighting included Lucite lamps of their own design and exposed-bulb reflector lamps. At one end of the room was a long library table with raised candle-stand-top legs; it was piled high with another smaller table and with plant stands holding a collection of oriental vases, jardinieres, and convex mirror reflectors framed with gilded fern leaves by French designer Line Vautrin. In the middle of the room, atop a tall fluted column, stood a Turkish bust. It was another of the decade's extraordinary exercises in mannerism and scale.

In another apartment, Zajac & Callahan demonstrated their ability to work with a more subdued palette—beiges, ochres, and siennas with accents of black, white, red, and blue—but the range of their textures was expansive. Glossy surfaces (Lucite and lacquer, silver and chrome, stone and steel, crystal and glass) were offset against rough textures (wools, wickers, woods, canes, and crackle lacquer as well as a glazed red-linen finish on a Chinese reproduction coffee table). In all of this, one pattern with variations—the basketweave—was used throughout. Typical as this was of the decade's multidirectional historicism, it was highly original in expression.

Denning & Fourcade

Along with many residential designs in the 1970s, Robert Denning designed a New York restaurant—Gertrude's. Though he designed it with some of his firm's trademarks, it was restrained by the heavy commercial traffic of the interior. Masters of the pattern-on-pattern, texture-on-texture, object-on-object technique of superimposition, Denning & Fourcade sheathed the walls in apricot-painted rough-hewn wood and with cut-and-painted mirrors in a sunburst pattern. A polished pressed-metal ceiling with a sunburst pattern reflected the pink-bulb light from steel-and-brass Neoclassical wall sconces that had fringed shades. (The latter had become one of Denning & Fourcade's trademarks.) Blue-and-green Chinese porcelain bowls, carafes, and ashtrays accented the blue tablecloths.

It was a scheme slightly more rustic than the suave Madison Avenue shop that the firm designed for Diane Von Furstenberg's line of cosmetics about the same time. The extreme of their pattern-on-pattern manipulation was in an apartment for Diane Von Furstenberg (see Figure 240). Denning & Fourcade also did highly controlled historical recreations of great country houses during the 1970s.

Mark Hampton

The designs of Mark Hampton first came to attention in the 1970s for his refreshed recreations of the eighteenth-century spirit. He worked in both informal and highly formal veins. Seven-coated lacquer walls, marbleized woodwork and moldings, huge coromandel screens, patterned wallpapers with elaborate borders—scallops, swags, and pennants—were typical of his work in residences.

Born in Plainfield, Indiana, Mark Hampton (1940–) attended De Pauw University and the London School of Economics. He received an M.F.A. from New York University's Institute of Fine Arts. He began his design career as David

240. Denning & Fourcade. Dining room, Diane Von Furstenberg apartment. New York City. 1975. *Photograph by Norman McGrath.*

Hicks's American representative, then worked for Mrs. Henry Parish II and as an associate of McMillen Inc. for the next six years. He opened his own practice in New York in 1976 and has since designed numerous residences as well as yachts, railroad cars, and offices.

John Saladino

John Saladino's designs came to national prominence in the 1970s for what he called "interior design as fine art" or "fantasies made real."

Born in Kansas City, Missouri, John Saladino (1939–) began his career not as a designer, but as a painter—first at Notre Dame University, where he received a B.F.A. in art history, and then at Yale University, where he received an M.F.A. in painting under Josef Albers. He then worked in Italy for architect Piero Sartogo (see Chapter 18) and returned to New York, where from 1963 to 1969 he worked with large space-planning firms—Saphier, Lerner, Schindler, and J.F.N. Associates. After a brief partnership with J. P. Maggio, he started his own practice in

New York in 1972. During the 1970s he designed numerous residences, offices, and pieces of furniture; the latter were put into production by Dunbar (see page 209ff.).

Saladino's designs combine Late Modern with traditional historical decorating and with Country Vernacular. His designs merge the elegant urbanity of the Machine Age with the domestic simplicity of country life. He blends the sleekness of Modern forms and detailing with the sensuousness of an art-oriented eye. "Oriented" is a key word for his style. He uses the colors and textures of oriental art—the aubergine of Japanese ceramic glazes, the celadon green of Chinese glazes, the mauve-pinks of the plum blossom—and actual artworks from the Orient in large measure. He is also fond of the simple materials that are associated with the Orient—wicker, bamboo, and unfinished wood.[8]

Against these elements, John Saladino sets the shapes and forms of the most refined Modern purity—frill-less corners, crisp and shimmering reflective sur-

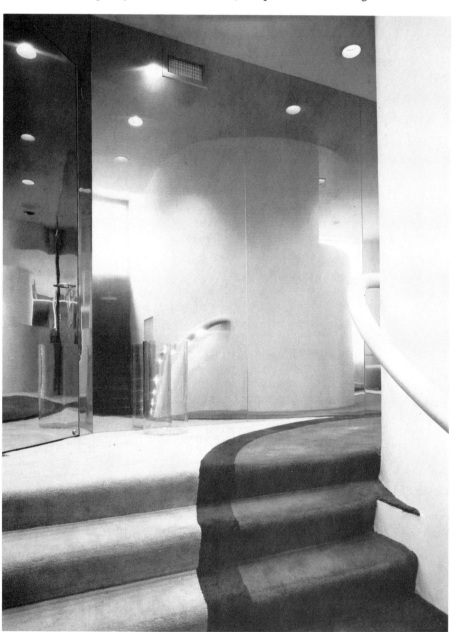

241. John Saladino. Physician's offices. New York City. 1974. *Photograph by James Mathews, courtesy John Saladino.*

faces, chunky sofas, and whimsical Post-Modern table bases, as well as built-in furniture and accessories of elegant precision and convenience. There is an air of simplicity and refinement about his work, an air of control and minimalism. Yet, overall, his interiors exhibit a painterly use of color that is delicate and sensuous.

His work has included residences, corporate offices, doctors' offices, and other interiors. One doctor's office designed in the mid-1970s combined crisp Art Deco–like carpet borders with mistily shimmering brushed-steel panels (see Figure 241) and a corridor of vibrant colors arranged progressionally—blue to yellow, to orange, to cream—that were run in diagonal bands around floor, walls, and ceiling.

His orchestrations of texture—stainless steel and wicker, wood and stone, velvet and plastic laminate—were balanced and rich. By the end of the decade he was using fabrics in quilted patterns, in flat hanging panels, in loose wind-wafted panels, and in a casual crumpled texture. In 1979 Saladino designed offices for the Almay cosmetics firm with a color palette derived not from the Post-Modern idiom, but contextually related to the tints and textures of the firm's products—pale apricot, peach, and similar tones covered the walls and upholsteries. Other interiors by Saladino sported lavender and pale blue, magenta and peach, cream and beige. It was a rich dessert of colors, textures, materials, and periods that he served.

Licensing for Interior Designers

In 1972 NSID and AID formed a joint committee to develop a common qualification examination and investigate licensing for interior designers. The National Council for Interior Design Qualification (NCIDQ) was the result. NCIDQ is governed by representatives of numerous organizations concerned with the profession of designing interiors: the American Society of Interior Designers, the Interior Design Educators Council, the Institute of Business Designers, the National Home Fashions League, and the Interior Designers of Canada.

The NCIDQ examination, which was developed with the aid of the Psychological Corporation and Educational Testing Service, was first given in 1974. It is designed to establish the core of interior design knowledge that is required to practice as a professional interior designer. The NCIDQ examination is also considered an essential first step in state-mandated legal licensing.

Throughout the decade these organizations continued to investigate licensing and examinations that would qualify interior designers. Throughout the decade, also, an interorganizational committee worked with the American Institute of Architects on a mutually agreed-upon standard contract for interior design services. In 1975 AID and NSID were consolidated as the American Society of Interior Designers—ASID. These activities, it was hoped, signaled the beginning of consolidation for the entire range of design professionals.

Suggested Reading

Abercrombie, Stanley. "The 70s Recap: Highlighting Events of the Decade," *AIA Journal.* January 1980, pp. 38–50.

Ambasz, Emilio. *Italy: The New Domestic Landscape.* New York: The Museum of Modern Art, 1972.

———. *The Architecture of Luis Barragan.* New York: The Museum of Modern Art, 1976.

Baird, George, and Charles Jencks. *Meaning in Architecture.* New York: Braziller, 1979.

Barthes, Roland. *Elements of Semiology.* New York: Hill & Wang, 1979.

Blake, Peter. *Form Follows Fiasco.* Boston: Little, Brown, 1977.

Broadbent, Bunt, and Charles Jencks. *Signs, Symbols and Architecture.* New York: John Wiley, 1980.

Drexler, Arthur. *Transformations in Modern Architecture*. New York: The Museum of Modern Art, 1979.

Filler, Martin. "The Plain, the Fancy, the Real, and the Unreal," *Progressive Architecture*. September 1977.

Five Architects: Eisenman, Graves, Gwathmey, Hejduk, Meier. 2nd ed. New York: Oxford University Press, 1975.

Charles Gwathmey & Robert Siegel: Residential Works, 1966–1977. New York: Architectural Book Publishing Co., 1977.

Jencks, Charles. *The Language of Post-Modern Architecture*. New York: Rizzoli, 1977.

———. *Late-Modern Architecture*. New York: Rizzoli, 1980.

Kron, Joan, and Susan Slesin. *High-Tech*. New York: Clarkson N. Potter, 1978.

Lévi-Strauss, Claude. *Myth and Meaning*. New York: Schocken Books, 1979.

Meier, Richard. *Richard Meier, Architect*. New York: Oxford University Press, 1976.

Meyer, Ursula. *Conceptual Art*. New York: E. P. Dutton, 1972.

Moore, Charles, and Gerald Allen. *Dimensions*. New York: Architectural Record Books, 1977.

Moore, Charles, Donlyn Lyndon, and Gerald Allen. *The Place of Houses*. New York: Holt, Rinehart and Winston, 1974.

Nuckolls, James L. *Interior Lighting for Environmental Designers*, 2d ed. New York: John Wiley, 1983.

Platner, Warren. *Ten by Platner*. New York: McGraw-Hill, 1975.

Ross, Michael Franklin. *Beyond Metabolism*. New York: Architectural Record Books, 1978.

Smith, C. Ray. "Alexander Girard's Offices for Irwin Miller," *Interiors*. February 1975, p. 60.

———, and Ruth Miller Fitzgibbons. "Workstations with Up and Down Lighting," *Interiors*. September 1975.

Stephens, Suzanne. "Playing with a Full Decade," *Progressive Architecture*. December 1979, p. 49.

Venturi, Robert, Denise Scott-Brown, and Stephen Izenour. *Learning from Las Vegas*. Cambridge: MIT Press, 1972.

Wheeler, Karen, and Peter Arnell, eds. *Michael Graves: Buildings and Projects, 1966–1981*. New York: Rizzoli, 1983.

Notes

1. Charles Moore, Donlyn Lyndon, and Gerald Allen, *The Place of Houses* (New York: Holt, Rinehart and Winston, 1974), pp. 124, 127. This book is a superb analysis of how to look at houses as well as a pioneering return to the importance of user response in interior design.

2. Adapted from C. Ray Smith's appraisal of Michael Graves's work in the encyclopedia *Contemporary Architects* (New York: St. Martin's Press, 1980), p. 305.

3. Michael Graves, quoted from an interview with C. Ray Smith and Allen Tate in New York City on November 3, 1982.

4. Adapted from C. Ray Smith's articles on the work of Bray-Schaible in *Architectural Digest* (November 1979 and October 1981).

5. This is the title of an article discussing this apartment design, written by C. Ray Smith as Editor of *Interiors* magazine (October 1974), p. 116R.

6. Billy Baldwin, quoted in *20th Century Decorating, Architecture, and Gardens*, ed. Mary Jane Pool (New York: Holt, Rinehart and Winston, 1980), p. 10.

7. Ibid., p. 11. See *House & Garden* (October 1985), pp. 136–39.

8. Adapted from C. Ray Smith's article on the work of John Saladino in *Avenue* magazine (March 1978), pp. 46–52.

Chapter 18

1980 to the Present: Today and Its Challenges

In the first half of the 1980s the interior design profession was still in transition, but its growth since the beginning of the century had been great. Professional interior design was being provided for medical facilities and schools, for hotels and restaurants, for commercial and institutional facilities, for retail sales boutiques and department stores, for theaters and museums, for offices and residences. Few types of interior spaces, in fact, were *not* being given careful professional attention. In addition, this interior design work by American designers was located not only within the United States; American designers of interiors were practicing around the world.

Employment for professional designers was at last available in numerous situations: as independent self-employed designers; as employees in interior design departments of large architecture or interior design firms; in the in-house design divisions of large corporations, large hospitals, and large hotel chains; in the interior design departments of department stores, retail and wholesale furnishings outlets; and in government agencies. More and more architecture firms began to establish their own departments of interior design. Other architects increasingly commissioned office-planning and other interior design firms to work with them on the interiors of their buildings. Interior design had grown to a $5-billion-a-year business.

Professional groups concerned with interior design were working steadily toward professional licensing and registration. The Foundation for Interior Design Education Research (FIDER) continued to develop national guidelines for interior design education. FIDER is now recognized by the federal government as the accrediting organization for educational programs in interior design. The National Council for Interior Design Qualification (NCIDQ) continued to promote its two-day examination to qualify members of professional organizations. In the early 1980s Alabama and Connecticut established legal licensing; there, use of the designation "interior designer" as a professional designation is restricted to those who have passed the two-day NCIDQ examination. Such legalities are intended to lead to required registration of professional interior designers in every state of the country. The aim is to make the profession as legally responsible (and respectable) as medicine and the law.

Designers of interiors from several different professions—architects, space planners, and interior designers—and from several different organizations whose members practice interior design—AIA, ASID, IBD—continued to sit jointly on the Interiors Committee of the American Institute of Architects to devise standard contract documents for all interior design professionals, as well as to conduct programs that would improve understanding, coordination, and management of interior design projects.

Directions at Mid-Decade

Energy and Conservation

Energy continued to be a prominent concern of interior designers, as it was for the rest of society; and the demands of the technology for energy conservation similarly increased demands on professional designers of interiors. Advances in other technologies—in office, medical, industrial, retailing, and even residential environments—created continuing needs for postgraduate professional education.

It became clear to most Americans that the Computer/Electronic Age was here. Designers of interiors were concerned with accommodating computers in offices and residences, with wide-screen television installations, and with other electronic devices. Whatever the degree of contribution to the process of design computers made, it was irrefutable that, as assists in doing repeat work—drafting, detailing, and the like—computers could increase speed, accuracy, and efficiency by many hours. Countless articles discussed the subject; but they focused primarily on the equipment, without due attention to making the new electronic environments satisfying or attractive to users or occupants. Among other notable technical advances that affected the field was the introduction of flat wiring in electrical systems. In construction technology, metal studs along with plasterboard and gypsumboard sheets had almost wiped out the plasterers' trade.

Professional journals as well as newspaper reporting on the interior design field all had undergone a considerable increase in numbers and quantity of reporting as well as quality. More of the complete range of interior design was presented by the journals—including historical interiors that had remained intact since their creation, restorations of the historical monuments of interior design, especially those from the 1920s and 1930s, as well as the new, the vanguard, and the stately homes from the eighteenth and early nineteenth centuries.

A Pluralism of Approaches

In the early 1980s the widest possible range of directions, approaches, styles, talents, and interests was at work in interior design. "Inclusiveness" and the "pluralism" of approaches were the terms used by analysts of this phenomenon, which was also labeled "confusion." This situation was expanded and complicated by unexpected combinations of one or more of the pluralistic possibilities; these combinations produced images of duality, multiplicity, and, sometimes, discontinuity. Historical eclecticism and mannered ornamentation were the single direction shared by most of the interior design professions—both in architecture and in decorating.

Post-Modernism was still the polemic idiom of the day, though there was little agreement on what it was. The prevailing definition or understanding was that it meant historicism and ornamentation, especially mannered classicism—games with classical ornament and scale. The AT&T Building in New York by Philip Johnson and John Burgee, Architects, with its superscale broken-pediment roofscape became the symbol of this school. Post-Modern interior designers seemed most indebted to the classically derived interior designs of Michael Graves. The Country "look," this time based on North American vernacular, furnishings, and folk art, for a short time held out hope of a new feeling for straightforward national realism; but American Country interiors soon gave way to the old Arts and Crafts romanticism.

The preservation movement began to focus more on treasured historical interiors. There were continuing revivals of neo-Deco and new revivals of neo-1950s. There were recalls and comments on art movements throughout the century—Abstract interiors, Conceptual interiors, and Constructivist interiors. There were also numerous recalls of early-twentieth-century designers, such as Hoffmann and Loos; and of later designers ranging from Aalto and Asplund, to Barragan, to SITE Inc.; and even recalls of Robert Venturi. Among the stylistic ventures of the first half of the 1980s were such combinations as Post-Modernism with Country; Minimalism within historical restoration; Country with Minimal; and so on.

As in every decade, there were vanguard innovative interiors, a few of which were truly innovative and others of which proffered imagery that was more meaningful to the designer than the concern for the client's activities or desires. In the middle were compromises and combinations that showed a confusion or uneasy compatibility of styles or ideas, muddled middle minds, and the like. And at the low end of the scale were shallow, glib glosses on style and function, on pretension and aspiration, that deserved the pejorative epithet "glitzy."

Preservation and Recycling

Preservation and recycling were accepted rationales for historicism and historical revivals, which were practiced by vanguard architects as well as traditional decorators. Lofts and other spaces from old industrial buildings were recycled into offices, shopping centers, residences, and any number of other functions for which they were not originally designed. It was beginning to look as if there might be a general recognition of the value of saving whatever old that was good and of preserving our design heritage. Since 1976, when laws began to make restoration economically advantageous, commercial organizations had begun to jump on the preservation train. Hotels, movie houses, and other commercial establishments began to capitalize on their historical advantages.

By the mid-1980s approximately one hundred major old hotels across the country had been restored instead of "renovated" to some contemporary state. Among them were Denver's Brown Palace Hotel of 1893, New York City's Plaza Hotel of 1907, Boston's Copley Plaza of 1912, Dallas's Adolphus Hotel of 1912, Seattle's Four Seasons Olympic Hotel of 1923, and Memphis's Peabody Hotel of 1925. In 1980 the Los Angeles Biltmore of 1923 was restored by Phyllis Lambert and Gene Summers, who furnished some of the old suites with Mies van der Rohe's classic furniture from the 1920s. In 1981 the Arizona Biltmore of 1929, designed by Albert Chase McArthur with the consultation of Frank Lloyd Wright, was restored to its original appearance. Also in 1981 the Villard houses in New York were saved and incorporated into the contrastingly overblown Helmsley Palace Hotel as its most elegantly designed reception rooms.

All this activity made clear the need for restoration designers who knew their history as well as the techniques for preservation and restoration.

Historical Revivals

The historicism of the decade was continued both as pure, academic restoration or recreation of period rooms, primarily eighteenth and nineteenth century as well as revivals with inclusions of twentieth-century mannerism such as scale manipulations. Architects continued to recall the work of early-twentieth-century architects. Cesar Pelli was designing mid-Victorian wall treatments for New York's Battery Park City complex that recalled London's Houses of Parliament and evoked

242. Zajac & Callahan. Apartment. New York City. 1983. *Photograph courtesy Zajac & Callahan Inc.*

again the spirit of the Great Exhibition at the Crystal Palace. Parish-Hadley and McMillen were doing more and more corporate and institutional work. The sixty-year career of Eleanor McMillen Brown was celebrated in a book published in 1982.

Albert Hadley redesigned the apartment of Mrs. Nelson Rockefeller after the death of her husband, rearranging the original Jean-Michel Frank furnishings (see Chapter 13). Mrs. Rockefeller needed a smaller apartment and, with Hadley's designing, she consolidated her collection into fewer rooms. The original living room, designed in 1937 by Wallace Harrison and Jean-Michel Frank (as "Louis XV—but modern," Nelson Rockefeller had said), was recast in the former dining room. Relocated were Jean-Michel Frank chairs; Christian Berard rugs and uphol-stered furniture; Giacometti's gilded consoles, sconces, and andirons; and a museum-quality collection of artworks. It was a fortuitous recycling—as well as an extension of the 1930s spirit—that was the essence of the history-oriented 1980s.

Historical revivalism also brought back some unexpected period styles: Zajac & Callahan manipulated 1880s frills for a Victorian house in Philadelphia. One apartment in New York by Zajac & Callahan exhibited a combination of the most recherché and unlikely—but beautiful—pieces of furniture, sculpture, painting,

243. Powell/Kleinschmidt. Apartment, One Magnificent Mile. Chicago, Illinois. 1984. *Photograph © Tony Soluri, 1984.*

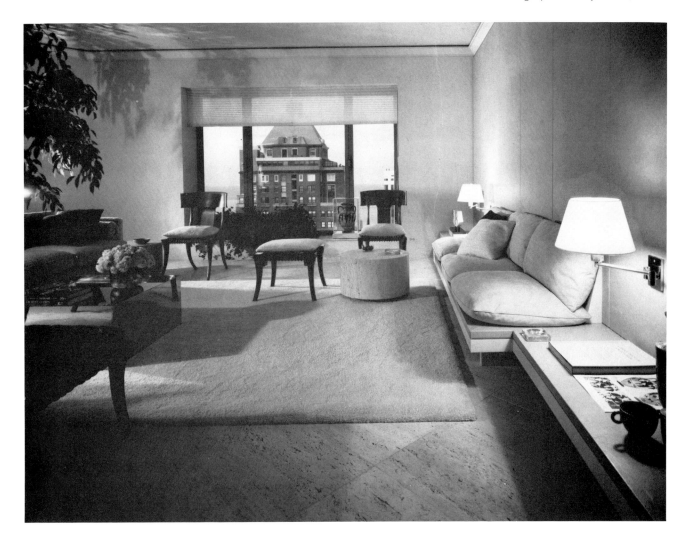

and decorative objects in a fresh and radiantly personal arrangement and atmosphere (see Figure 242). Powell/Kleinschmidt in Chicago continued variations on the Miesian idiom, updating it with colors that recalled color-field painting (see Figure 243). Sufficient time has not yet elapsed to determine whether this should be called Miesian revival, Miesian survival, or Late Modern. Furniture revivals, or survivals, included the furniture designs of Mies, Le Corbusier, Breuer, Aalto, Josef Hoffmann, and Eliel Saarinen; there was also a collectors' and commercial revival of Stickley and other Mission furnishings.

John Saladino was at a peak of popularity for his special color sense in blending mauves, pinks, apricots, ivories, pale grays, and taupes (it was the ice-cream palette of the decade); and for his sensitive juxtapositions of furniture—Machine Age, historical, Peasant, and his own soft and seductive, often channel-quilted upholstered pieces (see Figure 244).

Mark Hampton was doing more restoration design with his work on Gracie Mansion, New York City's mayoral residence (see Figure 245) and on Blair House in Washington, D.C.

244. John Saladino. Apartment. New York City. 1984. *Photograph © Peter Aaron/ESTO, 1984, courtesy Condé-Nast Publications, Inc.*

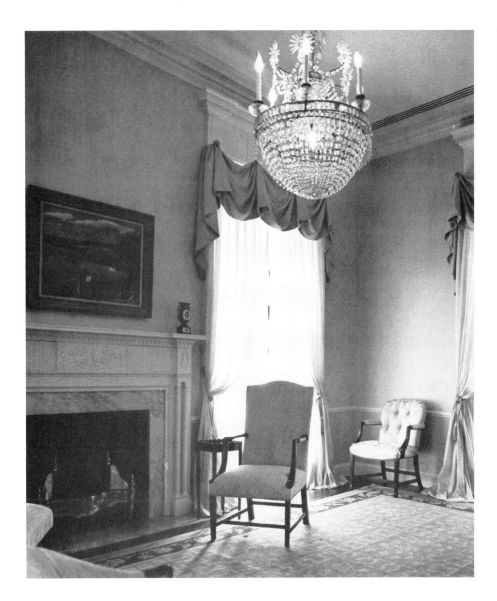

245. Mark Hampton. Restored room, Gracie Mansion. New York City. 1984. *Photograph © Stan Ries, 1984.*

Minimalism

A continued interest in stripped interiors with industrial-looking furnishings was also strong in the 1980s. A working-out of the goals of the Deutscher Werkbund since 1907, this approach also had overtones of prefab, found, and Pop. Among the designers working in the Minimal idiom were those continuing from the 1960s and 1970s—Benjamin Baldwin, Ward Bennett (see page 172ff.), William Machado, Joseph D'Urso (see page 184ff.), Bray-Schaible (see Figure 246 and page 175ff.), Robin Jacobsen and Scott Bromley, Norman Diekman, and Peter Andes (see Figure 247)—as well as a new generation from the 1980s who combined Minimalism with other influences.

In 1981 Benjamin Baldwin designed the interiors of the new Americana Hotel in Fort Worth, Texas, in his simple, Minimal idiom. Baldwin engaged Roger Ferri as assistant to design the ballroom and restaurant of the hotel. Ferri's large-scale sculptural elements were additions to the Minimal concept and were his first opportunity to adapt his plant-form concepts to commercial interiors.

Exemplary of the combinations, Joseph Paul D'Urso in 1983 redesigned the interiors of a turn-of-the-century house in Southampton, Long Island, as a com-

246. Bray-Schaible. Residence. New York City. 1982. *Photograph by François Hallard.*

247. Peter Andes. Apartment. New York City. 1980. *Photograph by Norman McGrath.*

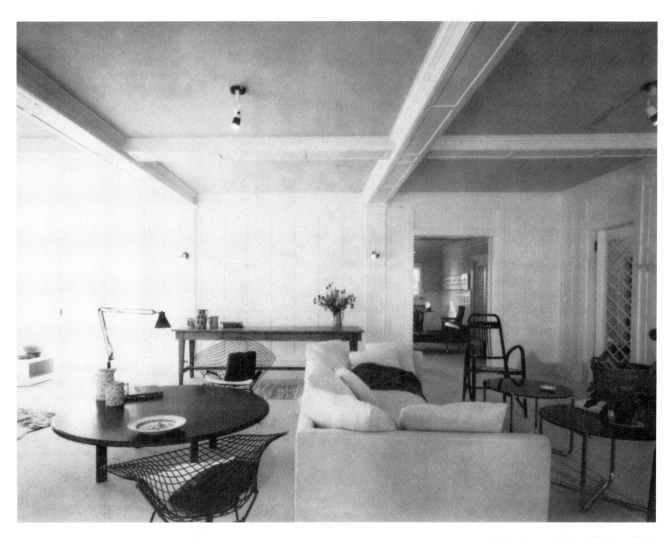

248. Joseph Paul D'Urso. Residence. Southampton, Long Island. 1982–83. *Photograph by Rick Barnes, courtesy D'Urso Designs Inc.*

bination of Industrial Minimalism with historical preservation (see Figure 248). The woodwork in the paneled and pilastered living room and dining room with their diamond-paned windows was restored and painted white; the ceilings were painted pale mauve; the dining room walls above the white wainscoting were painted a pale pink; and beige sisal carpeting was used throughout. Against this background D'Urso located white upholstered sofas and window seats with white cushions, and black tables and black metal chairs, and black-and-white industrial-looking lighting fixtures. Between these extremes he located furniture in natural wood tones that continued the palette of the sisal carpeting. The interplay of old and new, handcraft and industry, black and white, painted and natural, and of two versions of the diamond motif made a special synthesis of the decade's interests.

Post-Modernism

Post-Modern designers and architects continued to work out their manipulations of stripped classical ornamentation—what might better be called "mannered classicism"—in ice-cream colors (pale apricot, vanilla, and black raspberry). Although a definition of Post-Modernism had still not been broadly agreed upon, it was becoming clear that its primary components were historicism, classical ornamen-

249. Michael Graves. Plan, Sunar showroom. New York City. 1981. *Illustration courtesy Sunar/ Hauserman.*

tation, color, a pluralism of approaches, and sometimes simultaneity of multiple approaches, meanings, messages, historical inspiration, and emotional content.

Michael Graves (see page 190ff.) designed a series of eight showrooms in different cities for the Sunar furniture company, beginning in 1979. Their impact on other designers was immediate. Graves's technique of displaying fabrics as loosely draped and flowing yard goods, first thought so outrageous and inappropriate by many designers and display designers, was soon emulated widely. His muted, delicate, and seductive color palette—apricot, gray, French blue, taupe, ochre—was adopted by mainstream, established designers as well as by the vanguard young. Graves's concept for these showrooms was of contained, separate rooms, rather than flowing space; a hierarchical sequence of those rooms; and a three-part division of walls into base, middle, and top or, as Graves stresses the anthropomorphic classical background, "foot, body, and head."

In his second New York showroom for Sunar (1981), Graves integrated the working areas into the showroom space, forming both in his classically derived vocabulary—columns and capitals, pediments and vaulted ceilings, flutings and marbleizing (see Figure 249). In the third Chicago Sunar showroom (1982), colors were more somber and monumental; softly draped fabrics complemented hard surfaces in crisp forms; and Graves's Deco-Streamlined indirect lighting was subtle and captivating (see color plate 15). For Sunar, also, Graves began to design furniture in his personal vein of classical allusion.

Voorsanger & Mills, Architects, interpreted this direction (1982–84) with their designs for the New York restaurants Le Cygne and Nightfalls, with their offices for the New York chapter of the American Institute of Architects, and with the Janovic-Plaza paint store. And they had good company in the work of numerous other designers.

The architect-historian Robert A. M. Stern continued his multiple role of promoting Post-Modernism, rediscovering neglected designers and architects of the 1920s and 1930s, and designing buildings and interiors in the Post-Modern idiom with its multiple historical influences. One indoor swimming pool in a New Jersey residence (1982) was entered by Deco-Grecian stairs and was supported by columns that recreated the metal palm-tree capitals of John Nash's Brighton Pavilion of 1815–21. (In 1979, the influential architect Hans Hollein in Austria had called upon the same historical reference in a travel office in Vienna.) Elsewhere in the same residence, the furniture recreated the work of Mies and Le Corbusier and offered layered screens, Deco lighting effects, and at least one caryatid-decorated fireplace.

His other residential interiors, often within houses that were sensitive assemblies of motifs and elements from Shingle-Style buildings, showed the influence of Sir Edwin Lutyens, Stanford White, and other turn-of-the-century architects and designers. One of Stern's offices, for Dr. Herbert E. Walker, subtly reinterpreted the classicism of Stanford White. It contained furniture selected and specified by Peter Andes, that reinterpreted the classical-contemporary furniture that clients would recognize as being in the accepted idiom of other doctors' offices. Stern's showroom for Shaw-Walker furniture company in Chicago (1982) (see Figure 250) showed his manipulation of Hoffmann-inspired motifs—especially the grid—as integrated with Post-Modern circulation and the Post-Modern visual vocabulary.

Other Post-Modern designers indicated that "interiors as narrative" was their concept of the decade's direction. The theory was that designs should be reflective,

250. Robert A. M. Stern, Architects. Showroom for Shaw-Walker. Chicago, 1982. *Photograph © Peter Aaron/ESTO, 1982.*

expressive of their locale or content, of the client's background or history, or of some other interrelationship. Diana Agrest & Mario Gandelsonas, Architects, designed their Pink House as a discussion of the many kinds and uses of doors. "Contextualism" was the term used to denote this design attention and this basis for design. Some office designers adopted murals as a major communication technique for this aim: Photo murals in a variety of large-scale techniques and trompe l'oeil murals—some of them billboard size and building size by painter Richard Haas—became prevalent.

Abstract Interiors

A number of furniture and fashion showrooms as well as a few designers' own apartments were designed with homage to twentieth-century art movements such as Constructivism, Dadaism, or Surrealism. Abstract forms and bizarre selection and placement of furnishings suggested Magritte and other formalist dissociations.

Vignelli Associates (see page 212ff.) designed several showrooms in this vein, including one in Los Angeles in 1982 for the E. F. Hauserman Company, makers of partitioning systems and furniture. Their concept was to relate the story of Hauserman's wall-partition systems to the artwork of Dan Flavin with light and color. Flavin's work depends on lighting walls with colored fluorescent tubes. The Vignellis made this the envelope for the display of Hauserman's partitioning systems (see Figure 251). For their design of the Italcenter in Chicago (1982), a

251. Vignelli Associates with Dan Flavin. E. F. Hauserman showroom. Los Angeles, California. 1982. *Photograph by Toshi Yoshimi, courtesy Vignelli Associates.*

252A. Sartogo & Schwarting. Grid diagram, apartment. New York City. 1981. *Illustration courtesy Design Collaborative.*

252B. Sartogo & Schwarting. Apartment. New York City. 1981. *Photograph by Norman McGrath.*

showroom for a consortium of Italian furniture manufacturers, the Vignellis designed a series of low partition-like walls, finished to look like superscale stone texture, that were offset by a grid screen and massive sculptural forms such as an 8-foot-diameter sphere, a cylinder, and a pyramid, finished in the same texture but in different colors. It was a surreal landscape reminiscent of de Chirico, with motifs of Post-Modernism—the broken wavy line, the stepped wall, and the diagonal.

Conceptualism

Interiors as Conceptual Art was the approach of architects Piero Sartogo and Jon Michael Schwarting. Their apartments for a client in New York (1981) (see Figures 252A and B) and in Rome (1982), along with their Italian Trade Center in New York (1982) (see Figure 253), were elaborate conceptual overlays of this type. For the apartment in New York (see Figures 252A and B) Sartogo and Schwarting's concept was like a progressional nautilus shell. From room to room a series of columns and grids got larger but fewer. For the apartment in Rome, Sartogo's concept was that an identical plan of the apartment had been superimposed on the original one but a foot or so off alignment with the original. By painting the colors of each room along the lines of the imaginary, superimposed plan, the actual walls were considered as nonexistent; but looking along the juncture of the paint lines made it look as though the imaginary walls had been made real.

For the Italian Trade Center on Park Avenue, Sartogo and Schwarting envisioned an imaginary plan of the L-shaped space rotated over the actual plan; the intersections were indicated by changes of color and material. The effect was of one space that worked like two (see Figure 253).

253. Sartogo & Schwarting. Italian Trade Center. New York City. 1982. *Photograph by Norman McGrath.*

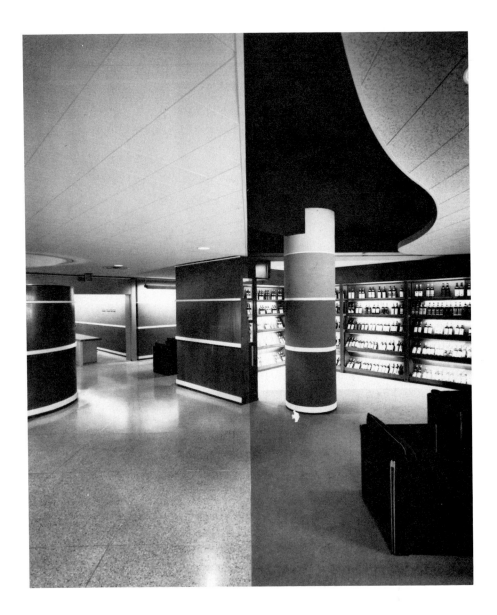

Mainstream Vanguard

Among interior designs by established architects, I. M. Pei's East Wing of the National Gallery of Art in Washington, D.C. (1980), showed the angular lengths to which establishment architects could go in their attempts to compose new interior imagery. Paul Rudolph continued to work out Futurist-Expressionist themes with vertigo-defying glass floors, glass bridges, and a transparent elevator in his own remodeled New York apartment (1980–85).

Other Combinations

A new school of young architects—including Friday Architects in Philadelphia, Arquitectonica in Miami, Taft Architects in Houston, and other firms—produced interiors as well as buildings that were a mix of Russian Constructivism, Art Deco, and 1950s motifs. Among their favorite motifs was the grid—as derived from Japanese traditional architecture, from Vienna in the 1900s—Loos, Hoffmann, et al.—and from Barragan and the 1950s.

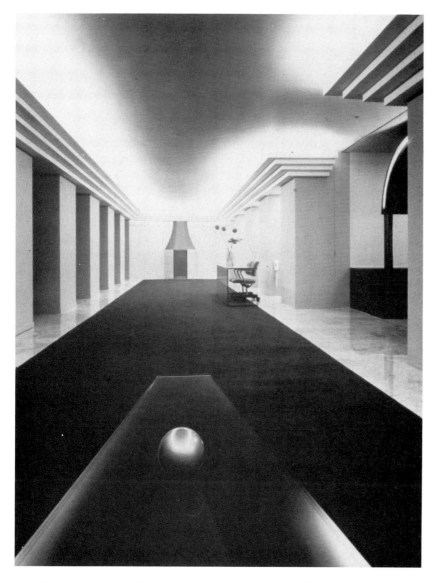

254. Arata Isozaki. E. F. Hauserman showroom. Chicago, Illinois. 1982. *Photograph by Barbara Karant, Sadin/Karant.*

Perhaps the paradigm of all these combined influences was devised by the poetic Japanese architect Arata Isozaki. Among his many attention-gathering interiors, he designed a showroom for E. F. Hauserman in Chicago (1982) (see Figure 254) that was the American introduction to his multiplicity of historical recalls— Post-Modern classicism, Streamlining, turn-of-the-century Vienna, Japanese traditions, Romanesque barrel vaults, Palladio, Mies, Kahn, and a list of other influences. No American designer combined so many inspirational devices in a single interior.

Problems of the Profession

Innovation

One critical question about the profession of interior design continually recurs throughout this history: If the most innovative designs have interested us as the significant contributions to the design world, why have those designs been received with less broad acceptance than (1) traditional designs, (2) ingrained eighteenth-century models, or (3) anonymously designed commercial products? The question is not about rivalry between designers or between the different design professions; it is more to the deep concern of all designers: Why are design innovation and progress not generally acceptable or desired?

Part of Modernist thinking has held that innovation is the ultimate goal—innovation of functional process as well as of formal shape. Modernists have felt that if designers or architects analyzed and thought carefully enough, they might, after six or eight months, devise a design that could be better than anything the world had ever seen for that purpose before. If you build a better mousetrap, the maxim goes, the world will beat a path to your door. By extension, if a good, thoughtful designer worked out a more efficient toilet, which also revolutionized the process of using it, then humankind ought to accept this innovative work of genius, perhaps even seek it out. It has not worked out that way.

The continued resistance to Modern design has made it increasingly clear that humankind cannot be swayed to give up a functional process that it has developed over a million years. Our race cannot easily reject a cultural tradition and adopt something that has just been worked out. Perhaps the battle between innovation and tradition, as between futurism and historicism, is ingrained.

Part of the answer to this question about innovation may be related to the desire for comfort. Why have the designs of innovators often been so uncomfortable? From Frank Lloyd Wright's furniture to Paul Rudolph's, from some of Le Corbusier's and Mies's to Richard Meier's? The question is strained by how many traditionally tried, proved, and accepted models from the past two centuries can be emulated. Those models have been approved of as comfortable by a majority of users.

Only on rare occasions have twentieth-century design innovators achieved comfort comparable to that of the most traditional furnishings. Charles Eames and, more recently, Donald Pettit, Charles Pollock, and Richard Schultz, have produced chairs that have been accepted as both handsome and truly comfortable. This question of comfort remains the core of the battle between the two schools of interior design—traditionalism and innovation—comfort to the body, and comfort to the accustomed eye. Was this question also raised in the eighteenth century? "We know what we like" really means "We like what we know."

Publishing Furniture Plans and Dates

Due to the concentration on surface and visual effects by both the majority of decorators and the shelter publications, furniture plans and sections are seldom presented along with the photographs of interior design projects. Without them, we cannot know whether innovative or even interesting placements of furniture, changes in level, or broader issues are addressed. Do we have any understanding of the plan of Jean-Michel Frank's salon for the de Noailleses? Or of Billy Baldwin's apartment for Cole Porter? For the profession to record its accomplishments, for individual designers to show the true strengths of their concepts, the plans and sections must be made an essential part of recorded presentations.

Dates are another essential element that is generally lacking in interior design records. Since early twentieth-century decorators did not have to file registered plans or other legal documents, there are numerous missing dates for design and construction. Can we ever know the dates of innovation in furniture finishing or other crafts endeavors? Furthermore, it is said that because of vanity many of the early "blue-haired lady decorators" would never let their birthdates be known. Ruby Ross Wood is a prime example. Nor have any of the books by the major decorators tried to provide more precise chronologies about their careers than specifying the decades—as opposed to the years—in which their projects were designed and installed. Establishing the facts is difficult enough in this situation; analyzing the time lags within this chronology is, at this stage of the profession, sometimes impossible.

The inclusion of more precise dates for interior design projects—more precise than assuming six months prior to a publication of the project—will be a greater requirement as the profession grows more professional. In later contract work, from the 1950s onward, this problem begins to vanish. But in residential work it lingers in the would-be perennially up-to-date pages of general-press journalism.

Getting Together

Will the different professions of interior design ever get together? The separation early in the 1900s of the architect-designer, who traditionally orchestrated a team of artists and artisans, from the decorator-designer, who served as art-and-object consultant and orchestrator of the assembly of those objects, set the two professions on divergent paths. Then in the 1960s, when many interior designers began to adopt the Modern idiom, the paths seemed to converge—except for the fact that vanguard designers were already turning away from Modernism to Post-Modernism.

Can the interior design professions ever come together at a single stylistic meeting point and agreement? Or are they destined to be—quite properly, numerous critics claim—separate and distinct because they focus on completely different things—architecture on ideas, space, and structure; interiors on vision and touch? Or are the professions merely different sides of the same coin, so that one cannot exist without the other? Architect-designer Warren Platner is said to have commented that the reason for architecture is interiors. Perhaps the overview of interior design history in this book will offer a new viewpoint.

Philosophy/Theory/Ideology

Why is there no aesthetic theory of interior design from interiors specialists? Why is it all from architects? Interior designers show no signs of having deep, overall philosophies about their work. They have generalized approaches that are governed by strong and individual points of view, and they have strong likes and dislikes. But those are not complete, developed philosophies. Interior designers seem not to develop complete systems of thought or ideology that stretch out to the intellectual frontiers of their work; they seem to have no cerebral methodologies that are all-pervasive—from overall approach to the most minute detail.

Architects, clearly, are not like that, have never been throughout history. The history of architecture is filled with critical works on architectural philosophy—from Vitruvius to Alberti and Serlio, from Viollet-le-Duc to Frank Lloyd Wright, from Le Corbusier to Camillo Sitte. Architects continue to write books about design theory and history. Decorators and interior designers seem only to write books for popular consumption to increase their fame or clientele.

Architects thrive on theories and philosophies—at times it seems as if they need such theories to keep their expanded visions expanded; at other times it seems as if theorizing and philosophy are all that architects have to concentrate on. Architects constantly take sides in great debates—which change from year to year—and these ideological issues seemingly condition their work, pervade it, and make it appear indivisible from those philosophies—if sometimes in contradiction. Louis Kahn mesmerized listeners at lecture after lecture with his mystical and mythical aesthetic philosophy; his was an almost complete mythology, as detailed in word and thought as it was in sketch and line.

It is not that all architects are verbal about their design philosophies. The practice of architecture and the professing of theory are not mutually dependent.

But the high points in the history of architecture do seem to have been made largely by those who have achieved high points of architectural theory. The same cannot be said for interior design and interior design theory. Some critics say that this difference in interest in design theory is due to the fact that architecture is, indeed, about ideas, whereas interiors are about vision and touch. This matter invites designers' convictions.

Design Morality

Today, the consideration of design morality relates not to the handmade versus the machine-made object. That battle was won long ago. Rather it concerns the original/individual item versus the mass-produced reproduction—in addition to design piracy, of course. This consideration of originality is complicated by the many stages of industrial production. The unique hand-carved chair is an original object; the hand-carved chair that is reproduced in multiples is considered a copy. A prototype chair intended for industrial production by Mies or Eames was a unique and original object; the chairs produced in multiples by industry are—originals or copies? This is the contemporary moral dilemma in design.

An analogy with culinary craft may be illuminating on this subject: To cook from scratch is the goal of purist chefs; opening a can or package of something already processed is rejected as unoriginal. Yet sugar and flour have already been processed, and serving fresh oysters is, essentially, a matter of opening a package and providing originality only in a sauce. Perhaps we should look at design for production—for reproduction—as a multistage process in which originality can be injected at any stage—in the conceptual stage, in the final form, in the material, in the process itself, or even in the final garnish or presentation.

Conclusions

As we look at the history of twentieth-century interior design as laid out in some detail, we recognize cycles of design emphasis, those continuous swings of the pendulum from one side to the other. But we also see the many different pendulums that constitute the totality of design choices:

- historical versus futurist
- classical versus romantic
- functional versus aesthetic
- geometric regularity versus biomorphic irregularity
- symmetrical versus asymmetrical
- clean versus messy
- vital versus static
- simple versus elaborate
- peasant versus palatial
- elaborated versus refined/purgative/stripped
- colorful versus monochromatic
- calm repose versus agitated excitement
- total/consistent/integral versus fragmented/layered/inconsistent

These seem to run in cycles of interest. The twentieth century has seen the ultimate aesthetic expression of the Industrial Revolution in its celebration of the imagery of the machine. Our century has also seen the working out of the Futurist vision of speed and light, of dematerialization and the ephemeral. What can we learn from an overview of these cycles or swings of the pendulum?

One fact seems clear: The great mistake is the tendency not to respect the existing, original conditions—client requirements, site, period, or original design. This leads to confusion of fashions in the cycles of design emphasis. Fashions become confused with the kind of timelessness that the best design must aim for.

Elaboration versus Refinement

In our century, also, each design revolution seems to be praised for its overthrow of the excesses of the past and its refinement of current design tastes. Refinement, along with white or light colors, seems to get the highest vote of praise in our age. Elsie de Wolfe simplified the Victorian interior; Jean-Michel Frank distilled the classical vision of the 1930s.

Yet, if everything that is good is simple and refined, what can be said positively for elaboration? And if everything that is good continues to be refined, will there ultimately be anything left to refine? Perhaps what is not explained by history is the disintegration of simplicity by popularization. What is initially refined by a vanguard visionary, then accepted and adapted by his or her colleagues, never stays as it was invented. Each adapter adds his or her own personality; each addition de-simplifies. Then, to be mass-producible and marketable, it must be changed—adapted to the available technology, modified to meet what the sales organization understands of marketable taste, then changed again by the inevitable copyists. As William Morris said, "There is always someone who is willing to debase a design to make it cheaper and sell it at a greater profit." In this way, it seems, both products and styles become elaborated rather than further refined. Soon, again, it will be time for another design revolution of refinement.

Time Lags

These cycles have come faster and faster, in our century, due to rapid transportation and to the instantaneous communications systems we have devised. Between 1921 and 1923, Mies van der Rohe drew his first visionary schemes of towers with all glass-and-metal curtain walls. It took thirty years for the available technology to catch up until such a building was made possible—in Mies's 1951 Lake Shore Drive Apartments in Chicago. In the next ten years, manufacturers of curtain-wall systems proliferated to accommodate the designs and demands of countless architects following in that idiom. By about 1961 professional critics were already calling such structures "boring"—just when the general public was beginning to see enough examples of glass architecture to become familiar with the idiom. Still, since then—now over twenty years—the glass-and-metal curtain wall has been the mainstream of building construction and technology around the world.

Meanwhile, of course, other cycles of design revolution have been going on, overlaid on this pyramid of acceptance that trickles down from the visionary designer to the profession and then to acceptance by the mass of population. And there are cycles that "trickle up" from nonacademic design circles—Peasant and Vernacular styles, Pop and Rock—to become high-style idioms. In this regard we cannot overlook the towering influence, throughout the century, of Picasso's and Matisse's Peasant or Primitive style on the field of interior design. Yet these simple styles by high-style artists further complicate the picture. All of these complicate our understanding of the cycles of design and the time lags inherent in those cycles.

Clients

In most books on design there seems to be so much to discuss about the problems, solutions, goals, techniques, and inventions of designers that several critical topics are usually omitted. One of these topics is the central role played by designers of fabrics and by upholsterers, drapers, and the many other contractors who build interiors. Another of these topics is the client. That is the case of this book also. A mass of information, sensitivity, and credit is due to every mention of the Vicomte and Vicomtesse de Noailles, the Mexican art patron Carlos de Bestigui, Nelson Rockefeller, Pauline Potter Baroness Philippe de Rothchild, Linda and Cole Porter, the Gilbert Millers, J. Irwin Miller, and countless other clients who made the work of the interior designers discussed in this history possible. The role of clients in the making of interiors is pivotal. For without the client, both the financing and the function are missing. It has often been rightly said that every great work of design requires a great client as well as a great architect or designer.

Interior design, as we must constantly bear in mind, is an applied art, not a fine art. It has a program of requirements—requirements for physical function, requirements for psychological function—that are or should be part of the goal of a designer. And it is a joint venture of client and designer that must set, pursue, modify, and express those goals. Both collaborators can foil the success. The designer can ignore the client's requirements and make a fine-art interior, with no regard for the client's requirements. The client can withhold understanding, agreement, cooperation, or funding, making it impossible for an interior designer to achieve the vision, the concept that he or she sees as fitting for that set of requirements, location, and the rest.

As much as an interior designer must maintain a personal vision—parameters, perseverance, and control to achieve the concept, and, ultimately, the total work of art—so too a client must maintain a commitment to the designer's talent and professionalism, as well as a commitment to the budget and the timetable. As much as the designer must maintain his or her vision, so must he or she also maintain a commitment to the functional and psychological requirements of the client, to the budget, and to the schedule.

In any work there are only three first and basic goals: to do the best job we can, to do it within the budget, and to do it on time. A failure in any one of these goals is a failure short of whatever perfection of professionalism a designer can have in mind in doing the best job he or she can do. Meeting these goals and creating appropriate and fitting interiors with a new and personal magic are the goals to which all designers of interiors aspire.

Glossary

aubergine   a purple-black color; the color of eggplant skin

chaise longue   (not "lounge") a chair with a long seat that one can stretch one's legs out on

chaise percée   a chair with a hole in the seat and a cabinet below to conceal a chamber pot

Churrigueresque   an elaborately ornamented genre of Spanish and Mexican baroque, named for José de Churriguera (1650–1725)

classical   (1) formal, stately, and composed; (2) based on Greek and Roman antiquities; (3) based on any ancient civilization, such as Egyptian, Mayan, Greek, Roman, and so forth.

Cromwellian   the period of Puritan revolt in England (1642–1660), named for Oliver Cromwell, when comparatively austere and undecorated furniture was adopted. American Colonial Puritans also adopted the style. Simplified rope-turnings on gate-leg tables and on square-backed, Spanish-inspired leather-upholstered chairs were produced chiefly in walnut, white oak, and maple.

Day-Glo   a series of vivid phosphorescent colors popularized in the 1960s

distressing   a technique of aging and weathering furniture and other objects to give them patina—such as streaks and gouges, dents and worm-holes

door buck   the frame built into a wall to support and enclose a door

fenestration   the placement and treatment of windows in building design

furred out/furred down   the building-out of a wall surface to meet a desired contour

intarsia   wood inlaid with ivory, metal, or other materials

knock-down   the name given to furniture that can be assembled and disassembled for production and for shipping

lambrequin   a horizontal drapery, such as a valance or pelmet, hanging on a fireplace shelf in the Victorian period; or, the drapery around the top of a bed

parquet de Versailles   a pattern of wood flooring popularized at the Palace of Versailles

plenum   a space in a wall or ceiling used for air supply or return

silver-bowl lamp   a lamp bulb that is silvered on its hemispherical end to produce a reflector

spline   a strip connecting or covering a long flat joint between elements, such as two panels

strié   a stripe-like texture or pattern in paint or fabric

tête-de-nègre   a rich red-cast chocolate brown; a color popularized in France

valance   a horizontal hanging or pelmet over a window or other opening

Victorian   common lumping of all nineteenth-century periods from 1840 to 1900, during the reign of Queen Victoria.

Pronunciation Guide

Andes AN-deez

Au Quatrième oh kah-tree-EHM

Bauhaus rhymes with out-house

Beaux-Arts bohz-arh

Berlage BEAR-lah-geh

Bijvoet BYE-foot

Breuer BROY-er

Castiglione cas-teel-YOH-neh

Chareau sha-ROH

Chiattone key-ah-TOH-neh

Cret kray

De Stijl in Dutch, somewhere between deh shtyle and deh shtale; in English, deh style

Der Blaue Reiter rhymes with dare-POWER-writer

Déscartes day-CART

Deutscher Werkbund DOYT-sher verk-boond

Die Bruecke dee BROOK-eh

ensembliers on-SAHM-blee-ay

Errazuris ehr-RAH-tsoo-ree

Foucault foo-COH

Fourcade foor-KAHD

Gesamtkunstwerk geh-ZAHMT-koonst-verk

Ghirardelli gear-arh-DELL-ee

Gris, Juan gree, wahn

Hejduk HAY-duck

La Jolla lah HOY-ah

Labrouste lah-BROOST

Loos lohs

Lutyens LUTCH-ens

Maire my-REH

Mairea my-RAY-ah

Maugham mawm

Mauna Kae moh-nah KAY-uh

Mielziner mill-ZEEN-er

Mies van der Rohe mees van dehr ROH-eh

Muthesius moo-TAY-zee-oos

Neutra NOY-trah

Noialles noh-EYE

parti par-TEE

Pei pay

Pfister FEES-ter

Poughkeepsie poh-KIP-see

Quitandinha key-tahn-DEEN-yah

Rietveld REET-velt

Sachlichkeit ZAHK-lick-kite

Scheebart SHAY-bart

Schnelle SHNEL-leh

Stoclet stock-LAY

Syon ZIGH-un

Taliesin tally-ESS-in

Terragni tear-RAHN-yee

trompe l'oeil trahmp LUH-ee or tromp LOY

Versailles vehr-SIGH

Vignelli veen-YELL-ee

Wasmuth VAHS-muht

Weyerhaeuser wear-HOW-zer

Wiener Werkstaette VEEN-er VERK-shtet-teh

Zajac zay-JACK

Index of Names

Index of Topics